THE HOLY
TRINITY

THE HOLY
TRINITY

In Scripture, History, Theology, and Worship

ROBERT LETHAM

P&R PUBLISHING

P.O. BOX 817 • PHILLIPSBURG • NEW JERSEY 08865-0817

Page design and typesetting by Lakeside Design Plus

Printed in the United States of America

Library of Congress Cataloging-in-Publication Data

Letham, Robert.
    The Holy Trinity : in Scripture, history, theology, and worship / Robert Letham.
        p. cm.
    Includes bibliographical references and indexes.
    ISBN-10: 0-87552-000-6 (pbk.)
    ISBN-13: 978-0-87552-000-1 (pbk.)
    1. Trinity. I. Title.

BT111.3.L48 2004
231'.044—dc22

                                      2004049273

For Joan

Contents

all of God is a model of the Trinity, p. 176-77

Part Four: Critical Issues

Islam, 432–446. Postmodernism, 446ff.

Appendixes

Preface

When approached by the publisher about writing this book, I was both delighted and awed—delighted, since for some time I had been planning a work such as this, but in many ways awed, for what an enormous challenge it is to write about the One who is utterly transcendent and incomprehensible! Karl Barth's thought as he sat in his study preparing his now famous Göttingen lectures crossed my mind too, more than once: "Can I do it?" However, the sage advice of Basil the Great in a letter to his friend, Gregory Nazianzen, is of constant encouragement. Basil recognized that our theological language is not adequate to convey our thoughts, and that, in turn, our thoughts pale before the reality. Yet we are compelled to give an answer about God to those who love the Lord. So he urged his friend to devote his energies to advocating the truth.[1]

This book interacts with theologians from widely differing backgrounds, from East and West, from Roman Catholicism as well as Protestantism. However, it is written from a Reformed perspective. As B. B. Warfield argued, Reformed theology is "Christianity come into its own." It is distinctively *Christian* theology. Its pedigree reaches back to the Fathers. This was the belief of, among others, Calvin, Bucer, and Zwingli. To be Reformed is to be truly catholic, biblical, evangelical, and orthodox. While our supreme authority is Holy Scripture, we should also listen seriously and attentively to the Fathers, as did Calvin, the Reformers, and John Owen. In a culture where rugged individualism flourishes, we need to be "submitting to one another out of reverence for Christ" (Eph. 5:21), recognizing that we are all liable to error.

Sadly, since the time of Calvin, little of significance has been contributed to the development of Trinitarian doctrine by conservative Reformed theologians. John Owen and Jonathan Edwards both wrote

---

1. Basil of Caesarea, *Letters* 7 (PG 32:244–45).

on the Trinity, and Owen's treatise *Of Communion with God the Father, Son, and Holy Ghost* is without peer in its treatment of communion with the three persons, but they did not contribute anything significant to the *advancement* of the doctrine. This dearth is evident from the lack of such sources quoted in this book, and it is in keeping with the neglect of the Trinity, until recently, in the entire Western church. Indeed, Calvin and Owen stand out by their focus on the persons of the Trinity, rather than the divine essence, which is more an Eastern emphasis than a Western one. This lacuna on the part of conservative Christianity is little short of tragic. A theology that declares that our chief purpose is "to enjoy [God] forever" needs to demonstrate it is doing just that.

In the last thirty years or so, there has been a veritable barrage of writing on the Trinity. Unfortunately, in a book of this scope, I have been able to consider only a small selection of that literature. On the other hand, the theologians I have chosen are in my estimation the most crucial ones. Much of this recent outburst has been of a pantheistic or panentheistic nature, beginning with human experience rather than God himself. Many of the criticisms I make of Rahner, Moltmann, and Pannenberg in chapter 14 are also applicable to those who follow further in this direction, like Catherine Mowry LaCugna, Elizabeth Johnson, and Robert Jenson.

I gladly acknowledge the help of a wide range of people, none of whom can be charged with any deficiencies in the following pages. I thank Mr. John Sundet and the committee of the Connecticut Valley Conference on Reformed Theology for their invitation to lecture on the Trinity in March 1997; the faculty of Mid-America Reformed Seminary for inviting me to give the annual guest lectures for 1999, which form the basis for two chapters and an excursus; and Dr. Carl Trueman, for asking me to contribute an article on the Trinity to *Themelios*, the substance of which forms the introduction. I also thank someone unknown to me who, upon reading my critical review of Robert Reymond's Trinitarianism in the first edition of his *New Systematic Theology of the Christian Faith*, encouraged the publisher to approach me about writing this book.

I am grateful to Mr. Allan Fisher of P&R Publishing, and to Barbara Lerch, Thom Notaro, and the rest of the staff, as well as copy editor Jim Scott, for their helpful assistance; the publishers of the *Mid-America Journal of Theology* for permission to use material from three articles: "Ternary Patterns in Paul's Letter to the Ephesians," *MJT* 13

(2002): 57–69, which is an excursus following chapter 3; "East Is East and West Is West: Another Look at the *Filioque*," *MJT* 13 (2002): 71–86, which forms the backbone of chapter 10; and "The Holy Trinity and Christian Worship," *MJT* 13 (2002): 87–100, much of which is incorporated in chapter 18; and the editors of the *Westminster Theological Journal* for permission to use material in my review of the book by Kevin Giles that appears in appendix 2.

I am appreciative for helpful interaction from the following: Sinclair Ferguson, Don Garlington, Paul Helm, Tony Lane, and John Van Dyk, for kindly reading draft chapters and making very useful comments; John Dishman and John Van Dyk, for important contributions on physics and chemistry, respectively; the Rev. George Christian, for his constant stimulus to thought on the Trinity; my colleague, the Rev. S. Edd Cathey, for checking a number of chapters for readability; Doug Latimer, for drawing my attention to the Syrian Antiochene Orthodox service book, which provides many of the Trinitarian collects at the end of chapters; and students in my Ph.D. class at Westminster Theological Seminary on Trinitarian Theology: Ancient and Modern, for stimulating contributions to debate. I am inevitably indebted (who is not?) to Grace Mullen of the Montgomery Library at Westminster Theological Seminary in Philadelphia, for locating and providing relatively inaccessible material, and for the indulgence of the staff while I removed boxes of books. I also thank the congregation of Emmanuel Orthodox Presbyterian Church in Wilmington, Delaware, for its interest in the progress of the book and its wonderful support for me and the ministry of the gospel.

Last, but certainly not least, come my children, Elizabeth, Caroline, and Adam, and the dedicatee, my wife Joan, who is a constant source of love and encouragement to me.

Moving beyond the sublunary realm, to the Father, the Son, and the Holy Spirit, ever one God, I offer this book with unspeakable gratitude, with the prayer of Augustine with which he concludes *De Trinitate*: "O Lord, the one God, God the Trinity, whatever I have said in these books that is from you, may your own people acknowledge; if anything of my own, may it be pardoned, both by you and by those who are yours. Amen."[2]

---

2. Augustine, *On the Trinity* 15.28.51 (my translation).

Abbreviations

ANF	*The Ante-Nicene Fathers*, ed. A. Roberts and J. Donaldson, rev. A. C. Coxe (reprint, Grand Rapids: Eerdmans, 1969–73)
AugStud	*Augustinian Studies*
C	The creed of Constantinople (called the Nicene Creed or the Niceno-Constantinopolitan Creed) (cf. "N" below)
CCSL	Corpus Christianorum: Series latina (Turnhout: Brepols, 1953–)
CD	Karl Barth, *Church Dogmatics*, ed. G. W. Bromiley and T. F. Torrance (Edinburgh: T & T Clark, 1956–77)
CO	John Calvin, *Opera quae supersunt omnia*, ed. Guilielmus Baum, Eduardus Cunitz, and Eduardus Reiss, 59 vols. Corpus Reformatorum, vols. 29–87 (Brunswick, 1863–1900)
CO²	*Ioannis Calvini opera omnia* (Geneva: Librairie Droz, 1992–)
CTJ	*Calvin Theological Journal*
DRev	*Downside Review*
ECR	*Eastern Churches Review*
EECh	*Encyclopedia of the Early Church*, ed. Angelo di Berardino, trans. A. Walford (New York: Oxford University Press, 1992)
EvQ	*Evangelical Quarterly*
GCS	Die griechische christliche Schriftsteller der ersten drei Jahrhunderte (Berlin, 1897–)

Greg	*Gregorianum*
HTR	*Harvard Theological Review*
JETS	*Journal of the Evangelical Theological Society*
JBL	*Journal of Biblical Literature*
JTS	*Journal of Theological Studies*
LSJ	Henry George Liddell and Robert Scott, *A Greek-English Lexicon*, rev. Henry Stuart Jones, 9th edition (Oxford: Clarendon Press, 1940)
LN	Johannes P. Louw and Eugene A. Nida, eds., *Greek-English Lexicon of the New Testament Based on Semantic Domains* (New York: United Bible Societies, 1988)
MJT	*Mid-America Journal of Theology*
N	The creed of Nicaea (cf. "C" above)
NPNF[1]	*A Select Library of the Nicene and Post-Nicene Fathers of the Christian Church*, [first series,] ed. P. Schaff (reprint, Grand Rapids: Eerdmans, 1978–79)
NPNF[2]	*A Select Library of the Nicene and Post-Nicene Fathers of the Christian Church*, second series, ed. P. Schaff and H. Wace (reprint, Grand Rapids: Eerdmans, 1979)
NT	New Testament
NTS	*New Testament Studies*
OCP	*Orientalia christiana periodica*
OS	*Joannis Calvini opera selecta*, ed. P. Barth and W. Niesel, 5 vols. (Munich: Chr. Kaiser, 1926–52)
OT	Old Testament
PG	Patrologia graeca, ed. J.-P. Migne *et. al.* (Paris, 1857–86)
PL	Patrologia latina, ed. J.-P. Migne *et. al.* (Paris, 1878–90)
RevScRel	*Revue des sciences religieuses*
SBET	*Scottish Bulletin of Evangelical Theology*

SCJ	*Sixteenth Century Journal*
Service Book	*Service Book of the Holy Orthodox-Catholic Apostolic Church*, comp. and trans. Isabel Florence Hapgood, 3rd ed. (Brooklyn, N.Y.: Syrian Antiochene Orthodox Archdiocese of New York and All North America, 1956)
SJT	*Scottish Journal of Theology*
ST	Thomas Aquinas, *Summa theologica*
StPatr	*Studia patristica*
StVladThQ	*St Vladimir's Theological Quarterly*
SwJT	*Southwestern Journal of Theology*
TDNT	*Theological Dictionary of the New Testament*, ed. Gerhard Kittel and Gerhard Friedrich, trans. and ed. Geoffrey W. Bromiley (Grand Rapids: Eerdmans, 1964–76)
Them	*Themelios*
TynBul	*Tyndale Bulletin*
WCF	Westminster Confession of Faith
WLC	Westminster Larger Catechism
WSC	Westminster Shorter Catechism
WTJ	*Westminster Theological Journal*

Citations from the English Bible, unless otherwise indicated, are from *The Holy Bible: English Standard Version* (Wheaton, Ill.: Crossway Bibles, 2001).

Citations from the Qur'an are taken from *The Meaning of the Holy Qur'an*, ed. 'Abdullah Yusuf 'Ali, 9th ed. (Beltsville, Md.: Amana Publications, 1997).

English translations of the church fathers are from *ANF* or *NPNF*[1] or *NPNF*[2], unless otherwise stated. In these and all other citations, capitalization of pronouns referring to God has been removed and brought into conformity with current usage.

Introduction

I believe it was Bernard Lonergan who once remarked that "the trinity is a matter of five notions or properties, four relations, three persons, two processions, one substance or nature, and no understanding."[1] In 1967, Karl Rahner famously drew attention to the then widespread neglect of the Trinity, claiming that "should the doctrine of the Trinity have to be dropped as false, the major part of religious literature could well remain virtually unchanged."[2] Since then, numerous works have appeared, but, as far as I can see, this torrent of activity has yet to percolate through to pulpit or pew. It is mainly confined to theological treatises, and often supports other agendas—ecumenical, ecological, egalitarian. For the vast majority of Christians, including most ministers and theological students, the Trinity is still a mathematical conundrum, full of imposing philosophical jargon, relegated to an obscure alcove, remote from daily life. I have been surprised over the years at the confusion prevalent in the most unexpected circles. Yet, as Sinclair Ferguson mentioned to me recently, "I've often reflected on the rather obvious thought that when his disciples were about to have the world collapse in on them, our Lord spent so much time in the Upper Room speaking to them about the mystery of the Trinity. If anything could underline the necessity of Trinitarianism for practical Christianity, that must surely be it!"[3]

Potential Problems for Trinitarianism

Part of the problem for the ordinary Christian may be that in its debates and struggles, the ancient church was forced to use extrabib-

---

1. This introduction is a slightly modified version of my article, "The Trinity—Yesterday, Today and the Future," *Them* 28, no. 1 (autumn 2002): 26–36.
2. Karl Rahner, *The Trinity*, trans. Joseph Donceel (New York: Crossroad, 1997), 10–11.
3. E-mail message, 4 April 2003 (cited by permission).

1

lical terms to defend biblical concepts. This was necessary because heretics misused the Bible to support their erroneous ideas. Athanasius provides a glimpse of what happened at the Council of Nicaea (A.D. 325), when the assembled bishops rejected the claim of Arius that the Son was not eternal, but was created by God, who thereby became his Father. Originally, the statement was proposed to the Council that the Son came "from God." This meant that he was not from some other source, nor was he a creature. However, those who sympathized with Arius agreed to the phrase, since in their eyes all creatures came forth from God. Consequently, the Council was forced to look for a word that excluded all possibility of an Arian interpretation.[4] Biblical language could not resolve the issue, for the conflict was over the meaning of biblical language in the first place. This reminds us that to understand an expression we have to consider it in a certain context, for its meaning cannot be derived by repeating the expression itself. A dictionary is an obvious example of this, for it explains the meanings of words in terms of other words and phrases. To think clearly about the Trinity, we must grapple with the history of discussion in the church.

Augustine, in his *De Trinitate*, writes that "in no other subject is error more dangerous, or inquiry more laborious, or the discovery of truth more profitable."[5] Helvellyn, a mountain in the English Lake District, contains a famous section known as Striding Edge. At that point, the path to the summit leads along a narrow ridge, the ground sloping away steeply on both sides. It is easily passable in good weather, despite "the nauseating feeling of height and fresh air on both sides." However, "many careful walkers have come to grief, as the memorials along the way will testify."[6] It "cannot be recommended to anyone afraid of heights."[7] Exploration of the Trinity has a similar feel to it, for one is always balanced precariously on a narrow path, with dangers looming on both sides—and many are those who fail to retain their balance.

The Eastern and Western churches have faced different tendencies toward imbalance on one side or the other. The East early on faced

4. Athanasius, *On the Decrees of the Synod of Nicaea* 19–21 (PG 25:447–54).
5. Augustine, *De Trinitate* 1.3.5 (PL 42:820–22).
6. www.antonytowers.btinternet.co.uk/001/indexalt.html.
7. www.onedayhikes.com/Hikes.asp?HikesID=4.

the danger of subordinationism, viewing the Son and the Spirit as some-how derivative, with their divine status not precisely clear. This was endemic until the fourth-century controversies. The terminology had yet to be developed by which God could be said to be three without detriment to his being one. Thereafter, beginning with a focus on the three persons, the East has sometimes tended to see the Father as the source not only of the personal subsistence of the Son and the Spirit but also of their deity. In this way, it is easy to see how the Son could be viewed as a little less divine than the Father, possessing his deity by derivation rather than of himself. The best of Eastern theology has avoided these dangers. However, with the recent reawakening of inter-est in Eastern theology in the West, a social model of the Trinity has arisen in the West that focuses on the distinctiveness of the three per-sons, often tending toward a loose tritheism.[8]

The West, for its part, has fallen more towards modalism. By this is meant the blurring or eclipsing of the eternal personal distinctions. This can come about either by treating God's self-revelation as the Father, the Son, and the Spirit as merely successive modes by which the one unipersonal God revealed himself (as Sabellius taught in the third century) or, alternatively, by a reluctance to recognize that God's revelation in human history tells us anything about who he is eternally. Either way, we are left without true knowledge of God, for what he says about himself in the Bible may not reflect who he actually is. Gen-erally—apart from these heretical extremes—Western Trinitarianism has been based on the priority of the one divine essence and has had some difficulty doing justice to the distinctions of the three persons.

Since most readers of this book are from the West, this modalis-tic tendency poses the most immediate threat. Augustine's dominant impact looms large. In the second half of *De Trinitate*, Augustine hes-itantly introduces some analogies for the Trinity, fully aware of their limitations.[9] However, these analogies have had a great impact over the years. They are based on the primacy of the essence of God over

---

8. Jürgen Moltmann, *The Trinity and the Kingdom: The Doctrine of God* (London: SCM, 1991) has been cited as possibly exemplifying this claim, but see Wolfhart Pannenberg, *Sys-tematic Theology*, trans. Geoffrey W. Bromiley (Grand Rapids: Eerdmans, 1991), 1:309–12, who rejects it.

9. Augustine, *De Trinitate* 8–15.

the three persons, for the unity of God is his starting point. He looks for reflections of the Trinity in the human mind. On this basis, Augustine finds it difficult to do full justice to the personal distinctions of the three. For example, he describes the Trinity in terms of a lover (Father), the beloved (Son), and the love that exists between them (Spirit). Does Augustine here impersonalize the Spirit? After all, love is a quality, not a person.

Later, Aquinas discusses *de Deo uno* (the one God) separately from *de Deo trino* (the triune God). In *Summa contra Gentiles*, he holds back discussion of the Trinity until book 4, after considering the doctrine of God in detail in book 1. In part 1 of *Summa theologia*, he discusses the existence and attributes of God in questions 1–25, turning to the Trinity only in questions 27–43. This pattern becomes standard in theological textbooks in the Western church. In Protestant circles, Charles Hodge spends nearly two hundred and fifty pages discussing the existence and attributes of God before at long last turning his attention to the fact that God is triune. Louis Berkhof follows the same procedure.[10] This tendency is exacerbated by the pressures of the Enlightenment. The whole idea of revelation is problematic in the Kantian framework. As a symptom of the malaise, Friedrich Schleiermacher restricts his treatment of the Trinity to an appendix in *The Christian Faith*. Even B. B. Warfield toys with a modalist position when he suggests, but then—happily—rejects, the possibility that certain aspects of the relation between the Father and the Son in human history may have been the result of a covenant between the persons of the Trinity and thus may not represent eternal realities in God.[11] J. I. Packer devotes a chapter in *Knowing God* to the Trinity, part of the way through the volume, but then continues as if nothing has happened.[12]

In keeping with the Enlightenment worldview, the focus of attention from the eighteenth century onward shifted away from God to

10. Charles Hodge, *Systematic Theology* (Grand Rapids: Eerdmans, 1977), 1:191–441 on the existence and attributes of God, 1:442–82 on the Trinity; Louis Berkhof, *Systematic Theology* (London: Banner of Truth, 1958), 19–81 on the existence and attributes of God, 82–99 on the Trinity.

11. B. B. Warfield, "The Biblical Doctrine of the Trinity," in *Biblical and Theological Studies*, ed. Samuel G. Craig (Philadelphia: Presbyterian and Reformed, 1952), 22–59, esp. 54–55.

12. J. I. Packer, *Knowing God* (London: Hodder and Stoughton, 1973), 67–75, out of 314 pages.

this world. Alexander Pope's famous lines sum it up: "Know then thyself, presume not God to scan, the proper study of mankind is man."[13] New academic disciplines emerge in the nineteenth century devoted to the study of man—psychology, sociology, and anthropology being the most prominent. In turn, there is a striking development of the historical consciousness. Biblical scholars search for the historical Jesus. Biblical theology, under pressure from the Kantian world to prescind from eternity and ontology, tends to limit the reference of biblical statements about the Father and the Son to the historical dimension only. A classic case is Oscar Cullmann's claim that the NT has a purely functional Christology.[14] The problem with this line of thought is that, if the reference of biblical statements is exclusively this-worldly, then God has not necessarily revealed himself as he eternally is.

Evangelicals have their own particular problems. Biblicism has been a strong characteristic. The post-Reformation slide into a privatized, individualist religion that neglects the church and the world has led many to downplay the ecumenical creeds in favor of the latest insights from biblical studies, whatever may be the motivation behind them.[15] Prominent aspects of the church's doctrine of the Trinity have often been derided or neglected as unbiblical speculation.[16] Opposition to the orthodox doctrine has often tended to come from those who stress the Bible at the expense of the teachings of the church.[17] These people forget that the church was forced to use extrabiblical language because biblical language itself was open to a variety of interpretations—some faithful, others not. We alluded above to Athanasius's remarks about the introduction of the words *ousia* and *homoousios* at Nicaea.

Today most Western Christians are practical modalists. The usual way of referring to God is "God" or, particularly at the popular level,

---

13. Alexander Pope, *An Essay on Man*, 2:1.

14. Oscar Cullmann, *The Christology of the New Testament* (London: SCM, 1959), 326–27; cf. [Cullmann,] "The Reply of Professor Cullmann to Roman Catholic Critics," trans. Robert P. Meye, *SJT* 15 (1962): 36–43, where he qualifies his earlier claims.

15. Robert Letham, "Is Evangelicalism Christian?" *EvQ* 67, no. 1 (1995): 3–33.

16. Robert L. Reymond, *A New Systematic Theology of the Christian Faith* (New York: Nelson, 1998). In the second edition of this work, Reymond happily corrects this tendency.

17. Gregory Nazianzen, *Orations* 28; 31.3 (PG 36:29–72, 136–37); John Calvin, *Institutes of the Christian Religion*, trans. Ford Lewis Battles, ed. John T. McNeill (Philadelphia: Westminster Press, 1960), 1.13.2–5.

"the Lord." It is worth contrasting this with Gregory Nazianzen, the great Cappadocian of the fourth century, who spoke of "my Trinity," saying, "When I say 'God,' I mean Father, Son, and Holy Spirit."[18] This practical modalism goes in tandem with a general lack of understanding of the historic doctrine of the Trinity. In a letter to the editor of the *Times* (London) in June 1992, the well-known evangelical Anglican, David Prior, remarked how he had looked for an appropriate illustration for a sermon on the Trinity for Trinity Sunday. He found it watching cricket on television, the Second Test Match between England and Pakistan. Ian Salisbury, the English leg spinner, bowled in quick succession a leg break, a googly, and a top spinner.[19] There, Prior exclaimed, was the illustration he needed—one person expressing himself in three different ways! We give full marks to Prior for spotting the importance of cricket—a pity about the theology. A perceptive correspondent wrote in reply that the letter should be signaled "wide."

Consider the following common analogies used to explain the Trinity. The generic analogy, of three men sharing a common humanity, considered and rejected by Gregory of Nyssa and others, was adopted recently by Robert Reymond in the first edition of his *Systematic Theology*, although he abandoned it in the revised edition. This analogy is false because, first, humanity is not restricted to three men. It is possible to conceive of one man or five trillion men. The Trinity consists of only three—no more, no less. Moreover, three men are separate personal entities, whereas the three persons of the Trinity share the identical divine substance, indwelling one another—occupying the identical divine space. The generic analogy leads to tritheism or a pantheon, not the Trinity. Other analogies of the Trinity are often used by evangelicals, such as that of a clover leaf, one branch with three leaves. However, each leaf is only one-third of the whole, while the three persons of the Trinity are both together and severally the whole God. This analogy destroys the deity of the three and reduces once again to modalism. As Gregory Nazianzen stresses at the end of his fifth theological oration, there are no analogies in the world around us that adequately convey the Christian doctrine of the Trinity.

18. Gregory Nazianzen, *Orations* 28; 38.8 (PG 36:29–72, 320).
19. These are three different ways in which a bowler of this type in cricket (equivalent to a baseball pitcher) can deliver the ball to the batsman (batter).

Colin Gunton has argued that the tendency toward modalism, inherited from Augustine, lies at the root of the atheism and agnosticism that has confronted the Western church in a way that it has not done in the East. Whatever the validity of his claim, Western Trinitarianism has found it difficult to break the shackles imposed by Augustine. Both Barth and Rahner, to cite but two examples, are strongly biased in that direction. In particular, Barth's statement on the Trinity that "God reveals himself as the Lord" and his triad of revealer, revelation, and revealedness have the flavor of unipersonality, although in fairness we must recognize that, like Rahner, he distances himself from modalism as such.[20]

For its part, the East has clearly seen the modalistic tendency of the West. As one prime example, the *filioque* clause[21] itself has, in their eyes, blurred the distinction between the Father and the Son by regarding them as sharing identically in the procession of the Spirit.[22] According to the East, since the Father is not the Son, and the Son is not the Father, how can the Spirit be said to proceed from both without differentiation or qualification? In the East's eyes, this lack of distinction casts a shadow on the overall doctrine of the Trinity in the West.

The West, in turn, has been quick to point out what it sees as the dangers of subordinationism, and even tritheism, in the East. In my own limited experience, many Westerners balk at reference to the relations of the persons, and appear to think that this challenges the equality or even the oneness of the three. In part, this may be due to the lack of attention given to the matter in conservative Protestantism.

Potential Benefits of Recovering Trinitarianism

It is my belief that a recovery of the Trinity at ground level, the level of the ordinary minister and believer, will help revitalize the life of the church and, in turn, its witness in the world.

1. Let us look first at its potential in worship. According to Paul, Christian experience is thoroughly Trinitarian, flowing from the

20. Karl Barth, *CD*, I/1: 295ff.

21. This is the Western addition to the Niceno-Constantinopolitan Creed: "and the Son" (*filioque*).

22. Thus, Augustine wrote of the Spirit proceeding from both "as from a single source." *De Trinitate* 15.17.27; 26.47 (PL 42:1079–80, 1092–96).

engagement of all three persons in planning and securing our salvation. The reconciliation effected by Christ has brought everyone in the church into communion with the Holy Trinity. Whether Jew or Gentile, we have access in or by the Holy Spirit through Christ to the Father (Eph. 2:18). Prayer, worship, and communion with God are by definition Trinitarian. As the Father has made himself known through the Son "for us and our salvation" in or by the Spirit, so we are all caught up in this reverse movement. We live, move, and have our being in a pervasively Trinitarian atmosphere. We recall too the words of Jesus to the Samaritan woman, that the true worshipers will from now on worship the Father in Spirit and in truth (John 4:21–24). How often have we heard this referred to inwardness in contrast to externals, to spirituality rather than material worship, to sincerity as opposed to formalism? Instead, with many of the Greek fathers, such as Basil the Great and Cyril of Alexandria, a more immediate and pertinent reference is to the Holy Spirit (all other references in John to *pneuma* are to the third person of the Trinity, except probably two—11:33 and 13:21) and to the living embodiment of truth, Jesus Christ (the way, the truth, and the life: cf. 14:6, 17; 1:15, 17; 8:32ff.; 16:12–15). The point is that Christian experience of God in its entirety, including worship, prayer, or what have you, is inescapably Trinitarian. How often have you heard that taught, preached, or stressed? The important point is that at the most fundamental level of Christian experience, corresponding to what Polanyi termed the "tacit dimension" of scientific knowledge,[23] this is common to all Christian believers. The need is to bridge the gap between this prearticulated level of experience and a developed theological understanding, so that this is explicitly, demonstrably, and strategically realized in the understanding of the church and its members. A necessary corrective to the ills I have mentioned must begin right here. If it begins here, many of the matters below will be enormously illuminated, for it is in worship that our theology should be rooted.

2. We need, second, to recapture and refashion a Trinitarian view of creation. Colin Gunton has produced some excellent work in this area. How can the unity in diversity and the diversity in unity, every-

23. Michael Polanyi, *The Tacit Dimension* (Chicago: University of Chicago Press, 1958).

where evident in the world around us and in the skies above, be explained without recourse to its Trinitarian origination? Instead of expending their energies fighting against Darwinism, conservative Christians need to construct a positive *theological* approach to creation—and thus to the environment—that expressly and explicitly accounts both for the order and coherence of the universe and for the distinctiveness of its parts. Precisely because it declares the glory of its Creator, the tri-personal God, the world is to be preserved and cultivated in thankful stewardship, not exploited as a plaything of fate or an accident of chance.

3. At a very basic level indeed, a clear outlook on the Trinity should deeply affect how we treat people. The Father advances his kingdom by means of his Son, the Son glorifies the Father, the Spirit speaks not of himself but of the Son, and the Father glorifies the Son.[24] All will call Jesus "Lord" by the Holy Spirit to the glory of the Father. Each of the three delights in the good of the others.

In Philippians 2:5–11, Paul urges his readers to follow the example of the incarnate Christ. Christ did not use his equality with God as something to be exploited for his own advantage. Instead he emptied himself, by taking human nature and so adding "the form of a servant." He was obedient to the point of death on a cross, so as to bring about our salvation. Thus, his followers are to shape their lives according to his—like that of the faithful, obedient, and self-giving Second Adam, in contrast to the grasping, self-interested First Adam. However, Paul's comments reach back to Christ's preincarnate state. His actions in his earthly ministry were in harmony with his attitudes beforehand. Being in the form of God, Jesus acted like that because he had always acted that way. In fact, all three persons of the Trinity always act like that. We are to live like that—looking to the interests of others—because that is what Christ did and also *because that is what God is like*. The contrast is stark: the whole tenor of fallen man is the pursuit of self-interest, but God actively pursues the interests of the other.[25]

---

24. Pannenberg, *Systematic Theology*, 1:308–27.

25. This is quite different from the case of a person who is persistently abused by another. In that case, either from unwillingness or enforced lack of opportunity, the one who is abused is unable to contend for his or her own interests, let alone actively to pursue the interests of the other.

4. A fully self-conscious and developed Trinitarian theology is indispensable for the future progress of evangelism and missions. We find ourselves face-to-face with a militantly resurgent Islam. I find it hard to see how Islam, or, for that matter, any religion based on belief in a unitary god, can possibly account for human personality or explain the *diversity* in unity of the world. Is it surprising that Islamic nations are associated with monolithic and dictatorial political systems?[26] If the Christian faith is to make headway after all these centuries, it must begin at the roots of Islam with the Qur'an's dismissal of Christianity as repugnant to reason due, among other things, to its teaching on the Trinity.[27] For historical reasons, the church in the East was on the defensive in the face of Islamic hegemony. For now and the future, we must recover our nerve, for this is the root of Islamic unbelief and also its most vulnerable point. Politically correct pluralists will do all they can to stop us.

In a somewhat different way, postmodernism is unable to account for *unity* in diversity. Islam is a militant and monolithic unifying principle, with no provision for diversity, but postmodernism is a militantly diversifying principle without any basis for unity. Its rejection of objective knowledge and absolute truth leaves it with no way to account for order in the world. Whereas Enlightenment rationalism imposed a man-made unity, the post-Enlightenment world has spawned a fissiparous diversity without unity. By its rejection of objective knowledge, it is unable to support science consistently, and so maintain the fight against microorganisms (has anyone told drug-resistant bacteria and viruses that they are simply engaged in a language game or in a manipulative bid for power?). Nor will it eventually be able to sustain the development of the weapons that our societies will need to defend themselves against aggressors who wish to overthrow them.

In politics, I have already suggested a connection between a unitary view of God and monolithic dictatorship. This is no new claim, for people like Moltmann have given it a good airing. A proper understanding of the triune God, to the extent of his revelation and our capacity, should lead to something quite different. Since God seeks the

26. The one notable exception, Turkey, is democratic because Mustafa Kemal secularized the state in 1923.
27. Qur'an 4:171; 5:73.

interests and well-being of the other, whereas in sin we seek first our own interests, only a Trinitarian-based society could achieve *in a very proximate fashion* an appropriate balance between rights and responsibilities, freedom and order, peace and justice.

What of the path to reclaiming God's triunity as an integral and vital part of Christian experience, witness, and mission? How are we to avoid the pitfalls of both Eastern and Western approaches, staying clear of the dangers of subordinationism on one side and modalism on the other? How can we spell out further these possible outcomes? In the following pages, I hope to suggest some lines of approach to these questions. This will include extensive discussion of the history of debate in the church. This is essential for two reasons. First, much of today's writing on the Trinity is in pursuit of particular agendas—ecumenical, ecological, and egalitarian-feminist. Often these writers build their case on an interpretation of past discussion. However, this is often culled from highly selective and tendentious readings of a limited range of sources. Without a wide and thorough historical underpinning, most readers are at the mercy of such selectivity. The feminist case then wins by default at this crucial point. Second, the lion's share of what we have to learn comes from listening to the voices of others, past and present. Since our chief end in life is "to glorify God and enjoy him," if we follow carefully and patiently the development of the church's understanding of God, it will surely bring great dividends in the ways we have already described.

I think I have said enough to alert you to the serious *lacunae* in contemporary Christian awareness of the triunity of God. At the same time, the prize is exceedingly great. Let us end with Augustine. This is a *dangerous* area of thought and belief, he said, because heresy is dangerously near on both sides. Wrong views of God can twist and corrupt our worship and ministry, the life and witness of the church, and ultimately the peace, harmony, and well-being of the world around us. A close study of the Trinity is also dangerous, for it must lead us to a closer and fuller sense of awe and worship. It imposes on us a huge responsibility and privilege to live godly lives. The Trinity is a mystery, as Calvin said, more to be adored than investigated. The study of it is *arduous*, for we are dealing with matters too great for us, before which we must bow in worship, recognizing our utter inadequacy. Barth's words are well taken when he writes that "correctness belongs exclusively to that about which we have thought and spoken, not to what we have thought and spoken."[28] Lonergan's reference to "no understanding" has a lot of truth to it, for these are matters beyond our capacity. However, contemplation of the Trinity is also (as Augustine added) *supremely rewarding*, for this is our God, who has truly made himself known to us (to the limits of what we are able to understand), giving himself to us, and thus by the Spirit granting through the Son access to the Father in the unity of his undivided being. This is eternal life, that we may know the Father and his Son Jesus Christ, whom he has sent, in the power and by the grace of the Holy Spirit. In his presence is life and joy forevermore, not simply for us, but for others beyond, for those yet to believe and for those not yet born, for generations to come and beyond that for eternity. Let us persevere, then, through the chapters that follow, amidst the dangers, for the great and wonderful prize of knowing our triune God better.

> *We praise you, O God; we acknowledge you to be the Lord.*
> *All the earth worships you, the Father everlasting.*
> *To you all angels cry aloud,*
> *the Heavens and all the Powers therein.*
> *To you Cherubim and Seraphim continually do cry:*
> > *Holy, holy, holy, Lord God of Sabaoth;*
> > *Heaven and earth are full of the majesty of your glory.*
> *The glorious company of the apostles praise you.*
> *The goodly fellowship of the prophets praise you.*
> *The noble army of martyrs praise you.*
> *The holy Church throughout all the world acknowledges you,*
> > *the Father of an infinite majesty,*
> > *your honourable, true, and only Son,*
> > *also the Holy Spirit the Comforter.*
>
> *You are the King of glory, O Christ.*
> *You are the everlasting Son of the Father.*
> *When you took upon yourself to deliver man,*
> *you did not abhor the Virgin's womb.*

28. Barth, *CD*, I/1: 432.

When you overcame the sharpness of death,
you opened the kingdom of heaven to all believers.
You sit at the right hand of God, in the glory of the Father.
We believe that you shall come to be our judge.[29]

---

29. *Te Deum laudamus* (Morning Prayer), *The Book of Common Prayer of the Church of England* (1662). Personal pronouns and verbal forms have been modernized.

Biblical Foundations

And when Jesus was baptized, immediately he went up from the water, and behold, the heavens were opened to him, and he saw the Spirit of God descending like a dove and coming to rest on him; and behold, a voice from heaven said, "This is my beloved Son, with whom I am well pleased." —Matthew 3:16–17

How much more will the blood of Christ, who through the eternal Spirit offered himself without blemish to God, purify our conscience from dead works to serve the living God. —Hebrews 9:14

If the Spirit of him who raised Jesus from the dead dwells in you, he who raised Christ Jesus from the dead will also give life to your mortal bodies through his Spirit who dwells in you. —Romans 8:11

And Jesus came and said to them, "All authority in heaven and on earth has been given to me. Go therefore and make disciples of all nations, baptizing them in the name of the Father and of the Son and of the Holy Spirit." —Matthew 28:18–19

The grace of the Lord Jesus Christ and the love of God and the fellowship of the Holy Spirit be with you all. —2 Corinthians 13:14

Old Testament Background

God in Genesis 1

"*In the beginning, God created the heavens and the earth.*" It takes the rest of the Bible to disclose the meaning concealed in this cryptic sentence. Even so, the first chapter of Genesis reveals much. It portrays the creation and formation of the world and the ordered shaping of a place for human beings to live. It presents man as the head of creation, in communion with God, his Creator. The act of creation itself is direct and immediate (vv. 1–2), distinct from the work of formation that follows.[1] The result is a cosmos that is formless, empty, dark, and wet—unfit for human habitation. The rest of the chapter describes the world's *formation* (or *distinction*) and *adornment*. God introduces order, light, and dryness, making it fit for life to flourish. First, God creates light and sets boundaries to the darkness (vv. 2–5). Second, he molds the earth into shape, so that it is no longer formless (vv. 6–8, 9–10). Third, God separates the waters and forms dry land, so that it is no longer entirely wet (vv. 9–10). Following this, he populates the earth, ending its emptiness (vv. 20–30), first with fish and birds, then with land animals, and finally, as the apex of the whole, with human beings made in his image. This God is not only almighty, but also a master planner, artist, and architect supreme.

1. Herman Bavinck, *In the Beginning: Foundations of Creation Theology*, ed. John Vriend and John Bolt (Grand Rapids: Baker, 1999), 100ff. See also the discussion in Thomas Aquinas, *ST*, Pt. 1a, Q. 66, art. 1–4 and the entire section QQ. 66–74 in general.

This order is clear from the parallels between the two groups of days, the first three and the second three.[2] On day one God creates light, while on day four he makes the moon and the stars. On day two he separates the waters, making the clouds and the seas, and forms the sky, while on day five he creates birds and fish to live there. On day three he forms the dry ground, and on day six he creates animals and humans, whose native element this will be. He shows his sovereign freedom in naming and blessing his creation, and sees that it is thoroughly good. At the end of it all comes the unfinished seventh day, when God enters his rest that he made to share with man, his partner, whom he created in his own image. Entailed in this is an implicit invitation to follow him.[3]

It is needless to elaborate on this, as it is so generally recognized. Especially striking is God's sovereign and variegated ordering of his creation. In particular, *he forms the earth in a threefold manner*. First, he issues direct fiats. He says, "Let there be light," and there is light (v. 3). By seemingly effortless command, he brings into being the expanse (v. 6), the dry ground (v. 9), the stars (vv. 14–15), and the birds and fish (vv. 20–21). It is enough for him to speak; his edict is fulfilled at once. Second, he works. He separates light from darkness (v. 4). He makes the expanse and separates the waters (v. 7). He makes the two great lights, the sun and the moon (v. 16), setting them in the expanse to give light on the earth (v. 17). He creates the great creatures of the seas and various kinds of bird (v. 21). He makes the beasts of the earth and reptiles (v. 25). Finally he creates man— male and female—in his own image (vv. 26–27). The thought is of focused, purposeful action by God, of divine labor accomplishing his ends. However, there is also a third way of formation, in which God uses the activity of the creatures themselves. God commands the earth to produce vegetation, plants, and trees (vv. 11–12). He requests the lights to govern the day and night (vv. 14–16). He commands the earth to bring forth land animals (v. 24). Here the creatures follow God's instructions and contribute to the eventual out-

2. This pattern was discerned at least as long ago as the thirteenth century. See Robert Grosseteste, *On the Six Days of Creation: A Translation of the Hexaëmeron*, trans. C. F. J. Martin (Oxford: Oxford University Press for the British Academy, 1996), 160–61 (5.1.3–2.1); Aquinas, *ST*, Pt. 1a, Q. 74, art. 1. See my article, "'In the Space of Six days': The Days of Creation from Origen to the Westminster Assembly," *WTJ* 61 (1999): 149–74.

3. Cf. Heb. 3:7–4:11.

come. This God who created the universe does not work in a mono-lithic way. His order is varied—it is threefold, but one. His work shows diversity in its unity, and unity in its diversity. This God loves order and variety together.

This reflects the chapter's record of God himself. The triadic man-ner of the earth's formation reflects the nature of its Creator. He is a relational being. This is implicit from the very start. Notice the dis-tinction between the God who creates the heavens and the earth (v. 1), the Spirit of God who hovers over the face of the waters (v. 2), and the speech or word of God who issues the fiat "Let there be light" (v. 3). Of course, it is unlikely that the author and original readers would have understood the Spirit of God in a personalized way, due to the heavy stress in the OT on the uniqueness of the one God. The Hebrew word *ruach* can mean spirit, wind, or breath. Many commentators understand it to refer to the energy of God—the divine force, the power that creates and sustains life (Driver), an awesome wind (Speiser), a mighty wind (Westermann), God's outgoing energy (Kidner), or the wind of God (Wenham). Wenham is sound when he suggests that this is a vivid image of the Spirit of God.[4] Driver recognizes that this pas-sage prepares for the personal use of the term "Word" in John's gospel and, by the same token, the later NT personalizing of the Spirit of God is a congruent development from this statement.

With the creation of man there is the unique deliberation, "Let us make man in our image," expressing a plurality in God (vv. 26–27). Von Rad comments that this signifies the high point and goal to which all of God's creative activity is directed. But what does it mean? A vari-ety of interpretations have been advanced to explain it. Some suggest that God is addressing the angels and placing himself in the heavenly court, so that man is made like the angels.[5] However, the agents addressed are invited to share in the creation of man, and this power is never attributed to angels elsewhere in the Bible. Second, Driver is one of those who suggest a plural of majesty, a figure of speech under-

4. S. R. Driver, *The Book of Genesis* (London: Methuen, 1926), 4; E. A. Speiser, *Genesis*, Anchor Bible (New York: Doubleday, 1981), 5; Derek Kidner, *Genesis: An Introduction and Commentary* (London: Tyndale Press, 1967), 45; Gordon J. Wenham, *Genesis 1–15*, Word Bib-lical Commentary (Waco, Tex.: Word, 1987), 15–17; Gerhard Von Rad, *Genesis: A Commen-tary*, rev. ed. (Philadelphia: Westminster Press, 1961).
5. Von Rad, *Genesis*, 57–59.

lining God's dignity and greatness.[6] However, this interpretation is no longer as favored as it once was. Among other reasons, plurals of majesty are rarely if ever used with verbs. Third, Westermann and many recent interpreters favor a plural of self-deliberation or self-encouragement. Yet few parallels support this view. Wenham puts forward a variant on the theme of the heavenly court, but he argues that God invites the angels to witness the creation of man, rather than to participate in it. He points to Job 38:4–7, where at creation the morning stars are said to sing together and all the sons of God (angels?) shout for joy.[7]

However, Scripture has a fullness that goes beyond the horizons of the original authors. Many of the Fathers saw in Genesis 1:26 a reference to the Trinity. While this was concealed from the original readers and from the OT saints as a whole, the Fathers were not at variance with the trajectory of the text. Rabbinical commentators were often perplexed by this passage and similar ones suggesting a plurality within God (Gen. 3:22; 11:7; Isa. 6:8). Philo thought they referred to subordinate powers assisting God in the creation of man. Puzzling over these passages, Jewish interpreters tried to see them expressing the unity of God.[8] The NT never refers to Genesis 1:26 with regard to the nature of God, but that does not make it unwarranted to see here a proleptic reference to the Trinity. The NT does not refer to everything, but it does give us the principle that the OT contains in seed form what is more fully made known in the NT. On that basis, we may reread the OT, just as we might reread the early chapters of a detective mystery, looking for clues that we missed the first time, but now are given fresh meaning by our knowledge of what comes later. In other words, in terms of the *sensus plenior* (the fuller sense or meaning) of Scripture, God's words here attest a plurality in God, a plurality later expressed in the doctrine of the Trinity. The original readers would not have grasped this, but we, with the full plot disclosed, can revisit the passage and see the clues there.

I have elsewhere commented on Genesis 1:26–27:

6. Driver, *Genesis*, 14.
7. Wenham, *Genesis 1–15*, 28.
8. Arthur Wainwright, *The Trinity in the New Testament* (London: SPCK, 1963), 23–26.

Man exists as a duality, the one in relation to the other. . . . As for
God himself . . . the context points to his own intrinsic relationality.
The plural occurs on three occasions in v. 26, yet God is also singular in v. 27. God is placed in parallel with man, made in his image as
male and female, who is described both in the singular and plural.
Behind it all is the distinction God/Spirit of God/speech of God in
vv. 1–3. . . . [T]his relationality will in the development of biblical revelation eventually be disclosed as taking the form of a triunity.[9]

I refer there to kindred comments by Karl Barth.[10]

In short, this God who made the universe—establishing an order
with a vast range of variety, with human beings as the crown of his
creation, representing him as his image bearers—is relational. Communion and communication are inherent to his very being. In creating the world, he has made us for himself, to enter into communion
with him in a universe of ravishing beauty and ordered variety. By his
creation of the seventh day, he ceased from his works in contemplation of their ordered beauty and goodness, and invites us to join him.
The first chapter of Genesis says to all who read it that Yahweh, the
God of Israel, the God of Abraham, Isaac, and Jacob, the God of
Moses, is also the Creator of all things. He who made his covenant
with his people Israel is not merely some territorial divinity, but the
one to whom all nations are accountable, for he is their maker. There
is a clear unity between creation and redemption. The mandate in
verses 26–29 to multiply and subdue the earth embraces the whole
creation, and it is also the basic building block for the unfolding structure of salvation after the Fall. Reflecting on this implicitly Trinitarian structure of Genesis 1, Athanasius writes of creation being in
Christ.[11] Since Genesis (no less than any other part of the Bible) is to
be read in the context of the whole of Scripture, we can see references
in the NT to the role of Christ and the Holy Spirit in creation as reinforcing this interpretation (Col. 1:15–20; Heb. 1:3; 11:3; John 1:1ff.).

This vital point is underlined by other—unmistakably poetic—
accounts of creation in the OT. In Psalm 33:6, creation is said to have
originated "by the word of the LORD . . . and by the breath of his

9. Robert Letham, "The Man-Woman Debate: Theological Comment," *WTJ* 52 (1990): 71.
10. Karl Barth, *CD*, III/1: 196.
11. Athanasius, *On the Incarnation* 1, 3, 12, 14 (PG 25:97–102, 115–22).

mouth." In Proverbs 8:22ff., a passage much used and abused in the early church debates, Wisdom is personified and eulogized as sharing with the Lord in the creation of the heavens and the earth. Job acknowledges that the Spirit of God made him (Job 33:4; cf. 26:13), and the psalmist also talks of God's Spirit as Creator (Ps. 104:30). It is impossible to think of creation (*this* creation, *this* multifaceted and coherent creation, the only one we know and the only one there is[12]) coming into existence apart from its maker being relational, and so in accordance with his full revelation as triune, as Bavinck so cogently argues.[13] Bavinck goes even further, arguing that "without generation [the generation of the Son by the Father] creation would not be possible. If in an absolute sense God could not communicate himself to the Son, he would be even less able, in a relative sense, to communicate himself to his creature. If God were not triune, creation would not be possible."[14] This is borne out by hints in the OT of distinction within the unity of the one God.

The Angel of the Lord

In the Pentateuch, there are a good number of passages where the angel of the Lord appears and is identified with God himself. They contain hints of plurality in God. In Genesis 16:7–13, an angel speaks as God, saying to Hagar, "I will surely multiply your offspring," and informing her of the impending birth of Ishmael and of the name he is to have. Hagar replies to the angel, calling the Lord who spoke to her "a God of seeing." Then, in Genesis 21:17–18, the angel again speaks to Hagar about her son, again using the voice of God: "I will make him into a great nation." In Genesis 22:11–18, when Abraham is about to offer Isaac on the altar, the angel of the Lord calls from heaven, making promises in line with the covenant that God has already established. The angel's words here are equivalent to the Lord's words in 12:1–3: "I will surely bless you, and I will surely multiply your offspring." Again, in Genesis 31:10–13, speaking to Jacob, the angel of the Lord identifies himself with the God of Bethel. In Exodus 3:2–6,

---

12. *Pace* theorists of parallel universes, for which there exists no evidence.
13. Bavinck, *In the Beginning*, 39–45.
14. Ibid., 39.

the angel of the Lord appears to Moses in a flame of fire out of the bush, while from the bush itself the Lord sees, speaks, and identifies himself as God.

Later, after the conquest of Canaan, the angel of the Lord in Judges 2:1–5 speaks in the name of Yahweh, saying, "I brought you up from Egypt. . . . I said, 'I will never break my covenant with you.' . . . But you have not obeyed my voice." Appearing to Gideon, the angel of the Lord (Judg. 6:12, 20, 21, 22) *is* the Lord (vv. 14ff., 23–24). Then, when he appears to Samson's parents, Manoah and his wife, in Judges 13:3–23, an angel of the Lord is equated by Manoah's wife at his first showing with a man of God (vv. 3–8), while the second time he is the angel of God, the Lord, and also a man (vv. 9–20). After this, in fearful awe the couple recognize that in seeing the angel of the Lord they have in fact seen God. In each instance, the angel appears as a man, but is simultaneously equated with God. Augustine discusses these matters at length in his great work *De Trinitate*. Here is a figure who is identified with God, yet is distinct from him. As yet in Scripture there is no explanation of how this can be, and the whole series of events is seen in the light of there being only one God.[15]

Theophanies

Closely related to the appearances of the angel of the Lord are those few occasions when God appears in bodily form (theophanies). Most notable is the visit by the three men or angels to Abraham, recorded in Genesis 18 and 19. The Lord appears to Abraham (18:1), yet in front of him stand three men (v. 2). He offers them the usual Semitic hospitality (vv. 3–8), including a meal. Then "the LORD" speaks, in words that only God could utter: "I will surely return to you about this time next year, and Sarah your wife shall have a son" (v. 10). Again, the narrative records that "the LORD" speaks to Abraham (v. 13).

Following this, the men set out, while the Lord speaks (vv. 16–21). The men turn to leave for Sodom, while the Lord speaks to Abraham (vv. 22ff.). Then the Lord leaves and Abraham returns home (v. 33),

---

15. See also Zech. 3:1–10, where the angel of the Lord is not explicitly identified with Yahweh, yet speaks the word of Yahweh.

while the two (no longer three) angels arrive at Sodom (19:1). These two angels announce to Lot that the Lord has sent them to destroy the place (19:13), but after Lot's precarious escape, it is the Lord who destroys it (19:24–25). Here there is a bewildering and continued juxtaposition of men, angels, and the Lord. It is as if boundaries have disappeared. This passage puzzled Augustine, who wondered whether it describes an appearance of the preincarnate Christ, of all three persons of the Trinity, or of angels. The point is that the one God presents himself in a way that poses questions. As Wainwright comments, this "mysterious oscillation" aroused a great deal of discussion among the rabbis, although it was not until Justin Martyr in the second century that Christians began to consider the implications of the incident.[16] However, not until then did the problem of the Trinity begin to emerge, and there were good reasons—rigorous Jewish monotheism and widespread pagan polytheism—why it could not be tackled any earlier.

Joshua's meeting with the commander of the army of the Lord in Joshua 5:13–15 deserves more attention than it has often received. This mysterious figure appears as a man, but is presumably an angel. However, Joshua worships him and is not reproved for it. This is strikingly different from the apostle John's experiences when he worships an angel (Rev. 19:10; 22:8–9), for both times he is sharply rebuked. Moreover, the commander of the Lord's army—and remember that Joshua was precisely that himself—speaks to him in the same language that the Lord used in addressing Moses at the burning bush. Both here and in Genesis, God appears as man, a personal agent speaks as God, and yet he is distinguished from him.

Israel's Rigorous Monotheism

Behind all these episodes is a pervasive monotheism. Israel was time and again taught that there is only one God—Yahweh, who had taken his people into covenant with him. Deuteronomy 6:4–5 was central to Israel's faith: "Hear, O Israel: The LORD our God, the LORD is one. You shall love the LORD your God with all your heart and with

---

16. Wainwright, *Trinity*, 26–29.

all your soul and with all your might." These words, and the whole law of which it is a part, trenchantly repudiate the polytheism of the pagan world. In the immediate context, Canaanite religions were the challenge to Israel, but this impressive declaration includes in its scope all pagan objects of worship mentioned in the historical and prophetic literature.

Israel's history was in many ways a conflict with idols, leading up to the Exile. This lesson is rammed home again and again, but is finally learned only through the painful tragedy of banishment to a far country.[17] Isaiah has many assertions of the uniqueness and sole deity of Yahweh:

> Thus says the LORD, the King of Israel and his Redeemer, the LORD of hosts: I am the first and I am the last; besides me there is no god. Who is like me? Let him proclaim it. Let him declare and set it before me, since I appointed an ancient people. Let them declare what is to come, and what will happen. Fear not, nor be afraid; have I not told you from of old and declared it? And you are my witnesses! "Is there a God besides me? There is no Rock; I know not any." (Isa. 44:6–8)

See also Isaiah 40:9–31; 42:8 and Zechariah 14:9. The creation account of Genesis was itself a powerful counter to the assumption of the ancient Near East that the gods of the nations were territorial deities, presiding over the area in which their devotees lived, but without jurisdiction beyond those boundaries. In this light, the conflict between the great king, Sennacherib the Assyrian, and the prophet Isaiah is crucial. Recorded three times in the OT, it is evidently considered an important example of the universal domain of Yahweh. In the vivid account of the confrontation between Assyria and Judah in 2 Kings 18–19, the central point is the duel between the word of the great king, backed up by all the political and economic muscle and all the military might of the greatest power on earth, and the word of Yahweh, whose human agents are utterly powerless, completely at the great king's mercy. There is simply no contest. The word of Yahweh triumphs with ease!

17. "All idolatrous worship had been abolished by that time." Jules Lebreton, *History of the Dogma of the Trinity: From Its Origins to the Council of Nicaea*, 8th ed., trans. Algar Thorold (London: Burns, Oates and Washbourne, 1939), 74.

It is in the light of this monotheistic faith, rammed home time and time again, that we should view the passages concerning the angel of the Lord and the various hints of distinction within God's being that come to light from time to time in the OT. These incidents were never remotely intended to accommodate the pagan supposition of a plurality of gods. They fitted into a monotheistic framework.

Distinction Within God

In a number of passages, Yahweh addresses Yahweh, not in self-deliberation, but apparently as distinct agents. Psalm 110:1 records: "The LORD says to my Lord: 'Sit at my right hand, until I make your enemies your footstool.'" Here Yahweh addresses a figure whom David calls his "Lord" (*Adonay*). In this enthronement psalm, David the king pays homage to a figure who appears as "more than royal."[18] This Lord receives authority and power greater than David's. He and Yahweh are fully at one. Yahweh's oracle is followed by an oath (v. 4), plus a pledge that he will never change his mind in his decree that the Lord is to be a priest forever according to the order of Melchizedek. This Melchizedek appears in Genesis 14 without any reference to his ancestry, birth, or death—all vital and essential features of the priests in Israel. As an everlasting priest, Melchizedek mediates an everlasting salvation. The psalm points forward to the person and power of Christ, and is cited frequently in the NT, both by Jesus of himself (Mark 12:36 and parallels) and by Peter of Jesus (Acts 2:33–35). The psalm stops short of explicitly identifying David's Lord with Yahweh, but the connection is as close as could be.

Then there is Psalm 45:6-7: "Your throne, O God, is forever and ever. The scepter of your kingdom is a scepter of uprightness; you have loved righteousness and hated wickedness. Therefore God, your God, has anointed you with the oil of gladness beyond your companions." Here, referring to a royal wedding, "royal compliments suddenly blossom into divine honours," and while some scholars attempt to evade the obvious point that the royal figure addressed as God in verse 6 is anointed by God in verse 7, "the Hebrew resists any

18. Derek Kidner, *Psalms 73–150: A Commentary on Books III-V of the Psalms* (London: Inter-Varsity Press, 1975), 392.

softening here."[19] Such language only makes sense in the light of the incarnation of the Son of God, but at the time the psalm was composed, this posed a mystery.

There is also a subtle series of ascriptions in Isaiah 63:8–14, where Israel's checkered past is in view. Yahweh became their deliverer (v. 8), the angel of his presence rescued them (v. 9), he loved, pitied, and carried them (v. 9), but they grieved his holy Spirit, and so he fought against them (v. 10). Then he remembered that he had put his holy Spirit in their midst (v. 11), and so the Spirit of the Lord gave them rest (v. 14). This series of oscillations brings the Spirit of God into rather clear relief, and so R. N. Whybray comments, "God's holy spirit . . . is here personified more clearly than anywhere else in the Old Testament, and is on its way to its later full development as a distinct hypostasis in late Jewish and in Christian thought."[20]

We also note Isaiah 6:3, where the prophet, in his vision of the exalted Yahweh, hears the trisagion "Holy, holy, holy" in the mouths of the seraphim. On the face of it, this is a threefold ascription of praise to God, but on further reflection, in the light of fuller NT revelation, it bears the impress of the three-personed God.

God as Father

While the distinctive covenant name of God, YHWH, occurs nearly seven thousand times in the OT, God calls himself "Father" only just over twenty times. Both the stress on monotheism and the commandment prohibiting images for worship underline God's transcendence over all creaturely comparisons. This helps explain why the name is so rarely used and also why there is an absence of feminine images and metaphors for God.[21] Indeed, the name Father usually refers to the covenantal relationship of Yahweh to Israel (Ex. 4:22–23; Hos. 11:1) and points to God's free choice, not to sexual activity and physical generation.[22] The

19. Derek Kidner, *Psalms 1–72: A Commentary on Books I-II of the Psalms* (London: Inter-Varsity Press, 1973), 170–71.

20. R. N. Whybray, *Isaiah 40–66*, New Century Bible Commentary (Grand Rapids: Eerdmans, 1975), 258.

21. Gerald O'Collins, *The Tripersonal God: Understanding and Interpreting the Trinity* (London: Geoffrey Chapman, 1999), 12.

22. Ibid., 14, 23; Wainwright, *Trinity*, 43.

various gods and goddesses of the ancient world were usually connected with procreation. Israel was hereby taught to avoid thinking of God in physical terms, especially in any terms drawn from human reproduction. Instead, as Father, Yahweh had freely chosen them in the history of salvation. His unconditional promise put him in an entirely different context,[23] that of a loving father, and thus we find "intimate closeness" expressed in, for example, Hosea 11:3–4:[24]

> Yet it was I who taught Ephraim to walk; I took them up by their arms, but they did not know that I healed them. I led them with cords of kindness, with the bands of love, and I became to them as one who eases the yoke on their jaws, and I bent down to them and fed them.

The Spirit of God

The Spirit of God is mentioned nearly four hundred times in the OT. In general, the Spirit is seen as the power of God at work, occasionally as an extension of the divine personality, but for the most part as little more than a divine attribute. Sometimes Hebrew poetic parallelism implies that the Spirit of God is identical to Yahweh (Ps. 139:7), but this simply begs the question, for there is not the slightest hint even here that the Spirit is to be understood as a distinct person. Rather, it is God's divine power or breath,[25] "God's manifest and powerful activity in the world."[26]

Frequently, anthropomorphic language is used. The Spirit has personal characteristics—guiding, instructing, being grieved. The Spirit, or breath, of God gives life (Gen. 1:2; Ps. 33:9; 104:29–30), coming upon the inert bones in Ezekiel's vision to reanimate them (Ezek. 37:8–10). The Spirit of God empowers people for various forms of service in God's kingdom (Num. 27:18; Judg. 3:10; 1 Sam. 16:13; Ex. 31:3; 35:31–34) and is the protector of God's people (Isa. 63:11–12; Hag. 2:5; 1 Sam. 19:20, 23), indwelling them (Num. 27:18; Deut. 34:7; Ezek. 2:2; 3:24; Dan. 4:8–9, 18; 5:11; Mic. 3:8) and resting upon and

23. O'Collins, *Tripersonal God*, 15–18.
24. Ibid., 17, 22.
25. Wainwright, *Trinity*, 30.
26. O'Collins, *Tripersonal God*, 32.

empowering the Messiah (Isa. 11:2–3; 42:1; 61:1). The most remark-able actions of the patriarchs and prophets are due to the Spirit of God, whether they be those of Gideon, Samson, Saul, or Joseph, who is able to interpret dreams because he is full of the Spirit of God (Gen. 41:38). However, there is no evidence that the Spirit was seen as a distinct per-son. In fact, everything points the other way. In view is not the Spirit's nature, but the Spirit's action.[27] Yahweh acts through the Spirit, as Wainwright comments.[28] To have suggested the contrary would have challenged the insistence of Deuteronomy that there is only one God, for no tools existed at that time to distinguish such a putative claim from the pagan polytheism that Israel was bound to reject. The Spirit is the power of God at work—no more than a distinctive attribute.

However, a development in the course of the OT helps pave the way for the Christian teaching. Generally, the Spirit comes only inter-mittently on the prophets and on select persons such as Samson and Saul, and his presence with his people in general is also intermittent (Ps. 51:11). However, later on the Spirit is seen as a permanent pos-session, with an increased focus on his ethical effect in terms of righ-teousness and justice (Isa. 11:2; Zech. 12:10).[29] The Spirit is also linked with the Messiah in three passages (Isa. 11:1–2; 42:1; 61:1), and the Spirit is expected to come as a future gift to all God's people (Joel 2:28ff.; Ezek. 11:19; 36:26; 37:12; Zech. 12:10). Thus, "the develop-ing idea of the Spirit provided a climate in which plurality within the Godhead was conceivable."[30]

At this point, B. B. Warfield's magisterial article, "The Spirit of God in the Old Testament," is important.[31] He considers the work of the Spirit in connection with the cosmos, the kingdom of God, and the individual, concluding that he is at work in the OT in all the ways that he works in the NT. However, there is a difference. What is new in the NT are the miraculous endowments of the apostles and the worldwide mission of the Spirit, promised in the OT, but only now realized. In

---

27. Lebreton, *Trinity*, 88.
28. Wainwright, *Trinity*, 31.
29. Ibid., 32.
30. Ibid., 32–33.
31. Benjamin Breckinridge Warfield, "The Spirit of God in the Old Testament," in *Biblical and Theological Studies*, ed. Samuel G. Craig (Philadelphia: Presbyterian and Reformed, 1952), 127–56.

addition and principally, since the OT was a preparation for the NT, the Spirit simply preserves the people of God in the OT, whereas in the NT he produces "the fruitage and gathering of the harvest."[32] Still, Warfield agrees, there is no evidence that he was considered to be a distinct person in OT times.

The Word and Wisdom of God

After the Exile, God is seen to work through a variety of heavenly figures, with divine attributes and powers—Wisdom and the Word, exalted patriarchs, or principal angels like Michael (Dan. 10:1–12:13). In particular, Wisdom and the Word provide the closest background for the eventual emergence of the doctrine of the Trinity.

Wisdom is mentioned in Job 15:7–8 and 28:12, implying preexistence, but hardly any personal distinction. In Proverbs 8 and 9 are two poems where Wisdom is the chief figure. In Proverbs 8:1ff., Wisdom addresses human beings, promising the same things that God gives.[33] In chapter 9, Wisdom presents herself apparently as a person, but more accurately as "a personified abstraction," in antithetical parallel with folly (v. 13ff). Since folly is merely personalized, the same might apply to Wisdom. However, in the famous section beginning at 8:22, more than metaphor is present, for Wisdom cries aloud, hates and loves, and is portrayed as God's master workman, "an effluence of God's glory" (Wainwright). Wisdom also advises and instructs and is even identified with God, yet also distinguished from him.[34] These themes are repeated in the intertestamental literature. Wisdom has a certain role in creation, is frequently identified with the law, and is also clearly distinguished from God.[35] While not directly connected with the Messiah, the idea of Wisdom is used by Paul and the early Christians to explain who Christ is.[36]

32. Ibid., 155–56.
33. Lebreton, *Trinity*, 91–92; O'Collins, *Tripersonal God*, 24.
34. Lebreton, *Trinity*, 92–94; Wainwright, *Trinity*, 33–34.
35. Lebreton, *Trinity*, 94–98.
36. See James D. G. Dunn, *Christology in the Making: A New Testament Inquiry into the Origins of the Doctrine of the Incarnation* (Philadelphia: Westminster Press, 1980), 163–212.

The psalmist presents the Word of God as active in creation, in parallel with God's Spirit (Ps. 33:6–9). When God communicates to man, he speaks (cf. Ex. 3:4ff.; Ps. 33:6–9). But this Word is never personified in the OT in the way that Wisdom is. It was Philo, under Hellenistic influence in Alexandria, who thought of the Logos in a personalized way.[37] Lebreton suggests that "if these various obscure and elementary conceptions are not sufficient of themselves to constitute a doctrine of the Trinity, they at least prepare the soul for the Christian revelation."[38]

The Expectation of the Coming Messiah

The prophets from time to time held out the prospect of a future deliverer. In fact, Yahweh himself was to come and save his people and bring them to an age of peace and prosperity. The sign that Isaiah gave to King Ahaz was the birth of a son to be called Immanuel (Isa. 7:14), which means "God with us." There is no clear contender for this accolade in Judah's immediate or later history, and since Hebrew children were regularly given names denoting some aspect of the character or action of Yahweh, no extraordinary significance may have been attached to this oracle at that time. However, Isaiah also spoke of a child, a son who would rule, whose dominion was to be of unending peace, security, and justice. This son is evidently portentous. He was to sit on the throne of David and be called, among other things, "Mighty God" (Isa. 9:6). Again, Micah foretells a ruler over Judah, born in Bethlehem, of superhuman origins, "whose origin is from of old, from ancient days" (Mic. 5:2–5a). This ruler is associated with God, but is not identical to him. In Daniel, the majestic figure of the Son of Man (Dan. 7:14) is given universal, everlasting, and impregnable dominion. Jesus was to call himself the Son of Man as his most common self-description. But the exact identity of this figure, presented in Daniel without recourse to any other source, is unclear. Neither the prophet's contemporaries nor later generations grasped the full meaning of these oracles. That was disclosed only by the coming

37. Wainwright, *Trinity*, 35–36; Lebreton, *Trinity*, 99–100.
38. Lebreton, *Trinity*, 81.

of Jesus. Then the NT writers could apply to him the prophetic statements referring to Yahweh.[39]

Summary

While the OT does not make explicit what is revealed by the coming of Christ and the writing of the NT, it does provide the essential foundation without which the full Christian doctrine of God could not exist. As O'Collins puts it, "The OT contains, in anticipation, categories used to express and elaborate the Trinity. To put this point negatively, a theology of the Trinity that ignores or plays down the OT can only be radically deficient,"[40] while from the positive angle "the NT and post-NT Christian language for the tripersonal God flowed from the Jewish Scriptures," for though deeply modified in the light of Jesus' life, death, and resurrection, naming God as Father, Son, and Spirit "found its roots in the OT."[41] This is not to say that by the first century there had emerged in Israel a clear and coherent picture of plurality within the one being of God. This was clearly not the case. These ideas in the OT were scattered and had not formed into anything like a coherent picture.[42] Notwithstanding, the OT provided the means both to distinguish and to hold together the roles of Son/Wisdom/Word and Spirit, since these were vivid personifications, not abstract principles. The ultimate acknowledgement by the church of the triunity of God was "providentially prepared" by these foreshadowings.[43] The OT personalizations helped lay the groundwork for the eventual leap to persons, for "the post-exilic Jews had an idea of plurality within the Godhead" and so "the idea of plurality within unity was already implicit in Jewish theology."[44]

On the other hand, there is no evidence in the OT that the question that the church had to answer had been raised. The problem was that Christ was not a mere emanation from God, and he was more than a personalized concept. He was a man with whom the apostles

---

39. Ibid., 101.
40. O'Collins, *Tripersonal God*, 11.
41. Ibid., 32.
42. Lebreton, *Trinity*, 102–3.
43. O'Collins, *Tripersonal God*, 33–34.
44. Wainwright, *Trinity*, 37.

conversed and with whom they worked. He had a real interaction with God, far more real than theirs. Indeed, they had eavesdropped on "an interaction within the divine personality," "a dialogue within the God-head," of which there is little if any trace in the OT. As Wainwright continues, "The idea of extension of divine personality is Hebraic. The idea of the interaction within the extended personality is neither Hebraic nor Hellenistic but Christian."[45] This is the great leap forward that the NT contains and which the church was to develop.

As so often, Gregory Nazianzen gives us a superbly appropriate summary, ingeniously pointing to the historical outworking of revelation, to explain its cautious, gradual, and progressive unfolding of who God is:

> The Old Testament proclaimed the Father openly, and the Son more obscurely. The New manifested the Son, and suggested the deity of the Spirit. Now the Spirit himself dwells among us, and supplies us with a clearer demonstration of himself. For it was not safe, when the Godhead of the Father was not yet acknowledged, plainly to proclaim the Son; nor when that of the Son was not yet received to burden us further . . . with the Holy Spirit. . . . [I]t was necessary that, increasing little by little, and, as David says, by ascensions from glory to glory, the full splendor of the Trinity should gradually shine forth.[46]

> *We adore the Father, as also his Son, and the Holy Spirit, the Holy Trinity in one Essence, crying with the Seraphim: Holy, holy, holy art thou, O Lord. Now, and ever, and unto ages of ages. Amen.*[47]

45. Ibid., 38–40.
46. Gregory Nazianzen, *Orations* 31.26 (PG 36:161).
47. Matins, *Service Book*, 29.

T W O

Jesus and the Father

Old Testament Expectation Realized

Immediately after the Fall, God cursed the serpent: "I will put enmity between you and the woman, and between your offspring and her offspring; he shall bruise your head, and you shall bruise his heel" (Gen. 3:15). This promised the woman's offspring that one day the damage inflicted by the serpent would be repaired. Eventually, it was fulfilled by Jesus Christ, who was born of a woman and who dealt a mortal blow to the devil. This earliest foreshadowing of the gospel is couched in the language of conquest. The victory was to be won by man (the seed of the woman), by Christ in his obedient and righteous humanity.[1] On the other hand, in the prophets there is a growing insistence that Yahweh himself will come in person to deliver his people. This is in line with a prominent theme in the Psalms that Yahweh alone can save and that it is vain to look to man for salvation (e.g., Ps. 146:1–2). The lesson of both Testaments is that this can only be

---

1. Derek Kidner points to there being good NT authority for seeing here the *protevangelium*, "the first glimmer of the gospel," referring to Col. 2:15; Rom. 16:20; Gal. 3:16; 4:4; Rev. 12:9; 20:2. See Derek Kidner, *Genesis: An Introduction and Commentary* (London: Tyndale Press, 1967), 70–71. Gordon Wenham agrees that, while it is wrong to suggest that this was the author's own understanding, the *sensus plenior* allows it, as was recognized as early as Justin and Irenaeus. See Gordon J. Wenham, *Genesis 1–15*, Word Biblical Commentary (Waco, Tex.: Word, 1987), 79–81. S. R. Driver agrees. See S. R. Driver, *The Book of Genesis* (London: Methuen, 1926), 48.

achieved by God himself living and acting *in* our humanity. Man cannot do it, for it requires greater strength than he could ever muster. Yet God alone cannot do it either! As the Heidelberg Catechism (1563) puts it, since man had sinned, man had to atone for sin. The angel announced the impending birth of Jesus in exactly these terms, telling Joseph to call the child Jesus, meaning "savior." God was bringing salvation through a human child. Yet, since salvation in the OT is consistently the work of Yahweh, this is reinforced with reference to the son foretold by Isaiah, Immanuel, or "God with us" (Matt. 1:21–23).

Towering over all else in the NT is Jesus' resurrection. The Resurrection discloses that Jesus is Lord, and from there the deity of Christ becomes "the supreme truth of the Gospel . . . the central point of reference consistent with the whole sequence of events leading up to and beyond the crucifixion."[2] At the center of the NT message is the unbroken relation between the Son and the Father.[3] It distinguishes the NT witness from intertestamental references to a range of heavenly figures, including the archangel Michael,[4] who carry out Yahweh's purposes.

Jesus and the Father

Father goes from being an occasional designation of God in the OT to his personal name in the NT in relation to Jesus Christ, his Son.[5] Bobrinskoy correctly says that "it is important to emphasize this mutual revelation of the Father and the Son throughout the Gospels, in some sort of reciprocity."[6] The relation between Jesus the Son and God the Father is unique. It is not to be understood on the pattern of human fatherhood. In neither Testament is God sexual, nor does he have a wife or mistress, as did many pagan deities. Human fatherhood derives

2. Thomas F. Torrance, *The Christian Doctrine of God: One Being, Three Persons* (Edinburgh: T & T Clark, 1996), 46; see also p. 52 and Peter Toon, *Our Triune God: A Biblical Portrayal of the Trinity* (Wheaton, Ill.: BridgePoint, 1996), 159.

3. Torrance, *Christian Doctrine of God*, 49.

4. Toon, *Our Triune God*, 114–15. See also the Letter to the Hebrews, where the author proves that Christ is superior to all human, superhuman, and angelic figures.

5. Arthur Wainwright, *The Trinity in the New Testament* (London: SPCK, 1963), 171–95. Paul uses the word *Father* forty times to designate God; John uses *Father* for *theos* ("God") 122 times.

6. Boris Bobrinskoy, *The Mystery of the Trinity: Trinitarian Experience and Vision in the Biblical and Patristic Tradition*, trans. Anthony P. Gythiel (Crestwood, N.Y.: St. Vladimir's Seminary Press, 1999), 64.

from God the Father and is to be measured by him, not vice versa (Eph. 3:15). The Father has a unique relation to the incarnate Son within the being of God. God's revelation as the Father does not refer to his general fatherhood with respect to all his creatures. Moreover, as Toon comments, the name *Father* is not merely a simile (as if God is simply *like* a father) or even a metaphor (an unusual use of language drawing attention to aspects of God's nature in surprising terms), but rather a definite personal name. In contrast, the term *mother*, when used in reference to God in the OT, is a simile, but never a metaphor,[7] and it is completely absent in the NT. *Father* is the proper name for God and does not merely describe what he is like.

Jesus refers to his relation to the Father throughout John's gospel and also in the Synoptics. At an early age, Jesus speaks of the temple, where Yahweh met with his people, as "my Father's house" (Luke 2:49). In turn, at Jesus' baptism the Father declares him to be his Son. The voice from heaven says, "This is my beloved Son, with whom I am well pleased" (Matt. 3:17), a conflation of Psalm 2:7 and Isaiah 42:1. There God the Father sets his seal upon him (John 6:27). When Jesus casts the tradesmen out of the temple, he again calls it "my Father's house" (John 2:16). Worship of God is worship of the Father, he tells the Samaritan woman (John 4:21–24).

Repeatedly Jesus asserts that he was sent into the world by the Father, and that he shares with the Father in giving life, in raising the dead, and in judging the world. These things the Father has given to the Son, and the Son consequently possesses them in himself. He understands what he came to do as having direct reference to the Father. All will honor him, just as all will honor the Father (John 5:23). He seeks nothing other than to do the will of the Father who sent him and to do his works (John 5:30, 36; 6:38–40; 8:16–18, 26, 49), to hear him and pass on what he heard to his disciples (John 15:15). The Father gives him his disciples and draws them to him (John 6:37–65). The Father knows him and loves him, and he fulfills the Father's charge (John 10:15–18).

In turn, Jesus prays to the Father (Matt. 6:9; John 17). "Abba" is his normal way of addressing God (Matt. 16:17; Mark 13:32 and

7. Toon, *Our Triune God*, 145–48.

par.; Luke 22:29–30). This is a familiar form of address, but it does not mean "daddy," as is popularly thought.[8] "Abba" was used by the early Christians in prayer. Paul refers to the practice (Rom. 8:15; Gal. 4:6), and he sees it as flowing from the Holy Spirit's indwelling of believers. This custom stems from Jesus' usual way of addressing God. His followers adopt it because they believe that they share his own natural relation to the Father.

In the garden of Gethsemane and on the cross, Jesus calls on the Father. Both are occasions of gravest crisis. In the garden, he asks the Father—submitting to his will—that the cup he is about to drink might pass from him. On the cross, at the pinnacle of his suffering, he commits his spirit into the Father's hands. Here is a clear distinction between the Son and the Father at the same time and in the same place, and it elicits our worship of the Son as Lord and God (Matt. 26:39–42 and par.; Luke 23:34).[9]

In his great prayer in John 17, Jesus prays to the Father, speaking of the glory he shared with him before creation, and looking forward to the renewal of that same glory (John 17:5, 22–24). He comments that he has completed the work that the Father gave him to do (v. 4). He reflects on the union, the oneness, the mutual indwelling that he has with the Father, and prays that his disciples might share in that union visibly in the world (vv. 20ff.). Earlier he defended his equality and oneness with the Father (John 10:30; 14:6–11, 20), a union so indivisible that his own word will be the criterion that the Father uses on the Day of Judgment (John 5:22–24; 12:44–50). After his resurrection, he tells Mary Magdalene that he will ascend to his Father, only now he can say that his God and Father is the God and Father of all his disciples too (John 20:17; cf. 16:10, 17, 28; 14:1–3). John himself recounts that the Father loves the Son and has given all things into his hand (John 3:35; cf. 16:15). In this, he simply repeats Jesus' own teaching (John 5:20; 15:9).

On the other hand, Jesus also says that he is less than the Father (John 14:28). This is evidently a reference to his incarnation. In becoming flesh, he restricted himself to human limitations. He was self-evidently a man. Later (in chapter 17) we will consider how far this reflects his

8. James Barr, "'Abba Isn't 'Daddy,'" *JTS* 39 (1988): 28–47.
9. Torrance, *Christian Doctrine of God*, 54.

eternal relations with the Father—something beyond the purview of the gospel text. What the Gospels do say is that Jesus the Son does nothing other than what he sees the Father doing (John 5:19). As the Father raises the dead, so the Son gives life to whomever he wills (John 5:21). As the Father has life in himself, so he has given to the Son to have life in himself and to exercise judgment (John 5:26–29). There is a sense in which the Son derives certain things from the Father. Yet, at the same time, Jesus puts this in the context of their indivisible oneness.

Thus, in response to Thomas, Jesus points out that to know him is to know the Father. And to Philip he says, "Whoever has seen me has seen the Father" (John 14:6–9). Behind this are his claims that he and the Father are one (John 10:30), and that he is, with the Father, the object of the disciples' faith (John 14:1). No one can come to the Father except through Jesus. Whoever has seen Jesus has seen the Father (John 14:6–9, 23–24; 15:23–24). Throughout John 14–16, Jesus refers to himself in relation both to the Father and to the Holy Spirit. In particular, he mentions the mutual indwelling of the three (cf. 14:20, "In that day you will know that I am in my Father"). Questions about the deity of Christ are intertwined with those about the Trinity. The Father will send the Holy Spirit at Pentecost in response to Jesus' own request (John 14:16ff., 26; 15:26). So the disciples' prayer to the Father is to be made in the name of Jesus (John 15:16).

In Matthew 11:25–27, Jesus claims mutual knowledge and sovereignty with the Father. H. R. Mackintosh describes this passage as "the most important for Christology in the New Testament," since it speaks of "the unqualified correlation of the Father and the Son."[10] It reads:

> At that time Jesus declared, "I thank you, Father, Lord of heaven and earth, that you have hidden these things from the wise and understanding and revealed them to little children; yes, Father, for such was your gracious will. All things have been handed over to me by my Father, and no one knows the Son except the Father, and no one knows the Father except the Son and anyone to whom the Son chooses to reveal him."

10. H. R. Mackintosh, *The Doctrine of the Person of Jesus Christ* (Edinburgh: T & T Clark, 1912), 27.

Jesus describes himself as "the Son." He shares knowledge and sovereignty with the Father. He thanks the Father for hiding "these things" (the things Jesus did and taught) from the wise, revealing them instead to babes. The Father is, he says, sovereign in revealing himself. However, Jesus immediately claims that he, the Son, has this sovereignty too. To know the Father is a gift given by the Son to whomever *he* chooses. As the Father reveals "these things" concerning the Son to whomever he pleases, so the Son reveals the Father—and "all things" the Father has committed to him—to whomever *he* pleases. Moreover, Jesus shares fully in the comprehensive knowledge of the Father. Only the Father knows the Son, and only the Son knows the Father. Jesus shares fully in the sovereignty of the Father, and his knowledge, like the Father's, is also comprehensive and mutual. On the other hand, in passages such as Matthew 24:36—where, concerning the timing of the *Parousia* (the second coming of Christ), Jesus says that the Son is ignorant of what the Father alone knows—he speaks of the voluntary restrictions that he has accepted in his incarnate state.

In short, Jesus as Son claims a relation to the Father of great personal intimacy, exclusive and unique, which is marked by full and willing obedience to the Father.[11] He is distinct from the Father, and yet one with him. The intimacy is one of "unusual familiarity," and is of intense interest and relevance to his followers. It distinguishes him from the prophets and, in the writings of Paul, entails his participation in God's attributes, sharing in his glory, so that he is "worthy to receive formal veneration with God in Christian assemblies."[12]

Paul, in his important statement about the Son[13] in Romans 1:3–4, distinguishes between the Son of God "of the seed of David according to the flesh" and as he is "appointed Son of God with power by the Holy Spirit since the resurrection of the dead."[14] Superficially it might seem that Jesus began to be the Son of God at the Resurrection, as the

---

11. D. R. Bauer, "Son of God," in *Dictionary of Jesus and the Gospels*, ed. Joel B. Green (Downers Grove, Ill.: InterVarsity Press, 1992), 769–75.

12. L. W. Hurtado, "Son of God," in *Dictionary of Paul and His Letters*, ed. Gerald F. Hawthorne (Downers Grove, Ill.: InterVarsity Press, 1993), 900–906.

13. On Jesus as the Son of God, see Donald Guthrie, *New Testament Theology* (Leicester: Inter-Varsity Press, 1981), 303–21; Richard Bauckham, "The Sonship of the Historical Jesus in Christology," *SJT* 31 (1978): 245–60.

14. My translation.

adoptionists of the early church held, thinking that the man Jesus was elevated to the status of Son as a result of his blameless life. However, both clauses refer to Jesus Christ as God's Son (v. 3). On the one hand, God's Son was descended from David by his incarnation; on the other hand, he was raised from the dead by the Holy Spirit to a new, transformed state—Son of God in or with power. Before the Crucifixion, he existed as God's Son in a condition of weakness, having taken "the form of a slave" (Phil. 2:7 [my translation]), but he was still God's Son. But when he arose from the dead, he was exalted to the right hand of God the Father (Acts 2:33–36; Phil. 2:9–11; Eph. 1:19–23; Col. 1:18; Heb. 1:3–4). He now reigns over the whole universe (Matt. 28:18), directing all things until all his enemies submit (1 Cor. 15:24–26), at which point death will finally be eliminated and he will hand back the kingdom to the Father (1 Cor. 15:24–28). Thus, while Jesus was always the Son, the Resurrection was still a unique and momentous event.

This focus on Jesus' sonship reveals a communion of life and love between the Father and the Son in the being of God—both a distinction and an identity. In Toon's words, "It is in the relation of 'the Father and the Son' and 'the Son and the Father' that the true identity of Jesus is known and salvation is available. To take away the words is also to take away the reality."[15] This biblical focus has important implications.

Jesus' Equality and Identity with God

Wainwright concludes that the evidence "favours the view that Jesus Christ was called God in Christian worship during New Testament times." The problem facing the apostles was to explain this in the context of Jewish monotheism, for "their faith outstripped their reason, and they were able to give joyful utterance to a belief which they felt incapable of expounding."[16] Wainwright is correct that the experience of the infant church was of a work of salvation coming from God, overpoweringly demonstrated in Jesus' resurrection. It was

15. Toon, *Our Triune God*, 171. This is done by feminist theologians in abandoning the vocabulary of Christian Trinitarianism, drawn from the Scriptures, in favor of impersonal epithets such as *creator, redeemer, sanctifier*, or *parent, child, spirit*, or some such human construction.

16. Wainwright, *Trinity*, 68–69; see also 54–72.

expressed in worship. His assessment is sound that the exposition of this great reality was to be a challenging and daunting one.

First, Jesus asserts his identity in the face of opposition from the Jewish leaders. In John 5:16–47, they try to kill him for breaking the Sabbath and for calling God his Father, thereby making himself equal with God. Jesus denies the charge of blasphemy, citing in his support the plurality of witnesses required by Jewish law—John the Baptist, the works given to Jesus by the Father, the Father himself, and the Scriptures all testify to the truth of his testimony. His claim to be equal with God is true, not false. He then turns the tables on his accusers, charging them with failure to believe Moses' testimony concerning him (vv. 45–47).

In John 8:58, Jesus tells his accusers, "Before Abraham was, I am." For his audience, his claim to have lived prior to Abraham is monstrous. Later, they charge him with blasphemy for identifying himself with God, when he says that both he and the Father grant eternal life and preserve his disciples from perishing, for he and the Father are one (John 10:25–39). His opponents threaten to exact the penalty for blasphemy, death by stoning. However, Jesus denies that he is blaspheming, not by withdrawing his claim as false, but by reinforcing it as true (vv. 34–39).

In keeping with this, in John 14:1 Jesus coordinates himself with God as the object of faith—"Believe in God; believe also in me." It is not certain in the original Greek whether he uses imperatives or indicatives here, for *pisteuete* could be either, but this does not affect the point. The context favors two imperatives, but in either case Jesus regards himself as equal with God as the proper object of his disciples' faith. Along the same lines, John refers to him as "God" in John 1:18 at the start of his gospel, and has Thomas confessing him as "my Lord and my God" in John 20:28 at the end—like frames enclosing a picture.

Paul, in Romans 9:5, probably follows John in expressly designating Jesus Christ as "God," although the punctuation of the Greek text has occasioned much discussion. The overwhelming balance of evidence indicates that we have in this verse not an independent doxology addressed to God ("God be blessed forever"), but an ascription of praise and deity to Christ ("Christ, who is God, blessed forever").[17] In Philippians 2:5ff.,

17. See C. E. B. Cranfield, *A Critical and Exegetical Commentary on the Epistle to the Romans*, International Critical Commentary (Edinburgh: T & T Clark, 1979), 464–70; William Sanday, *A Critical and Exegetical Commentary on the Epistle to the Romans*, International Crit-

Paul refers to Christ's preincarnate state, saying that he did not regard his status of being "in the form of God" as something to be exploited for his own advantage, but instead "humbled [*or* emptied] himself."[18] The present participle "being" (*hyparchōn*) denotes continuance, so that Christ's being in the form of God neither ends nor is curtailed by his incarnation, but rather continues. Incidentally, as we shall see later in the book, this attitude of loving self-abasement reflects the character of God. Moreover, this attitude continues, for by his incarnation he adds the form of a servant (humanity) and becomes obedient to death itself, even the death of the cross. Thus, he empties himself by addition, not subtraction, by adding his human nature with all that that entails, not by abandoning his deity. In turn, at his resurrection the incarnate Christ is exalted by the Father to his right hand and is given the name that is above every name, the name of Lord (*kyrios*), the Greek equivalent of Yahweh.[19]

The author of Hebrews, too, in his argument for Christ's supremacy, cites Psalm 45 to establish that the incarnate Son possesses divine status (Heb. 1:8–9). As we saw in chapter 1, this psalm distinguishes God from God. God who occupies the throne is anointed by God. Thus, Hebrews considers that the Son is the anointed and enthroned king who is also God. This is underlined in the rest of the chapter. The Son is the brightness of the Father's glory, the express image of his being. All angels are to worship him. Psalm 102, referring to the Creator of the universe, is applied directly to Christ.[20] As T. F. Torrance puts it, Christ is "not just a sort of *locum tenens*, or a kind of 'double' for God in his absence, but the incarnate presence of *Yahweh*."[21]

---

ical Commentary (Edinburgh: T & T Clark, 1905), 233–38; B. M. Metzger, "The Punctuation of Rom. 9:5," in *Christ and Spirit in the New Testament: Studies in Honour of C. F. D. Moule,* ed. B. Lindars (Cambridge: Cambridge University Press, 1973), 95–112.

18. We shall consider later in the chapter whether Paul has personal preexistence in mind, which has been disputed by James D. G. Dunn. Meanwhile the old but sage words of Lightfoot are worth recalling here: "Though μορφή is not the same as φύσις or οὐσία, yet the possession of the μορφή involves participation in the οὐσία also: for μορφή implies not the external accidents but the essential attributes." See J. B. Lightfoot, *Saint Paul's Epistle to the Philippians: A Revised Text with Introduction, Notes, and Dissertations* (London: Macmillan, 1881), 170. Bobrinskoy comments that μορφή occurs only here in Paul and "implies a way of being that belongs to God and cannot be limited to a form external to the very being of God." Bobrinskoy, *Mystery,* 122.

19. Paul refers to Christ as "the image of the invisible God" in Col. 1:15.

20. See P. E. Hughes, "The Christology of Hebrews," *SwJT* 28 (1985): 19–27.

21. Torrance, *Christian Doctrine of God,* 51.

Paul's characteristic name for Jesus Christ is "Lord" (*kyrios*).[22] This is the Greek word used to transliterate the tetragrammaton, YHWH, the covenant name of God in the OT. In applying it to Jesus Christ, not on an occasional or casual basis, but pervasively, Paul shows that he regards Jesus as having the status of God, fully and without the slightest abridgment. This is particularly clear in Philippians 2:9–11, but it so pervades his letters that the only conclusion possible is that he took it for granted. Moreover, he makes no attempt to explain or defend it. He uses it so unself-consciously that, as Hurtado comments, it must have been regular, everyday currency among the early Christians. Paul's letters are the earliest NT documents, and so this title testifies to belief in the full deity of Jesus Christ from the very beginning of the Christian church, as its basic axiom, not as a point of contention. It was assumed as given in Palestinian Christianity. This, Hurtado points out, is confirmed by the Aramaic acclamation that Paul cites in 1 Corinthians 16:22—*marana' tha'*, "Our Lord, come!" He uses this expression in a Gentile context without any explanation or translation. Jesus Christ is here addressed in a form of corporate, liturgical prayer, with the reverence shown only to God. Moreover, the roots of this prayer are obviously Palestinian, yet widely familiar beyond its original source and quite probably pre-Pauline.[23] This fits well with the thesis of Seyoon Kim that the origins of Paul's gospel go back to the very earliest days of Christianity, a thesis that he has recently defended strongly against his critics, particularly Dunn.[24] Hurtado produces a range of citations where Paul applies the tetragrammaton to Christ through the title *kyrios* "without explanation or justification, suggesting that his readers were already familiar with the term and its connotation."[25] In Witherington's words, referring to John,

22. See Guthrie, *New Testament Theology*, 291–301; Wainwright, *Trinity*, 757–92; Gerald O'Collins, *The Tripersonal God: Understanding and Interpreting the Trinity* (London: Geoffrey Chapman, 1999), 54–59; Jules Lebreton, *History of the Dogma of the Trinity: From Its Origins to the Council of Nicaea*, 8th ed., trans. Algar Thorold (London: Burns, Oates and Washbourne, 1939), 267–80, 303–6; and from an Eastern perspective, Bobrinskoy, *Mystery*, 114ff.

23. L.W. Hurtado, "Lord," in *Dictionary of Paul and His Letters*, ed. Gerald F. Hawthorne (Downers Grove, Ill.: InterVarsity Press, 1993), 560–69.

24. Seyoon Kim, *The Origin of Paul's Gospel* (Grand Rapids: Eerdmans, 1982); Seyoon Kim, *Paul and the New Perspective: Second Thoughts on the Origin of Paul's Gospel* (Grand Rapids: Eerdmans, 2002).

25. Certainly in these passages: Rom. 4:8 (Ps. 32:1–2); 9:28–29 (Isa. 28:22; 1:9); 10:16 (Isa. 53:1); 11:34 (Isa. 40:13); 15:11 (Ps. 117:1); 1 Cor. 3:20 (Ps. 94:11); 2 Cor. 6:17–18 (Isa. 52:11;

he "is willing to predicate of Jesus what he predicates of the Lord God, because he sees them as on the same level."[26]

Jesus' Works as Creator and Judge

In the prologue of his gospel (John 1:1–18), John declares that Jesus Christ is identical with the eternal Word who made all things, who is with God and who is God. Jesus is the Word who became flesh. Not one thing came into existence apart from that Word. The Word, who was "in the beginning" (note the allusion to Genesis 1:1), was "with God" (directed toward God) and indeed "was God." Jehovah's Witnesses point to the absence of a definite article before "God" and argue that John means that the Word is "a god." However, when nominative predicate nouns precede the verb, as is the case here, they normally lack the definite article. The issue is one of Greek syntax. John points to the unity, equality, and distinction of the Word (*logos*) and God (*theos*). He then underlines that the Word is the creator of all things (vv. 3–4), and that he became flesh (v. 14). To cap it all, he is the only begotten God (v. 18).[27]

John's description of Christ as Creator is echoed by Paul in Colossians 1:15–20, where he says that Christ made all things and sustains his creation in being. The author of Hebrews says the same thing in Hebrews 1:1–4, where he says that the Son is the one through whom the world was made and the one who directs it toward his intended goal. In 1 Corinthians 8:6, Paul couples God the Father, "from whom are all things," and the Lord Jesus Christ, "through whom are all things," evidently referring to their respective work in creation. In this light, we can appreciate many incidents in the Gospels. In Matthew 14:22–36, Jesus' walking on water is the action of Yahweh, the God of Israel, described in the OT as the one whose path lies through the waters (Ps. 77:19; Job 9:8). Moreover, Yahweh has the power to calm the raging storm (Job 26:11–14; Pss. 89:9; 107:23–30). Hence, Jesus

---

2 Sam. 7:14); probably in these: Rom. 10:13 (Joel 2:32); 1 Cor. 1:31 (Jer. 9:23–24); 10:26 (Ps. 24:1); 2 Cor. 10:17 (Jer. 9:23–24); and possibly in a range of others. See Hurtado, "Lord," 563.

26. B. Witherington III, "Lord," in *Dictionary of the Later New Testament and Its Developments*, ed. Ralph P. Martin and Peter H. Davids (Downers Grove, Ill.: InterVarsity Press, 1997), 672.

27. Although the manuscript tradition is divided at John 1:18; on Christ as Creator in the NT, see Wainwright, *Trinity*, 130–54.

displays the functions of deity, in sovereign charge of the elements. As a consequence, note the change in the disciples. When they first see Jesus striding across the lake, they are filled with fear and terror (Matt. 14:26). On realizing who he is, and seeing the effects of his command of nature, they declare, "You are the Son of God" (v. 33). It is worth noting that Jesus greets them with the statement "I am" (*egō eimi*), a declaration of deity (v. 27). (The NIV and ESV limply paraphrase this as "It is I.") In addition, there are a host of records of Jesus' miraculous power over sickness and disease, his creation of food to sustain thousands at one sitting, and the like. While the Synoptic Gospels present these as evidence of the coming of the kingdom of God, pointing to Christ's lordship over the world, they also lend support to our general argument here.

In John 5:22–30, Jesus describes himself as the judge at the Last Judgment. The judge of all the world can only be God; therefore, Jesus claims to be equal to and identical with God. He makes this claim in a different form in Matthew 25:31–46, where he uses his characteristic self-description as Son of Man. As the Son of Man in Daniel 7:14 is connected with the final judgment, so Jesus as the Son of Man will decide between the sheep and the goats, judging the nations with righteousness—a Messianic function—and deciding their final and irreversible destiny. In Mark 8:38, he also speaks of himself as the judge. Paul is emphatic about this, connecting Christ's return with the final judgment in 1 Thessalonians 3:13; 5:23 and most emphatically in 2 Thessalonians 1:7–10. We must all appear before the judgment seat of Christ (2 Cor. 5:10).

Jesus as Savior

As we have seen, the OT stresses that deliverance for God's people can only come from Yahweh, not from man.[28] In Psalm 146, Israel is urged, in verses 3, 5–6, "Put not your trust in princes, in a son of man, in whom there is no salvation. . . . Blessed is he whose help is the God of Jacob, whose hope is in the LORD his God, who made heaven and earth, the sea, and all that is in them." The name *Jesus*, which the

---

28. See ibid., 155–70, on Christ as Savior.

angel told Joseph to call Mary's son, means "savior." He was to save his people from their sins (Matt. 1:21). Jesus' healings, including resurrections, demonstrate him to be the Lord of life, for he is life itself. The cumulative impact of his creative and healing miracles points to deliverance from all that enslaves. T. F. Torrance correctly and forcibly describes Jesus' whole ministry as anticipating and demanding the Resurrection. Beyond that, his work expressly delivers from sin and death.[29] Since salvation is a work of God himself, the apostle Paul's consistent description of Jesus as Savior implicitly attributes deity to him (Titus 2:11–13; cf. Titus 1:4; 3:6; Phil. 3:20; 2 Tim. 1:10; for Peter, see 2 Peter 1:11). Moreover, in Titus 2:11–13 Paul expressly calls Jesus Christ "our great God and Savior." Peter also calls him both "God" and "Savior" in 2 Peter 1:1.

Worship of Jesus

Following all this, a number of NT passages express praise to Jesus Christ. They have in common a strongly hymnic meter. Whether composed by the writer or borrowed from existing church use, they indicate Christ to be an object of worship in the early church. In view of the strict monotheism impressed on Israel, this entails the recognition that Jesus Christ is one with God. These passages all focus on Jesus' significance and his saving work. Into this category come, for example, John 1:1–18, Hebrews 1:3–4, Colossians 1:15–20, Philippians 2:5–11, and 2 Timothy 2:11–13. However, James Dunn argues that these passages are *about* Jesus, rather than addressed *to* him, and that only in the book of Revelation (e.g., Rev. 5:8–10) do we find hymns explicitly addressed to him.[30] This may be so, but the way Jesus is described in the passages about which Dunn expresses reserve requires that hymns be addressed to him. Moreover, since they assume wide, if not universal, agreement in the church, there is good reason to believe that the hymns in Revelation were based on a practice already in existence. In addition, the close link in Revelation between the strug-

29. See Robert Letham, *The Work of Christ* (Leicester: Inter-Varsity Press, 1993), esp. chaps. 7, 10, and 11.
30. James D. G. Dunn, *The Partings of the Ways: Between Christianity and Judaism and Their Significance for the Character of Christianity* (Philadelphia: Trinity Press International, 1991).

gling churches in Asia Minor and the church triumphant around the throne of God in heaven assumes a correlation between heavenly and earthly worship. Wainwright lists a number of NT doxologies addressed to Christ, two of which he considers "clear examples" (2 Peter 3:18; Rev. 1:5b–6) and two very probable (Rom. 9:5; 2 Tim. 4:18).[31]

Prayer is also offered to Christ. Stephen calls out to the Lord Jesus as he is being stoned to death (Acts 7:59–60). His cry, "Lord Jesus, receive my spirit," parallels Jesus' own words, "Father, into your hands I commit my spirit!" which Luke also records in Luke 23:46. The Lord Jesus is the one on whom to call in prayer at the point of death every bit as much as the Father is. Paul also prays to the Lord (as we saw, his usual title for the risen Christ) that his thorn in the flesh be removed (2 Cor. 12:8–9). He refers to an apparently common cry, "Our Lord, come!" (1 Cor. 16:22; cf. Rev. 22:20). It is striking that this is an Aramaic phrase (*marana' tha'*), originating in Palestine, since Corinth was Greek speaking. Paul cites it without comment, assuming it to be common coinage, known to all without need for translation or explanation. This shows that the phrase originated in the very earliest days after the Resurrection. Jesus was recognized as Lord, equal in status to Yahweh, right from the start. Moreover, Paul also appeals to both "our God and Father" and "our Lord Jesus" to direct his way, so that he can return to Thessalonica (1 Thess. 3:11–12). At his conversion, he called on the name of the Lord Jesus (Acts 9:14, 21; 22:16), following the OT phrase, "calling on the name of Yahweh," which implies Jesus' identical status with God. He also declares salvation to consist of confessing Jesus Christ as *kyrios* (Lord or Yahweh) in Romans 10:9–13, 1 Corinthians 12:1–3, and Philippians 2:9–11, probably in a context of public Christian worship. While there is evidence that in first-century Judaism prayers were offered to angels as intermediaries, these prayers are all made to Christ in his own right and distinguish him clearly from any intermediate beings, placing him on the same level as the Father.[32] In turn, prophecy is received from the exalted Christ concerning his churches in Asia Minor (Rev. 1:17–3:22).

31. Wainwright, *Trinity*, 93–97.
32. See ibid., 100–101.

Jesus' Preexistence

Based on our discussion so far, we must revise the consensus, held until recently, that belief in Christ's personal preexistence was a gradual development, crystallizing only relatively late in the composition of the NT. Certainly the later NT contains much material along these lines. In Hebrews 1:3–4, the Son is said to be "the radiance of the glory of God." In the same chapter, the author cites Psalm 45:6–7, God's address to his Son as God, and applies it to Christ as the Son. Peter says that Christ existed *with* God before the creation, not merely in the mind of God (1 Peter 1:20). 1 John 1:1–4 is a passage not without ambiguity, but in the end it clearly refers to Jesus Christ. The exalted Christ is depicted in Revelation 1:17 as the first and the last, implying pretemporal existence, while the similar statement in 22:13 links protology and eschatology. Revelation 3:14 points to Christ as the origin or cause of creation.[33]

Typical of this consensus is James D. G. Dunn. Dunn argues that a full view of Christ's personal preexistence is not found in Paul, but only in Hebrews and John, which he regards as significantly later documents. In particular, he argues, the *locus classicus*, Philippians 2:5ff., does not refer to the claimed pretemporal existence of Christ at all. Paul here contrasts Christ with Adam. Adam wanted to be like God and, in self-assertiveness, grasped the prize of the forbidden fruit. In utter contrast, Christ refused to act like this. Dunn concludes that since Paul compares Christ with the temporal Adam, there is no need to seek any pretemporal reference in the passage.[34] Opposed to Dunn is Kim, who considers Paul to be the author of the teaching of preexistence.[35] Martin also favors the claim that Paul teaches pre-existence here.[36] Hurtado points out that, while Dunn makes some evocative points, it is a logical fallacy to assume that even if Paul refers to Adam, preexistence is thereby precluded. Moreover, he claims that the Adamic reference is not explicit, and points out that the majority of exegetes hold that preexistence is in view.[37] Dunn

---

33. D. B. Capes, "Pre-Existence," in *Dictionary of the Later New Testament and Its Developments*, ed. Martin and Davids, 955–61.

34. James D. G. Dunn, *Christology in the Making: A New Testament Inquiry into the Origins of the Doctrine of the Incarnation* (Philadelphia: Westminster Press, 1980), 117ff.

35. Kim, *Origin*.

36. Ralph Martin, *Philippians*, New Century Bible (Grand Rapids: Eerdmans, 1980), 94–96.

37. L. W. Hurtado, "Pre-Existence," in *Dictionary of Paul and His Letters*, ed. Hawthorne, 743–46.

fails to do justice to the force of the language, Hurtado comments. The remarkable conclusion that follows Hurtado's evaluation is that, if this passage is an early Christian hymn, as is commonly supposed and as is probable, then most likely its liturgical use was widespread. It follows that its teaching was widely accepted a considerable time before Paul wrote Philippians. Thus, Hurtado concludes that belief in Christ's preexistence originated "remarkably early" and was "an uncontested and familiar view of Christ in Paul's churches."[38]

This puts other Pauline passages in a different light. With the evaporation of Dunn's argument, statements such as Paul's in Romans 8:3 and Galatians 4:4 can be seen afresh to refer to the coming of the *preexistent* Christ for our salvation. Together with the great prologue to the gospel of John and the exalted introduction to Hebrews, they reflect a belief that was present in the church from the very start, that Jesus' birth at Bethlehem was the coming into the world of God the Son as man. Paul was not foisting a novelty on the church, but giving voice, clarity, and development to what it already believed.

Conclusion

These developments are crucial for the Christian doctrine of God. In Lebreton's words,

> they show us very clearly that, in all the theses presented by the Christian religion from the very first days, there was something new and something traditional; the belief in Christ, the worship of Christ appear in the foreground, and yet the ancient faith in Jahve is not supplanted by this new belief, nor is it transformed into it, nor placed side by side with it; Christian worship is not addressed to two Gods or to two Lords, and yet it is offered, with the same confidence and the same love to Jesus and his Father.[39]

Again he writes:

> The two terms of θεός and κύριος are to him [Paul] equally divine names. . . . [T]hey have, moreover, become personal names, indi-

38. Ibid., 746.
39. Lebreton, *Trinity*, 277.

cating respectively the Father and the Son. . . . This definite attribution was not the work of a single day or of a single man. . . . This usage, however, was never so exclusive that the name of Lord was not sometimes given to the Father, and the name of God to the Son.[40]

Hurtado argues that the treatment of Christ as an object of worship began in Jewish-Christian circles within the earliest years of the Christian movement, a development "almost explosively rapid in the first few years." Consequently, "elaborate theories of identifiable stages of Christological development leading up to a divine status accorded to Christ are refuted by the evidence."[41]

As T. F. Torrance says, we rely for our belief in the deity of Christ not on various incidents recorded in the Gospels or on particular biblical texts, but

upon the whole coherent evangelical structure of historical divine revelation given in the New Testament Scriptures. It is when we indwell it, meditate upon it, tune into it, penetrate inside it, and absorb it in ourselves, and find the very foundations of our life and thought changing under the creative and saving impact of Christ, and are saved by Christ and personally reconciled to God in Christ, that we believe in him as Lord and God.[42]

Consequently, Torrance continues, we pray to Jesus as Lord, worship him, and sing praises to him as God.

The evidence is overwhelming. We could go on and on. It is no wonder that Thomas, confronted with the tangible evidence of Jesus' resurrection, could say in response, "My Lord and my God!" (John 20:28). As Josiah Conder wrote:

Thou art the everlasting Word, the Father's only Son;
God manifestly seen and heard, and heaven's beloved one:
Worthy, O lamb of God, art thou that every knee to thee should bow.

40. Ibid., 278.
41. L. W. Hurtado, "Christology," in *Dictionary of the Later New Testament and Its Developments,* ed. Martin and Davids, 178–79.
42. Torrance, *Christian Doctrine of God,* 53.

In thee most perfectly expressed the Father's glories shine;
of the full deity possessed, eternally divine:
Worthy, O lamb of God, art thou that every knee to thee should bow.

In the words of the Syrian Antiochene Orthodox liturgy for Epiphany, Antiphon III, Tone I:

When in Jordan thou wast baptized, O Lord, the worship of the Trinity was made manifest. For the voice of the Father bare witness unto thee, calling thee his beloved Son, and the Spirit, in the form of a dove, confirmed the steadfastness of that word. O Christ our God, who didst manifest thyself, and dost enlighten the world, glory to thee.[43]

43. *Service Book,* 188.

The Holy Spirit and Triadic Patterns

Explicit Binitarianism and Implicit Trinitarianism

The early church was characterized by the way it regarded Jesus Christ. In the NT, he is given the devotional attention reserved in the OT for Yahweh alone. However, in no sense did the church see this as conflicting with OT worship. Nor was it thought of as in any sense polytheistic. The church understood its worship of Jesus as within the boundaries of OT monotheism. This worship began at a very early stage of the church's existence. Hurtado sees it less as a development from OT monotheism and more as a mutation resulting from the life and ministry of Jesus, his resurrection, and Jewish opposition that forced the church to articulate its distinctive beliefs about him. Hurtado detects a basic binitarianism in the NT.[1]

There is little doubt that the explicit focus of worship was binitarian. The overwhelming significance of Jesus Christ and the impact of his resurrection brought into focus a unified concentration of worship of God the Father and the Lord Jesus Christ. This is clearly evident in the NT. Paul's customary greetings follow this pattern: "in the name of God the Father and Jesus Christ our Lord" (Rom. 1:1, 7; 1 Cor. 1:1–3; 2 Cor. 1:1–2; Gal. 1:1–5; Eph. 1:1–2; Phil. 1:1–2; Col. 1:1–2; 1 Thess. 1:1; 2 Thess. 1:1–2; 1 Tim. 1:1–2; 2 Tim. 1:1–2; Titus 1:4; Philem. 3). He thanks God through Jesus Christ (Rom. 1:9) or

---

1. Larry W. Hurtado, *One God, One Lord: Early Christian Devotion and Ancient Jewish Monotheism* (Philadelphia: Fortress, 1988).

through Jesus Christ our Lord (Rom. 7:25; 16:27). From a slightly different angle, he says that the fruit of righteousness comes to God through Jesus Christ (Phil. 1:11), where Christ is an intermediary between Christians and the Father. It is not entirely clear in this passage whether Paul considers Christ simply as a man, in the sense of 1 Timothy 2:5, where he refers to the one mediator between God and man, *the man* Christ Jesus. It is in this light that he writes of the righteousness of God being given to us through the faithfulness of Jesus Christ (Rom. 3:21–22), where the obedience of Christ on our behalf in submitting to God's law as man is the ground of our salvation. From this we are justified by God's grace through faith in the redemption that is in Jesus Christ (Rom. 3:23–24).

More obviously indicative of Christ's divine status are Paul's comments that God has reconciled us to himself through or in Christ (2 Cor. 5:16–21), that the grace of God has been given to us in Jesus Christ (1 Cor. 1:4), and that the glory of God has shone on us in Christ (2 Cor. 4:6)—this latter passage self-consciously reflecting on the work of God in creation, when he said, "Let there be light." Our justification is based on God having raised Jesus our Lord from the dead (Rom. 4:24–25; 6:4; 10:9), so that we have peace with God through our Lord Jesus Christ (Rom. 5:1) and are now alive to God in Jesus Christ (Rom. 6:11, 23). God leads the apostles in triumph in Christ (2 Cor. 2:14–17). God called us into the fellowship of his Son, Jesus Christ our Lord (1 Cor. 1:9). Grace is mediated to us by the Lord Jesus (1 Cor. 16:22–24), since Christ dwells in us (Col. 1:27).

Christ is God (Rom. 9:5). Jesus is Lord (Rom. 10:9, 12–13; 14:5–9; 2 Cor. 4:5; 12:8–10; Phil. 2:9–11 [expressly after the Resurrection]; Col. 2:6; 1 Tim. 6:3; Titus 2:13 [where he is called God and Savior]; Heb. 1:3–14). Christ is the image of God (2 Cor. 4:4; Col. 1:15), in the form of God (Phil. 2:5). The fullness of God dwells in him (Col. 1:19; 2:9). He is in God (Col. 3:3). God and Christ are often coupled together (2 Cor. 10:4–6; Col. 2:2; 1 Tim. 5:21; 2 Tim. 4:1; Heb. 13:20), as is the Lord Jesus Christ with our God and Father (Rom. 15:5–7, 8; 1 Cor. 8:6;[2] 2 Cor. 1:3; 11:31; Eph. 1:3; Col. 1:3; 1 Thess. 3:11, 13; 5:23; 2 Thess. 1:5–10; 2:16; 3:5).

---

2. On this passage, see Paul A. Rainbow, "Monotheism and Christology in 1 Corinthians 8:4–6" (D.Phil. thesis, University of Oxford, 1987).

In another vein, God is the head of Christ (1 Cor. 11:3), where Paul may refer to the incarnate Christ during his earthly ministry. At the consummation of his mediatorial kingdom, Christ the Lord will deliver the kingdom to God the Father (1 Cor. 15:24–28). Meanwhile our confession of Jesus as Lord is to the glory of God the Father (Phil. 2:11).

Outside the writings of Paul, a similar pattern is clear, with differing nuances. James brings together God and the Lord Jesus Christ in his greeting (James 1:1). Peter connects the Father, Christ, and God (1 Peter 1:17–21), God and Christ (1 Peter 5:10), God and the Savior (2 Peter 1:1), and God and Jesus our Lord (2 Peter 1:2). In all these passages, and the ones from Paul, reference to God is specifically to the Father, and the title "Lord" is reserved for Christ the Son. On the other hand, John, in his letters, sticks to the terms that Jesus used. He distinguishes between the Father/God and the Son/Jesus Christ (1 John 1:1–2:1), the Father and the Son (1 John 2:22–24), and God and his Son (1 John 5:20). In 2 John, he speaks of God the Father and Jesus Christ, the Father's Son (2 John 3), or of the Father and the Son (2 John 9). Jude's preference is for God the Father and Jesus Christ (Jude 1), or God and the Lord Jesus Christ (Jude 4), while he addresses his doxology to God our Savior through Jesus Christ our Lord (Jude 24–25).

All these patterns bespeak a binitarian frame of reference. There is no mention of the Holy Spirit in any of them. On the surface, it might appear that the church is strongly biased toward binitarianism. However, this pattern emerges out of a gradually developing revelation of God in the OT, reaching its climax in his incarnate revelation in Jesus Christ. God appeared *as man*, in a form and a manner that humans could appreciate. The status of the risen Christ is clearly at the center of the church's attention. In a moment, we shall see that this is fully in line with the activity of the Holy Spirit, who does not draw attention to himself, but to Christ. At this point, we can find help from the epistemology of Michael Polanyi. Polanyi points out that human knowledge operates at different levels. At the most basic level, we know things that we are as yet unable to articulate. This he calls tacit knowledge.[3] If knowledge were confined to what could be explained, it would

---

3. Michael Polanyi, *The Tacit Dimension* (Chicago: University of Chicago Press, 1958).

be impossible to search for fresh knowledge. Either we would know and could explain a matter and would not need to search for it, or we could not explain something and so could not know it and could not even know how to go about searching for it. In our present case, following Polanyi's important insight, there may be more than meets the eye when we consider the church's new understanding of God. This finds further support when we recall not only the focus of the Holy Spirit's work, but also his invisible nature, belonging to a realm alien to our physicality. Moreover, the Spirit did not become incarnate, and his ministry is basically in the background. Jesus had been with the apostles as a human being, whereas the Spirit had not.

Toon agrees with Hurtado that the earliest Christian confession may have been binitarian, but he also contends that underlying it was a basic Trinitarian consciousness, something Hurtado's thesis does not exclude.[4] In chapter 2, we saw that the deity of Christ is crucial for the NT. However, explicit awareness of the status and role of the Holy Spirit is not on the surface to the same extent, since he is "invisible and anonymous."[5] Nonetheless, this awareness is still there. Toon cites the striking statistic that while the Hebrew *ruach* is used roughly 90 times for the Spirit of God in the entire OT, Paul alone uses *pneuma* for the Holy Spirit 115 times in his letters, which occupy only a small fraction of the space taken up by the OT. Toon correctly concludes that the Holy Spirit was a real and present reality in the lives of Paul and the early Christians.[6] It is self-evident that Pentecost was a momentous event for the church. The presence of the Spirit is overwhelmingly clear in Acts. The church is not as yet a developed institution in the modern sense. Its power is not human direction or bureaucratic efficiency (if there is such a thing), but the overwhelming power of the Holy Spirit. Toon concludes that "an explicit binitarianism and an implicit trinitarianism can therefore be seen to belong to the same Faith. For only a dogmatic binitarianism denies a trinitarian consciousness and an implicit trinitarianism."[7]

---

4. Peter Toon, *Our Triune God: A Biblical Portrayal of the Trinity* (Wheaton, Ill.: Bridge-Point, 1996), 117ff.
5. Ibid., 122.
6. Ibid., 123.
7. Ibid., 125. Note that Toon is commenting on the NT and does not himself advocate merely an implicit Trinitarianism.

The Holy Spirit

Due to the invisibility and anonymity of the Spirit, his presence is not normally noted, even though it may be known that he is present. His presence is known by what he does. Even so, there is a vast increase in references to the Holy Spirit in the NT, compared with the OT. The Holy Spirit is mentioned more times by Paul than in the entire OT. The NT, while never explicitly calling the Holy Spirit "God," ascribes to him divine characteristics. Among other things, fellowship with one another, and with the Father and the Son, is by the Holy Spirit. The Spirit sanctifies, gives joy in sufferings, opens people's minds to believe, enables us to worship, and brings about union with Christ.

The NT portrays the Holy Spirit as active at every stage of redemption, especially in the life and ministry of Jesus Christ, from conception to ascension.[8] Jesus is conceived by the Holy Spirit. An angel of the Lord tells Joseph that Mary's shocking pregnancy is the result of the work of the Spirit (Matt. 1:20). More expansively, Gabriel informs Mary that "the Holy Spirit will come upon you, and the power of the Most High will overshadow you; therefore the child to be born will be called holy—the Son of God" (Luke 1:35). The angel compares the Spirit's role in Jesus' conception to his work in creation, where he brooded over the primeval waters (Gen. 1:2). Jesus was to be the author of a new creation, begun, as the first, through the overshadowing action of the Spirit of God. In turn, the holiness of the child is the result of his conception by the Holy Spirit.

In Luke's account, the Holy Spirit surrounds the events at the Nativity. Bobrinskoy writes of "an exceptional convergence between the outpouring of the Spirit and the birth of Christ." Indeed, the Holy Spirit is "the Spirit of the incarnation, the One in whom and through whom the Word of God breaks into history."[9] When Mary visits her

8. On the Holy Spirit in the NT, see Donald Guthrie, *New Testament Theology* (Leicester: Inter-Varsity Press, 1981), 510–72; Jules Lebreton, *History of the Dogma of the Trinity: From Its Origins to the Council of Nicaea*, 8th ed., trans. Algar Thorold (London: Burns, Oates and Washbourne, 1939), 252–58, 280–84, 314–31, 352–54, 398–407; Arthur Wainwright, *The Trinity in the New Testament* (London: SPCK, 1963), 199–234; Toon, *Our Triune God*, 175–94; Boris Bobrinskoy, *The Mystery of the Trinity: Trinitarian Experience and Vision in the Biblical and Patristic Tradition*, trans. Anthony P. Gythiel (Crestwood, N.Y.: St. Vladimir's Seminary Press, 1999), 95–136.
9. Bobrinskoy, *Mystery*, 87.

cousin, Elizabeth is filled with the Holy Spirit and her baby leaps for joy in her womb (Luke 1:41–44). Elizabeth's husband, Zechariah, is also filled with the Holy Spirit when he prophesies concerning his son, John the Baptist (Luke 1:67ff.). After Jesus' birth, when his parents take him to the temple for the ritual of purification, the Holy Spirit is upon Simeon as he receives them. Simeon had been informed in advance by the Spirit that he would see the Christ in person and on that day he entered the temple "in the Spirit" (Luke 2:25–28).

Later, at the outset of Jesus' public ministry, the Holy Spirit pervades all that happens. John the Baptist announces that the one who is to come will baptize "with the Holy Spirit and with fire" (Luke 3:16). At Jesus' baptism, the Spirit descends on him in the form of a dove (Luke 3:22 and par.; John 1:32–33). Bobrinskoy calls this "a revelation of the eternal movement of the Spirit of the Father who remains in the Son from all eternity." The Savior's entire being is defined "in a constant, existential relation with the Father in the Spirit."[10] The descent of the dove manifests the eternal rest of the Spirit on the Son.[11] Jesus returns from the Jordan "full of the Holy Spirit" and is led by the Spirit into the wilderness to be tempted by the devil (Luke 4:1). After this great ordeal, which is self-evidently under the direction of the Spirit of God, Jesus returns to Galilee "in the power of the Spirit" (Luke 4:14). There in the synagogue of Nazareth he reads a passage from the prophet Isaiah that refers to the Spirit of the Lord resting on the Messiah for his work (Luke 4:16–19), and he declares that this is now fulfilled in him (v. 21). Luke is telling his readers that Jesus himself was governed and directed by the Holy Spirit in all that he did. His ministry as the Christ, the Anointed One, was empowered by the Spirit. Behind that, Jesus from his earliest days was in all his human development (cf. Luke 2:40–52) under the immediate leading of the Spirit.

All this does not of itself establish that the Holy Spirit is a third person in addition to the Father and the Son. There are obvious circumstantial reasons for leading us in that direction, but they stop short of direct proof at this point. His divine status becomes clearer when we examine Jesus' teaching in John 14–16 on the coming of the Holy Spirit at Pentecost, where he links the Spirit expressly with the Father

10. Ibid., 88, 91.
11. Ibid., 94, 99.

and the Son, entailing identity of status and consequently of being. Here he calls the Spirit "another *paraclētos* (paraclete)" (John 14:16)— another like himself. The word *paraclētos* has often been translated as "comforter" or "counselor" here (the ESV prefers "Helper"), but there is no one word in English that accurately captures its meaning. It refers to someone like a defense attorney, one who speaks on our behalf in opposition to an accuser, represented by the *diabolos* (devil).[12] Jesus' comments here bring the Spirit into the closest possible conjunction with the Father and the Son. The Father will send the Spirit in response to the Son's request (John 14:16, 26). Jesus identifies the Spirit's coming with his, for it is as if Jesus himself is to come in person (John 14:18). This reminds us of John's earlier comment that the Spirit can come only when Jesus has been glorified (John 7:37–39; cf. 16:7). When the Spirit comes, he will enable the disciples to know and recognize the mutual indwelling of the Father and the Son (John 14:20). The Spirit's coming to those who love Jesus is the equivalent of the Father and the Son coming (John 14:21, 23). The Holy Spirit will bring to the disciples' minds all that Jesus has said to them (John 14:26). So close is the connection here that Jesus can say that the presence of the Holy Spirit is interchangeable with that of the Father and the Son.

This interchangeability is also clear when Jesus says that it is he who sends the Holy Spirit from the Father (John 15:26; cf. 16:7), rather than the Father sending the Spirit in response to his request. Later, Jesus will breathe the Spirit on his disciples, commissioning them to go into the world as the Father sent him into the world (John 20:21–23). In the earlier utterance, Jesus also refers to the Spirit proceeding from the Father. This is distinct from his impending coming at Pentecost, for it is a continuous procession (present tense). In view of this close—inseparable—union in working, one of the tasks that the Spirit will perform after Pentecost is to convince the world of sin, righteousness, and judgment (John 16:8–11). Each of these results is seen in connection with the Father and the Son. The Spirit convicts the world of sin because it does not believe in the Son. His ministry is to speak of the Son and, in so doing, to expose resistance and opposition where it occurs, thus displaying the nature of sin as unbelief in the Son

12. Bertrand de Margerie, *The Christian Trinity in History*, ed. Edmund J. Fortman (Petersham, Mass.: St. Bede's Publications, 1982), 32–34.

of God. He also convicts the world of righteousness, seen in the Son going to the Father. This refers to the resurrection, ascension, and glorification of Jesus Christ the Son, and the correlative approval and vindication given him by the Father. Only one whose status is identical to that of the Father and the Son could ever do that. Finally, the judgment facing the world following the judgment of the ruler of the world cannot be detached from the Father or the Son. John has already spoken of the prince of this world being cast out in connection with the cross of Jesus (John 12:31–32). The ruler of this world, the world in rebellion against God, the world that refused to receive the Word made flesh (John 1:9–14), the world for which the Father gave his only begotten Son (John 3:16), has been dethroned. Jesus the Son has done it by his cross. God the Father has shown his immeasurable love for this wicked world by giving his Son. Yet the world faces judgment if it continues to be impenitent. And of this the Holy Spirit convicts it.

He is thus "the Spirit of truth" (John 16:12–15). He would guide the apostles into all truth. He would teach them what Jesus could not teach them, since they were as yet unable to understand. He was not to teach his own things, but those he heard from the Father concerning the Son. "He will glorify me, for he will take what is mine and declare it to you. All that the Father has is mine; therefore I said that he will take what is mine and declare it to you" (vv. 14–15).

This identity Jesus makes explicit in his final instructions to the apostles before his ascension (Matt. 28:18–20). The Great Commission includes his instructions on baptism. Baptism in particular, and the ministry of the church in general, are to be integral to the spread of the kingdom of God in the ages to follow. Thus, the church is to make disciples in all the nations, beginning with baptism. This baptism is to be "into the name of the Father, and of the Son, and of the Holy Spirit" (my translation). Behind this statement lies the fact that at every stage of the outworking of God's covenant, he names himself. In the Abrahamic covenant, he names himself El Shaddai, "God Almighty" (Gen. 17:1). In the Mosaic covenant, he reveals his name Ehyeh, "I Will Be Who I Will Be" (Ex. 3:14; cf. 6:3). Matthew shows how Jesus fulfilled all the successive covenants that God made. He brought into effect the new covenant promised through the prophets (Matt. 26:27–29). Not only Israel, but all nations, participate in this through faith (cf. Matt. 8:11–12). Hence, in this ultimate, climactic revelation of the new covenant in Christ, God reveals his covenant name in its fullness, the *one* name of the Father, the Son, and the Holy Spirit. The Spirit is on an equal footing with the Father and the Son. Moreover, the Spirit shares in the one being of God. Thus the Spirit is not only equal to, but of an identity with, the Father and the Son.

Paul also refers to the Holy Spirit in the same breath as the Father and the Son, and thus as God. In writing of the gifts of the Spirit, he refers to "the same Spirit," "the same Lord," and "the same God" (1 Cor. 12:4–6). Here the Spirit is on a par with both God (the Father) and the Lord (the Son). A similar pattern is present in Ephesians 4:4–6 (see the excursus that follows). Most obvious of all in Paul's letters is his apostolic benediction in 2 Corinthians 13:14 (v. 13 in Greek), where he associates "the fellowship of the Holy Spirit" with "the grace of the Lord Jesus Christ" and "the love of God [the Father]." While we are thinking of Paul's letters, it is worth mentioning Romans 8:9–11, where he connects the resurrection of Jesus with our resurrection on the Last Day. Both are works of the Father accomplished by the Holy Spirit. What gives us assurance of our future resurrection is not only that Jesus Christ has already been raised from the dead, but also that the Spirit who raised him and will also resurrect us in the future actually lives within us. Given to the church at Pentecost, he indwells God's people. Therefore, we are already in intimate union with the one who is the agent of the resurrection. We live in the sphere of resurrection life here and now, while simultaneously going about our everyday business in the world that is affected by sin and under judgment. This activity of the Holy Spirit is infinitely greater than that of some angelic intermediary. It is the work of God.

These conclusions are reinforced by the personal characteristics attributed to the Holy Spirit throughout the NT. He grieves over human sin (Eph. 4:30), persuades and convicts (John 14–16), intercedes for us with groanings that cannot be uttered (Rom. 8:26–27), testifies (John 16:12–15), cries (Gal. 4:6), speaks (Mark 13:11 and par.), creates (Gen. 1:2; Luke 1:35), judges, leads Jesus throughout his life and ministry (Luke 1:35–4:22), and tells evangelists like Philip and apostles like Paul what to do (Acts 8:29, 39; 16:6–10). He has a mind (Rom. 8:27) and so does not lead us in ways that detour our own intellectual faculties (1 Cor. 12:1–3). He can be blasphemed (Mark 3:28–29; 12:32 and par.), which requires his identity with God. Peter places him in parallel with God when confronting Ananias: lying to the Holy Spirit is lying to God (Acts 5:3–4). He is self-effacing, for he draws attention to Christ the Son, not to himself (John 16:14–15; cf. 13:31–32; 17:1ff.). He creates the confession that Jesus is Lord (1 Cor. 12:3). He is invisible, unlike Jesus, for unlike the Son he does not share our nature.

Moreover, the Holy Spirit is mentioned in triadic statements linking him with the Father and the Son (Rom. 15:30; 1 Cor. 12:4–6; 2 Cor. 13:14; Gal. 4:4–6; Eph. 2:18; Col. 1:3–8; 2 Thess. 2:13–14; Titus 3:4–7). He is called "the Spirit of Christ" (Rom. 8:9; 1 Pet. 1:11) and "the Spirit of [God's] Son" (Gal. 4:6). He is personally distinct from the Father and the Son, while having divine status himself, since he reveals them, and only God reveals God. It is possible, but not probable, that he is called *kyrios* (Lord) on one occasion (2 Cor. 3:17), due to his identity in action with the Son in the history of salvation.[13] T. F.

---

13. Richard B. Gaffin Jr., *The Centrality of the Resurrection: A Study in Paul's Soteriology* (Grand Rapids: Baker, 1978), 92–97, argues that Paul identifies Christ and the Holy Spirit, not ontologically, but "in terms of their redemptive activity." He claims that all five previous references in the passage to *kyrios* (Lord) refer to Christ. However, he takes care to avoid equating their personal identities. In contrast, P. E. Hughes denies that there is a direct reference to the Holy Spirit, although the Spirit is implicit in Paul's argument. Hughes thinks Paul is referring to the dynamic liberty of the spirit, in contrast to the letter that kills, although he allows that this is a fine distinction and one unlikely to be resolved. See Philip Edgcumbe Hughes, *Paul's Second Epistle to the Corinthians*, New International Commentary on the New Testament (London: Marshall, Morgan & Scott, 1961), 116–17. Toon presents two alternatives without committing himself to either. First is the idea that the Lord Jesus is the "spirit," with a consequent focus on the spiritual action of Christ. Here there is (as in Hughes's position) no reference to the Holy Spirit and no equation of the two in any way. Second, he suggests the possibility that "the Lord" (Yahweh) is equated with the Holy Spirit; that is, the Spirit is said to be so close to Christ in his work that it seems to us that they are one and the same person. See Toon, *Our Triune God*, 189–90. J. D. G. Dunn sees an identification between Yahweh and the Holy Spirit, so that the Lord = the Spirit = the Spirit of the Lord. As the result of his resurrection, Jesus is now equated with the Spirit. This equation is evident from the perspective of believers, although the exalted Christ, God, and the Spirit are not equivalent in themselves. See James D. G. Dunn, *Christology in the Making: A New Testament Inquiry into the Origins of the Doctrine of the Incarnation* (Philadelphia: Westminster Press, 1980), 143–46. Dunn is close to Gaffin. From another angle, Furnish takes an agnostic stance. There is nothing precise here about the relation between Christ and the Holy Spirit. In the context, the Lord is God, the God of Jesus Christ. The Lord is the God of the new covenant, which operates through the Spirit, not the letter. The passage "sheds very little light on Paul's view of the Spirit. It certainly sheds no light on his Christology." See Victor Paul Furnish, *II Corinthians*, Anchor Bible (New York: Doubleday, 1984), 235–36. I would suggest that "the Lord" refers to the preceding OT citation, where Yahweh is

Torrance considers that, in 1 Corinthians 2, Paul views the Spirit as one "who dwells in the depths of God's being."[14]

On top of all that, the final comment of Jesus in the baptismal formula of Matthew 28:19, noted above, must have had an ongoing and powerful effect on the entire church. Whenever baptisms were administered—which was frequently and continually—there was a reminder to the whole church, particularly to those being baptized, that the God they worshiped and served is the Father, the Son, and the Holy Spirit. This was a constant pointer to the reality that God the Father, God the Son, and God the Holy Spirit "are the transcendent Communion of personal Being which God is in himself."[15]

Recognition of the divine status of the Holy Spirit sprang at root from Christian experience. The power of God displayed in the gift of faith, his grace on a daily basis, support in the face of opposition and suffering, the deep sense of communion with God, and the knowledge that the risen Christ shared in the being of God were all overwhelming and inescapable realities of Christian experience in the early days of the church. On the other hand, four factors had a cautionary impact and restrained an immediate, outright, and bald statement of the Spirit's deity. First, there was the overwhelming importance attached to the unity of God, from the OT background and the hard lessons learned by Israel in the past. Second, the danger of misunderstanding in the Gentile world was very real. Paganism dealt in polytheism, with a wide selection of divinities on offer in Graeco-Roman civilization. Third, there is what Torrance calls the "diaphonous self-effacing nature of the Holy Spirit . . . enlightening transparence. . . . We do not know the Holy Spirit directly in his own personal Reality or Glory. We know him only in his unique spiritual mode of activity and transparent presence in virtue of which God's self-revelation shines through to us in Christ, and we are made through the Spirit to see the Father in the Son

---

in view, in which case Paul is saying that the Holy Spirit, who unveils our face to recognize the glory of Christ (cf. 4:4–6), is Yahweh. Donald Guthrie (*New Testament Theology*, 570–71) agrees, considering it "sound exegesis" to interpret "Lord" in v. 17 in terms of "Lord" in the previous verse. He also points out that Paul's use of the phrase "the Spirit of the Lord" in the same context "is proof that he maintained a distinction between the Spirit and the Lord."

14. Thomas F. Torrance, *The Christian Doctrine of God: One Being, Three Persons* (Edinburgh: T & T Clark, 1996), 61–62.

15. Ibid., 62.

and the Son in the Father."[16] The point is that only the Son became incarnate and so shares our nature. The Holy Spirit did not become flesh. There are irreducible distinctions between the persons. Therefore, in his personal identity the Holy Spirit is altogether different from the realm in which we live. Fourth, if it is suggested that the NT writers were wary about attributing personality to the Spirit, we must reply that personality as we know it was not understood then (and do *we* really understand it?). The concept of the person actually developed *after* the doctrine of the Trinity. It did not precede it. However, while Warfield overstates the case in saying that the doctrine of the Trinity is there in the NT "already made,"[17] it is nonetheless true that the NT "exhibits a coherent witness to God's trinitarian self-revelation imprinted upon its theological content in an implicit conceptual form."[18] While the overt pattern of Christian worship was at first binitarian, behind it lay a tacit Trinitarianism.

Triadic Patterns

So much is evident in the NT passages where God acts toward us in a threefold manner.[19] A triadic pattern is obvious in the initiatory rite of baptism that introduces all to the Christian church. However, as Wainwright argues, there is a further development within the NT from a Trinitarian pattern toward the recognition of what he calls a Trinitarian problem. We shall come to this in a moment, but for now let us focus on this feature of a threefold pattern.

By "a Trinitarian pattern," Wainwright means "a strong body of evidence which shows that the writers of the New Testament were influenced in thought and expression by the triad 'Father, Son, and Holy Spirit.'" However, there are no doctrinal comments in these passages on the relations of the three and how this fits into the received teaching of monotheism. In each case, the writer assumes that the readers will know what he means without giving any explanation. Into

16. Ibid., 66.
17. B. B. Warfield, "The Biblical Doctrine of the Trinity," in *Biblical and Theological Studies*, ed. Samuel G. Craig (Philadelphia: Presbyterian and Reformed, 1952), 30.
18. Torrance, *Christian Doctrine of God*, 49.
19. Wainwright, *Trinity*, 237–47.

such a category Wainwright places, among many other passages, the baptismal formula.[20]

Other such passages include Paul's comment in 1 Corinthians 12:4–6:

> Now there are varieties of gifts, but the same Spirit; and there are varieties of service, but the same Lord; and there are varieties of activities, but it is the same God who empowers them all in everyone.

He uses a similar form of words in Ephesians 4:4–6 (see the excursus following this chapter). In Galatians 4:4–6, there is an even more striking example:

> But when the fullness of time had come, God sent forth his Son, born of woman, born under the law, to redeem those who were under the law, so that we might receive adoption as sons. And because you are sons, God has sent the Spirit of his Son into our hearts, crying, "Abba! Father!"

These triadic patterns are pervasive in Paul.[21] In the introduction to his letter to the Romans, he describes himself as "an apostle, set apart for the gospel of God . . . concerning his Son, who . . . was declared to be the Son of God in power according to the Spirit of holiness by his resurrection from the dead" (Rom. 1:1–4). In describing the consequences of salvation by God's grace, he says, "We have peace with God through our Lord Jesus Christ" and "God's love has been poured into our hearts through the Holy Spirit" (Rom. 5:1, 5). Entailed in this is the fact that we have "died to the law through the body of Christ . . . in order that we may bear fruit for God . . . [serving] in the new life of the Spirit" (Rom. 7:4–6). The eighth chapter of Romans is full of such references. "There is therefore now no condemnation for those who are in Christ Jesus. For the law of the Spirit of life has set you free in Christ Jesus from the law of sin and death. For God has done what the law . . . could not do" (Rom. 8:1–3a). By sending his own Son, God has condemned sin and enabled us to fulfill the righteous require-

---

20. Ibid., 245–46.
21. See the excursus entitled "Ternary Patterns in Paul's Letter to the Ephesians," at the end of this chapter.

ment of the law as we walk according to the Spirit (Rom. 8:3b–4). Consequently, Christian believers "live according to the Spirit," "set their minds on the things of the Spirit," are "in the Spirit," for "the Spirit of God dwells in [them]." The Spirit is "the Spirit of Christ," and so Christ dwells in them. The Spirit is also called "the Spirit of him who raised Jesus from the dead," an obvious reference to the Father, who will also raise us from the dead "through his Spirit who dwells in you" (Rom. 8:5–11). The rest of the chapter, right up to verse 30, continues in a similar vein. The following section on Israel's privileges (Rom. 9:1–5) also makes reference to Christ as God and to the Holy Spirit. Later Paul describes the kingdom of God as "righteousness and peace and joy in the Holy Spirit," for "whoever thus serves Christ is acceptable to God" (Rom. 14:17–18). He describes himself as "a minister of Christ Jesus . . . in the priestly service of the gospel of God, so that the offering of the Gentiles may be acceptable, sanctified by the Holy Spirit" (Rom. 15:16). Then he appeals to his readers "by our Lord Jesus Christ and by the love of the Spirit, to strive together with me in your prayers to God on my behalf" (Rom. 15:30).

To the Corinthians, Paul characterizes his ministry as centered in "Jesus Christ and him crucified . . . in demonstration of the Spirit and . . . the power of God" (1 Cor. 2:1–5). God has revealed his hidden wisdom to us by the Spirit, granting us the mind of Christ (1 Cor. 2:9–16). He writes of the one foundation of the church as Jesus Christ, the church itself being a temple of God, with God's Spirit living in it (1 Cor. 3:11–17). The kingdom of God consists of those who are "justified in the name of the Lord Jesus Christ and by the Spirit of our God" (1 Cor. 6:11). Thus, our bodies are members of Christ, temples of the Holy Spirit whom we have from God (1 Cor. 6:12–20). In the wilderness, God was not pleased with Israel, despite the fact that they fed on spiritual food and drank spiritual drink, which originated from the Spirit and which Paul describes as Christ (1 Cor. 10:1–5). The Spirit of God leads people to confess Jesus as Lord (1 Cor. 12:3), baptizes us into the body of Christ, and is given to us to drink (1 Cor. 12:13).[22] God has established us in Christ, and has anointed and sealed us by the Holy Spirit (2 Cor. 1:21–22). In the new covenant, ministers of

---

22. This is possibly a reference to baptism and the Lord's Supper.

Christ have a ministry of the Holy Spirit (2 Cor. 3:4–18). The Spirit produces in us a yearning for the resurrection and, with it, our complete redemption and unbroken presence with the Lord (2 Cor. 5:1–10).

Elsewhere Paul brings together the work of the Spirit and union with Christ as the fulfillment of the promises of God (Gal. 3:1–4:6). The fruit of the Spirit and living by the Spirit are the equivalent of belonging to Christ, putting on Christ, and inheriting the kingdom of God (Gal. 5:16–26; cf. Rom. 13:9ff.). Fulfilling the law of Christ is also sowing to the Spirit (Gal. 6:2, 7–9). Worshiping by the Spirit of God is the same as glorying in Christ Jesus (Phil. 3:3). In Colossians, Paul instructs his readers to "let the word of Christ dwell in you richly" (Col. 3:16), while in the parallel passage in Ephesians he calls this being filled with the Holy Spirit, giving thanks to God the Father in the name of our Lord Jesus Christ (Eph. 5:18–20). He speaks of the gospel coming to Thessalonica "in power and in the Holy Spirit" and remarks on the church's "steadfastness of hope in our Lord Jesus Christ" as he himself remembers them "before our God and Father" (1 Thess. 1:3–5). Later he gives thanks to God for them, calling them "brothers beloved by the Lord, because God chose you . . . to be saved, through sanctification by the Spirit" (2 Thess. 2:13). In a possible hymn, he refers to the church of God and its center as the confession of Christ, who was "vindicated by the Spirit" (1 Tim. 3:15–16). God our Savior saved us by, among other things, "renewal of the Holy Spirit, whom he poured out on us richly through Jesus Christ" (Titus 3:4–6). Thiselton aptly comments that "an overreaction against an earlier naïve dogmatics has made us too timid in what we claim for Paul's respective understandings of Christ, the Holy Spirit, and God."[23]

The author of Hebrews considers the Cross in a triadic context. "How much more [than the OT sacrifices] will the blood of Christ, who through the eternal Spirit offered himself without blemish to God, purify our conscience from dead works to serve the living God" (Heb. 9:14). Does "eternal spirit" mean the human spirit or the Holy Spirit? The mention of Christ and God, evidently the Father, supports a reference to the Holy Spirit. The human spirit can hardly be called eternal. There is little else on the Holy Spirit in Hebrews, although the for-

---

23. Anthony C. Thiselton, *The First Epistle to the Corinthians: A Commentary on the Greek Text*, New International Greek Testament Commentary (Grand Rapids: Eerdmans, 2000), 1238.

mula in 3:7 refers to the Spirit speaking in Scripture, in particular in Psalm 95. In the background of 9:14 may conceivably be the Gospels' stress on the Holy Spirit supporting Christ's humanity from infancy onward.

Peter's introduction to his first letter is triadic. He calls his recipients "elect exiles . . . according to the foreknowledge of God the Father, in the sanctification of the Spirit, for obedience to Jesus Christ" (1 Peter 1:1–2). His first main paragraph has a triadic structure, referring to the God and Father of our Lord Jesus Christ (v. 3), Jesus Christ (vv. 3ff.), and the Spirit of Christ and the Holy Spirit (vv. 11–12). The church is "a spiritual house"—not a house with spiritual qualities, but rather a house built and indwelt by the Holy Spirit—offering spiritual sacrifices acceptable to God through Jesus Christ (1 Peter 2:4–5). In 2 Peter, attestation of Christ comes as "men spoke from God as they were carried along by the Holy Spirit" (2 Peter 1:16–21). John writes that the Father commands that we believe in the name of his Son, and has given us the Spirit (1 John 3:21–24). The Holy Spirit grants us the capacity to distinguish truth from error, for he enables us to believe that Jesus Christ has come from God (1 John 4:1–6). The Father sent his Son to be the Savior, and it is by the Spirit that we know we belong to him (1 John 4:13–15). Jesus Christ came by the water (baptism) and the blood (the Cross). The Spirit testifies to this, God having borne witness to his Son (1 John 5:6–12). Jude urges his readers to "pray in the Holy Spirit; keep yourselves in the love of God, waiting for the mercy of our Lord Jesus Christ" (Jude 20–21). Finally, there is a clear and full triadic greeting in Revelation 1:4–5:

> Grace to you and peace from him who is and who was and who is to come, and from the seven spirits who are before his throne, and from Jesus Christ the faithful witness, the firstborn of the dead, and the ruler of kings on earth.

The words "him who is and who was and who is to come" most likely point to the Father. And since numerology is important in Revelation and the number seven indicates perfection, the phrase "the seven spirits who are before his throne" must mean the Holy Spirit. This theme continues in chapters 2 and 3, where each of the letters from the exalted

Christ to the seven churches concludes with the refrain, "He who has an ear, let him hear what the Spirit says to the churches." Later in the book, there are places where Christ and the Holy Spirit are also closely associated (Rev. 14:12–13; 22:17).

These patterns vary. The most prominent one, which was developed the most by the Fathers, is the pattern *from the Father through the Son in or by the Holy Spirit*. This is clear in the work of salvation and in the baptismal formula. From our side, in response to being saved by God, in prayer, worship, and the whole Christian life, there is the reverse pattern *by the Holy Spirit through the Son to the Father* (cf. Eph. 2:18).

However, these are not the only such triads. Paul's apostolic benediction runs *Son—Father—Holy Spirit* (2 Cor. 13:14). This suggests the Johannine model of the Son revealing the Father and promising the gift of the Spirit to follow. In 1 Corinthians 12:4–6 and Ephesians 4:4–6, Paul writes of *the Holy Spirit—the Son—the Father*. John refers in Revelation 1:4–5 to *the Father—the Holy Spirit—the Son*. This pattern follows the revelation at the Jordan, where the Spirit proceeded from the Father and came to rest on the Son. It also mirrors the Messianic passage quoted by the Father at that time (Isa. 42:1), and the pattern at Jesus' conception. It was followed by the Syrian tradition.[24] In short, there is no settled pattern in the NT. Understanding unfolds from the Christian experience of salvation; conceptualization follows later. The expression of the Trinity is rooted in personal salvation and Christian experience, not abstract speculation. Bobrinskoy suggests that the most common formula, Father-Son-Holy Spirit, points to the need for the Orthodox to reflect on the fact that the Son is not only the one on whom the Spirit rests, but also the one who gives the Spirit as well. On the other hand, he argues that this formula should be balanced by the one from the Jordan, "by the vision of Christ as the One on whom the Spirit rests, the One who is obedient to the Spirit, the One who is sent by the Spirit, who speaks and acts by the Spirit."[25] That there is no one settled pattern shows that there is, in Torrance's

---

24. See Emmanuel Pataq Siman, *L'expérience de l'Esprit par l'église d'après la tradition syrienne d'Antioche* (Paris: Beauchesne, 1971), cited by Bobrinskoy, *Mystery*, 67.

25. Bobrinskoy, *Mystery*, 70. The whole section, pp. 65–72, is particularly stimulating. Bobrinskoy calls for a balance between what he terms *filioquism* and *Spirituque*, a participation and presence of the Spirit in the Father and the Son.

words, "an implicit belief in the equality of the three divine Persons." Torrance considers that it was the baptismal formula, in accordance with the "irreversible relation of the Father to the Son," that established the Trinitarian order regularly used in the church's proclamation, worship, and tradition, and that while these triadic patterns do not give us an explicit doctrine of the Trinity, "they do more than pave the way for it, for they give expression to the three-fold structure of God's astonishing revelation of himself through himself."[26] Thus, in the light of the Cross, the Resurrection, and the sending of the Holy Spirit at Pentecost, we can see that God is inherently triune.[27]

Trinitarian Questions

Wainwright sees an awareness of a Trinitarian problem as coming later. Paul, the author of Hebrews, and particularly John were aware of it.[28] It entailed the question of the relations of the three and the difficulties of placing them in a monotheistic setting. Granted that the Son and the Holy Spirit are fully God, how can they—together with the Father—be one God? Moreover, how is one related to the other? The problem focused on the relation of the Father and the Son, and it would do so for several centuries. The Spirit did not pose such difficulties. Although they did not call the Spirit God, the NT writers saw him as a distinct person and his relation to the Son and to the Father was not an evident problem for them. It also seems clear that if a second shares the divine nature, there should be no insuperable difficulties in a third doing so, too.

That Paul is aware of the matter is indicated in 1 Corinthians 8:5–6. However, John's gospel is the only place in the NT where the threefold problem is clearly understood and an explanation is attempted.[29] The Synoptics stress the triad without attempting to solve any questions arising from it. Matthew frames the gospel with clear triadic statements—at the baptism of Jesus (the voice of the Father, the Holy Spirit descending on the Son) and the baptismal formula (in the

26. Torrance, *Christian Doctrine of God*, 71–72.
27. Ibid., 54.
28. Wainwright, *Trinity*, 248ff.
29. Ibid., 250.

name—singular, the covenant name—of the Father, and the Son, and the Holy Spirit). So does Luke—from the birth announcement in 1:35 of the Son of God to be conceived by the Holy Spirit, to the Holy Spirit as the promise of the Father in 24:49. Acts uses the formula and makes a deliberate attempt to describe the activity of the three—see 2:33–39, for instance. Hebrews calls Jesus God and Lord, the Creator and the object of worship, but it does not tackle the problem of the Holy Spirit. It does not recognize a threefold problem. Paul consistently exhibits a threefold pattern, but does not trace a threefold problem. It is John who spells this out.

Wainwright suggests that there is sufficient connectiveness in John's account of the relations of the three for it to be regarded as one of the major themes of his gospel.[30] That he starts and ends the gospel by equating Jesus with God (1:1–18; 20:31) shows that there is nothing accidental or unpremeditated. The Word who is "in the beginning" (note the allusion to Genesis 1:1) is "with God" (or "directed toward God") and, moreover, equated with God. John is pointing to the unity, equality, and distinction of the Word (*logos*) and God (*theos*). He then underlines that the Word is the creator of all things (vv. 3–4) and that he became flesh (v. 14). To cap it all, he is the only begotten God (v. 18).

The "I am" sayings, and the consistent emphasis on the relation between the Father and the Son, support this. The Holy Spirit is prominent in John, and is clearly distinct from the Father and the Son, especially in the Paraclete sayings in chapters 14–16. True worship is to be directed to the Father in Jesus, the truth (cf. 1:17, 14:6), by the Spirit (John 4:21–24).

In summary, the Father loves the Son, sends the Son, and glorifies the Son. He also sends the Holy Spirit in Jesus' name, in response to his request, and is worshiped in the Son and in the Spirit. He and the Son indwell one another. He has life in himself and has given to the Son to have life in himself. He is the judge and has committed judgment to his Son.

The Son was with God in the beginning, in the bosom of the Father, and was and is God. He made all things. He was sent by the Father, became flesh, and lived among men. He obeys the Father, prays to the

30. Ibid., 264–65.

Father, and after his resurrection ascends to the Father. He asks the Father to send the Holy Spirit, sends the Holy Spirit himself, and breathes out the Spirit on his disciples. He and the Father indwell one another. He receives from the Father life in himself and the right to judge.

The Holy Spirit proceeds from the Father, is sent by the Father on the Day of Pentecost in response to the Son's request, and is also sent at that time by the Son. He is breathed out by the Son. He bears witness of the Son and brings glory to him.

The three work together in harmony. Through the Holy Spirit, they come together to the disciples, who as a consequence live in the Father and in the Son.

As C. K. Barrett writes: "More than any other writer he [John] lays the foundations for a doctrine of a co-equal trinity." Wainwright concludes that John is not merely aware of the problem, but provides an answer to it. There is no formal statement of the doctrine of the Trinity in the Bible as we find it made at the later church councils. However, an answer to the problem is there. "The problem of the trinity was being raised and answered in the New Testament."[31] It arose because of Christian experience, worship, and thought. It was based upon the life and ministry of Jesus, and his reception of the Holy Spirit, and then upon his resurrection and subsequent impartation of the Spirit to his church.[32]

> *Glory to the Father, and to the Son, and to the Holy Spirit.*
> *Through the Holy Spirit unto all men come adoration, good will,*
>   *wisdom, peace and blessing:*
> *For equally with the Father and the Son he hath effectual power.*
> *Now, and ever, and unto ages of ages. Amen.*[33]

> *Come, O ye people, let us worship the Godhead in three Persons,*
> *the Son in the Father with the Holy Spirit. For the Father before time*
> *was begat the Son, who is coeternal and is equally enthroned, and*
> *the Holy Spirit who was in the Father, and was glorified together*
> *with the Son; one Might, one Essence, one Godhead. Adoring the*

31. Ibid., 266.
32. See Toon, *Our Triune God*, 197–246; Lebreton, *Trinity*, 408–14; de Margerie, *Christian Trinity*, 8–56.
33. The Order for the Burial of the Dead (Priests), *Service Book*, 398.

same let us all say: O Holy God, who by the Son didst make all things through the cooperation of the Holy Spirit: O Holy Mighty One, through whom we have known the Father, and through whom the Holy Spirit came into the world: O Holy Immortal One, the Spirit of comfort, who proceedest from the Father, and restest in the Son: O Holy Trinity, glory to thee.

Glory to the Father, and to the Son, and to the Holy Spirit, now, and ever, and unto ages of ages. Amen. O heavenly King, the Comforter, Spirit of Truth, who art in all places and fillest all things; Treasury of good things and Giver of life: Come, and take up thine abode in us, and cleanse us from every stain; and save our souls, O Good One.[34]

34. Pentecost, At the all-night vigil, *Service Book*, 245, 249.

Ternary Patterns in Ephesians

Written to the Ephesians?

As is well known, the words "in Ephesus" in Ephesians 1:1 are not found in the best early MSS (ℵ, B, p⁴⁶) or in references to the letter in the second-century church fathers.[1] The writer does not seem familiar with the readers, whereas Paul knew the Ephesian church well, having planted it. Hence, the suggestion has gained ground that this was a circular letter with the destination left blank, to be filled in appropriately for each church as the courier delivered it. However, taken as a whole the great body of the Fathers assume it to have been directed to Ephesus. Chrysostom's *Homilies on Ephesians*, for example, do not even discuss the question. Moreover, the phrase *tois ousin* ("to those") would stand alone awkwardly if a blank space followed. C. E. Arnold has argued that if we assume the reliability of ℵ, B, and p⁴⁶ here, no satisfactory account can be given for the state of the original text.[2] Finally, even if this were a circular letter, there seems no good reason why it could not have been intended for Ephesus, even as the principal destination.

1. This excursus was originally a lecture delivered at Mid-America Reformed Seminary on 9 November 1999. It was subsequently published in *MJT* 13 (2002): 57–69, and is reprinted with permission.
2. C. E. Arnold, "Ephesians," in *Dictionary of Paul and His Letters*, ed. Gerald F. Hawthorne (Downers Grove, Ill.: InterVarsity Press, 1993), 238–49.

Written by Paul?

Until the nineteenth century, all agreed that Paul wrote the letter. Today, most critical scholars consider it pseudopigraphic, written by an unknown author to unknown recipients. It is claimed that the language differs from agreed Pauline writings. However, pseudopigraphy is exceedingly rare in early Christian circles, and the Fathers all assumed that Paul was the author. Besides, who was the unknown genius who wrote it, if not Paul—and why do we have no other examples of his creative artistry? As for the language, do we have enough instances of Paul's writing to say definitively that he could not have written in the manner he displays in Ephesians? The theory appears to rest on a basic fallacy that a person must write in a limited number of ways on each and every occasion he takes up a pen. We should not forget that Paul on occasions used an amanuensis, and so it is not improbable that he could have entrusted this or others of his writings to such a person while ensuring that the thought and details were in accord with his wishes.[3]

The Trinity in Ephesians?

The dogma of the Trinity was not established until the Councils of Nicaea (325) and Constantinople (381). This was a development from the New Testament. Arthur Wainwright considers that in the New Testament there is what he calls a "threefold pattern" in relation to God, something evident in Paul, while in its later writings there develops an awareness of a "threefold problem" of how—if Christ and the Holy Spirit are God—Jewish monotheism is preserved. This latter element he sees as present in John, but not yet in Paul.[4] On the other hand, the Dutch Reformed New Testament scholar Herman Ridderbos, in his compendious volume on Paul's theology, has not a single reference to "God" or to the "Father" in his index of principal subjects. Neither does he refer in his 550 pages to any of the texts we shall cite![5]

3. For a fuller discussion, see Arnold, "Ephesians," who defends Pauline authorship.
4. Arthur Wainwright, *The Trinity in the New Testament* (London: SPCK, 1963).
5. Herman Ridderbos, *Paul: An Outline of His Theology* (Grand Rapids: Eerdmans, 1975).

Most discussions of the underlying basis in the Bible for the later development of the doctrine of the Trinity consider only isolated texts (e.g., Matt. 28:19), or else follow particular themes across the New Testament, such as Christ as the Son of God. It is exceedingly rare to find the discussion focus on the content of a particular book. This is made worse in the case of Ephesians by the critical claim that Paul did not write it.

In the context of this excursus, I shall be using the term "Trinity" in connection with a threefold pattern, as Wainwright describes it, not in terms of the later developed doctrine as the church unfolded it. I shall argue that in Ephesians Paul pervasively thinks of God in a ternary, or triadic, form, all the more significant for its being so unself-conscious and artless. He gives no consideration to relations between the three, nor any awareness of problems that might arise from such a view of God. In itself, this buttresses the claim that Ephesians was written early, before John's gospel had introduced such questions, and so in turn it gives further support to Pauline authorship. However, I shall seek to establish that Paul brings it into connection with everything on which he writes, and so it is the underlying base of his whole view of the Christian faith.

This argument runs counter to much recent comment on Ephesians. Lincoln pays some attention to a threefold pattern in the writer's understanding of God[6]—and he considers him to have lived much later than Paul—but most others ignore the point. Schnackenburg thinks the writer has a basically monotheistic view of God, and passes over such passages as 2:18 without any significant comment. The Holy Spirit is simply "the power that comes from Christ."[7] Ralph Martin recognizes that the writer has "a rudimentary trinitarian faith" and sees the triadic patterns as "suggestive," but he does not elaborate further.[8]

The Trinity and the Plan of Salvation

We shall concentrate here on two major sections in which Paul unfolds the purpose of God for the salvation of his church.

6. Andrew T. Lincoln, *Ephesians* (Dallas: Word, 1990).

7. Rudolf Schnackenburg, *Ephesians: A Commentary* (Edinburgh: T & T Clark, 1991), on 2:18 and 3:17.

8. Ralph P. Martin, *Ephesians, Colossians, and Philemon* (Atlanta: John Knox Press, 1992), on 1:13–14 and 4:1–6.

1:3–14. This is, of course, one huge sentence—"the most monstrous sentence conglomeration that I have encountered in Greek," in the words of the early twentieth-century German scholar E. Norden. Here is a clear case where the reality shapes and bursts the boundaries of the language. The flow of thought is from the pretemporal (v. 4) to the past historical (vv. 3, 7) to appropriation in the past (vv. 13–14), on to the present (v. 7) and thence to the future (v. 14). There is also an overlap between the present and the future (vv. 10, 14). In short, the sentence encompasses everything from the eternal purpose of God to a sweep through human history and on to the ultimate fulfillment.

Underlying all God's blessings described here is the action of the Trinity. The Father is the origin of all the blessings we receive in Christ (v. 3), the first of which are election (v. 4) and predestination (v. 5). The Son is the one in whom we have redemption (v. 7), and it is he who will head up all things (v. 10). Indeed, all God's blessings from beginning to end are given in Christ, the Son. Each element in the whole sentence is given "in Christ" or "in him." The Holy Spirit is the one who sealed us when we believed (v. 13) and who is the guarantor of our inheritance (v. 14). Thus, the whole panorama is of a sweeping movement of God's grace toward us: from the Father, in or through the Son, and by the Holy Spirit.

Paul presents the Father as the source of all God's grace. He is "the God and Father of our Lord Jesus Christ" (v. 3). In relation to the Son, he is Father. Since these are evidently relations within God, it is a reasonable inference to conclude that they are eternal. This is corroborated by the reference in verse 4 to election "before the foundation of the world." The Father has brought to fruition his covenant with Abraham. Back in Genesis, God promised to bless Abraham and his seed—in terms of land and progeny, and also in general. Now "every spiritual blessing" has been given, in fulfillment of that ancient promise. These blessings are given by the Holy Spirit, for they are "spiritual" blessings. The singular "blessing" denotes the unity of the whole. These are not so many disparate and disconnected blessings, but are part of one movement of God's grace begun with Abraham and now fulfilled "in Christ." This phrase (*en Christō*) indicates that the Father's blessing is given by the Holy Spirit and in the Son. We hinted above that this theme is right at the heart of the whole sentence.

Eternal election is the first work of the Father to be distinguished. The Father is its source or origin. His action in choosing us was before creation. As such, it transcends time. It was a decision by the Father into which we had no input whatsoever. In accord with the previous statement, it was a decision made *en Christō*—a reality that exists not merely at some future point in world history, or in the life experience of particular persons, but at the point of election itself. Elsewhere in the New Testament, the Son claims the right to choose us (John 16:15), and so too the Holy Spirit chooses Saul and Barnabas for the missionary task described in Acts (Acts 13:1ff.). However, Paul considers election to be supremely a work of the Father, although not apart from the Son, in whom he chose us, nor from the Spirit, who is the one by whom the blessing comes (cf. v. 3). Indeed, since this is the first of all, the rest of the blessing by the Holy Spirit flows from here. So much is clear by reason of the fact that the purpose of election is that we be holy and blameless before him (the Father).

Foreordination to adoption as sons is also a work of the Father. It is the Father who foreordained us through the Son to be his. This is through the Son (*dia Iēsou Christou*), since we can only be adopted in union with the natural Son. Christ is the Son and we were chosen in him as sons by adoption. Thus, election, foreordination, and adoption are all founded in the relation between the Father and the Son in eternity, a relation that takes fully into account the Holy Spirit by whom these realities are effected.

In Christ, the Son, we have redemption through his blood. We have deliverance from slavery by the power of God on the payment of a price (v. 7). This redemption occurred at the cross. Christ's death secured our release. As a payment, it could only be offered to the Father, for the devil had no rights or authority over the human race. Again, the relation between the Father and the Son is in the background, echoing Paul's comments in Romans 8:32, where he refers to the Father not sparing his Son, but giving him up for us all, and in Romans 4:25, where he comments that Jesus was "delivered up" to the cross for our trespasses.

In the Son, the Father's cosmic purpose will be realized, whereby he is made the head of all created things (v. 10). The phrase *ta panta* (all things) can only refer to the entire universe. Paul proceeds to define it as "things in heaven and things on earth." The Father's will is realized in Christ the Son, bringing the creation together into a unity, restoring harmony under his leadership. Thus, the Father makes Christ head of both the church (see later) and the cosmos.

The Holy Spirit seals us (v. 13). The Spirit, we have seen, effects the blessing promised to Abraham, and thus is dynamically active in all the elements of the Father's plan that we have already considered. However, it is particularly in the aspects here in verses 13–14 that he comes to more prominence. The verb *sphragizein* denotes putting a seal on something either for security, or to indicate ownership, or again to assure of authenticity. These ideas are all closely related, and it is hard to be dogmatic as to which is preferable here. Certainly the idea of security is in the foreground, and for that reason may be close to the author's intention. This action of the Spirit occurs concurrently with faith—the aorist participle is most likely a participle of attendant circumstance. If so, it is not so much a specific action of the Holy Spirit that Paul has in mind as the person of the Spirit himself who seals believers.

The Holy Spirit is the guarantor of our future inheritance (v. 14). The word *arrabōn* meant "down payment," confirming a transaction, making it legally binding and so leaving no room for a change of mind. In turn, it was part of a greater whole that was yet to come when the remainder of the payment was made. It followed that it was of the same kind as the rest. It guaranteed that the rest would follow. Here the future inheritance is in view. The Holy Spirit, who seals all believers, establishes that the Father will give them the full possession of their eternal inheritance in Christ his Son.

According to this monstrous sentence conglomeration, the plan of salvation, promised to Abraham, fulfilled by Christ, is an engagement of the Father, the Son, and the Holy Spirit together, by which they, in unbreakable unity, from before creation and through the whole panorama of human history, secure our eternal inheritance in Christ. This pattern remains in a second passage where Paul focuses more precisely on deliverance from sin.

2:4–10. The background is the hopeless and utterly helpless condition in which the human race finds itself as a result of sin. Paul describes this as a situation of "death," from which we are incapable of rescuing ourselves. Only outside help will avail, only the help of God himself. Mercifully, he has acted in power and grace.

God the Father raised us up together with Christ the Son (vv. 5b–6a). As Pannenberg points out, in the New Testament *theos* invariably refers to the Father.[9] Here the Father has made us alive, where previously we were "dead in sins" (v. 1). In turn, he has raised us up with Christ. This is sovereign action by the Father. Moreover, we are not raised up in isolation. The verbs in verses 5 and 6 consistently have *syn* prefixes (meaning "with"). We are brought to life in conjunction with others, as part of a corporate body. Even more, we are given life in connection and union with Christ, whom the Father raised from the dead. So we too share in his resurrection. If we bear in mind Paul's comments in Romans 8, the Holy Spirit is also actively engaged in the resurrection of Christ and so in our participation in it—the Father effects it by the Spirit.

God the Father enthroned us with Christ the Son in the heavens (v. 6b). Here is the continuation and consequence of what we just considered. Christ ascended into heaven and is now seated at the right hand of God. In union with him, we are seated together with him (and in him) in heaven. The point again is that the Father continues to be the subject of this clause.

To sum up thus far: the plan of salvation in its entirety, as well as in its details, is a fulfillment of God's covenant with Abraham, was prepared from before the creation, is focused corporately in Christ and—above all—is an engagement of the Father, the Son, and the Holy Spirit, who have one purpose, one will, and one effect.

The Trinity and Our Knowledge of God

According to Paul in Ephesians, what shape does our knowledge of God take? Is there a reflection from our side of the movement of God's grace that expresses itself in the threefold pattern we have recognized? A number of sections of the letter are relevant.

1:17. Knowledge of God is a gift of God the Father. Paul prays that the Father will give the readers a knowledge of himself. This gift

---

9. Wolfhart Pannenberg, *Systematic Theology*, trans. Geoffrey W. Bromiley (Grand Rapids: Eerdmans, 1991), 1:326.

he considers to be continuous throughout life. As Thomas Goodwin described it, it is "a prayer for grown Christians." The source of this knowledge is the Father—"the God of our Lord Jesus Christ, the Father of glory." Here the noun *doxēs*, "of glory" (in the genitive), has adjectival force. Glory is thus the mode of the Father's being. The Father is Father in relation to our Lord Jesus Christ, who is the Son. The Father reveals himself in the Son.

The noun *pneuma* is used by Paul consistently of the Holy Spirit, with or without the article (see Eph. 3:5; Col. 1:9; 1 Cor. 2:6–16). The stress of the text is on the creative function of the Holy Spirit, his giving of faith, revelation, and wisdom. The Father of Christ, the Son, thus gives knowledge of himself by the efficacy of the Holy Spirit.

The knowledge the Father gives is not some superficial notional knowledge. Paul uses *epignōsis* to denote a real, deep, personal knowledge, in contrast to superficial acquaintance. Personal communion with God is clearly in view. This knowledge of God comes from the Father, through the Son, and by the Holy Spirit, and is continuous and progressive. Moreover, it is of first importance on Paul's agenda for the church. It is the first category on his prayer list, the single most important thing he mentions.

2:18. Paul has stressed that Christ has secured access to God by the Cross. In the Old Testament, there was a distance between God and the people. The priesthood and sacrificial system stood between God and the people. To the Holy of Holies there was no general access. Moreover, the Gentiles were excluded from the temple, effectively on penalty of death. However, now that Christ has come, we have open access to God. We are reconciled through the Cross. This reconciliation also has effect between Jew and Gentile.

Martin points to the immediately obvious reference—the temple balustrade barring Gentiles from the temple enclosure. This is now set aside by the one perfect sacrifice of Christ that renders the temple ritual obsolete. However, he considers the point of the writer to be the Mosaic law with its scribal interpretation. Either way, Christ has set aside the law and so destroyed that which distinguished Israel and so kept Jew and Gentile apart.

This is the background for the key statement in verse 18. Both Jews and Gentiles now have access to the Father. The Father's rich mercy has delivered us from sin, raised us with Christ, and reconciled us through Christ's death. Salvation can therefore be seen as access to, and consequently fellowship with, the Father. This access is *di' autou*, through Christ. He is the one who made peace and who is our peace (v. 14). The access is effected *en heni pneumati*, referring to the Holy Spirit.

Consequently, while the plan of salvation is brought about *from the Father through the Son by the Holy Spirit*, from our side we experience a reverse movement *by the Holy Spirit through the Son to the Father*. The Spirit gives faith (cf. 2:8–9) and is the source of all the ways in which we respond to the grace of God. He enables us to trust Christ, and through him and his mediation we have fellowship with the Father. Christian experience is therefore Trinitarian through and through. Lincoln recognizes this when he comments on his putative author, "How naturally his thought expresses itself in the trinitarian pattern of 'through Christ in the Spirit to the Father.'"[10] Indeed, it is the unself-conscious nature of this statement that underlines it as an integral part of Paul's thinking. Unfortunately, Ridderbos does not even mention this statement anywhere in his volume.

3:14–17a. There is no reference to this passage in Ridderbos either! This is another prayer for the readers based upon the preceding content (although the precise reference of *toutou charin* is ambiguous). He asks the Father to strengthen the readers through his Spirit (vv. 15–16). In turn, he describes this as Christ dwelling in your hearts through faith (v. 17).

The Father, he says, is "rich in glory." The stress is on the Father's greatness as the source of this blessing. He is the Creator and Lord of all family groups. These families are named *ex hou*. Naming denoted sovereignty in the ancient world, so here the sovereign authority of the Father over all peoples is in view.

The Holy Spirit has already been described as the seal of our salvation (1:13) and the one who indwells the church (2:22). Here the strengthening power of the Holy Spirit is parallel with the indwelling

10. Lincoln, *Ephesians*, on 2:18.

of Christ in the hearts of the faithful. The result is that they will be rooted and grounded in love, with further consequences that Paul spells out in the following clauses. Faith, strengthening, and love—all features of the life of Christian believers—are seen by Paul as the fruit of the concerted engagement of the three.

5:18–20. We merely note that Paul's request to the church to be filled with the Spirit (v. 18) anticipates as an inseparable corollary the singing of psalms to the Lord (v. 19), *kyrios* being his consistent term for the post-Resurrection Christ. In turn, they will give thanks for everything "to God the Father in the name of our Lord Jesus Christ" (v. 20). Once again, Paul sees Christian experience as thoroughly Trinitarian. His formula is not smooth, but this feature demonstrates the natural way he recognizes the reality and also points to his writing early in the church's development.

6:10–11. Note the threefold pattern in this famous section. Be strong in the Lord, Paul urges (v. 10). To do this, the readers must put on the whole armor of God (v. 11). The one piece of offensive equipment is "the sword of the [Holy] Spirit, which is the word of God" (v. 17).

Let us summarize what we have found here. In response to the grace of God, planned and effected in the threefold pattern we described earlier, Christian believers are taken up, enveloped, and empowered by a corresponding threefold pattern—this time *by the Holy Spirit through the Son to the Father.* The air they breathe is, so to speak, Trinitarian.

The Trinity and the Church

Finally, we shall look at two sections of Ephesians where Paul considers the church in some detail.

2:20–22. Here Paul describes the church as a temple, built on the foundation of the apostles and prophets, with Christ Jesus as the cornerstone. There is some debate as to whether Paul considers Christ to be the cornerstone, laid down before the rest of the structure is built, or instead whether he has a capstone in view, in which case Christ would be the final part of the building, setting it off and completing it. The imagery seems to favor the former, for the structure grows upwards after the apostolic foundation is set in place and so after Christ founded it. If he were the final capstone, the developing building would be without Christ for the entirety of its construction, an obvious incongruity.

The picture is of harmonious growth and development. The building is a living one, composed of people, not stone. It grows organically. The implication is that its development, like the existing temple in Jerusalem—or, we may add, like the construction of many an ancient cathedral—is a long process. It is growth in holiness—its goal is to become a holy temple (*auxei eis naon hagion*), one belonging to God. Moreover, this holy temple is such "in the Lord" (*en kyriō*). The church's identity is in Christ and not for one instant outside. This temple is a dwelling place of the Father by the Holy Spirit (*eis katoikētērion tou theou en pneumati*). Thus, Paul brings all three persons into direct connection with the church. The church itself reveals the Trinity, for it exists in Christ and the Father indwells it by the Holy Spirit.

4:4–6. Paul's attention at this point has moved from the church as a growing temple, indwelt by the Holy Spirit, to its unity. There are hints beneath the surface of a disunity that he is trying to correct (4:1–3).

The section before us has a strong hymnic or creedal feel to it. There are "seven acclamations of oneness," as Lincoln puts it, divided into two groups of three each, together with one concluding statement which is itself arranged in a threefold form.[11] The main point of this citation (if citation it be) is the need to maintain unity at Ephesus. This is the only course consistent with the foundational unities—the unity of the church, the unity of the Christian faith, the unity of God himself. Let us look at it in more detail.

Verse 4. "One body" is presumably a reference to the church, the body of Christ. This will be the central theme of the following paragraph and is, of course, a point spelled out in great measure by Paul in his first letter to Corinth. "One Spirit" obviously means the Holy

11. Ibid., on 4:4–6.

Spirit. "One hope that belongs to your call" looks back to 1:18, where Paul prays that the Ephesians would know what is the hope of their calling and where it points to the final eschatological fulfillment of God's plan of salvation, the cosmic unity that will be realized in Christ. This has added significance if, as chapter 2 indicates, there was a mixture of Jewish and Gentile Christians in the church, for it would then underline that, whatever the ethnic differences, the unity Christ established in his church transcends them.

Verse 5. "One Lord" means Jesus Christ, the Son who is the cornerstone of the church (2:20). "One faith" in turn points to the unity of the content of the Christian gospel, possibly, as some have argued, the faith confessed by baptismal candidates on their conversion from paganism. "One baptism": only one, since in baptism we are united with Christ in his death and resurrection, and, as there is only one Christ, and only one Cross and Resurrection, baptism can occur but once.

Verse 6. "One God and Father of all." God the Father is in view, and he is "over all," transcendent over his entire creation, "through all" and "in all"—both phrases pointing to his thorough immanence. This threefold description of the Father in relation to all things cannot be taken as a reference to the Trinity as such, although its threefold aspect may possibly reflect Paul's consistent understanding of God in threefold terms.

Here in this passage, Paul stresses that the unity of God takes a threefold pattern. More than that, since the Lord and the Spirit share with the Father in the qualities of God, they are equally personal. Paul's threefold pattern is a definitely personal one, although he does not of course use those terms, which were to emerge later over the course of time. The Holy Spirit is in view in verse 4, the Son in verse 5, and the Father in verse 6. From this flows the unity of the faith and the unity of the church. We should note that this is a unity in diversity. Perhaps *plurality* might be a better word. As he goes on to expound it, Paul sees the unity of the church consisting of a diversity of persons with a diversity of gifts (vv. 7–16). This is of a piece with his view of God, who is not a solitary monad, but whose unity evidences a threefold pattern of personal activity. There is no reference to this passage in Ridderbos.

Conclusion

1. Paul consistently views God as one, his unity evidencing a three-fold pattern of personal activity. As Donald Guthrie wrote, shortly before his death, "It may be said that Paul does not work with a conceptual framework which would lead naturally to speculations about the essence of God. . . . Yet the evidence lays foundations for the later developed doctrine. The problems which that later doctrine grappled with had their roots in the New Testament itself."[12]

2. However, he has not reached the stage John reached, which was to consider the relations *between* the Father, the Son, and the Holy Spirit, and how these were compatible with the rigorous Old Testament monotheism. This may be another argument in support of Pauline authorship of Ephesians, for it argues strongly for an early date for the letter.

3. The manner in which Paul handles the matter is instructive for, apart from the hymnic or creedal section in 4:4–6, he refers to the triadic pattern in a natural, unforced, and unself-conscious way. This indicates that it was a deeply held conviction that he did not believe required extensive elaboration, for it was recognized widely, if not universally, among his readership.

4. Not only is this triadic, or ternary, pattern clearly evident, but it comes to expression in all the key areas of the letter. It is *pervasive*. As such, it underlies all Paul says, whether about the plan of salvation and its implementation, our own knowledge of God, or the church. It impinges too on the practical consequences of Christian faith, expressed in the unity of the church and in how Christian believers interact with one another. We may therefore say that it is *at the very center* of Paul's theology in the letter to the Ephesians.

---

12. Donald Guthrie and Ralph P. Martin, "God," in *Dictionary of Paul and His Letters*, ed. Hawthorne, 367.

PART TWO

Historical Development

We believe in one God the Father Almighty, maker of heaven and earth and of all things visible and invisible; And in one Lord Jesus Christ the Son of God, the Only-begotten, begotten by his Father before all ages, Light from Light, true God from true God, begotten not made, consubstantial with the Father, through whom all things came into existence, who for us men and for our salvation came down from the heavens and became incarnate by the Holy Spirit and the Virgin Mary and became man, and was crucified for us under Pontius Pilate and suffered and was buried and rose again on the third day in accordance with the Scriptures and ascended into the heavens and is seated at the right hand of the Father and will come again with glory to judge the living and the dead, and there will be no end to his kingdom; And in the Holy Spirit, the Lord and life-giver, who proceeds from the Father, who is worshiped and glorified together with the Father and the Son, who spoke by the prophets; And in one holy, catholic, and apostolic Church; We confess one baptism for the forgiveness of sins; We wait for the resurrection of the dead and the life of the coming age. Amen.

—Niceno-Constantinopolitan Creed, A.D. *381*

Early Trinitarianism

After the completion of the NT, Christian writers saw it as their task to defend and explain how Jesus is one with God, while maintaining that there is only one God. The NT triads impressed themselves on the church's mind, especially the baptismal formula of Matthew 28:19.[1] However, in postapostolic times the implications were rarely addressed. Usually the triad was simply asserted. The most graphic example is Ignatius's imagery of the faithful as stones lifted into place in God's temple by the cross of Christ as a crane and the Holy Spirit as the rope![2] Ignatius also taught that the Son has been coexistent with the Father from before time.[3]

The Logos Christology

In the second century, the apologists (Justin, Tatian, Athenagoras, Theophilus of Antioch) began to explore the relation of the preexistent Christ to the Father. They used the idea of the divine Word or Logos, from the Jewish philosopher Philo. By this, they saw Christ as the Father's thought, expressed in creation and revelation. Two things were stressed—his eternal oneness with the Father, as the Word immanent in God, and also his appearance in human history, as the

1. Justin, *Apology* 1.61, 65 (PG 6:419–22, 427–28). See *Didache* 7.1–3.
2. Ignatius, *To the Ephesians* 9; Ignatius, *To the Magnesians* 13 (PG 5:739–42, 671–74).
3. Ignatius, *To the Magnesians* 6.1; 7.2.

Word emitted or expressed[4]—but without reference to a distinct personal identity.

However, we need to avoid anachronism—reading an author in terms of knowledge that only developed at a later date, of which he could not be aware. J. N. D. Kelly warns that it is anachronistic to judge the apologists in terms of a later, more sophisticated, and developed Trinitarianism.[5] They lacked the conceptual tools forged in subsequent battles and did not face the questions posed by later heresies. They thought according to the light available to them. We must evaluate them in terms of their own times. The main issue for them was the unity of God. In that light, Theophilus of Antioch made a significant contribution in writing about God, who "having his own Word internal within his own bowels, begat him, emitting him along with his own wisdom before all things."[6] The Word was a helper in creation, a governing principle and ruler of all that was made. The OT theophanies were appearances of the Word. Theophilus seems to conflate the Word and what he calls "the Spirit of God." Theophilus was the first to use the term *trias* (triad) for God. The first three days of the creation account in Genesis 1, he said, are "types of the trinity (*trias*), of God, and his Word, and his Wisdom."[7] However, it is with Irenaeus that we find the most significant thought in the second century.

Irenaeus

Originally from Asia, Irenaeus (130–200) became bishop of Lyons—in Gaul—where, because of migration, the church was mostly Greek. He is best known for his work *Against Heresies*.[8] The church in the West was threatened by a form of Gnosticism, an amorphous movement of a broadly religious and philosophical kind, laying claim to special insight or knowledge (*gnōsis*). Like a computer virus, Gnos-

4. J. N. D. Kelly, *Early Christian Doctrines* (London: Adam & Charles Black, 1968), 95–101.
5. Ibid., 100–101.
6. Theophilus of Antioch, *To Autolycus* 2.10 (PG 6:1064).
7. Ibid., 2.15 (PG 6:1071).
8. Robert M. Grant, *Irenaeus of Lyons* (London: Routledge, 1997); A. Benoit, *Saint Irénée: Introduction à l'étude de son théologie* (Paris: Presses Universitaires, 1960); J. Fantino, *La théologie d'Irénée. Lecture des Écritures en réponse à l'exégèse gnostique: Une approche trinitaire* (Paris: Cerf, 1994); J. Lawson, *The Biblical Theology of St. Irenaeus* (London: Epworth, 1948).

ticism could attach itself to a range of different religious beliefs and so corrupt them. The brand of gnostic spirituality that Irenaeus opposed was associated with Valentinus, a long-standing resident of Rome. One of the main thrusts of Gnosticism was the idea that the supreme being, such as it was, must be radically separate from the material world. Interposed between this supreme being and matter were a complicated series of lesser beings, emanating one from the other. In the case of Valentinian Gnosticism, let us hear Irenaeus describe it:

> He stated that there is an ineffable Duality consisting of the Inexpressible and Silence. Later this Duality emitted a second Duality, Father and Truth. This Tetrad bore as fruit Logos and Life, Man and Church, thus constituting the first Ogdoad. From Logos and Life ten powers were emitted, as we have said; from Man and Church were emitted twelve, one of which, leaving (the Pleroma) and falling into distress, made the rest of creation. He has two Limits: one, between the Abyss and the Pleroma, separates the generated Aeons from the uncreated Father, while the other separates their Mother from the Pleroma. The Christ was not emitted by the Aeons of the Pleroma, but was borne by the Mother, when she was outside it, according to the memory she had of the powers above, though with a certain shadow. As this Christ was masculine, he cut off the shadow from himself, and returned to the Pleroma. Then the Mother, abandoned with the shadow and emptied of spiritual substance, emitted another Son: this is the Demiurge, omnipotent master of those beneath him. Along with him was emitted an Archon of the left, as in the system of those falsely called "Gnostics."
>
> Jesus was sometimes said to be emitted by Theletos, the Aeon separated from their Mother and united with the others, sometimes by Christ, who ran upward again into the Pleroma, and sometimes by Man and Church. And the Holy Spirit was emitted by Truth for testing and fructifying the Aeons; it enters them invisibly, and by it the Aeons fructify the plants of Truth. Such is the doctrine of Valentinus.[9]

Well might we say with Irenaeus, "Iou iou! Pheu pheu!"[10]

---

9. Irenaeus, *Against Heresies* 1.11.1 (PG 7:559–64), as translated in Grant, *Irenaeus of Lyons*, 72–73.

10. Irenaeus, *Heresies* 1.11.4 (PG 7:565–66).

Another threat was Marcion, who, starting with the law-gospel dualism that he found in Paul, held to dual gods, the creator characterized by justice and the other characterized by love. In doing this, he radically separated the OT from the NT. Since the OT was full of law and justice, it had no place for the Christian. The greater part of the NT fared little better. Only Paul's letters were of use, together with Luke and Acts (written by Paul's colleague Luke), since he had disentangled himself from Jewish superstitions.[11] Both Marcion and the gnostics, in differing ways, kept the supreme being from contact with the material world. Both sharply separated Jesus Christ from the creator and, in turn, from the supreme god. The threat they posed to the Christian gospel is unmistakable.

Irenaeus, in combating them, identifies the one true God with the creator of the world, the God of the OT, and the Father of the Logos. He proves the existence of the Father, the Son, and the Holy Spirit from events in human history. However, he does not discuss in any detail the relations of the three, nor does he use Theophilus's term *trias*.

Irenaeus's Main Points

According to Irenaeus, there is one God the Father, who created *ex nihilo* (from nothing) by his Word—standard teaching already, but needing reemphasis in this context.[12] There is one Lord Jesus Christ. The gnostics held that the Jesus who lived a human life and suffered was different from the Christ, who descended on him and then left him and ascended. In contrast, Irenaeus identifies Jesus with the Christ and the Son of God. The Son of God was himself born of a virgin and is identical with Christ the Savior.[13] Paul (who was acceptable to Marcion) knew of no other Christ than he who was born, suffered, was buried, and rose again, and whom he speaks of as a man.[14]

Irenaeus says that the relation of the Son and the Father is ineffable. Isaiah 53:8, "Who shall declare his generation?" (KJV), a favorite text of later church fathers, underlines the impossibility of us under-

---

11. Adolf von Harnack, *Marcion: The Gospel of the Alien God*, trans. John E. Steely (Durham, N.C.: Labyrinth Press, 1990).

12. Irenaeus, *Heresies* 2.2.4; 3.16.6; 4.20.2 (PG 7:714–15, 925–26, 1032–33).

13. Ibid., 3.16.2 (PG 7:921–22).

14. Ibid., 3.18.3; see also 3.16.6–8 (PG 7:933–34, 925–27).

standing the Father's generation of the Son, contrary to gnostic claims of special knowledge. No human analogy is possible, for these are "unspeakable mysteries of God." Irenaeus uses a variety of terms for the generation of the Son (production, generation, calling, revelation), for language cannot encapsulate the reality, and so no one metaphor is adequate. The gnostics had described his generation "as if they themselves had assisted at his birth, thus assimilating him to the word of mankind formed by emissions."[15] In truth, only the Father who begat and the Son who was begotten know what this means. What we can and do know is that God is revealed through the Son, and that the Son is in the Father and has the Father in himself.[16] Irenaeus reflects Johannine language and gropes toward the later doctrine of the mutual indwelling of the three persons. In sum, the Son was with the Father from the beginning, and dispenses the Father's grace in human history, in the "economy" of salvation.[17]

Returning to the theme of creation, so vital in this context, Irenaeus uses a striking image that points to a triadic view of creation. He repeatedly writes of the Father having created by his "two hands." Alluding to Genesis 1:26 and asserting creation *ex nihilo*, Irenaeus states that God stood in need of no angel to help him, "as if he did not possess his own hands. For with him were always present the Word and Wisdom, the Son and the Spirit, by whom and in whom, freely and spontaneously, he made all things, to whom also he speaks, saying 'Let us make man after our image and likeness.'"[18] The Son and the Spirit are both coeternal with the Father, and one with him, for they share in what is exclusively a work of God. So, "the Father plans and gives commands, the Son performs and creates, while the Spirit nourishes and increases."[19]

Irenaeus extends this metaphor to the creation of Adam in particular and also to the incarnation of the Second Adam. "For never at any time did Adam escape the *hands* of God, to whom the Father speaking said, 'Let us make man in our image, after our likeness.' And for this reason in the last times . . . his hands formed a living man, in

---

15. Ibid., 2.28.5–6 (PG 7:808–9); Irenaeus, *The Demonstration of the Apostolic Preaching* 47.

16. Irenaeus, *Heresies* 3.6.2 (PG 7:861).

17. Ibid., 4.20.7 (PG 7:1037).

18. Ibid., 4.20.1 (PG 7:1032).

19. Ibid., 4.38.3 (PG 7:1107–8).

order that Adam might be created [again] after the image and likeness of God."[20] The translation of Enoch and Elijah followed a similar pattern, for "by means of the very same hands through which they were molded at the beginning, did they receive this translation and assumption. For in Adam the hands of God had become accustomed to set in order, to rule, and to sustain His own workmanship, and to bring it and place it where they pleased."[21] So for Irenaeus God's whole work of creation, providence, and grace is carried out by his two hands, the Son and the Holy Spirit. At first sight, this seems to subordinate the Son and the Spirit as merely God's agents. Indeed, before the Council of Nicaea (325) some form of subordination was endemic. However, in most cases the subordination was clearly within the being of God. So, with Irenaeus, the two hands are not external to God. They are unmistakably divine, always with the Father. There is but one God, while the Son "was always with the Father; and . . . the Spirit, was present with him, anterior to all creation."[22] However, the Father has first place, and salvation focuses on union with him.[23]

Irenaeus does not consider at length the relations of the Son and the Spirit with the Father, nor their preexistence.[24] However, he does make a start, at the place often thought best to begin, the Jordan—with the baptism of Jesus. There the Holy Spirit, as a dove, descended on Jesus. Receiving the Spirit as a gift from the Father, Jesus then imparted him to his followers, sending the Spirit upon all the earth.[25] Centuries before the *filioque* controversy, Irenaeus says unreflectingly that the Father gives the Spirit to the Son, who then pours him out on his people as a gift. For our part, we receive by the Spirit the image of the Father and the Son. Jesus' anointing at the Jordan reveals the triad, for we see him who anoints (the Father), the Son who is anointed by the Spirit, and the Spirit who is the anointing.[26] Irenaeus roots his tri-

20. Ibid., 5.1.3 (PG 7:1123).
21. Ibid., 5.5.1 (PG 7:1134–35).
22. Ibid., 4.20.2–4 (PG 7:1032–34); Irenaeus, *Demonstration* 5.
23. Basil Studer, *Trinity and Incarnation: The Faith of the Early Church*, trans. Matthias Westerhoff, ed. Andrew Louth (Collegeville, Minn.: Liturgical Press, 1993), 64.
24. Boris Bobrinskoy, *The Mystery of the Trinity: Trinitarian Experience and Vision in the Biblical and Patristic Tradition*, trans. Anthony P. Gythiel (Crestwood, N.Y.: St. Vladimir's Seminary Press, 1999), 204; Studer, *Trinity and Incarnation*, 62.
25. Irenaeus, *Heresies* 3.17.1–3 (PG 7:929–31).
26. Ibid., 3.18.2–3 (PG 7:932–34).

adic view of God in the Bible and redemptive history, in contrast to the bizarre speculations of the gnostics.

Indeed, Irenaeus prepares the way for a thoroughgoing Trinitarian approach to the whole of God's dealings with the world. "The Father bears creation and his own Word simultaneously, and the Word borne by the Father grants the Spirit to all as the Father wills." The Father is above all and is the head of Christ, the Word is through all things and is head of the church, while the Spirit is in us all and is the living water that the Lord grants to all who rightly believe in him and love him. The creator of the world is the Word of God, our Lord, "who in the last times was made man, existing in this world, and who in an invisible manner contains all things created, and is inherent in the entire creation, since the Word of God governs and arranges all things."[27]

There is a triadic pattern in our salvation, too, for in the kingdom of heaven we shall see God "paternally . . . the Spirit truly preparing man in the Son of God, and the Son leading him to the Father, while the Father, too, confers [upon him] incorruption for eternal life."[28] Salvation is life, and this life is found "in fellowship with God; but fellowship with God is to know God, and to enjoy his goodness." Through bearing his Spirit in us, we can see God, for sanctification is central to the Spirit's work.[29] In this way, God reveals himself to us, "for God the Father is shown forth . . . the Spirit indeed working, and the Son ministering, while the Father was approving, and man's salvation being accomplished."[30] There is a descent in grace from the Father through the Son to the Spirit, with a reverse movement in us from the Spirit through the Son to the Father.[31] Bobrinskoy rightly points to the pervasive Trinitarianism of Irenaeus's approach to salvation.[32]

This Trinitarian pattern in salvation is integrally tied to human history, for Jesus, the incarnate Son, recapitulates and corrects the history of Adam, leading to the Cross. This famous recapitulation

27. Ibid., 5.18.1–3 (PG 7:1172–75).
28. Ibid., 4.20.5 (PG 7:1034–36).
29. Ibid., 5.18.2 (PG 7:1173–74).
30. Ibid., 4.20.5–6 (PG 7:1034–37); Irenaeus, *Demonstration* 6.
31. Irenaeus, *Heresies* 3.17.1–2; 4.20.5, 33.7; 5.18.2, 36.2 (PG 7:929–30, 1034–36, 1076–77, 1173–74, 1223–24); Irenaeus, *Demonstration* 5ff.
32. Bobrinskoy, *Mystery*, 204.

theory is permanently associated with Irenaeus. The Word of God, became man, the Son of God became the Son of man, "so that what we had lost in Adam . . . we might recover in Jesus Christ,"[33] "that man, having been taken into the Word, and receiving the adoption, might become the Son of God." It is by union with the incorruptible and immortal one that we attain to immortality and incorruption.[34] The Son of God, our Lord, the Word of the Father, the Son of Man, repaired Adam's disobedience through a tree by his own obedience on the tree, and then ascended to the height above, "offering and commending to his Father that human nature which had been found, making in his own person the first-fruits of the resurrection of man; that, as the Head rose from the dead, so also the remaining parts of the body."[35] The Incarnation is integral to salvation.[36] For this, contrary to the gnostics, Jesus truly suffered on the cross.[37]

Irenaeus's Contribution

Irenaeus answers his opponents on each of their main points. He stresses the oneness of God. The Word and Wisdom, the Son and the Spirit, are fully God, but yet in no way detract from the divine unity. They work in union and harmony in creation, providence, and salvation, for they are in each other prior to creation. God has direct contact with all creation. He brought it into being himself directly—not through a range of intermediaries. God is distinct from his creation, but is not apart from it. Irenaeus sets his face against ontological dualism.

He roots this triadic view of God firmly in the Bible and in the history of salvation, in contrast to the philosophical speculation of his opponents. These matters directly affect our salvation, Irenaeus says. This triadic view of God, God's eternity, and human history, intimately connected by the work of God himself, is a clear and lasting contribution to theology.

33. Irenaeus, *Heresies* 3.18.1 (PG 7:932).
34. Ibid., 3.19.1; see also 3.18.7 (PG 7:937–40).
35. Ibid., 3 19.3; see also 5.14.2, 21.1–2 (PG 7:941, 1161–62, 1177–78).
36. Ibid., 3.19.1–3 (PG 7:938–41).
37. Ibid., 3.18.4–5 (PG 7:934–36).

Moreover, Irenaeus takes a few tentative steps toward considering the relations of the Father, the Son, and the Holy Spirit. Again, he does this from a biblical perspective, in his reflections on Jesus' baptism. The Father gifts the Spirit to the Son, who gives him to his people.

Tertullian

This stress on one God could lead in one of three directions. It could lead to a doctrine of the Trinity. Failing that, Christ and the Holy Spirit could be held to be of lesser status, subordinate to God, some kind of intermediate beings (*subordinationism*). But if Christ were less than God, he could not save us and his claims to be one with the Father would be false. Third, if the Son and the Spirit were accorded divine status, they could be simply temporary manifestations of the one God (*modalism*), not eternal personal distinctions in the one divine being. In that case, the revelation of God in human history as the Father, the Son, and the Holy Spirit would not accurately reflect who God is in himself, and so we would have no true knowledge of God.

Tertullian (*ca.* 160–220), a layman who was once thought to be a lawyer and a convert to the Montanist sect, opposes this latter error in his treatise *Against Praxeas*.[38] We know nothing elsewhere of Praxeas. We understand that he stressed that God is one—the Father, the Son, and the Holy Spirit being identical, not eternally distinct. This was modalism writ large. Tertullian directs his energies to asserting the distinctions of the Father, the Son, and the Holy Spirit.

Tertullian's Argument

Tertullian summarizes the catholic doctrine of the Trinity as it stood around A.D. 210–215. There is only one God. In this, the church agrees with Praxeas. However, this one God has a Son: "his Word, who pro-

---

38. Tertullian, *On Modesty* 21 also has a brief summary of the Trinity; see B. B. Warfield, "Tertullian and the Beginnings of the Doctrine of the Trinity," in *Studies in Tertullian and Augustine* (New York: Oxford, 1930), 1–109; Kelly, *Doctrines*, 110–15; J. Moingt, *Théologie trinitaire de Tertullien* (Paris: Aubier, 1966).

ceeded from himself (*qui ex ipso processerit*), by whom all things were made." He was sent by the Father into the Virgin and was born of her, and so is both man and God. Tertullian presents a statement of faith similar to the Apostles' Creed, including belief "in the Paraclete, the sanctifier of the faith of those who believe in the Father, and in the Son, and in the Holy Ghost." This rule of faith has come down "from the beginning of the gospel." Praxeas's heresy supposes that one can believe in the one God only by holding that the Father, the Son, and the Holy Spirit are identical. To the contrary, the catholic faith holds that God's unity is a trinity (Tertullian is the first to use the word *trinitas*). The three are three, "not in condition, but in degree; not in substance, but in form; not in power, but in aspect; yet of one substance (*unius autem substantiae*), and of one condition, and of one power, inasmuch as he is one God."[39] This is of great interest from a number of angles. It shows what was believed in the early third century. Moreover, Tertullian coins a new vocabulary, a lasting legacy to the Western church. Terms like *Trinity*, *person*, and *substance* will direct discussion permanently.

Tertullian gets to his argument at once. The one God exists in three distinct persons. The names *Father*, *Son*, and *Holy Spirit* are not ciphers, referring to the one God under different guises, but represent real, eternal distinctions. This Trinity does not subvert the monarchy (single rule). "The numerical order and distribution of the Trinity they [his opponents] assume to be a division of the Unity; whereas the Unity which derives the Trinity out of its own self is so far from being destroyed, that it is actually supported by it." Even the word *monarchy* does not preclude the governor from having a son or from ruling by whatever agents he chooses. If the monarch has a son, and the rule is shared, it remains a monarchy, since the two are inseparable. In the case of God, the Son and the Spirit are so closely joined with the Father in his substance (*tam consortibus substantiae Patris*) that his monarchy cannot be overthrown.[40] The monarchy is preserved in the Son, since it was committed to him by the Father. The same applies to the

39. Tertullian, *Against Praxeas* 2 (PL 2:180). Christopher Stead, *Divine Substance* (Oxford: Clarendon, 1977), 203, argues that in this work Tertullian connects *substantia* with *spiritus* for divine stuff composed of spirit.

40. Tertullian, *Praxeas* 3 (PL 2:181). Warfield, *Tertullian and Augustine*, 77–79, argues that Tertullian uses this famous analogy to say that the personal distinctions penetrate into the God-head itself, "a recognition of an ontological basis . . . for this manifested Trinity."

third degree in the Godhead, since the Spirit proceeds from the Father through the Son.[41]

Tertullian sees here an ordering of the persons (he is the first to use the term *persona*, meaning by it a concrete individual, rather than an actor's mask, as in prior secular usage[42]) of first, second, and third. The Son is second to the Father, while the Spirit is third from the Father and the Son.[43] This makes us wonder how far Tertullian, in combating modalism, is veering toward subordinationism, with the Son and the Spirit less than the Father. He suggests this when he considers how, before all things were made, God was alone—yet not alone, for he had with him his own reason (*ratio*), which he possessed in himself, that is, his own thought, which the Greeks call *logos*. Technically, Tertullian argues, God did not have his Word (*sermo*) at this time, only reason. God sent out his Word at creation. This seems suspiciously as if the Word came into existence only at creation and so had no preexistence. Moreover, was reason a distinct ontological reality? Was it a person or merely an attribute? The answer seems to be that Tertullian adopts the apologists' distinction between the immanent Word and the emitted Word. The Word was always inherent in reason, and reason was within God, but is explicitly a person only from creation.[44] This sounds, and probably is, subordinationist. In the rest of the work, he insists on the real personal distinctions of the three, and that they all share fully in the one being of God. Yet, although they are inseparable and indivisible, they are also first, second, and third, for the Trinity is "flowing down from the Father."[45]

Tertullian proves the distinction of the Father and the Son from their different names,[46] and from a number of OT passages (Psalms, Isaiah, and Gen. 1:26) where there are a plurality of persons, but one substance.[47] The key for him is "another . . . on the ground of personality, not of substance—in the way of distinction, not of division."[48]

41. Tertullian, *Praxeas* 4 (PL 2:182–83).
42. G. L. Prestige, *Fathers and Heretics* (London: SPCK, 1940), 84; Roy Kearsley, *Tertullian's Theology of Divine Power* (Carlisle, U.K.: Paternoster, 1998), 135–38.
43. Tertullian, *Praxeas* 7–8 (PL 2:184–87).
44. Ibid., 5; Kelly, *Doctrines*, 112–15.
45. Tertullian, *Praxeas* 8: "Ita trinitas per consertos et connexos gradus a Patre decurrens" (PL 2:187).
46. Ibid., 10 (PL 2:188–89).
47. Ibid., 12–13 (PL 2:191–94).
48. Ibid., 12 (PL 2:191–92).

The Father is invisible, but the Son has been visible—not only during his incarnate life, but in the OT as well.[49] This clear Father-Son distinction is yet an undivided and inseparable union, for the Son is to be reckoned as being in the Father, even when he is not specifically named.[50] In the NT, where the Father and the Son are distinct, but equal and united, this conjunction is clear in the Father's becoming visible in the Son's mighty works.[51] Similarly, the Holy Spirit is distinct from the Father and the Son in terms of personal existence, while one and inseparable in the divine being.[52]

Tertullian's conclusions can best be summed up in his own words, when he expounds the saying of Jesus, "I and my Father are one," in John 10:30—

> Here, then, they take their stand, too infatuated, nay, too blind, to see in the first place that there is in this passage an intimation of two beings—"*I and my Father*;" then that there is a plural predicate, "*are*," inapplicable to one person only; and lastly, that (the predicate terminates in an abstract, not a personal noun)—"we are one thing" *unum*, not "one person" *unus*. For if he had said "one person," he might have rendered some assistance to their opinion. *Unus*, no doubt, indicates the singular number; but (here we have a case where) "two" are still the subject in the masculine gender. He accordingly says *unum*, a neuter term, which does not imply singularity of number, but unity of essence, likeness, conjunction, affection on the Father's part, who loves the Son, and submission on the Son's, who obeys the Father's will. When he says "I and my Father are one" *in essence—unum*—he shows that there are two, whom he puts on an equality and unites in one.[53]

Tertullian's contributions are clear and important. The first to use *Trinitas* and *persona*, he sets the agenda for the Western church and is not superseded until Augustine. He is clear, ahead of his time. In writing of the Son as from the substance of the Father (*de substantia Patris*) and of the Holy Spirit as sent from the Father through the

49. Ibid., 16 (PL 2:198–99).
50. Ibid., 18 (PL 2:200–201).
51. Ibid., 21–25 (PL 2:203–12).
52. Ibid., 25 (PL 2:211–12).
53. Ibid., 22 (PL 2:207).

Son (*a Patre per Filium*), he coins phraseology later developed to consider the relations between the three.[54] In particular, by demonstrating the real personal distinctions in the Trinity, he sets up a barrier to modalism.

However, Tertullian has significant weaknesses, too. There is the subordinationist strain that we noted. Did the Word come into existence at creation? Was the Word personally coeternal with the Father? These are open questions. He seems to hold that the Son is a derivation or a portion of the Father's substance, the Father being the whole, although he does not mean that the Father's substance is divided, for it is inseparably one.[55] This tendency is exacerbated by his imagery of the intra-Trinitarian relations. The Son goes forth from the Father as a ray of light from the sun, with the Spirit as the apex of the light beam. The three can be compared to a root, a shoot, and its fruit, or to a spring, a river, and an irrigation canal. In each case, what proceeds is second to that from which it proceeds, while inseparably conjoined.[56] However, some form of subordinationism is standard, with Nicaea still a century in the future. For Tertullian, these relations refer to matters within the Godhead, with no implications of inferiority of status; they refer to origin, not to any inequality of being. As yet, the concepts are not present that can resolve this problem. However, the failings of both the Logos speculation and the monarchy theme are clear, for they carry a bias toward subordination and modalism, respectively.[57]

Origen

Origen (185–254), in contrast to Tertullian, is an Eastern theologian. He writes in Greek, not Latin. Unfortunately, most of his work has been destroyed, and we depend to a great extent on rather questionable Latin translations by his disciple Rufinus. He is also a highly

54. Ibid., 4 (PL 2:182–83).

55. Ibid., 9: "Pater enim tota substantia est: (b) Filius vero derivatio totius et portio" (PL 2:187); Kelly, *Doctrines*, 114; Johannes Quasten, *Patrology*, vol. 2, *The Ante-Nicene Literature After Irenaeus* (Westminster, Md.: Christian Classics, 1992), 326; J. Moingt, "Le problème de Dieu unique chez Tertullian," *RevScRel* 44 (1970): 337–62; Bertrand de Margerie, *The Christian Trinity in History*, trans. Edmund J. Fortman (Petersham, Mass.: St. Bede's Publications, 1982), 82–83.

56. Tertullian, *Praxeas* 8 (PL 2:186–87).

57. Warfield, *Tertullian and Augustine*, 88–109; Kearsley, *Tertullian*, 132–35.

controversial figure—long regarded as bordering on heresy, but in recent years enjoying something of a posthumous rehabilitation.[58] He writes at length on the Trinity in his major systematic work, *On First Principles*, which is directed against modalism, adoptionism, and gnostic docetism.[59] In particular, the old Marcionite dualism of OT and NT still lingers, separating the just Creator of the OT from the good Father of Jesus Christ. Origen responds by asserting that there is only one God, who created all things out of nothing, appeared to the OT saints, promised through the prophets to send his Son, and in due time sent him. In the preface, he summarizes the apostolic teaching.[60]

The most noteworthy—and controversial—element of Origen's Trinitarianism is his doctrine of the eternal generation of the Son by the Father. This is not entirely new, for we saw that Irenaeus teaches it, too. However, it is central to Origen's view of the relation between the Father and the Son.[61] He calls the Son "Wisdom." He does not imply by this that he is impersonal. Rather, he argues that God the Father never existed without his Wisdom, which was ever a particular *hypostasis* or *substantia* (substance). "Wherefore we have always held that God is the Father of his only-begotten Son, who was born indeed of him, and derives from him what he is, but without any beginning, not only such as may be measured by any divisions of time, but even that which the mind alone can contemplate within itself. . . . And therefore we must believe that Wisdom was generated before any beginning that can be either comprehended or expressed."[62] This generation is incomparable, for human generation is quite different. It does not happen by any outward act, but according to God's own nature[63] and eternally (not in time), having no beginning other than in God. There is no point at which the Son is nonexistent or the Father is with-

---

58. If such a thing can be enjoyed!

59. Charles Kannengiesser, in "Divine Trinity and the Structure of *Peri Archon*," in *Origen of Alexandria: His World and His Legacy*, ed. Charles Kannengiesser (Notre Dame: University of Notre Dame Press, 1988), 231–49, describes it as "Origen's greatest achievement as a theologian" and as "a ruling category in Origen's vision." Studer (*Trinity*, 79), on the other hand, cautions that this is an early work preserved only partially in the Latin translation made by Rufinus.

60. Origen, *On First Principles* pref. (PG 11:115–21).

61. Peter Widdicombe, *The Fatherhood of God from Origen to Athanasius* (Oxford: Clarendon, 1994), 90–92.

62. Origen, *On First Principles* 1.2.2 (PG 11:131).

63. Ibid., 1.2.4 (PG 11:132–33).

out the Son.[64] This distinguishes the Son from all creatures, which have a beginning as the result of an act of the Father's will. It follows that the generation of the Son is continuous; the Father communicates his divinity to the Son at every instant.[65]

Here Origen encounters and avoids a conundrum. He argues that this occurs by the will of the Father.[66] Here he distances himself from gnostic speculations, in which the divine nature is divided into parts by a series of emanations, and also from any necessity constraining God, with the Son's begetting happening according to nature. If that were so, he would be less than God, subject to a higher force over which he had no control. Therefore, Origen seems to suggest that the generation of the Son is a free act of the Father's will. However, if the generation were entirely free, the Son might not have been, and would be in the same category as the creatures. Origen has to balance these poles, will and nature, for either will subvert his central intention. How does he avoid this dilemma? This is where the *eternal* character of the generation is so vital. It places the relation between the Father and the Son entirely outside the realm of creaturely phenomena, beyond comparison or analogy, and so obviates the logical problem that would otherwise put an end to the whole argument. Hence, he can say that the Son is generated out of the Father's goodness as a counterweight to the Father's will. It is an act of divine freedom, but one that could never fail to be, for it comes out of the *essential* goodness of the Father (the goodness of the Father's being), not out of any *accidental* goodness (a goodness that is derivative or that might not have been).[67]

Following this, the Son is the image of the Father. This means for Origen that the Father and the Son have unity of nature (what they are like) and of substance (what they actually are). The Son (as God) is the invisible image of the invisible Father, the glory of his light, illuminating the whole of creation. It is a property of bodies to be visible, and of intellectual beings to know, so therefore the Father and the Son, since they are not material, are invisible and do not see each other, but know each other. However, we see the divine light of the Father in the

---

64. Ibid., 1.2.9, 2.11 (PG 137–38, 142–43). Widdicombe, *Fatherhood*, 69–70, points to the generation of the Son correlating with the fatherhood of God and thus being eternal.

65. Origen, *Homilies on Jeremiah* 9.4 (PG 13:356–57).

66. Origen, *On First Principles* 1.2.6 (PG 11:134–35).

67. Ibid., 1.2.13 (PG 11:143–45).

incarnate Son, for he is a perfect image on our level of the greatness of the Godhead.[68] The whole of Origen's doctrine of God thus focuses on the eternal Father-Son relation.[69]

The Father and the Son have unity of nature and substance,[70] and share one and the same omnipotence,[71] for there is no unlikeness between them.[72] Moreover, the Son is in the Father, and the Father is in the Son. This points toward the later development of the doctrine of the mutual indwelling of the three persons in the one divine being.[73]

What Origen says of the Son applies also, *mutatis mutandis*, to the Holy Spirit. He finds no evidence in Holy Scripture that the Spirit was created.[74] There is a distinct order in our knowledge of God, for it is by revelation of the Son through the Holy Spirit. As the Son, "who alone knows the Father, reveals him to whom he will, so the Holy Spirit, who alone searches the deep things of God, reveals God to whom he will." However, the Spirit does not know by revelation from the Son, for then he would pass from a state of ignorance to one of knowledge. Instead, he is one of the Trinity.[75] This is why we attain salvation only with the cooperation of the whole Trinity, and why we cannot become partakers of the Father or the Son apart from the Holy Spirit. Whereas the Father and the Son work in both the animate and inanimate creation, in both saints and sinners, the Spirit works only in those persons "who are turning to a better life."[76] So the Holy Spirit is eternally in the Trinity, and there is nothing in the Trinity that can be called greater or lesser. This is an important point, for it shows that for Origen the eternal begetting of the Son and also the position of the Spirit do not affect the place of either in the Trinity, nor diminish their status. These differences in their work—what will later be called *appropriations*—make no difference to their status. There is no difference in the Trinity, "but that which is called the gift of the Spirit is made

68. Ibid., 1.2.6–8; see 1.1.8 (PG 11:134–37, 128–29).
69. Widdicombe, *Fatherhood*, 63–92, esp. 78.
70. Origen, *On First Principles* 1.2.6 (PG 11:134–35); Kannengiesser, "Structure," 242.
71. Origen, *On First Principles* 1.2.10 (PG 11:138–42).
72. Ibid., 1.2.12 (PG 11:143).
73. Origen, *Commentary on the Gospel of John* 22.18 (PG 14:817–21).
74. Origen, *On First Principles* 1.3.3 (PG 11:147–48).
75. Ibid., 1.3.4 (PG 11:148–50).
76. Ibid., 3.1.5 (PG 11:253–56).

known through the Son, and operated by God the Father."[77] In short, the Father gives existence to all things, the Son grants a rational nature to his creatures, and by partaking of the Spirit we are made holy and cleansed from pollution and ignorance. Creation, providence, and salvation are all works of the entire Trinity. "In this way, then, by the renewal of the ceaseless working of Father, Son, and Holy Spirit in us, in its various stages of progress, shall we be able at some future time perhaps, although with difficulty, to behold the holy and blessed life."[78]

Major Questions

Origen is frequently labeled a subordinationist.[79] It is said that his doctrine of eternal generation, apart from its allegedly speculative nature, makes the Son secondary to the Father. In addition, he does not reflect at length on the Holy Spirit, implying a correspondingly lower status for him, too. Parts of the preface of *On First Principles* lend support to that charge. Rehearsing the catholic teaching, he says that it is not clear whether the Spirit is "born or not born" (*natus an innatus*). But in this preface he also says that the Spirit is accorded the same honor and dignity as the Father and the Son. We noted his insistence that there is no greater and no lesser in the Trinity, and that there is no biblical evidence that the Spirit was created. This is a subordination of *glory*, since the Father is the Father of the Son and the Spirit. While he uses the verb *egeneto*, meaning "created" or "made," in commenting on John 1:3, this cannot be used as evidence that he regarded the Spirit as a creature, for, until the Council of Nicaea in 325, the verbs *ginomai* (to make) and *gennaō* (to beget), together with their derivatives with one *n* or two, were used interchangeably. Crouzel points out that Origen uses *subsistentia* (an individual being) for the Spirit, which, since other terms were not available at the time, clearly indicates his status as a person.[80] Origen wrote relatively little on the Holy Spirit because he lived in the early third century. Only in 360 was

77. Ibid., 3.1.7 (PG 11:259–60).
78. Ibid., 3.1.8; see also 1.6.4; 2.2.2 (PG 11:261–62, 169–70, 187).
79. Kelly, *Doctrines*, 131, writes of "the thoroughgoing subordinationism which is integral to Origen's Trinitarian scheme." J. Nigel Rowe, *Origen's Doctrine of Subordination: A Study in Origen's Christology* (Berne: Peter Lang, 1987) takes the same position, but the author is transparently unable to understand basic Christian doctrine.
80. Henri Crouzel, *Origen*, trans. A. S. Worrall (Edinburgh: T & T Clark, 1989), 200.

the church called upon to expound and defend the place and work of the Spirit, and we shall see how Athanasius, Basil, and others were equal to the task, but until then there was no call for extensive reflection on the third person. Doctrine develops, for we are creatures of history. In this case, the development still lay ahead. Even so, there is enough to see Origen's basic orthodoxy.[81]

However, Origen is a research theologian, advancing ideas for consideration and discussion as well as for official teaching. He has a clear strand of thought in which the Son derives his deity from the Father. This flows from a hierarchy in the Trinity, according to which the Father works in the entire creation, the Son works among rational creatures, and the Spirit works among the saints. Neither the Son nor the Spirit is *autotheos* (God of himself), for they share in the Father's deity by derivation.[82] Indeed, in one famous passage Origen says that while the Son and the Holy Spirit are far greater than creatures, the Father surpasses them to an even greater degree. Yet he refers to the Son and the Spirit having the same glory as the Father.[83] Again, while he speaks of the Son as created (in a fragment carefully preserved by his enemies!), in the same breath he asserts that he was never nonexistent.[84] J. Rebecca Lyman concludes that while "his insistence on the uniqueness and eternity of the relation of the Father, Son, and Spirit precludes the extreme subordinationism sometimes attributed to him, the core of their unity remains the relation to the Father, the source of existence."[85] Origen's ambiguity,

---

81. Kannengiesser, "Structure," 246–47, points to "three first principles in one Godhead," wanting to have his extensive discussion later in the work "framed by a substantial dogmatic statement on divine Trinity . . . considered in itself and in view of . . . salvation." The work was in effect "a theological synthesis Peri Triados." See John Behr, *The Way to Nicaea* (Crestwood, N.Y.: St. Vladimir's Seminary Press, 2001), 185; Studer, *Trinity*, 84–85.

82. Origen, *On First Principles* 1.2.13 (PG 11:143–45); Origen, *Against Celsus* 5.39 (PG 11:1243–44); Bobrinskoy, *Mystery*, 192–93; Behr, *Way*, 188.

83. Origen, *John* 13.25 (PG 14:411–14).

84. G. L. Prestige, *God in Patristic Thought* (London: SPCK, 1952), 133. Prestige's treatment of Origen is well nuanced; Kelly, *Doctrines*, 128–36, is rather harsh and does not pay sufficient attention to the contexts of the passages that he cites. Crouzel, *Origen*, 203–4, argues for Origen's essential orthodoxy, warning against casting into heresy "the whole Church of the martyrs, for virtually all the Fathers of that period can be accused of subordinationism." See Henri Crouzel, "Les personnes de la Trinité sont-elles de puissance inégale selon Origène Peri Archon I, 3, 5–8?" *Greg* 57 (1976): 109–25.

85. J. Rebecca Lyman, *Christology and Cosmology: Models of Divine Activity in Origen, Eusebius, and Athanasius* (Oxford: Clarendon, 1993), 51. Bobrinskoy, *Mystery*, 212–13, recognizes that Origen follows the movement of the Trinity from the Father through the Son by the Spirit, and the reverse in prayer, by the Spirit through the Son to the Father.

occasioned by his propensity to think on his feet, would create problems for the East in the next century. Stress on the subordination of the Son and the Spirit would lead to the denial of their deity (by the Arians and the *pneumatomachii*), while the assertion of their deity in that context would foster allegations of tritheism (which Gregory of Nyssa would rebut).

In defense of Origen, he did not equate derivation of substance with inferiority. That was for a later time. Nor, in his day, was there a clear distinction between derivation and creation. Confusion reigned about the meanings of *created* (*genetos*) and *uncreated* (*agenetos*), and *begotten* (*gennetos*) and *unbegotten* (*agennetos*). In this linguistic and conceptual mire, Origen makes a crucial distinction between God uncreated (*agenetos*), applicable to all three persons, and God unbegotten (*agennetos*), only to be said of the Father. In addition to this verbal similarity, a further problem is that Gnosticism and much Greek thought equated creation and generation—hence, the system of emanations of Valentinus. Origen, on the other hand, distinguishes them, enabling the Son's begottenness to be understood in the sphere of deity, so paving the way for greater clarity in the next century through Athanasius. Widdicombe observes that Origen's aim is to stress both the Son's real individual existence and also his sharing of the Father's divine nature. He aims to keep a balance between these two fundamental ideas.[86]

Is Origen a forerunner of Arius? This portentous figure will surface in the next chapter, so the answer is best deferred until then. However, Origen several times makes a statement that Arius and his friends openly contradict, and the orthodox strongly assert. This statement, "There was not when he was not," maintains that the Son did not come into existence at some point, for he has always been and always will be. His relations with the Father are eternally in the context of the undivided Trinity. That is the crucial point that Arius would deny.[87]

86. Widdicombe, *Fatherhood*, 85–86.
87. Origen, *On First Principles* 1.2.9: "never at any time non-existent" (PG 11:138). See Origen, *Commentary on the Epistle to the Romans* 1.5 (PG 14:848–51); Caroline P. Hammond Bammel, *Der Römerbriefkommentar des Origenes: Kritische Ausgabe der Übersetzung Rufins: Buch 1–3* (Freiburg: Verlag Herder, 1990), 53; W. Marcus, *Der Subordinatianismus als historiologisches Phänomen* (Munich: M. Hueber, 1963), explores and distinguishes pre-Nicene subordinationism from that of the Arians.

F   I   V   E

The Arian Controversy

Beneath the surface of the third-century debate were problems ticking like time bombs, destined to explode sooner or later. The chief of these was how to reconcile the unity of God with the status of Jesus Christ within the framework of either the monarchian paradigm or the Logos Christology. For those who were determined to maintain the unity of God and resist anything savoring of two or three deities—the monarchians—there was a danger of regarding the Son and the Holy Spirit as identical to the Father, as different appearances of the one God at different times. This blurred any distinctions among the three, for they were at root not three, but one. This was modalism. We saw this with Praxeas, whom Tertullian opposed. Modalism continued after Tertullian, with Paul of Samosata being condemned by the Council of Antioch in 268. Earlier, Sabellius held that the only God, the Father in the OT, had become the Son in the NT, and sanctified the church as the Holy Spirit after Pentecost. The three were merely successive modes of the unipersonal God. Modalism is often called Sabellianism, and some think that Sabellius may have been Praxeas.[1] With modalism, God's revelation in human history as the Father, the Son, and the Holy Spirit does not reveal who he is eternally, and so we have no true knowledge of God. Moreover, the net effect is to under-

---

1. Bertrand de Margerie, *The Christian Trinity in History*, trans. Edmund J. Fortman (Petersham, Mass.: St. Bede's Publications, 1982), 85–87; Boris Bobrinskoy, *The Mystery of the Trinity: Trinitarian Experience and Vision in the Biblical and Patristic Tradition*, trans. Anthony P. Gythiel (Crestwood, N.Y.: St. Vladimir's Seminary Press, 1999), 217–20.

mine God's faithfulness, for we cannot rely on him if what he disclosed of himself in Jesus Christ does not truly reflect who he is eternally.

On the other side of the spectrum were those influenced by the Logos speculation. They recognized the distinctions of the three, and understood this by according a lower status to the Son and the Spirit, maintaining the unity of God with the Father imparting deity to the Son and Spirit. This was subordinationism. Many have thought that Origen exemplifies this view, but it was endemic at this time, for the conceptual and linguistic resources did not exist to distinguish between the way God is one and the way he is three. For now, this tendency was generally held within bounds by placing the relations of the three firmly within the Godhead.

However, this was an unstable and explosive situation. It only needed further pressure from one side or the other to erupt into open conflict. Modalism was suppressed at Antioch in 268, but the subordinationist question was still unresolved. Suddenly, bursting on the scene came an Alexandrian cleric named Arius. Around 318 he advanced criticisms of the theology of his bishop, Alexander. Examining these criticisms, Alexander concluded that Arius's position was heretical. The crux was his belief that the Son was not coeternal with the Father, came into existence out of nothing, and was in fact a creature. Such teachings would undermine the Christian faith. Jesus Christ could not then be the revelation of the one true God. Moreover, Arius was an effective propagandist. He attracted a large following, drawn by a range of popular choruses that he composed. The dangers for the church were great.

Arius

Arius was born around 256 in Libya. We have very little from his hand—three letters, a fragment of a fourth, and a scrap of a song, the *Thalia*. Otherwise, there are reports of what he is alleged to have taught, much of which may be biased against him. Ironically, while the crisis of the next sixty years is forever associated with his name, he was strikingly insignificant in it. M. R. Barnes and D. H. Williams summarize the situation well:

Perhaps the most central finding in the last fifteen years of renewed research . . . has been to show how peripheral the person of Arius was to the actual debates which occupied the church for most of the century . . . the name of Arius appears hardly at all in the literature of the first generation of "Arians," and the paucity of Arius' own writings seems to argue against his supposed importance. Later on, those accused of being followers of Arius either denied they were "Arians" or disavowed any formal connection to Arius. Arius himself, therefore, had only a minor role in the theological debates which were reputed to be a conflict over his views and which eventually bore his name.

Indeed, "few Greek polemicists, even if they are clearly pro-Nicene, bother to refute Arius."[2]

The compilers of the First Creed of the Council of Antioch in 341 began by saying, "We are not the followers of Arius (for how could we bishops follow a presbyter?)." Maurice Wiles emphasizes that even though Athanasius militantly attacked Arius, he had no confrontation with him personally, for "Arius was dead before Athanasius embarked on any large scale theological debate of the issues that Arius had raised. And then his real quarrel was with the living. The dead Arius was not even a whipping boy, but a whip."[3] Arius belonged to the past, to the world of the third century and its problematics, Athanasius to the fourth and a new way of thought.[4] He was not a significant writer, nor was he regarded as such by the people of his own day. He was hardly ever quoted by friend or foe.[5] He was never seen as a founding father of a movement. The polemics that arose later in the fourth century were directed at others than he. His name is simply a term of theological abuse. The controversy over his views subsided after Nicaea. Not until 357 did the crisis erupt in clearly articulated form. In Han-

2. M. R. Barnes, introduction to *Arianism After Arius: Essays on the Development of the Fourth Century Trinitarian Conflicts*, ed. M. R. Barnes (Edinburgh: T & T Clark, 1993), xvii.

3. Maurice Wiles, "Attitudes to Arius in the Arian Controversy," in *Arianism After Arius*, ed. Barnes, 43.

4. C. Kannengiesser, *Arius and Athanasius: Two Alexandrian Theologians* (Aldershot, U.K.: Variorum, 1991), 4:392.

5. R. P. C. Hanson, *The Search for the Christian Doctrine of God: The Arian Controversy 318–381* (Edinburgh: T & T Clark, 1988), 123.

son's words, he "was the spark that started the explosion, but in himself he was of no great significance."[6]

A common myth is that Arius challenged the orthodox doctrine, leaving Athanasius as the sole defender of the faith, *Athanasius contra mundum*. As with many such idealized portrayals of particular epochs, this is far from the truth. For one thing, "there was not as yet any orthodox doctrine for if there had been the controversy could hardly have lasted sixty years before resolution."[7] Theologians were feeling their way, differences and tensions existed, and no definitive statements had yet been made. After Nicaea, the situation was confused to the extent that detailed consideration of the differences—theological, political, personal, and ecclesiastical—is enough to make one's head spin. Nor was the controversy created by the supposed intrusion of Greek thought into the domain of biblical faith, although Greek concepts were used. It arose out of questions basic to the Christian gospel—belief in one God, together with the recognition that Jesus Christ is divine. "The theologians of the Christian Church were slowly driven to a realization that the deepest questions which face Christianity cannot be answered in purely biblical language, because the questions are about the meaning of biblical language itself."[8]

A Summary of Arius's Claims

Arius's views can be summarized as follows:

1. God is solitary, the Father unique. (This shows Arius's concern to maintain the unity of the one God.)

2. The Son had an origin *ex nihilo* (out of nothing). There was a time when he did not exist. He was created, existing by the will of God. Before he was created, he did not exist. (The logic here is that since everything created came into being out of nonexistence, and the

6. Ibid., xvii.
7. Ibid., xviii-xix.
8. Ibid., xxi. On the conflict, see also de Margerie, *Christian Trinity*, 87–91; J. N. D. Kelly, *Early Christian Doctrines* (London: Adam & Charles Black, 1968), 226–31; Bobrinskoy, *Mystery*, 220–21; Basil Studer, *Trinity and Incarnation: The Faith of the Early Church*, trans. Matthias Westerhoff, ed. Andrew Louth (Collegeville, Minn.: Liturgical Press, 1993), 103–5; Robert C. Gregg, *Early Arianism—a Way of Salvation* (Philadelphia: Fortress Press, 1981), 1–129; Kannengiesser, *Arius*; Rowan Williams, *Arius: Heresy and Tradition*, 2nd ed. (Grand Rapids: Eerdmans, 2001).

Word of God is a creature, so the Word of God also came into being out of nonexistence. Thus, God was not always Father, for before he created the Son he was solitary.)

(3.) God made a person (Word, Spirit, Son) when he wanted to create. In short, he created by an intermediary.

(4.) The Word has a changeable nature, and he remains good by exercising his freewill only so long as he chooses.

(5.) The *ousiai* (substances or beings) of the Father, the Son, and the Spirit are divided and differ from one another. The Father is the Son's origin, and the Son's God. There are two wisdoms, one that existed eternally with God, the other the Son who was brought into existence in this wisdom. Thus, there is another Word of God besides the Son, and it is because the Son shares in this that he is called, by grace, Word and Son.[9]

Gregg and Groh have argued that Arius was primarily concerned about the doctrine of salvation, not about the nature of God or cosmology. There is some truth to this, as Hanson and Kopecek agree.[10] According to this argument, it was necessary that the preexistent Christ be a creature to secure the closest possible link with his fellow creatures who were to be saved. Thus, he had free moral choice, advanced in virtue and obedience, and became a perfected creature, always in subordinate dependence on God. The text John 10:30, where Jesus says "I and the Father are one," was taken to mean a unity in harmonious agreement of will, not identity of essence. Thus, for Arius, will is primary, rather than essence. The Son was an assistant to the Father, operating under orders. Thus, the monarchy of God was preserved, since the Son was not, and is not, true God.[11]

From his opponents' perspective, the main problem was that Arius's attempt to identify the Son with human beings severed his connection with God. In particular, they were concerned with his idea that the Son came into existence from nonexistence. This clearly taught that the Son was a creature. After ecclesiastical maneuverings, Arius's

9. See Athanasius, *Of Synods* 16, for Arius's profession of faith.

10. Thomas A. Kopecek, *A History of Neo-Arianism* (Cambridge, Mass.: Philadelphia Patristic Foundation, 1979), 1:21.

11. Gregg, *Early Arianism*, 1–129.

views were outlawed by the Council of Nicaea in 325. Its creed will follow shortly.

Early Arianism

Those who followed Arius (we can hardly call them Arius's followers!) held the following tenets:

1. God was not always Father, for there was not always a Son. Prior to the Son, God was simply God. (Athanasius refers to the early Arians' habit of confronting a man in the street and asking him if he was a father before the birth of his son, following with the clinching point that neither was God always Father. Here we see their assumption that divine substance and generation were to be understood in a material sense, according to the analogy of human fatherhood and generation.)

2. The Son or Logos is a creature, made out of nonexistence. (This follows from the first point and the assumptions that underlie it.)

3. The Son is variable—changeable—by nature, and is stable by the gift of God.

4. The Son's knowledge of God and of himself is imperfect.

5. The Son was created by God as an instrument by which he created the world.

6. The Trinity, such as it is, is of unlike *hypostases*. Any unity is purely moral, not ontological, dependent on will, not essence.

The "Arians" (for want of a better word) wanted to protect God from involvement in creation, from human experiences and suffering. Jesus' human limitations showed that he was inferior to God. So he should not be worshiped. In the Incarnation, the Son took a human body, but not a human soul or mind (this had not been a matter of consideration hitherto and was not to arouse opposition until later in the century, when Apollinarius propounded it as a major theme and was condemned as a heretic at the Council of Constantinople in 381).

Arians wanted a God who could suffer, but, at the same time, it was inconceivable to them that the one God, the Father, could himself suffer. Revelation and redemption (and so the suffering entailed) had to be by one less than fully divine, since God could not come into contact with the creation without either deifying it or destroying it. They held to a nature-grace dualism, like Gnosticism, which kept God at a distance from any contact with the material creation. Thus, they needed a god of lesser status than the Father, one less than fully divine.[12] If this crisis involved Greek dualism, it was through Arius and his successors that it appeared, with their insistence on this radical split between the material and the spiritual. Hanson, accepting the broad lines of argument advanced by Gregg and Groh, suggests that the Arians "held their cosmological idea about Christ because of their convictions about his redemptive acts, and they were able to support their views about his redemptive acts with confidence because they thought they could satisfactorily relate them to their whole concept of God." In other words, theirs was a theology of salvation as much as a theory of the inner relations of the Trinity.[13]

Origen and Arius

The wide differences between Arius and Origen can be clearly seen:

1. Origen does call the Son a creature—but that is more than balanced by his stress on his being eternal and one with the Father. For Arius, the Son was created out of nonexistence, even if before time, and is part of the creation.

2. For Origen, subordination exists within the Godhead. Such subordination was *de rigeur* before Nicaea. For Arius, the Son is created by the Father, by the Father's will, and is external to the Father.

3. Origen sees the relation of the Son to the Father within the divine essence, whereas Arius considers the Son to be a product of God's will.

4. For Origen, the human soul of the incarnate Christ is crucial. For Arius, the incarnate Christ had no human soul.

5. Origen's doctrine of eternal generation is in utter contrast to Arius's claim that the Son was created by the Father. For Origen, "There never was when he was nonexistent," but for Arius, "There was when he was not."

Hence, apart from some minor similarities, it is a mistake to see Arius as following in the line of Origen or as inheriting his theology.[14]

12. Hanson, *Search*, 100–101.
13. Ibid., 26. Kannengiesser, *Arius*, 2:470, points to methodological and hermeneutical flaws in the Gregg-Groh thesis. See also R. Williams, "The Logic of Arianism," *JTS* 34 (1983): 56–81.
14. Hanson, *Search*, 70; Gregg, *Early Arianism*, 110–11; Kannengiesser, *Arius*, 2:472.

Williams agrees that "the confident ancient and modern judgment
that Arius represents a development within an 'Origenist' theological school cannot be sustained in any but a radically qualified
sense."[15] Indeed, it is hard to find any specific forerunners of Arius.
He strongly opposed any hint of Sabellianism, and this pushed him
to an extremely subordinationist position. Kannengeisser suggests
that Arius was a Christianized adapter of Plotinus, since he was basically a philosopher.[16] Both wanted to get their theology from the
Bible.[17] Opponents of the Cappadocians were to make the same cry
later in the century.

The Creed of Nicaea 325 AD

There is little that can be learned of the proceedings of the Council of Nicaea, at which Arius was condemned and exiled. One of the
few items of which we have clear and certain evidence is the creed that
was produced.[18] This is not what is today known as the Nicene Creed
(C), which is the product of the Council of Constantinople of 381,
although that is clearly based on the creed of Nicaea (N). This earlier
creed is as follows:

> We believe in one God Father Almighty maker of all things, seen and
> unseen:
>
> And in one Lord Jesus Christ the Son of God, begotten as only-
> begotten of the Father, that is of the substance (*ousia*) of the Father,
> God of God, Light of Light, true God of true God, begotten not made,
> consubstantial with the Father, through whom all things came into
> existence, both things in heaven and things on earth; who for us men
> and for our salvation came down and was incarnate and became
> man, suffered and rose again the third day, ascended into the heav-
> ens, is coming to judge the living and the dead:
>
> And in the Holy Spirit.

---

15. Williams, *Arius*, 148.
16. Kannengiesser, *Arius*, 1:38–39.
17. Hanson, *Search*, 126–28.
18. R. E. Person, *The Mode of Theological Decision Making at the Early Ecumenical Councils: An Inquiry into the Function of Scripture and Tradition at the Councils of Nicaea and Ephesus* (Basel: Friedrich Reinhardt Kommissionsverlag, 1978), 116n1, lists a wide range of works
that discuss the council.

> But those who say, "There was a time when he did not exist,"
> and "Before being begotten he did not exist," and that he came into
> being from non-existence, or who allege that the Son of God is of
> another *hypostasis* or *ousia*, or who is alterable or changeable, these
> the Catholic and Apostolic Church condemns.[19]

The reference to the Son being "of the substance (*ousia*) of the
Father" is an innovation. Athanasius tells us how it got included. When
it was proposed that the Son was "from God," the Arians agreed, since
they accepted that all creatures come from God. Therefore, in order
to say that the Son is indivisible from the substance of the Father,
always in the Father (and the Father always in the Son), the bishops
were forced to use extrabiblical terms to convey "the sense of Scripture," realizing that biblical language alone could not distinguish it
from the false teaching they were combating.[20] With the allied expression "consubstantial (*homoousios*) with the Father," this phrase would
create a mountain of ambiguity and prove to be a major bone of contention in the following decades. The problem was the range of meanings that *ousia* had at the time. It could have in view generic nature
(what is common to the three), asserting that the Son is of the same
nature as the Father. On the other hand, it could refer to a specific
individual nature (what is peculiar to one of the three), meaning that
the Son is of the same *hypostasis* as (identical to) the Father, which
would be Sabellian, erasing any distinctions between them. The final
anathema seems to reinforce this latter possibility, for it repudiates the
claim that the Son is of a *hypostasis* or *ousia* other than that of the
Father. Here the terms *ousia* and *hypostasis* are apparently synonyms,
as they were generally at that time and would be for decades afterwards. The Council of Constantinople (381) would use *hypostasis* for
the three, so Nicaea's assertion that the Son is of the same *hypostasis*
as the Father was by that time rejected. On a central, but less disputed
point, the phrase "begotten, not created" opposed the Arian claim that
the Son was a creature, by distinguishing generation from creation,
contrary to the Arians. The word *homoousios* was used because the

19. Translation by Hanson from the Greek text printed by G. L. Dosetti, *Il simbolo di Nicaea
e di Constantinopoli*, 1967, 226f., quoted in *Search*, 163.
20. Athanasius, *On the Decrees of the Synod of Nicaea* 19–21 (PG 25:447–54).

Arians could not apply it to the relationships of creatures to the Father, but this word would still be a problem for some time to come.[21]

Not surprisingly, the monarchians, led by Marcellus of Ancyra, were the happiest with N. The creed would be widely condemned in the following years. Marcellus and his supporters maintained that there is one *hypostasis* in God, a claim that struck many at the time as outrageously Sabellian and modalist. Later in the century, when *hypostasis* would be reserved for the three and distinguished from the one being or essence (*ousia*), such a claim would be condemned. That time had not yet come. Of course, Marcellus was content with a creed that seemed to affirm that the Father and the Son are of the same *ousia* or *hypostasis*, treating the terms as synonyms! However, while this seems to be the case, as Hanson observes, "the ancients did not suffer from the same passion for exact accuracy which modern scholarship displays."[22] Moreover, Nicaea's main achievement was to place on record once and for all that the being of the Son is identical to the being of the Father, dealing a mortal blow to subordinationism.

Yet Eusebius of Caesarea, who supported Arius, signed the document! For him and others, the phrase "begotten not made" distinguished the Son from the other creatures made through the Son. For him, the Son is probably a creature, but is not to be called something made. The anathemas at the end simply condemn nonbiblical terms, and Eusebius was a biblicist. He defended the condemnation of "Before he was begotten he did not exist" on the ground that everyone accepted that the Son existed before the Incarnation (which was when he considered him to have been begotten).[23]

The anathemas condemned the view that the Son "is of another *hypostasis* or *ousia*" than the Father. This is ambiguous and confusing. It would be heretical in the terminology of the Council of Constantinople (381), since by that time it was recognized that the Son must have a *hypostasis* (person) different from that of the Father. This Nicene anathema sounds Sabellian, erasing the distinctions between the Father and the Son. However, is it really Sabellian? One reason why this is unlikely is that many members of the Council vig-

21. Person, *Decision Making*, 92–94.
22. Hanson, *Search*, 164.
23. Ibid., 165–66.

orously opposed Sabellianism. It was probably understood to say
that the Son came from the Father's person, since the Father begat
the Son and the two are of the same substance. However, it would
be a major source of confusion. The creed did not end the Arian crisis—it confirmed its existence. For its part, the word *homoousios*
may, as some have suggested, be a Greek translation of Tertullian's
"of one substance," although Latin documents containing N do not
translate it this way, and few Western bishops were present at Nicaea.
In fact, *homoousios* was open to a wide variety of interpretations at
that time, so, by using it, the Council allowed a variety of people to
accept N, from the virtually Sabellian Marcellus of Ancyra to the
Arian sympathizer Eusebius of Caesarea. Behind it lurked the powerful presence of Emperor Constantine, who was determined to
achieve as widespread agreement as possible for the sake of imperial unity. No questions would be raised about *homoousios* for almost
twenty years, so it could not have been a matter of controversy at
Nicaea as it would become later.[24] It can be read as affirming either
divine unity or the equal deity of the Son, and the ambiguity may
not be accidental.[25] However, we lack knowledge of the detailed discussions and backstage politicking at Nicaea, and so definitive conclusions are precluded.

Terminological Inexactitude

The creed of Nicaea bequeathed to the church a lexical minefield
that would cause many casualties in the decades ahead. Hanson
remarks that "people holding different views were using the same
words as those who opposed them, but, unawares, giving them different meanings from those applied to them by their opponents."[26] If
we add the bewildering speed of events—ecclesiastical, political, and
theological—mixed with skullduggery on all sides, it is no wonder that
the mess would take so long to clear up. For this reason, what follows
may appear confusing and difficult. However, any attempt to simplify

24. Ibid., 169–70.
25. Person, *Decision Making*, 94–105; de Margerie, *Christian Trinity*, 90–100; Studer, *Trinity*, 101–14.
26. Hanson, *Search*, 181.

the perplexing problems of terminology or the variety of competing claims will not be true to the circumstances of the fourth century. Those were muddled times. To appreciate the work of Athanasius and the Cappadocians, to say nothing of what was to follow in successive centuries, we first need to know something of the crosscurrents of doctrine that they helped to calm.

Hypostasis/Ousia

The terms *hypostasis* and *ousia* were used interchangeably in Greek and by the Greek fathers. For many, they were synonyms. The technical theological meanings that eventually developed ("person" and "substance" [or "being"], respectively) were *not* what anyone understood by them for most of the fourth century, and it is anachronistic to project those meanings back to an earlier time when they simply did not apply. There was not at that time a single word for what God is as three that could command wide, let alone universal, agreement. The word *hypostasis* in Greek philosophy from 50 B.C. onward had different meanings for Stoics than it had for Neoplatonists, although in general it meant "realization turning into appearance."[27] In the NT, it means "confidence," but on one occasion (Heb. 1:3) it refers to the Son as the "exact imprint of the nature" of God. According to Prestige, it refers to "that which gives support," and thus to an individual entity. Hence, it is a reference to individuality, whereas *ousia* is reserved for a single object, the individuality of which is disclosed by means of internal analysis.[28] However, he focuses on the eventually agreed meanings and misses the point that for most of this time the two were used interchangeably.[29] Stead argues that *ousia* had a wide variety of meanings at this time, referring to existence, category, status, substance, stuff or material, form, definition, and truth.[30] Tertullian's use of *substantia* was a material one—with Stoic influence—and the Easterners involved in this controversy recoiled from such an idea. Hanson's pithy remark is to the point: "Tertullian may well have sup-

27. Ibid., 182.
28. G. L. Prestige, *God in Patristic Thought* (London: SPCK, 1952), 162–76.
29. Christopher Stead, *Divine Substance* (Oxford: Clarendon, 1977), 160–61.
30. Ibid., 133–56.

plied the West with its Trinitarian vocabulary; he certainly did not sup-
ply the East with its Trinitarian theology."[31]

Thus, at the time of the Council of Nicaea, (1) *hypostasis* and
ousia could be synonyms and could describe either what God is as
three or what he is as one, (2) *hypostasis* could refer to the three and
ousia could be either ignored or rejected, (3) *hypostasis* could be used
for "distinct existence" and *ousia* for "nature," or (4) uncertainty
could prevail. Sometimes single writers move from one to the other
meaning. A few (Hanson cites Arius and Asterius[32]) do clearly distinguish them.

According to N, the Son is from the *ousia* of the Father and is
homoousios with the Father. The creed condemns those who say
that the Son is from a different *ousia* than the Father. Stead thinks
that this means that the Son is from God, not from any external
source, and that it does not necessarily denote equal status. The
same applies to the anathema. He cites a range of sources to show
that they recognize three possible origins for the Son—from nonexistence, from an external source, and from the Father.[33] This assumes
that the words are used synonymously.[34] Hanson concludes that,
even for those who distinguish the terms, the concept "of what each
person of the Trinity is in his existence and proper form distinct
from the others had not yet been distinguished from the concept of
what all of them were as full and equal (or even as partial and
unequal) members of the Godhead."[35] Not only is there no commonly agreed term for the three, but the concept itself has barely
appeared on the theological radar.

Homoousios

In the third century, this term sounded gnostic, for very good
reasons. The gnostics used it, and it never indicated equality or identity.[36] Even worse, it was associated with Paul of Samosata and was
cited in his condemnation by the Council of Antioch in 268. Athana-

31. Hanson, *Search*, 184.
32. Ibid., 187.
33. Stead, *Divine Substance*, 233–42.
34. Prestige, *God*, 177.
35. Hanson, *Search*, 190.
36. Ibid., 190–91.

sius, who later championed the term, would be forced to recognize this unpalatable fact and would try to extricate himself by saying that Paul used the word in a different sense than N. The problem for us is that it is impossible to know how Paul used it![37] Whatever the case, it did not have a happy history before Nicaea. Moreover, it does not seem to have acquired a steady and recognized meaning. It hardly means "shared being,"[38] let alone "identity of being." Hanson suggests that it was used in N because Arius disliked it, but people like Eusebius of Caeasarea signed N, so we can be reasonably sure it was not intended to teach the numerical identity of the Father and the Son.[39] In fact, it may have been used merely to unite everyone who was opposed to Arius, by denying that the Son came from a source other than God.[40]

Genetos/Gennetos, Agenetos/Agennetos

Genetos (having come into existence, and thus created) and *agenetos* (that which has never not existed, never had a beginning, for it has existed eternally) are one pair of antonyms, as are the almost matching *gennetos* (generated, begotten) and *agennetos* (ingenerate, unbegotten). The close similarity of spellings and meanings is another source of confusion and contention. We saw that in the third century there was never a clear distinction between something created and something generated, although Origen began this process of distinction.[41] Arius and the Arians used the two pairs interchangeably for Christ, for they saw him as a creature. Athanasius, in an early work, was also confused.[42] The anti-Arians had to say that the Son was both *agenetos* (eternal) and *gennetos* (begotten of the Father)—*gennetos non genetos* (begotten, not created). The terms *prosōpon* (Greek) and *persona* (Latin), which came to refer to person, do not feature in the controversy.

37. Ibid., 195; Stead, *Divine Substance*, 216–17.
38. Prestige, *God*, 209–11.
39. Hanson, *Search*, 202.
40. Stead, *Divine Substance*, 233–42; Person, *Decision Making*, 92–105.
41. Kopecek, *Neo-Arianism*, 1:242–66; Prestige, *God*, 37–52.
42. Athanasius, *Orations Against the Arians* 1.30–31 (PG 26:73–78).

The Contending Parties in the Decades after Nicaea

The details, historical and theological, of the period following the Council of Nicaea are bewildering. We have neither space nor inclination to enter the labyrinthine complexities of this period. Hanson's volume describes these machinations in their often sordid detail. We will identify contending parties only for our convenience. In practice, the situation was fluid, and the various parties were not nearly as clear-cut as our classification implies.

Marcellus of Ancyra and the Miahypostatic Theologians

The most emphatic belief of Marcellus of Ancyra and the *miahypostatic* theologians was that God is one *hypostasis* in one *ousia*. The Son is only a word (Logos). The Logos is united to God, eternal, "put forth" (but not begotten—*begotten* is too anthropomorphic an expression), one and the same thing as God, and silent in the Father. The Logos was only called Son after the Incarnation. While God is called by the names Father and Son, there is only one *hypostasis* and only one *ousia*. *Homoousios* means for him "of identical being." He interprets the Nicene anathema literally. Thus, the Spirit is not a separate *hypostasis*. The three are names only. The flesh of Christ cannot be associated permanently with the Logos, and so it will be discarded at the end of Christ's reign, when the Logos returns to the Father, as Marcellus interprets 1 Corinthians 15:28. This sounds, and in reality is, Sabellian. He was regarded as Sabellian by Eusebius of Caesarea. He considered Nicaea (approvingly) Sabellian, due to its apparent equation of *hypostasis* with *ousia*. In short, there is only one person in the Godhead, and there are apparently no distinctions within it.[43]

This group's intent was to avoid any idea of the subordination of the Son to the Father. All biblical texts usually understood as referring to the preexistent Son, which imply a lower status than that of the Father, Marcellus instead applies to the incarnate Logos. Consequently, Marcellus and those who think like him fail to distinguish between the Father and the Son. Prestige suggests that Marcellus's posi-

43. Eusebius of Caesarea, *Against Marcellus* 1.1.4–5; 2.2.39–41 (GCS 14:4, 42–43); Marcellus, "Die Fragmente Marcells" (GCS 14:183–215); Marcellus of Ancyra (?), *Expositio Fidei* (PG 25:199–208).

tion encouraged many of different persuasion to adopt a hostile position toward N, in line with the Arians.[44] Whatever later modifications
he may have made (and these are open to doubt, due to the sketchi-
ness of the evidence[45]), he holds unflinchingly to his refusal to see distinctions in God. In this he could claim that he and his followers were
in line with Nicaea. As we have said, this position is hard to distinguish from modalism.

Anomoeans or Eunomians

At the opposite subordinationist end of the spectrum from Marcellus were the Anomoeans or Eunomians, who became prominent
after 355. Their main spokesmen are Aetius and, after him, Eunomius
(against whom the Cappadocians would write). They followed broadly
in the path of Arius.[46] For them, in effect, the Son is *unlike* the Father,
although there is no evidence they actually said that. The Father is
absolutely transcendent, the sole ingenerate (unbegotten) one. The
Son, who is generated, differs from the Father in both *hypostasis* and
substance. He is inferior and is not from eternity. These people are dis-
inclined to call the Son begotten. The Son is the sole being created by
the Father's will to be his minister in the creation of the world. He participates in the Father's perfections at a lower level. He is like the Father
in operation, but not in substance. They give a prominent place to late
Platonic philosophy and Aristotelian logic. They think knowledge of
God is open to everyone, and that it is easily and comprehensively
available. In turn, Eunomius raises the question of the Holy Spirit, the
most excellent of creatures created by the Son. Any notion of the Trinity is absent from Eunomius's writings. We will meet Eunomius in more
detail in chapter 7.

Homoousians

The term *homoousios* was originally used by Marcellus's sympathizers to counter the Arians. After Nicaea, it fell into disfavor due
to the ambiguity of *ousia*, which we have noted. Besides, it has a strong

44. Prestige, *God*, 222.
45. Hanson, *Search*, 231.
46. Kopecek, *Neo-Arianism*, esp. 133–61, 402-53.

flavor of Sabellian modalism, for it seems to blur all distinction between the Father and the Son. The homoousians insisted that the Son is of the same (identical) being as the Father. Athanasius revived the term in mid-century, but only when Basil the Great produced a new definition of *ousia* as the single substance or divine nature common to the three *hypostases*. By then, Basil had coined a new vocabulary to account for the one and the three. Using these new tools, the homoousians defended the unity of substance of the Father and the Son without being susceptible, in appearance or reality, to charges of eroding the distinctions between them.

Homoiousians

A reaction against the dominance in the late 350s of the homoian Arians (see below) quickly developed. Led at first by Basil of Ancyra, who succeeded Marcellus when the latter was deposed, the homoiousians are sometimes unfairly called semi-Arians. They never used the word *homoiousios*—so much for Gibbon's theory that all the fuss was over one Greek letter! Since they claimed that the Son is of similar or like substance (*homoiousios*) to the Father, they were anti-Arian, but wanted to avoid the Sabellianism that they saw inherent in the Nicene *homoousios*. This group gained strength after 355 in opposition to monarchianism (Marcellus of Ancyra) and the homoian Arians, as the Sabellian and Arian tendencies of both groups became clearer.

According to the homoiousians, the Son is *like* the Father, with full divinity and personal distinction. Likeness of *ousia*, it was felt, preserves against the twin dangers of seeing the Son as a creature, on the one hand, and of confusing the Son with the Father, on the other. The distinction is that the Father generates and the Son is generated. The Father and the Son are father and son in a *real* sense, and the Son is coeternal with the Father.

Basil of Ancyra attacked N for identifying the *ousiai* of the Father and the Son (understood in a Sabellian sense), and he also opposed those who said that their *ousiai* are unlike. He began to coin terms for God as one (*ousia*) in distinction from God as three (*prosōpon*).[47] He considered that *homoousios* blurs the distinction between the Father

---

47. Epiphanius, *Panarion* 73.10.1–11.10 (GCS 37:280–84); Hanson, *Search*, 355.

and the Son by identifying them. The letter of George of Laodicea (possibly cowritten with Basil of Ancyra) clearly states the distinct existence of all three persons and uses *hypostasis* for each. There is one ultimate principle (*archē*), but there are three persons (*prosōpon*). He attacks the neo-Arians for focusing on the ingenerate/generate distinction instead of the biblical Father/Son distinction, which entails relations and a shared nature.[48]

It is from the ranks of the homoiousians that the main forces for the Trinitarian settlement emerged—Basil the Great and the other Cappadocians. The foundations were laid by Basil of Ancyra and George of Laodicea, although they stressed the subordination of the Son to the Father. This had to be eradicated before any settlement of the crisis could be achieved. Athanasius acknowledged in his *Tomus ad Antiochenos* that of primary importance is not the precise form of words, but the meaning and intention behind those words. Hence, a rapprochement between the homoousians and the homoiousians was possible.

Homoian Arians

The homoian Arians were midway between the homoiousians and the Eunomians. Led by Acacius of Caesarea and Mark of Arethusa, they taught that Christ is simply "like" the Father. They avoided the term *ousia* for the relation between the Father and the Son. Their plan was to stick to biblical terms. Neither *homoousios* nor *ousia* occurs in the Bible. One writer said they did not call the Holy Spirit "God" since the Bible does not do so. Truth is to be found in reliable proof texts from Scripture.[49] In keeping with such a hermeneutic, they had a doctrinaire belief that they alone were right.

According to the homoian Arians, Jesus' weakness, ignorance, and disavowal of goodness point to the Son being a creature. The Son's subordination to the Father is evident from 1 Corinthians 15:28. All this is in the context of the uniqueness of the Father. In turn, the Spirit is subordinate to the Son as the Son is to the Father. The Father is incomparable and supreme. They stressed as much the dissimilarity of the three as any "likeness." There are clear distinctions of being. On

48. Epiphanius, *Panarion* 73.16.1–4 (GCS 37:288–89); Hanson, *Search*, 368–70.
49. Hanson, *Search*, 559–61.

the other hand, the Son was not created *ex nihilo*, but from the Father's will, not his nature, so they conceded that he could be called either created or begotten. If created, his creation must be distinguished carefully from the creation of everything else, since all other things were created *ex nihilo*. The subordination of the Son to the Father is drastic. The Father is the God of the Son. Eudoxius, perhaps facetiously, called the Father "impious" and the Son "pious," since the Son worships the Father, while the Father renders worship to none. Athanasius charges them with belief in two gods. "One could call this a Trinity; but it consists of a high God who does not mingle with human affairs, a lesser God who does, and a third—what?"[50] The Spirit is as rigorously subordinated to the Son, as the Son is to the Father. The Spirit worships the Son, as the Son worships the Father. In the mid-fourth century, it was possible to entertain the notion of varying degrees of deity. Many saw the matter as the Son being like the Father in power or activity, but not in substance.[51] They deeply opposed the Sabellian (and Marcellian) confusion of the three. Those who accepted Nicaea, they thought, were lapsing into Sabellianism, for the *homoousios* entails that the three are identical. The homoians were weak, for their formula was as much an attempt at political compromise as anything. They rose to prominence in the Second Creed of Sirmium in 357, briefly dominated, but after 362 split and dissolved. However, they staged a minor recovery in Italy in the 380s, causing problems for Ambrose around the time of Augustine's conversion.[52]

So the skirmish at Alexandria between Arius and Alexander was to cause quite unanticipated convulsions. Arius may have been unimportant in himself, but, as Rowan Williams remarks, "he stirred an intellectually careless Church into a ferment of conceptual reconstruction."[53]

50. Ibid., 570.
51. Ibid., 574.
52. See chapter 9.
53. Williams, "Logic."

Athanasius

Athanasius (295?–373), the five-times exiled archbishop of Alexandria who succeeded Alexander in 328, was controversial for the way he used his episcopal power. He was accused of diverting the vital grain supplies controlled by Alexandria as an anti-Antiochene tactic. He was also implicated in the alleged assassination of an ecclesiastical opponent and of using the unfortunate rival's severed hand for magical purposes. Fortunately for Athanasius, the murdered cleric was produced alive at a synod, with his hand attached.[1] Athanasius has been venerated by history as the one who stood alone for the truth against the forces of heresy. The reality is not entirely what romanticized hindsight might suggest. There was no definitively settled orthodoxy before 381, and Athanasius was not alone in defending the truth. Nevertheless, we can hardly exaggerate his contribution to the refinement and crystallization of Trinitarian dogma.

The Trinity Within Athanasius's Overall Theology

In order to understand Athanasius's Trinitarianism, we must consider how it fits into his overall theology.[2] This is doubly important

1. R. P. C. Hanson, *The Search for the Christian Doctrine of God: The Arian Controversy 318–381* (Edinburgh: T & T Clark, 1988), 239–73; Alvyn Petterson, *Athanasius* (London: Geoffrey Chapman, 1995), 10.

2. Khaled Anatolios, *Athanasius: The Coherence of His Thought* (London: Routledge, 1998); Basil Studer, *Trinity and Incarnation: The Faith of the Early Church*, trans. Matthias Westerhoff, ed. Andrew Louth (Collegeville, Minn.: Liturgical Press, 1993), 115–19; Martin Tetz, *Athanasiana: Zu Leben und Lehre des Athanasius* (Berlin: Walter de Gruyter, 1995); Frances

because of his strategic significance in developing the doctrine of the Trinity. There are three basic axes to his theology—creation, incarnation, and deification. Athanasius relates his view of God closely to salvation. In the early work *On the Incarnation*, possibly written in the 330s, he regards salvation in Christ as the renewal of creation:

> It is, then, proper for us to begin the treatment of this subject by speaking of the creation of the universe, and of God its artificer, that so it may be duly perceived that the renewal of creation has been the work of the self-same Word that made it at the beginning. For it will appear not inconsonant for the Father to have wrought its salvation in him by whose means he made it.[3]

His view of creation is clearly Trinitarian. The Word, Jesus Christ our Lord, was the agent in making all things out of nothing.[4] This extends to providence as well, for the Father through the Word orders all things, all things are moved by him, and in him they are quickened.[5] The Word by his own providence makes the Father known to all, so that through him they might know God.[6] In turn, man was created in Christ. Since Christ *is* the image of God, and man was created *in* the image of God, man was made in Christ:

> He did not barely create man . . . but made them after his own image, giving them a portion even of the power of his own Word; so that having as it were a kind of reflection of the Word, and being made rational, they might be able to abide ever in blessedness, living the true life which belongs to the saints in paradise.[7]

Thus, God "did not leave them destitute of the knowledge of himself," for "he gives them a share in his own image," so that they might get an idea of the Father, by such grace perceiving the image (the Word of the Father) and knowing their maker, so living a happy and truly

Young, *From Nicaea to Chalcedon: A Guide to the Literature and Its Background* (London: SCM, 1983), 69–83.
   3. Athanasius, *On the Incarnation* 1; see also 14 (PG 25:97–98, 119–22).
   4. Ibid., 3 (PG 25:99–102).
   5. Ibid., 1 (PG 25:95–98).
   6. Ibid., 12 (PG 25:115–18).
   7. Ibid., 3 (PG 25:99–102).

blessed life. God made us out of nothing, but also "gave us freely, by the grace of the Word, a life in correspondence with God."[8] If Adam and Eve had remained good, they would "by the grace following from partaking of the Word . . . have escaped their natural state."[9] Athanasius here brings together creation, providence, the Trinity, man, Christ, and salvation into an integrated whole in the first few pages. That, of course, was not the whole story, for sin entered and death gained a legal hold over us.[10] Since we could not be restored by repentance alone, which was insufficient to guard the just claim of God,[11] what was needed was the Word of God, who at the beginning made all things out of nothing. Again, salvation is re-creation.

Athanasius then explains the purpose of the Incarnation.[12] The Word was not far from us before, "for no part of creation is left void of him: he has filled all things everywhere, remaining present with his own Father." In becoming man, he took a body, no different from ours, giving it up to death on behalf of all, and offering it to the Father, so that, since all have died in him, the ruin of the human race might be undone (since its power was fully spent in his body). Moreover, he turns us from corruption to incorruption, quickening us from death by the Resurrection.[13] So the renewal of man made in God's image is by the image of God himself, our Lord Jesus Christ.[14]

Protestants are accustomed to think of an exchange occurring at the cross, where Christ took our sins and we received his righteousness. For Athanasius, an exchange of a different, although related, kind took place in the Incarnation. In becoming man, Christ received and assumed what is ours and, in doing so, sanctified (deified) it, making it fit for fellowship with God. In turn, he gave to humanity the grace of partaking of the divine nature.[15] This exchange in the Incarnation is the basis for Athanasius's teaching on deifica-

8. Ibid., 11 (PG 25:113–16).
9. Ibid., 5 (PG 25:103–6).
10. Ibid., 6 (PG 25:105–8).
11. Ibid., 7 (PG 25:107–10).
12. Ibid., 8 (PG 25:109–10).
13. Ibid., 9 (PG 25:111–12).
14. Ibid., 13 (PG 25:117–20).
15. Athanasius, *Orations Against the Arians* 1.42; 2.74; 3.40 (PG 26:97–100, 303–6, 407–10); Athanasius, *On the Incarnation* 9 (PG 25:111–12).

tion (*theōsis*)—"He was made man that we might be made God."[16]
Behind this lies NT teaching such as 2 Peter 1:4 (we "become partakers of the divine nature") and much in the writings of John. He
no more means that we cease to be human and become God than
he implies that, in the Incarnation, the Word ceased to be God and
changed into man. Rather, the idea is that of union and communion, just as the deity and humanity in Christ remain what they are,
but are in unbreakable personal union. At that time, the word *God*
had a degree of elasticity that can cover these possibilities:

> For therefore did he assume the body originate and human, that hav-
> ing renewed it as its framer, he might deify it in himself, and thus might
> introduce us all into the kingdom of heaven after his likeness. For man
> had not been deified if joined to a creature, or unless the Son were very
> God; nor had man been brought into the Father's presence, unless he
> had been his natural and true Word who had put on the body.[17]

Here Athanasius connects the central themes of incarnation and deification with the deity of the Word. The identity of Jesus Christ is crucial for salvation, he says. Similarly, he comments that the Son "has
become man that he might deify us in himself,"[18] and "we are deified
. . . by receiving the body of the Word himself" in the Eucharist.[19] Just
as creation and the Incarnation raise the question of the deity of Christ
and his oneness with the Father, so in turn deification points to the
oneness of the Holy Spirit with the Father and the Son.[20]

The Humanity of Christ

For some time, scholars have questioned whether Athanasius had
a significant place for a human soul in Jesus. Grillmeier follows this
line in acknowledging that, whereas after 362 Athanasius accepted
that Jesus had a human soul, in practice he attached no theological
significance to it. Quasten goes further, casting doubt even on what

16. Athanasius, *On the Incarnation* 54 (PG 25:191–94).
17. Athanasius, *Against the Arians* 2.70 (PG 26:295–96).
18. Athanasius, *Letters* 60.4.
19. Ibid., 61.2.
20. Athanasius, *Letters to Serapion on the Holy Spirit* 1.24–33 (PG 26:585–608); Athanasius, *To Epictetus* 6–7 (PG 26:1059–62).

Grillmeier allows.[21] A number of factors support this claim. First, Athanasius usually writes of the incarnate Christ in terms of a union of the Logos with a body, implying that the assumed humanity is physical only. Second, while death was seen at the time as a separation of soul from body, Athanasius talks of Christ undergoing a separation of the Logos from the body. Hanson even describes him as having a "space-suit Christology," the Word's relation to the body being no closer than an astronaut's body to his space suit.[22] Third, one of his closest collaborators against the Arians was Apollinarius of Laodicea, who was condemned in 381 at Constantinople for teaching that the Logos took the place of a human soul in Christ. This the church (both East and West) saw as an incomplete humanity, jeopardizing salvation. After all, how can human nature be soulless? In mitigation, all recognize that, unlike Apollinarius, Athanasius never denies that Jesus had a human soul. Moreover, while Athanasius does not devote much attention to this point, this is not where the battle was raging.

On the other hand, a number of passages written by Athanasius after 362 point to his recognition of Jesus' full humanity. In that year, in his synodal *Letter to the Antiochenes*, he writes:

> For they confessed also that the Savior had not *a body without a soul*, nor without sense or intelligence; for it was not possible, when the Lord had become man for us, that his body should be without intelligence: nor was the salvation effected in the Word himself a salvation of body only, but of soul also.[23]

Grillmeier suggests the phrase "lifeless body," but agrees this will not do, but Quasten misreads him and says that he accepts it.[24] Quasten is one-sided here, for the final clause in the sentence can only

21. Aloys Grillmeier, *Christ in Christian Tradition*, vol. 1, *From the Apostolic Age to Chalcedon (451)*, 2nd ed., trans. John Bowden (Atlanta: John Knox Press, 1975), 308–28; Johannes Quasten, *Patrology*, vol. 3, *The Golden Age of Greek Patristic Literature from the Council of Nicaea to the Council of Chalcedon* (Westminster, Md.: Christian Classics, 1992), 72–76; J. Roldanus, *Le Christ et l'homme dans la théologie d'Athanase d'Alexandrie: Étude de la conjonction de sa conception de l'homme avec sa Christologie* (Leiden: E. J. Brill, 1968), 252–76, 359–73; Charles Kannengiesser, *Arius and Athanasius: Two Alexandrian Theologians* (Aldershot, U.K.: Variorum, 1991), 7:108–10.

22. Hanson, *Search*, 448.

23. Athanasius, *To the Antiochenes* 7 (PG 26:803–4).

24. Grillmeier, *Christ*, 324; Quasten, *Patrology*, 3:74.

with difficulty be rendered "not of body only but of life also," and additionally reflects back on the earlier phrase. Moreover, the phrase in question is a direct rebuttal of the Arian denial of a human soul in Jesus.

Quasten, in referring to the *Third Oration against the Arians* (written between 339 and 345, according to Hanson), fails to mention sections where Athanasius teaches that Christ's humanity was a whole; instead, he points only to where he says that the death of Christ involved only the Logos and the body. But this speech has plenty of material belying Quasten's argument. Athanasius discusses at length Jesus' advance in human traits like wisdom and his emotional distress at the time of his death, and he also refers to his human weakness.[25] Besides, these speeches were composed before 362, before Athanasius gained a better awareness of the humanity of Christ.

Quasten also cites the *Letter to Epictetus*, which was to acquire almost canonical status and be quoted by the Council of Chalcedon (451). He quotes paragraphs 5–6, where Athanasius omits to mention the departure of Christ's soul from his body at all. However, Quasten does not refer to paragraph 7, where Athanasius insists that salvation extends to the whole person, body and soul, and so

> the Saviour having in very truth become man, the salvation of the whole man was brought about. For if the Word were in the body putatively, as they say, and by putative is meant imaginary, it follows that both the salvation and the resurrection of man is apparent only. . . . But truly our salvation is not merely apparent, nor does it extend to the body only, but the whole man, body and soul alike, has truly obtained salvation in the Word himself. That then which was born of Mary was according to the divine Scriptures human by nature, and the body of the Lord was a true one; but it was this, because it was the same as our body, for Mary was our sister inasmuch as we are all from Adam.

"Body" here is equivalent to the whole person, and Christ's likeness with the rest of us is very clear.[26]

25. Athanasius, *Against the Arians* 3.52–57 (PG 26:431–44); Quasten, *Patrology*, 3:72–76.
26. Athanasius, *To Epictetus* 7 (PG 26:1061–62); Quasten, *Patrology*, 3:72–76.

Frequently Athanasius says that Christ took a human nature just like ours[27] and points to the common practice of Scripture to call human beings "flesh."[28] Jesus' advance in wisdom occurred as his humanity advanced in divine wisdom.[29] As a result, since Christ's advance was for the sake of all, people then advance. This growth in wisdom is humanity's deification—not becoming less human, but more so. According to the flesh, the Logos (as man) is ignorant, demonstrating that his humanity is genuine and that the Logos *qua* Logos is not the unqualified subject.[30] This is integrally connected to Athanasius's soteriology—Christ's ignorance, fear, and thirst free us from these things by divinization. The Logos becomes man, a man like all others, at once knowing and ignorant. Finally, Athanasius constantly reiterates the Nicene formula—the Logos, in becoming flesh, became man—a rebuttal of the Arian denial of a human soul in Jesus. Moreover, while the Arians cited Proverbs 8:22 to prove that the Logos was a creature, Athanasius consistently interpreted it as referring to the humanity of Christ.[31]

However, for Athanasius the decisive fulcrum is the Incarnation. As a result, the Cross has diminished significance. Hanson likens his theory of salvation to a sacred blood transfusion that almost does away with a doctrine of the Atonement.[32] Athanasius lacks reasons why Christ should have died. For him, corruption consists in fallenness, rather than in sin.

The Son, One in Being with the Father

As we have seen, the key point in the fourth-century controversies was the relationship of the Son to the Father. Athanasius strenuously supports the Council of Nicaea and defends its use of *homoousios* in this connection. Knowledge of the Trinity, he consistently maintains, comes through the Son. In his short work on Luke 10:22 (*In illud omnia*), he sums up his teaching on this vital matter.

27. Athanasius, *To Epictetus* 5 (PG 26:1057–60); Athanasius, *Incarnation* 34 (PG 25:153–56); Athanasius, *Against the Arians* 2.61 (PG 26:275–78).

28. Athanasius, *Against the Arians* 3.30 (PG 26:387–88).

29. Ibid., 3.52–53 (PG 26:431–36).

30. Ibid., 3.46 (PG 26:419–22).

31. Athanasius, *Against the Arians* 2.8ff. (PG 26:161ff.); Widdicombe, *Fatherhood*, 215ff.

32. Hanson, *Search*, 450–51.

The divine essence (being) of the Word is united by nature to his own Father. Whatever is in the Father is in the Son. Since the Father is not a creature, neither is the Son. The will of the Father and the will of the Son are one, since they are indivisible. The Son is an exact seal of the Father. The triad is one and indivisible, without degrees; there is no first, second, or third God. This is a complete rebuttal of all in the Arian camp.[33]

As is his custom, Athanasius springs to the defense of the Council of Nicaea. The expression in its creed, "from the essence (*ousia*) of the Father," was inserted, he claims, expressly to distinguish the Son from creatures. The Word alone comes from the being of the Father, and is emphatically not a creature.[34] The Son is consubstantial with the Father, existing out of the being of the Father. Whatever the Father has, the Son has.[35]

T. F. Torrance correctly points to Athanasius's movement from the saving acts of God in the incarnation of the Son, by way of the Nicene formula, to the ultimate ground of the Trinity in the eternal relations and distinctions of the persons in the one being of the Godhead.[36] Thus, the Son is inseparable from, and proper to, the Father's essence (being). He and the Father are one being. He is not a creature, as Arius had claimed and as Aetius and Eunomius were alleging. Created things have a beginning. However, the Word comes from the Father, who is without beginning. So too the Son is without beginning, as the offspring of the Father. The bishops at Nicaea were compelled to use extrabiblical terms "to collect the sense of Scripture," to rewrite more distinctly what was in Scripture. Since the Son is one with the Father, he is "very God . . . one in essence with the Father." He is the expression of the Father's person, "light from light," the very image of the Father's essence. As Photius, the ninth-century patriarch of Constantinople, was to say, in *The Mystagogy of the Holy Spirit*, the expression "light from light" shows the consub-

33. Athanasius, *On Luke 10:22 (Matthew 11:27)* 4–6 (PG 25:215–20); Thomas F. Torrance, *Trinitarian Perspectives: Toward Doctrinal Agreement* (Edinburgh: T & T Clark, 1994), 8ff.
34. Athanasius, *On the Decrees of the Synod of Nicaea* 19 (PG 25:447–50).
35. Athanasius, *Serapion* 2.5 (PG 26:616).
36. Torrance, *Trinitarian Perspectives*, 9–10.

stantiality of the Son with the Father.[37] Since the Father is everlasting, so is the Son.[38]

Hence, the Son had no beginning, but was eternally begotten. In
his early work, the *Statement of Faith*, Athanasius talks of the Father's
deity passing to the Son without flow or division. This has the feel of
subordination in the sense of the Son receiving his deity from the Father,
as almost a secondary manifestation of God. However, Athanasius
stresses in the immediately preceding context that there are two distinct objects (the Father and the Son), but also cautions that "as the
well is not a river, nor the river a well, but both are one and the same
water which is conveyed in a channel from the well to the river," so
the Father's deity passes without division into the Son.[39] Athanasius is
grappling with a form of expression to convey the unity of being, but
at that early stage has not found one that was adequate to the task.

However, building on Origen, Athanasius consistently thereafter
points to eternal generation as exemplifying the Son's oneness with
the Father, and opposing the idea that he is a creature. According to
the Arians, if the Son is coeternal with the Father, he is his brother,
not his Son. Athanasius responds by saying that the Father and the
Son were not generated from some preexisting origin, "but the Father
is the origin of the Son and begat him; and the Father is Father, and
not born the son of any; and the Son is Son, and not brother." He is
eternal, "for where it is proper to men to beget in time, from the imper-
fection of their nature, God's offspring is eternal, for his nature is ever
perfect."[40] Indeed, the Son is the proper offspring from the Father's
being. If the Son were not with the Father from everlasting, then the
triad would not be from everlasting. Instead, there would be a monad
first and afterwards by addition a triad, consisting of alien essences.
That obviously will not do.[41] Rather, the Son is the offspring of the
Father, eternal and coexistent with him. "The divine generation must
not be compared to the nature of men, nor the Son considered [merely]

37. Photius, *On the Mystagogy of the Holy Spirit*, trans. Holy Transfiguration Monastery
(n.p.: Studion Publishers, 1983), 92–93, 170.

38. Athanasius, *On the Decrees* 20 (PG 25:449–54); Athanasius, *Against the Arians* 2.57;
1.9, 13 (PG 26:68–69, 28–32, 37–40).

39. Athanasius, *Statement of Faith* 2 (PG 25:203–4).

40. Athanasius, *Against the Arians* 1.14 (PG 26:41–42).

41. Ibid., 1.16–17 (PG 26:44–48).

to be part of God, nor the generation to imply any passion whatever."
God is not composed of parts. This generation was impassable and
eternal.[42] God begets not as man begets, but as God. He does not
make man his pattern.[43] Men beget and are begotten in succession. A
man, begotten by his father, in turn begets a son and becomes a father
to him. But it is not so with God, for the Father is not from a father,
nor does he beget one who will become a father. In the Godhead, the
Father is properly Father, and the Son is properly Son. In them and
in them only is it true that the Father is ever Father and the Son is
ever Son. These are eternal and unchangeable distinctions.[44] We may
call a man a maker although he has not yet made anything, but he
cannot be called a father unless a son exists. In stark contrast, the
Son, not being a work, but being proper to the Father's essence, must
always be.[45]

Following this, Athanasius stresses that language about God is
analogical. What we speak about God, we speak with regard to his
existence in a mode appropriate to him. Thus, this generation is unlike
human generation. We must not conceive of the things of God in a
human way, or we will fall into error. We understand the terms in different senses for God and men, for humans are incapable of self-
existence and are enclosed in place, whereas God is self-existent and
encloses all things.[46] So the Son's generation is inseparable from the
nature of the Father. He and the Father are ever one—the Word ever
in the Father, and the Father in the Word, as the radiance is to the
light.[47] Again, God does not, like man, beget a son by division of himself. The Father is not himself from a father as a human father is, nor
is the Son a part of the Father. Nor does the Son beget as he has been
begotten, but is the "whole image and radiance of the whole" (*holos
holou*). The Father is eternally Father, and the Son is eternally Son.
The Father can never be a son, nor can the Son ever be a father. The
Son is Son of the Father.[48]

42. Ibid., 1.27–28 (PG 26:68–72).
43. Ibid., 1.23 (PG 26:60).
44. Ibid., 1.21, 34 (PG 26:56–57, 81–84).
45. Ibid., 1.29 (PG 26:72–73).
46. Athanasius, *On the Decrees* 10–11 (PG 25:431–36).
47. Ibid., 20 (PG 25:449–52); Athanasius, *Serapion* 1.16 (PG 26:568–69).
48. Athanasius, *Serapion* 1.16 (PG 26:568–69).

Underlying this analogical language is the relationship between words and reality. The words we use are to be governed by the reality that they are intended to signify. "For terms do not disparage his nature; rather that nature draws to itself those terms and changes them. For terms are not prior to essences, but essences are first, and terms second." When the essence is a creature, the words "he made" are used, but when the essence is an offspring or Son, "he made" or "he created" are not proper to it. "For nature and truth draw the meaning to themselves."[49] With the priority of the reality recognized, he writes later to the Antiochenes, urging a certain flexibility in the use of words, providing the intention behind those words is acceptable. He counsels that those who explain and hold the truth aright should "not . . . fight about words to no useful purpose."[50] On the other hand, some terms are more appropriate to the reality than others; it is more pious and accurate to name God in connection with his Son and call him Father, than to name him from his works and call him Unoriginate. The latter relates to all God's works, but *Father* has its significance only from the Son.[51] This is a strikingly relevant commentary on trends in our own day, when feminist theologians want to rename God so as to eradicate the male names of the Father and the Son. What transpires from these attempts, at best, is a depersonalizing of God by such names as Creator, Provider, or Redeemer.

Let us recall briefly the striking phrase that Athanasius uses of the Son, *holos theou*[52] (cf. *holos holou*[53]). The Son is "whole God." Athanasius explains this further. He who looks at the Son, he says, sees the Father. In turn, the Father's Godhead is in the Son and is seen in the Son. The Father is in the Son. The being of the Son is the proper offspring of the Father's being. For the Son is such as the Father is, since he has all that is the Father's. He who worships and honors the Son, in the Son worships and honors the Father, for the Godhead is one. Therefore, the worship and honor is one that is given to the Father in and through the Son. He who thus worships, worships one God. The expression in the *Letters to Serapion*, "whole of whole," he explains as fol-

49. Athanasius, *Against the Arians* 2.3–4 (PG 26:151–56).
50. Athanasius, *To the Antiochenes* 5–8 (PG 26:799–806).
51. Athanasius, *Against the Arians* 1.34 (PG 26:81–84).
52. Ibid., 3.6 (PG 26:333–34).
53. Athanasius, *Serapion* 1.16 (PG 26:568–69).

lows. The Father, being one and only, is Father of a Son who is one and only. The Son is not part of the Father, and so does not himself beget, "but is whole image and radiance of the whole." Shapland argues in his note on the phrase that it signifies the perfection and totality of the image. The Son is not a picture of the Father, emanating from him, but is the perfect expression of all that God is. The use of *holos* excludes the notion of partiality and defect. The Son is not part of God, nor is he less than God. Athanasius does not use analogy in the way that the Arians do, referring to a reproduction of an original.[54] In short, we may say, Athanasius asserts the Son's *identity in being* with the Father. All that the Father is, the Son is, except for being Father. Nothing could be further removed from subordinationism. This is of a piece with his vaunted defense of *homoousios*, "the controlling centre of his thought," on which the truth of the gospel depends.[55] From this, to know the incarnate Son is immediately to know the Father, for there is no gap between the being of the Father and the being of the Son.[56]

Athanasius also guards against another possible modification of his teaching. He argues that there is no external development of the Father's essence.[57] If there is anything about or surrounding him that completes the essence, so that when we say "Father" we do not signify the invisible and incomprehensible essence "but something about it" (*peri auton*), we would be blaspheming. When we say "Father," we denote his essence itself. This point would not be remembered too well, for the East was to develop the idea that we know God's energies, that which he puts forth in creation and redemption, but not his essence, which is unknowable.[58]

54. Athanasius, *The Letters of Saint Athanasius Concerning the Holy Spirit*, trans. C. R. B. Shapland (London: Epworth Press, 1951), 102–3; Athanasius, *Against the Arians* 1.20–21 (PG 26:53–57).

55. Torrance, *Trinitarian Perspectives*, 10–12. In agreement is J. Rebecca Lyman, *Christology and Cosmology: Models of Divine Activity in Origen, Eusebius, and Athanasius* (Oxford: Clarendon, 1993), 147–48, who says that the essential identity of the Father and the Son is "an axiom of [Athanasius's] thought." Peter Widdicombe, *The Fatherhood of God from Origen to Athanasius* (Oxford: Clarendon, 1994), 188ff., sees this as the basis of his theology of creation and salvation. But see the qualifications made by Christopher Stead, *Divine Substance* (Oxford: Clarendon, 1977), 260–61.

56. Widdicombe, *Fatherhood*, 205.

57. Athanasius, *On the Decrees* 22 (PG 25:453–56).

58. See chapter 11, where we will consider the theology of John of Damascus and Gregory Palamas.

The Persons of the Trinity, Indivisible

Referring with approval to the words of Dionysius, a predecessor at Alexandria, Athanasius states that the Father and the Son are not separated, "but in their hands is the Spirit, who cannot be parted either from him that sent or from him that conveyed him." The monad is extended indivisibly into the triad, and the triad is gathered together without diminution into the monad.[59] This insistence that the persons of the Trinity cannot be separated is a constant theme for Athanasius. The Father, possessing his existence from himself, begat the Son as a river from a well, as a branch from a root, as brightness from a light—all things that nature knows are indivisible.[60]

The Son is consubstantial with the Father, out of the being of the Father. Whatever the Father has, the Son has.[61] The Trinity is indivisible, so wherever the Father is mentioned, the Son should also be understood. Thus, where the Father is mentioned, his Word and the Spirit who is in the Son are also included. If the Son is named, the Father is in the Son, and the Spirit is not outside the Word. One grace is fulfilled through the Son in the Holy Spirit.[62] If there is such unity in the holy triad, who can separate the Son from the Father, or the Spirit from the Son or the Father?[63] The oneness and indivisibility of the triad destroys any notion of subordination, for the triad is without degrees, "united without confusion . . . distinguished without separation."[64]

With Athanasius we see the beginnings of the doctrine of the mutual indwelling of the three persons (later to be called perichoresis). The Father is in the Son, and the Son is in the Father, Athanasius states, following the language of John's gospel. This is not to be understood as if they were emptied into each other, as if neither were complete in himself. Nor is it akin to the sense in which God comes into the saints to strengthen them, for the Son is not Son by participation, but by being the Father's offspring. Nor is the Father in the Son in the sense of the aphorism "In him we live

59. Athanasius, *Defence of Dionysius* 17 (PG 25:503–6).
60. Athanasius, *Statement of Faith* 4 (PG 25:203–6).
61. Athanasius, *Serapion* 2.5 (PG 26:616).
62. Ibid., 1.14, 17 (PG 26:564–65, 569–72).
63. Ibid., 1.20 (PG 26:576–80).
64. Athanasius, *On Luke 10:22 (Matthew 11:27)* 6 (PG 25:217–20); Athanasius, *Serapion* 1.33; 3.5–6 (PG 26:605–8, 632–33).

and move and have our being," for the Son himself is life and gives life. This is mutual indwelling, for the whole being of the Son is proper to the Father's essence, as radiance from light. The Son is what is from the Father and proper to him. The form and Godhead of the Father constitute the being of the Son, and from this it follows that the Father is in the Son and the Son is in the Father. The identity of the Godhead and the unity of being (essence) is shown by this. The Father and the Son are not two separate beings, but neither are they one being named twice. They are two, for the Father is eternally Father and not the Son, and the Son is eternally Son and not the Father. Later theologians will use the term *hypostasis* (person) for this distinction. But, concurrently, their nature is one, in the identity of the one Godhead. The Godhead of the Son is the Father's and thus is indivisible, so there is one God. So "the same things are said of the Son which are said of the Father, except his being said to be the Father." The Godhead of the Father is the being of the Son, and so the Son is "whole God." He who looks at the Son sees the Father. The Son is what the Father is, since he has all that is the Father's, for he is one in being with the Father.[65] From this, the Father and the Son know each other fully and mutually delight in each other.[66] So, *mutatis mutandis*, the Holy Spirit is in the Son as the Son is in the Father.[67]

On the other hand, we ourselves are also considered to be "in God." The central idea of deification bears witness to this. Athanasius is aware of a possible confusion here, and so he demonstrates that this differs markedly from the way in which the Son is in the Father. The Son does not merely partake of the Spirit or receive the Spirit as we do, for he actually supplies the Spirit. Nor does the Spirit unite the Son to the Father as he unites us to the Father, but he receives from the Father. The Son is in the Father by nature eternally, but we by nature are distant from God and our being in the Father is not ours, but the Spirit's, who is in us.[68] We creatures are enabled by the Spirit

65. Athanasius, *Against the Arians* 3.1–6; see also 1.9; 3.19–25 (PG 26:321–34, 27–32, 361–78); Athanasius, *On the Decrees* 20 (PG 25:449–54); Athanasius, *On Luke 10:22 (Matthew 11:27)* 5 (PG 25:217–18).

66. Widdicombe, *Fatherhood*, 206–7, citing Athanasius, *Against the Arians* 1.20, 38; 2.56, 82 (PG 26:53–54, 89–92, 265–68, 319–22).

67. Athanasius, *Serapion* 1.14 (PG 26:564–65); Torrance, *Trinitarian Perspectives*, 10, 16–18, 20.

68. Athanasius, *Against the Arians* 3.24 (PG 26:373–76).

to commune with God and be united to him, but the Son and the Spirit are by nature one with the Father from eternity.

The Spirit in Relation to the Father and the Son

Athanasius's *Letters to Serapion on the Holy Spirit* are the first extensive treatment of the Holy Spirit in the history of the church, written between 355 and 360 and antedating Basil the Great's famous treatise. These letters are written against the *tropicii* (trope mongers) who, while accepting the deity of the Son, balked at ascribing the same status to the Spirit. In line with what we have seen, Athanasius considers the Spirit to be inseparably united to the Father and the Son. Since he proceeds from the Father, he is ever in the hands of the Father, who sends him, and of the Son, who conveys him.[69] He is united to the Godhead of the Father and the Son. So, in the days of Moses, God led the people through the Word in the Spirit.[70] The Spirit is in Christ as the Son is in the Father. What is spoken from God is said through Christ in the Spirit.[71] Against the argument of the *tropicii* that if the Spirit is from the Father he must be a second son and a brother to the Son, Athanasius replies that there is no other father than the Father, and no other son than the Son. Hence, the one and only Father is the Father of a Son who is one and only.[72] The Spirit cannot change, fills all things, and in the Word is present in all things.[73]

Athanasius turns to one of the most fruitful biblical accounts for an understanding of the relation between the Son and the Spirit, that of the baptism of Jesus in the river Jordan. There Jesus was anointed with the Holy Spirit, and in turn supplied the Spirit to his church. Since he sanctified himself for our sake, the descent of the Spirit at the Jordan was a descent upon us because Jesus bore our body. When he was washed in the Jordan, we were washed in him and by him. When he received the Spirit, we received it through him. The flesh that he assumed was anointed, and this for us. Only the Son could unite us to the Holy Spirit, for the Spirit is his. Athanasius affirms repeatedly that

---

69. Athanasius, *Statement of Faith* 4 (PG 25:203–6).
70. Athanasius, *Serapion* 1.12; 2.5 (PG 26:560–61, 616).
71. Ibid., 1.14 (PG 26:564–65).
72. Ibid., 1.16 (PG 26:568–69).
73. Ibid., 1.26 (PG 26:589–93).

the Son is the giver of the Spirit. "Through whom and from whom behoved it that the Spirit should be given but through the Son, whose also the Spirit is? . . . [T]herefore have we securely received it, he being said to be anointed in the flesh; for the flesh being first sanctified in him, and he being said as man, to have received for its sake, we have the sequel of the Spirit's grace, receiving out of his fulness."[74]

As the Father is light and the Son is his radiance, we see in the Son the Spirit by whom we are enlightened. In turn, when the Spirit enlightens us, Christ in him enlightens us. As the Father is the fountain and the Son is called a river, we are said to drink the Spirit. When we drink the Spirit, we drink of Christ. Since Christ is true Son, when we receive the Spirit we are made sons. When the Spirit is given to us, God is in us. When God is in us, the Son is in us. When we are quickened by the Spirit, Christ lives in us.[75] The perichoretic relations of the three persons underlie their inseparable involvement in the one work of God for our salvation. The Spirit is never apart from the Word, the Son—a point that Athanasius repeats time and time again.[76]

So, for Athanasius, the Spirit is the image of the Son, proper to the Son, distinct from the creatures and not alien from God. That which joins creation to the Word cannot belong to the creatures, and that which bestows sonship upon creation cannot be alien from the Son. He belongs to the Godhead of the Father, and in him the Word makes things originated divine. But he in whom things are made divine cannot be outside the Godhead of the Father.[77] So too, the Spirit is indivisible from the Son.[78] As the Son is in the Spirit, as in his own image, so also the Father is in the Son.[79] The Trinity is indivisible, and so just as it is true that wherever the Father is mentioned, the Son is also understood, so also is it true that wherever the Son is, the Holy Spirit is also, in him.[80]

Moreover, as the Son has his particular property in relation to the Father, so does the Holy Spirit in relation to the Son.[81] The Son is the image of the Father, and so also is the Holy Spirit the image of the

74. Athanasius, *Against the Arians* 1.46–50 (PG 26:105–18).
75. Athanasius, *Serapion* 1.19 (PG 26:573–76).
76. Ibid., 1.14, 17, 20, 31; 3.5; 4.4 (PG 26:564–65, 569–72, 576–80, 600–605, 632–33, 641–44).
77. Ibid., 1.24–25 (PG 26:585–89).
78. Ibid., 3.5 (PG 26:632–33).
79. Ibid., 1.20; 3.1 (PG 26:576–80, 624–28).
80. Ibid., 1.14 (PG 26:564–65).
81. Ibid., 3.1 (PG 26:624–28).

Son.[82] Athanasius denies the obvious rejoinder that there are consequently two sons, maintaining the distinctiveness of the Holy Spirit in doing so, but the fact that he feels obliged to make such a point indicates how close he understands the relation of the Son and the Spirit to be. Indeed, the Holy Spirit has the same order or rank (*taxis*) and nature (*physis*) relative to the Son as the Son has relative to the Father. The Son is in the Father, and the Father is in the Son; similarly, the Holy Spirit is in the Son, and the Son is in the Holy Spirit. Thus, the Spirit cannot be divided from the Word.[83] So also the Spirit is in God the Father and from the Father.[84] As the Son comes in the name of the Father, so the Holy Spirit comes in the name of the Son.[85] There is one efficacy and action of the Holy Trinity, for the Father makes all things through the Word by the Holy Spirit.[86]

Similarly, the Spirit receives from the Word, while the Word gives to the Spirit, and whatever the Spirit has, he has from the Word. Whatever the Word has in the Father, he wishes it to be given to us through the Spirit.[87] Nothing could be clearer than the intimate, unbreakable relation between the Son and the Holy Spirit in Athanasius's thought. The three persons indwell one another; they are in each other. This applies as much to the Son and the Spirit as to the Son and the Father or the Father and the Spirit.

These relations being what they are, Athanasius understands the procession and giving of the Spirit to occur in the indivisible oneness of the triad. Later disagreement over the procession of the Holy Spirit (see chapter 10) might have been avoided if sufficient attention had been paid to his *Letters to Serapion*. The Spirit, he says, proceeds from the Father, since it shines forth, is sent, and is given from the Word, who is from the Father. The Son sends the Spirit. The Son glorifies the Father. The Spirit glorifies the Son. So, in order of nature, the Spirit bears the same relation to the Son as the Son to the Father. As the Son, who is in the Father (and the Father is in him), is not a creature, so it is wrong to rank the Spirit with the creatures, since he is in the Son (and the Son is in him).[88] On the

---

82. Ibid., 4.3 (PG 26:640–41).
83. Ibid., 1.20–21 (PG 26:576–81).
84. Ibid., 1.25 (PG 26:588–89).
85. Ibid., 1.20 (PG 26:576–80).
86. Ibid., 1.20, 28, 30 (PG 26:576–80, 593–600).
87. Athanasius, *Against the Arians* 3.24–25; see also 3.44 (PG 26:373–78, 415–18).
88. Athanasius, *Serapion* 1.20–21 (PG 26:576–81).

contrary, the Spirit is proper to the Word, and is of the holy triad. "There is, then, a triad, holy and complete, confessed to be God in Father, Son, and Holy Spirit. . . . The Father does all things through the Word in the Holy Spirit. Thus the unity of the holy Triad is preserved. . . . It is a Triad not only in name . . . but in truth and actuality. For as the Father is he that is, so also his Word is one that is and God over all. And the Holy Spirit is not without actual existence, but exists and has true being. Less than these (persons) the catholic Church does not hold."[89] Hence, the *homoousios* is applicable to the Holy Spirit as well as to the Son.[90] In terms of our salvation, we are sealed by the Spirit, and so made partakers of the divine nature, as Peter puts it, and thus all creation partakes of the Word in the Spirit.[91]

The gifts of the Holy Spirit are also given from the Father through the Son. For all things of the Father are of the Son also, and so those things given from the Son in the Spirit are gifts of the Father. These gifts are given in the triad, from the Father, through the Son, in the Holy Spirit. When we partake of him, we have the love of the Father and the grace of the Son, and the communion of the Spirit himself. Once again, the activity of the triad is one, for all is originated and effected through the Word in the Spirit, for the Spirit is indivisible from the Word.[92] Referring to John 4:21–24, Athanasius says that true worshipers worship the Father in the Spirit and in the Truth (the Lord himself), confessing the Son and in him the Spirit.[93]

Athanasius's Contribution

Torrance suggests that Athanasius brought about "a profound revision of the meaning of being," both of *ousia* and *hypostasis*, leading to an agreement at the Council of Alexandria in 362 that God is one being (*ousia*) and three persons (*hypostasis*)—the first time the latter term means anything definite for him.[94] God alone is *ousia*,

89. Ibid., 1.27–28 (PG 26:593–96).
90. Ibid., 1.14, 16–33; 2:2 (PG 26:564–65, 568–612).
91. Ibid., 1.23 (PG 26:584–85).
92. Ibid., 1.30–31 (PG 26:597–605).
93. Ibid., 1.33 (PG 26:605–8).
94. Torrance, *Trinitarian Perspectives*, 15. See also G. L. Prestige, *God in Patristic Thought* (London: SPCK, 1952), xxix, 168ff., 188; Thomas F. Torrance, *Theology in Reconciliation* (Grand Rapids: Eerdmans, 1975), 218ff., 226ff., 231ff.; Hanson, *Search*, 444–45.

strictly speaking—one eternal being in the indivisible reality of his intrinsic personal relations as the Holy Trinity. This development, Torrance argues, is based on God as he has named himself (I am), personal and active, not as an impersonal essence or generic being. He reveals himself as possessing the coinherent relations of the three persons, in indivisible oneness and identity of being, as the Father, the Son, and the Holy Spirit. Moreover, in terms of the monarchy, Athanasius calls the Father the "origin" (*archē*) of the Son, begetting the Son. The Son is *homoousios* with the Father, but Athanasius never says that the Father is *homoousios* with the Son. The Father is the fountain, the Son is the stream; the Father is the source of light, and the Son is the ray. But due to the coinherent relations of the three, the Son and the Spirit are both associated with that origin. Thus, he defines the oneness of God not in terms of the Father, but in terms of the whole Godhead. The Father is the Father of the Son, but the three are completely coequal and mutually coinherent. This, Torrance contends, had the potential to cut behind the later *filioque* problem.[95] Moreover, Athanasius had the breadth of mind to recognize that what matters is right belief and intention, even if words and phrases are not precisely what one might want. This he brought out very effectively at the Council of Alexandria (362), when he allowed that *ousia* and *hypostasis* could be used in different senses, and that it is possible to speak of three *hypostases* and be orthodox.[96] This was a major breakthrough, paving the way for resolution of the crisis.

While the eventual settlement would be due more precisely to the work of the three great Cappadocians, Athanasius's contribution to the theology of the Trinity can scarcely be overestimated. His elaborations of the full deity of the Son and the Spirit in the one being of God, and of the relations of the three in their mutual coinherence, were quantum advances in understanding and huge milestones on the path to a more accurate view of the Trinity. In addition, he rooted his Trinitarianism in his doctrines of creation and salvation, and turned discussion away from philosophical speculation and back to a biblical and theological basis. These were no mean achievements.

---

95. Torrance, *Trinitarian Perspectives*, 20. See also Lyman, *Christology*, 150.
96. Athanasius, *To the Antiochenes* 5–8 (PG 26:799–806); Hanson, *Search*, 644–45.

The Cappadocians

We encountered Eunomius (d. 394) in chapter 5. He and his followers—the Eunomians—were rationalists, confident in the extensive capacities of human logic. By logic, they maintained, we are able to comprehend God. They assumed there to be a univocal relation between the divine mind and the human mind (a correspondence between divine and human thought, such that meaning is identical for both). For them, the Son is absolutely unlike the Father. God is absolute being, and generation cannot be attributed to him. Because of the identity between the mind of God and human reasoning, the Son's generation is to be understood in terms of human generation. Since eternal generation is inconceivable, the generation of the Son must have had a beginning. Hence, there was a time when the Son did not exist. The Son was the first created being, and was the instrument by which God created the world. The Holy Spirit is even further removed from God.

Eunomius's views were therefore much like those of the Arians. Opponents described him as "the leader of Arius' theatrical dancing-floor."[1] His rationalism is evident in his assertion that "God does not know anything more about his own essence than we do, nor is that essence better known to him and less to us; rather, what we ourselves know about it is exactly what he knows, and, conversely, that which he knows is what you will find without change in us."[2] The creed he

---

1. Richard Paul Vaggione, ed., *Eunomius: The Extant Works* (Oxford: Clarendon Press, 1987), 179 (Fragment iii).
2. Ibid. (Fragment ii). See also Graham A. Keith, "Our Knowledge of God: The Relevance of the Debate Between Eunomius and the Cappadocians," *TynBul* 41 (1988): 60–88.

cites at the start of his *Apology* is the creed that Arius presented to Alexander.[3] God is one, and has sole supremacy. He is unbegotten essence. God is prior to the Son, and thus the Son is subordinate to the Father, a creature, subject to the Father in essence and will, neither *homoousios* nor *homoiousios* with the Father. He was made. He came into existence, with a beginning,[4] begotten by the will of God; the Father is the cause of his existence. The Son is the minister of creation. So the Son and God (the Father) are of different essences. The Holy Spirit is third in order and nature, and is not the only begotten, but was brought into existence by the command of the Father and the action of the Son, a thing made by the Son and subject to Christ.[5]

For the Eunomians and others in the Arian tradition, the line between God and all other beings came between the Father and the Son, whereas the supporters of Nicaea placed it between the triad and all other beings.[6] There was general agreement that the Son is the offspring of the Father, but that raised the question whether he was a creature, as Eunomius claimed, or of the same being as the Father, as the Nicene supporters maintained. The Eunomians used Proverbs 8:22 in support, focusing on the weakness of Christ.[7] But Eunomius did not think that the Son was a creature like all others, for he created all others.[8] In short, Arians of all shapes froze the triad into a hierarchy, the one God who became the Father, plus two different, subordinate and noneternal beings.

The Macedonians, or *pneumatomachii* (fighters against the Spirit), accepted the deity of the Son (in many cases), but regarded the Spirit as less than God (though eternal) and so not to be worshiped. Being biblicists, they argued that Scripture nowhere calls the Spirit "God" and opposed any extrabiblical arguments. The movement was named for Macedonius (d. 362), who was bishop of Constantinople

3. Eunomius, *Apology* 4–5 (in Vaggione, *Eunomius*, 38–39).

4. Eunomius, *The Fragments* i; Eunomius, *Apology* 7–15, 17, 20–23, 26–27; Eunomius, *An Apology for the Apology* 1.ii.b; 2.v; 3.ii-iii, vi-vii, xi; Eunomius, *The Confession of Faith* 2–3 (in Vaggione, *Eunomius*, 40–55, 60–63, 70–71, 102–3, 112, 116–18, 122, 126, 150–53, 177).

5. Eunomius, *Apology* 15–27; Eunomius, *An Apology for the Apology* 3.iii-vii; Eunomius, *Confession* 3–4; Eunomius, *Fragments* i (in Vaggione, *Eunomius*, 52–71, 117–22, 152–57, 177).

6. Richard Paul Vaggione, *Eunomius of Cyzicus and the Nicene Revolution* (Oxford: Oxford University Press, 2000), 123–24.

7. Ibid., 107–11.

8. Ibid., 124–26.

from 342 until his deposition in 360, but there is no concrete evidence that he had anything to do with it.[9]

Basil the Great

A native of Cappadocia who became bishop of Caesarea, Basil the Great (330–379) is noteworthy for his organizational skill and his development of monastic life. He wrote a volume *Against Eunomius* in 364,[10] but his mature thought on the Holy Spirit and the Trinity is found in his *magnum opus*, the treatise *On the Holy Spirit*, which he wrote against the pneumatomachians around 376.[11] His writing was probably aimed at his former mentor, Eustathius, who had been recently teaching the subordination of the Holy Spirit. This work is a staunch defense of the Spirit's deity. Basil has often been thought to have been hesitant in affirming this, but Larson has undermined such an interpretation.[12] Some have pointed out that Basil does not speak of the Spirit as *homoousios* with the Father and the Son,[13] in marked contrast to his friend Gregory Nazianzen.[14] However, Larson marshals evidence that Basil says the same thing in other words. Again, scholars have noted that he never explicitly identifies the Spirit as God.[15]

9. R. P. C. Hanson, *The Search for the Christian Doctrine of God: The Arian Controversy 318–381* (Edinburgh: T & T Clark, 1988), 760–72.

10. For a detailed discussion of Eunomius's theology and Basil's response, in addition to the literature cited above, see Thomas A. Kopecek, *A History of Neo-Arianism* (Cambridge, Mass.: Philadelphia Patristic Foundation, 1979), vol. 2.; Milton V. Anastos, "Basil's Κατα Ευνομιου, a Critical Analysis," in *Basil of Caesarea: Christian, Humanist, Ascetic: A Sixteen-Hundredth Anniversary Symposium*, ed. Paul Jonathan Fedwick (Toronto: Pontifical Institute of Medieval Studies, 1981), 67–136, considers this work at length, which has never been published in a critical edition nor translated into a modern language. On Basil, see Philip Rousseau, *Basil of Caesarea* (Berkeley: University of California Press, 1994); Volker Henning Drecoll, *Die Entwicklung der Trinitätslehre des Basilius von Cäsarea* (Göttingen: Vandenhoeck & Ruprecht, 1996); Johannes Quasten, *Patrology*, vol. 3, *The Golden Age of Greek Patristic Literature from the Council of Nicaea to the Council of Chalcedon* (Westminster, Md.: Christian Classics, 1992), 204–36, esp. 230–33.

11. See Basil Studer, *Trinity and Incarnation: The Faith of the Early Church*, trans. Matthias Westerhoff, ed. Andrew Louth (Collegeville, Minn.: Liturgical Press, 1993), 148–51, for a perceptive summary.

12. Mark J. Larson, "A Re-Examination of *De Spiritu Sancto*: Saint Basil's Bold Defence of the Spirit's Deity," *SBET* 19, no. 1 (spring 2001): 65–84.

13. Thomas F. Torrance, *The Christian Doctrine of God: One Being, Three Persons* (Edinburgh: T & T Clark, 1996), 126; Quasten, *Patrology*, 3:232.

14. Gregory Nazianzen, *Orations* 31.10 (PG 36:144).

15. Quasten, *Patrology*, 3:231; Larson, "A Re-Examination," 67–69.

However, his comments belie this claim, and Gregory Nazianzen's critical remarks to that effect may well apply to an earlier time.[16]

Basil points to the liturgical origin of the dispute. Opponents had attacked him for the prepositions he used in the doxology, where he was accustomed to say "to the Father *with* the Son *together with* the Holy Spirit," besides their approved form, "to the Father *through* the Son *in* the Holy Spirit." They considered his addition a novelty, extrabiblical, and contradictory. Their preferred form allowed a clear subordinationist understanding, unlike Basil's.[17] For his part, Basil distinguishes the *hypostases*, to demonstrate that the Father and the Son are distinct and not to be confused.[18] This is a development from Nicaea, where *hypostasis* and *ousia* were apparently interchangeable, and the Father and the Son were said to be of the same *hypostasis*! This is the first recorded instance of Basil using *hypostasis* to denote the way God is three, thereby opening the way to speak of the Trinity in clearer language. Basil strongly defends the Son as inseparable from the Father, against the pneumatomachian refusal to recognize the Son or the Spirit as being together with the Father.[19] The Son is with the Father in nature, Basil insists; his will is in indissoluble union with the Father's.[20]

The commonly accepted doctrine concerning the Holy Spirit, Basil continues, is that he is of "the supreme nature . . . an intelligent essence, in power infinite, in magnitude unlimited, unmeasured by times or ages . . . perfecting all other things, but itself in nothing lacking . . . supplier of life . . . omnipresent . . . filling all things with its power," and so on—all terms and descriptions that only God can possess. Those who are cleansed he makes spiritual by fellowship with himself and conveys the gifts of "joy without end, abiding in God, the being made like to God, and, highest of all, the being made God."[21] He is ranked by our Lord with the Father and the Son in the baptismal formula (Matt. 28:19). What more intimate conjunction can there be than this?

16. Basil of Caesarea, *On the Holy Spirit* 16.37; 19.49; 21.52 (PG 32:133, 155–60, 164–65); Larson, "A Re-Examination."

17. Basil of Caesarea, *Holy Spirit* 1.3–4; see further to 4:6 (PG 32:72–77).

18. Ibid., 5.7 (PG 32:77–81).

19. Ibid., 6.13–14 (PG 32:88–89).

20. Ibid., 7.16–8.20 (PG 32:93–105).

21. Ibid., 9.22–23 (PG 32:108–9).

Our salvation is established through the Father and the Son and the Holy Spirit.[22] Thus, the Spirit is ranked with God, inseparable from the Father and the Son "on account of natural fellowship."[23] This fellowship is evident in the work of creation. Here the original cause of all created things is the Father, the creative cause is the Son, and the perfecting cause is the Holy Spirit. However, the first principle of existing things is "One . . . creating through the Son and perfecting through the Spirit." The work of all three (the Lord, the Word, the Spirit) is lacking in nothing, whether taken singularly or together.[24] The inseparable conjunction of the Holy Spirit with the Father and the Son is seen in that, referring to 1 Corinthians 2:8–11, "he is said to have the same relation to God which the spirit in us has to each of us."[25] He is to be numbered *with* the Father and the Son, not under them as the heretics allege.[26]

This does not mean that there are three gods, for while the persons are distinct, they are not additions in a numerical sequence. We confess "the distinctions of the persons, and at the same time abide by the monarchy." These are distinct persons, but there is only one object of worship, the one God. The Holy Spirit is one "conjoined to the one Father through the one Son . . . completing the adorable and blessed trinity."[27] However, the Spirit in his relations with the Father is distinct from the Son. The Holy Spirit is "from God," not in the way that all things are from him, but "as proceeding out of God, not by generation, like the Son, but as breath of his mouth." Basil is not speaking of human realities, but of those appropriate to God. The mode of generation is beyond our understanding. Styled "Spirit of Christ," he has a close relation to the Son as well as to the Father.[28] He proceeds from the Father and is God, not something created or a mere minister of God.[29] Thus, according to nature there is a movement from the Father through the Son to the Spirit, seen

22. Ibid., 10.24–26 (PG 32:109–13).

23. Ibid., 13.30; 16.37; cf. 11.27; 23.54 (PG 32:120–21, 133, 113–16, 168–69).

24. Ibid., 16.38 (PG 32:136–40).

25. Ibid., 16.40 (PG 32:141–44).

26. Ibid., 17.41–43 (PG 32:144–48); Basil of Caesarea, *Letters* 125, 159.2 (PG 32:545–52, 620–21).

27. Basil of Caesarea, *Holy Spirit* 18.45 (PG 32:152); Basil of Caesarea, *The Hexaemeron* 2.6 (PG 29:41–44).

28. Basil of Caesarea, *Holy Spirit* 18.46 (PG 32:152–53).

29. Basil of Caesarea, *Letters* 125, 159.2 (PG 32:545–52, 620–21).

in creation and grace, while in terms of our knowledge of God we move in the reverse direction from the Spirit through the Son to the Father. At the same time, the monarchy is not lost, for this order is not to be understood as three separate beings in a hierarchy, which would be tantamount to polytheism.[30] Basil argues on the basis of both the titles given to him in Scripture and the nature of his works that the Holy Spirit has the status of God, for he has the same titles and shares the same works as the Father and the Son.[31] At the other end of the spectrum, Basil's use of the preposition *with* in his doxology refutes Sabellianism by distinguishing the *hypostases*. The preposition affirms simultaneously "uninterrupted conjunction" and "distinction."[32] "He who fails to confess the community of the essence . . . falls into polytheism [and] he who refuses to grant the distinction of the *hypostases* is carried away into Judaism." Merely enumerating the persons is insufficient; we must confess each person to have a natural existence in real *hypostasis*.[33] Thus, Basil moves back and forth from the oneness in being of the Spirit with the Father and the Son, to the distinctness of the three *hypostases*. He insists that none of the three is subordinate to the others, but the Father is still the source or ultimate principle.

Finally, Basil returns to where he started, with worship and sanctification. In a remarkable figure of speech, he says that the Holy Spirit is "the place of them that are being sanctified . . . the special and peculiar place of true worship." Referring to John 4:21–24, he argues that the place of Christian worship is the Holy Spirit, for "the Spirit is . . . the place of the saints and the saint is the proper place for the Spirit, offering himself as he does for the indwelling of God, and called God's temple." The Spirit is in the saints in different kinds of ways, but in relation to the Father and the Son he is not so much in them as with them.[34] Thus, even in our own worship the Holy Spirit is inseparable from the Father and the Son.

Basil insists, in a letter to Gregory Nazianzen, that no theological terminology is adequate to express the thought of the speaker, for

30. Basil of Caesarea, *Holy Spirit* 18.47 (PG 32:153).
31. Ibid., 19.48–49; see 21.52; 23.54 (PG 32:156–60, 164–65, 168–69); Basil of Caesarea, *Letters* 90.2 (PG 32:473–76).
32. Basil of Caesarea, *Holy Spirit* 25.59 (PG 32:176–77).
33. Basil of Caesarea, *Letters* 210.5 (PG 32:773–77).
34. Basil of Caesarea, *Holy Spirit* 26.62–64 (PG 32:184; see also 181–85).

language is too weak to act in the service of objects of thought. And, in turn, our thought is too weak to comprehend the reality. Nevertheless, we are compelled to give an answer about God to those who love the Lord. So devote the intellectual energies that God gives you to advocating the truth, he urges his friend.[35] Basil's recognition of the limitations of human thought and language contributes to the relaxation of the technical terminology that had bedeviled the Trinitarian question. Like Athanasius, he recognizes that the claims of truth are paramount, and that human language and logic must bow before it.

Thus, he makes the vital move of disengaging *ousia* from *hypostasis*.[36] He writes to Count Terentius that "*ousia* has the same relation to *hypostasis* as the common has to the particular." *Ousia* is common, like goodness or Godhead, "while *hypostasis* is contemplated in the special property of Fatherhood, Sonship, or the power to sanctify." These are perfect, complete, and real *hypostases*, while the *homoousion* is preserved in the unity of the Godhead.[37] This is a major step forward, and it will help in finding a way out of the conceptual maze. However, by his comparison of general to particular, Basil leaves the door open for a generic view of God, and a comparison to three men sharing a common human nature, with the unfortunate entailments of that analogy. Writing to his friend Amphilochius, he says, "The distinction between *ousia* and *hypostasis* is the same as that between the general and the particular." With God we confess one essence, but a particular *hypostasis*, so that our conception of Father, Son, and Holy Spirit may be without confusion and clear. If we have no idea of the separate characteristics of fatherhood, sonship, and sanctification, but form our conception of God from the general idea of existence, we cannot give a sound account of our faith. We must therefore confess the faith "by adding the particular to the common."[38]

Another significant hostage to fortune is his assertion that we know the attributes of God (his power, wisdom, goodness, providence, and justice), which are within our reach, but that the essence of God

---

35. Basil of Caesarea, *Letters* 7 (PG 32:244–45).

36. Occasionally Basil writes of *physis* rather than *ousia*, and *prosōpon* rather than *hypostasis*.

37. Basil of Caesarea, *Letters* 214.4 (PG 32:789).

38. Ibid., 236.6 (PG 32:883–84). See Hanson, *Search*, 691–92, 696–99; Studer, *Trinity*, 142–43; Bertrand de Margerie, *The Christian Trinity in History*, trans. Edmund J. Fortman (Petersham, Mass.: St. Bede's Publications, 1982), 99–104.

(who he *is*) is beyond us, and so we do not try to approach that. We do not comprehend the essence, but we do comprehend that the essence exists.[39] Here Basil departs from Athanasius and prepares the way for later developments in the East, which will claim that we know only God's energies, not his essence (being). This will draw into question ✓ the reality of our knowledge of God. On these assumptions, we cannot know God as he is, but only as he reveals himself, and what God reveals of himself is not to be understood of who he is. As this notion would be elaborated by Gregory Palamas, it would undermine the doctrine of the Trinity (see chapter 11). Is Basil overreacting to Eunomian rationalism? He is certainly a clear defender of the deity of the Spirit, and contributes greatly to the eventual Trinitarian settlement, but he leaves behind some unresolved legacies as well.[40]

Gregory of Nyssa

Basil's brother Gregory (*ca.* 335/340–394/400), the most brilliant of the three great Cappadocians and the most systematic thinker, became bishop of Nyssa in 372 and was present at the Council of Constantinople in 381.[41] His large work *Against Eunomius* used to be dated prior to the council, but some recent scholarship places most of the work after it.

Gregory joins Athanasius and Basil in stressing the oneness of the Son with the Father. It is preferable, he argues, to speak of the "Father," rather than the "Ingenerate"—Eunomius's term. By using that word, Eunomius set the Son in opposition to the Father, as generate to ingenerate. By contrast, the title "Son" expresses identity of being with the Father, and thus personhood, rather than a mere

39. Basil of Caesarea, *Letters* 234.1–2 (PG 32:868–69).

40. Claims of Platonist influence on Basil (and Gregory Nazianzen) are dismissed by John M. Rist, "Basil's 'Neoplatonism': Its Background and Nature," in *Basil of Caesarea*, ed. Fedwick, 137–220.

41. Anthony Meredith, "The Idea of God in Gregory of Nyssa," in *Studien zu Gregor von Nyssa und der christlichen Spätantike*, ed. Hubertus R. Drobner and C. Klock (Leiden: E. J. Brill, 1990), 127–47; G. Christopher Stead, "Why Not Three Gods? The Logic of Gregory of Nyssa's Trinitarian Doctrine," in *Studien zu Gregor von Nyssa*, ed. Drobner and Klock, 149–63; Hanson, *Search*, 715–30, 784–87; J. N. D. Kelly, *Early Christian Doctrines* (London: Adam & Charles Black, 1968), 261–62; G. L. Prestige, *God in Patristic Thought* (London: SPCK, 1952), 252–55, 260; Quasten, *Patrology*, 3:254–96.

energy.[42] In turn, "Son" is on a different level from all other titles given to him. These other names must be purged of all connotations that detract from his glory. The title "Son" stands alone, since it has no need of such analogical adjustment.[43] Regarding the eternal generation of the Son, Gregory points out that the divine nature is not divided, contrary to a materialist understanding. Thus, the Son is of identical nature to the Father, coeternal, so that he is all that the Father is, except for being Father.[44] The Word of John 1 is as great as God is.[45] Gregory follows Athanasius in relating Proverbs 8:22ff. to the human nature of the incarnate Son. He also distinguishes biblical references to the only begotten, which concern the eternal Son, from references to the Son as the firstborn of all creation (Col. 1:15), which apply to his incarnate state.[46]

Gregory also affirms Basil's vital distinction between *ousia* and *hypostasis*. In particular, Letter 38, which has been traditionally attributed to Basil and listed as his, but is now recognized to be by Gregory, is especially important. He follows Basil's comparison of general (*ousia* or *physis*) and particular (*hypostasis* or occasionally *prosōpon*). These correspond to the incomprehensible essence and the recognizable manifestation in the particular persons. The three are distinct but inseparable in equality, unity, and indissoluble communion.[47]

Thus, God is one in essence, three in persons, divided without separation, and united without confusion. In essence, he is incomprehensible and impossible to circumscribe. The persons are relational, for "Son" entails a Father, and the Father is Father in relation to the Son.[48] In a work entitled *On the Holy Trinity and of the Godhead of the Holy Spirit to Eustathius*, probably written in the year before Con-

---

42. Gregory of Nyssa, *Against Eunomius* 2.12. This vast work is found in PG 45:248–1121. A discussion of Trinitarian personhood in Gregory of Nyssa, which argues against interpreting it in terms of individualism or a social doctrine of the Trinity, is found in Sarah Coakley, "'Persons' in the 'Social' Doctrine of the Trinity: A Critique of Current Analytic Discussion," in *The Trinity: An Interdisciplinary Symposium on the Trinity*, ed. Stephen T. Davis (Oxford: Oxford University Press, 1999), 123–44.

43. Gregory of Nyssa, *Against Eunomius* 1.37; 3.7.

44. Ibid., 1.25; 2.6–7.

45. Ibid., 4.1.

46. Ibid., 2.8, 10; 3.2.

47. Basil of Caesarea, *Letters* 38 (PG 32:325–40). This is now believed to be a composition of Gregory of Nyssa.

48. Gregory of Nyssa, *Against Eunomius* 2.2–3; 7.4.

stantinople, Gregory argues in similar vein, saying that we know God, not from his essence, but from his works. The works of the three persons are one, and so we conclude that their nature is one. These works are inseparable for it is impossible to separate the Holy Spirit from any work of the Father and the Son. The Trinity is one Godhead. It follows that the Son is inseparable from the Holy Spirit.[49] In *On the Holy Spirit Against the Followers of Macedonius*, written at about the same time, he says that the Holy Spirit has the same rank as the Father and the Son, is exactly identical with them, and so should receive equal honor with the other two persons. The three are inseparable, a perfect Trinity, eternally distinct, but mutually indwelling.[50] Neither here nor elsewhere does he use *homoousios* of the Spirit (for that matter, neither does the Council of Constantinople).[51] But he says all that needs to be said to reach that conclusion, and both Kelly and Studer accept that he does so regard the Spirit.[52]

This assessment is fully compatible with the view that Gregory has of the relations of the three. Here he preserves the monarchy, for the Father is the fountain of power, while the power of the Father is the Son, and the Holy Spirit is the spirit of that power. Thus, creation began with the Father, was advanced through the Son, and was completed in the Spirit, while grace comes from the Father, through the Son, and in the Holy Spirit. So the Spirit is third in sequence, but in inseparable union with the Father and the Son.[53] In *Against Eunomius*, he says that there is one first cause, the Father. The relations of the three he likens to a causal chain of dependence, although he qualifies this by adding that there is no interval between them, for they exist simultaneously like the sun and a ray of light streaming from it. There is no difference between one light and the other, for both are completely perfect. Hence, there is a very clear order,[54] but one admitting no thought of discord, for the three are coeternal, mutually indwelling one another.[55] Indeed,

49. Gregory of Nyssa, *Dogmatic Treatises, Etc.*, in NPNF², 5:326–30 (PG 46:235 [in 32:683–94 it is erroneously listed as Letter 189 of Basil]).
50. Ibid., 5:315–19 (PG 45:1301–33).
51. Hanson, *Search*, 786.
52. Studer, *Trinity*, 152; Kelly, *Doctrines*, 261–63.
53. NPNF², 5:320–23.
54. Gregory of Nyssa, *Against Eunomius* 1.34–36.
55. Ibid., 1.42; 2.2.

the expressions "light from light" and "true God from true God" in the creed refer to the Son "being what the other is, except being that Father," pointing simultaneously to personal distinctions and to identity of being. Since Gregory writes this within two years after the Council of Constantinople, it is a valuable commentary on phrases that will embed themselves in the consciousness of the church, both East and West. This order (*taxis*) is fully compatible with the Trinity's oneness of being.[56] So much is clear, too, from Gregory's teaching on the full mutual relations of the Father and the Son. "Thus we conceive no gap between the anointed Christ and his anointing . . . but as there is contemplated from all eternity in the Father the Son . . . so there is contemplated in him the Holy Spirit. . . . For which reason we say that to the holy disciples the mystery of godliness was committed in a form expressing at once union and distinction."[57]

This finds expression in worship, where the corollaries of the full mutual indwelling of the three in the one being of God are evident. When the Father is worshiped, so are the Spirit and the Son. Since the Spirit has the same status as the Father and the Son, we worship all three simultaneously. Again, in their mutual indwelling each of the three seeks the glory of the others. There is "a revolving circle of glory from like to like. The Son is glorified by the Spirit; the Father is glorified by the Son; again the Son has his glory from the Father; and the Only-begotten thus becomes the glory of the Spirit. . . . In like manner . . . faith completes the circle, and glorifies the Son by means of the Spirit, and the Father by means of the Son."[58] Worship of any of the three is worship of all three and thus worship of the one.[59]

Because of his focus on the three, it is not surprising that Gregory was accused of tritheism. He felt obliged to defend himself against the slur in his short but intriguing work On "Not Three Gods" to Ablabius, which Stead considers to have been written after the Council of Constantinople.[60] Gregory responds to Ablabius's suggestion that the Trinity

56. Ibid., 3.4. Gregory refers to a creed, citing wording common to Nicaea and Constantinople. However, he omits, as the latter does, the Nicene phrase "God of God."

57. Ibid., 2.2; see also 4.8.

58. NPNF[2], 5:324.

59. On mutual indwelling, see Verna Harrison, "Perichoresis in the Greek Fathers," *StVladThQ* 35 (1991): 53–65.

60. Stead, "Why Not Three Gods?" 149–63; See Gregory's work in NPNF[2], 5:26–27, 331–36 (PG 45:115–36).

is comparable to three men sharing a common human nature. This analogy follows the generic definition of *ousia* and *hypostasis* that Basil propounded and Gregory himself accepted. The problems are obvious. There are a vast number of men, but only three and ever three persons of the Trinity—no more, no less. Moreover, the Trinitarian persons indwell one another, which human beings cannot do, for they are separate and autonomous personal entities. The analogy points to tritheism, not the Trinity. That Gregory qualifies the idea, while toying with it, is due to his strong Platonic realism, by which universals have not only a reality, but even a primacy over particulars. This keeps him from focusing on the three to the detriment of the one divine being. Of all the Cappadocians, he was the most conversant with Platonism, especially Plotinus, although he used it rather than being mastered by it.[61] He explains the weaknesses of the analogy further in his treatise *Against the Greeks (about common notions)*,[62] but here he insists to Ablabius that the works of the Trinity are indivisible. Not one of the persons works by himself in isolation from the others. Every work of God originates from the Father, proceeds through the Son, and is perfected in the Holy Spirit. However, these are not three different things, but one and the same work of God. Moreover, this united action precludes any possibility of referring to God in the plural. While the Father is the cause, this does not refer to the essence of God, but rather to "the difference in manner of existence." We do not divide the essence, but simply point to the fact that the Son exists by generation and the Father without generation. So "the idea of cause differentiates the Persons of the Holy Trinity," while the divine nature (essence, being) is "unchangeable and undivided" and is to be referenced in the singular.[63]

Gregory of Nazianzus

Gregory of Nazianzus (*ca.* 330–391) is called by the Eastern church "the theologian," a title he shares with the apostle John alone.[64]

---

61. Michael Azkoul, *St. Gregory of Nyssa and the Tradition of the Fathers* (Lewiston, N.Y.: Edwin Mellen Press, 1995).

62. PG 45:180–81. The analogy is effectively refuted by Gregory Nazianzen, *Orations* 31.15 (PG 36:149).

63. NPNF[2], 5:336; see also 333–36. See Studer, *Trinity*, 143–44.

64. For the first biography of Gregory in English, see John A. McGuckin, *St. Gregory of Nazianzus: An Intellectual Biography* (Crestwood, N.Y.: St. Vladimir's Seminary Press, 2001).

A friend of Basil, Gregory had a wide-ranging education. Ordained in 361 against his will, often shrinking from his responsibilities in search of seclusion ("We cannot acquit him of pusillanimity"[65]), he was briefly bishop of Constantinople, presiding for a while at the Council. Around that time, the Arians hired a man to murder him. In 381 he preached five sermons (the *Theological Orations*) at Constantinople that permanently established his reputation. As one biographer put it, "Critics have rivalled each other in the praises they have heaped upon them, but no praise is so high as that of the many theologians who have found in them their own best thoughts."[66]

In his first theological oration, against the Eunomians, Gregory discusses the principles for talk about God. The Arians had fostered cheap and easy theological gossip to spread their ideas among the masses. For Gregory, only those who practice Christian virtue are qualified to talk about God. "Not to everyone, my friends, does it belong to philosophize about God; not to everyone; the subject is not so cheap and low; and I will add, not before every audience, not at all times, nor on all points; but on certain occasions, and before certain persons, and within certain limits." It belongs to those who are masters in meditation, who are free from all external defilement, and for whom the subject is of real concern. We must also philosophize within our proper bounds, unlike the Eunomian rationalists, while looking to ourselves "to polish our theological self to beauty like a statue."[67] In the second discourse, he says it is impossible for anyone fully to grasp the nature (essence or being) of God. "It is difficult to conceive God but to define him in words is an impossibility." To comprehend such a great subject is quite impossible and impracticable. It is one thing to be persuaded of the existence of God and quite another to know what he is.[68] On the other hand, God has revealed himself to mankind, to Abraham, Isaiah, and Paul, so an apophatic approach[69]

The volume contains an extensive bibliography of secondary sources. On Gregory's doctrine of the Trinity, in addition to the general works already cited, see Thomas F. Torrance, *Trinitarian Perspectives: Toward Doctrinal Agreement* (Edinburgh: T & T Clark, 1994), 21–40; Quasten, *Patrology*, 3:236–54.

65. Hanson, *Search*, 706.

66. H. W. Watkins, cited in *NPFN*[2], 7:280.

67. Gregory Nazianzen, *Orations* 27.3–7 (PG 36:13–21).

68. Ibid., 28.4–17 (PG 36:29–49).

69. When taking an apophatic approach, one speaks only of what God is *not*, without asserting anything about what he is.

is ruled out. Gregory shows no sign of following Basil's distinction between the essence and the attributes or energies of God, with the difficulties that was to create.[70] Our knowledge of God is true knowledge, but it is not direct knowledge of God's essence, for the properties of the persons do not affect God's essence.[71] Moreover, our bodily existence prevents us from grasping nonphysical realities.[72] Our inability to know God's essence should keep us from pride, increase our valuation of the knowledge of God, and sustain us in the trials of life by directing us to its attainment in the hereafter as a reward for faithful service now.[73] Here Gregory opposes Eunomian rationalism and establishes the limits of human knowledge.

The third and fourth orations are on the Son. Now Gregory unfolds his own teaching. He starts by affirming the monarchy. The Cappadocians have been criticized for making the Father the cause of the deity of the Son and the Holy Spirit, so that the Father is the source of the divine essence. Nothing could be further from Gregory's mind. The monarchy "is not limited to one person," and so, although the persons are numerically distinct, "there is no severance of essence." Here is a major advance that offsets any possible tendency to subordinate the Son and the Spirit to the Father. The Father is the begetter and emitter, the Son is the begotten, and the Holy Spirit is the emission, but this concerns the relations of the persons and is in the context of equality of nature, of identity of being.[74] The begetting of the Son occurred when the Father was not begotten, while the procession of the Spirit took place when the Son was begotten and not proceeding—beyond time and above reason—for there never was when the Father, the Son, and the Spirit were not. The Son and the Spirit are from the Father, but not after the Father.[75] To be begotten and to proceed are concurrent with being.[76] This is beyond our comprehension, best honored by silence. Yet such silence does not negate the truth, any more than we reject God's existence because we cannot comprehend

70. Torrance, *Trinitarian Perspectives*, 37–40.
71. Gregory Nazianzen, *Orations* 29.12 (PG 36:89).
72. Ibid., 28.13 (PG 36:41–44).
73. Ibid., 28.17–31 (PG 36:48–72).
74. Ibid., 29.2; 31.13–14; 39.12 (PG 36:76, 148–49, 348).
75. Ibid., 29.3 (PG 36:77).
76. Ibid., 29.9 (PG 36:84–85).

him.[77] So the begetting of the Son by the Father establishes their identity of nature, for the offspring is of the same nature as the parent.[78]

Gregory continues to maintain the incomprehensibility of God's essence against Eunomian rationalism. Perhaps at some point in the future we may know "when this darkness and dullness is done away."[79] The thing to note, he says, is that the distinction of Father and Son is "outside the essence." Begetting and being begotten (and, by inference, procession) are properties of the persons (the *hypostases*), not of the one essence.[80] This is in line with Gregory of Nyssa's observation in *On "Not Three Gods" to Ablabius*. It is another major contribution, for by placing the properties in the realm of the relations of the persons, all connotations of subordination are removed. This is so since these characteristics, strictly properties of the persons, do not define God's being. Thus, the name *Father* does not denote the essence of God, "but the relation in which the Father stands to the Son" and also the identity of nature between the Father who begets and the Son who is begotten.[81] The Son is called *Son* to denote this identity of nature, as well as because he is of the Father in terms of *relatio*.[82] Thus, there never was when the Father was without the Son, nor the Son without the Father.[83] In *Oration 40 on Holy Baptism*, Gregory says that while he would like to say that the Father is greater, in that "from him flows both the equality and the being of the equals . . . I am afraid to use the word *origin*, lest I should make him the origin of inferiors, and thus insult him by precedencies of honor."[84] So the Son is *homoousios* with the Father, the living image of the living one, the whole copy of the whole.[85]

Since his opponents customarily cited biblical passages attributing weakness and subordination to the Son, Gregory (following Athanasius) points to the Incarnation as the occasion for such descriptions. "What is lofty you are to apply to the Godhead . . . but all that

77. Ibid., 29.8 (PG 36:84).
78. Ibid., 29.10 (PG 36:85–88).
79. Ibid., 29.11 (PG 36:88–89).
80. Ibid., 29.12 (PG 36:89).
81. Ibid., 29.16 (PG 36:93–96).
82. Ibid., 30.20 (PG 36:128–32).
83. Ibid., 29.17 (PG 36:96–97).
84. Ibid., 40.43 (PG 36:420–21).
85. Ibid., 30.20 (PG 36:128–32).

is lowly to the composite condition of him who . . . was incarnate."[86]
He remained God while adding human nature.[87] His humanity was
united to God and became one person, so that we might be made God
so far as he is made man. He concludes with a shot across the bows
of the rationalists. "When we leave off believing, and protect ourselves
by mere strength of argument, and destroy the claim the Holy Spirit
has upon our faith by questionings . . . elegance of language makes
void the cross of Christ."[88] In the fourth oration, Gregory continues
to answer the charges of weakness and subordination. Many times
Scripture refers to Christ fulfilling the Father's will. These are explained
in terms of the Incarnation and the work of salvation on our behalf.[89]

The fifth and final discourse, on the Holy Spirit, is the jewel in
Gregory's crown. Here the *pneumatomachii* are the problem. Their
tactic, common to heretics at various times, is biblical literalism. The
Arians, Eunomians, and Macedonians all appeal to Scripture, contending that the pro-Nicenes use unscriptural terms. "Over and over
again you turn upon us the silence of Scripture," Gregory complains.
He points out that the Fathers, in their handling of the Bible, "have
gone beneath the letter and looked into the inner meaning."[90] But the
heretics' "love for the letter is but a cloak for their impiety."[91] Scripture uses metaphors and figures of speech. Slavery to a literal interpretation is an erroneous exegetical and theological method.[92] In fact,
the heretics favorite terms for God, "unbegotten" and "unoriginate,"
are not in the Bible at all![93]

Gregory argues for the Spirit's deity from deification. In salvation we are made God, but if the Holy Spirit is not from eternity, how
can he make me God, or join me with the Godhead?[94] Confusion over
the status of the Spirit was rife: "But of the wise men among us, some
have conceived of him as an activity, some as a creature, some as God;
and some have been uncertain which to call him, out of reverence for

86. Ibid., 29.18 (PG 36:98).
87. Ibid., 29.19 (PG 36:100).
88. Ibid., 29.21 (PG 36:101–4).
89. Ibid., 30.5 (PG 36:108–9).
90. Ibid., 31.21 (PG 36:156–57).
91. Ibid., 31.3 (PG 36:136–37).
92. Ibid., 31.21–24 (PG 36:156–60).
93. Ibid., 31.23 (PG 36:157–60).
94. Ibid., 31.4 (PG 36:137).

Scripture, they say, as though it did not make the matter clear either way. And therefore they neither worship him, nor treat him with dishonor, but take up a neutral position, or rather a very miserable one, with respect to him."[95] His opponents had asked Gregory to give clear definitions, supposing human logic capable of unfolding the truth about God. He responds that with the procession of the Spirit, as the begetting of the Son, language about God cannot be understood in a univocal sense.[96] Consequently, we cannot define the procession of the Spirit and the generation of the Son: "What then is procession? Do you tell me what is the unbegottenness of the Father, and I will explain to you the physiology of the generation of the Son and the procession of the Spirit, and we shall both of us be frenzy-stricken for prying into the mystery of God."[97] How then do the Father, the Son, and the Spirit differ from one another? Their properties (unbegotten, begotten, proceeding), which concern their relations, have given them their names (Father, Son, Holy Spirit), "that the distinction of the three persons may be preserved in the one nature . . . of the Godhead." These properties affect their relations, not the one identical *ousia*.[98] Gregory, reflecting the language of John's gospel, here coins a new word (*procession*) for the distinctive property of the third person. "What then? Is the Spirit God? Most certainly. Well then, is he consubstantial (*homoousios*)? Yes, if he is God."[99] Where Basil and his brother had a reluctance to say this openly, possibly for fear of alienating potential supporters, there is no hesitation with Gregory.

Appropriately, Gregory now turns to consider worship. The Spirit is the one in whom we worship and pray. Thus, prayer to the Spirit is, in effect, the Spirit offering prayer or adoration to himself. The adoration of the one is adoration of the three, because of the equality of honor and deity among the three.[100] The questions of the deity of the Son and the Holy Spirit are connected—once we acknowledge the former, the other follows.[101] "To us there is one God, and all that pro-

95. Ibid., 31.5 (PG 36:137).
96. Ibid., 31.7 (PG 36:140–41).
97. Ibid., 31.8 (PG 36:141).
98. Ibid., 31.9; 39.11–13 (PG 36:141–44, 345–49).
99. Ibid., 31.10 (PG 36:144).
100. Ibid., 31.12 (PG 36:145–48).
101. Ibid., 31.13 (PG 36:148).

ceeds from him is referred to one, though we believe in three persons. For one is not more and another less God; nor is one before and another after; . . . but the Godhead is . . . undivided in separate persons. . . . When we look at the Godhead, or the first cause, or the monarchia, that which we conceive is one; but when we look at the persons in whom the Godhead dwells . . . there are three whom we worship."[102] This point, that no one of the three is more divine than the others, is vital, for Gregory undercuts any idea that because the Father is the first principle, the Son and the Spirit derive their deity from him. He avoids the idea of a causal chain of dependence that Basil and his brother implied. The monarchy, the first cause, is the Godhead, and is one. So, as Calvin would point out (see chapter 12), each is God in himself. "Each of these persons possesses unity, not less with that which is united to it than with itself, by reason of the identity of essence."[103]

Gregory ingeniously points to the progressive historical outworking of revelation to explain the comparative reticence of Scripture on the Spirit. "The Old Testament proclaimed the Father openly, and the Son more obscurely. The New manifested the Son, and suggested the deity of the Spirit. Now the Spirit himself dwells among us, and supplies us with a clearer demonstration of himself. For it was not safe, when the Godhead of the Father was not yet acknowledged, plainly to proclaim the Son; nor when that of the Son was not yet received to burden us further . . . with the Holy Spirit."[104] Now, worship and baptism establish the Spirit's deity, for "we worship God the Father, God the Son, and God the Holy Spirit, three persons, one Godhead, undivided in honor and glory . . . for if he is not to be worshiped, how can he deify me by baptism? But if he is to be worshiped, surely he is an object of adoration, and if an object of adoration he must be God."[105] Gregory has a clear grasp of the distinct persons, while holding firmly to the unity of the undivided Godhead. For him, the Trinity is not an abstract puzzle, but the heart of the Christian faith and the center of true worship. "But when I say God, I mean Father, Son, and Holy Spirit."[106]

102. Ibid., 31.14 (PG 36:148–49).
103. Ibid., 31.16 (PG 36:149–52).
104. Ibid., 31.26 (PG 36:161).
105. Ibid., 31.28 (PG 36:164–65).
106. Ibid., 38.8 (PG 36:320).

We conclude with a passage that Calvin, in his *Institutes*, says "vastly delights me,"[107] from Gregory's *Oration on Holy Baptism*. We note first that each person is God in himself, obviating any idea that the deity of the Son and the Spirit is derived from the Father. Second, entailed in this is the idea of the complete mutual indwelling of the three. Third, his method of refocusing from the unity of God to the trinity of persons and back again, making knowledge of the one and the three coincident, is a vital principle to which we will return. This is in contrast to the West's movement from the one being of God to the three persons, and to the East's movement in the reverse direction.

> This I give you to share, and to defend all your life, the one Godhead and power, found in the three in unity, and comprising the three separately; not unequal, in substances or natures, neither increased nor diminished by superiorities or inferiorities; in every respect equal, in every respect the same; just as the beauty and the greatness of the heavens is one; the infinite conjunction of three infinite ones, each God when considered in himself; as the Father, so the Son; as the Son, so the Holy Spirit; the three one God when contemplated together; each God because consubstantial; one God because of the *monarchia*. No sooner do I conceive of the one than I am illumined by the splendour of the three; no sooner do I distinguish them than I am carried back to the one. When I think of any one of the three I think of him as the whole, and my eyes are filled, and the greater part of what I am thinking escapes me. I cannot grasp the greatness of that one so as to attribute a greater greatness to the rest. When I contemplate the three together, I see but one torch, and cannot divide or measure out the undivided light.[108]

The Contribution of the Cappadocians

The three Cappadocians together brought about an open recognition of the deity of the Spirit, as well as of the Son, and thus cleared the decks for a definitive settlement of the Trinitarian crisis engendered by Arius. This they did by clarifying the real, eternal, personal distinc-

107. John Calvin, *Institutes of the Christian Religion*, trans. Ford Lewis Battles, ed. John T. McNeill (Philadelphia: Westminster Press, 1960), 1.13.17.
108. Gregory Nazianzen, *Orations* 40.41 (PG 36:417).

tions of the three and setting these in the context of their relations to each other. God is one undivided being, yet three persons in communion and union. At the same time, while the Father is, in terms of the relations of the three, the principle, the fount, even the first cause, Gregory Nazianzen in particular took care to specify that this does not affect the being of God, and so all three persons are God in themselves. None is more and none is less God than the others. Hence, Kelly comments that "as stated by the Cappadocians, the idea of the twofold procession from Father through Son lacks all trace of subordinationism, for its setting is a wholehearted recognition of the homoousion of the Spirit."[109] Catherine LaCugna points out that this means that in Cappadocian theology each person "is the divine *ousia*; the divine *ousia* exists hypostatically, and there is no *ousia* apart from the *hypostases*. To exist as God is to be the Father who begets the Son and breathes forth the Spirit." Moreover, the idea of relations of origin "makes it impossible to think of a divine person 'unto itself,' disconnected either from other persons or from the divine essence," and so "*it is impossible to think of the divine essence in itself or by itself.*"[110] However, a cloud the size of a man's hand emerged with Basil's distinction between the knowable divine attributes and the unknowable divine essence. This would develop later to darken the sky, and would threaten to obscure our knowledge of God. We cannot hold Basil responsible for this, and debate surrounds the question of exactly how far the later Palamite developments accurately reflect Cappadocian theology.[111]

The terms used by our trinity of theologians for the divine properties can be summarized by this table originally presented by K. Holl in 1904:

Basil: Fatherhood, Sonship,—(i.e., nothing much)
Gregory of Nyssa: Ingenerateness, Only begotten, "through the Son"
Gregory Nazianzen: Ingenerateness, Generateness, Procession[112]

109. Kelly, *Doctrines*, 263; see also Torrance, *Trinitarian Perspectives*, 27–32.
110. Catherine Mowry LaCugna, *God for Us: The Trinity and Christian Life* (San Francisco: Harper, 1991), 69–70.
111. See chapter 11.
112. Cited by Hanson, *Search*, 787.

Vaggione comments that the Constantinopolitan settlement was made possible by two developments that the Cappadocians facilitated. First, there was a narrowing of the gap between ordinary and expert language. In this case, expert language became more ordinary. In many ways, this was a freeing of theological language from its philosophical background. Second, and in direct connection with this, there was a relaxation of precision by Athanasius and then Basil. Exact, technical definition of terms was replaced by a new fluidity, as the reality of the nature of God was allowed to reshape language and refashion it to represent the reality better. This led to a widespread acceptance of a new way of speaking about God. In the 330s and 340s, the ambiguity of the creed of Nicaea made defense of that creed appear modalist, and so made the charge of Sabellianism plausible.[113] This proved to be a barrier to the acceptance of the Nicene formula.[114] A more flexible vocabulary, developing around 362, allowed terms like *homoousios*, *ousia*, and *hypostasis* to be reformulated in a way that opened the door to a new understanding of the Trinity. At the same time, language was freed from previous philosophical assumptions.[115] We saw in passing how the Cappadocians used a variety of terms to express both what is one in God and what is three, and we have noticed how Athanasius came to realize that what is being affirmed is more important than the precise language with which it is affirmed. All told, between 360 and 381 a decisive breakthrough occurred, which would leave an indelible mark on the whole church. To a consideration of the Council of Constantinople in 381 we now turn.

---

113. Vaggione, *Eunomius of Cyzicus*, 364–65.

114. Ibid., 376–78.

115. Ibid., 364–67. However, we must recognize that the Cappadocians used a range of terms (*physis* and *theotēs* as well as *ousia*) to refer to the way God is one, as well as a similar range (*idiotētēs* and *prosōpon* as well as *hypostasis*) to refer to the way God is three. See Joseph T. Lienhard, "*Ousia* and *Hypostasis*: The Cappadocian Settlement and the Theology of 'One Hypostasis,'" in *Trinity*, ed. Davis, 99–121.

The Council of Constantinople

Early in 381, the new emperor Theodosius I called a council of the Eastern church at Constantinople in an attempt to unite it on the basis of the Nicene faith. The council met in May, June, and July. Unfortunately, no official records of its proceedings survive. Its composition was not ecumenically representative, nor was it recognized as an ecumenical council at once. There was no representation of the Western church, and in particular none from Rome. At first the only bishops present were from Asia Minor, western Syria, and Palestine, although later some arrived from Egypt, notably Alexandria, and a few from Illyricum. However, by 550 it was universally regarded as ecumenical.

Since the largest and most powerful representation was from Antioch, its bishop, Meletius, presided. He was militantly opposed to the *pneumatomachii*. However, he died shortly after the start of the council. He was replaced by Gregory Nazianzen, who had been appointed bishop of Constantinople after the withdrawal of the previous incumbent, an Arian who had refused Theodosius's demand to accept the Nicene faith. Gregory was a hopeless leader—politically inept, inflexible, and pusillanimous. He preferred monastic seclusion to the maelstrom of public business. A great scholar and preacher, he was at sea in the turmoil of church politics. Not surprisingly, the council began to lurch into chaos. Seeing the drift of conciliar sentiment to be against him, Gregory stunned his fellow bishops by suddenly resigning as president of the council and also as bishop of Constantinople. After a brilliant and caustic farewell oration, handing in his official resignation

to the emperor and other assembled dignitaries in such style as to provoke a standing ovation, he returned to Nazianzus. He disapproved
of the creed and held the council in some contempt, but in seclusion
he wrote a defense of his flight and edited his orations so as to provide the eventual definitive commentary on the theological issue of the
day.[1] In this way, he foreshadowed Winston Churchill, who confidently
predicted during the Second World War that history would paint him
in a favorable light since he himself would be writing it![2]

A crucial issue for the council was the relationship with the Macedonians or *pneumatomachii*. Some have argued that Theodosius
wanted the council to adopt a conciliatory tone so as to secure the
broadest possible unity for the church, an important factor in maintaining the cohesion of his empire in the face of threats from the Goths.
In the end, whether or not this was so, conciliation proved impossible
to secure. The council passed four important canons. Bishops' activities were to be limited to their dioceses. Maximus the Cynic was condemned. The bishop of Constantinople was proclaimed second in
honor to the bishop of Rome, for "Constantinople is the new Rome."
The first canon was on theology, reaffirming the dogma of Nicaea,
and condemning the Eunomians, Anomians, Arians, Eudoxians, Macedonians, Sabellians, Marcellians, Photinians, and Apollinarians.

The Creed

To this day, what is popularly but wrongly called the Nicene Creed,
and is more accurately described as the Niceno-Constantinopolitan
Creed, is recited throughout the Eastern and Western churches. This
creed (C) is associated with this council. However, it raises the vexing
question whether the council ever produced such a creed. The first mention of C is no earlier than in 451. The minutes of the Council of Chalcedon of that year record the archdeacon of Constantinople reading it
to the assembled bishops as the faith of the 150 fathers who met at
Constantinople. Until the middle of the twentieth century, the great

1. John A. McGuckin, *St. Gregory of Nazianzus: An Intellectual Biography* (Crestwood,
N.Y.: St. Vladimir's Seminary Press, 2001).
2. See, *inter alia*, Roy Jenkins, *Churchill: A Biography* (New York: Farrar, Straus and Giroux,
2001), 819.

majority of scholars disputed its purported origin.[3] There is no record
of it being worked on at the council of 381—although, since no minutes of it are extant, that proves less than might at first sight be supposed. However, the church historians closest to the events—Socrates
and Sozomen, of the early fifth century—do not mention it. Indeed,
from 381 to 451 silence reigns, not only from councils, but also from
theologians. Some have pointed to a virtually identical creed cited by
Epiphanius in a work composed in 374, but later scholarship considers this creed to be closer to the creed of Nicaea (N) than to C.

However, Kelly produces powerful arguments that support the
Constantinopolitan origin of C.[4] Why, he asks, did the fathers at Chalcedon accept the explanation of its origin presented to them by the
archdeacon? They were known to be opposed to the making of unnecessary creeds. No one cast doubt on it at that time. As Hanson argues,
we should expect the archdeacon of Constantinople to know what
was done by the council in his own city.[5] Moreover, the hostility of
Rome and especially Alexandria to the claims of Constantinople to be
second in honor only to Rome, advanced at the council, helps to explain
why its creed may have been suppressed for a time by its jealous rivals.
The expression "the faith of Nicaea," used pervasively down the years,
was not always applied to the Council of Nicaea as such, but to all
who followed in the general orbit of its teaching. Given this practice,
it is easy to see why a formulary that followed in the ethos of Nicaea
might have remained in the background for a while. The Council of
Constantinople would not have seen itself as promulgating a new teaching, but rather endorsing Nicaea, only with a different formulary. The
teaching of Nicaea, rather than its precise words, was considered
important.[6] It could well be that C was already in existence—the flow
of its language suggests liturgical use—and that the council then
adopted it, perhaps using it at the baptism of Nectarius, Gregory
Nazianzen's successor at Constantinople. Kelly suggests that the Nicene
faith was ratified in the shape of C, arguing that it was used to try to

3. J. N. D. Kelly, *Early Christian Creeds* (London: Longman, 1972), 305–12.
4. Ibid., 312–31.
5. R. P. C. Hanson, *The Search for the Christian Doctrine of God: The Arian Controversy
318–381* (Edinburgh: T & T Clark, 1988), 813.
6. Hanson, *Search*, 820, agrees.

win over the Macedonians (hence Gregory Nazianzen's strictures at its theological temporizing), while at the same time endorsing Gregory's doctrine of the Holy Spirit in all but words. I might also suggest that there is a hint of a very early reference to C in the third book of Gregory of Nyssa's *Against Eunomius*, where he refers to the phrases "light of light, true God of true God" in "our simple and homespun statement of faith," as confessing the identity of the substance of the Son with that of the Father. These phrases are present in both N and C, but two factors may point to a reference to C. We know that Gregory read parts of this work to a select gathering immediately before the council, but this consisted of the first two books, for he did not write the rest until two years afterwards. Additionally, Gregory omits the phrase "God of God" from N, which is also left out by C. If so, this is the very earliest attestation we have for C, and it would be a most reliable one, for Gregory was present throughout the council and played a leading role in it.[7]

What is the connection of C to the synodical letter issued the following year? The principal difference is the moderate tone of C concerning the Holy Spirit—there is no reference to his being *homoousios* with the Father and the Son, nor is he called God—compared with the clear and unambiguous assertions of the letter, which state precisely these points that C sidestepped. The most common thesis is that the council attempted to secure as wide an acceptance as possible and so held back on terms that might offend some, particularly the Macedonians. By the following year, so the theory goes, these people had shown themselves to be so hostile to the council that further temporizing was unnecessary, and the value of restraint no longer existed. This is based on the assumption that C was an attempt to win over the Macedonians. However, there are good reasons why this is a misreading of the creed. It also overlooks the fact that the Macedonians left the council early, rejecting the course it was taking. The breach between them and the Nicenes had already occurred, and it was not postponed until after the council had ended.[8]

---

7. Gregory of Nyssa, *Against Eunomius* 3.4 (my translation). See McGuckin, *St. Gregory of Nazianzus*, 349–50; Johannes Quasten, *Patrology*, vol. 3, *The Golden Age of Greek Patristic Literature from the Council of Nicaea to the Council of Chalcedon* (Westminster, Md.: Christian Classics, 1992), 254–96.

8. Hanson, *Search*, 817–18.

From another angle, what is the relationship between C and N? C has often been thought to be simply an expansion and updating of N. This is not so. C omits a wide range of words and phrases in N, while introducing a further series of statements that have no counterpart in its predecessor. Only about one-fifth of the words of C can be traced to N. The biggest difference is a larger section in C on the Holy Spirit. Kelly correctly states that C is an entirely new document, not merely a revision, although its compilers would not have thought of it as new, since they were concerned less with verbal precision and more with theological compatibility.[9] The two key formulae of N are omitted—"from the *ousia* of the Father" and "God from God." Some of the words and phrases introduced by C are important. For instance, the phrase "whose kingdom shall have no end" clearly counters Marcellus of Ancyra's Sabellian-sounding idea that the Son's kingdom would end when he hands over the kingdom to the Father. There are also a large number of trivial differences between the two creeds that would hardly have been introduced if the compilers of C had simply wanted to update N. In short, the council either constructed or adopted as its own the only creed that is truly ecumenical, confessed in both Eastern and Western churches, "one of the few threads by which the tattered fragments of the divided robe of Christendom are held together."[10]

The following are the words of the Niceno-Constantinopolitan creed, probably dating from the Council of Constantinople (381), which brought to a resolution the convulsions of the fourth century:

> We believe in one God the Father Almighty, maker of heaven and earth and of all things visible and invisible;
>
> And in one Lord Jesus Christ the Son of God, the Only-begotten, begotten by his Father before all ages, Light from Light, true God from true God, begotten not made, consubstantial with the Father, through whom all things came into existence, who for us men and for our salvation came down from the heavens and became incarnate by the Holy Spirit and the Virgin Mary and became a man, and was crucified for us under Pontius Pilate and suffered and was buried and rose again on the third day in accordance with the Scriptures

9. Kelly, *Creeds*, 301–5, 325; Hanson, *Search*, 820.
10. Kelly, *Creeds*, 296.

and ascended into the heavens and is seated at the right hand of the
Father and will come again with glory to judge the living and the
dead, and there will be no end to his kingdom;

And in the Holy Spirit, the Lord and life-giver, who proceeds
from the Father, who is worshipped and glorified together with the
Father and the Son, who spoke by the prophets;

And in one holy, catholic and apostolic Church;

We confess one baptism for the forgiveness of sins;

We wait for the resurrection of the dead and the life of the
coming age. Amen.[11]

The Theology of the Creed

We noted that C is significantly different from N. In the first place,
there are a number of additions. The phrase "by the Holy Spirit and
the Virgin Mary" has been thought to be an anti-Apollinarian insertion, but this is highly unlikely, for Apollinarius could accept this without demur. He readily accepted the virgin birth of Jesus and his conception by the Spirit. It was the reality of a human soul that he denied.
Indeed, there is no ready explanation for this addition, other than that
the words were already in a preexisting formula that the council
adopted. We have seen that the expression about Christ, "and there
will be no end to his kingdom," was directed against Marcellus of
Ancyra. The other additions, with one exception, are all trivial and so
point to a different base for this creed than N. The one nontrivial addition is the third article, on the Holy Spirit. This is explained by the
controversies caused by the Macedonians. The council, whatever else
it did, had no option but to respond to these questions.

The omissions from N require some comment. The single most
obvious one is the phrase "from the substance (*ousia*) of the Father,"
referring to the Son. On the basis of this omission, Harnack claimed
that C is a homoiousian, not a homoousian, document. The council,
in his estimation, was not prepared to assert that the Son is of the identical substance (*homoousios*) of the Father. However, this argument is
nowhere near so strong as Harnack imagined. As Hanson points out,

---

11. Translation by Hanson from the Greek text printed by G. L. Dosetti, *Il simbolo di Nicaea
e di Constantinopoli*, 1967, 244f., quoted in *Search*, 815–16.

the homoiousians, while objecting to the term *homoousios*, actually found the expression in question acceptable. It was not a bone of contention.[12] The most reasonable conjecture for the omission of the phrase is that C may have originated as a formula for liturgical purposes—it has a rhythmic flow to it—and so the council may not have considered it necessary to repeat the precise phraseology of N.

Moving from the details of the creed to its theology, we recall that the particular needs of the time required a more extensive reference to the Holy Spirit. We were skeptical about the council's adopting, whether under imperial pressure or by design, a conciliatory line toward the Macedonians on this issue. A year later, the *homoousion* of the Spirit was clearly asserted in the synodical letter. As Hanson suggests, the clause on worshiping the Holy Spirit together with the Father and the Son was unacceptable to the Macedonians. They considered the Spirit to be some kind of creature and so not to be worshiped. The clause in question was designed to exclude them, not conciliate them.[13]

Overall, however, C intends to teach the deity of the Holy Spirit in guarded language, giving as little offense as possible. A number of factors support this view. First, the title "Lord" is applied to the Spirit: "the Lord and life-giver." *Kyrios* (Lord) is the Greek word customarily used for YHWH, the God of Israel. Second, the statement that the Spirit is "worshipped and glorified together with the Father and the Son" reproduces Athanasius's comments in his letters to Serapion.[14] The phrase highlights the real personal distinctions, but unites the worship, which is one and the same. It places the Holy Spirit without question on the side of deity. While he is not specifically called *homoousios* as such, all that goes with that term is present, whether explicitly or by direct entailment.[15] While not everyone in the orthodox ranks as yet felt completely at ease about calling the Holy Spirit "God" in so

---

12. Hanson, *Search*, 817–18.

13. Ibid., 818.

14. Athanasius, *Letters to Serapion on the Holy Spirit* 1.31 (PG 26:601). See also Basil of Caesarea, *Letters* 90.2 (PG 32:473).

15. Bertrand de Margerie, *The Christian Trinity in History*, trans. Edmund J. Fortman (Petersham, Mass.: St. Bede's Publications, 1982), 105–6; Basil Studer, *Trinity and Incarnation: The Faith of the Early Church*, trans. Matthias Westerhoff, ed. Andrew Louth (Collegeville, Minn.: Liturgical Press, 1993), 157.

many words (remember Gregory Nazianzen's comments about the diversity of opinion at the time), the synodical letter that followed in 382 removed all ambiguity. It said, "We believe that there is one substance (*ousia*) of the Father and of the Son and of the Holy Spirit in three most perfect *hypostases* or three perfect Persons (*prosōpois*)."[16] Moreover, despite—or perhaps even because of—the disastrous role played by Gregory Nazianzen at the council, the creed was destined to be interpreted through his lens, definitively abandoning Basil's silence concerning the deity of the Spirit.[17]

The creed asserts indirectly the monarchy of the Father, since the Holy Spirit proceeds from the Father.[18] At the same time, this statement counters and contradicts the Macedonians, who maintained that the Spirit was a creation of the Son. That he is said to proceed from the Father—and by implication from the Father's *ousia*—places him completely outside those things made by the Son.[19] In addition, the personality of the Spirit is implied by the reference to his speaking through the prophets.[20] As de Margerie indicates, the creed introduces a new dimension, since no longer is heresy confined to what is said or taught; now it also applies to what is *not* said or taught. Failure to teach that the Spirit is to be worshiped together with the Father and the Son is placed beyond the pale of the Christian faith.[21]

The Holy Spirit is also coordinate with the Father and the Son in creation and grace. The Father is the maker of all things, while the Lord Jesus Christ is the one through whom all things came into existence, and the Holy Spirit is the Lord and giver of life. Creation is a work of the whole Trinity; all three persons are actively involved in the creation of all that is made. Moreover, in being the Lord and giver of life, creating all things together with the Father and the Son, the Spirit is again placed unequivocally in the category of what is God.

16. De Margerie, *Christian Trinity*, 107, citing J. Alberigo, *Conciliorum oecumenicorum decreta* (Rome: Herder, 1962), 24. See Studer, *Trinity*, 158.

17. De Margerie, *Christian Trinity*, 106: "The council made its own the doctrine that we already saw set forth by St. Gregory of Nazianzus."

18. Boris Bobrinskoy, *The Mystery of the Trinity: Trinitarian Experience and Vision in the Biblical and Patristic Tradition*, trans. Anthony P. Gythiel (Crestwood, N.Y.: St. Vladimir's Seminary Press, 1999), 249–50.

19. Studer, *Trinity*, 157.

20. Ibid., 157–58; Bobrinskoy, *Mystery*, 249–50.

21. De Margerie, *Christian Trinity*, 107.

On the other hand, there are notable omissions. As McGuckin indicates, in addition to the absence of the *homoousion* of the Spirit and of any direct reference to his being God, there is no mention of the mutual indwelling of the three persons, to which Athanasius and the Cappadocians had borne witness. Nor does the creed refer to the points made by the two Gregorys, that the properties of the persons concern their relations and do not affect the one divine essence. McGuckin, who tends to accentuate Gregory Nazianzen's short-term failure, considers this to be a triumph of the theology of the timid Basil and his brother, and a rejection of Gregory Nazianzen,[22] but Kelly, Hanson, Studer, Bobrinskoy, and de Margerie disagree with him. If Kelly's thesis is correct, and he marshals a powerful array of evidence in its favor, we must conclude that the council was not going out of its way to be innovative. It was content to adopt a previous formula. The synodical letter of 382 gives more of a clue as to what its intentions really were, and these were more in line with the theology of Gregory Nazianzen.

Indeed, McGuckin agrees that the creed has been and is interpreted in accordance with the views of Gregory Nazianzen in any case:

> In the subsequent history of the ancient Church these five Orations [of Gregory] . . . were . . . adopted as the ultimate statement of Trinitarian orthodoxy despite what the conciliar creed of 381 had to say. It is a providential irony that the creed, which was itself a clear and explicit rebuke of Gregory's boldness in teaching the consubstantiality of the Spirit, has come in the subsequent history of theology to be so strictly interpreted in terms of Gregory's Orations. . . . He could hardly have envisaged the manner in which his work would become established as the foundations of Christian orthodoxy. . . . For centuries after him, this sheaf of Orations became the chief trinitarian curriculum of all the Eastern schools, and of almost as great importance to the West.[23]

Implications of the Trinitarian Settlement

From the Trinitarian settlement, it is apparent that there are a number of parameters to be held in balance as equally ultimate. Violation of any one leads to major problems.

---

22. McGuckin, *St. Gregory of Nazianzus*, 350–69; but see Hanson, *Search*, 818–19.
23. McGuckin, *St. Gregory of Nazianzus*, 277.

One Being, Three Persons

That God is one being (essence, from *esse*, "to be") is, from the biblical background, axiomatic. That the one being of God consists eternally of three distinct persons is a matter that the Fathers considered to be essential to salvation, for if it were not so, the truth and reliability of God's revelation would be destroyed. Creation and salvation are presented in the Bible as works of God. Since the Son and the Holy Spirit are, together with the Father, direct and distinct personal actors in both realms, it follows that all three have the status of deity. A more precise explanation awaited the church's prolonged reflection, catalyzed by proposals that on consideration proved unacceptable.

Since all three persons are God, the question could be approached from two opposite directions. It could be said either that God is one being who exists as three persons (this was to prove the preferred route in the West) or, alternatively, that he is three persons who are simultaneously one undivided being (which tended to be the approach favored in the East). However, both approaches are equally valid. From one side, God is one being, three persons, while from another angle, he is three persons, one being.[24] To see why this is so, the following discussion may be helpful.

When the church says that the Son or the Holy Spirit is fully God, it means that the whole being of God, without remainder, is in each person. All that is God, all that can ever be said to be God, without dilution or subtraction, constitutes the person of the Son, and in turn the person of the Spirit, just as it is with the person of the Father. Each person of the Trinity, when considered in himself, is absolutely, one hundred percent God, and at the same time one hundred percent of God is in each person. The whole God is in each person, and each person is the whole God.

At the same time, the one being of God is simple, not divisible. It is impossible to cut off and detach part of God, leaving the rest behind, as can be done with any created being. It is possible, for instance, to remove a human kidney from its original owner and trans-

---

24. See Thomas F. Torrance, *The Christian Doctrine of God: One Being, Three Persons* (Edinburgh: T & T Clark, 1996), 112–67, for a developed exposition of this point.

plant it into another person. Such a thing is not possible with God. He cannot be divided. That is why the Father, the Son, and the Holy Spirit comprise all of God, both severally and together. God cannot be apportioned to the several persons in amounts less than the whole of who he is. Consequently, the whole of God is in each person, and each person is the whole God.

It follows from this that there is no more of God in the whole three persons than there is in any one of them. This is so because there is but one divine essence or being. Therefore, when we contemplate God the Father, we are contemplating one who is wholly and completely God. At the same time, we are considering the whole of God, who infinitely transcends our own capacities, for there is nothing more of God than there is in the Father. Similarly, when we contemplate God the Son, we are again contemplating one who is wholly and completely God. We are considering the whole of the infinite God, who transcends the greatest human capacities, for again there is nothing more of God than there is in the Son. Finally, when we contemplate God the Holy Spirit, we are once again contemplating one who is wholly and completely God. We are considering the whole of the infinite God, who transcends the greatest human capacities, for there is nothing more of God than there is in the Holy Spirit. Since there is only one God, we should by now realize that we should immediately revert to the one undivided being of God, who is eternally the Father, the Son, and the Holy Spirit. It is no wonder that Gregory Nazianzen most commonly referred to the Trinity in terms of a blazing, dazzling light.

Consubstantiality

It follows from this that the one identical divine being is shared by the Father, the Son, and the Holy Spirit. All three persons are of one substance (*consubstantial*). All three are of the identical being (*homoousios*). There is only one essence or being of God, which all three persons share completely. Furthermore, each person is God in himself. There is nothing in the creed (C) to suggest that the Son or the Holy Spirit derives his deity from the Father. If this idea was present in Origen or others, by the time of the Council of Constantinople it had been corrected. While at times Gregory of Nyssa appears to suggest a chain of causal dependency,

Gregory Nazianzen corrects him, and both stress that the relations of origin (begetting and procession) refer to the relations between the persons, not to the essence or being of God. The theme present in Athanasius, taken up by the two Gregorys, that the Son is all that the Father is, except for being the Father, entails the full status of deity *a se* (of himself). Gregory Nazianzen could not have been more emphatic on the point.[25] Even statements ("light of light," "true God of true God") taken by some to refer to remnants of subordination are understood by contemporaries and the tradition to refer to the *homoousion*.[26]

Perichoresis

Although the precise word *perichoresis* was not used for some time yet, the truth it signifies was already widely accepted. Athanasius and the Cappadocians, in particular, had brought to the forefront the concept of the full mutual indwelling of the three persons in the one being of God. Although C does not explicitly express the concept, it is entailed by all that C openly declares. It follows from the homoousial identity of the three and the undivided divine being. Since all three persons are fully God and the whole God is in each of the three, it follows that the three mutually contain one another. As Gerald Bray puts it, all three occupy the same divine space.[27]

This idea would be developed further by John of Damascus. It was already implied by the pervasive reference to the three persons as inseparable. Their union is unbreakable, and the three are inseparable. Not one of them occupies space, so to speak, that the others do not. Here divine and human persons differ, as the Leiden Synopsis explains. Human persons do not exist in one another, as the divine persons do.[28] As human beings, we are not only distinct, but apart. We act differently, we go our separate ways, and some live longer than others. Moreover, there are a huge number of different human beings, and the sum total increases or diminishes as time goes by. But the divine persons are three in number, no more and no less, and are so eternally

25. Gregory Nazianzen, *Orations* 30.20; 31.14, 16; 40.43 (PG 36:128–32, 148–52, 420–21).

26. Gregory of Nyssa, *Against Eunomius* 3.4; Photius, *On the Mystagogy of the Holy Spirit*, trans. Holy Transfiguration Monastery (n.p.: Studion Publishers, 1983).

27. Gerald Bray, *The Doctrine of God* (Leicester: Inter-Varsity Press, 1993), 158.

28. Doctorum et Professorum in Academia Leidensi: Iohannes Polyandrus, Andreas Rivetus, Anthonius Walaeus, Anthonius Thysius, *Synopsis purioris theologiae* (Leiden, 1625), 77.

without change. That is why the analogy of three men sharing a common human nature could never even remotely approximate the Holy Trinity. It is far more suited to tritheism or even polytheism.

The Order of the Persons

In terms of the relations between the three persons, there is a clear order (*taxis*[29]): *from the Father through the Son by the Holy Spirit.* These relations cannot be reversed—the Son does not beget the Father, nor does the Father proceed from the Holy Spirit. In this sense, the Father is the first, the Son is the second, and the Holy Spirit is the third. But in what sense is the Father primary? In particular, is it proper to speak of the *monarchy* of the Father? Some Eastern theologians, following hints in Basil and Gregory of Nyssa, refer to the Father as the source or origin of the deity of the Son and the Spirit—language with subordinationist overtones. However, Gregory Nazianzen taught that the monarchy should be seen as that of the whole Trinity, rather than of the Father alone. T. F. Torrance supported this view, arguing that all three persons are coequally God, while retaining their distinctive relations, and his position recently became a basis for agreement between Orthodox and Reformed churches.[30]

However, the three persons are not identical to one another. They are eternal and distinct. It was modalism that confused them, and this still resurfaces whenever the personal distinctions are in any way blurred or confined to human history. The particular relations that the three persons sustain to each other are inseparable from their identity and so are eternal and unchangeable.

Thus, the Father is the Father of the Son, and the Son is the Son of the Father. The Father begets the Son, and the Son is begotten by the

29. The Greek word *taxis* has a range of meanings. It was often used in military contexts and had the idea of rank, implying a hierarchy of some kind. This fitted in well with the Arian view of a gradation between the Father and the Son, with the latter having a lower and subordinate status. However, the word was also used of role, office, class, orderliness and regularity of the stars, order in the church or monastery, or an ordered constitution. It is in the sense of order, not rank, closer to what is fitting and suitable than to rank or hierarchy, that the orthodox use the term. See G. W. H. Lampe, ed., *A Patristic Greek Lexicon* (Oxford: Clarendon Press, 1961), 1372–73.

30. Gregory Nazianzen, *Orations* 29.2; 31.13–16; 39.12 (PG 36:76, 148–52, 348); Torrance, *Christian Doctrine of God*, 168–202; Thomas F. Torrance, *Trinitarian Perspectives: Toward Doctrinal Agreement* (Edinburgh: T & T Clark, 1994).

Father. This relation is not interchangeable, nor can it be reversed—it is eternal and unchangeable. *Mutatis mutandis*, the Holy Spirit proceeds from the Father (the West adds "and the Son"—the *filioque* clause added to C), while the Father (and the Son, according to the West) spirates the Spirit. Again, this is never reversed. The Father is not begotten, nor does he proceed; the Son does not beget, nor does he proceed; the Spirit neither begets nor spirates. These relations exist in the context of the mutual indwelling of the three (perichoresis). Indeed, the Spirit is the Spirit of the Son, and the Father is the Father of the Son. Also, the relation of the Father and the Son is in the midst of the perichoretic relations of the three, and thus in the Holy Spirit. Hence, there are distinctions (not divisions) among the three as they distinctly and yet together constitute the one undivided being of God and, at the same time, among them in their eternal and distinct personal relations.

Since there is only one being of God, which all three persons share completely, when it is said that the Son is begotten by the Father or that the Spirit proceeds from the Father, the generation and procession have to do with the relations of the persons. However, since the Father's essence is the one essence of God, the monarchy can be said to be that of the whole Trinity.

Torrance points to the foundational work done by Gregory Nazianzen on this matter. He brought about a shift from the concept of "modes of being," as found in Basil, to a view of "interrelations that belong intrinsically to what Father, Son, and Holy Spirit are coinherently in themselves and in their mutual objective relations with and for one another . . . [relations that are] just as substantial as what they are unchangeably in themselves and by themselves. . . . 'Person' is an onto-relational concept."[31] Calvin sums this up when he says that the Son is God of himself (*ex seipso esse*), whereas in terms of his personal subsistence he is from the Father (*ex Patre*).[32]

Here we note Van Til's suggestion that God is one person.[33] He is concerned to avoid any notion of an impersonal divine essence, such as crept into Western Trinitarianism later. This is a laudable motive. How-

31. Torrance, *Christian Doctrine of God*, 157.

32. John Calvin, *Institutes of the Christian Religion*, trans. Ford Lewis Battles, ed. John T. McNeill (Philadelphia: Westminster Press, 1960), 1.13.25. Cf. 1.13.17–19.

33. Cornelius Van Til, *An Introduction to Systematic Theology* (Phillipsburg, N.J.: Presbyterian and Reformed, 1974), 220, 229.

God's not "a person."

ever, Torrance, while recognizing that God is "fulness of personal being," warns against calling him a person.[34] The reasons for this should be clear, for the persons of the Trinity are relational. They are persons in relation to others (*ad alios*). The Father is Father in relation to the Son. Hence, if the one being of God were a person in the same sense that the three are persons, we would have to ask, in relation to whom? The answer could only be one of three possibilities, each heretical. First, the being of God would be in relation to the three, and so would be a fourth, forming a quaternity. Or, second, he would be in relation to some other being, and we would have a pantheon, not a trinity. Or, third, the three persons would be reduced to attributes of the one absolute person. However, if God is not one person in the same way that the three are persons, a different term is needed to express the way he is one, which is exactly what the Fathers used. Van Til's intention is clearly orthodox and positive; his problems are posed by the limitations of language.

The Aftermath

By the sixth century, C became the sole baptismal creed of the East. In addition, it became the universal creed at the Eucharist, quickly in the East, more gradually in the West. Since its origin, over fifty generations of the church in both East and West have confessed their faith using its words. This alone should give pause to those who wish to jettison it. The Protestant Reformation asserted the supreme authority of Holy Scripture, but the Reformers to a man wanted to keep this creed, for they respected the historic teaching of the church and accorded it an authority of its own. In this they have good biblical precedent, for the apostle Paul urged his readers to be "submitting to one another out of reverence for Christ" (Eph. 5:21).

In answering the question of whether the journey from the opening verses of Mark's gospel to the creed of Constantinople was really necessary, R. P. C. Hanson replies strongly in the affirmative, concluding that "a consideration of the whole history of the gradual formation of this doctrine must convince students of the subject that the doctrine of the Trinity is a development which in its shape . . . is true

---

34. Torrance, *Christian Doctrine of God*, 102–3, 155–61.

and authentic."[35] J. N. D. Kelly sums up the profound achievements of the fourth century, culminating in C:

> What is not always noticed, however, is the profound intellectual revolution which the triumph of the new orthodoxy at the two great councils implied. To make my point as clearly and as simply as I can, prior to Nicaea the accepted Christian doctrine of God was an Origenistic one of a holy Triad, of an ineffable Godhead with two subordinate and, in the last resort, disparate hypostases; but after Nicaea the pressure group which pushed through the introduction of the *homoousion* dragged, if you will forgive the crude metaphor, these two inferior hypostases within the divine essence. During the four or five decades following Nicaea the predominant view in the church continued to be Origenistic, pluralistic. . . . But once the creed of Constantinople both reaffirmed and supplemented the Nicene creed proper, there could be no future for such pluralism. The Son and the Spirit were "one in being" (as we now translate *homoousion*) with the Father, and the Godhead was an indivisible unity expressing itself in three eternal modes differing only in their relations. The Nicene creed, in its original form N and its more mature development C, symbolised this far-reaching revolution.[36]

However, this does not mean that C is without limitations. Subsequent history, as Basil Studer indicates,[37] has disclosed at least two such shortcomings, explained as much as anything by the inevitability of future surprises, to which we all are subject. The council can hardly be blamed for being human and time-bound! First, Studer points out that the council did not explore the meaning of *ousia* and *hypostasis* very far. This was to have damaging consequences after the Christological debates of the next century. It led to an outbreak of tritheism in the sixth century. The Christological debates produced the conclusion that the incarnate Christ was one person or *hypostasis*, with two natures or *physeis* (a word used interchangeably with *ousia* in the fourth-century Trinitarian debates). Thus, the focus came to be on the one *hypostasis* of Christ, the one person consisting of two

35. R. P. C. Hanson, "The Doctrine of the Trinity Achieved in 381," *SJT* 36 (1983): 57.
36. J. N. D. Kelly, "The Nicene Creed: A Turning Point," *SJT* 36 (1983): 38–39.
37. Studer, *Trinity*, 159–60.

natures, the deity uniting with a human nature. When applied to Trinitarian thought, this had an adverse effect. Since the focus of Christological thought was on the *hypostasis* of Christ, rather than the two natures, the focus of Trinitarian thought shifted to the *hypostases* rather than the nature or being of God. In time, the sixth-century John Philiponus (d. after 600) was accused of tritheism. He was answered, so it is claimed, by an unknown seventh-century writer, pseudo-Cyril, whose treatise *De sacrosancte Trinitate* is bound with the works of Cyril of Alexandria by J.-P. Migne.[38] However, it has recently been demonstrated by V. S. Conticello that this is a compilation of the fourteenth-century Joseph the Philosopher,[39] and so made no contribution to the development of doctrine, but was entirely derivative. Credit for countering tritheism and introducing the technical term *perichōrēsis* into Trinitarian discussion now goes to John of Damascus. Allied with this problem is the lack of clarity over exactly what *hypostasis* means and the differences and similarities between divine and human persons. Again, this is asking a lot at this stage, when the language had only recently been coined to distinguish between the ways in which God is three and one.

A second limitation of C, in Studer's estimation, is its inability to press further the question of generation and procession. This was to ignite the *filioque* controversy, which has divided the church down to the present day (see chapter 10). However, that would lie in the future. Meanwhile, we move across to the Western church, where in the next century Augustine would appropriate the Constantinopolitan theology and give it his own distinctive and far-reaching imprint.

> *Glory to the Holy, Consubstantial, Life-giving and Undivided Trinity, now, and ever, and unto ages of ages.*[40]

---

38. Ibid., 232–33; G.L. Prestige, *God in Patristic Thought* (London: SPCK, 1952), 263–95; Elmer M. Colyer, *The Promise of Trinitarian Theology: Theologians in Dialogue with T. F. Torrance* (Lanham, Md.: Rowman & Littlefield, 2001), 316.

39. Vassa S. Conticello, "Pseudo-Cyril's *De sacrosancte Trinitate*: A Compilation of Joseph the Philosopher," *OCP* 61 (1995): 117–29; Walter Kaspar, ed., *Lexikon für Theologie und Kirche*, 3rd ed. (Freiburg: Herder, 1993–2001), 8:707–8.

40. Collect for Easter, *Service Book*, 226.

Augustine

Augustine (354–430) wrote his great work *On the Trinity* between 400 and 420. It was to have a profound and lasting impact on the Western church. However, he wrote extensively on the Trinity in other works throughout his career, notably in Tractate 20 of his *Tractates on the Gospel of John*, Letter 11 to Nebridius, and Letter 169 to Bishop Evodius, as well as in *The City of God* and the *Confessions*.[1]

There is little doubt of Augustine's debt to Tertullian. On the other hand, he was not aware of all that had gone on in the East. However, he did learn from Hilary of Poitiers, who, after returning from exile in Cappadocia, wrote a treatise on the Trinity and introduced much of the debate to Latin speakers in the West.

It has been widely assumed that Augustine was influenced by Neoplatonism. From this, it is claimed, came his stress on the unity of the divine essence and his great difficulties recognizing real distinctions for the three persons. As a result of his legacy, modalism has been an ever-present threat in the Western church. Colin Gunton has made a particularly devastating attack on Augustine's Trinitarianism along

---

1. Many of Augustine's biographers mention little or nothing of his writing on the Trinity. Among them are Peter Brown, *Augustine of Hippo: A Biography* (London: Faber and Faber, 1967) and Gerald Bonner, *St. Augustine of Hippo: Life and Controversies* (Norwich: Canterbury Press, 1986). Serge Lancel, *Saint Augustine*, trans. Antonia Nevill (London: SCM Press, 2002), 368–87, is a notable exception. See further Basil Studer, *The Grace of Christ and the Grace of God in Augustine of Hippo: Christocentrism or Theocentrism?* (Collegeville, Minn.: Liturgical Press, 1997), 104–9, and Bertrand de Margerie, *The Christian Trinity in History*, trans. Edmund J. Fortman (Petersham, Mass.: St. Bede's Publications, 1982), 110–21.

these lines.[2] Similarly, Prestige asserts that Augustine's "attention [is] firmly riveted on the essential unity," so that he has an "essentially different" doctrine from that of the Greeks.[3] Bray, like de Margerie, argues for the influence of the Neoplatonism of Porphyry, mediated by Marius Victorinus, although he does not rule out impact from the Cappadocians mediated by Hilary. Augustine, he says, is contradictory and confusing, moving close to modalism, with "a trinitarianism quite different from the Cappadocians."[4]

In contrast, Basil Studer adopts a more positive attitude.[5] In turn, M. R. Barnes carefully undermines the received notion of Neoplatonic influence. Read in context, it is in terms of Nicene theology that Augustine should be understood. He calls the received view "dead wrong." There is definite continuity with the previous tradition in his Trinitarianism. The great problem has been the habit of reading Augustine in dismembered form, with bits and pieces extracted from his writings and read piecemeal, without regard to the historical and theological context. Barnes thinks the best single study is by Studer (1997). In fact, there are few proper historical-theological studies of Augustine's Trinitarianism, yet "this lack of productivity . . . has not visibly stopped anyone in the field of Systematics from saying whatever they wanted to say about Augustine's trinitarian theology." Moreover, the assertion of Neoplatonic influence stems from an understanding of Neoplatonism as a historical phenomenon that is no longer viable. It also fails to reflect the doctrinal content of the texts.[6] Rowan Williams agrees with Barnes that Augustine's contact with homoian Arians in Milan is the background to much of his Trinitarian writing, right through to his final years.[7]

2. Colin Gunton, "Augustine, the Trinity, and the Theological Crisis of the West," *SJT* 43 (1990): 33–58.

3. G. L. Prestige, *God in Patristic Thought* (London: SPCK, 1952), 237.

4. Gerald Bray, "The *Filioque* Clause in History and Theology," *TynBul* 34 (1983): 115–16; de Margerie, *Christian Trinity*, 110–21.

5. Basil Studer, *Trinity and Incarnation: The Faith of the Early Church*, trans. Matthias Westerhoff, ed. Andrew Louth (Collegeville, Minn.: Liturgical Press, 1993), 167–85; Studer, *Grace of Christ*, esp. 104–9.

6. Michel René Barnes, "Rereading Augustine on the Trinity," in *The Trinity: An Interdisciplinary Symposium on the Trinity*, ed. Stephen T. Davis (Oxford: Oxford University Press, 1999), 145–53.

7. Rowan Williams, "De Trinitate," in *Augustine Through the Ages*, ed. Allan D. Fitzgerald (Grand Rapids: Eerdmans, 1999), 845–51; Lancel, *Saint Augustine*, 79–82.

The Catholic Doctrine of the Trinity

Augustine provides a succinct summary of the Catholic doctrine of the Trinity in Letter 169 to Bishop Evodius. There is "one God, the Father, and the Son, and the Holy Spirit. . . . [The Son is not the Father, the Father is not the Son, and neither the Father nor the Son is the Holy Spirit.] . . . [T]hese are equal[8] and co-eternal, and absolutely of one nature . . . an inseparable trinity, yet . . . a trinity . . . in inseparable union . . . distinctively and in mutual relation to each other . . . presenting the three to our attention separately . . . but in no wise separated."[9] God is one substance, existing as three persons. Since "to be a substance is to be something," God is "a sort of substance." Whatever the Father is because he is God, so also is the Son, and so also is the Holy Spirit. But the Father is called Father, not in reference to himself, but in reference to the Son. So the Son in himself is God, but in relation to the Father he is Son. We refer to human persons, such as Abraham and Isaac, in the plural. "Not so in things divine," for while the Father is God and the Son is God, they are not Gods but God, in the singular. Being of the same substance, they are equal ("entirely and without differentiation equal" as Williams points out[10]), but not plural.[11] Thus, God is God thrice, not three gods.[12] Augustine writes in terms that foreshadow the misnamed Athanasian Creed (the *Quicunque vult*).[13]

The Son, of the Same Substance as the Father

Crucial to Augustine is the fact, established by the fourth-century Trinitarian controversy, that the Son is of the same essence as the

8. Basil Studer, "Augustin et la foi de Nicée," *Recherches Augustiniennes* 19 (1984): 133–54, demonstrates that Augustine understands by this the idea of consubstantiality that the Eastern controversies had vindicated.

9. Augustine, *Letters* 169, in *NPNF*[1], 1:540 (PL 33:742–48).

10. Williams, "De Trinitate," 845.

11. Augustine, *On Psalm 69*, 5, in *NPNF*[1], 8:301 (PL 36:870); Augustine, *On the Trinity* 1.4.7 (PL 42:824); Augustine, *Tractates on John 39*, in *NPNF*[1], 7:222–23 (PL 35:1681–84).

12. Augustine, *Tractates on John 6*, in *NPNF*[1], 7:39 (PL 35:1425–35). For another short summary of Trinitarian doctrine, see Augustine, *On Christian Doctrine* 1.5, in *NPNF*[1], 2:524 (PL 43:21). Note that Augustine sees the Trinity taught as early as Genesis 1:1–2. *Confessions* 13.4.5, in *NPNF*[1], 1:191 (PL 32:846–47); *City of God* 11.24, in *NPNF*[1], 2:218–19 (PL 41:337–38).

13. Augustine, *Trinity* 7.3.6 (PL 42:938–39).

Father.[14] Since they are one in being, the Son and the Father are indivisible in their person and work—this is a constant *leitmotiv* in his thought[15]—while to us the persons and works of the Trinity are revealed sequentially, for we cannot understand the true simultaneity of being and action.[16] In the important Tractate 20 in his *Tractates on the Gospel of John*, Augustine argues this at length. The inseparability of the works of the Trinity follows from the inseparability of the persons, "because the Father and the Son are not two Gods, but one God . . . and the Spirit of charity also one, so that Father, Son, and Holy Spirit is made the Trinity." Thus, creation is by the Father through the Son in the Holy Spirit, not three separate actions.[17] Hence, God has one will, one power, and one majesty.[18] We saw this line of thought in Gregory Nazianzen.

A question from Augustine's friend Nebridius is important at this point. In the context of debate in the 380s and the issues raised by the homoian Arians, Nebridius asked why, since the works of the Trinity are indivisible, and so all three persons are engaged in all the works of God, only the Son became incarnate and not the Father and the Spirit also. It was at this time, in 389, early in his Christian experience, when Augustine would have been most susceptible to Neoplatonic influence, that he first expounded a Trinitarianism that was to change little in the decades ahead. Augustine replies to Nebridius that all three persons are indeed involved in all the works and ways of God. The three do nothing in which all do not have a part. Nevertheless, each work is appropriately applied to one of the persons. In particular, the Son alone is the subject of the Incarnation, but not without the direct engagement of the Father and the Holy Spirit. The works of the divine persons are inseparable, but distinct. It was most suitable that the Son became incarnate—although Augustine cannot explain satisfactorily why this is so.[19] He says much the same thing in a sermon on

14. Ibid., 1.6.9 (PL 42:825); Augustine, *Tractates on John* 6, in NPNF¹, 7:39 (PL 35:1425–35).

15. Augustine, *Trinity* 1.6.12, 8.15–17, 12.25–27 (PL 42:827, 829–32, 838–40); Augustine, *Letters* 169.2.5, in NPNF¹, 1:540 (PL 33:744); Studer, *Grace of Christ*, 104.

16. Augustine, *Trinity* 4.21.30 (PL 42:909–10).

17. Augustine, *Tractates on John* 20, in NPNF¹, 7:131–37 (PL 35:1556–64).

18. Augustine, *Tractates on John* 22, in NPNF¹, 7:150 (PL 35:1574–82). See *Tractates on John* 77, in NPNF¹, 7:339 (PL 35:1833–35).

19. Augustine, *Letters* 11, in NPNF¹, 1:228–30 (PL 33:75–77).

Matthew 3:13, proving that the works of creation and grace are under-
taken by all three persons, while applied to one in particular. There is
"a distinction of persons, and an inseparableness of operation."[20]
Hence, when one person is named, sometimes all three persons are
understood.[21]

The Holy Spirit, Consubstantial with the Father and the Son

It follows from all this that Augustine considers the Holy Spirit
to be consubstantial with the Father and the Son. The three persons
are clearly and basically equal.[22] The Spirit is "a certain unutterable
communion of the Father and the Son"[23] and "consubstantial love of
the Father and the Son."[24] This full acknowledgment of the Spirit's
coequal and consubstantial deity enables Augustine to develop his
teaching on the twofold procession of the Spirit from the Father and
the Son:[25]

> . . . yet there is good reason why in this trinity we call none Word of
> God but the Son, none Gift of God but the Holy Spirit, none of whom
> the Word is begotten and from whom the Holy Spirit originally (*prin-
> cipaliter*) proceeds, but God the Father. I add the word "originally",
> because we learn that the Holy Spirit proceeds also from the Son.
> But this is part of what is given by the Father to the Son, not as already
> existing without it, but given to him as all that the Father gives to
> his only-begotten Word, in the act of begetting. He is begotten in
> such a manner that the common gift proceeds from him also, and
> the Holy Spirit is Spirit of both.[26]

So the Spirit proceeds from the Father *principaliter*, but in common
from both the Father and the Son. Here are the seeds of the fateful *filioque* controversy that will bedevil the church (see chapter 10). What

20. Augustine, *Sermon on Matthew 3:13*, in NPNF¹, 6:259–66, esp. 262 (PL 38:354–64).
21. Augustine, *Trinity* 1.9.18–19 (PL 42:832–34).
22. Ibid., 1.6.13; 7.3.6 (PL 42:827–28, 938–39); J. N. D. Kelly, *Early Christian Doctrines*
(London: Adam & Charles Black, 1968), 272–73; Studer, *Trinity*, 174, 176.
23. Augustine, *Trinity* 5.11.12 (PL 42:918–19).
24. Augustine, *Tractates on John* 105, in NPNF¹, 7:396 (PL 35:1904–8).
25. Augustine, *Trinity* 1.12.25 (PL 42:860–61).
26. Ibid., 15.26.47; see also 15.26.45, 27.48 (PL 42:1092–96).

exactly is Augustine saying? First, he carefully safeguards the place of the Father as the sole origin of the Holy Spirit.[27] Again, he does not assert that the Spirit proceeds from two sources, as if from two parents (contrary to what Photius will allege[28]), for it is from a single source that the procession occurs. Yet the procession is not from an indistinguishable unity,[29] since the Spirit is *principaliter* from the Father. Nor does the Father give the Spirit to the Son to pass on; instead, he gives his own life to the Son, which includes the outpouring of the Spirit. In this way, the Holy Spirit is eternally and simultaneously given by the Father and the Son together. The Father as giver is not exhausted by being the Father of the Son, for in begetting the Son there is an excess of gift, and this excess is given to the Son to give in turn.[30]

On the other hand, Augustine's talk of the Spirit as the communion of the other two,[31] and as the mutual love uniting them,[32] raises a major question as to whether the Spirit is in fact subordinate. We will focus on this question later, when we discuss the Trinitarian analogies (better, illustrations) that he is so fond of using. The answer here must be negative. He has stressed the Spirit's consubstantiality at length and in almost the next section writes of him as the "consubstantial communion" of the Father and the Son.[33]

The Incarnation

Augustine considers at length the differences between the OT theophanies and the Incarnation. In particular, he contrasts the voice of the Father and the descent of the Spirit as a dove at the baptism of Jesus with the Incarnation of the Son. The first two were temporary appearances, while the Incarnation was permanent, entailed personal union, and brought about our salvation, for "by joining therefore to us the likeness of his humanity, he took away the unlikeness of our

27. Ibid., 4.20.29 (PL 42:908–10); Williams, "De Trinitate," 847.

28. Photius, *On the Mystagogy of the Holy Spirit*, trans. Holy Transfiguration Monastery (n.p.: Studion Publishers, 1983).

29. *Contra* Stylianopoulos and many Eastern apologists; see Augustine, *Trinity* 15.17.29 (PL 42:1081).

30. Williams, "De Trinitate," 850.

31. Augustine, *Trinity* 15.27.50 (PL 42:1096–97).

32. Ibid., 15.17.27 (PL 42:1079–80).

33. Ibid., 15.27.50 (PL 42:1096–97).

unrighteousness; and by being made the partaker of our mortality, he made us partakers of his divinity."[34] While the Son is sent and the Father sends, they are equal. This is not a relation of greater and lesser, but of Father and Son, begetter and begotten.[35] We have noted Augustine's comment that the Incarnation is appropriate to the Son. He anticipated the contours of the Christological settlement at Chalcedon (451). Both Studer and Barnes point to the vital connection in Augustine's thought between the Trinity and the Incarnation. Christ is at the heart of his entire theology.[36] This undermines Gunton's trenchant claims. As Leithart observes, while Gunton charges Augustine with a lack of biblical exegesis, there is vastly more biblical exegesis in the early books of *De Trinitate* than in the whole of the Gunton corpus.[37] Moreover, Studer's point is well taken that those books are "a dogmatic description of what is believed about the Trinity as this emerges from the traditional understanding of the biblical passages in question. In any case, it is the Nicene faith in the identical essence of the Father, Son, and Spirit and in their common action that Augustine makes his starting point."[38]

Relations Between the Father, the Son, and the Holy Spirit

Augustine also considers the relations of the three persons. The Father begat, the Son is begotten; the Father sent, the Son was sent. Both are one. The Holy Spirit proceeds from the Father, and also from the Son, since he is called the Spirit of the Son as well as the Spirit of the Father. The Father is the beginning (*principium*) of the whole divinity, and so the Spirit who proceeds from both the Father and the Son is referred back ultimately to the Father.[39] Thus, as Studer correctly states, the Father is called God in the proper sense, while the Son, the Spirit, and the whole Trinity are called God in the common sense. The Father is "God who is from no one."[40] In this sense, Augustine has a

34. Ibid., 4.2.4; see 4.2.4–19:26 (PL 42:889–906).
35. Ibid., 4.20.27–30 (PL 42:906–10).
36. Barnes, "Rereading," 154–68; Studer, *Grace of Christ*; Studer, *Trinity*, 168–85.
37. Peter J. Leithart, "'Framing' Sacramental Theology: Trinity and Symbol," *WTJ* 62 (2000): 1–16, esp. 2–4.
38. Studer, *Grace of Christ*, 106.
39. Augustine, *Trinity* 4.20.28–29 (PL 42:907–9); Augustine, *Tractates on John* 39, in *NPNF*[1], 7:222–23 (PL 35:1681–86).
40. Studer, *Grace of Christ*, 104–5.

degree of commonality with the Greeks. However, how can these relations be understood, allowing for the indivisibility and inseparability of the Trinity? This is a question that Augustine tackles in book 5.

God is a substance or essence, in line with Exodus 3:14, where Yahweh names himself "I am." On the other hand, he has no accidents.[41] Augustine here draws on the distinction in Aristotelianism between substance and accidents. The *substance* of a thing is what that individual thing really is, its intrinsic nature. On the other hand, *accidents* are incidental characteristics, related not to a thing's inner nature, but more to what it may appear to be, or to something adventitious that could be withdrawn without altering that thing's substance. Since God does not change, he has no accidents.

At this point, Augustine responds to an Arian argument that aimed to deny the Son's deity, using as ammunition passages that declare the Son to be less than the Father. For the Arians, whatever is said of God cannot be said concerning accidents, and so must refer to God's substance or essence. Therefore, these passages teach that the Son is of a different essence than the Father.[42] In response to this, Augustine makes the vital point that not all that is said about God is said about his substance.[43] Some things are said about his *relations*.[44] Whatever is said about God's substance is said about each person and about the Trinity.[45] All other things are said *relatively*, about the persons and their relations with each other.[46] Hence, a range of biblical passages refer to the Son in relation to the Father and so speak of his being sent, or of the Father as the beginning,[47] and do not refer to the essence of God as such. For example, what is said of God being in time is said relatively, not accidentally.[48] So all three persons are equal in essence.[49] God is a Trinity—the Father alone, the Son alone, and the Spirit alone are neither less nor greater

41. Augustine, *Trinity* 5.2.3 (PL 42:912).
42. Ibid., 5.3.4 (PL 42:912–13).
43. Ibid., 5.4.5 (PL 42:913).
44. Ibid., 5.5.6 (PL 42:913–14).
45. Ibid., 5.8.9–9.10 (PL 42:916–18).
46. Ibid., 5.11.12 (PL 42:918–19).
47. Ibid., 5.13.14–14.15 (PL 42:920–21). See the comments of W. G. T. Shedd in *NPNF*[1], 3:95n6.
48. Augustine, *Trinity* 5.15.16–16.17 (PL 42:921–23).
49. Ibid., 6.2.3–5.7 (PL 42:924–28).

than the three together[50]—an important statement of what the creed of Constantinople entailed. So "in that highest Trinity one is as much as the three together, nor are two anything more than one. And they are infinite in themselves. So both each are in each, and all in each, and each in all, and all in all, and all are one."[51] Shedd's comments are particularly helpful on this. He remarks that each person is as great as the Trinity, if reference be had to the essence, but not if reference be had to the persons.[52] Thus, Augustine can say that God sent God.[53] Each person, with respect to essence, is fully, completely, and identically God. But each person, in relation to the others, differs according to the particular properties of each, entailing sending and being sent, begetting and being begotten, and emitting and proceeding. Indeed, no person exists in respect to himself alone—each exists relatively, one to the other. Thus, the Father and the Son are together one essence, but they are not together one Word.[54] There is thus a kind of asymmetry and inequality in the relations of the persons.[55]

Augustine turns to the question of language. The Greeks speak of three *hypostases*. The Latins had reacted in horror, since the Greek *hypostasis* could only be translated into Latin as *substantia* (substance), leading to the intolerable notion that God is one being and three substances. Thus, they prefer Tertullian's term *persona* (persons).[56] These differences in language and terminology, Augustine says, must be seen in context, as referring to a reality greater than human language or thought can encompass. We must use such terms—from the necessity of speaking—while recognizing that they refer to things that cannot be uttered, for God is more truly thought than uttered and exists more truly than he is thought.[57]

Augustine, in passing, demolishes the analogy of three men.[58] We need to think of the three persons as other than three cases of a genus

50. Ibid., 6.7.8–8.9 (PL 42:928–30).
51. Ibid., 6.10.11 (PL 42:931–32).
52. See NPNF¹, 3:101n2 and n3.
53. Augustine, *Tractates on John* 14, in NPNF¹, 7:97–99 (PL 35:1301–8).
54. Augustine, *Trinity* 7.1.2–2.3 (PL 42:934–36).
55. Williams, "De Trinitate," 847.
56. See the clear discussion in Lancel, *Saint Augustine*, 378–80.
57. Augustine, *Trinity* 7.4.7–6.11 (PL 42:939–45).
58. Ibid., 7.6.11 (PL 42:943–45).

that can be added to one another in cumulative fashion. Three men are more than one man, but the three persons of the Godhead are not more than any one person.[59]

Is the Son Less Than the Father?

In dealing with biblical passages that appear to teach that the Son is inferior to the Father, Augustine follows the pro-Nicene rule of Athanasius and the Cappadocians, that anything in the Bible describing the Son as less than the Father refers to his incarnate state, to his assumed humanity. Augustine uses the Pauline contrast in Philippians 2:5ff. between Christ "in the form of God" and Christ "in the form of a servant" to distinguish his eternal status from his lowly incarnate position. This approach holds true for such passages as 1 Corinthians 15:28 and John 14:28.[60] Yet this is not the complete picture for Augustine. There are actually three ways in which the Son is spoken of in Scripture. First, he is said to be in the form of God, in which he is equal to the Father. Second, he is said to have taken the form of a servant in the Incarnation, in which he is less than the Father. Third, he is spoken of as the Son, making him equal to the Father, but from him, as God of God and light of light. In this third sense, he is equal to the Father and indivisible from him (in being), but in terms of personal relations there is an order, from the Father to the Son.[61] For Augustine, this is not a matter of inequality, but of birth, for "the Son is not less than, but equal to the Father, but yet . . . from him." The working of the Father and the Son is indivisible and equal, "but it is from the Father to the Son."[62] The same applies, *mutatis mutandis*, to the Holy Spirit.[63] The Son and the Holy Spirit are not less than the Father

59. Ibid., 5–6; Williams, "De Trinitate," 848.

60. Augustine, *Trinity* 1.7.14, 8.15, 10.20, 11.22, 12.23–24, 13.28–31 (PL 42:828–30, 834–38, 840–44).

61. Ibid., 2.1.2–3 (PL 42:845–47).

62. Ibid., 2.1.1–3 (PL 42:845–47). See *NPNF*[1], 3:38n2. See also Augustine, *Tractates on John* 20.4–8, in *NPNF*[1], 7:133–35 (PL 35:1556–1564), where he says that "the power of the Son is of the Father, therefore also the substance of the Son is of the Father," and "because he is not Son from himself, therefore he is not able from himself." However, he adds, this does not entail inequality or mean that the Son is less than the Father. The works of the Father and the Son are inseparable, made by the Father through the Son, for "if he is a Son, he was begotten; if begotten, he is from him of whom he is begotten. Nevertheless the Father begat him equal to himself."

63. Augustine, *Trinity* 2.3.5 (PL 42:847–48).

because they are sent by him,[64] for the three work indivisibly in all things. The Son is sent, the Father sends—never the reverse—but they are ontologically equal. This is not a matter of greater and lesser, of superior and inferior, but of Father and Son, of begetter and begotten. It precedes the Incarnation. "For the Son is from the Father, not the Father from the Son. And . . . the Son is not only said to have been sent because 'the Word was made flesh,' but therefore sent that the Word might be made flesh." So the Word "was sent that it might be made man; because he was not sent in respect to any inequality of power, or substance, or anything that in him was not equal to the Father; but in respect to this, that the Son is from the Father, not the Father from the Son." "What wonder, therefore, if he is sent, not because he is unequal with the Father, but because he is 'a pure emanation issuing from the glory of the Almighty God?' For there, that which issues, and that from which it issues, is of one and the same substance."[65] The relations of the three persons, which involve distinctions, completely coexist with the equality and identity of the three in the one divine essence. As Williams indicates, there is no ontological inferiority of the Son to the Father.[66]

The Sendings of the Son and the Spirit Versus Theophanies

Next Augustine discusses the differences between the Incarnation and the OT theophanies.[67] His axiom has been that the entire Trinity is invisible.[68] So was it one particular person who was the subject of the theophanies, such as the Son, or did the Trinity appear indiscriminately? What seems clear to him is that the entire Trinity appeared through the changeable creature,[69] being seen in the appearance of the three men to Abraham, in the burning bush to Moses, in the cloud and fire at Sinai, and to Daniel.[70] The Trinity appeared in bodily form by means of an angel.[71] He reaffirmed this of the preincarnate appear-

64. Ibid., 2.5.7–9 (PL 42:848–51).
65. Ibid., 4.20.27 (PL 42:862–63).
66. Williams, "De Trinitate," 847.
67. Augustine, *Trinity* 2.7.12–18.35 (PL 42:857–68).
68. Ibid., 2.8.14–9.16 (PL 42:854–55).
69. Ibid., 2.10.17–19 (PL 42:855–58).
70. Ibid., 2.11.20–18.33 (PL 42:858–67).
71. Ibid., 3.11.21–27 (PL 42:881–86).

ances.[72] This is in obvious contrast to the Incarnation itself. The entire Trinity was involved in the theophanies—through created mediation. For Augustine, all three persons share the transcendence ascribed in the Eastern church to the Father[73]—in line with the basing of his Trinitarian doctrine on the one divine essence, rather than the person of the Father.

In Letter 169 to Bishop Evodius, Augustine discusses the uniqueness of the Incarnation. The difference between the voice of the Father, the appearance of the Holy Spirit as a dove, and the Incarnation of the Son is that the first two were temporary, rather than permanent, and were simply symbols, in contrast to the Incarnation, in which human nature was assumed permanently in a real union. As a consequence of the Incarnation, some things are said of the Son according to his human nature, and some are said according to his deity.[74]

In *De Trinitate* he explains this further. The Spirit did not beatify the wind, the fire, or the dove—any of the material elements in which he appeared—nor did he join them forever to himself and to his person. These physical things were themselves changed and adapted for the purpose of making him known. Thus we cannot call the Spirit both God and a fire, or God and a dove. On the other hand, we rightly call the Son both God and man. Moreover, the fire and the dove appeared simply for the purpose of signifying the Holy Spirit, then to disappear. The Incarnation was both real and permanent.[75]

In view of arguments like this, Gunton's strictures are surprising. It hardly appears that Augustine had little interest in the distinctions of the persons, or that he was averse to the full import of the Incarnation. Studer, for one, demolishes such ideas. These discussions were precisely for that purpose.

Trinitarian Illustrations

In the second half of *De Trinitate*, in books 8–15, Augustine considers whether there is in humans some discernible trace of the Trinity. However, this is not some new interest, but one that he pursued through-

72. Ibid., 4.21.31 (PL 42:910).
73. Williams, "De Trinitate," 847.
74. Augustine, *Letters* 169.2.7, in *NPNF*[1], 1:540–41 (PL 33:745).
75. Augustine, *Trinity* 2.6.11 (PL 42:851–52).

out his career, ever since his reply to Nebridius in 389. In Tractate 23 of his *Tractates on the Gospel of John*, he refers to the likeness of the human mind to God,[76] and he also develops the idea in Letters 11 and 169, his volume on the Psalms, the *Confessions*, and *The City of God*.

In book 8, following his conviction that love, not intellectual knowledge, is of primary importance in our knowledge of God, he says that there are three things in love—the lover, the one loved, and love itself.[77] However, this poses immediate problems, for while the lover and the one loved are real personal entities, love is not. This illustration draws into question the personal status of the Holy Spirit. It also implies that the Father and the Son need to be united, for love "seeks to couple together some two things."[78] This is in sharp contrast to the accepted teaching of the full mutual indwelling of all three persons, which Augustine does not seem to have grasped.

In book 9, he introduces the triad of mind, knowledge, and love. This, if effective as an illustration, would prove modalism, not orthodoxy. These are all abstract qualities, not concrete persons,[79] and they are also qualities of a single mind. Again, how is the triad of memory, understanding, and will in book 10 (his favorite illustration) different from modalism?[80] Nor does the troika of things seen, things impressed on the sight of the seer, and the purpose of will combining the two (book 11) leave any place for mutual indwelling,[81] while the third element is not a personal entity distinct from the second. Similar objections apply to the proposed triads of wisdom, rational knowledge, and animal knowledge (book 12), and memory, thought, and will (book 13). Augustine himself recognizes that these are unsuccessful.[82] He returns to the triad of memory, understanding, and will in book 14. The mind remembers, understands, and loves itself.[83] This, he claims, is "a certain kind of trinity."[84] But he is close to modalism

76. Augustine, *Tractates on John* 23, in *NPNF*[1], 7:155 (PL 35:1582–92).

77. Augustine, *Trinity* 8.10.14 (PL 42:960).

78. Ibid., 8.10.14.

79. See the comments of W. G. T. Shedd in *NPNF*[1], 3:126n2, 127, 129n1, 131n1, 133n3.

80. See Shedd's remarks in *NPNF*[1], 3:143.

81. See Shedd in ibid., 3:145.

82. Augustine, *Trinity* 13.20.26 (PL 42:1034–35).

83. Cf. Shedd in *NPNF*[1], 3:189. See also Augustine, *Letters* 169.2.6, in *NPNF*[1], 1:540 (PL 33:744–45).

84. Augustine, *Trinity* 14.8.11 (PL 42:1044–45).

again, for these three things are activities, not personal entities, and are attributes of a single mind. Augustine has his "attention riveted on the essential unity,"[85] and so the persons are not "objective realities in their own right, but expressions of real relations inherent in the divine being."[86]

Augustine is prepared to recognize all this. In his *Confessions*, he says concerning the triad of being, knowledge, and will, that "these three are far other than the trinity"—a dim illustration, not an analogy.[87] He repeatedly distances himself from Sabellianism,[88] although Harnack thought that this was merely assertion, and that nothing else would lead the reader to recognize a difference. Harnack's assessment is far too harsh, for in his positive dogmatic statements Augustine clearly regards the three as distinct within the unity of God.

While he considers there to be "footprints" of the Trinity in creation[89] and "certain trinities" in man,[90] these are very difficult,[91] for they are an "inadequate image."[92] He puts these illustrations in context[93] and recognizes that they are modalistic.[94] They are "very far removed from him [God]"[95] and "imperfect."[96] He has no illusions about their serious limitations.[97]

Augustine gives an extensive explanation of these illustrations and their limits in a brilliant sermon on Matthew 3:13.[98] They give "some vestige of the trinity . . . very different from its model." They provide "a distant resemblance," "very far removed from each other,

85. Prestige, *God*, 236.
86. Bray, "Filioque," 115.
87. Augustine, *Confessions* 13.11.12, in *NPNF*[1], 1:193 (PL 32:849–50); Augustine, *Of Free Will* 3.7 (PL 32:1225); Augustine, *On True Religion* 13 (PL 34:128–29).
88. Augustine, *Trinity* 7.11 (PL 42:943–45); Augustine, *City of God* 10.24, in *NPNF*[1], 2:194–95 (PL 41:300–302); Augustine, *On Psalm 5*, 3, in *NPNF*[1], 8:11 (PL 36:83–84); Augustine, *On Psalm 68*, 36, in *NPNF*[1], 8:297 (PL 36:865).
89. Augustine, *City of God* 11.28, in *NPNF*[1], 2:221 (PL 41:341–42).
90. Augustine, *Trinity* 15.2.2–3 (PL 42:1057–58).
91. Ibid., 15.5.7, 7.11–12 (PL 42:1061–62, 1065–66).
92. Ibid., 9.2.2 (PL 42:985–86).
93. Ibid., 15.17.28–29 (PL 42:1080–81).
94. Ibid., 15.22.42–24.45 (PL 42:1089–93).
95. Augustine, *City of God* 11.26, in *NPNF*[1], 2:220 (PL 41:339–40).
96. Augustine, *Letters* 169, in *NPNF*[1], 1:540 (PL 33:740–48).
97. Kelly, *Doctrines*, 278.
98. In *NPNF*[1], 6:259–66 (PL 38:354–64).

as the lowest from the highest." His intention behind this line of investigation is simply to find "three things which are separately exhibited whose operation is yet inseparable." The Father, Son, and Holy Spirit are revealed distinctly, yet their operation is inseparable. Memory, understanding, and will, in turn, are distinct, but not one can operate without the other two. He does not identify memory with the Father, or understanding with the Son. "I do not say that these things are in any sort to be equalled with the Holy Trinity, to be squared after an analogy; that is, a kind of exact rule of comparison. This I do not say. But what do I say? . . . I have discovered . . . three things, which are exhibited separately, whose operation is inseparable."[99] This ties in exactly with Nebridius's question to which Augustine replies in Letter 11. As Barnes argues, this is the context in which to understand the Trinitarian illustrations. This was the question open for debate in the closing years of the fourth century, which Augustine took over in order to show how the persons of the Trinity are distinct, and particular actions are attributable to particular persons, while, at the same time, the being (and work) of the Trinity is indivisible.

Augustine and His Legacy

However, Augustine's legacy is a different thing. Succeeding generations in the West would develop a powerful focus on the divine essence, driven by the psychological illustrations. Here Gunton's criticisms have weight. Inherently modalistic—all are within the human mind—they make the one being primary and the three persons problematic. Gunton claims that an intellectualizing, an assumption that the mind is specially privileged in comparison with the body, combined with a corresponding distancing of God from the material creation.[100] Bobrinskoy points to "what, in Augustine, only had an illustrative character, became a systematic criterion of later theological thought, with Anselm and in Thomism."[101] This problem is present in Augustine himself. He admits that when he begins with the essence of God,

---

99. Augustine, *Letters* 169, in *NPNF*[1], 1:541 (PL 33:740–41).

100. Gunton, "Augustine."

101. Boris Bobrinskoy, *The Mystery of the Trinity: Trinitarian Experience and Vision in the Biblical and Patristic Tradition*, trans. Anthony P. Gythiel (Crestwood, N.Y.: St. Vladimir's Seminary Press, 1999), 284.

AUGUSTINE 199

he has difficulty thinking of the persons. "When the question is asked, 'What three?' human language labors under great poverty of speech. The answer, however, is given 'three persons' not that it might be completely spoken, but that it might not be left wholly unspoken."[102] The persons are relations, and the Father is real only in relation to the Son and the Spirit. On the other hand, the essence is simple and is not problematic in this way, but for that very reason it tends toward the impersonal. Whereas the Cappadocians began with the Bible and the Christian experience of salvation, Augustine was driven by the Aristotelian category of relations.[103] LaCugna is in general agreement with this thesis when she remarks that Augustine's "focus on the individual apart from its personal and social relations flows directly from the ontology that begins from substance rather than person." She goes on to say that "even if Augustine himself intended nothing of the sort, his legacy to Western theology was an approach to the Trinity largely cut off from the economy of salvation."[104]

Augustine's first main achievement was to stress that the activity of the Trinitarian persons, flowing from their unity, was inseparable. In fact, as Barnes argues, "the unity of the trinity is found in its inseparable activities or operations."[105] The inseparability of the persons in both being and action, in turn, is a reflection of their complete equality. All elements of subordination are pruned away. Studer observes "how much more closely the immanent Trinity and the threefold work in salvation history are interrelated in the Augustinian theology than is admitted by many even to this day," for "it can be taken for granted that Christ is at the center of Augustinian theology."[106] Studer also points to Augustine's revolutionary concept of person, his reflection on the differences between the sending of the Son and the sending of the Spirit, the sharpness with which he works out the concept of *relatio*, and the "not unbiblical" notion of the Spirit as the love between the Father and the Son.[107] It is this last point to which de Margerie

102. Augustine, *Trinity* 5.9.10 (PL 42:894–95).
103. Richard Haugh, *Photius and the Carolingians: The Trinitarian Controversy* (Belmont, Mass.: Norland, 1975), 198–200.
104. Catherine Mowry LaCugna, *God for Us: The Trinity and Christian Life* (San Francisco: Harper, 1991), 102.
105. Barnes, "Rereading," 154.
106. Studer, *Trinity*, 175–77.
107. Ibid., 173–83.

devotes attention, when he says that Augustine was the first theologian to elaborate the doctrine of the Spirit as the bond of love between the Father and the Son. However, de Margerie is enamored with the strengths of this insight, and does not appear to be aware of its weaknesses.[108] For one thing, it obscures the mutual indwelling of the three persons, of which Augustine scarcely appears aware.[109] Perhaps, as Barnes suggests, part of the problem is that modern theology has worked on the premise of a division between Trinitarianism and Christology that was alien to Augustine. For him, theology is shaped by the intersection of the common activity of the Trinity and the Son as the revealer of the Trinity.[110]

If we do recognize drawbacks in what the West has made of Augustine, this can only be a by-product of his immense achievements. It seems to me incontestable that he operated within the Christian tradition bequeathed by the Cappadocians. His prime motive was to defend and develop it against challenges that had arisen in the wake of the Constantinopolitan settlement. However, while doing so, he took a significantly different turn that would open up a chasm between East and West. We will consider these developing differences in the next two chapters.

Meanwhile, how better could we end than with Augustine's prayer at the conclusion of *De Trinitate*?

> O Lord the one God, God the Trinity, whatever I have said in these books that is of thine, may they acknowledge who are thine; if anything of my own, may it be pardoned both by thee and by those who are thine. Amen.[111]

108. De Margerie, *Christian Trinity*, 110–21.
109. Kelly, *Doctrines*, 285.
110. Barnes, "Rereading," 168n32.
111. Augustine, *Trinity* 15.28.51.

East and West:
The *Filioque* Controversy

The Eastern and Western churches had their origins in the ethnic
and linguistic divisions in the Roman Empire.[1] The Western church,
based in Rome, today includes the Roman Catholic Church and the
churches that broke with Rome at the Reformation. The Eastern
church, originally based at Constantinople, today consists of a number of autocephalous jurisdictions rooted in Russia, the eastern
Mediterranean, and southeastern Europe. Communion between the
East and the West was ruptured in 1054, and the rupture was confirmed after the collapse of the Byzantine empire in 1453. A number
of serious disagreements had developed, some relating to the jurisdiction of the Roman church and papal authority, others including the
use of leavened bread in the Eucharist, clerical marriage (which the
East allowed), and a range of theological issues. Of the latter, by far
the most important single question of all was, and is, the *filioque* clause
added by the West to the Niceno-Constantinopolitan Creed (C).[2] In

---

1. Much of this chapter was originally a lecture given at Mid-America Reformed Seminary
on 10 November 1999, subsequently published in *MJT* 13 (2002): 71–86, and now republished
with permission.

2. The best place to begin consideration of this important matter is, in support of the East,
the excellent article by Nick Needham, "The *Filioque* Clause: East or West?" *SBET* 15 (1997):
142–62, and, in support of the West, Gerald Bray, "The *Filioque* Clause in History and Theology," *TynBul* 34 (1983): 91–144. Bray's article is an extensive historical discussion with penetrating theological comment. A valuable collection of essays, from Orthodox, Roman Catholic,
and Protestant perspectives, is *Spirit of God, Spirit of Christ: Ecumenical Reflections on the Fil-*

1965, as a sign of a new movement in a long path toward rapprochement, Pope Paul VI and Patriarch Athenagoras I withdrew the anathemas of 1054.

The *Filioque* Clause

C states that the Holy Spirit "proceeds from the Father." There
is no mention of his proceeding from the Son as well. However, in
Spain, due to the threat of a continued Arianism, in localized liturgies
an addition crept in—*a patre filioque*—"from the Father *and the Son.*"
This addition of *filioque* spread and was adopted by local councils,
particularly the Council of Toledo (589),[3] and was accepted by the
French church in the late eighth century, but was not inserted into the
Creed by Rome until 1014 under Pope Benedict VIII. The Fourth Lat-
eran Council of 1215 mentioned it, and the Council of Lyons in 1274
proclaimed it as dogma.

The East objected to this development on ecclesiastical grounds.
Such a change (more a development, since C did not deny the *filioque*,
but simply did not comment on it, as it was not an issue) requires an
ecumenical council akin to Nicaea, Constantinople, and Chalcedon,
it maintained. As Stylianopoulos puts it, "Can a clause deriving from
one theological tradition simply be inserted in a creed deriving from
another theological tradition without council?"[4] The East also objected
on theological grounds. We shall examine the reasons for this in a
moment. Since East and West understand the Trinity differently, on
Eastern premises this Western development appears to undermine the
church's teaching on the Trinity.

---

ioque Controversy, ed. Lukas Vischer (London: SPCK, 1981). The most comprehensive and
recent work on the whole issue is Bernd Oberdorfer, *Filioque: Geschichte und Theologie eines
Ökumenischen Problems* (Göttingen: Vandenhoeck & Ruprecht, 2001).

3. But see Richard Haugh, *Photius and the Carolingians: The Trinitarian Controversy* (Belmont, Mass.: Norland, 1975), 160–61, who questions this explanation and argues that it "first
entered the Ecumenical Creed in the Latin West by a simple method of transposition and not by
any willful act of interpolation in conscious violation of the Ecumenical decrees." Sergei Bulgakov rightly argues that the phrase was unnecessary, for Arianism could have been rebutted
quite readily without it; "pour rejeter l'arianisme et reconnaître l'équi-divinité et la consub-
stantialité du Fils au Père, on n'a nul besoin de cette surérogation." Sergei Nikolaevich Bulgakov,
Le Paraclet, ed. Constantin Andronikof (Paris: Aubier, 1946), 125.

4. Theodore G. Stylianopoulos and S. Mark Heim, eds., *Spirit of Truth: Ecumenical Perspectives on the Holy Spirit* (Brookline, Mass.: Holy Cross Orthodox Press, 1986), 32.

To appreciate the significance of this question and not to dismiss it as sterile, one must, as Dietrich Ritschl observes, "let one's thought sink into the classical trinitarian modes of argumentation."[5] Stylianopoulos comments: "At stake was not an abstract question but the truth of Christian salvation."[6] In Pelikan's terms, the Greek fathers and the early councils did not construct a science of divine ontology, but one of divine revelation.[7] The key question is whether the clause is consistent with Scripture and C.

Biblical Teaching on the Procession of the Holy Spirit

In the *locus classicus*, John 15:26, Jesus says he will send the Paraclete (a reference to Pentecost, the historical sending), who in turn *proceeds from* (*ekporeuetai*) the Father—denoting a continuous procession. Much modern NT scholarship argues that the procession here refers to economic activity only—the relations between the Father, the Son, and the Holy Spirit in human history—and not at all to eternal, antecedent realities in God himself. Robert L. Reymond thinks that referring this to immanent realities in God is to go beyond the bounds of Scripture. But de Margerie rightly calls this restriction to the temporal mission "a simplistic exegesis that lacks a theological background."[8] It effectively undermines the reality and truthfulness of God's revelation by positing that what God does economically does not necessarily reveal who he is.

The Spirit proceeds from the Father. The question in dispute, however, concerns whether this procession is from the Son also. Jesus refers to the Father's sending of the Spirit at Pentecost, in response to his request or in his name (John 14:16, 26). However, Jesus also says that he himself will send the Spirit at Pentecost (John 16:7), and later

---

5. Dietrich Ritschl, "Historical Development and the Implications of the *Filioque* Controversy," in *Spirit of God, Spirit of Christ*, ed. Vischer, 46.

6. Theodore Stylianopoulos, "The Biblical Background of the Article on the Holy Spirit in the Constantinopolitan Creed," in *Études Théologiques: Le IIe Concile Oecuménique* (Chambésy-Genève: Centre Orthodoxe du Patriarcat Oecuménique, 1982), 171.

7. Jaroslav Pelikan, *The Christian Tradition*, vol. 2, *The Spirit of Eastern Christendom* (Chicago: University of Chicago, 1974), 33.

8. Robert L. Reymond, *A New Systematic Theology of the Christian Faith* (New York: Nelson, 1998), 331–32; Bertrand de Margerie, *The Christian Trinity in History*, trans. Edmund J. Fortman (Petersham, Mass.: St. Bede's Publications, 1982), 169.

he breathes on the disciples and says, "Receive the Holy Spirit" (John 20:22). So he shares with the Father in the sending of the Spirit. Moreover, he says that he and the Father are one (John 10:30). So it may be asked whether the Son does not also share with the Father in spirating the Spirit in that eternal manner to which John 15:26 refers.

Overall, the Bible paints a complex picture of the relations of the Spirit to the Father and to the Son. We saw this vividly in chapter 3. The Holy Spirit hears the Father, receives from the Father, takes from the Son and makes it known to the church, proceeds from the Father, is sent by the Father in the name of the Son, is sent by the Son from the Father, rests on the Son, speaks of the Son, and glorifies the Son. The relation between the Spirit and the Son is not one-directional, but mutual and reciprocal. The Spirit plays an instrumental role in the coming of Christ and in his resurrection. The Spirit is active throughout the earthly life of the incarnate Son. So while Christ sends the Spirit, he himself lives in union with the Spirit and—as far as his incarnate existence is concerned—in dependence on the Spirit.[9] The Spirit is called the Spirit of God, referring to the Father, but he is also the Spirit of Christ, the Spirit of God's Son, and the Spirit of the Lord.

The Trinity According to the Eastern Church

The dominant influences in Eastern Trinitarianism, the Cappadocians and John of Damascus, place primary stress on the Father as the source of the personal subsistence of the Son and the Holy Spirit. The Father is the guarantor of unity in the Godhead—the sole principle, source, and cause of the Son and the Spirit. Thus, the Holy Spirit proceeds from the Father. Gregory Nazianzen corrected this emphasis with his teaching that the monarchy is the whole Trinity, not the Father alone, but this primary stress remains.

The Trinity According to the Western Church

Augustine has exerted an overpowering influence in the Western church up to the present day. We saw how he makes the divine essence,

9. John 16:7, 13–15; 15:26; 14:26; cf. Mark 1:10; Luke 3:22; 1:34–35; Matt. 1:18–20; Luke 4:1, 14; Rom. 1:3–4; 8:11.

not the person of the Father, the foundation for his doctrine of the Trinity. Western theology has followed by starting from the one essence. The continued threat of Arianism in the West, particularly in Spain, led the church to lay extra stress on the consubstantiality of the Father and the Son. The *filioque* was intended to undergird this: the Holy Spirit's procession from the Father *and the Son* served in Western eyes to safeguard the identity of substance of the Son and the Father. In turn, following Augustine's psychological analogy, the Spirit was seen as the bond of union between the Father and the Son.[10]

The Western Church According to Photius

Photius, patriarch of Constantinople (858–867, 880–886), confused the situation further.[11] He insisted that the Holy Spirit proceeds from the Father *alone*, the Son having no part to play, although he did not require this to be accepted by Rome. His intent was not to deny the intimate relations between the Son and the Spirit, but to make very clear that the Father alone causes the existence of the Son and the Spirit. In turn, Photius attributed to the Western church the arrangement whereby the Holy Spirit proceeds from the Father and the Son as from two separate principles. He regarded this as heresy, since two separate principles in the Trinity would destroy the unity of God.

The Origin of the Western View in Augustine

However, Photius's understanding of Western Trinitarianism had been explicitly repudiated by Augustine four hundred and fifty years earlier:

> . . . yet there is good reason why in this trinity we call none Word of God but the Son, none Gift of God but the Holy Spirit, none of whom the Word is begotten and from whom the Holy Spirit originally (*principaliter*) proceeds, but God the Father. I add the word "originally", because we learn that the Holy Spirit proceeds also from the Son.

10. See Vischer, *Spirit of God, Spirit of Christ*, 12–16, for a clear and incisive evaluation of these differences.

11. Photius, *On the Mystagogy of the Holy Spirit* (PG 102:280–391).

But this is part of what is given by the Father to the Son, not as already existing without it, but given to him as all that the Father gives to his only-begotten Word, in the act of begetting. He is begotten in such a manner that the common gift proceeds from him also, and the Holy Spirit is Spirit of both.[12]

For Augustine, the Holy Spirit proceeds from the Father and the Son *as one principle of origination*. The Father is the sole principle of deity, the Son is begotten by the Father, and *from their common love proceeds, as a single principle*, the Holy Spirit *a patre filioque*.[13] The Holy Spirit thus proceeds first from the Father and by the Father's gift at no temporal interval from both in common.[14] Photius rejects this also, for reasons we will mention later. As Ritschl suggests, Augustine's beginning with the Trinity itself, rather than with the Father, as the Cappadocians had done, together with his stress on the divine simplicity, made the *filioque* almost inevitable.[15]

The Western View According to the Eastern Apologists

Despite Photius, the chief Eastern objection to the *filioque* is not that it implies two separate sources for the Holy Spirit. As we saw, Augustine taught that the Spirit proceeds from the Father and the Son as from a single source. Nor is it that the clause might subordinate the Holy Spirit to the Son—another point of issue for Photius—since the Western affirmations of consubstantiality offset that possibility. The main concern is that the *filioque* posits that not only the Father, but also the Son, is a source or origin or cause of the Holy Spirit. Thus, the Western view, in Eastern eyes, compromises the monarchy of the Father. The Greek fathers held that the Holy Spirit is the treasure and the Son is the treasurer—the Son receives and manifests the Spirit, but he does not cause its existence as such, since only the Father is the source or origin or cause of both the Son and the Holy Spirit through ineffably different but united acts.

12. Augustine, *De Trinitate*, 15.26.47 (PL 42:1092).
13. Ibid., 15.17.27 (PL 42:1079–80).
14. Ibid., 15.26.47 (PL 42:1092).
15. Ritschl, "*Filioque* Controversy," 60–61.

Another related problem in Eastern eyes is that the clause confuses the Father and the Son. The Father is not the Son. This is evident in that the Father begets the Son, while the Son is begotten by the Father. Thus, the relation between the Spirit and the Father differs from the relation between the Spirit and the Son. Since the Son and the Father are not the same, their respective relations to the Holy Spirit cannot be the same either. Therefore, to talk of the Spirit proceeding from the Father *and* the Son without differentiation is to confuse the two. This is underlined by Augustine's teaching that the Spirit proceeds from both as from a common source. By avoiding the suggestion that there are two separate sources of the Spirit (which would divide the Trinity), the West confuses the distinctiveness of both the Father and the Son. According to the East, all three persons are one God by consubstantial union and mutual indwelling, but are never to be confused in their personal distinctiveness (as in the modalistic heresy).

What can we say to this? With respect to the monarchy, the West has never intended to compromise the monarchy of the Father and has consistently affirmed it. The monarchy is not a point in dispute, although it has come to expression in differing ways in East and West. The *filioque* was never directed against this. Stylianopoulos agrees, but adds that "the *que* (and) of the *filioque* does not seem to relinquish the 'monarchy' of the Father in the Augustinian context but unintentionally does relinquish it in the Cappadocian context."[16] However, the claim that the *filioque* confuses the Father and the Son is, I submit, of greater weight. We will consider it shortly. One other objection can be dismissed quickly. According to some Eastern apologetes, the *filioque* led in the West to ecclesiasticism, authoritarianism, and the dogma of the pope.[17] This is as far-fetched as some Western polemics.

The Eastern View According to Western Apologists

According to the West, the Eastern repudiation of the *filioque* leaves no clear relation between the Son and the Holy Spirit. This is in odd con-

---

16. Theodore Stylianopoulos, "The Filioque: Dogma, Theologoumenon or Error?" in *Spirit of Truth*, ed. Stylianopoulos and Heim, 50.

17. Timothy Ware, *The Orthodox Church* (London: Penguin Books, 1969), 222–23.

trast to the patristic teaching of perichoresis, whereby the persons of the Trinity indwell and interpenetrate one another. The West holds that this exhibits subordinationist tendencies reaching back as far as Origen, for in the East the Son and the Holy Spirit are commonly said to receive their deity from the Father, and so both seem to be derivative. In contrast, the *filioque* affirms the intimate relation between the Son and the Spirit. This, the West claims, has led to a gulf in the East between theology and piety. Speculative theology, grounded on the Logos, has been separated from worship, mediated by the Holy Spirit. Thus, Eastern piety, so Western observers like Bavinck claim, is unduly dominated by mysticism.[18]

Neither of these two arguments bears much scrutiny. In the first place, let us examine the claim that the East, by rejecting the *filioque*, holds apart the Son and the Holy Spirit. This is simply wrong. Throughout, the Eastern church has accepted terminology such as "from the Father through the Son" as a valid expression of the intent of C. It maintains a mediating role for the Son in the procession of the Spirit, while insisting that the Father is the sole source, cause, or origin. Again, the East argues that the Holy Spirit rests on the Son (as at Jesus' baptism) and is received by him, and in turn is sent by the Son.[19] In saying that the Spirit proceeds from the Father, the East presupposes the relation existing in the Trinity between the Father and the Son, for the Father is the Father of the Son, the Son is eternally in and with the Father, and the Father is never apart from the Son.[20] For Western theologians to make this claim ignores the Cappadocian teaching on mutual indwelling, first taught by Gregory of Nyssa. This is a crowning affirmation of the close relations of the Son and the Holy Spirit, as we shall see in a moment. Besides, C minus the *filioque* clause (the original version of C) is not silent on the relation of the Holy Spirit and the Son, for the Spirit is worshiped and glorified together with the Father and the

18. Herman Bavinck, *The Doctrine of God* (reprint, Edinburgh: Banner of Truth, 1977), 313–17.

19. Wolfhart Pannenberg, *Systematic Theology*, trans. Geoffrey W. Bromiley (Grand Rapids: Eerdmans, 1991), 1:317–19.

20. See the references to Athanasius below. Jürgen Moltmann's proposal that the Spirit proceeds "from the Father of the Son" assumes a consensus would form in the East in support of it; see Jürgen Moltmann, *The Trinity and the Kingdom: The Doctrine of God* (London: SCM, 1991), 185–87.

Son, and is the author and giver of life together with the Father and the Son, "by whom [the Father] made the worlds." In short, the East consistently affirms that the Son participates in the Holy Spirit's procession from the Father, both immanently and economically.

On the second point, one of the most famous elements of Eastern piety, the Jesus prayer, is thoroughly Christocentric—"Lord Jesus Christ, Son of God, have mercy on me a sinner" can hardly be more evangelical or Christological in tone. That the East has no monopoly on unbridled mysticism is evident by the Toronto blessing and similar phenomena, which are distinctly Western in effect. This claim is, in short, akin to the Eastern argument about a supposed connection between the *filioque* and the papacy. There are reductionist dangers in attributing all perceived ills to a single cause.

A third objection, however, carries much greater weight. Following John of Damascus, the East tends to consider that the essence of God is unknowable, only God's energies or operations being revealed, that is, the things around him ("all that we can affirm concerning God does not shew forth God's nature, but only the qualities of his nature").[21] This dichotomy is used to offset some of the biblical evidence for the joint and coordinate involvement of the Son in relation to the Holy Spirit. As a sympathetic critic like T. F. Torrance argues, it drives a wedge between the inner life of God and his saving activity in history, ruling out any real access to knowing God in himself.[22] It also departs from earlier Greek patristic thought, which rejected this distinction.[23] Besides opening a yawning chasm between the economic Trinity and the ontological Trinity, the tendency seems to be toward a quaternity rather than a Trinity—the unknowable divine essence plus the three revealed persons.

The Early Eastern View

According to Basil the Great, true religion teaches us to think of the Son together with the Father.[24] The good things that come from

---

21. John of Damascus, *The Orthodox Faith* 1.4 (PG 194:797–800).

22. Thomas F. Torrance, *The Christian Doctrine of God: One Being, Three Persons* (Edinburgh: T & T Clark, 1996), 187.

23. Athanasius, *On the Decrees of the Synod of Nicaea* 22 (PG 25:453–56).

24. Basil of Caesarea, *On the Holy Spirit* 14 (PG 32:88–89).

God reach us "through the Son."[25] The Son's will is in indissoluble union with the Father's.[26] Thus, the Holy Spirit is in all things inseparable from the Father and the Son.[27] Moreover, "the way of the knowledge of God lies from one Spirit through the one Son to the one Father, and conversely the natural goodness and the inherent holiness and the royal dignity extend from the Father through the only-begotten to the Spirit."[28] Hence, the Spirit shares in the works of the Father and the Son.[29] In short, the Father is the sole principle of deity. From the Father, the Holy Spirit proceeds through the Son. The deity communicates itself from the Father through the Son to the Holy Spirit.

John of Damascus, in his *De orthodoxa fidei*, teaches that the Spirit of God is "the companion of the Word and the revealer of his energy . . . proceeding from the Father and resting in the Word, and shewing forth the Word, neither capable of disjunction from God in whom it exists, and the Word whose companion it is . . . being in subsistence the likeness of the Word."[30] Never at any time was the Father lacking in the Word, nor the Word in the Spirit. The Holy Spirit proceeds from the Father and rests in the Son, is communicated through the Son, is inseparable and indivisible from the Father and the Son, possessing all the qualities the Father and the Son possess, except that of not being begotten or born. Both the Son and the Spirit have their being from the Father. The three are in each other, having the same essence and dwelling in each other, being the same in will, energy, power, authority, and movement. They cleave to each other and have their being in each other, without coalescence or commingling. The Son and the Spirit, therefore, do not stand apart. It is like three suns cleaving to each other without separation and giving out light mingled and conjoined into one. The Spirit is manifested and imparted to us through the Son.[31]

De Margerie points out that Photius ignores all this, and he cites Bulgakov, who comments, "It is stupefying that the very learned patriarch, who knew the Greek Fathers much better than many of his prede-

---

25. Ibid., 19 (PG 32:101–2).
26. Ibid., 20 (PG 32:103–5).
27. Ibid., 37 (PG 32:133).
28. Ibid., 47 (PG 32:153).
29. Ibid., 53 (PG 32:166–67).
30. John of Damascus, *The Orthodox Faith* 1.7 (PG 194:805).
31. Ibid., 1.8 (PG 194:808–833).

cessors and contemporaries, did not know that the patristic doctrine of the procession of the Holy Spirit . . . differed radically from his own."[32]

Problems of East and West

The positions of both the East and the West regarding the *filioque* face problems.

(1.) Criticism has been made that the *filioque* debate centers on the persons understood in terms of relations of origin. In contrast, Pannenberg points to the rich complexity in the NT that indicates these relations are far more subtle than the simple formulas of East and West give us to believe. This is true, and we have seen something of this complexity in passing. However, there seems to me no good reason why relations of origin should be excluded from consideration.

(2.) Western theology has often said that the East exhibits a tendency toward tritheism by starting with the Father rather than the one divine essence. There is little evidence for this. The monarchy of the Father (or of the whole Trinity in the case of Gregory Nazianzen), consubstantiality, and perichoresis are the preservatives.

(3.) On the other hand, the Eastern split between God's essence and his energies is a reality, certainly after John of Damascus. In this case, the earlier criticisms we made apply. In this way, Eastern apologists can say that references to the Son sending the Spirit apply only to the energies, to the purely economic. Jürgen Moltmann answers this with great clarity when he says we can speak of only one Trinity and of its economy of salvation, and so "the divine Trinity cannot appear in the economy of salvation as something other than it is in itself. Therefore one cannot posit temporal trinitarian relations within the economy of salvation which are not grounded in the primal trinitarian relations." Thus, Moltmann continues, this relation between the Son and the Holy Spirit cannot be restricted to the temporal sending. If this were so, there would be a contradiction in God. This cannot be, for God remains true to himself. He is faithful and trustworthy. What holds true in his revelation is true in his being.[33]

---

32. De Margerie, *Christian Trinity*, 166; Bulgakov, *Paraclet*, 102.
33. Jürgen Moltmann, "Theological Proposals Towards the Resolution of the Filioque Controversy," in *Spirit of God, Spirit of Christ: Ecumenical Reflections on the Filioque Controversy*, ed. Lukas Vischer (London: SPCK, 1981), 165–66.

④ In the West, the danger of modalism is very real, evident in all Western theology down to Barth and Rahner. Later chapters will provide evidence for this. If we start with the divine unity, the persons become problematic as real, personal, permanent, irreducible, and eternal ontological distinctions. Colin Gunton has argued forcibly that the Augustinian model has bred atheism and agnosticism.[34] Indeed, most Western Christians are practical modalists. Certainly, the Trinity is little more than an arithmetical conundrum to Western Christianity.

⑤ The *filioque* clause is misleading for three possible reasons. First, if the Spirit were to proceed from two separate sources, the monarchy of the Father would be undermined. That is not the way it has been understood, but, having said that, it must be admitted that the clause lends itself to that kind of untutored interpretation. Second, if in the Augustinian sense (the way the West has consistently understood it) the Spirit proceeds from the Father and the Son *as a single source*, the distinction between the Father and the Son is blurred. The Son is not the same as the Father—he is begotten, and the Father is not. The Son is forever the Son, and the Father is forever the Father. Thus, the Son does not have the identical relation to the Holy Spirit that the Father has. The doctrine of the procession of the Holy Spirit must take this distinction into account. Third, there appears to be *some* evidence of a *tendency* to subordinate the Holy Spirit if the *filioque* is needed to support the consubstantiality of the Son. If the deity of the Son requires him to be the spirating source of the Holy Spirit, where does that leave the Spirit, who is the source of no other *hypostasis*? The argument for the *filioque* comes with a price, a subtle undermining of the Trinity. In this connection, is not a basic principle of Trinitarian theology flouted by the West? The attributes of the divine nature are shared by all three persons, while the divine properties are held by one person. But here a property (spiration) is shared by two persons while the third is excluded.[35]

From all this it is clear that both the Western and the Eastern lines of approach have serious weaknesses. These are highlighted when both

34. Colin Gunton, "Augustine, the Trinity, and the Theological Crisis of the West," *SJT* 43 (1990): 33–58.

35. Photius argues that "everything not said about the whole, omnipotent, consubstantial, and supersubstantial Trinity is said about one of the three persons. The procession of the Spirit is not said to be common to the three, consequently it must belong to one of the three." Photius, *Holy Spirit* 36.

are exposed to dialog with the other, as has been the case in recent decades—something that has never seriously happened before. As a result, the question is now arising as to whether there is some way to transcend this great divide, to preserve the best intentions of both sides while avoiding their damaging weaknesses.

Toward Solutions

Mutual Recognition

For a resolution of this long-standing problem to occur, the East will need to recognize that the *filioque* was used in the West in support of teaching that the East fully accepts—the consubstantial unity of the Trinity, the deity of the Son, and the intimacy between the Son and the Holy Spirit. For its part, the West must recognize that Augustine's teaching that the Father and the Son are the common cause of the eternal being of the Holy Spirit unintentionally compromises the monarchy of the Father in the eyes of advocates of the Cappadocian paradigm.

Historical Reconstruction

When one gets lost while walking in the countryside, it helps to retrace one's steps to the last place where one's location was precisely known. Then progress can be made toward the intended destination. On the *filioque*, help can be found by turning not to Cappadocia or Hippo, where the paths diverge, but instead to Alexandria. Before the Cappadocians and Augustine set the stage for future discussion, Athanasius made some crucial points, which were forgotten in the ensuing conflict. He was followed in a similar direction the following century by Cyril of Alexandria.

In his four *Letters to Serapion on the Holy Spirit*, Athanasius deals at length with the Trinitarian relations. The Son is consubstantial with the Father, out of the being of the Father. Whatever the Father has, the Son has.[36] The Trinity is indivisible, so wherever the Father is mentioned, the Son should also be understood, and—by the same token—where the Son is, the Holy Spirit is in him.[37] The Spirit is never

---

36. Athanasius, *Letters to Serapion on the Holy Spirit* 2.5 (PG 26:616).
37. Athanasius, *Serapion* 1.14 (PG 26:566).

apart from the Word, the Son, a point Athanasius repeats time and time again.[38]

Moreover, as the Son has his particular property in relation to the Father, so does the Holy Spirit in relation to the Son.[39] The Son is the image of the Father, but so also is the Holy Spirit the image of the Son.[40] Athanasius denies an obvious rejoinder that there are consequently two sons, maintaining the distinctiveness of the Holy Spirit in doing so, but the fact that he feels obliged to make such a point indicates how close he understands the relation of the Son and the Spirit to be. Indeed, the Holy Spirit has the same order and nature toward the Son as the Son has toward the Father. The Son is in the Father, and the Father is in the Son, and so also is the Holy Spirit in the Son and the Son in the Holy Spirit. Thus, the Spirit cannot be divided from the Word.[41] So also the Spirit is in God the Father and from the Father.[42] As the Son comes in the name of the Father, so the Holy Spirit comes in the name of the Son.[43] There is one efficacy and action of the Holy Trinity, for the Father makes all things through the Word by the Holy Spirit.[44]

Nothing could be clearer than the intimate, unbreakable relation between the Son and the Holy Spirit in Athanasius's thought. The three persons indwell one another, are in each other. This applies as much to the Son and the Spirit as to the Son and the Father or to the Father and the Spirit.

Similar lines of thought are evident in Cyril. In *Dialogue II on the Holy and Consubstantial Trinity*, he explains that the whole divinity is common to each person, so the Father, the Son, and the Holy Spirit are of one, identical essence. The Son and the Spirit are no less than the Father, equal in all things except for their relations, in which, *inter alia*, the Spirit proceeds from the Father, flowing or pouring forth *through* the Son.[45] In his *Thesaurus on the Holy and Consubstantial Trinity*, he unfolds his thinking on the matter at length. The Holy Spirit

38. Ibid., 1.14, 17, 20, 31; 3.5; 4.4 (PG 26:565–66, 572, 576–77, 601, 632–33, 641).
39. Ibid., 3.1 (PG 26:625).
40. Ibid., 4.3 (PG 26:640–41).
41. Ibid., 1.20–21 (PG 26:580).
42. Ibid., 1.25 (PG 26:588).
43. Ibid., 1.20 (PG 26:580).
44. Ibid., 1.20, 28, 30 (PG 26:580, 596, 600).
45. Cyril of Alexandria, *De sancta et consubstantiali Trinitate, Dialogus II* (PG 75:721–23).

is, according to nature, God, from the being of the Father. The creation was made through the Son by the Holy Spirit.[46] The Spirit is not alien to the divine essence, for he is of the essence, for he *inexists* (*enhypostatos*), proceeding from it and remaining in it.[47] So the Spirit is from the Father *and* the Son, since it is clear that he is of the divine being, proceeding *in* it and *from* it.[48] Hence, the Spirit is from the being of the Son as well as the being of the Father.[49] While he naturally proceeds from the Father,[50] because of his enhypostatic relations he is *in* the Son and *from* the Son[51] and so can be said to proceed from the Father *in* the Son.[52] Cyril also says that the Spirit is sent from the Father *through* the Son (citing both John 15:26 and 14:26!)[53] and that he proceeds from the Father *and* the Son.[54]

Recent Developments

Renewed interest in the matter was generated by the modest attention given to it by Karl Barth.[55] Since then, a range of Western theologians have expressed dissatisfaction with the *filioque*. Among them are Jürgen Moltmann and Wolfhart Pannenberg. Moltmann attempts to bridge the divide by his proposal that the Spirit proceeds *from the Father of the Son*. He points to the Son being both conceived by the Spirit and baptized by the Spirit in salvation history. Here the Spirit precedes the Son. Moltmann stresses the reciprocal relations of the persons. He wants to preserve the procession of the Spirit from the Father, while recognizing that this does not occur apart from the Son's participation. Overall, he seems to concede the case to the East, and from the West's perspective does not adequately express the role of the Son.[56] Pannenberg rejects the *filioque* on the grounds that it implies

46. Cyril of Alexandria, *Thesaurus de sancta et consubstantiali Trinitate* (PG 75:565).
47. Ibid. (PG 75:577).
48. Ibid. (PG 75:585).
49. Ibid. (PG 75:587, 589).
50. Ibid. (PG 75:597).
51. Ibid. (PG 75:581).
52. Ibid. (PG 75:577).
53. Ibid. (PG 75:581).
54. Ibid. (PG 75:585).
55. Karl Barth, *CD*, I/1: 546–57.
56. Moltmann, *Trinity*, 178–90.

the subordination of the Holy Spirit, and also because Scripture says the Son receives the Spirit from the Father, so undermining the idea that the relation of the Son and the Spirit is unilateral.[57]

On the other hand, Gerald Bray has some far-reaching points in defense of the *filioque*. Different positions here, he argues, indicate differing views of salvation. In particular, the East has failed to express adequately a connection between the Spirit and the Son. This is directly connected to its soteriology, in which deification by the Spirit is at the heart, while for the West the work of Christ is central—the Cross and Resurrection, applied by the Holy Spirit.[58] In other words, under Western eyes the Eastern paradigm undermines the gospel by its failure to place the atoning work of Christ in center stage and to integrate it with the work of the Spirit. Bray's point is crucial. We saw how Athanasius has little to say about the Atonement. The Cross is not integral to his soteriology. The key for him is Christ, in the Incarnation, assuming our humanity and uniting it with God, thus healing it. As Hanson pithily describes it, for Athanasius salvation is by means of a kind of sacred blood transfusion.[59] This is characteristic of Eastern soteriology. For the East, death is the great enemy, bringing about the disorder of sin. Sin is subordinate to death. Christ's resurrection defeats death. Salvation is a conquest of mortality, the risen Christ bringing life in its place. The Cross is not ignored, but it is seen from the standpoint of the Resurrection. The idea of sin as a transgression of the law of God, for which Christ on the cross makes atonement, is found hardly at all. Whereas for the West salvation is at its root moral and ethical, for the East it is cosmic. For the West, a holy God delivers his people from sin, while for the East the risen Christ delivers the human race from death.[60] The gulf between East and West, according to Bray (and his thesis is sound), is wider than the *filioque* in itself. Referring to Calvin, he suggests that "the work of the Holy Spirit is to remake us in the image of Christ, so that we might enjoy the benefits of Christ's relationship to the Father," and so "He is remaking us in the image of

---

57. Pannenberg, *Systematic Theology*, 1:319–21.
58. Bray, "Filioque," 139–44.
59. R. P. C. Hanson, *The Search for the Christian Doctrine of God: The Arian Controversy 318–381* (Edinburgh: T & T Clark, 1988), 450–51.
60. Ware, *Orthodox Church*, 230–34; John Meyendorff, *Byzantine Theology: Historical Trends and Doctrinal Themes* (New York: Fordham University Press, 1979), 159–65.

Christ's *person* . . . [to do which he] must share in the hypostasis of
the Son, and therefore proceed from him." Thus, Bray argues, "without a living appreciation of the *Filioque* clause within the context of
a personal as opposed to a natural theology, Evangelical faith becomes
incomprehensible." The clause is both integral and necessary to
Reformed and evangelical Christianity.[61] Barth reinforces these criticisms by taking Eastern Trinitarianism to task for isolating individual
verses of the Bible (he has John 15:26 in mind) from many others that
speak of the Spirit of the Son. It also isolates God's self-revelation from
who he is eternally and antecedently in himself.[62]

It is clear that both atonement for sin and conquest of death
should be prominent in any theology that seeks to be faithful to the
Bible, and so, for all the merits of the Eastern position, the implication of the *filioque* cannot be discarded.[63] Discussions of the *filioque*
must extend further afield. However, Bray's argument is powerful
against the extreme monopatrism of Photius that excludes the Son
from the procession of the Spirit. It is also of great weight when we
consider the clause *from the Father through the Son*, widely accepted
in the East, which can imply a certain subordination of the Son to the
Father and also contains an inherent ambiguity, to which both Bulgakov and Bobrinskoy point.[64] On the other hand, if all the parameters we proposed at the end of chapter 8 are positively recognized,
these perils should be avoidable. Moreover, Bray overlooks the rich
reflection in the East on the baptism of Jesus. Here the Spirit descends
from heaven, from where the Father's voice comes, and rests upon the
Son, who in turn breathes him out on his disciples. In Staniloae's words,

> The sending of the Spirit by the Son to men rather signifies that the
> Spirit rests in those who are united with the Son, since he rests in the
> Son. The Spirit does not go beyond the Son, even when we say
> improperly that he is sent to men. The Son is the only and ultimate
> resting place of the Spirit. The Spirit dwells in us insofar as we are

61. Bray, "*Filioque*," 142–43.
62. Barth, *CD*, I/1: 480.
63. See Robert Letham, *The Work of Christ* (Leicester: Inter-Varsity Press, 1993), esp.
chap. 7.
64. Boris Bobrinskoy, *The Mystery of the Trinity: Trinitarian Experience and Vision in the
Biblical and Patristic Tradition*, trans. Anthony P. Gythiel (Crestwood, N.Y.: St. Vladimir's Seminary Press, 1999), 302–3; Bulgakov, *Paraclet*, 93.

raised up in the Son. This saves us from a theological rationalism on
the one side and a purely sentimental enthusiasm on the other.[65]

At this point, we note the 1991 Agreement between Orthodox
and Reformed Churches.[66] This historic agreement is limited in its
scope. The Western representatives were from the World Alliance of
Reformed Churches, one particular strand of Reformed theology. There
was no one from other Protestant bodies, nor any from Rome. Moreover, the documents indicate that there was no adequate representation of Augustinian Trinitarianism. The Reformed participants were
already sympathetic—though not uncritically—to the East. The leading figure, T. F. Torrance, had already adopted the Athanasian soteriology, refracted through his reading of Calvin and Barth and his interaction with modern physics. That said, the agreement does represent
progress. Torrance's commentary indicates a thorough recognition of
all the main theological parameters that we specified in chapter 8: the
homoousion of all three persons; their full mutual indwelling, the perichoresis; the equal ultimacy of the one being of God and the three persons; the rejection of an impersonal divine essence and a concurrent
recognition of the living, dynamic, personal being of God; and the
order and relationality of the persons. Thus (as Gregory Nazianzen
taught), the monarchy is that of the whole Trinity, not the Father alone.
As a result, the monopatrism of Photius is undermined and, at the same
time, any idea of subordinationism is eliminated. The procession of
the Holy Spirit is seen in the light of the full homoousial and perichoretic relations of the three persons in the one divine essence. So the
Spirit proceeds from the being of God, inseparably from the Father
and the Son.

If all these factors are given due recognition, can this not avoid
the dangers of which Bray rightly warns? On the other hand, if the

65. Dumitru Staniloae, "The Procession of the Holy Spirit from the Father and His Relation
to the Son, as the Basis for Our Deification and Adoption," in *Spirit of God, Spirit of Christ*,
ed. Vischer (London: SPCK, 1981), 179.

66. For the official text, see Thomas F. Torrance, *Theological Dialogue Between Orthodox
and Reformed Churches*, vol. 2 (Edinburgh: Scottish Academic Press, 1993), 219–32, or "Agreed
Statement on the Holy Trinity Between the Orthodox Church and the World Alliance of Reformed
Churches," *Touchstone* 5, no. 1 (winter 1992): 22–23. For commentary on the agreement, see
Thomas F. Torrance, *Trinitarian Perspectives: Toward Doctrinal Agreement* (Edinburgh: T &
T Clark, 1994), 110–43.

filioque were understood in the full light of these parameters, might we ask what the remaining objections from the East might be? In chapter 3, we alluded to Bobrinskoy's comment that suggests a blending of what he calls (from an Eastern perspective) an appropriate *filioquism*, recognizing the inseparable union of the Spirit and the Son, and also a *Spirituque*, in which, considering the eternal generation of the Son, the equally inseparable union of the Spirit and the Father should be brought into focus. In short, Bobrinskoy points to the perichoretic relations of the three as providing a way out of the dilemma.[67] The alternative phrase *from the Father through the Son* certainly has the merit of a biblical foundation and is acceptable to the East. However, it can still imply ideas of pre-Nicene subordination, the Father being the prime source, and the Son secondary.[68] Moltmann, we saw, suggests *from the Father of the Son*. This is so since the Father is the Father only in relation to the Son, in the eternal begetting of the Son. It is as the Father of Jesus Christ that he reveals himself, not as a universal father of all creation. Neither is he the Father of the Spirit, for his being the Father is in relation to the Son. Therefore, the eternal procession of the Spirit from the Father presupposes the eternal begetting of the Son by the Father. Hence, the Spirit's procession occurs in the eternal presence of the Son.[69] Dumitru Staniloae gives a cautious welcome to this as something worth considering, although he expresses misgivings about Moltmann's additional speculation that the Spirit receives his image from the Son.[70] The Cyrillian phrase *from the Father in the Son* seems to me to express the mutual indwelling of the three, avoids any residual subordination, and also directs us to Jesus' baptism. It also avoids a focus on the Spirit apart from Christ, for we receive the Spirit *in Christ*. The West's concern for the relation between the Son and the Spirit is maintained, and the confusion of the *filioque* is avoided. The monarchy of the Father is also clear. Moreover, the focus is on the persons, rather than the essence, a move greatly needed so as to avoid the West's tendency to the impersonal.

67. See chap. 3, n. 23, referring to Bobrinskoy, *Mystery*, 65–72.
68. See note 62 above.
69. Moltmann, "Proposals," 167–69.
70. Staniloae, "Procession," 184–86.

We have seen how the differences between East and West over the *filioque* are symptoms of underlying and alternative ways of understanding the Holy Trinity. In the next chapter, we will examine further their divergent paths.

When we say "Father", the Son and the Holy Spirit come from him. When we say "Son", the Father and the Holy Spirit are recognized through him. When we say "Spirit", the Father and the Son are perfect in him. The Father is the Creator, unbegotten; the Son is begotten and does not beget; the Holy Spirit proceeds from the Father and receives from the Son the person and being of the Father. (Prayer for Pentecost, Syrian Orthodox Church of South India)[71]

Come, O ye people, let us worship the Godhead in three Persons, the Son in the Father with the Holy Spirit. For the Father before time was begat the Son, who is coeternal and is equally enthroned, and the Holy Spirit who was in the Father, and was glorified together with the Son; one Might, one Essence, one Godhead. Adoring the same let us all say: O Holy God, who by the Son didst make all things through the cooperation of the Holy Spirit: O Holy Mighty One, through whom we have known the Father, and through whom the Holy Spirit came into the world: O Holy Immortal One, the Spirit of comfort, who proceedest from the Father, and restest in the Son: O Holy Trinity, glory to thee.

For unto thee are due all glory, honour and worship, to the Father, and to the Son, and to the Holy Spirit, now, and ever, and unto ages of ages. Amen.

Glory to the Father, and to the Son, and to the Holy Spirit, now, and ever, and unto ages of ages. Amen. O heavenly King, the Comforter, Spirit of Truth, who art in all places and fillest all things; Treasury of good things and Giver of life: Come, and take up thine abode in us, and cleanse us from every stain; and save our souls, O Good One.[72]

71. Moltmann, "Proposals," 171, who cites *Die syrisch-orthodoxe Kirche der südindischen Thomas-Christen: Geschichte, Kirchenverfassung, Lehre*, by Navakatesh J. Thomas (Würzburg: Augustinus-Verlag, 1967), 67.
72. Pentecost, At the all-night vigil, *Service Book*, 245, 249.

East and West: The Paths Diverge

The differences over the *filioque* clause arose, as we saw, from differing approaches to the Trinity in the Eastern and Western churches. As the centuries passed, these differences became entrenched, all the more so because of increasingly restricted contact and mutual suspicion. In particular, the hegemony of Islam in the East kept a tight check on theological progress and placed a high premium on holding tenaciously to the tradition. In this chapter we will look briefly at some important Latin and Greek representatives.

Three Western Representatives

Anselm of Canterbury

Anselm (1033–1109) wrote *De fide Trinitatis et de incarnatione Verbi* (*On Faith in the Trinity and the Incarnation of the Word*) after being wrongly accused by the monk Roscelin of teaching that the three persons were three "things," or that the Father and the Holy Spirit were incarnate with the Son.[1] He completed the final version in 1094, after becoming archbishop of Canterbury in 1093. In it he proves in his own inimitable way that neither the Father nor the Spirit could have become incarnate. He insists on the vital distinction between the

---

1. G. R. Evans, *Anselm* (London: Geoffrey Chapman, 1989), 57.

being of God and the relations of the three persons. He asks, "How will someone whose mind is too darkened to distinguish between his horse and its color be able to distinguish between the one God and his several relations?"[2] In each of the persons, there is that which is common to all three and that which is proper to the one person. What is common is to be God. However, the personal names "Father" and "Son" are predicated in opposition to each other. Thus, the relations of the Father and the Son are two things, while their substance is one.[3] A relation exists in God in terms of the differences of the persons from each other.[4] He proves that the relations are fully compatible with the equality of the persons. He is working within the tradition bequeathed by Augustine to the Western church.

Anselm then launches into his proof that it was only fitting that the Son be incarnate and that this was not possible for either of the other two persons. If the Holy Spirit had been incarnate, he would have been the son of a human being. So there would have been two sons in the Trinity. One would be the Son of God, the other the son of a human being. The two would be unequal.[5] Moreover, if the Father had taken a human nature into union with his person, not only would there again be a plurality of sons, but both the Father and the Son would be grandsons. The Father would be the grandson of the Virgin's parents, while the Son would be the grandson of the Virgin. Therefore, "since it is impossible for there to be even any small unbefittingness in God, no person of God other than the Son ought to have been incarnate."[6] Additionally, it is fitting that the Son became incarnate since he was to pray on behalf of the human race. Our minds understand it to be more suitable for the Son to supplicate the Father, even though this is done not by his divinity but by his humanity to his divinity.[7] Therefore, none of the three persons of God more fittingly "emptied himself and took on the form of a servant" than did the Son.[8]

2. Anselm, *De fide Trinitatis et de incarnatione Verbi*, in *Anselm of Canterbury*, ed. and trans. Jasper Hopkins and Herbert Richardson (Toronto: Edwin Mellen Press, 1975–76), 3:13 (PL 158:265).

3. Ibid., 3:15–16 (PL 158:267).

4. Ibid., 3:19 (PL 158:270).

5. Ibid., 3:27 (PL 158:276).

6. Ibid., 3:28 (PL 158:276).

7. Ibid. (PL 158:277).

8. Ibid., 3:29 (PL 158:277).

There is also a congruity between the person of the Son and the humanity assumed in the Incarnation. In Christ, the divine being is not one individual and the human being another, for the same being who is human is also divine. The Word assumed a human nature, not a human person.[9] Consequently, the Word and the assumed human nature have the same collection of distinguishing properties.[10]

Thus, the three persons are distinct eternally. "The Father is never identical with his Son, and he who proceeds is never identical with him from whom he proceeds. Rather, the Father is always different from the Son, and he who proceeds is always different from him from whom he proceeds. . . . Therefore, when God is begotten of God or when God proceeds from God, the substance cannot lose its singularity nor the relations their plurality."[11] In view of this argument, it is extraordinary that scholars can accuse Anselm of modalism (without any documentation to back it up), when actually he had been charged by Roscelin with tritheism![12]

Anselm's treatise on the procession of the Holy Spirit (*De processione Spiritu Sancto contra Graecos*) was composed at the request of Pope Urban, addressing the Greeks in defense of the *filioque*. This is a closely reasoned, scholastic document, but, as Evans agrees, more relaxed than the other, since Anselm's own teaching is not at stake. It is, of course, a thoroughgoing defense of the contentious clause, and we will not repeat all his points. For our purposes, Anselm introduces an important defense of how the relations of the persons are compatible with their full equality. Does the begetting of the Son, his existing from the Father, entail that he is less than the Father? How can one thing exist from another without that other one somehow existing "more principally and more valuably," and without the thing which exists from this other somehow existing inferiorly and secondarily? Anselm's reply is that this is far different than in other cases. We cannot and ought not to judge God's begottenness and procession in the manner of creation. In God, "that which is begotten and that which proceeds is no other than

9. Ibid., 3:30 (PL 158:278).
10. Ibid., 3:31 (PL 158:279).
11. Ibid., 3:36–37 (PL 158:283–84).
12. See Evans, *Anselm*, 56–60, for a summary of the context of this work.

that from which it proceeds or is begotten." Since God is not greater or lesser than himself, there is nothing greater or lesser than the three persons, "and no one of them is what he is any more or any less than is another of them, even though it is true that God exists from God by proceeding and by being begotten."[13] Yet each is distinguished from the others. The Father alone exists from no one else and is he from whom two others exist. The Holy Spirit exists from two others and is he from whom no one exists. The Son alone exists from one other and is he from whom one other exists. It is common to the three that each one stands in relation to both of the others. "Thus, each [of the three persons] possesses his distinguishing properties."[14] This is without detriment to their being wholly God, for God exists from God by being begotten, and God exists from God by proceeding. Since there is nothing external to God, when God is begotten from God or when God proceeds from God, the one who proceeds or is begotten does not pass outside of God, but remains within God.[15] Since God has no parts, but is wholly whatever he is, it follows inescapably that the Father is God as a whole, the Son is God as a whole, and the Holy Spirit is God as a whole—and they are one and the same God. When God exists from God, God is within God and there is only one God.[16] But he who exists from another cannot be one and the same as the other from whom he exists, and so the three persons retain a plurality.

Evans concludes that Anselm is dry and limited in scope. We find no sense of the Trinity as a wonder. This is rigorous logic and relentless argumentation. However, his arguments are original, and he advances the discussion significantly.[17] While superficially true, Evans's assessment should be qualified by the fact that Anselm here as elsewhere is guided by his own principle of *fides quaerens intellectum* (faith seeking understanding), placing his work in the context of prayer and monastic discipline. He assumes faith and piety, and his logic flows out of these. From a thoroughly Augustinian

13. Anselm, *De processione Spiritu Sancto contra Graecos*, in *Anselm of Canterbury*, ed. and trans. Hopkins and Richardson, 3:224–25 (PL 158:320).
14. Ibid., 3:228 (PL 158:323).
15. Ibid., 3:229 (PL 158:324).
16. Ibid. (PL 158:325).
17. Evans, *Anselm*, 65–66.

base,[18] he makes a good and developed argument for the distinctions of the three.

Richard of St. Victor

Of Scottish origin, Richard of St. Victor (d. 1173) joined and eventually became prior of the Abbey of St. Victor in Paris. His treatise *De Trinitate* (*The Trinity*) is, like Anselm's, thoroughly rationalistic.[19] He aims to unfold the doctrine of the Trinity "clearly from reason."[20] We find more help from reason than from the Fathers, he claims. Following Augustine, he starts from the one essence, for "first of all, it seems that we should inquire whether there is true plurality in that true and simple Divinity."[21] He assumes the unity of God, and the threeness is something to be proved by reason. Both in this premise and in his overall argument, Richard shows Augustine's influence. He develops the latter's teaching that the Holy Spirit is the bond of love between the Father and the Son and also his comparison of the Trinity with a lover, the one loved, and love. In this sense, Richard shares the problematics that affected Augustine, which raise the question of the status of the Holy Spirit and the reality of the three persons.

His argument. Where there is supreme goodness, there is love, for nothing is better than love (charity), Richard insists. Love, by definition, is directed toward another. Therefore, love (or charity) cannot exist where there is not a plurality of persons. Supreme love is not directed toward creation, since a created person is not worthy of supreme love. So, "in order that charity be supreme and supremely perfect, it is necessary that it be so great that nothing greater can exist and that it be of such a kind that nothing better can exist."[22] The lan-

---

18. In his *Monologion*, he uses Augustine's idea of the image of the Trinity in the human soul, as memory, understanding, and love. See G. R. Evans, "Anselm of Canterbury," in *Augustine Through the Ages*, ed. Allan D. Fitzgerald (Grand Rapids: Eerdmans, 1999), 23–24.

19. W. J. Hill, *The Three-Personed God* (Washington, D.C.: Catholic University of America Press, 1982), 225–32; Michael C. O'Carroll, *Trinitas: A Theological Encyclopedia of the Holy Trinity* (Collegeville, Minn.: Liturgical Press, 1987), 197–98.

20. Richard of St. Victor, *The Trinity* 3.1 (PL 196:915–16). The translation is from Richard of St. Victor, *The Twelve Patriarchs; the Mystical Ark; Book Three of the Trinity*, trans. and ed. Grover A. Zinn (New York: Paulist Press, 1979).

21. Richard of St. Victor, *Trinity* 3.1 (PL 196:915–16).

22. Ibid., 3.2 (PL 196:916–17).

guage of Anselm's famous ontological argument is clear. Richard continues by arguing that, in order for fullness of charity to exist in God, it is necessary that a divine person be related to an equally worthy person, who is for this reason divine:

> Certainly God alone is supremely good. Therefore God alone ought to be loved supremely. A divine person could not show supreme love toward a person who lacked divinity. However, fullness of Divinity could not exist without fullness of goodness. But fullness of goodness could not exist without fullness of charity, nor could fullness of charity exist without a plurality of divine persons.[23]

An argument from the fullness of happiness demonstrates the same conclusion.[24] This love must be mutual. One who loves wishes much to be loved by the one loved much. Therefore, for true and supreme happiness, it is necessary that the love be mutual, that there be both one who gives and one who returns love. For that fullness of happiness, a plurality of persons is necessary. Since supreme happiness is divinity itself, in true divinity a plurality of persons cannot be lacking.[25] Similar conclusions follow a consideration of divine glory.[26] Moreover, it is necessary that divine persons exist eternally and that an eternal person have a coeternal person—it is impossible for divine persons not to be coeternal.[27] True happiness cannot exist without true unchangeability, nor the latter without eternity. Thus, a coeternity of persons is necessary.

Moreover, true charity demands equality of persons. Each person must give and return supreme love, and that means equal power, wisdom, goodness, and so forth.[28] This means that each possesses one and the same substance in common, with substantial unity in that plurality of persons and a personal plurality in that unity of substance.[29] While in human nature there is unity of person and plurality of substance (body and soul), in the divine nature there is unity of substance

23. Ibid.
24. Ibid., 3.3 (PL 196:917–18).
25. Ibid., 3.3 (PL 196:917–18).
26. Ibid., 3.4 (PL 196:918).
27. Ibid., 3.6 (PL 196:919).
28. Ibid., 3.7 (PL 196:919–20).
29. Ibid., 3.8 (PL 196:920–21).

and plurality of persons.[30] However, in the divine there is full likeness and supreme equality, whereas there is much unlikeness and inequality in human nature.[31]

Thus, the perfection of charity requires a trinity of persons—true trinity in true unity, and true unity in true trinity.[32] In order for charity to be true, it requires a plurality of persons; in order for charity to be perfected, it requires a trinity of persons.[33] The reason for this is that, for love to be shared, there cannot be less than three persons. If there were only two persons, charity could not be shared.[34] Wisdom and power can dwell in a single heart, but love requires another.[35] The fulfillment of happiness cannot subsist without a pair of persons.[36] But the supreme level of generosity would have no place if a third person were lacking, for there would be no one with whom either of the two could share their delight. Thus, the consummation of true and supreme goodness cannot subsist without the completion of the Trinity.[37]

Consequently, a glimpse of the Trinity can be detected in shared love—not just any shared love, but supremely shared love—that a creature could never merit from the Creator.[38] Concordant and united love is never found anywhere in isolated individuals.[39]

There is supreme equality in that Trinity, in which it is necessary for all to be equally perfect.[40] In that supremely simple being, there can be only one omnipotence, only one essence.[41] In that Trinity, that supreme and simple being that belongs to one person also belongs to each other person.[42] Therefore, any one person in the Trinity will not be something greater or better in the Trinity than any other, since one and the same substance is simultaneously in each. Any two persons

30. Ibid., 3.9 (PL 196:921).
31. Ibid., 3.10 (PL 196:921–22).
32. Ibid., 3.11 (PL 196:922–23).
33. Ibid., 3.13 (PL 196:923–24).
34. Ibid., 3.14 (PL 196:924–25).
35. Ibid., 3.16 (PL 196:925–26).
36. Ibid., 3.17 (PL 196:926).
37. Ibid., 3.18 (PL 196:926–27).
38. Ibid., 3.19 (PL 196:927).
39. Ibid., 3.20 (PL 196:927–28).
40. Ibid., 3.21 (PL 196:928).
41. Ibid., 3.22 (PL 196:928–29).
42. Ibid., 3.23 (PL 196:929).

will not be greater than any one person alone, nor will all three together be greater than any two or any one by itself.[43]

Assessment. Richard makes a strong argument for a plurality of persons, but he cannot convincingly explain why there should be only three persons, not four or more. If supreme love is shared love, what is to limit it to three persons only? Moreover, the three are to be proved by reason. He shows no interest in a biblical starting point, in which the three are given as revealed. The impression he gives is that the Trinity is logically necessary, something to be proved by a process of human reasoning. How true is that to the biblical teaching on the Trinity?

On the other hand, this approach has the great merit of undermining belief in a unitary deity, by demonstrating that such a being must be less than perfect, insofar as it will be unable to love. There can be no basis for personality in a monad, nor any ontological grounding for human love. Instead, the deity is reduced to power and will—such a being is supreme simply because it is able to impose its will on all other beings. This leads on the human level to a philosophy of might makes right and monolithic tyranny. In the religious, political, and military situation at the start of the third millennium, Richard's argument—appropriately modified and contextualized—offers the church a powerful apologetic and missionary tool as it faces the challenge of Islam.[44]

Thomas Aquinas

Brian Davies suggests that, for Thomas Aquinas (1225–1274), "the heart of Christian teaching is the doctrine of the Trinity."[45] It is necessary for a right view of creation, for it excludes any idea of necessity—that God needed the world—and also for a right view of salvation.[46] This may be so, but, as has often been remarked, Aquinas sep-

43. Ibid., 3.24 (PL 196:929–30).
44. See also Hill, *Three-Personed God,* 225–32; O'Carroll, *Trinitas,* 197–98.
45. Brian Davies, *The Thought of Thomas Aquinas* (Oxford: Clarendon Press, 1992), 185. This is in contrast to Catherine Mowry LaCugna, *God for Us: The Trinity and Christian Life* (San Francisco: Harper, 1991), 158ff., who argues that Aquinas creates a chasm between the triune God and God the Creator. This view may be due, in part, to LaCugna's almost pantheistic relational idea of the Trinity, in which God is to be understood only in relation to his creatures. By this yardstick, the vast majority of past theology is deficient.
46. Thomas Aquinas, *ST,* Pt. 1a, Q. 32, art. 1.

arates discussion of the Trinity from that of the existence, being, and attributes of God. Moreover, he attributes creation to the one God, to the whole Trinity, leaving unclear the extent to which the persons contributed distinctly to it.

The Trinity, reason, and revelation. In stark contrast to Richard of St. Victor, Aquinas maintains that it is impossible to attain knowledge of the Trinity by natural reason. By reason, we can attain knowledge of the unity of the divine essence, but not of the distinction of persons. Attempts to prove the Trinity by natural reason actually undermine faith. The object of faith is invisible realities that are beyond the reach of human reason. Besides, weak arguments provoke ridicule by unbelievers. Instead, we rest upon authority, that of the sacred Scripture. Nevertheless, we can still use reason to prove that God is one and to confirm the Trinity after we have accepted it by faith.[47] So "though the doctrine of the Trinity cannot be rationally demonstrated, it can still be rationally discussed."[48] The doctrine can be set forth, and objections can be answered.[49] According to G. E. M. Anscombe and P. T. Geach, the personal distinctions are demonstrably undecidable by reason.[50] God is inherently and pervasively mysterious, beyond our understanding, and this applies not only to the Trinity, but to everything about him. "Aquinas recognizes that philosophy can take us so far and no further."[51] In this sense, he consciously places limits on the extensive rationalism we saw in Anselm and Richard of St. Victor.[52]

However, these parameters point to Aquinas's separation of *de Deo uno* from *de Deo trino*, for the way we approach these two elements is significantly different. In his *Summa contra Gentiles*, he dis-

47. Ibid., Pt. 1a, Q. 32, art. 1; Thomas Aquinas, *Compendium theologiae* 36; Thomas Aquinas, *On Boethius* 1.4; 3.4.

48. Davies, *Aquinas*, 191.

49. Ibid., 192.

50. G. E. M. Anscombe, *Three Philosophers* (Oxford: Clarendon Press, 1973), 118ff., cited by Davies, *Aquinas*, 189.

51. Davies, *Aquinas*, 190. See the section beginning on p. 188.

52. See also F. C. Copleston, *Aquinas* (London: Penguin, 1963), 54–56; Ralph McInerny, ed. and trans., *Thomas Aquinas: Selected Writings* (London: Penguin, 1998), 122–26, for a translation of art. 4 of Aquinas's *On Boethius*, where he considers the question, "Is the human mind sufficient of itself to reach knowledge of the divine Trinity?" On Aquinas overall, see also Hill,

cusses at length the existence and essence, the nature and attributes, of the one God in part 1, while he holds back consideration of the Trinity and the relations of the persons until the final section, part 4. The separation is less radical in his *Summa theologica*, but still real. In part 1a, he discusses the one God in questions 2–26, while only with question 27 does he turn to the Trinity. Aquinas follows the tradition established by Augustine in proceeding from the axiomatic basis of the one divine essence. He does discuss the persons and their relations at length, for this is where the problem for Aquinas lies.

His discussion in the Summa theologica. Here we shall summarize the most salient features of Aquinas's discussion of the Trinity before we move on to examine his teaching critically.

Procession. Since God is above all creatures, we should understand what is said about him in terms of the highest creatures, recognizing that even these fall far short of what is true of him. Thus, procession is not to be understood in physical terms, but as an intelligible emanation, like a word proceeding from a speaker, yet remaining in him.[53] The Word proceeds from within the same nature, since in God understanding and existence are the same, due to his absolute simplicity.[54] The Word receives his divine existence in proceeding, but this does not mean that he is from anything other than the divine nature. With both the Word and the Holy Spirit, "all that exists in God, is God," the divine nature being communicated by every internal procession.[55] There is a distinction between the procession of love in God (the Spirit) and that of the Word, and so, while the latter is generation, the former is spiration.[56] Here the model of word, will, or love comes from Aquinas's reading of John 1, influenced by Augustine.[57]

Relations. Following Augustine, the relations in God are real, not accidental.[58] They refer to what is relatively opposed, implying a real

---

Three-Personed God, 62–78, and Bertrand de Margerie, *The Christian Trinity in History*, trans. Edmund J. Fortman (Petersham, Mass.: St. Bede's Publications, 1982), passim.

    53. Thomas Aquinas, *ST*, Pt. 1a, Q. 27, art. 1.

    54. Ibid., Pt. 1a, Q. 27, art. 2 (referring back to Q. 14, art. 4).

    55. Ibid., Pt. 1a, Q. 27, art. 3.

    56. Ibid., Pt. 1a, Q. 27, art. 4.

    57. Thomas Aquinas, *Commentary on the Gospel of St. John* (Albany: Magi Books, 1980), 23ff.

    58. Thomas Aquinas, *ST*, Pt. 1a, Q. 28, art. 1.

distinction, but not pertaining to the essence.[59] There are only four real relations—paternity, filiation, spiration, and procession.[60]

Persons. Aquinas follows Boethius's generic definition of *person* as "an individual substance of a rational nature." However, since in Latin *substantia* is ambiguous and can represent either *hypostasis* or *ousia* in Greek, Aquinas prefers to use the term *subsistentia* (subsistence), meaning that which exists in itself and not in another.[61] The word *persona* (person) is appropriate to God since it refers to what is perfect in all nature (a subsistent individual of a rational nature), but it is applied to God differently than to creatures, since his essence is perfect. We have to use extrabiblical terms, because "the urgency of confuting heretics made it necessary to find new words to express the ancient faith about God." What matters is to follow "the sense of Scripture."[62] When we talk of a human person, we mean a particular individual, distinct from others. With God, however, distinction is only by relation of origin, and relation is not an accident (as in humans), but is the divine essence itself. Therefore, "a divine person signifies a relation as subsisting" in the divine nature.[63] Aquinas here identifies the divine persons with relations, which seems to weaken his point that they are real persons—a matter we will discuss below. He goes on to affirm that there are three persons in God.[64] In God there is not triplicity, which denotes inequality, but trinity, which entails unity of order and essence.[65] We must not understand number here in the sense that it is applied to creaturely things, as one man is simply part of a sequence of two men, and two of three, for "this does not apply to God, because the Father is of the same magnitude as the whole Trinity."[66] Aquinas is saying that the persons of the Trinity are not sequential members of a class, as are human individuals, for divinity cannot be exemplified by individual members of a class. He opposes here a form of "tritheism, according to which Father, Son, and Spirit are three individuals sharing a nature in the sense that Peter, Paul, and John are

59. Ibid., Pt. 1a, Q. 28, arts. 2–3.
60. Ibid., Pt. 1a, Q. 28, art. 4.
61. Ibid., Pt. 1a, Q. 29, arts. 1–2.
62. Ibid., Pt. 1a, Q. 29, art. 3.
63. Ibid., Pt. 1a, Q. 29, art. 4.
64. Ibid., Pt. 1a, Q. 30, arts. 1–4.
65. Ibid., Pt. 1a, Q. 31, art. 1.
66. Ibid., Pt. 1a, Q. 30, art.1.

three individuals sharing a (human) nature."[67] We must avoid the error
of Arius and terms like *separation* or *division*, while also steering clear
of Sabellianism by refraining from words like *confusion* and *singularity*. Thus, the Son is other than the Father, as he is another person,
but he is not something else, since he is of the identical essence.[68]

   Notions. The various relations between the persons are differentiated by the defining characteristics of the persons, called *properties* or
notions. There are four notions that characterize relations: paternity, filiation, common spiration, and procession. There is also a fifth notion
that does not characterize a relation: innascibility (unoriginatedness).
Whereas the essence and persons are real, the notions are simply descrip-
tive ideas. Different ideas are compatible with right faith, if someone
"does not mean to uphold anything at variance with the faith."[69]

   The Father. The Father is the *principle* of the Trinity. The word
means only "that whence another proceeds." *Principle* must be distinguished from *cause*. It is improper to talk of the Father as cause,
for that would mean diversity of substance, and the other two persons
would be dependent. Neither of these problems exists with the term
principle. Although we attribute some authority to the Father because
he is the principle, "we do not attribute any kind of subjection or inferiority to the Son, or to the Holy Ghost, to avoid any occasion of error,"
since the word *principle* "does not signify priority but origin."[70] Here
Aquinas denies that the Son and the Spirit are subordinate to the Father
or dependent on him for their being. Procession neither implies nor
entails dependence or subordination. Aquinas continues by saying that
the Father is properly so called, since paternity distinguishes him from
the other two persons.[71] He is also characterized by common spiration
and by innascibility (unbegottenness), since, as the principle of others, he is from no one.[72]

   The Son. The Son, or Word (for that is his proper name), is to be
completely identified with God.[73] He is the image of God, which is

67. Davies, *Aquinas*, 187.
68. Thomas Aquinas, *ST*, Pt. 1a, Q. 31, art. 2.
69. Ibid., Pt. 1a, Q. 32, art. 4.
70. Ibid., Pt. 1a, Q. 33, art. 1.
71. Ibid., Pt. 1a, Q. 33, art. 2.
72. Ibid., Pt. 1a, Q. 33, art. 4.
73. Ibid., Pt. 1a, Q. 34, arts. 1–3.

properly said of the Son, but not of the Holy Spirit also, as the East had held.[74]

The Holy Spirit. The Spirit proceeds from the Son, as well as from the Father. The Greeks recognize that the procession of the Spirit has a connection with the Son. While this is not explicit in Scripture, "we do find it in the sense of Scripture." It is a rule of Scripture that whatever applies to the Father also applies to the Son, except what applies to the opposite relations. The Nestorians introduced the error that the Spirit does not proceed from the Son. It can be rightly said, as some in the East do, that he proceeds from the Father through the Son. The Father and the Son are one principle of the Holy Spirit, since there is no relative opposition between them as the principle of the Holy Spirit—here Aquinas follows and cites Augustine.[75] Aquinas follows Augustine and the Western position, but wants to bridge the divide with the Greeks, if at all possible. Love is the proper name of the Spirit (following Augustine), and so he is the bond of love between the Father and the Son. He is the love of the Father for the Son.[76] The name of the Spirit is also "gift," for he is given and is the gift. Before a gift is given, it belongs only to the giver, but when it is given, it is his to whom it is given. So the Spirit is "the gift of God giving," but when he is given, he is "a gift bestowed on man."[77]

The persons in relation to the essence. The essence is the same as the persons, due to the divine simplicity, yet the persons are really distinguished from each other. God's essence is the form of the three persons, since the persons are multiplied, but the essence is not. So the three persons are of one essence. Thus, the names denoting God's essence (God) can be applied to the persons as well as to the essence.[78] On the other hand, abstract names (essence) cannot stand for the persons. The essence does not beget the essence, but the Father begets the Son. Whereas "God" signifies the divine essence in him that possesses it, the word "essence" cannot stand for the person, because it signifies the essence in an abstract form.[79] However, while adjectival terms

74. Ibid., Pt. 1a, Q. 35, arts. 1–2.
75. Ibid., Pt. 1a, Q. 36, arts. 1–4.
76. Ibid., Pt. 1a, Q. 37, arts. 1–2.
77. Ibid., Pt. 1a, Q. 38, arts. 1–2.
78. Ibid., Pt. 1a, Q. 39, arts. 1–4.
79. Ibid., Pt. 1a, Q. 39, art. 5.

cannot be predicated of the essence, substantive terms can, owing to the real identity of essence and person. The divine essence is really the same as one person, and also the same as the three persons.[80] Thus, the essential attributes (power, wisdom, and so on) can be appropriated to each of the three persons.[81]

The persons compared to the relations or properties. The properties are the same as the persons, although they differ in concept. However, differences of opinion exist on this point. It is important here to recognize not only the unity of essence, but also the distinctions between the persons. They agree in essence, but are distinguished by relations. Since the essence is not divided, they are distinguished by the distinguishing properties—paternity for the Father, filiation for the Son. So it is better to say that they are distinguished by the relations (Father-Son) than by origin (begetter-begotten). They are not distinguished by being, nor by anything absolute (essence), but by something relative—hence, relation suffices for their distinction.[82]

The persons in reference to the notional acts. The notional acts (paternity, filiation, spiration, procession) differ from the persons only in their mode of signification, and in reality they are the same. For example, it is the Father's nature to beget the Son. He does not do so as an act of his will, except as there is a unity of divine will in eternity (the will of concomitance).[83]

Equality of the persons. The three persons are equal because they are of one essence.[84] Thus, the Son is coeternal with the Father, and so "the generation of the Son is not . . . in time, but in eternity." It is best to say with Gregory and Augustine, "He is ever born," rather than with Origen, "He is ever being born."[85] However, there is a natural order of persons in God, without priority.[86] This order is compatible with equality, for the Son is equal to the Father in greatness. "For the Father and Son have the same essence . . . which exists in the Father by the relation of giver, and in the Son by the relation of receiver."[87]

80. Ibid., Pt. 1a, Q. 39, art. 6.
81. Ibid., Pt. 1a, Q. 39, art. 7.
82. Ibid., Pt. 1a, Q. 40, arts. 1–2.
83. Ibid., Pt. 1a, Q. 41, arts. 1–2.
84. Ibid., Pt. 1a, Q. 42, art. 1.
85. Ibid., Pt. 1a, Q. 42, art. 2.
86. Ibid., Pt. 1a, Q. 42, art. 3.
87. Ibid., Pt. 1a, Q. 42, art. 4.

The missions of the persons (the sending of the Son and of the Spirit in history) correspond to their eternal relations, which accord with equality, not inferiority.[88] Mission and giving relate to the temporal; generation and spiration relate to what is eternal.[89]

Summary. Aquinas pays considerable attention to the persons and their relations. The Islamic threat was a real one in the thirteenth century, and the challenge of Arab interpreters of Aristotle posed crucial questions to Christian apologists. However, Aquinas begins with the one essence, greatly delaying his discussion of the Trinity—a very significant fact, in LaCugna's estimation[90]—and he accepts and follows Augustine's focus. He does not challenge the Islamists at root. Furthermore, his identification of the persons with the relations of paternity, filiation, and procession casts a large question mark over whether they have real ontological distinction. The persons are obviously relational, and their relations are real—that is to say, they belong to the nature of God. As Christopher Hughes argues, the relations constitute, as well as individuate, the divine *hypostases*. Thus, Aquinas "means that *being the Father of the Son* is something real in the Father, and that *being the Son of the Father* is something real in the Son," and he "concludes that *being the Father of the Son* is just the Father himself; and likewise, *being the Son of the Father* is just the Son himself." Hughes then argues that for Aquinas these relations are something real in God, not simply how we think about God.[91]

Some, like John Frame, have thought that Aquinas is very close to modalism.[92] However, Aquinas is as concerned with the errors of Sabellius as he is with those of Arius, and he insists that the persons of the Trinity are distinct in a real sense. The Son is other than the Father, since he is another person and another *hypostasis*, while he is not alien to the Father, since they are of the same essence.[93] Frame's suggestion, following Cornelius Plantinga, that Aquinas regards the persons merely as

88. Ibid., Pt. 1a, Q. 43, art. 1.
89. Ibid., Pt. 1a, Q. 43, art. 2.
90. LaCugna, *God for Us*, 147.
91. Christopher Hughes, *On a Complex Theory of a Simple God: An Investigation in Aquinas' Philosophical Theology* (Ithaca: Cornell University Press, 1989), 196–97. See the section on pp. 187–239.
92. John M. Frame, *The Doctrine of God* (Phillipsburg, N.J.: P&R Publishing, 2002), 701–3.
93. Thomas Aquinas, *ST*, Pt. 1a, Q. 31, art. 2.

notions in our own minds, is not true to the evidence.[94] Plantinga, with his strong predilection for a social Trinity, is at the far end of the spectrum from Aquinas, and none too sympathetic to him. Both Frame and Plantinga appear here to confuse Aquinas's teaching on notions and persons. Notions are, for Aquinas, abstract terms signifying the relations by which the persons are distinguished. The notions are our own mental constructs, merely signifiers, but the relations and the persons are real. Aquinas is clear about this, and the two ought not to be confused.[95]

Notwithstanding, Aquinas's full-scale use of the Augustinian model does entail a strong bias in a modalist direction. Above all, his powerful doctrine of the simplicity of God drastically inhibits his Trinitarianism. Aquinas holds God to be identical with his essence, nature, and attributes, and to be without composition (internal distinction). It becomes very difficult for him to conceive of three distinct persons while maintaining such a powerful idea of simplicity, for three persons imply complexity and counteract absolute simplicity.[96] This is as much a conflict between an Aristotelian doctrine of God and a biblical one, but the impact of Augustine adds to the tension. Hughes concludes: "For Aquinas, God is the simplest possible being, in whom there is no distinction between person and nature, or part and whole, or subject and attribute. Now, it is on the face of it incredible that such a being could have enough structure to be three persons in one nature."[97] Significantly, Hughes thinks it is possible for the divine simplicity, in Aquinas's view, to fit a Sabellian doctrine in which the divine persons are all the same as one another, for "the full-strength account of divine simplicity . . . describes a God who could not possibly be triune."[98] In Aquinas, there are therefore "two incompossible Gods."[99]

Another weakness in Aquinas, in the *Summa theologica* and in the *Summa contra Gentiles*, is his lack of focus on the events of the history of salvation, and a corresponding failure to treat them historically. Notwithstanding, Aquinas's whole theology is an outworking

94. Frame, *The Doctrine of God*, 702.
95. Thomas Aquinas, *ST*, Pt. 1a, Q. 32, art. 2.
96. I am grateful to Paul Helm for his suggestions at this point and for directing me to the book by Christopher Hughes.
97. Hughes, *On a Complex Theory*, 239.
98. Ibid., 240.
99. Ibid., 269.

of his Trinitarianism. The Trinity matters. It is not "a complicated exercise in speculative celestial physics," but a wonderful truth full of implications for human beings. Its significance is that we may come to share in its life.[100]

Three Eastern Theologians

John of Damascus

In his *magnum opus*, *The Orthodox Faith*, John of Damascus (ca. 675–753)—the last great father of the Eastern church—starts at once with God, and moves without delay to discuss the Trinity—in stark contrast to Aquinas, for all that the latter saw in the Trinity as central and crucial to the Christian faith. Here its place at the very start of the treatise expressly demonstrates that centrality in a way that Aquinas was unable to do. Moreover, he discusses the three persons and their perichoretic relations in great detail—in the very first section of his work. Nothing emphasizes more strongly the dominant position that the Trinity should occupy in the faith and worship of the church, nor its respective positions in the faith and worship of the Eastern and Western churches.[101]

The knowledge and incomprehensibility of God. God is ineffable and incomprehensible. No one has ever known him, except insofar as he has revealed himself. However, he has not left us in ignorance. He has implanted the knowledge of his existence in all nature. More than that, in the Law and the Prophets and, later, in Christ, he disclosed himself as far as it is possible for us to grasp. Therefore, we seek for nothing further than those things delivered to us in Scripture.[102]

Thus, not all things about God are knowable; neither are all things unknowable. On things above us, we express ourselves according to

---

100. Davies, *Aquinas*, 207.

101. On John of Damascus, see Jakob Bilz, ed., *Die Trinitätslehre des Hl. Johannes von Damaskus* (Paderborn: Ferdinad Schöningh, 1909); G. L. Prestige, *God in Patristic Thought* (London: SPCK, 1952), 263–64, 280; O'Carroll, *Trinitas*, 139–40; Andrew Louth, *St. John Damascene: Tradition and Originality in Byzantine Theology* (Oxford: Oxford University Press, 2002).

102. John of Damascus, *The Orthodox Faith* 1.1; see also 1.3 (PG 194:789–97).

our limited capacity. We confess that God is, among other things, eternal and unchangeable,

> and that God is . . . one essence (*ousia*); and that he is known, and
> has his being in three subsistences . . . and that the Father and the
> Son and the Holy Spirit are one in all respects, except in that of not
> being begotten, that of being begotten, and that of procession. . . .
> But neither do we know, nor can we tell, what the essence (*ousia*) of
> God is, or how it is in all. . . . It is not within our capacity, therefore,
> to say anything about God or even to think of him, beyond the things
> which have been divinely revealed to us, whether by word or by man-
> ifestation, by the divine oracles at once of the Old Testament and of
> the New.[103]

So what God is in his being and nature (essence) is incomprehensible and unknowable. We know that he does not have a body, that he is infinite, invisible, simple (not compound), and immutable, and that he fills the universe. But these things give an idea only of what he is not, not of what he is. To explain the essence of anything, we must speak in positive terms, but in the case of God it is impossible to explain what he is. "For he does not belong to the class of existing things: not that he has no existence, but that he is above all existing things . . . even above existence itself." So, all we can affirm concerning God "does not show forth God's nature, but only the qualities of his nature. For when you speak of him as good, and just, and wise, and so forth, you do not tell God's nature but only the qualities of his nature [τα περι την φυσιν]."[104] John opposes Athanasius at this point. In doing so, he introduces a deep agnosticism about our knowledge of God, which will echo down the centuries in the Eastern church. We will be returning to this matter shortly.

The being and persons. That God is one, is clear to all who believe the Holy Scriptures.[105] As for the Son, there never was a time when God was not Word—he ever possesses his own Word. He has his Word "ever existing within himself . . . possessed of all the attributes of the

---

103. Ibid., 1.2 (PG 194:792–793). The English translation used here is that of *NPNF²*.
104. John of Damascus, *The Orthodox Faith* 1.4 (PG 194:797–800).
105. Ibid., 1.5 (PG 194:800–801).

Begetter." As our word, proceeding out of the mind, is neither completely identical with the mind nor utterly different from it, so "the Word of God in its independent subsistence is differentiated from him from whom it derives its subsistence: but inasmuch as it displays in itself the same attributes as are seen in God, it is of the same nature as God."[106]

In turn, the Word possesses the Spirit. The Spirit of God is "the companion of the Word and the revealer of his energy." The Spirit is not to be compared merely to the breath of our mouth, for it is

> an essential power, existing in its own proper and peculiar subsistence, proceeding from the Father and resting in the Word, and shewing forth the Word, neither capable of disjunction from God in whom it exists, and the Word whose companion it is, nor put forth to vanish into nothingness, but being in subsistence in the likeness of the Word, endowed with life, free volition, independent movement, energy . . . having no beginning and no end. For never was the Father at any time lacking in the Word, nor the Word in the Spirit.[107]

The Trinity. John follows in the next section with an extensive exposition of the doctrine of the Trinity. There is one God who "does not derive his being from another . . . being himself the fountain of being to all that is . . . made known in three perfect subsistences and adored with one adoration . . . united without confusion and divided without separation." He relies largely on the language of C.

The Son is "everlastingly and without beginning begotten of [the Father]." Since the Father is eternally the Father, there never was a time when the Son was not. It is impious to speak of the generation of the Son in temporal terms, for he is generated from the Father's nature. Unless we grant that the Son coexisted with the Father from eternity, we introduce change into the Father's subsistence. "For generation means that the begetter produces out of his essence offspring similar in essence. But creation . . . [means] that the creator . . . produces from what is external, and not out of his essence, a creature of an absolutely dissimilar nature." Thus, there is a great gulf between man's begetting

---

106. Ibid., 1.6 (PG 194:801–4).
107. Ibid., 1.7 (PG 194:805).

and God's. Human generation is temporal, passionate, and sexual. In contrast, divine generation is eternal, passionless, and nonsexual. So the Son is begotten of the Father and is ever in him, without separation, having a proper subsistence of his own. Distinct from this, the procession of the Holy Spirit from the Father is not generative in character, and so is a different mode of existence, but it is still as incomprehensible, yet similarly involves no difference of essence. To say that the Father is the origin of the Son suggests no superiority in anything except causation. We mean that the Son is begotten by the Father, and the Father is not begotten by the Son, just as light proceeds from fire, not fire from light. So in the Father's creating through the Son, the Son is not a mere instrument, but the Father's subsistential force.

The Holy Spirit proceeds from the Father and rests in the Son, being equally glorified with the Father and the Son since he is coessential and coeternal, proceeding from the Father and communicated through the Son, inseparable and indivisible from both, possessing all the qualities that the Father and the Son possess, except that of being begotten or born. For the Father is without cause and unborn, the Son is derived from the Father by generation, and the Spirit is derived from the Father by procession (not generation). The generation of the Son and the procession of the Holy Spirit are simultaneous. "All then that the Son and the Spirit have is from the Father, even their very being."[108]

The perichoresis of the three persons. John writes:

> For in these hypostatic or personal properties alone do the three holy subsistences (hypostases) differ from each other, being indivisibly divided not by essence but by the distinguishing mark of their proper and peculiar subsistence. . . . one simple essence existing in three perfect subsistences.[109]

The subsistences, or persons, are *in* each other[110]—that we may not introduce a multitude of gods. Owing to the three subsistences, there is no compoundness or confusion; owing to their having the same

108. Cf. Gregory Nazianzen, *Orations* 25 (PG 35:1193–1225).
109. This and the following is from John of Damascus, *The Orthodox Faith* 1.8 (PG 194:808–33).
110. Cf. Gregory Nazianzen, *Orations* 1; 37 (PG 35:395–402; 36:279–308).

essence and dwelling in one another, we recognize the indivisibility and unity of God. John carefully contrasts this with the faulty analogy of three men sharing human nature. The three human subsistences do not exist one within the other. Each is separate, having many points that divide it from the other—in space, time, thought, power, shape, form, habit, temperament, dignity, pursuits, and, above all, in that they do not dwell in one another, but are separate. Thus we speak of two, three, or many men. In the case of the Trinity, it is the reverse. The three are coeternal, of identical essence, one in energy, goodness, will, power, and authority. "For each one of them is related as closely to the other as to itself. . . . [T]he Father, the Son, and the Holy Spirit are one in all respects, save those of not being begotten, of birth and of procession." For, citing John 14:11, they dwell in one another, cleaving together. "For they are made one not so as to commingle, but so as to cleave to one another, and they have their being in each other (*perichōrēsin*) without any coalescence or commingling. . . . For the Deity is undivided amongst things divided . . . and it is just like three suns cleaving to each other without separation and giving out light mingled and conjoined into one." There follows a passage that is effectively a paraphrase of Gregory Nazianzen.

This is an important stage in the history of the doctrine of the Trinity. It has been thought that John is using here the work of the anonymous seventh-century monk pseudo-Cyril, who purportedly countered a tritheistic outbreak associated with John Philoponos. However, V. S. Conticello has demonstrated that pseudo-Cyril is in fact the fourteenth-century Joseph the Philosopher, so we can now recognize John as the first to use the term *perichoresis* of the mutual indwelling of the three persons. The idea is present earlier, but John gives it a more developed treatment.[111]

We note in passing John's comment, referring to Exodus 3:14, that the most proper of names given to God is "he that is," conveying the idea of God's existence and his nature or essence. The second name of God is *ho theos*, which suggests the idea of energy.[112]

111. Verna Harrison, "Perichoresis in the Greek Fathers," *StVladThQ* 35 (1991): 53–65; Vassa S. Conticello, "Pseudo-Cyril's *De Sacrosancte Trinitate*: A Compilation of Joseph the Philosopher," *OCP* 61 (1995): 117–29; Walter Kaspar, ed., *Lexikon für Theologie und Kirche*, 3rd ed. (Freiburg: Herder, 1993–2001), 8:707–8.

112. John of Damascus, *The Orthodox Faith* 1.9 (PG 194:833–37).

This has implications for the later Eastern distinction between the essence and the energies of God.

In summary, for John (and, in view of his strategic significance for Orthodoxy, for the East in general) the Trinity is central in theology and so in practice. John gives prominence to the three persons, not because he has to prove their existence rationally from the one divine essence—as in the West—but because the three are a given of revelation. He follows the Cappadocian tradition, and so is able to develop the doctrine in a more biblical and doxological direction, rather than a rationalistic one.

Photius

Photius (ca. 810–ca. 895), the controversial patriarch of Constantinople, produced in his *Mystagogy of the Holy Spirit*, the main arguments against the West on the *filioque*.[113] These disclose the major differences of approach between the East and the West on the Trinity. Unfortunately, he wrote in exile, where he lacked access to the writings of the Latin fathers, and possibly had to use Greek sources from memory. Nor were his Western contemporaries able to read it. So, despite his wide learning, Photius could not strike home as incisively as he might have liked. Bulgakov describes the result of this treatise as "a victory without a fight from Latin thought."[114] Research has shown that he was not systematically opposed to the West, but rather took the theological issue with great seriousness.[115]

It is important to grasp that for Photius, the divine properties belong *either* to the nature (essence) *or* to the *hypostases* (persons).

113. Photius, *On the Mystagogy of the Holy Spirit*, trans. Holy Transfiguration Monastery (n.p.: Studion Publishers, 1983), 67–116 (in English), 153–91 (in Greek). Bobrinskoy comments that this work "constitutes the foundation of the dogmatic teaching of the Orthodox schools." Boris Bobrinskoy, "The Filioque Yesterday and Today," in *Spirit of God, Spirit of Christ: Ecumenical Reflections on the Filioque Controversy*, ed. Lukas Vischer (London: SPCK, 1981), 134. For further reading on Photius, see F. Dvornik, *The Photian Schism* (Cambridge: Cambridge University Press, 1948); Joseph Hergenröther, *Photius, Patriarch von Constantinopel*, 3 vols. (Regensburg: G. J. Manz, 1867–69); Richard Haugh, *Photius and the Carolingians: The Trinitarian Controversy* (Belmont, Mass.: Norland, 1975).

114. Sergei Nikolaevich Bulgakov, *Le Paraclet*, ed. Constantin Andronikof (Paris: Aubier, 1946), 102.

115. John Meyendorff, *Byzantine Theology: Historical Trends and Doctrinal Themes* (New York: Fordham University Press, 1979), 60.

The personal properties are incommunicable and singular. Therefore, the Father is the unique cause of the Son and the Holy Spirit, and the Spirit's procession is from the person of the Father, and thus from a property the Son cannot share.[116] For the West to say that the Spirit proceeds also from the Son is, in Photius's eyes, to say that the Son shares the personal properties of the Father. In short, it is the modalist heresy.

For Photius, first, the *filioque* subverts the monarchy of the Father, something crucial for the East. By starting with the essence, the West in effect makes it the monarchy, rather than the Father. This, Photius contends, establishes an impersonal ground for the Trinity. It also reduces the persons to mutual relations within the divine essence, rather than the starting point for our knowledge of God, as in the Cappadocian and Eastern tradition.

Second, the Western doctrine subordinates the Holy Spirit. According to Photius and the East, the Son is begotten *immediately* by the Father, but for the West the Spirit proceeds from the Father *remotely*, since he also proceeds from the Son, who is himself begotten. Thus, the Spirit's procession is subsequent to the begetting of the Son, since these cannot occur at the same time or else the Spirit would also be begotten by the Son. This argument is reinforced by the Western teaching on the Spirit (following Augustine) as the bond of love between the Father and the Son, which gives him subpersonal status. This we saw as a grave danger in Augustine's Trinitarian analogies, but it also surfaced, as Photius indicates, in his discussion of the relations. The point is that when the focus is placed on the essence, the persons and their relations become problematic. Photius sees the Western doctrine as rationalist, rather than one resting on biblical revelation.

Third, the Western approach is tantamount to modalism, since the distinctiveness of the *hypostases* is clouded. This is so because the Spirit is said to proceed from both the Father and the Son, as from a single source. This blurs the *hypostases* of the Father and the Son, Photius contends. We noted this in chapter 10.

Another point that Photius makes is that, since distinctive characteristics belong either to one of the persons or to the nature (essence) and so are common to all three persons, the West errs in giving pro-

116. Photius, *On the Mystagogy of the Holy Spirit*, 11.

cession to two persons, while excluding the third. However, the tables could be turned on Photius by countering that the East ascribes to two persons, but not to the third, a common origin from the Father!

For his part, Photius (like Irenaeus) points to the baptism of Jesus as crucial. There the Spirit proceeds from the Father and abides in the Son. Hence, the Spirit can rightly be called the Spirit of the Son. There is no separation between the Son and the Holy Spirit, but the monarchy of the Father is maintained. Moreover, the effect of Photius's approach is to treat the three persons as revealed, as given, not as objects to be proved by logical argument.

Photius recognizes a distinction between the eternal procession of the Spirit and his sending in the course of time in the economy of salvation. In this latter sense, the Spirit is sent by the Father through the Son. The scene at the Jordan gives rise to this view. Since the Spirit rests on Jesus, his deified humanity is then the link with the church and the creation. This is also how he opposes the *filioque*, by restricting the role of the Son in this sense to the economic sphere only.[117]

Owing to the inaccessibility of Western writings when he wrote his *Mystagogy*, Photius failed to deal with the crucial question of how the Spirit is related to the Son. He did not address the issue properly, and so both sides became increasingly like the proverbial ships passing in the night.[118]

Gregory Palamas

Born in Constantinople, Gregory Palamas (1296–1359) was a monk who was ordained a priest at the age of thirty. Much of his time was taken up by polemics and ecclesiastical turmoil. In 1347 he was elected archbishop of Thessalonica. After his death, he was proclaimed a saint by the Synod of Constantinople in 1368. Palamas wrote his *Triads* against Barlaam, a Byzantine philosopher with a positive estimate of Greek philosophy who regarded education and human knowledge as necessary to know anything about God. For Barlaam, God's essence is unknowable. His energies are created, and so what is left to man is a dialectical knowledge that stops short of a knowledge of God

117. Ibid., 21–23; John Meyendorff, *Byzantine Theology*, 60–61.
118. Gerald Bray, "The *Filioque* Clause in History and Theology," *TynBul* 34 (1983): 125.

himself in his essence. Direct knowledge of God is not possible for the human mind. God can only be known indirectly by contemplation of his works in nature. Barlaam was strongly intellectualist and believed it necessary to mortify all passions, rather than to transform them and devote them to the service of God, as Palamas maintained.[119] Barlaam's views were condemned by successive councils in Constantinople in 1341. Following this, he went into exile in Italy. Gregory, in opposing these ideas, supported the *heyschasts*, hermits who engaged in continuous prayer and contemplation. The famous Jesus prayer was central to their spirituality. Because of their practice of gazing downward at their bodies while repeating the prayer over and over again, Barlaam mockingly called these monks "people-whose-soul-is-in-their-navel."[120] Gregory's defense of the *heyschasts* was accepted by the Orthodox.

The essence and energies of God. For Gregory, as for the East in general, deification is central to the Christian message, for the saints are made partakers of the divine nature, as Peter says in 2 Peter 1:4. As Meyendorff observes, Gregory sees this as given to all Christians through baptism and continuous participation in the Eucharist.[121] The Incarnation is crucial for this. In becoming flesh, the Son of God united human nature to himself. It became God's humanity, filled with the divine energy. In union with Christ, we in our humanity are transformed, body as well as soul. A real knowledge of God is possible in Christ through communion with his *uncreated* energies.

Gregory affirms that there is only one unoriginated and eternal essence—the essence of God. Since the divine essence possesses his powers, they are also unoriginate. However, they themselves are not essences, but exist *in* the divine essence. The essence of God is therefore not the only reality that is unoriginate.[122] Not only the divine powers, but also

119. Gregory Palamas, *The Triads*, ed. John Meyendorff, trans. Nicholas Gendle (New York: Paulist Press, 1983), 154n119.
120. Ibid., 8. For this reason, it is mystifying to read Bray's description of the difference between the Eastern and the Western concepts of man and his salvation as, on the part of the East, "a denial of the Son's saving love in the life of the Christian, or at best a relegation of that love to second place." Bray, "*Filioque*," 128.
121. Meyendorff, *Byzantine Theology*, 77.
122. Gregory Palamas, *Triads* 3.2.5.

some works of God, have no beginning: his providence, will, and fore-knowledge. These are not identical with the essence of God, but are clearly pretemporal and have no beginning.[123] God himself infinitely transcends his uncreated works—whether his uncreated goodness, holiness, or virtue. These are themselves not the superessential essence of God. These are what he calls the energies of God. We might think of these energies as "existentially perceivable manifestations" in an Aristotelian sense, but applied here as the appearance of the coinherent (perichoretic), tripersonal life of God. Thus, since God is entirely present in each of the divine energies, we name him from each of them, although it is clear that he transcends them all.[124]

However, there are some energies of God that have both a beginning and an end. All the divine energies are uncreated, but not all are without a beginning. These are those energies that are directed toward created things. Since creation had a beginning, so do those energies of God related to creation. Here the distinction between the energies and the essence of God is most clear. Thus, the superessential essence of God is not to be identified with his energies, even with those without beginning. The divine essence transcends all energies whatsoever and transcends them to an infinite degree and an infinite number of times.[125] Essence and energy are therefore not identical in God. The energies exist, not in him, but around him.[126] So it is impossible, as the Fathers said, to find a name to express the nature of the uncreated Trinity. Rather, the names belong to the energies. He who is beyond every name is not identical with what he is named.[127]

The energies of God—created or uncreated? Barlaam had claimed that the divine energies were created. God granted existence to them. Hence, he held that a great gulf exists between the unknowable essence and the knowable created energies, from which it follows that we can have no direct knowledge of God. In response, Gregory refers to Gregory Nazianzen (*Oration* 28:31) and argues that it is impermissible to identify the eternal glory of God, which is visible in some way, with

123. Ibid., 3.2.6.
124. Ibid., 3.2.7; John Meyendorff, *Byzantine Theology*, 185–86.
125. Gregory Palamas, *Triads* 3.2.8.
126. Ibid., 3.2.9.
127. Ibid., 3.2.10.

his essence, in which we cannot participate. Since the eternal glory of God is visible in some way, we may participate in it, even though the essence is beyond participation.[128] Spiritual contact and union are possible with the spiritual and divine light, which is neither sensible nor intelligible, distinct from all creatures in its transcendence, an energy of the superessential, which is the object of vision and the power by which we see.[129] The good angels contemplate this eternal glory and do so eternally, and so it is not created, natural, or intellectual, but rather eternal, spiritual, and divine.[130] On the other hand, the fallen angels have had this power removed from them, so it is not natural to the angels.[131] It is a divinizing energy that is inseparable from the energizing Spirit. It is unknowable to the spiritually immature and incapable of remaining with those inclined to evil.[132] God spoke personally to the OT patriarchs—to Abraham and Moses. Since then, the Lord himself has saved us, and the Spirit of God has instructed us in all truth. The Incarnation transformed the scene radically. It is not possible to see the light without seeing *in* the light. It is not the divine essence that is accessible and visible, but the glory of the Father and the grace of the Holy Spirit.[133] Barlaam, in contrast, assumes that only the essence of God is uncreated, the energies being created, and so if this reality is uncreated, it must be identical to the essence of God.[134]

Can God be known? A critical assessment. Gregory's argument appears to raise questions about the person of Christ and then about the Trinity. He identifies the two natures of Christ with energies. He attacks the implications of Barlaam's claim that the energies of God are created. Barlaam is in effect saying, Gregory insists, that the divine nature of Christ was created, and so his opponent is worse than a monothelite or a Manichee.[135] It appears that for Gregory the human

128. Ibid., 3.2.13.
129. Ibid., 3.2.14.
130. Ibid., 3.2.15.
131. Ibid., 3.2.16.
132. Ibid., 3.2.17; Gregory Palamas, *The Triads*, ed. John Meyendorff, 150n61.
133. Gregory Palamas, *Triads* 3.3.5; Gregory Palamas, *The Triads*, ed. John Meyendorff, 17–18.
134. Gregory Palamas, *Triads* 3.3.6.
135. Ibid., 3.3.7. The Manichees held that the universe is dualistic, with two competing principles—good and evil.

nature of Christ is an energy, and so this (human) energy was united with a divine energy. In taking this position, Gregory appears to regard the person of the Son as a divine energy. This is confirmed by the fact that he does not talk about the person of the Son. He restricts his discussion to the energies. However, he has already listed such things as foreknowledge, goodness, virtue, and will as energies of God. Is he not reducing the person of the Son to a divine attribute? In doing so, what is left of the Trinity? Are the three persons merely divine energies? If not, and they belong to the divine essence, are they not, according to his theology, unknowable and beyond participation on our part? It is not clear how the relationship between the essence and the energies of God is compatible with an orthodox position on Christology and the Trinity, nor how he can get around this dilemma.[136]

So much is reinforced by his argument that deified man—the saints in union with and transformed by God—participates in the uncreated energies of God, rather than his essence.[137] These energies are in God and remain invisible to the created faculties. Yet the saints see them because they have transcended themselves with the help of the Spirit.[138] Knowledge of God by experience comes from the grace that grants man the likeness of God. We know this is deification because man becomes entirely God in soul and body through grace, and through the divine radiance of the blessed glory he is made entirely resplendent. This is the radiance of God, an uncreated energy.[139] This, however, takes place in communion with the energies, by grace and not by nature. The sharp distinction between essence and energies safeguards against any possible confusion between Creator and creature.

There is an answer to this problem. We noted how deification is brought about by the Incarnation—a theme at least as old as Athanasius—and takes place at the level of the divine energies, so preserving the Creator-creature distinction. The essence of God, always unknowable to us, is of course tripersonal—Gregory is an Eastern theologian and works within the tradition that gives pride of place to the three persons. The energies, such as will, foreknowl-

---

136. Gregory Palamas, *The Triads*, ed. John Meyendorff, 17–20.
137. Gregory Palamas, *Triads* 3.3.8.
138. Ibid., 3.3.10.
139. Ibid., 3.3.13.

edge, and providence, are not forces detached from God, nor divine emanations, nor something of lesser status than God himself. They are the divine life and should be seen in that context.[140] In turn, as Bray indicates, in their eternal relations the three persons are unknowable, but, in his manifestation by the Son, the Holy Spirit is knowable as the divine energy at work in the world.[141] In this, Gregory follows Photius's distinction between the Holy Spirit proceeding from the Father in terms of his hypostatic existence and the Holy Spirit being sent by the Father through the Son in terms of his mission in history, as divine energy.[142]

However, as we have remarked, and as Laats also suggests, the East "has had to introduce a special entity for linking the divine and human—the so-called divine energy. It took the place of the Holy Spirit in bridging the gap between God and the creature."[143] In Trinitarian dogma, the Son himself bridges this gap in the Incarnation, and the Spirit unites us with the Son. This is obscured by Gregory, for whom the persons are eclipsed by the energies and absorbed into the ineffable divine essence. The problem here is the gulf this posits between human beings and the unknowable essence. Ultimately, the result is a form of invincible agnosticism. God as he has revealed himself is different from God as he is. Additionally, the three persons are lost in the unknowable superessential essence. At best, Gregory allows an indirect knowledge of God through the energies, but this is not a knowledge of God as he is. If indeed we can have this indirect knowledge, how do we know that it is true knowledge, if we cannot know God's essence? Moreover, at the heart of Palamite theology is nonsense. If the divine essence is unknowable, how does Gregory know it? ie. that it's unknowable.

That this is a radical departure from the Cappadocians is clear. For them, as LaCugna points out, "God's *ousia* exists *as* Father, Son, Spirit. The three persons do not *have* a common *ousia*; they *are* the divine *ousia*. . . . Further, as Rowan Williams points out, the doctrine of the Trinity means the identification of *ousia* with *energeiai*." With

140. John Meyendorff, *Byzantine Theology*, 77–78.
141. Bray, "*Filioque*," 134.
142. Gregory Palamas, *Capita physica theologica* (PG 150:1145).
143. Alar Laats, *Doctrines of the Trinity in Eastern and Western Theologies: A Study with Special Reference to K. Barth and V. Lossky* (Frankfurt am Main: Peter Lang, 1999), 163–64.

Gregory, the energies, not the persons, enter into communion with the creature. The essence and persons are inaccessible to us, and the essence (*ousia*) is beyond the persons.[144] Gregory has in effect abandoned historic Trinitarianism. He has certainly "removed the Trinity from our salvation."[145]

The Differences Between East and West—A Summary

As we have noted, the East and West have two significantly different concepts of the Trinity.

The West

- The West, ever since Augustine, has consistently started from the essence of God, which has precedence over the persons. Consequently, the essence tends to be impersonal and the three persons are problematic, the subjects of lengthy discussion and proofs. Moreover, again following Augustine, the persons are simply mutual relations within the one essence.
- Since the Holy Spirit is seen as the bond of love between the Father and the Son, the question remains as to whether he is in effect subordinate. This was acute in Augustine's Trinitarian analogies and has been passed down in the tradition ever since. Indeed, if the Spirit is understood in this way, it may be asked whether he is properly considered to be a person in his own right.
- A tendency toward modalism is therefore endemic in Western Trinitarianism. We shall see how this remains even in more recent theology.
- The Trinity has been increasingly divorced from the life and worship of the church. For the overwhelming majority of Western Christians, it is considered more of a mathematical conundrum than a vital matter of everyday faith and worship.

144. LaCugna, *God for Us*, 192.
145. Ibid., 197. On Palamas, see also Rowan Williams, "The Philosophical Structures of Palamism," *ECR* 9 (1977): 27–44; D. Wendebourg, "From the Cappadocian Fathers to Gregory Palamas: The Defeat of Trinitarian Theology," *StPatr* 17, no. 1 (1982): 194–98.

The East

- The East consistently starts with the three persons. In Christian faith, the Son and the Holy Spirit are encountered as divine agents of salvation. Consequently, God is at once one and three, as Gregory Nazianzen so graphically portrayed it.
- The monarchy of the Father is a key factor. The Father, rather than the divine essence, is the origin or cause of the divine nature in the Son and the Spirit.
- How far has the relation between the Son and the Spirit been made clear? It seems to many Westerners to be a consequence of opposition to the *filioque* that there is a less than clear connection between the work of Christ and the work of the Holy Spirit.
- The danger of tritheism has been recognized from the fourth century; the monarchy of the Father is the safeguard.
- Ontological subordinationism was eliminated at Nicaea and Constantinople, but a "Biblical and Orthodox subordinationism"[146] is maintained, with the Father being the origin of all divine being and action.
- The Eastern doctrine, as it developed, distinguishes between the immanent Trinity and the economic Trinity, between God in himself and God as he has revealed himself, between essence and energies. This threatens our knowledge of God with a profound agnosticism. It also defies rational discourse. The acme of the Christian life is mystical contemplation, rather than *fides quaerens intellectum*. As Barth says, "It goes beyond revelation to achieve a very different picture of God 'antecedently in himself.'"[147]
- The Trinity is more central to the life and worship of the church than in the West, as Orthodox service books clearly indicate.

146. Meyendorff, *Byzantine Theology*, 183.
147. Karl Barth, *CD*, I/1: 480.

John Calvin

How New Is Calvin's Trinitarianism?

As one reads John Calvin's treatment of the Trinity in the 1559 (definitive) edition of his *Institutes*, one is struck by the difference from Aquinas. Rather than making a rigorous argument in syllogistic terms, based on the premise of the unity of the divine essence, and asking how the one God can also be three persons, Calvin presents a biblically based exposition in straightforward language that largely avoids philosophical terminology. It is the Trinity in plain Latin. Moreover, his discussion is largely concerned with the deity of the Son and the Holy Spirit, treated in order. The difference in manner and content is striking. It leads at once to the question of how far Calvin (1509–1564) was an innovator. For now, we note that Bray considers him, in common with the Protestant Reformers generally, to have "a vision of God which was fundamentally different from anything which had gone before, or which has appeared since."[1] He considers it a tragedy that modern historical theology has not recognized "the revolutionary character of Calvin's trinitarianism."[2] Reymond argues that he departs from "Nicene trinitarianism."[3] Dowey considers his Trinitarianism to be "exclusively biblical in origin."[4]

On the other hand, many scholars argue for his continuity with the tradition. Wendel considers him as "carefully avoiding anything

1. Gerald Bray, *The Doctrine of God* (Leicester: Inter-Varsity Press, 1993), 197.
2. Gerald Bray, "The *Filioque* Clause in History and Theology," *TynBul* 34 (1983): 143.
3. Robert L. Reymond, *A New Systematic Theology of the Christian Faith* (New York: Nelson, 1998). In the second edition, Reymond corrects this claim.
4. Edward A. Dowey Jr., *The Knowledge of God in Calvin's Theology* (Grand Rapids: Eerdmans, 1994), 125–26, 146.

that could have been considered an innovation," for while the Trinity is an essential part of his theology, he is "devoid of originality."[5] Niesel considers that "he took over from the early church fathers the doctrine of the Trinity with all the theological equipment that accompanied it." He is not original and his whole purpose at this point is to secure the biblical message.[6] O'Carroll finds Calvin, of all Protestants, to have "the fullest, most evidently traditional and orthodox trinitarian theology."[7] Parker agrees that from as early as 1536 he was "perfectly orthodox" and that, as he went on, he found that "the orthodox doctrine of the Trinity said precisely what he himself wanted to say."[8]

We begin with the 1559 *Institutes* in order to gain a basic grasp of his teaching, bearing in mind that this work needs to be read in conjunction with the commentaries, in historical progression.[9] This is Calvin's own express intention. However, from this definitive edition of the *Institutes* we gather that the Trinity *is* his doctrine of God. It contains nothing expressly on God other than a section on the Trinity. Here is a major departure from Aquinas's separation of his discussion of the one God from his discussion of the Trinity; this is more in line with Peter Lombard's approach in his *Sentences*. So much is the Trinity integral to his understanding of God, that the whole work has a Trinitarian structure. Indeed, the Apostles' Creed became more explicitly the structural basis of the *Institutes* as edition succeeded edition—and the Creed is, of course, patterned on the Trinity. Butin

5. François Wendel, *Calvin: The Origin and Development of His Religious Thought*, trans. Philip Mairet (London: Collins, 1963), 168–69.

6. Wilhelm Niesel, *The Theology of Calvin*, trans. Harold Knight (Grand Rapids: Baker, 1980), 54–57.

7. Michael C. O'Carroll, *Trinitas: A Theological Encyclopedia of the Holy Trinity* (Collegeville, Minn.: Liturgical Press, 1987), 194.

8. T. H. L. Parker, *The Doctrine of the Knowledge of God: A Study in the Theology of John Calvin* (Edinburgh: Oliver and Boyd, 1952), 61–62. See also Jan Koopmans, *Das altkirchliche Dogma in der Reformation* (Munich: Chr. Kaiser Verlag, 1955), 66–75; W. Nijenhuis, "Calvin's Attitude Towards the Symbols of the Early Church During the Conflict with Caroli," in *Ecclesia Reformata: Studies on the Reformation*, by W. Nijenhuis (Leiden: E. J. Brill, 1972), 73–96; Benjamin Breckinridge Warfield, "Calvin's Doctrine of the Trinity," in *Calvin and Augustine*, ed. Samuel G. Craig (Philadelphia: Presbyterian and Reformed, 1974), 187–284; Philip Walker Butin, *Revelation, Redemption, and Response: Calvin's Trinitarian Understanding of the Divine-Human Relationship* (New York: Oxford University Press, 1995).

9. Elsie A. McKee, "Exegesis, Theology, and Development in Calvin's *Institutio*: A Methodological Suggestion," in *Probing the Reformed Tradition: Historical Studies in Honor of Edward A. Dowey, Jr.*, ed. Brian G. Armstrong (Louisville: Westminster/John Knox, 1989), 154–72.

argues extensively for a strong soteriological concern in Calvin's Trinitarianism, and in turn his treatment of soteriology is pervasively Trinitarian.[10] Parker outlines the growth of a pervasively Trinitarian cast
to Calvin's theology, based on the Apostles' Creed and enriched by
increasing familiarity with, and quotation of, the Fathers.[11]

Calvin in Relation to East and West

Whatever we may conclude about Calvin's relationship to the
tradition he inherited, his focus on the three persons rather than the
one essence is more like the Eastern approach than the Western. In
much of what he writes, Calvin combines elements of both East and
West. His use of the baptismal formula is reminiscent of Basil. He
insists that God is not truly known unless he is distinctly conceived
as triune, and that the fruit of baptism is that God the Father adopts
us in his Son and through the Spirit re-forms us into righteousness.[12]
Butin comments on the influence of the baptismal formula on both
Calvin and Basil,[13] and also notices the weakness of Warfield on the
Eastern church, for, like the vast majority of Protestants until recently,
Warfield took little or no notice of Eastern theology.[14] This focus of
Calvin on the three does not undermine the unity of God, for his
being is one. The three persons imply a distinction, not a division.[15]

Calvin's Focus on the Persons

The bulk of Calvin's substantive discussion in the *Institutes* concerns the eternal deity of the Son[16] and the Holy Spirit.[17] Moreover, he

10. Butin, *Revelation*, 13, 19, 25, 27, 30, 40ff., 137n14, 145n106.

11. Parker, *Knowledge of God*, 61–69.

12. John Calvin, *Calvin's Commentaries: A Harmony of the Gospels Matthew, Mark and
Luke*, vol. 3, *and the Epistles of James and Jude*, trans. A. W. Morrison, ed. David W. Torrance
and Thomas F. Torrance (Edinburgh: Saint Andrew Press, 1972), on Matt. 28:19; John Calvin,
Calvin's Commentaries: The Gospel According to St John 11–21 and the First Epistle of John,
trans. T. H. L. Parker, ed. David W. Torrance and Thomas F. Torrance (Edinburgh: Oliver and
Boyd, 1961), on John 17:21, 24.

13. Butin, *Revelation*, 43–45, 128–29, 157n15, 158n21, 159n25.

14. Ibid., 163n46.

15. John Calvin, *Institutes of the Christian Religion*, trans. Ford Lewis Battles, ed. John T.
McNeill (Philadelphia: Westminster Press, 1960), 1.13.17.

16. Ibid., 1.13.7–13.

17. Ibid., 1.13.14–15.

begins this straightaway, after a few introductory chapters, without a
lengthy consideration of the existence, nature, or attributes of God.
In short, this is his doctrine of God. This is in marked contrast to
Augustine and Aquinas. In addition, his exposition is based almost
entirely on the Bible, rather than on reason or on ecclesiastical authorities, as with Aquinas. This is not to say that Calvin ignores either reason or the Fathers. He cites the latter frequently in controversy, and
his argument is nothing if not orderly. However, he refers to a wide
variety of passages from both Old and New Testaments in support of
Christ's eternal deity. The deity of both the Son and the Spirit is the
same as that of the Father, he insists. There is no gradation in the Godhead. Commenting on Romans 8:9, referring to the Spirit, Calvin
stresses this utter equality in a passage that shows evidence of both
Western and Eastern influence. The Spirit, he says, "is sometimes
referred to as the Spirit of God the Father, and sometimes as the Spirit
of Christ without distinction. This is not only because his whole fulness was poured on Christ as our Mediator and Head, so that each
one of us might receive from him his own portion [note here the Eastern turn of thought, traceable all the way back to Irenaeus], but also
because the same Spirit is common to the Father and the Son [here he
speaks the language of Augustine], who have one essence, and the same
eternal deity."[18] Perhaps in view of his unusually strong assertions of
the absolute deity of the Son, to which we will refer in a moment,
Calvin has some difficulty with the old problem passage, 1 Corinthians
15:27–28, and his comments on it have a definitely Nestorian ring to
them. At the conclusion of his mediatorial kingdom, Calvin says, Christ
will hand the kingdom back to God. He will not abdicate his kingship
in any way, "but will transfer it in some way or other from his humanity to his glorious divinity." This seems to imply a division in the person of Christ. Indeed, he goes on to say that we will then see God
plainly in his majesty, "and the humanity of Christ will no longer be
in between us to hold us back from a nearer vision of God."[19] This

18. John Calvin, *Calvin's Commentaries: The Epistles of Paul the Apostle to the Romans
and to the Thessalonians*, trans. Ross Mackenzie, ed. David W. Torrance and Thomas F. Torrance (Edinburgh: Oliver and Boyd, 1961), on Rom. 8:9; cf. also on Rom. 14:11.

19. John Calvin, *Calvin's Commentaries: The Epistle of Paul the Apostle to the Corinthians*,
trans. John W. Fraser, ed. David W. Torrance and Thomas F. Torrance (Edinburgh: Oliver and
Boyd, 1960), on 1 Cor. 15:27.

astonishing statement appears to conflict with Calvin's otherwise strong, and definitely orthodox, focus on the Incarnation. It is as if in attempting to guard against any diminution of Christ's full deity, he has momentarily lost his grasp of the union of the two natures of the incarnate Christ. Even if this is so, it simply serves to underline the centrality of his emphasis on the true and eternal deity of the Son, and, in turn, of the Holy Spirit.

The Son as *Autotheos* (God of Himself)

As we have hinted, later in his career Calvin was forced by disputes with Italian anti-Nicenes to assert the deity of the Son and the Holy Spirit in as strong terms as possible. His critics were Michael Servetus, George Blandrata, and Valentine Gentile. In his *Impietas Valentini Gentilis detecta et palam traducta*, most commonly known as *Expositio impietatis Valentini Gentilis*, he frequently refers to the Son as *autotheos*, "God of himself."[20] In this way, he opposes any idea that the Son receives his deity from the Father. Rather, he has his deity from himself, just as the Father does. This is in opposition to Gentile's teaching that the Father alone is *autotheos*, so that the Son and the Holy Spirit are of a different essence than the Father. Gentile used the expression exclusively of the Father, and Calvin, in rebutting him, applies it also to the Son—and by implication to the Spirit. Thus, it is not original with Calvin and arose in controversy after the final edition of his *Institutes* had been published. He uses the term nowhere else.

Calvin's claim raised some significant opposition in Roman Catholic circles. However, Rome's leading apologist of the sixteenth century, Robert Bellarmine, took a more measured view. He recognized that, in the terms of classic Trinitarian dogma, Calvin was orthodox. Calvin's novelty was simply in his terminology, his manner of speech (*modus loquendi*). Even in that, Bellarmine acknowledged that Calvin was defending the true doctrine.[21] Other Roman Catholic critics alleged that Calvin was failing to distinguish the Son from the Father, and so was falling into the Sabellian heresy, or else—if distinguishing

20. Calvin, CO, 9:368–70.
21. Robert Bellarmine, "Secunda controversia generalis de Christo," in *Disputationum de controversiis Christianae fidei adversus haereticos* (Rome, 1832), 1:307–10.

them—was arguing for another *principium* (beginning) than the Father, thereby coming close to Manichaeism. Calvin, Bellarmine says, has erred in his manner of speech, particularly in *Institutes* 1.13.19, 23 and in his treatise against Gentile, where he calls the Son *autotheos* and refers to the phrase in N, "God of God," as a hard saying. "However, when I examine the matter and carefully scrutinize Calvin's thoughts I am not so bold to pronounce him to be in error, since he teaches the Son to be of himself in respect of essence, not of person, and he is seen to speak well that the person is begotten by the Father, and the essence not begotten . . . but to be from itself." The reason why Calvin says the Son is *autotheos*, Bellarmine suggests, is that he was driven to it by Gentile, who constantly pronounced that the Father alone is *autotheos*, meaning that he alone has the uncreated, divine essence, the Son and the Spirit being of a different essence produced by the Father.[22] Bellarmine goes on to make some heavy criticisms of Calvin and his followers, but on these vital points he pronounces him in error only in terms of his way of speaking.

What did Calvin mean by this term? On the premise of the orthodox Trinitarian teaching that God is one and indivisible, it follows that all three persons share in the one identical and undivided being of God. Thus, the Son cannot be said to derive his deity from the Father. In contrast, Gentile had argued that only the Father has deity of himself, and thus that the other two persons are of a different essence than the Father. As Warfield recognizes, Calvin did not introduce anything radically new, for, as we shall see, he reinforced his opposition to Gentile with references to the Fathers.[23] However, it is right to acknowledge that Calvin does give expression in the strongest possible way to the full, eternal deity of the three persons.

The Essence and the Persons

Where does that leave the classic teaching that the Son is begotten by the Father from eternity, and also the eternal procession of the Holy Spirit? Gentile maintained that Calvin could not have his cake

22. Ibid., 1:307–8.
23. Warfield, "Calvin's Doctrine," 241ff.

and eat it too—he could not hold Christ to be *autotheos* and also confess the Niceno-Constantinopolitan faith, which asserts that he is "light of light, true God of true God." According to his thinking, eternal generation and procession are incompatible with the Son and the Spirit being *autotheos*. Here Calvin has recourse to the equally classic teaching of Gregory Nazianzen, followed by Augustine, that the creedal phrases describe characteristics of the persons, not of the essence. These are spoken of the relations and are peculiar to the several persons. They are not shared equally and identically by all three, since they do not refer to the essence as such. Calvin declares:

> Indeed, if we hold fast to what has been sufficiently shown above from Scripture—that the essence of the one God is simple and undivided, and that it belongs to the Father, the Son, and the Spirit; and on the other hand that by a certain characteristic the Father differs from the Son, and the Son from the Spirit—the gate will be closed not only to Arius and Sabellius but to other ancient authors of errors.[24]

Thus, for the Son, "with respect to his deity his being is from himself," and "whoever says that the Son has been given his essence from the Father denies that he has being from himself." The anti-Nicenes held that the Father alone has the being of God and imparts this essence to the Son. However, Calvin says, there is with respect to the essence no distinction between the Father and the Son.[25] Yet Calvin also says that we can still hold to the distinct, eternal relations between the persons, since we do not separate the persons from the essence, but rather distinguish them while they remain within it. He concludes:

> Therefore we say that deity in an absolute sense exists of itself; whence likewise we confess that the Son since he is God, exists of himself, but not in respect of his Person; indeed, since he is the Son, we say that he exists from the Father. Thus his essence is without beginning; while the beginning of his person is God himself.[26]

24. Calvin, *Institutes*, 1.13.22.
25. Ibid., 1.13.23.
26. Ibid., 1.13.25. Here Calvin cites Augustine in support, from his commentary on Psalm 109:13 (110:13 in English); see *NPNF*[1], 8:542ff. (PL 37:1457), and Augustine, *De Trinitate*, book 5.

Hence, the Word was eternally hidden in God before he was revealed in the creation of the world, but his *hypostasis* was distinct from the Father while he was of the same essence as the Father, "concealed in God."[27] Christ the Son is also distinct from the Spirit.[28] Thus, there is a distinction of persons in God. Unity of essence requires that what is of the essence of God is as much the Son's as the Father's, and so what belongs to God is common to both, but this "does not prevent each having the property of his own person." The Father's glory is invisible to us until it shines forth in Christ. Indeed, the Father's substance is "in some way engraven on Christ." So the Son "is one God with the Father, yet is nonetheless to be distinguished in such a way that each has his own subsistence."[29]

This entails an order among the three that is in full harmony with their autotheotic status. As Warfield puts it, Calvin's conception of the Trinity "included a postulation of an 'order' in the Persons of the Trinity, by which the Father is first, the Son second, and the Spirit third. And it included a doctrine of generation and procession by virtue of which the Son as Son derives from the Father, and the Spirit as Spirit derives from the Father and the Son."[30] Whenever the name of God is mentioned, the Son and the Spirit are included as well as the Father. On the other hand, "where the Son is joined to the Father, then the relation of the two enters in; and so we distinguish among the persons." In doing so, the peculiar properties of the three persons carry an order within them. Since the Father is the beginning and the source, where he is mentioned together with the Son or the Spirit, the name of God is peculiarly applied to him.[31] This is why the Father is called the Creator—"it is by reason of the order between the persons." For this reason, it is improper (*improprie*) to call Christ the Creator in terms of the

27. John Calvin, *Calvin's Commentaries: The Gospel According to St John 1–10*, trans. T. H. L. Parker, ed. David W. Torrance and Thomas F. Torrance (Edinburgh: Oliver and Boyd, 1959), on John 1:1–3.

28. Ibid., on 14:16.

29. John Calvin, *Calvin's Commentaries: The Epistle of Paul the Apostle to the Hebrews and the First and Second Epistles of St Peter*, trans. William B. Johnston, ed. David W. Torrance and Thomas F. Torrance (Edinburgh: Oliver and Boyd, 1963), on Heb. 1:2–3.

30. Warfield, "Calvin's Doctrine," 244.

31. Calvin, *Institutes*, 1.13.20.

persons. Rather, he is to be called Creator when speaking of the divine essence.[32]

The Father as the *Principium*

In keeping with patristic and medieval teaching, Calvin regarded the Father as the *principium* (beginning) or *origo*. To him "is attributed the beginning of activity, and the fountain and well-spring of all things; to the Son, wisdom, counsel, and the ordered disposition of all things; but to the Spirit is assigned the power and efficacy of that activity." In all God's works, the three work together (a dominant theme in Augustine), and in these activities there is this clear order. Behind this lies a relational order. The Father is first, from him is the Son, and from both is the Spirit. For this reason, "the Son is said to come forth from the Father alone; the Spirit, from the Father and the Son at the same time."[33] Thus, it is permissible to say that "in respect to order and degree the beginning of divinity is in the Father."[34] "The Father is first in order . . . the beginning and fountainhead of the whole of divinity."[35] As we saw, this is in respect to the persons.

This is very clear in Calvin's catechetical work, *Le catechisme de l'église de Genève*, or in its Latin translation, *Catechismus ecclesiae Genevensis*, published in 1545, in question 19. Here he calls the Father the beginning or origin, the first cause. Again, he is speaking of the relations of the persons, not of the one divine essence or being.[36] In the draft he produced for the *French Confession* in 1559—a draft which was followed almost entirely, except for his first few chapters, of which this is one—he says that the name of God is sometimes applied in par-

32. "Cur ergo creator dicitur pater, et hoc titulo seorsum ornatur? Nempe ratione ordinis, dum respicitur ad personas. . . . Si vere creator est Christus, neque id personae respectu: sequitur necessario referri hoc ad essentiam." CO, 9:369.
33. Calvin, *Institutes*, 1.13.18.
34. Ibid., 1.13.24.
35. Ibid., 1.13.25.
36. "Pource qu'en une seule essence divine nous avons à considerer le Pere, comme le commencement et origine, ou la cause première de toutes choses," and, in translation, "Quoniam in una Dei essentia patrem intueri nos convenit, tanquam principium et originem, primamve rerum omnium causam." OS, 2:76–77; CO, 6:13–14.

ticular to the Father, "since he is the principle and origin of his Word and his Spirit."[37]

The Eternal Generation of the Son

The distinction between the Father and the Son is not confined to creation and redemption. Nor is language referring to the Father begetting the Son to be limited to the economic sphere only, although it is true that Calvin's focus normally lies there. Biblical passages referring to the generation of the Son usually point to the incarnate Son's resurrection, but nevertheless before this "it is manifest that he was the only-begotten 'in the bosom of the Father.'"[38] Indeed, he is the Son "because the Word was begotten by the Father before all ages."[39] At the same time, Calvin is averse to speculating on what eternal begetting entails. Like Gregory Nazianzen, he regards this as a matter that is beyond our capacities to explain. These thoughts profit little and involve useless trouble. The idea of Origen that there is a "continuous act of begetting" is foolish, since the relation is eternal.[40] Calvin's focus is on the economic activity of the divine persons. Thus, the citation of Psalm 2:7 in Acts 13:33 refers to the resurrection of Jesus, by which he was generated visibly before human eyes. Nevertheless, this in no way negates the hidden generation (*illa arcana generatio*) that happened in eternity.[41] In his high priestly prayer in John 17, Christ indicates that since his glory is eternal, he always was. In so doing, he expresses a distinction between himself and the Father, "from which we infer that he is not only the eternal God but also the eternal Word of God begotten of the Father before the ages."[42] Also in

37. "Et combien que le nom de Dieu soit quelque fois attribué en particulier au Pere, d'autant qu'il est principe et origine de sa Parole et de son Esprit." *OS*, 2:312. See also *Expositio impietatis Valentini Gentilis*, in CO, 9:369.

38. Calvin, *Institutes*, 1.13.17.

39. Ibid., 1.13.23–25.

40. Ibid., 1.13.29. Warfield is wrong to say that all the "Nicene fathers" were "accustomed to explain" eternal generation. We have noted how many, such as Gregory Nazianzen, recognized this as an impenetrable mystery; see Warfield, "Calvin's Doctrine," 247.

41. John Calvin, *Calvin's Commentaries: The Acts of the Apostles 1–13*, trans. John W. Fraser and W. J. G. McDonald, ed. David W. Torrance and Thomas F. Torrance (Edinburgh: Oliver and Boyd, 1965), on Acts 13:33; *Ioannis Calvini opera exegetica*, vol. 12/1, *Commentariorum in Acta Apostolorum liber primum*, ed. Helmut Feld (Geneva: Droz, 2001), 389.

42. Calvin, *The Gospel According to St. John 11–21*, on John 17:5: "Sed aeternum quoque Dei sermonem ex Patre ante secula genitum."

Le catechisme de l'église de Genève, 22, he says that the eternal Word was begotten by the Father before all ages.[43]

Calvin brings this into focus most acutely in the very work where he stresses the Son as *autotheos*, the *Expositio impietatis Valentini Gentilis*. Christ is the Son of God, since he is the Word of God begotten by the Father before all ages (*ante secula a patre genitus*), who is now made known in the flesh. The eternal Word, relative to the Father, is the Son of God; considered apart from the relations, he is at the same time God.[44] In a crucial passage in which he reflects on the words of N, "God of God" (dropped by C), Calvin weighs the views of the Fathers, particularly Athanasius, and concludes that the creed is speaking of the personal relations and does not imply any communication of essence or concomitant subordination:

> But the words of the Council of Nicaea resound "God of God." This is a hard saying, I acknowledge. However, no one is better able to remove any ambiguity or a more capable interpreter than Athanasius who composed it. And certainly the counsel of the fathers was no other than that the Son in terms of origin is led out from the Father, in respect of his person, and in no way to oppose his being of the same essence and deity. And so, according to essence, he is the word of God without beginning, according to his person however the Son has a beginning from the Father.[45]

Again, shortly afterwards, he says that the Son "has his origin from the Father, as he is the Son; an origin not of time, nor of essence, both of which would be most absurd, but an origin strictly of order (*sed ordinis duntaxat*). Thus everything is said to be from the Father, insofar as the relations of the persons are concerned."[46] Calvin would have had no quarrel with Gentile if he had been saying only that the Son

43. *OS*, 2:77; *CO*, 6:15–16.
44. *CO*, 9:370.
45. "Sed verba consilii Nicaeni sonant, Deum esse ad Deo. Dura loquutio, fateor, sed ad cuius tollendam ambiguitatem nemo potest esse magis idoneus interpres, quam Athanasius, qui eam dictavit. Et certe non aliud fuit patrum concilium, nisi manere originem quam ducit a patre filius, personae respectu, nec obstare quominus eadem sit utriusque essentia et deitas: atque ita, quoad essentiam, sermonem esse Deum absque principio: in persona autem filii habere principium a patre." Ibid., 9:368.
46. Ibid., 9:369.

has his origin from the Father in terms of begetting. At issue, however, was Gentile's denial that the Son is without origin in terms of the one divine essence.[47] In his *Defensio* (1545), written in reflection on the Caroli controversy, Calvin remarks that in terms of relation he has "continually proclaimed" that the Son is of the Father.[48] This, as he remarks in his draft of the French Confession, is because the persons have that which is characteristic of each, while the unique essence is indivisible.[49] To sum up Calvin's thoughts on the question, since the Son is God, he exists of himself, "but not in respect of his Person; indeed, since he is the Son, we say that he exists from the Father."[50]

The Eternal Procession of the Holy Spirit

Calvin accepts the eternal procession of the Holy Spirit from the Father and the Son, a teaching that he says "appears in many passages, but nowhere more clearly than in chapter 8 of Romans."[51] We noticed above the blend of Eastern and Western approaches to the procession of the Holy Spirit in his comments on Romans 8:9, but when it comes to the question of the *filioque*, Calvin is clearly Western and Augustinian. Bray argues that this is at the heart of his theology and central to evangelical Protestantism. Both Christ and the Spirit are called by the same name, *paraclētos*, "Comforter," for it is an office common to both to comfort, exhort, and guard us by their patronage. As long as he lived in the world, Christ was our patron. Then he committed us to the patronage of the Holy Spirit. However, Christ is still our patron, although no longer in a visible manner, for he guards us by his Spirit.[52] Christ sends the Spirit from the heavenly glory and, while he names the Father as the one from whom the Spirit proceeds, he does so because he wants us to contemplate the Spirit's divinity, not because he wants to exclude himself from that role.[53]

---

47. Ibid., 9:375.
48. Ibid., 7:323–24.
49. "D'autant que chacun ha tellement ce qui luy est propre, quant à la Personne, que l'essence unique n'est point divisee." *OS*, 2:312.
50. Calvin, *Institutes*, 1.13.25.
51. Ibid., 1.13.18.
52. Calvin, *The Gospel According to St. John 11–21*, on John 14:16.
53. Ibid., on John 15:26.

After all, it is Christ who communicates his life to us "by the power of his Spirit."[54]

The Mutual Indwelling of the Persons

In each *hypostasis*, the whole divine nature is understood. Referring to John 14:10, Calvin states that "the Father is wholly in the Son, the Son wholly in the Father."[55] He says the same in commenting on John 17:3, for "we learn that [Christ] is wholly in the Father and the Father wholly in him. In short, whoever separates Christ from the divinity of the Father does not yet know him who is only true God."[56] Torrance points to Calvin's use of the phrase *in solidum*, which was originally used by Cyprian in an ecclesiastical context referring to the corporate interconnectedness of bishops within the one episcopate, but which Calvin adopts to attest the three persons' sharing completely and equally in the one being of God.[57] This entails their mutual indwelling (perichoresis) or containment.[58]

Calvin and the Early Church Councils and Fathers

Calvin concludes his formal discussion of the Trinity in the 1559 edition of the *Institutes* by stressing that his teaching in the controversy against the Italian anti-Trinitarians has the full backing of the Fathers. He cites Justin, Ignatius, the Council of Nicaea, and Augustine.[59] Augustine took for granted the doctrine that the anti-Nicenes were attacking, Calvin maintains. In the preceding section, he also cites Irenaeus, Tertullian, Hilary, and Gregory Nazianzen.[60]

This is of some significance in view of the Caroli controversy. Pierre Caroli had identified himself with the Reformation, had become

54. Ibid., on John 17:21.
55. Calvin, *Institutes*, 1.13.19.
56. Calvin, *The Gospel According to St. John 11–21*, on John 17:3; cf. on John 14:10. Cf. also Warfield, "Calvin's Doctrine," 229; Butin, *Revelation*, 42–43, 130.
57. Thomas F. Torrance, *The Christian Doctrine of God: One Being, Three Persons* (Edinburgh: T & T Clark, 1996), 201–2.
58. Ibid., 194–202. See also Verna Harrison, "Perichoresis in the Greek Fathers," *StVladThQ* 35 (1991): 53–65.
59. Calvin, *Institutes*, 1.13.29.
60. Ibid., 1.13.16–29; cf. *OS*, 3:129–51.

pastor at Lausanne, but then wavered and eventually reverted to Rome. He attacked Calvin during the latter's first period at Geneva (1536–38). In particular, Caroli accused Calvin and others of Arianism and demanded that they subscribe to the Nicene Creed. This Calvin refused to do. Ever after, his Trinitarianism was held in some suspicion in circles hostile to him. There were good practical and political reasons why Calvin did not acquiesce to Caroli's demand.[61] Among other things, Warfield suggests that his refusal is "not in the least because he did not find himself in accord with [the ancient creed's] teaching, but solely because he was determined to preserve for himself and his colleagues the liberties belonging to Christian men." He was not even misunderstood by Caroli as repudiating them.[62] However, this episode has given some people reason to suppose that he did not hold firmly to the decisions of the ecumenical church.[63]

While Calvin insisted that all doctrine must be founded on the teaching of Scripture, he did not see himself as breaking with the Catholic doctrine of the Trinity in any respect. He supported the Fathers' use of extrabiblical language, such as the terms *hypostasis* and *ousia*, in order to defend biblical teaching.[64] He frequently cited the Fathers, especially Augustine, and a range of medievals in support of his teaching.[65] In Warfield's words, Calvin considered the terminology used by the councils to be "the best expressions for stating and defending the doctrine" and as the language by which alone heresies can be confounded.[66] In its complete formulation, it is the basis for his whole argument.[67] In short, Warfield argues that "in his doctrine of the Trinity Calvin departed in nothing from the doctrine which had been handed down from the orthodox Fathers."[68] So far is he from

61. See Nijenhuis, "Symbols," 73–96.
62. Warfield, "Calvin's Doctrine," 207.
63. On the Caroli controversy, see Karl Barth, *The Theology of John Calvin*, trans. Geoffrey W. Bromiley (Grand Rapids: Eerdmans, 1995), 309–45; Nijenhuis, "Symbols," 73–96.
64. Calvin, *The Gospel According to St. John 1–10*, on John 1:1.
65. See Koopmans, *Altkirchliche Dogma*, esp. 54–57, 86–97, 108–15, 121–30, 132–37, 141–47; Hughes Oliphant Old, *The Patristic Roots of Reformed Worship* (Zurich: Theologischer Verlag, 1975), 149–51, 338–41; Anthony N. S. Lane, *John Calvin: Student of the Church Fathers* (Grand Rapids: Baker, 1999). That Calvin is not uncritical toward Augustine is evident from his dismissal of the latter's finding an image of the Trinity in the human soul as "by no means sound." Calvin, *Institutes*, 1.15.4.
66. Warfield, "Calvin's Doctrine," 210.
67. Ibid., 215.
68. Ibid., 229.

rejecting the Nicene Creed, or even the assertion that the Son is "God of God" (which C dropped), that he explicitly teaches the eternal generation of the Son before all time. His criticisms of that creed affect its form, not its content.[69]

In his *Expositio impietatis Valentini Gentile*, he cites Athanasius in support of calling the Son *autotheos* and goes on to defend the Council of Nicaea (not Constantinople, but the much more difficult earlier council) in the important passage we quoted above in note 45. In his *Defensio* (1545), in which he demonstrates his agreement with the church's theological resolution of the fourth-century Trinitarian crisis, Calvin cites both Augustine and Cyril in support of the Son existing of himself (*a se ipso*) because he is God.[70] His *Responsionum ad quaestiones Georgii Blandratae* is an emphatic defense of the Niceno-Constantinopolitan theology.[71] In his *Antidote to the Council of Trent*, Calvin passes over the first decree of Trent—on the Apostles' Creed—pausing only to ridicule the assembled dignitaries for taking over one month to affirm the creed.[72] This was a matter on which there was no dispute between Calvin and Rome. Writing to Cardinal Sadolet, Calvin insisted that "our agreement with antiquity is far greater than yours, but all that we have attempted has been to renew that ancient form of the church . . . [that existed] in the age of Chrysostom, and Basil, among the Greeks, and of Cyprian, Ambrose, and Augustine, among the Latins."[73] Most significantly, in his draft of the French Confession, 2, he states, concerning the Trinity, "We receive what was determined by the ancient councils, and we hate all sects and heresies which were rejected by the holy doctors from the time of St. Hilary and Athanasius until St. Ambrose and Cyril."[74] Parker, in outlining the growth of a pervasively Trinitarian cast to Calvin's theol-

---

69. Ibid., 248–49.

70. CO, 7:322–24.

71. Ibid., 9:325–32.

72. John Calvin, "Antidote to the Council of Trent," in *Selected Works of John Calvin: Tracts and Letters*, ed. Henry Beveridge (Grand Rapids: Baker, 1983), 3:61–63; CO, 7:407–8.

73. John Calvin, "Reply to Sadolet," in *Selected Works of John Calvin: Tracts and Letters*, ed. Beveridge, 1:37–38.

74. "Et en cela nous avons ce qui a esté determiné par les anciens Conciles, et detestons toutes sectes et heresies qui ont esté reiettees par les saincts docteurs depuis S. Hilaire, Athanase, iusqu'à S. Ambroise, et Cyrille." CO, 9:739–42; OS, 2:312.

ogy, explains that this development was based on the Apostle's
Creed and was enriched by his increasing familiarity with, and quotation of, the Fathers.[75]

T. F. Torrance argues that Calvin has a close theological kinship
to Gregory Nazianzen. Many of his characteristic nuances can be
detected to some extent in Gregory.[76] Calvin famously cites this passage from Gregory's *Oration on Holy Baptism*, saying it "vastly
delights me":

> No sooner do I conceive of the one than I am illumined by the splen-
> dour of the three; no sooner do I distinguish them than I am carried
> back to the one. When I think of any one of the three I think of him
> as the whole, and my eyes are filled, and the greater part of what I
> am thinking escapes me. I cannot grasp the greatness of that one so
> as to attribute a greater greatness to the rest. When I contemplate
> the three together, I see but one torch, and cannot divide or measure
> out the undivided light.[77]

A. N. S. Lane pours cold water on this thesis, producing evidence that
Calvin hardly read Gregory and often cited the Fathers as weapons in
debate rather than from thorough firsthand knowledge of their work
in context.[78] This may well be true. However, by Calvin's own admis-
sion, Gregory's words here delighted him, whether he had read them
in context or not.

Conclusion

We started by posing the question of how far Calvin is an innovator on the doctrine of the Trinity. Clearly, he breaks significantly
from the late medieval scholastic approach and restores a thoroughly

75. Parker, *Knowledge of God*, 61–69; see also H. H. Esser, "Hat Calvin eine 'Leise Modal-
isierende Trinitätslehre'?" in *Calvinus Theologus*, ed. W. H. Neuser (Neukirchen-Vluyn:
Neukirchener Verlag, 1976), 20–24. See also Butin, *Revelation*, 46–49; S. M. Reynolds, "Calvin's
View of the Athanasian and Nicene Creeds," *WTJ* 23 (1960–61): 33–37.

76. See especially his chapter on "The Doctrine of the Holy Trinity in Gregory Nazianzen
and John Calvin," in *Trinitarian Perspectives: Toward Doctrinal Agreement* (Edinburgh: T &
T Clark, 1994), 21–40.

77. Gregory Nazianzen, *Orations* 40.41, cited by Calvin, *Institutes*, 1.13.17.

78. Lane, *Calvin*, 1–13, 83–86.

biblical exposition. He eschews speculation. Again, he shows a noticeable openness to the East and is prepared to borrow certain themes
from the Cappadocians. He admires the work of Gregory Nazianzen,
however limited his knowledge of it may be. His focus on the three
persons is more of an Eastern than a Western characteristic. Calvin is
like a breath of fresh air in these respects.

However, at root his Trinitarianism is deeply conservative. He
becomes increasingly conscious of following in the tradition of the
early church councils. His argument is not with the Fathers, but with
the late medievals with whom he has come into conflict, particularly
with the theologians of the Sorbonne. Thus, even where he evidences
a certain kinship with the Greek fathers, he firmly retains his allegiance
to Augustine—the father he most frequently cites. For instance, where
he borrows a theme from the Eastern teaching on the Holy Spirit, he
still remains committed to the *filioque* clause and all that it entails. Far
from being a reviser of the doctrine of the Trinity, Calvin both preserves and develops the inheritance he receives.

Modern Discussion

Error and confusion are not the prerogative of small minds, and to be able candidly to examine the points of incoherence in a theologian's work should be a testimony to what the student has learned from that theologian at his greatest and best.

—Rowan Williams, "The Philosophical Structures of Palamism"

Karl Barth

The doctrine of the Trinity suffered increasing neglect in Western theology after the Reformation. In keeping with the worldview of the Enlightenment, attention shifted from God to this world. Alexander Pope's famous lines sum it up: "Know then thyself, presume not God to scan, the proper study of mankind is man."[1] A batch of new academic disciplines emerged in the nineteenth century devoted to the study of man, such as psychology, sociology, and anthropology. In turn, there was a striking development of the historical consciousness. Biblical scholars searched for the historical Jesus. Biblical theology, pressured by the Kantian world to prescind from eternity and ontology, tended to restrict and limit the reference of biblical statements concerning the Father and the Son to the historical dimension only. A classic case was Oscar Cullmann's claim that the NT has a purely functional Christology.[2] The problem with this line of thought is that, if the reference of biblical statements is exclusively this-worldly and restricted to human history, then God has not necessarily revealed himself as he is eternally in himself.

On top of all this, the pattern set by Aquinas of delaying discussion of the Trinity until after a full consideration of the doctrine of God, became commonplace. As a result, the Trinity was increasingly

---

1. Alexander Pope, *An Essay on Man*, 2:1.
2. Oscar Cullmann, *The Christology of the New Testament* (London: SCM, 1959), 326–27; [Cullmann,] "The Reply of Professor Cullmann to Roman Catholic Critics," trans. Robert P. Meye, *SJT* 15 (1962): 36–43, where he qualifies his earlier claims.

viewed as an addition to the doctrine of God, as something for advanced thinkers, rather than at the heart of the Christian faith. Charles Hodge, in his *Systematic Theology*, spends 250 pages on the existence, nature, and attributes of God and only then turns to the Trinity. Schleiermacher relegates the Trinity to an appendix in *The Christian Faith*. The effects of this are far-reaching. All aspects of theology are related to all others. As Alar Laats comments, "It is not impossible that the reduction of the role of Christ to a moral teacher in the liberal theology of the last [nineteenth] century happened because of the eclipse of the doctrine of the Trinity."[3]

Then came Karl Barth (1886–1968), and it is from him that the recent revival of interest in the doctrine of the Trinity has its genesis. As R. W. Jenson puts it, "[It is] from Barth that twentieth-century theology has learned that the doctrine of the Trinity has explanatory and interpretative use for the whole of theology; it is by him that the current vigorous revival of trinitarian reflection was enabled."[4] The translator of the first half-volume of Karl Barth's *Church Dogmatics* suggests that his treatment of the Trinity in that volume is the most significant since Augustine. While this claim is exaggerated, there is little doubt that Barth's work has had a seminal effect. As Bromiley comments, God is the theme of theology for Barth, for "even Christ's centrality is meant to point to (and not away from) the centrality of the triune God."[5]

The Early Barth

Scripture and Dogma

In the first volume of his *Church Dogmatics*, Barth states that Scripture is the basis, not for the Trinity, but for *the doctrine* of the Trinity.[6] While the dogma is not in the Bible as such, we must test it by whether it is a good interpretation of the Bible.[7] Its basis lies in revelation, since

---

3. Alar Laats, *Doctrines of the Trinity in Eastern and Western Theologies: A Study with Special Reference to K. Barth and V. Lossky* (Frankfurt am Main: Peter Lang, 1999), 160.

4. R. W. Jenson, "Karl Barth," in *The Modern Theologians*, ed. D. F. Ford (Oxford: Blackwell, 1989), 1:42, cited in Laats, *Doctrines of the Trinity*, 15.

5. Geoffrey W. Bromiley, *An Introduction to the Theology of Karl Barth* (Grand Rapids: Eerdmans, 1979), xi.

6. Karl Barth, *CD*, I/1: 295.

7. Ibid., I/1: 310.

we are dealing with God himself and not, "as Modalists in all ages have thought, with an entity distinct from him."[8] Revelation, then, is not the basis of the Trinity, but the basis of *the doctrine* of the Trinity.[9] Since the Bible is the basis of the doctrine, the problems that developed in the doctrine of the Trinity during the course of the church's history are not alien to the Bible, but are at least prefigured there.[10] Moreover, the doctrine of the Trinity is foundational. It is at the head of dogmatics,[11] for "the doctrine of the Trinity is what basically distinguishes the Christian doctrine of God as Christian."[12] This is a vital point that nineteenth-century liberalism forgot. Here Barth sets himself against Schleiermacher and his ilk. Von Balthasar argues that Barth's placing of the Trinity in the prolegomena of dogmatics establishes God's full sovereignty and excludes Schleiermacher's theology of consciousness. God is not accountable to man but, since he reveals himself as triune, he is free.[13] By making his doctrine of the Trinity his doctrine of God, Barth, like Calvin, stands apart from the Western tradition after Aquinas. This foundational role of the Trinity is evident in many ways in Barth's theology. In particular, in this very volume, the threefold form of the Word of God takes on distinctively Trinitarian lines. The Word of God revealed, written, and preached has threefold form, but a basic unity, the three elements indwelling and permeating each other in a perichoretic manner.

Is Barth's Doctrine in CD, I/1, Unipersonal?

Barth argues that the doctrine of the Trinity is an outflow of the proposition that "God reveals himself." "God reveals himself through himself, and reveals himself."[14] Later he explains this by affirming that God reveals himself as the one he is.[15] Revelation is God's self-unveiling

8. Ibid., I/1: 311.

9. Ibid., I/1: 312; Laats, *Doctrines of the Trinity*, 17, 23. We leave untouched the debatable connection in Barth between the Bible and revelation.

10. Barth, *CD*, I/1: 314.

11. Ibid., I/1: 300–302.

12. Ibid., I/1: 301.

13. Hans Urs von Balthasar, *The Theology of Karl Barth: Exposition and Interpretation*, trans. Edward T. Oakes (San Francisco: Ignatius, 1992), 87; David Ford, *Barth and God's Story: Biblical Narrative and the Theological Method of Karl Barth in the "Church Dogmatics"* (Frankfurt am Main: Peter Lang, 1981), 154; Bromiley, *Karl Barth*, 10.

14. Barth, *CD*, I/1: 296.

15. Ibid., I/1: 396.

to human beings, who are incapable of receiving God's Word due to their sinful condition. God does what man cannot do.[16] Rowan Williams points out that the idea that man is incapable of hearing the Word is nonsense, for it supposes that he knows what the Word is from which he is alienated. What Barth means, he suggests, is that "it depends entirely upon God's creative address to man, the Word spoken out of his freedom, his decision."[17] Moreover, God is concealed even in his revelation,[18] which is historical, not mythical.[19] Thus, there is a unity between the self-revealing God, his revelation, and his being revealed—a union with no barriers separating the three forms of his being: subject, predicate, and object. However, this unity takes the form also of a differentiation, for the names Christ and Holy Spirit are unexchangeable.[20] Jüngel observes that the doctrine of the Trinity "had to lay down the fact that God as the subject of his being is also the subject of his being known and becoming known. This is why for Barth the doctrine of the Trinity stands at the beginning of his *Dogmatics*."[21]

As a further expansion on this theme, Barth states that the proposition that "God reveals himself as the Lord" is the root of the doctrine of the Trinity.[22] God's lordship is prior to his revelation, but his revelation is the root of the doctrine of the Trinity. Thus, his lordship is in some sense prior to the Trinity. His sovereignty is paramount. This will have far-reaching consequences. God "is the same in unimpaired unity and yet also the same thrice in different ways in unimpaired distinction," or "the Father, the Son and the Holy Spirit in the biblical witness to revelation are the one God in the unity of their essence, and the one God in the biblical witness to revelation is the Father, the Son and the Holy Spirit in the distinction of his persons."[23]

Immediately, the question arises as to the subject of the Trinity. Barth's stress is on the oneness of God. It is "himself" he reveals. He is

16. Ibid., I/1: 320.

17. Rowan Williams, "Barth on the Triune God," in *Karl Barth: Essays in His Theological Method*, ed. S. W. Sykes (Oxford: Clarendon Press, 1979), 147–48.

18. Barth, *CD*, I/1: 322–23.

19. Ibid., I/1: 323–29.

20. Ibid., I/1: 299.

21. Eberhard Jüngel, *The Doctrine of the Trinity: God's Being Is in His Becoming* (Edinburgh: T & T Clark, 1976), 42.

22. Barth, *CD*, I/1: 306–7.

23. Ibid., I/1: 307–8.

God in threefold repetition. This is a strongly Western model, with obvious roots in Augustine. Laats argues that it is a linear, unipersonal model and the evidence appears to support him. Laats thinks that Barth has the Father as the divine subject, although, as he points out, Moltmann considers it to be the divine essence.[24] Rowan Williams sees it as "the order of a 'repetition' of *one* divine subject."[25] However, Barth departs from his earlier discussion of the Trinity in his lectures at Göttingen of April 1924-October 1925. At that time, "he had no difficulties in affirming the existence of *three* divine subjects,"[26] for in these lectures he was opposing Sabellianism.[27] While holding to a clear distinction between the economic Trinity and the immanent Trinity, he nevertheless insisted that there could be no distinction in content between them, or one would lapse into Sabellianism.[28] With the changes in the first volume of the *Church Dogmatics*, he abandons his support for three divine subjects. His *bête noire* becomes tritheism, and so we must ask a further question.

Is Barth a Modalist?

Because of his discussion in the first volume of the *Church Dogmatics*, it is not surprising that some have charged Barth with modalism.[29] However, despite the unipersonal sound of Barth's root premise, he consistently opposes modalism. He attacks it in discussing the *vestigium Trinitatis*.[30] In considering the divine unity, he excludes "a mere unity of kind or a mere collective unity."[31] He holds to the doctrine of the immanent Trinity.[32] The three moments, the Father, Son, and Holy Spirit, are not alien to God's being as God, and he clearly affirms the distinctiveness of Christ and the Holy Spirit.[33] He is fully aware of the danger of Sabellianism in neo-Protestant theology, which

24. Laats, *Doctrines of the Trinity*, 37.
25. Williams, "Barth," 166.
26. Bruce L. McCormack, *Karl Barth's Critically Realistic Dialectical Theology: Its Genesis and Development, 1909–1936* (Oxford: Clarendon Press, 1995), 355–56.
27. Ibid., 358.
28. Ibid., 352–58.
29. Jürgen Moltmann, *The Trinity and the Kingdom: The Doctrine of God* (London: SCM, 1991), 143; Catherine LaCugna, *God for Us* (San Francisco: Harper, 1991), 252.
30. Barth, *CD*, I/1: 343.
31. Ibid., I/1: 350.
32. E.g., ibid., I/1: 358, 499, 542; II/1: 16, 208–50.
33. Ibid., I/1: 451–53.

had limited itself to an economic Trinity of revelation, with God himself in the background as absolute personality. However, his main concern is to avoid tritheism, and this raises the question of how far this concern arises from an equal exaggeration in the other direction. The Trinity, he says, is not three objects. As we saw, he identifies the lordship of God with God's essence.[34] The unity of God consists in the threeness of the persons, but it is not threefold essence or deity. Rather, the one God is in threefold repetition.[35] This *sounds* both unipersonal and modalist. On the other hand, God's unity is not singularity or isolation, for it includes distinction or order.[36]

In his discussion of the concept of "person," these questions reoccur. Barth reflects on Augustine's recognition that neither "person" nor any other term can adequately express the threeness in God.[37] Following Augustine, he states that "person" is not used to say that the three in God are persons in the same way that we are persons, but is simply a help to say that there are three in God. The modern concept of the person as a center of self-consciousness muddies the waters further, for Barth sees in this, if applied to the Trinity, a recipe for tritheism, with three separate beings, each an "I." Melanchthon, among others, veered very close to this, he argues.[38] If that were true of God, there would be three I's, which is definitely not what classic theology meant by "person."[39] Therefore, "we do not use the term 'person'." What, then, does Barth use in its place? His preference is for the German term *seinsweise*, translatable into English as "mode (or way) of being." By this he hopes to express the same thing as "person" in classic Trinitarianism, while avoiding the problems that modern usage creates. This idea is not new, he says, but an auxiliary concept used from the very beginning. The statement "God is one in three ways of being" means that "the one God . . . is what he is not just in one mode but . . . in the mode of the Father, in the mode of the Son, and in the mode of the Holy Ghost."[40] We note at this point that *seinsweise* can mean

34. Ibid., I/1: 349.
35. Ibid., I/1: 350.
36. Ibid., I/1: 354–55.
37. Ibid., I/1: 355–56.
38. Ibid., I/1: 359.
39. Ibid.; see also I/1: 350ff.
40. Ibid., I/1: 359.

"way of being" or "mode of being." Barth's translator, Geoffrey Bromiley, renders it almost uniformly as "mode of being." For casual readers, this at once conjures up the specter of modalism. Bromiley himself rightly regards such a claim as absurd, for Barth "stays very close to the orthodox formularies," and his polemic against the term "person" "aims to defend rather than subvert the orthodox position."[41]

This is very true, for Barth both here and in many other places rejects modalism.[42] He is constantly aware of its danger and steadfastly turns away from it. What he means by *seinsweise* is "the mode of being of an existent."[43] He cites Calvin's definition favorably,[44] as well as those of the Reformed scholastics Wolleb and Burmann, who refer to "divine substance in a particular manner of subsistence" or "the being of God in a certain manner of being or subsistence." These ways of being are distinct and unexchangeable and cannot be confounded. So "this one God is God three times in different ways, so different that it is only in this threefold difference that he is God."[45] This threefold way of being is essential to him and irremovable. The Father and the Son are irreducible to the other. If we were to deny the threefoldness in God, we would be referring to another God than the God revealed in Holy Scripture.[46] These modes of being are *distinctive* modes of being, not to be equated with divine attributes nor relegated to three departments of the divine essence.[47] They are distinguished by their distinctive relations to one another. "Father, Son, and Spirit are distinguished from one another by the fact that without inequality of essence or dignity, without increase or diminution of deity, they stand in dissimilar relations of origin to one another."[48] This is far from modalism.

However, more significant than Barth's use of *seinsweise*, let alone its translation into English, is his basic model of the Trinity: "God reveals himself as the Lord," or as "revealer, revelation and revealedness," both of which imply unipersonality. His refusal to use the term

41. Bromiley, *Karl Barth*, 16, 21.
42. Barth, *CD*, I/1: 382.
43. Ibid., I/1: 360.
44. John Calvin, *Institutes of the Christian Religion*, trans. Ford Lewis Battles, ed. John T. McNeill (Philadelphia: Westminster Press, 1960), 1.13.6.
45. Barth, *CD*, I/1: 360.
46. Ibid., I/1: 360.
47. Ibid., I/1: 361.
48. Ibid., I/1: 363.

person appears to support this. Although he avoids modalism, Barth cannot be entirely exonerated from the charge of unipersonality. His obvious intention is to follow in the line of ecclesiastical orthodoxy, and his extensive exposition of the creed of Constantinople (C) proves this. But he is wedded to the Western and Augustinian model, in which the persons are problematic.

Leonard Hodgson argues that Barth's refusal to call the persons of the Trinity "persons" in the full sense of the word "seems to me to be in flat contradiction to the biblical evidence." Barth's rationale, in Hodgson's estimation, is his fear of tritheism. In turn, he is governed by rationalistic considerations rather than biblical ones, and so makes the biblical evidence conform to an *a priori* conception of unity. Hodgson concludes: "I must emphatically dissent from the judgment of his English translator who finds in his work the greatest contribution to the exposition of the doctrine of the Trinity in modern theology."[49]

Jürgen Moltmann makes some incisive criticisms of Barth at this point. He sees him as following German idealism in its interpretation of the divine *monas* as the absolute, identical subject, with God as the subject of his own being and his own revelation. Thus, with Barth, "the early church's trinitarian formula: *una substantia—tres personae* [is] now replaced by the formula: one divine subject in three different modes of being." If there is only one divine subject, Moltmann argues, then the three persons are degraded to modes of being of that one subject. It is "a late triumph for Sabellian modalism."[50] The problem is of Barth's own creation, for he has given the lordship of God precedence over the Trinity. God's essence is his sovereignty. In this way, "it is impossible to go on talking about 'three Persons,'" and the only remaining possibility is to talk about "three modes of being" in God. Moreover, "to understand God's threefold nature as eternal repetition or as holy tautology does not yet mean thinking in trinitarian terms. The doctrine of the Trinity cannot be a matter of establishing the same thing three times."[51] In this scheme, the Holy Spirit is merely the common bond of love linking the Father with the Son. There is no need for a third per-

49. Leonard Hodgson, *The Doctrine of the Trinity: Croall Lectures, 1942–1943* (London: Nisbet, 1943), 229.
50. Moltmann, *Trinity*, 139.
51. Ibid., 140–41.

son in the Trinity. The Spirit is only the unity of what is separated.[52] The principle that "God reveals himself as the Lord" means, strictly, that the Father is the one divine personality.[53] This is why Barth "argues polemically against a 'tritheism' which has never existed."[54]

On the other hand, it is impossible not to appreciate Barth's basic conservatism. On the relations of the three, he is thoroughly ortho-dox,[55] as on the appropriations (attributions of works to specific persons),[56] and also on perichoresis, where he cites John of Damascus to the effect that "the life of God would appear to be a kind of uninterrupted cycle of the three modes of being."[57] Perichoresis is, he maintains, the sum of the doctrine of *unitas in trinitate* and *trinitas in unitate*.[58] He asserts, as a direct implication, that a focus on one of the three to the detriment of the other two is forbidden.[59] Yet the distinctions are real. He clearly distinguishes the Father from the Son. There is a certain subordination there, for reconciliation is a second divine act that follows creation. Thus, the Son irreversibly follows the Father, not vice versa. This is emphatically not a distinction of being (essence), but of mode of being.[60] He has an extensive and appreciative commentary on the clauses of the creed of Constantinople (C).[61] In passing, he calls the Holy Spirit "he." He is not identical to Jesus Christ and the Son.[62] The Spirit guarantees man participation in revelation.[63] He is the communion of the Father and the Son—an obviously Augustinian comment.[64] In a similar vein, he staunchly defends the *filioque*. The Holy Spirit is not a creature, but God, differentiated from the Father and the Son, although there is no possibility of our defining the distinction between generation and procession, for only God can do so.[65]

52. Ibid., 142.
53. Ibid., 143.
54. Ibid., 144.
55. Barth, *CD*, I/1: 363–65.
56. Ibid., I/1: 373.
57. Ibid., I/1: 370.
58. Ibid., I/1: 370–71.
59. Ibid., I/1: 395.
60. Ibid., I/1: 413.
61. Ibid., I/1: 414ff.
62. Ibid., I/1: 451.
63. Ibid., I/1: 453.
64. Ibid., I/1: 469–70.
65. Ibid., I/1: 473ff.

Vestigium Trinitatis

Barth's negative attitude toward natural theology seems to preclude the possibility of *vestigium Trinitatis* (evidence of the Trinity)
being found in creation. He has some serious questions to ask of its
advocates. Only the form of the Trinity taken by God in revelation is
true, he claims.[66] This is necessary because of the inability of human
language to capture the truth of who God is. However, this provides
no grounds for pessimistic agnosticism, for revelation enters the picture. We cannot attain to God, but he has revealed himself to us. So
"it was now found for the first time, not that the language could grasp
the revelation, but that revelation . . . could grasp the language."[67]
Consequently, people did not try to explain the Trinity by the world
around them, but on the contrary "they tried to explain the world by
the Trinity in order to be able to speak about the Trinity in this world."
In short, they had confidence that the Trinity could reflect itself in
things.[68] To reason from creation to God is dangerous and also futile.
In doing so, we depart from revelation. Here Barth is of course critical of Augustine and his legacy of psychological analogies or illustrations of the Trinity.[69] God provides the true *vestigium Trinitatis*—the
twice single voice of the Father, the Son, and the Holy Spirit.[70]

A Change in the Later Barth?

Around 1936, after the publication of the first volume of the
Church Dogmatics, Barth changed his theology in some significant
ways. He foreshadowed these changes in volume I/2, acknowledging
that earlier he had given insufficient attention to the historical roots
of revelation. From then on, he declared, he would try to do justice to
the reality of John 1:14, the Word made flesh.[71] In keeping with this,
Barth thereafter paid increasing attention to Calvin and Reformed
orthodoxy, as well as the history of theology as a whole. McCormack
argues that the change came into effect with his revision of the doc-

66. Ibid., I/1: 339.
67. Ibid., I/1: 340.
68. Ibid., I/1: 341; see also II/1: 230.
69. Ibid., I/1: 343–45.
70. Ibid., I/1: 347.
71. Ibid., I/2: 50.

trine of election in 1936.[72] This differed from the change from dialectic to analogy, which Hans Urs von Balthasar saw occurring in 1931 with Barth's book on Anselm.[73]

Barth now connects God's lordship with love. God is the one who loves in freedom.[74] This opens the door to a possibility that Barth may have more room for the three persons, for love in God entails more than one personal entity. However, it still seems that there is only one divine person. Barth still affirms that "God is who he is . . . subject, predicate and object; the revealer, the act of revelation, the revealed; Father, Son and Holy Spirit." This is the same model as before. Again, he identifies God's being and God's act. The being of God is an event—the event of his action.[75] Barth insists that the definition of a person—a knowing, willing, acting "I"—can have meaning only in the person of God declared in his revelation of the one who loves and who as such is *the* person (Barth's emphasis). God alone is a person in this way. Man is a person only insofar as he becomes one by being loved by God and loving God in return. God is "the personifying person." Here it is the one essence that is the I.[76] Barth emphasizes this further by saying that "everything depends on the statement that God is the One who loves. But nothing at all depends on the statement that he is or he has personality." This is because God is not a thing, but a person, the speaking and acting subject, the original and real I. Referring to his earlier rejection of the word *person*, he claims that the Christian church has never taught that there are three persons and therefore three personalities in the sense of a threefold subject, which he says would be tritheism. God is always the One. Personality is properly ascribed only to the whole Trinity, not to the individual aspects by themselves. The one triune God is not threefold, but thrice, "and therefore the One . . . personality."[77] While Barth makes changes in his theology, some of which

72. "With the material modification of his doctrine of election in 1936, Barth's theology had arrived at a new stage of consistency with itself. Henceforth, his theology would not only be Christologically grounded in theory but in practice as well." McCormack, *Barth*, 462.

73. Von Balthasar, *Barth*, passim.

74. Barth, CD, II/1: 275, 322.

75. Ibid., II/1: 262–63.

76. Ibid., II/1: 284–85.

77. Ibid., II/1: 296–97.

are significant, Laats overstates his case by suggesting two quite different models, the first unipersonal and the second centered around an I-thou relationship,[78] for the problems of the later Barth are surprisingly similar to those of Barth in the first volume.

How Far Are There Three Persons?

We agree with Barth that the doctrine of the Trinity does not admit that the three are separate centers of self-consciousness, as the post-nineteenth-century idea of human personality understands persons. This would indeed be tritheism. Barth is right to point this out. However, his reservation of the term *person* to the one being of God is problematic. Its effect is to reduce the three to little more than divine attributes. At the very least, it creates a great deal of ambiguity. As T. A. Smail points out,

> In so far as one can understand . . . Father and Spirit, and Son and Spirit are distinct from each other as modes of being of the one God. . . . Barth does not explain further and, while it is clear that he affirms the Spirit as a hypostatically distinct mode of the divine being, the way in which he understands this distinctness remains in a certain obscurity, as it has always done in the Augustinian tradition that Barth follows very closely here. . . . His typically Western interest in the oneness of God and his tendency to see the Spirit as functionally subordinate to the Son makes this almost inevitable.[79]

For our part, we may say that the crucial point in the doctrine of the Trinity must be the effect of the Incarnation (see chapter 17). Here the Son has eternally united himself to human nature, which the Father and the Holy Spirit have not done. There is something quite different, and eternally so, about the Son when he is considered in relation to the other two. At the same time, all three in mutual indwelling exhaustively contain one another and are contained in the one being of God.

---

78. Laats, *Doctrines of the Trinity*, 68.
79. Thomas A. Smail, "The Doctrine of the Holy Spirit," in *Theology Beyond Christendom: Essays on the Centenary of the Birth of Karl Barth, May 10, 1886*, ed. John Thompson (Allison Park, Pa.: Pickwick Publications, 1986), 106.

On the other hand, there are seemingly countervailing aspects to Barth's teaching. For instance, he famously remarks that the divine essence does not exist in itself, "for Godhead, divine nature, divine essence does not exist and is not actual in and for itself."[80] What Barth means here is that the one being of God is never to be considered in itself, for God is the Father, the Son, and the Spirit. "Even Godhead exists only in and with the existence of Father, Son and Holy Ghost. . . . Only the One who is God has Godhead." There is no fourth thing in addition to the three. There is no divine remainder after the three are considered individually and together. The one who exists and is actual is "God the Father, Son and Holy Ghost."[81] Moreover, he regards the Father and the Son as distinct. In God there is both proximity and remoteness in irresolvable unity, no proximity without remoteness and no remoteness without proximity, which is why we can talk of God as love.[82] Von Balthasar goes further and suggests that this "intradivine distance between the Persons in the Trinity" is the deepest foundation of the distance between God and the creature.[83] Notwithstanding, Barth is talking here of the relations of the Father and the Son in abstract terms, which conveys the impression that the two are somewhat less than personal.

In creation, the power and wisdom of God were in the beginning specifically the power and wisdom of Jesus Christ. His existence as the Son of God the Father was in some sense the inner divine analogy and justification of creation. Passages in the NT declare that it is not only God the Father, but also the Son, Jesus Christ, who is the Creator of all things.[84] This distinction in God is mirrored in the creation of man as male and female, for "this being in differentiation and relationship" in fellowship with God is as "a copy and imitation of God," for "man is no more solitary than God." Man reflects God's image, "a copy and imitation of his Creator as such."[85] In his incarnation and all that follows, the Son is distinct from the Father. It is he and neither the Father nor the Holy Spirit who becomes flesh.[86] It is the Son who goes into

80. Barth, *CD*, IV/2: 65.
81. Ibid.
82. Ibid., II/1: 462; see II/2: 76–77, 116–17, 145, 175.
83. Von Balthasar, *Barth*, 292.
84. Barth, *CD*, III/1: 55–56.
85. Ibid., III/1: 185–86.
86. Ibid., IV/2: 42–43.

the far country and makes atonement as a substitute for us, the judge judged in our place.[87] This irreducible distinction of the Son continues, for "it is not merely that he was once 'touched with the feeling of our infirmities'; he is so still."[88]

Eternity and Time

Another element of change in the later Barth is a pronounced historicizing. This is ironic in view of many conservatives' criticism of him as prescinding from history. His commitment to the identity of God's being and act enables him to absolutize the Incarnation. Thus, God's self-revelation is exhaustively found in Christ. Divine election is *in Christ* and is not to be understood in terms of a decree by God in himself concerning man in himself.[89] The hypostatic union is from eternity, so that the Son is never considered by God apart from the humanity assumed in the Incarnation. Hence, the *logos asarkos*, the eternal Son considered apart from the flesh, is an abstraction. Barth insists, for this reason, that the NT passages that speak of the ontological connection between Christ and creation do not refer to the *logos asarkos*, the eternal preincarnate Son of God. On the other hand, the *logos asarkos* is an indispensable concept for dogmatic inquiry, and Barth does not dispense with it. He rejects it only if it leads to a Christ other than the one who is revealed. But, he argues, the NT does not speak expressly about the eternal Son or Word, but about the Jesus Christ who existed before the world was, who in the eternal sight of God had already taken on himself our human nature. Colossians 1, Hebrews 1, and John 1 speak of the incarnate Christ. From all eternity, God wanted to see and know and love his only begotten Son as the mediator—the Word incarnate. These NT passages say that the creative wisdom and power of God were in the beginning specifically the wisdom and power of Jesus Christ.[90] Thus, "the self-revelation of God as our Creator consists in the fact that in Jesus Christ he gives himself to us to be recognized as the One who has made our cause his own before it was or could be ours, who does not stand aloof from the contra-

87. Ibid., IV/1: 75, 222.
88. Ibid., IV/3: 394–95; see IV/2: 341–46.
89. Ibid., II/2, 3–506, esp. 3–194.
90. Ibid., III/1: 54–56.

diction of our being as a stranger, who has willed to bear it himself, and has in fact borne it from all eternity."[91] Following from this, "it is not merely the eternal but the incarnate Logos and therefore the man Jesus who is included in this circle." Jesus' participation in the God-head is not the dissolution, but the foundation, of his humanity. John's gospel shows that the eternal, divine Logos was this man Jesus, and this man Jesus was in the beginning with God. His participation in the divine is the basis of his humanity. He is the Son of God as he is man, and he is man as he is the Son of God.[92]

Barth's orthodox Christology points him in this direction.[93] His commitment to the classic dogma of *anhypostasia* is a case in point. This dogma, affirmed at the Second Council of Constantinople in 553, teaches that the human nature assumed by the Son in the Incarnation has no independent existence outside that union. It is often, rather unfortunately, called the doctrine of the impersonal humanity. The twin dogma of *enhypostasia*—also propounded at the same council—asserts that the personal center of the incarnate Christ is that of the Son of God, the humanity personalized by the Son, since it has no distinct existence apart from that union. By means of these dogmas, Barth can say that Jesus is a real man only as the Son of God. This is the only form his humanity takes. The concept of *enhypostasia* "is quite unavoidable." So the existence of the Son of God became and is the existence of a man.[94] As a result, in the hypostatic union the Son causes his divine existence to be the existence of the man Jesus.[95] It is also only as the Son of God that Jesus Christ also exists as man.[96] As a consequence, "what Jesus Christ does as the Son of God and in virtue of his divine essence, and what he does as the Son of Man and in exercise of his human essence, he not only does in the conjunction but in the strictest relationship of the one with the other. The divine expresses and reveals itself wholly in the sphere of the human, and the human serves and attests the divine."[97] Divine

91. Ibid., III/1: 380ff.

92. Ibid., III/2: 64–66.

93. His commitment to a human soul in the incarnate Christ, to the impersonal humanity (*anhypostasia*), to the Son of God being the subject (*enhypostasia*), and to the two wills (*dyotheletism*) are all impeccably orthodox Christological teachings.

94. Barth, CD, IV/2: 49–50; see also IV/1: 204.

95. Ibid., IV/2: 51.

96. Ibid., IV/2: 90–91.

97. Ibid., IV/2: 115–16.

and human are and remain as different as God and man, not interchangeable, the divine still above, the human below. But in Jesus Christ
they work together. So the human and divine wills in Christ (Barth's
dyotheletism is both correct and orthodox) are coincident.[98] This compatibility enables the divine person to be the subject in Christ—the dogma
of *enhypostasia*[99]—and means that we learn about God only from Christ
in the flesh.[100]

Nevertheless, Barth is also committed to the reality of the immanent (or ontological) Trinity. This is important, since many more recent
theologians dismiss the immanent Trinity as speculation, and so merge
God with human history in one cosmic process.[101] This Barth does not
do. He urges Moltmann not to shape his theology on an abstract principle of hope, but instead "to accept the doctrine of the immanent trinity."[102] God is objectively *immediate* to himself, but objectively *medi-
ate* to us.[103] He opposes Melanchthon's reduction of the doctrine of
God to the *beneficia Christi*, the benefits of salvation that Christ has
won for us.[104] His discussion of God himself as the basis of love underlines his belief that God is prior to his creation, his revelation to us,
and the reconciliation he has made.[105] After all, God loves in freedom,
and he would not be free if he were dependent on creation in some
way for his being. As Molnar remarks, for Barth "God exists eternally
as the Father, Son and Holy Spirit and would so exist even if there had
been no creation, reconciliation or redemption."[106]

Is the Holy Spirit a Person?

Before taking our leave of Barth, we note some tendencies in his
thought that point in the opposite direction from the modalism of

98. Ibid., IV/2: 166ff.
99. Ibid., IV/3: 38ff.
100. Ibid., IV/1: 177.
101. See Paul D. Molnar, *Divine Freedom and the Doctrine of the Immanent Trinity: In Dialogue with Karl Barth and Contemporary Theology* (Edinburgh: T & T Clark, 2002).
102. Karl Barth, *Letters, 1961–1968*, trans. and ed. Jürgen Fangemeier and Geoffrey W.
Bromiley (Grand Rapids: Eerdmans, 1981), 175.
103. Barth, *CD*, II/1: 16.
104. Ibid., II/1: 257–60; see also II/1: 285, 663.
105. Ibid., IV/2: 756–68.
106. Molnar, *Divine Freedom*, 63; see Barth, *CD*, II/1: 260–61.

which he has been accused. Following Augustine again, he regards the Holy Spirit as the bond of love between the Father and the Son. This at once raises the specter of a fragile unity between the Father and the Son, if it requires a third to unify them. It also has the typically Augustinian weakness of making the Spirit an attribute or a quality, rather than a person. It points to a duality rather than a trinity.

It is Barth's consistent teaching that the Holy Spirit unites different entities. "The work of the Holy Spirit . . . is to bring and hold together that which is different and therefore . . . disruptive in the relationship of Jesus Christ to his community, namely, the divine working, being and action on the one side and the human on the other." "His work is to bring and to hold them together . . . to co-ordinate them, to make them parallel, to bring them into harmony and therefore to bind them into a true unity." Thus, in the Lord's Supper the Holy Spirit brings about the church's unity with its heavenly Lord and the receiving of his body and blood.[107] Before that, the Holy Spirit is "the bond of peace" between the Father and the Son.[108] He unites the divine and the human in the incarnate Christ,[109] and constitutes and guarantees the unity in which Christ is one with God and with his earthly body.[110] He mediates between the man Jesus and other men.[111] He brings about the existence and unity of church, for he "constitutes and guarantees the unity of the *totus Christus*."[112] He unifies man as body and soul,[113] and as husband and wife in marriage.[114]

All this flows from the *filioque* and Barth's Augustinian view of the Trinity, for if the Spirit proceeds from the Father and the Son, his role is that of a mediating force between them, and so also in creation and redemption. But this role serves only to lend credence to the idea that Barth's view of God is unipersonal, since the Holy Spirit is reduced merely to the love between the Father and the Son. At the same time, it implies a distance between the Father and the Son, if a third force is needed to secure a unity that would otherwise not be there. This is also

107. Barth, *CD*, IV/3: 761.
108. Ibid., IV/3: 760.
109. Ibid., III/2: 193ff.
110. Ibid., IV/3: 760–62.
111. Ibid., IV/2: 343.
112. Ibid., IV/3: 760.
113. Ibid., III/2: 354.
114. Ibid., IV/2: 746ff.; see also III/4: 184.

Moltmann's criticism. He states that "the Spirit is merely the common bond of love linking the Father with the Son . . . [so] there is no need for a third person in the trinity. . . . [T]he Spirit is only the unity of what is separated. The reflection trinity of absolute subject is a duality."[115] He believes that this persistent Western point, handed down from Augustine, "contradicts the tradition in which the Spirit is the third person of the trinity, not merely the correlation of the other two persons." Barth's principle, "God reveals himself as the Lord," means, strictly speaking, that the Father is the one divine personality.[116] So we are back where we began.

Williams agrees, observing that "Barth seems to be saying that, although no 'person' of the Trinity is an independent centre of consciousness in the modern sense, yet the Father and the Son more nearly approximate to it than does the Spirit." Again, "If the Spirit is the communion or love between Father and Son, the implication is that there are two subjects and one 'operation' or, perhaps, 'quality' involved." Williams concludes that, for Barth, the Trinity is a society of two, not three.[117] While he admits that Barth is more pluralist in IV/1 than in I/1,[118] nevertheless "problems begin to appear in Barth's Trinitarian scheme when the controlling model of revelation or self-interpretation proves difficult to apply to a theology of the Holy Spirit." What Williams calls the "linear model," evident as early as I/1, is of no help at all. "Not very much sense can be made of 'modes' relating to each other in love." This becomes even more serious when we consider the Cross.[119] As for Barth's comparison of the Trinity as unity in distinction to man as male and female, it would be odd to consider human persons as simply 'modes' of being.[120]

Ambiguous Opposition to Modalism

Barth continues to oppose modalism at every opportunity. The theme of proximity and remoteness underlines this.[121] He talks of God

115. Moltmann, *Trinity*, 142.
116. Ibid., 143.
117. Williams, "Barth," 170–71.
118. Ibid., 175.
119. Ibid., 181.
120. Barth, *CD*, III/2: 64, 246–48, 274ff.; IV/2: 343.
121. Ibid., II/1: 462.

as one "even in the distinctions of the divine persons of the Father, the Son and the Holy Spirit," and insists that the divine simplicity must be understood in the context of the Trinity and Christology.[122] In fact, God is eternally the Father, eternally the Son, and eternally the Spirit, and due recognition must be given to the inner movement of the begetting by the Father, the being begotten of the Son, and the procession of the Holy Spirit from both.[123] Barth certainly does not consider himself to be a modalist. This is clear again when he firmly opposes any refusal to see that God's self-revelation grants us access to God himself. "For if in his proper being as God God can only be unworldly, if he can be the humiliated and lowly and obedient One only in a mode of appearance and not in his proper being, what is the value of the true deity of Christ?"[124] Yet he continues to repeat his earlier refrain that in God there is but one subject, not three, "the one God in self-repetition . . . in three different modes the one personal God."[125] There is this persistent ambiguity at the heart of Barth's Trinitarianism that does not change. If he is not modalistic, he will escape from the charge of unipersonality only with the greatest difficulty.

There is another glaring unresolved question. As we saw, Barth's consideration of the Father and the Son in terms of proximity and remoteness requires the Holy Spirit to unite them. Thompson points to another problem here, that thinking of them in isolation from the Spirit is an abstraction.[126] It also suggests a lack of union between the Father and the Son that flies in the face of the doctrine of perichoresis that Barth affirms in I/1. Smail offers some sustained criticism along these lines. Barth's defense of the *filioque* leads him to see the Holy Spirit as dependent on the Son in a one-way relation, and so, Smail contends, he misses the complexity and reciprocity that the NT presents.[127] As a result, he fails to give sufficient weight to the priority of the Father as the *fons et origo totius divinitatis* (source and origin of the whole divinity). Barth rejects this two-way relation on the grounds that it applies only to Christ's humanity. But, as Smail argues, "if what

122. Ibid., II/1: 445.
123. Ibid., II/1: 615.
124. Ibid., IV/1: 196–97.
125. Ibid., IV/1: 205.
126. John Thompson, "On the Trinity," in *Theology Beyond Christendom*, ed. Thompson, 30.
127. Smail, "Holy Spirit," 106ff.

happens to the human Christ has no reference to the eternal Son, Barth's whole doctrine of revelation is attacked at its heart." He should have paid more attention to the baptism of Jesus. The Western doctrine of the *filioque* leads to a depression of the role and the person of the Spirit in relation to the Son, and pneumatology merges into Christology.[128]

In this chapter, we may have given the impression that we are going around in circles, often returning to the same themes, but from a slightly different angle. In this, we are actually faithful to Barth himself, who adopts a spiral method in his *Church Dogmatics*, constantly circling around the central themes.

128. Ibid., 108.

Rahner, Moltmann, and Pannenberg

Karl Rahner

Karl Rahner (1904–1984), one of the most prominent Roman Catholic theologians of the twentieth century, played a leading role in theological discussion following Vatican II. Soon after the council ended in 1967, he wrote *The Trinity*. There he describes the current state of affairs—"We must be willing to admit that, should the doctrine of the Trinity have to be dropped as false, the major part of religious literature could well remain virtually unchanged."[1] As Catherine LaCugna recognizes in her introduction to the 1997 English edition, it is to Rahner himself that credit is due that this is no longer the case. In this book, Rahner attempts to answer a number of important questions. He operates within the Western paradigm followed by the Roman Catholic magisterium, but critically so. He is interested in the distinctiveness of the three and is open, in a way that Barth was not, to the insights of the East.

The Identity of the Economic Trinity and the Immanent Trinity

Rahner probes the relationship between the Trinity and the Incarnation. After Augustine, in contrast to the older tradition, it was assumed by theologians in the West that any person of the Trinity could have become incarnate.[2] This is mirrored by the common perception

---

1. Karl Rahner, *The Trinity*, trans. Joseph Donceel (New York: Crossroad, 1997), 10–11.
2. But see our discussion of Anselm (chapter 11), who argues otherwise.

that God in a general sense became man. If that were so, Rahner insists, the incarnation of the Son would tell us nothing distinctive about the Son himself.[3] Instead, he argues that salvation comes from the incarnate Word, not simply from the God-man. It is precisely and particularly the Son (not God in general) who became man.[4] The separation of discussion of the one God from the Trinity, *de rigeur* since Aquinas, helped foster this misconception and so caused a blur in the collective consciousness of the distinctions among the three.[5] This leads Rahner to the heart of his argument, the axiomatic unity of the economic Trinity and the immanent Trinity.[6] The basic thesis that establishes that the Trinity is a mystery of salvation and not simply a doctrine is that "*The 'economic' Trinity is the 'immanent' Trinity and the 'immanent' Trinity is the 'economic' Trinity.*"[7] This entails the unity of the Trinity with the history of salvation and will root it in the experience of that history recorded in the Bible. The distinctiveness of Jesus Christ the Son and of the Holy Spirit in our salvation reflects real distinctions.

Rahner elaborates this thesis with reference to the Incarnation. Jesus is God the Son, and so there is at least one mission that is not simply appropriated to the Son, "but is proper to him." This is not just a work of the Trinity that is especially the part of the Son, but in which the other two share. Rather, this is something that belongs to the Logos alone, which can be predicated of one person only.[8] It is unique, and is not an example of a general situation or principle, as if there are many more or less equally relevant examples of which the Incarnation is merely a more pronounced or heightened type.[9] It cannot be demonstrated that any person of the Trinity could have become incarnate and, furthermore, it is false to claim that they could.[10] If any person could have become incarnate, there would be no connection between the missions and the intra-Trinitarian life, and so "that which God is for us would tell us absolutely nothing about that which he is in himself, as triune." So "we cling to the truth that the Logos is really as he appears

3. Rahner, *Trinity*, 11.
4. Ibid., 12.
5. Ibid., 15–21.
6. Ibid., 21ff.
7. Ibid., 22.
8. Ibid., 23.
9. Ibid., 24–28.
10. Ibid., 28–30.

in revelation, that he is *the one* who reveals to us (not merely *one* of those who might have revealed to us) the triune God."[11] Rahner does not mean to deny that the Father and the Spirit share in their distinctive ways in the Incarnation, or to question that the work of the Trinity is indivisible. What he means is that it is only the Son who actually became man, and that this is the way it had to be. Rahner goes on to apply the dogmas of *anhypostasia* and *enhypostasia* to the question, concluding that the Logos reveals himself in and through his humanity.[12] Thus, "each one of the three divine persons communicates himself to man in gratuitous grace in his own personal particularity and diversity."[13] The self-communication of God has a threefold aspect.[14] Economic Sabellianism is false.[15] So we may seek access to the Trinity through Jesus and his Spirit as we experience them through faith in salvation history. In these two persons, the immanent Trinity is already given. The Trinity is not merely a doctrine—it is rooted in experience. The reality of which they speak is bestowed upon us.[16]

Rahner shows a more positive appreciation for the Eastern approach than Barth. He also wants to follow the biblical order of events.[17] However, like Barth, he sees the biggest danger as tritheism, not modalism.[18] This is a clue to the problems that he will run into himself. He shares Barth's reservations about the term *person*; however, he concedes that there is no better word, and so he uses it, with appropriate qualifications. However, he does not begin with the persons, but with the one God.[19] The element of consciousness inherent in the modern concept of person is not part of the classic teaching or the dogma of the magisterium.[20] There is in God only one power and will and outward activity, and the idea of three subjectivities must be kept away from the concept of person in the current context.[21] When

11. Ibid., 30.
12. Ibid., 31–33.
13. Ibid., 34–35.
14. Ibid., 36.
15. Ibid., 38.
16. Ibid., 39.
17. Ibid., 40–42.
18. Ibid., 43.
19. Ibid., 44; see also 56–57.
20. Ibid., 75.
21. Ibid., 75–76.

an activity is appropriated to one person, it is also implicitly attributed to the other two, but this does not imply that God's outward relations can exist only in a way that is common to all three persons.[22] The understanding of the immanent Trinity comes by way of the economic Trinity.[23] It follows that the Father, Son, and Holy Spirit are identical with the one Godhead, but relatively distinct from one another.[24]

God's Self-Communication and the Identity of the Three Persons

Therefore, the economic Trinity discloses two distinct, yet related, ways of God's self-communication, by Jesus Christ and by the Spirit. These are two "moments" of the one self-communication of God.[25] Gunton, cited by Molnar, comments that this term has overtones of emanation.[26] There follows a lengthy and rather obscure discussion of what this self-communication is, under four pairs of concepts: origin-future, history-transcendence, invitation-acceptance, and knowledge-love. It seems to me that Rahner falls into the same trap as Barth. When the term *person* is rejected or heavily qualified, one ends up with abstractions that are less than personal. Rahner evidently wants to embrace some Eastern insights and is critical of Western leanings, but he is unable to break free. As LaCugna says,

> Rahner's theology is an anthropology based on the idea that the structure of the human person in some essential way corresponds to or is an image of God's own being. The quadriform that Rahner composes to describe the economy has an explicit twofoldness that resembles the two activities of knowing and loving: origin-future, history-transcendence, invitation-acceptance, knowledge-love. By the end of this work, Rahner's criticisms of Augustine are rather muted.[27]

22. Ibid., 76–77.
23. Ibid., 65–66.
24. Ibid., 72.
25. Ibid., 83–85.
26. Paul D. Molnar, *Divine Freedom and the Doctrine of the Immanent Trinity: In Dialogue with Karl Barth and Contemporary Theology* (Edinburgh: T & T Clark, 2002), 85.
27. Catherine Mowry LaCugna, *God for Us: The Trinity and Christian Life* (San Francisco: Harper, 1991), 109.

This is painfully clear when he eventually tries to arrive at some conclusions about the identity of the three. He argues that the term "person" is not absolutely constitutive of our knowledge of the Father, Son, and Holy Spirit. "It attempts to generalize once more that which is absolutely unique."[28] He is right in this—Augustine and others have recognized the weakness of human language. We remember also the tortuous struggles in the fourth century over terminology. So, Rahner continues, we may not speak of three persons as we do elsewhere. The three are not a "group-building multiplication of the essence nor an 'equality' of the personality of the three persons."[29] We must instead return to the original experience of salvation history. There are not three spiritual centers of activity or subjectivities in God. Rather, one consciousness subsists in a threefold way.[30] What would an explanatory concept be that explains and correctly interprets the concept of "person"? Rahner comes up with this: "The one God subsists in three distinct manners of subsisting."[31] Any one person, then, would be "God as existing and meeting us in this determined distinct manner of subsisting. . . . This-there is what subsists."[32]

This nonsensical phrase graphically emphasizes the impersonal consequences of abandoning the word "person." Rahner recognizes difficulties with this definition, but suggests that it expresses the unity of God in a way that "person" nowadays cannot do.[33] His bogeyman is tritheism, but this is a bogus threat, and he seems less aware of the more pressing danger of modalism. To be fair, he intends by "distinct manner of subsisting" to say the same thing as "person" formerly did, and he agrees that we should not give up the classic term. He intends only for his proposal to be used as an explanatory tool.[34]

Problems with Rahner's Trinitarianism

The question remains as to how three "distinct manners of subsisting" can love each other. Attempts to improve on the word *person*

28. Rahner, *Trinity*, 104.
29. Ibid., 105.
30. Ibid., 106–7.
31. Ibid., 109.
32. Ibid., 110.
33. Ibid., 111.
34. Ibid., 115.

lead inexorably to a less than personal conclusion. In turn, this undercuts any connection with human persons, made in the image of God.
Is Rahner himself, and are you, the reader, a "distinct manner of subsisting"? What does that mean? Is it any clearer? Could not the phrase
"divine persons" be used with a corresponding explanation of how
they are different from human persons? Rahner makes a heroic effort
to do justice to the problem within the bounds of church dogma. However, he veers toward modalism.

On the other hand, Rahner is extremely suggestive on the uniqueness of the Son and the Incarnation. His main thesis, connecting and
identifying the economic Trinity with the immanent Trinity, is vital
when appropriately understood and applied. If the axiom is held to
reflect the fact that God's self-revelation as triune in the work of creation, providence, and grace is a true revelation of who he is eternally,
then it expresses a truth at the heart of the Christian faith. It points to
the faithfulness of God. It demonstrates that there is only one Trinity.
God is free and did not need to create us, nor to make himself known
to us. But, having chosen to do so, his own faithfulness requires that
he reveal himself in a manner that reflects who he is. A bifurcation
between the economic Trinity and the immanent Trinity undermines
our knowledge of God. Our salvation depends on God's revelation of
himself in the history of salvation being true and faithful to who he is
in himself. But is this what Rahner means by his axiom? Or is he instead
using it to avoid considering the immanent Trinity? Does this not absolutize history and time, leading toward pantheism, where God is
dependent on his creation?

Here we note Colin Gunton's criticism of Rahner's Christology
for approaching the person of Christ by means of a transcendent
anthropology.[35] His is a Christology "from below," based on the
human life of Jesus, on his supreme human qualities. The result, Gunton concludes, is a Christ who is not quite God and not quite man.
Here Rahner suggests either that the humanity of the Logos is "precisely that which comes into being when the Logos expresses himself
into the non-divine," or that human nature should ultimately be
explained "through the self-emptying self-utterance of the Logos him-

---

35. Colin E. Gunton, *Yesterday and Today: A Study of Continuities in Christology* (Grand
Rapids: Eerdmans, 1983), 11–15.

self."[36] This appears to be a blurring of the Logos, the humanity of the Logos, and humanity in general. The general drift is in the direction of modalism and pantheism. This is in keeping with the thrust of Rahner's theology. Molnar argues that Rahner begins with the premise that knowledge of God comes through our experience, rather than from God's free self-manifestation.[37] Our experience of our own limits and of transcendence is then inseparable from our knowledge of God.[38] From this comes Rahner's reliance on the four polarities mentioned above (origin-future, history-transcendence, invitation-acceptance, knowledge-love). The result is the merger of universal human experience with revelation, and so a powerful tendency to make God part of creation. Rahner indeed says that God willed to become non-God, and so remains as man forever, so that "all theology is therefore eternally an anthropology," and man is "the articulate mystery of God."[39] The end product of the axiom, as used by Rahner and particularly by those influenced by it, is that talk of the immanent Trinity is a mirage, and that all is reduced to human history and human experience. This is particularly noticeable in other works by Rahner.[40] In Molnar's words, "As long as it is thought that our self-transcending experiences provide a point of departure for knowing the true God, Christian theologians will always have difficulty actually distinguishing God from their ideas about God."[41] The fourfold schematism of God's self-communication expounded in *The Trinity* entails that universal human experience gives us access to the Trinity. This follows whenever abstractions are used in preference to God's own identity as the Father, the Son, and the Holy Spirit. The result is close to pantheism—and Gordon Kaufmann, Robert Jenson, Jürgen Moltmann, various feminists such as Catherine LaCugna and Elizabeth Johnson, and others travel to varying extents along the route charted by Rahner. As Molnar points out, this is very different from

36. Rahner, *Trinity*, 31.
37. Molnar, *Divine Freedom*, 85–86.
38. Ibid., 85–92.
39. Karl Rahner, *Theological Investigations*, vol. 4, *More Recent Writings*, trans. Kevin Smyth (Baltimore: Helicon Press, 1966), 116.
40. Karl Rahner, *Foundations of Christian Faith: An Introduction to the Idea of Christianity*, trans. William V. Dych (New York: Seabury Press, 1978), 44–55; Rahner, *Theological Investigations*, 4:41–65.
41. Molnar, *Divine Freedom*, 85.

the road Barth used. It goes astray by neglecting or rejecting the immanent Trinity. For Barth, God is prior to creation, which is something
he freely determined to bring into existence. Thus, our experience is
determined by God's free, sovereign revelation. With Rahner, since
human experience is the yardstick, situated in history, the immanent
Trinity is collapsed into the economic Trinity, which in turn is founded
on the human experience of limits and transcendence. History is absolutized and general human experience is the basis for an understanding of God.[42] Either a monistic modalism or a social doctrine of the
Trinity that veers into tritheism follows. In turn, this merges the Creator and the creature into one cosmic process. God is as dependent
on the world as the world is on God. The result is pantheism or panentheism. This is seen in Catherine LaCugna, one of the many who have
been influenced by Rahner. Molnar cites her as arguing—and this is
central to her thesis in *God for Us*—that "economy and theology are
two aspects of *one* reality: the mystery of divine-human communion,"
[43] and again, "The doctrine of the Trinity is not ultimately a teaching
about 'God' but a teaching about *God's life with us and our life with
each other.*"[44]

Jürgen Moltmann

In *The Crucified God*, first published in 1973, Jürgen Moltmann
(1928–) focuses on a dialectical interpretation of the cross and resurrection of Jesus. He places this in the framework of the doctrine of the Trinity. At the heart of his argument is the statement that "the theology of
the cross must be the doctrine of the Trinity and the doctrine of the Trinity must be the theology of the cross."[45] The Cross was an event between
Jesus and the Father, and to understand it we must approach it in Trinitarian terms. "The Son suffers dying, the Father suffers the death of the

42. Ibid., 1–25. Molnar presents a thorough and penetrating exposition of the importance
of the doctrine of the immanent Trinity, together with a devastating exposure of the weaknesses
of Rahner's approach and of those who take his axiom further along the road toward pantheism and panentheism. It is essential reading for anyone interested in exploring contemporary
Trinitarian theology.

43. LaCugna, *God for Us*, 222.

44. Ibid., 228.

45. Jürgen Moltmann, *The Crucified God: The Cross of Christ as the Foundation and Criticism of Christian Theology* (Minneapolis: Fortress Press, 1993), 241.

Son . . . the Fatherlessness of the Son is matched by the Sonlessness of the Father. . . . God . . . suffers the death of his Fatherhood in the death of the Son."[46] This event contains community between Jesus and the Father in separation, and separation in community. The Father and the Son are deeply separated, and John the evangelist sees the very existence of God in this event of love. What proceeds from this event is the Spirit, which justifies the godless and includes them in the death in God.[47] In short, God is known in his identification with the godless and godforsaken, as he in death suffers in love. The impact of Hegel's dialectic is unmistakable. The Cross is a dialectical event in which God identifies with what contradicts him in order to overcome the contradiction in suffering love. "The Trinity is therefore a dialectical historical process."[48]

Throughout, Moltmann correlates God and the world. With strong echoes of Hegel, he follows and further develops Rahner's axiom. God experiences a history with the world, both affecting the world and being affected by the world.[49] This is clear in his Trinitarian approach to the Cross, but it is pervasive throughout his entire theology. In close connection with this is his eschatology, especially from his early work, *Theology of Hope*.[50] This is a direction to the future, to the kingdom of God. It entails, meanwhile, a continuous process of change. This future-directed hope is based on the resurrection of Jesus Christ and takes the form of promise, contradicting and counteracting our present experience of suffering and abandonment. Hegel's impact is again clear, in the overcoming of the antithesis of suffering by the synthesis of the promise.

Meanwhile, God identifies with the world in its suffering. The Cross is the event of divine love. It demonstrates God's own nature as suffering love. In Bauckham's words, "The cross does not solve the problem of suffering, but meets it with the voluntary fellow-suffering of love."[51] This is not simply a choice that God makes; it is a need he

---

46. Ibid., 243.

47. Ibid., 244.

48. Richard Bauckham, *The Theology of Jürgen Moltmann* (Edinburgh: T & T Clark, 1995), 155.

49. Ibid., 6, 173–74.

50. Jürgen Moltmann, *Theology of Hope: On the Ground and the Implications of a Christian Eschatology*, trans. James W. Leitch (London: SCM, 1967).

51. Bauckham, *Moltmann*, 12.

has, for his very being is love, and love must suffer.[52] God's Trinitarian history is intertwined with, and utterly inseparable from, the history of the world, and so is a history of fellow suffering.[53]

In turn, Moltmann has a pronounced orientation toward political theology. Since God is suffering love, suffering in solidarity with the oppressed, Moltmann has a predilection for political movements that he believes express this concern. In the 1960s, Marxism appealed to him with "its vision of a new society of freedom." More recently Moltmann has stressed human rights, founded on the created dignity of human beings and the eschatological destiny of humanity as the image of God.[54] I will contend that his theological conclusions match his political acumen.

Reciprocal Relationship with the World

For Moltmann, God has a reciprocal relationship with the world in which "his love for the world not only affects the world but is affected by it." The Trinitarian history of the world is a real history for God, as well as for the world.[55] This is a clear consequence of the path trod by Rahner. As Moltmann himself puts it, "God 'needs' the world and man. If God is love, then he neither will nor can be without the one who is his beloved."[56] The Creator has to make the space in which creation can exist. He must take time for the creation and allow it freedom.[57] He creates the world *ex nihilo*, but by this Moltmann does not mean the classic Christian belief that God brought the universe into existence out of nothing, but rather that he concedes a primordial space through his self-limitation, a nothingness to which he exposes himself, a godforsakenness which he pervades with his presence, and it is out of this nothingness that he creates the world.[58] Borrowing the language of Isaac Luria, Moltmann describes this as "made

52. Jürgen Moltmann, *The Trinity and the Kingdom: The Doctrine of God* (London: SCM, 1991), 32ff.; Jürgen Moltmann, *God in Creation: A New Theology of Creation and the Spirit of God* (San Francisco: HarperSanFrancisco, 1991), 108ff.; Molnar, *Divine Freedom*, 200.

53. Bauckham, *Moltmann*, 13.

54. Ibid., 18–19.

55. Ibid., 15.

56. Moltmann, *Trinity*, 58.

57. Ibid., 59.

58. Moltmann, *God in Creation*, 89–91.

possible through a shrinkage process in God."[59] Thereupon, the history of God is the history of the world. God and creation are bound together in a process in which they are both reciprocally related, utterly correlative. This is what underlies *The Crucified God*. The Cross is central to the Trinity. It determines the life of God. Historical events determine God's being. The economic Trinity not merely reveals the immanent Trinity, but determines it retroactively.[60]

Panentheism

It follows that God is subject to necessity. Bound together with the creation, the latter is a necessary outflow of his being. The result is unmistakable panentheism. Following the early twentieth-century Anglican, C. E. Rolt, Moltmann argues:

> Through his understanding of God's self-love as his self-sacrifice, Rolt's trinitarian interpretation of God's eternal self-love leads to a doctrine of the Trinity which is open to the world. Love has to give, for it is only in the act of giving that it truly possesses, and finds bliss. That is why God has to give himself; and he cannot possess himself apart from this act of serving. God has to give himself completely; and it is only in this way that he is God. He has to go through time; and it is only in this way that he is eternal. He has to run his full course on earth as servant; and it is only in this way that he is Lord of heaven. He has to be man and nothing but man; and it is only in this way that he is completely God. So God's divinity is not cut off from his humanity, and his humanity is not cut off from his divinity: "It was necessary for God to be Man, for only so could he be truly God."[61]

Molnar contends that this pantheism and emanationism is essential to Moltmann's doctrine of creation and the Trinity.[62] Moltmann's thesis is that creation is an overflow of the love that is God's own being. The eternal generation of the Son and the creation of the world are both nec-

59. Moltmann, *Trinity*, 109.
60. Ibid., 160–61; Roger Olson, "Trinity and Eschatology: The Historical Being of God in Jürgen Moltmann and Wolfhart Pannenberg," *SJT* 36 (1983): 217–18.
61. Moltmann, *Trinity*, 33.
62. Molnar, *Divine Freedom*, 220.

essary acts. They are also simultaneous acts. He cites Meister Eckhart
approvingly to the effect that the Father brings forth the Son in the soul
in the same way he does in eternity.[63] However, as Molnar points out,
Eckhart was condemned for his views in 1329. He argued that God created the world at the same time as he generated the Son. This was rejected
on the grounds that to make creation coeternal with the Son was a denial
of the Christian doctrine of creation *ex nihilo*.[64] Molnar is correct in
arguing, against Moltmann, that to say as he does that God *must* create to be true to himself, means that there is no distinction between God's
self-sufficient love as the Father, Son, and Holy Spirit and his free will
to create a world distinct from himself. Instead, for Moltmann, creation
is inherent in the Father's necessary love for the Son.[65] In turn, the suffering of the Holy Spirit is identical to the world's suffering, while the
Holy Spirit is identical with the cosmic spirit. God and creation are not
identical. Everything is not God. But God is everything.[66] Or again, "An
ecological doctrine of creation implies a new kind of thinking about
God. The centre of this thinking is no longer the distinction between
God and the world. The centre is the recognition of the presence of God
in the world and the presence of the world *in* God."[67] Thus there is no
need for a doctrine of the immanent Trinity since, with this emanation-
ist view of creation, God needs the creatures and does not exist without
them.[68] Hence, "All created things are individuations of the community
of creation and manifestations of the divine Spirit."[69] When we consider
"the evolution of the cosmos and of life from the contingency of events,
dynamic pantheism seems much more plausible" than theism, which
distinguishes between God and the world.[70] The Trinitarian concept of
creation that Moltmann is advocating "integrates the elements of truth
in monotheism and pantheism." It will seek to integrate God and nature
into the same vista.[71]

63. Moltmann, *Trinity*, 236.
64. Molnar, *Divine Freedom*, 210ff.
65. Ibid., 213–14.
66. Moltmann, *God in Creation*, 102–3.
67. Ibid., 13.
68. Molnar, *Divine Freedom*, 231.
69. Moltmann, *God in Creation*, 100.
70. Ibid., 212.
71. Ibid., 98.

Divine Passibility

Moltmann's early stress on the crucified God, in which the doctrine of the Trinity is the theological interpretation of the history of Jesus, with the Cross being an event between the Father and the Son, both exhibits and demands a doctrine of divine passibility (God's capacity to suffer). This is in opposition to the classic doctrine of divine impassibility (the doctrine that God cannot suffer). For Moltmann, suffering is not only not alien to God, but indeed defines who he is. "A God who cannot suffer cannot love either. A God who cannot love is a dead God."[72] Since he is love, and love cannot be without suffering, it follows that God himself is quintessentially suffering love. This is played out, of course, in history, which is at the same time Trinitarian history. Since suffering is integral to God, and is the principle that encompasses God's being, he cannot overcome it.[73] He is powerless to change it, for his power consists in suffering in love.

Recently, Thomas Weinandy has carefully exploded this spurious and debilitating idea, accepted without question by so many for the last generation or so, that God himself suffers. Weinandy's treatment of the question is masterful. Carefully, step by step, with meticulous precision and careful scholarship, he demolishes the theological consensus that has argued, in Bonhoeffer's memorable phrase, that "only a suffering God can help" in the face of atrocities and the devastation of human suffering. This he does by a thorough investigation of the classic Christian tradition and equally secure biblical and theological argument.

God, who is sovereign over creation, acts within creation to reveal himself as over creation. Only a God who *cannot* suffer can help us. For it is through the Incarnation, in which the Son lives *as man*, that he experiences human suffering *as man* and deals with the root cause—sin—by his death and resurrection. It would be of no help to us if God suffered divinely as God. On the one hand, he would be unable to help us, for he would be at the mercy of hostile forces in his creation. On the other hand, he would have no capacity to understand or deal with *human* suffering. Precisely because he does

---

72. Moltmann, *Trinity*, 38.
73. Molnar, *Divine Freedom*, 203.

not and cannot suffer as God, he is able (through the Incarnation) to suffer *in a human way* and, having made atonement for sin (the cause of human suffering), to bring about its ultimate removal. To turn Bonhoeffer on his head, only the God who as God cannot suffer, can help and so put love into action.[74]

Correlation of God with Human Experience

Moltmann's correlation of God and the world, his panentheism, goes hand in hand with his abandonment of the traditional distinction between the immanent Trinity and the economic Trinity. Here he follows Rahner and takes him a stage or two further.[75] Since God is intertwined with the creation, he changes. His relationships with the world change as he suffers, and his relationships in himself also undergo change. Thus, we can adopt only a narrative form as a history of God's changing Trinitarian relationships in himself and simultaneously with the world. Indeed, our experience of love and thus of ourselves is the same as our experience of God.[76]

Moltmann comes close to identifying the creation with the Trinity at this point. Indeed, he does identify our experience with experience of the Trinity as such:

> [A person] perceives that the history of the world is the history of God's suffering. At the moments of God's profoundest revelation there is always suffering. . . . If a person once feels the infinite passion of God's love which finds expression here, then he understands the mystery of the triune God. God suffers with us—God suffers from us—God suffers for us: it is this experience of God that reveals the triune God. It has to be understood, and can only be understood, in trinitarian terms. Consequently, fundamental theology's discussion about access to the doctrine of the Trinity is carried on today in the context of the question about God's capacity or incapacity for suffering.[77]

74. Thomas G. Weinandy, *Does God Suffer?* (Notre Dame, Ind.: University of Notre Dame Press, 2000).

75. Bauckham, *Moltmann*, 16, 155–56; Molnar, *Divine Freedom*, 198–99; Moltmann, *Trinity*, 151ff.

76. Bauckham, *Moltmann*, 159.

77. Moltmann, *Trinity*, 4–5.

Molnar sees this as a direct outflow of Moltmann's emanationism and panentheism.[78] According to Bauckham, Moltmann makes the same mistake as Hegel—that of making world history the process by which God realizes himself.[79]

Mutual Reciprocity among the Persons of the Trinity

Bauckham points out that Moltmann's understanding of God "could be said to hinge on a concept of dynamic relationality." The Trinity is "three divine subjects in mutual loving relationship."[80] Moltmann, over the course of his career, has developed a social doctrine of the Trinity, in stark contrast to Barth and the Western tradition. Instead of a single divine subject in three modes—or ways—of being, for Moltmann the three divine persons are three subjects in relationship to one another.

There is no fixed order between the three, for their "relationship" (the word consistently used in English translation) is that of mutual, reciprocal love in freedom. There is emphatically no subordination. The three exist in "trinitarian fellowship."[81] This follows Moltmann's complete rejection of lordship and authority. As Bauckham observes, "His disagreement with Barth [is] pivotal."[82] Whereas Barth placed lordship at the heart of his doctrine of God, Moltmann wants to banish it from view entirely. Thus, the unity of God is a "unity of persons in relationship," open to include the world within itself, with the ultimate goal of uniting all things with God, "a trinitarian and eschatological panentheism."[83] In contrast to "monotheism," which holds to the lordship of God Almighty, Trinitarianism "grounds relationships of freedom and equality." Moltmann quotes a thinker who profoundly influenced him, the Marxist Ernst Bloch: "Where the great Lord of the universe reigns, there is no room for liberty."[84] This view of a changing set of mutual, reciprocal relationships between three divine subjects in a Trinitarian fellowship raises the question of tritheism, which we will consider in a moment, and also opens the door for a feminist understanding of the Trinity.

78. Molnar, *Divine Freedom*, 218.
79. Bauckham, *Moltmann*, 25.
80. Ibid., 15.
81. Ibid., 16, 162.
82. Ibid., 173; see also 176; Molnar, *Divine Freedom*, 199.
83. Bauckham, *Moltmann*, 17.
84. Moltmann, *Trinity*, 203.

So important is the concept of relationality for Moltmann, that Molnar concludes that for him "relationality is the subject and God is the predicate instead of the other way round."[85] Thus, in direct opposition to Barth, "God reveals his Son. . . . God does not reveal 'himself.' He reveals 'his Son.' The Son is not identical with God's self. He is a subject of his own."[86] God is not a single identical subject, as Barth taught. God has open Trinitarian relationships of fellowship. There is an eternal perichoresis of Father, Son, and Holy Spirit. It corresponds "to a human fellowship of people without privileges and without subordinances."[87] Thus, the Spirit is "an independent subject," along with "the divine subjects of the Father and the Son."[88]

Unbridled Speculation

Bauckham accuses Moltmann of undisciplined speculation and hermeneutical irresponsibility in his later work.[89] He constantly refers to biblical texts without any exegesis to support his use of them. One example will suffice. In asserting his view of Christ's abandonment on the cross, he cites Hebrews 2:9, "when it says χωρὶς θεοῦ—far from God or, perhaps better, without God 'he tasted death for us all.'"[90] In his footnote, he refers to O. Michel, who favors this reading over the normally accepted χάριτι θεοῦ (by the grace of God) on the grounds that the latter was a substitution and correction.[91] However, while Moltmann's preferred reading has a range of Fathers to support it, the manuscript attestation for χάριτι θεοῦ is far superior, including p[46], ℵ, B, C, and D. The variant was probably inserted to ensure that θεὸς was excluded from the things subjected to man in the citation of Psalm 8 in verses 5–8.[92] Moltmann simply avoids this question and presents his position as if it were unassailable.

85. Molnar, *Divine Freedom*, 227.
86. Moltmann, *Trinity*, 86.
87. Ibid., 156–57.
88. Moltmann, *God in Creation*, 97.
89. Bauckham, *Moltmann*, 167.
90. Moltmann, *Trinity*, 78.
91. Ibid., 233.
92. Bruce M. Metzger, *A Textual Commentary on the Greek New Testament* (London: United Bible Societies, 1971), 664.

More to the point is Moltmann's "pseudo-biological" idea[93] about God the Father as the "motherly father." On the basis of a gratuitous and unsubstantiated assertion, Moltmann says that if the Son proceeds from the Father, this entails not only a begetting but a birth, and thus the Father "is a motherly father too. He is no longer defined in unisexual, patriarchal terms but . . . bisexually or transexually. He is to be understood as the motherly Father of the only Son he has brought forth, and at the same time as the fatherly Mother of his only begotten Son."[94] In support of this bizarre and self-evidently unbiblical speculation, Moltmann cites the Council of Toledo (675), which spoke of the Son as "begotten or born out of the Father's womb."[95] Here he is elevating a rare metaphorical allusion in a nonecumenical council, a *theologoumenon*, to the level of doctrine. Besides the fact that the Bible does not depict God as a sexual being, and that references to the Father are not to be understood in terms of sexuality, Jesus did not pray to a transexual Father. Enough said.

Moltmann also frequently uses the concept of perichoresis. However, whereas John of Damascus used the term to refer to the mutual indwelling of the three persons in God, which precludes natural knowledge, with Moltmann it becomes a principle applicable right across the board. He argues that "all relationships which are analogous to God reflect the primal, reciprocal indwelling and mutual interpenetration of the trinitarian perichoresis," and concludes that "it is this trinitarian concept of life as interpenetration or perichoresis which will therefore determine this ecological doctrine of creation."[96] Once again, this is pure speculation.

Tritheism?

Molnar cites a number of scholars who accuse Moltmann of tritheism, including George Hunsinger, who responds to Moltmann's claim that there has never been a Christian tritheist by saying that "one can only conclude that Moltmann is vying to be the first. . . . *The Trinity and the Kingdom* is about the closest thing to tritheism that any of us

---

93. Bauckham, *Moltmann*, 169.
94. Moltmann, *Trinity*, 164.
95. Ibid., 165.
96. Moltmann, *God in Creation*, 16–17.

are ever likely to see."[97] But isn't the focus on three persons truer to the tradition than a focus on one supreme individual, asks Bauckham?[98] Yes, it is closer, but in the East it comes with a balancing focus on the one God and with a defense of the immanent Trinity—while Moltmann correlates God and creation and collapses the immanent Trinity.

For Moltmann, the Trinity is not one subject, but a fellowship of three subjects. Moltmann compares it to a human family, an analogy we saw the Cappadocians toy with, but then reject for good and necessary reasons. It led to tritheism. It is no wonder that Moltmann likes it, for it speaks of three independent subjects. "The image of the family is a favourite one for the unity of the Triunity: three Persons—one family. The analogy is not just arbitrary," for it points to the fact that we must seek the image of God not merely in human individuality, but "with equal earnestness in human sociality."[99] This comes to expression particularly at the Cross, where "the Father and the Son are so deeply separated that their relationship breaks off."[100]

If we want to be kind to Moltmann, we can point out that while he drifts uncomfortably close to tritheism, he draws salutary attention to the fact that God is God in three irreducibly different ways. As a result, "no single, univocal concept of person is applicable to the Father, the Son, and the Spirit," and "we cannot apply the concept of person to the Father, the Son, and the Spirit in exactly the same way."[101] The Father, the Son, and the Holy Spirit are eternally distinct. Each is different from the others, and will ever be so. Yet God is one undivided being. As Bauckham sagely observes, "We should certainly not reduce these three to three ways in which a single, identical divine subject repeats or relates to himself: to make this point is the merit of Moltmann's argument for social trinitarianism."[102] Thus, as Bauckham argues, we can recognize that the Incarnation is appropriate to the Son, and not to the Father or to the Spirit, while inspiration and indwelling the world are appropriate to the Spirit and not to the Father or the Son. Indeed, to flatten and equalize these differences is to drift towards modalism.

97. Molnar, *Divine Freedom*, 201–2.
98. Bauckham, *Moltmann*, 25.
99. Moltmann, *Trinity*, 199.
100. Ibid., 82.
101. Moltmann, *God in Creation*, 97.
102. Bauckham, *Moltmann*, 179.

Yet there is also an opposite and surprising danger in Moltmann—that of modalism. He says that as Christ suffered in time, so the Father must have suffered in eternity—*c'est son métier*. Patripassianism, the claim that the Father suffered on the cross, was an early heresy. Barth and Rahner both reject it, but Moltmann embraces it.[103] In this way, the sufferings of the Son and the Spirit are the sufferings of the Father.

Molnar, as usual, is on solid ground when he says that our approach to the doctrine of the Trinity must not overemphasize the one being of God, nor instead the three persons, as Moltmann has done. Instead, we are to proceed from the fact that the triune God is simultaneously one and three, which are equally ultimate.[104] We shall argue for this later, when we address the basic problems that the East and the West have faced. Molnar's primary concern, one flouted by Moltmann, is that where the doctrine of the immanent Trinity is blurred or rejected, an inevitable collapse occurs into some form of pantheism or panentheism. Here again, Moltmann provides a classic object lesson.

God the Pauper?

"If you will pardon me," wrote Karl Barth to Moltmann, "your God seems to me to be rather a pauper."[105]

Moltmann has an obvious and deep-seated problem with authority—with human authority in the political arena, and above all with the authority of God. Obedience to God is slavish, for utter dependence is abhorrent. "The idea of the almighty ruler of the universe everywhere requires abject servitude, because it points to complete dependency in all spheres of life."[106] And, in Bloch's words, "Where the great Lord of the universe reigns, there is no room for liberty."[107] This is alarmingly contradictory to the whole Christian tradition, to say nothing of Scripture. Moltmann has construed God as a fellowship of free and reciprocal persons, in codependency with the world which he was bound to create, which is correlative to himself. In this

---

103. Moltmann, *The Crucified God*, 241ff.; Moltmann, *Trinity*, 32ff.
104. Molnar, *Divine Freedom*, 232–33.
105. Letter dated 17 November 1964, in Karl Barth, *Letters, 1961–1968*, trans. and ed. Jürgen Fangemeier and Geoffrey W. Bromiley (Grand Rapids: Eerdmans, 1981), 176.
106. Moltmann, *Trinity*, 192.
107. Ibid., 203.

cosmic process, he is a loving and suffering participant, unable to remove the suffering, but expressing solidarity with his creation. Human beings are in a reciprocal, mutual, and free fellowship with their cosuffering Creator—mutually victims in a cosmic tragedy, moving toward an eschatological hope. In this there is no place for subordination or authority. In contrast, Moltmann might have paid heed to the wise Collect for Peace, in the order for Morning Prayer in the 1662 *Book of Common Prayer*, "O God, who art the author of peace and lover of concord, in knowledge of whom standeth eternal life, *whose service is perfect freedom*; defend us thy humble servants in all assaults of our enemies; that we, surely trusting in thy defence, may not fear the power of any adversaries, through the *might* of Jesus Christ our Lord. Amen [emphasis added]." Obedience to Christ, and service of him, is freedom. Moreover, this world is such that we need his might to govern and protect us. Moltmann could also have considered the apostle Paul, who often describes himself as the *doulos* (servant) of Christ, who in turn willingly took the form of a slave (*en morphē doulou*) to be our Savior (Phil. 2:5–7).

In Moltmann's own words, referring approvingly to Rolt, "The sole omnipotence which God possesses is the almighty power of suffering love."[108] Again, this time citing Studdert Kennedy, he explicitly denies that God the Father is almighty.[109] God creates by withdrawing himself, making room for creation, "lowering himself into his own impotence."[110] Power is thus removed from God. Moltmann's Christian political system would have a massive power vacuum at its heart.[111] However, this is not the way the world works, because it is not the way God made us. All human societies need leadership to succeed—firm leadership, but wise and loving, and behind that the power and authority to lead. Moltmann is naïve in the extreme when he says, "It is not the monarchy of a single ruler that corresponds to the triune God; it is the community of men and women, without privileges and without subjugation."[112]

108. Ibid., 31.
109. Ibid., 35.
110. Ibid., 110.
111. Ibid., 198.
112. Ibid.

What, we may speculate, was the effect on Moltmann of being raised in Hitler's Germany, with its horrific outcomes? Truth is evidently a problem for people like Derrida, Barthes, Foucault, Lyotard, and other French postmodernists, for truth was the plaything of manipulative power in occupied France and open to great ambiguity thereafter. Was the Vichy regime saving France from disaster or a treasonable betrayal? Who belonged to the resistance and who was a collaborator? How could you tell, when some who appeared to be collaborators were secretly aiding the resistance, and when the resistance itself was deeply divided? The rejection of objective truth has behind it some acute historical issues. Is it permissible to ask this question of Moltmann? His almost pathological abhorrence of power is everywhere evident. He even claims that monstrous tyrannies (the existence of which we do not for one moment deny) are the consequence of belief in the lordship of God. Yet he makes no reference at all to the development of constitutional monarchy in Britain and the Scandinavian countries, nor to the emergence of freedom in a federal form in the United States, all of which occurred in countries where a strong belief existed in the authority of God. The deplorable record of continental Europe in these matters, and Germany in particular, should not be allowed to govern theology. Still less can we for a moment allow Moltmann's dubious admiration for Marxist socialism, the record of which he equates with that of liberal democracies![113] With blinding political ineptitude, writing before the collapse of Communism, he thinks it vitally necessary for the two systems to converge.[114] Since Moltmann places *his own* stress on political theology, we must ask whether we should place as much credence in his theological speculations as in his political ones.

The Impact on Feminist Theology

Moltmann's wife, Elisabeth Moltmann-Wendel, is a prominent feminist theologian. It is little surprise that Moltmann's Trinitarianism is a fruitful base for feminist reconstructions of the doctrine of God. Moltmann is staunchly opposed to patriarchy and, as we have seen, to all forms of authority. This is connected with his concept of the Trinity.

113. Ibid., 199.
114. Ibid., 200.

For Moltmann, the persons of the Trinity are independent subjects who relate in a mutual and reciprocal manner. There are no elements of subordination between them, not only in terms of their participation in deity (uniformly accepted in the Trinitarian dogma), but
in the relations (Moltmann prefers "relationships") of the three persons. In the mutual, perichoretic relationships of the persons there is
no order. The three are independent subjects. Their relationships are
open to change. God and the world are mutual partners in the Trinitarian history of the world. These free, mutual relationships, without
any order or precedence, are the basis of a free, mutual, and reciprocal
relationship between men and women. There is no question of remnants of patriarchal order.

If anything, Moltmann's Trinitarianism encourages a reversal of
patriarchal structures and attitudes. His view of God as suffering love,
cosuffering with the world, is that of a weak bystander who can do
nothing to change the situation. He simply suffers. God is a feminized
God, indeed a transexual deity, a motherly Father and a fatherly
Mother. In turn, Moltmann's Christian society is a feminized society
of persons in relationship, devoid of authority. One might call it a cas-
trated theology. It is a mixture of Christian teaching and paganism.
Whatever else one might say, it is certainly "politically correct."

Wolfhart Pannenberg

Wolfhart Pannenberg (1928–), throughout his work, exhibits
prodigious scholarship and great care. In contrast to Moltmann, he
has an absence of unbridled speculation. However, in the end he occupies very similar territory. If he does not go quite as far as Moltmann,
he heads in the same direction.

Jesus, History, and the Resurrection

For Pannenberg, Christology is grounded in universal history.
Jesus' deity is established retroactively by his resurrection. In his early
work, *Jesus—God and Man* (1964), he goes so far as to argue that the
existence of God is to be established only by the eschatological resurrection. One dense but pregnant passage sums it up:

. . . that an element of God's becoming and being in the other, in the reality differentiated from himself, is one with his eternity requires that what newly flashes into view from time to time in the divine life can be understood at the same time as having always been true in God's eternity. This can be expressed in the form of the concept that the "intention" of the incarnation had been determined from all eternity in God's decree. However, the truth of such an assertion is dependent upon the temporal actuality of that thing, thus in this case the incarnation. *What is true in God's eternity is decided with retroactive validity only from the perspective of what occurs temporally with the import of the ultimate* [italics added]. Thus, Jesus' unity with God—and thus the truth of the incarnation—is also decided only retroactively from the perspective of Jesus' resurrection for the whole of Jesus' existence on the one hand . . . and thus also for God's eternity on the other. Apart from Jesus' resurrection, it would not be true that from the very beginning of his earthly way God was one with this man. That is true from all eternity *because* of Jesus' resurrection. Until his resurrection, Jesus' unity with God was hidden not only to other men but above all . . . for Jesus himself also. It was hidden because the ultimate decision about it had not been given.[115]

Much of this work is taken up by arguing that the resurrection of Jesus is to be established on the basis of general history, and thus by the methodology of historical research.

In his *Systematic Theology*, Pannenberg denies that the Son of God is antecedently the Son of God in himself. For Pannenberg, Christ's eternal deity is a reflection of his humanity. The Easter event does not simply *disclose* who Jesus was in his relation to God, but *determines* the meaning of his pre-Easter history. The Resurrection determines Jesus' identity, rather than merely disclosing it.[116] Pannenberg implies that the Son needed to become incarnate in order to actualize his eternal sonship.[117] Thus, it is Jesus' message, not his person, that is central. With unmistakable echoes of Harnack, Pan-

---

115. Wolfhart Pannenberg, *Jesus—God and Man*, trans. Lewis L. Wilkins (Philadelphia: Westminster Press, 1968), 321.
116. Wolfhart Pannenberg, *Systematic Theology*, trans. Geoffrey W. Bromiley (Grand Rapids: Eerdmans, 1991), 2:345–46; Molnar, *Divine Freedom*, 153–54.
117. Pannenberg, *Systematic Theology*, 2:325, 367.

nenberg claims, "In the debate about the figure of Jesus it is of decisive importance that we should not put his person at the center. The center, rather, is God, the nearness of his rule, and his fatherly love."[118] Jesus' claim and message needed confirmation by the Resurrection, since during his earthly ministry Jesus did not have this confirmation.[119] Pannnenberg acknowledges the eternal deity of the Son and recognizes that this preceded the Incarnation,[120] yet he claims that Jesus' identity is dependent on the Resurrection.[121] Statements that refer to the eternal deity are only possible in the light of the Resurrection.[122]

Criticism of the Tradition

In the first of the three volumes of his *Systematic Theology*, Pannenberg has an extensive discussion of Trinitarian theology in the history of the church, before turning to his own constructive proposals. He is particularly critical of Augustine. Any derivation of the plurality of the Trinitarian persons from the essence of the one God—whether it be viewed as spirit or love—leads to the problem of either modalism or subordinationism, he maintains.[123] Instead, we must begin with the way in which Father, Son, and Spirit come on the scene and relate to one another in the event of revelation. We must begin with the revelation of God in Jesus Christ.[124] Barth saw this with great clarity. Here Pannenberg reiterates his earlier theme that history provides the basis for the doctrine of God and Christology. While he applauds Barth here, his method is radically different.

Pannenberg is also critical of the Cappadocians for making the Father the source of deity. While there is nothing in the NT that expressly formulates the doctrine of the Trinity, it speaks of the deity of the Son and the Holy Spirit. However, it is unclear how this relates to the Father. Problems exist if the Father is the sole subject of deity, for the Son and the Spirit are then subordinate. We must begin with

118. Ibid., 2:335.
119. Ibid., 2:337.
120. Ibid., 2:367.
121. Ibid., 2:345.
122. Ibid., 2:371.
123. Ibid., 1:298.
124. Ibid., 1:299–300.

the relation of Jesus to the Father, a prominent theme in the Gospels, which is the presupposition for understanding the Spirit as a third figure.[125] From this unfolds the reciprocal self-distinction of the Father, Son, and Spirit as the concrete form of Trinitarian relations.[126]

Pannenberg also distances himself from the older Protestant dogmatics, which considered statements where Jesus distinguishes himself from the Father to refer to his human nature. This, Pannenberg says, was an "evasion." According to the canons of classical Christology, these passages refer to the person of Christ, the incarnate Son, and not just his human nature. This "evasive answer" misses the point that Jesus shows himself to be the Son of God precisely in his self-distinction from God.[127] By subjecting himself to God's will, he showed himself to be the Son of God. This is the way he glorifies the Father. As the one who corresponds to the fatherhood of God, Jesus is the Son. "Hence self-distinction from the Father is constitutive for the eternal Son in his relation to the Father."[128]

Mutual, Reciprocal Relations

The Son's self-distinction from the Father entails full mutual reciprocity. Athanasius argued that the Father would not be the Father without the Son. So in some way the deity of the Father depends on his relation to the Son, although not in the same way that the Son's deity is dependent on the Father. While the Father is not begotten by the Son or sent by him, for "these relations are irreversible,"[129] nevertheless "the Father made his deity dependent on the success of the mission of the Son."[130] This dependence of the Father on the Son is the basis of true reciprocity between them.[131] However, as Molnar comments, this cannot be *free* reciprocity, since it depends on what happens in history, with the result that "God is no longer the free subject of his own internal and external relations."[132]

125. Ibid., 1:301–5.
126. Ibid., 1:308ff.
127. Ibid., 1:309–10.
128. Ibid., 1:310.
129. Ibid., 1:312.
130. Ibid., 2:391.
131. Ibid., 1:312.
132. Molnar, *Divine Freedom*, 152.

The handing over of the rule and the power of the Father to the Son defines the intra-Trinitarian relations between the two, as does their handing back by the Son to the Father (cf. 1 Cor. 15:28). These acts interpenetrate one another. Thus, the kingdom of the Son does not end when he hands lordship back to the Father. Rather, his own lordship is consummated in this act. Pannenberg argues that we see a mutuality in this handing over and handing back that we do not see in the begetting.[133] Due to his stress on the mutuality of relations, Pannenberg dismisses the *filioque*. It does not do justice to the fellowship of both Father and Son with the Spirit.[134] Both East and West have a problem, since they see the Trinitarian relations as relations of origin. On this basis, "one cannot do justice to the reciprocity in the relations,"[135] and even perichoresis could have a limited impact.

As with Moltmann, Pannenberg's idea of mutual reciprocity between the persons drives him in the direction of tritheism, as all social doctrines of the Trinity in some way must. Because the relations are those of mutual self-distinction, "they must be understood . . . as living realizations of separate centers of action." Here he cites Moltmann in support, besides Staniloae and Robert Jenson.[136] Against Rahner, he asserts that "a divine consciousness subsists in a threefold mode,"[137] and "each of the three persons relates to the others as others and distinguishes itself from them."[138] These cannot be reduced to relations of origin.

> Relations among the three persons that are defined as mutual self-distinction cannot be reduced to relations of origin in the traditional sense. The Father does not merely beget the Son. He also hands over his kingdom to him and receives it back from him. The Son is not merely begotten of the Father. He is also obedient to him and he thereby glorifies him as the one God. The Spirit is not just breathed. He also fills the Son and glorifies him in his obedience to the Father, thereby glorifying the Father himself. In so doing he leads into all truth (John 16:13) and searches out the deep things of the Godhead (1 Cor. 2:10–11).[139]

133. Pannenberg, *Systematic Theology*, 1:312–13.
134. Ibid., 1:318.
135. Ibid., 1:319.
136. Ibid.
137. Ibid.
138. Ibid., 1:320.
139. Ibid.

A "richly structured nexus of relationship" constitutes the different distinctions of the persons.[140]

From this, "the question arises whether we might not define the relational nexus of the perichoresis more accurately, and also show how it relates to the unity of the divine life."[141] The different structure of the persons comes out more clearly, Pannenberg suggests, if we consider the full complexity of the relations among the Father, Son, and Spirit "and do so precisely in respect of the different forms of their mutual self-distinction."[142] Only of the Son may it be said that the other person from whom he distinguishes himself—the Father—is for him the only God and that his deity is grounded in the fact that he subjects himself to the deity of the Father. For his part, the Spirit shows his deity by teaching us to recognize and confess the Son as Kyrios (Lord). "Thus the form of the self-distinction of the Spirit from the Son and the Father is different from that of the Son in relation to the Father. Again the self-distinction of the Father from the Son and Spirit with respect to the deity of both takes yet another form."[143] The Father does not recognize the one God in the Son in distinction from himself, but hands over his lordship to the Son.[144] Again he cites Athanasius, who says that the Son is a condition of the deity of the Father—in contrast to the common view, which holds that the deity of the Father is unconditional and ascribes deity to the Son and Spirit only derivatively. Thus, the Father's deity is dependent on the Son, and so all three persons are fully reciprocally related, although in different ways.[145] Pannenberg believes that by this he has avoided the error of the Cappadocians. With their stress on the Father as the fountain of deity, they sometimes came close (against their best intentions) to ascribing ontological inferiority to the Son and the Spirit, since they do not expressly add that the Father is the fountain of deity only from the perspective of the Son.[146] From the Western side, Augustine reduced the mutual

140. Ibid.
141. Ibid., 1:320–21.
142. Ibid., 1:321.
143. Ibid., 1:321–22.
144. Ibid., 1:322.
145. Ibid.
146. Ibid., 1:322–23.

relations to an identical participation of each in the undifferentiated unity of the divine essence.[147]

On the other hand, Pannenberg stresses, the mutuality of the persons does not mean that the monarchy of the Father is destroyed. Rather, it is established through the work of the Son and the Spirit. The Father's monarchy or kingdom does not exist without them, but only through them.[148] "The Son is not subordinate to the Father in the sense of ontological inferiority, but he subjects himself to the Father. In this regard he is himself in eternity the locus of the monarchy of the Father. Herein he is one with the Father by the Holy Spirit. The monarchy of the Father is not the presupposition but the result of the common operation of the three persons."[149] Pannenberg distances himself from Moltmann in this; the perichoretic unity of the three persons requires the monarchy of the Father as the source of deity. The monarchy of the Father cannot be in competition with the life of the Trinity.[150] In the NT, the word *God* almost without exception means the Father.[151] We should note that Pannenberg does not share Moltmann's deep aversion to power and authority. This saves him from tritheism. While moving toward the same destination, he is able to correct some of Moltmann's worst excesses.[152] Thus, "we need not surrender the basic truth that the Father, Son, and Spirit work together in creation, reconciliation, and redemption because we accept the possibility of distinguishing the persons in these works."[153] And despite his overwhelming reliance on history, Pannenberg is prepared to recognize a distinction between the economic Trinity and the immanent Trinity, although the immanent Trinity must not be seen in detachment from his revelation and work in the world and in the economy of salvation.[154]

Economic Trinity and Immanent Trinity

However, we must ask how far the distinction between the economic Trinity and the immanent Trinity is an effective working dis-

147. Ibid., 1:324.
148. Ibid.
149. Ibid., 1:324–25.
150. Ibid., 1:325.
151. Ibid., 1:326.
152. See Olson, "Trinity and Eschatology."
153. Pannenberg, *Systematic Theology*, 1:326.
154. Ibid., 1:327.

tinction for Pannenberg. He shows the same tendencies as Moltmann. He makes God dependent on history and thus on his creation. By creating the world and by sending his Son and the Spirit to work in it, God has made himself dependent on the course of history.[155] He adds with approval, "The dependence of the deity of the Father upon the course of events in the world of creation was first worked out by Jüngel and then by Moltmann, who illustrated it by the crucifixion of Jesus."[156] He is somewhat equivocal on the effect that events in history have on God. He refutes the idea that there is a divine becoming in history, since the identity of the economic Trinity and the immanent Trinity requires the existence of the immanent Trinity to give the economic Trinity significance,[157] but differentiating the eternal Trinity from all temporal change makes Trinitarian theology one-sided and detaches it from its biblical basis.[158] Indeed, the Resurrection not only provides knowledge that Jesus is the Son of God, but actually *decides* this by retrospective confirmation.[159] Again, the eschatological consummation is the locus of the decision that the Trinitarian God is always the true God from eternity to eternity.[160] The immanent Trinity belongs to the future and is decided by the present, rather than belonging to eternity and so transcending time.

Persons and Essence in Pannenberg's Social Doctrine

Pannenberg's social doctrine is clear. Today we cannot adopt the traditional derivation of the persons from the Father (the Cappadocians and the East) or from the divine essence (Augustine and the West), because they entail either subordinationism or Sabellianism. The unity of Father, Son, and Spirit finds expression in mutual self-distinction and joint working. This expresses the unity of the divine essence, which is "the epitome of the personal relations among Father, Son, and Spirit."[161] The divine essence is thus bound up with the relations, but has no precedence, for "as forms of the eternal God, Father,

155. Ibid., 1:329, 296.
156. Ibid., 1:329.
157. Ibid., 1:331.
158. Ibid., 1:333.
159. Ibid., 1:331; Pannenberg, *Jesus—God and Man*, 321.
160. Pannenberg, *Systematic Theology*, 1:331.
161. Ibid., 1:334.

Son, and Spirit cannot be derived from anything else. They have no genesis from anything different from themselves. The unity of the essence may be found only in their concrete life relations."[162] While the Father is primary to the Trinity for the Cappadocians, and the divine essence is primary for Augustine, Pannenberg holds that the three persons are primary. He has a less precarious grip than Moltmann on the divine unity (he reproves Moltmann for his onslaught against monotheism[163]), but it is still a unity of three persons working together. Instead of a subordinationist danger with the Cappadocians, or a modalist danger with Augustine and the West, Pannenberg's social Trinity exhibits a tritheistic danger. This becomes alarmingly clear when he talks about the Son distinguishing himself from the deity of the Father in the Incarnation, with the result that he "moves out of the intratrinitarian life of God."[164] Indeed, the Son is the one of the three "most clearly distinct from the divine essence." He does not represent the Godhead as a whole because he partakes of eternal deity "only through his relation to the Father and as filled by the Spirit of the Father."[165]

This clearly tritheistic tendency flows from Pannenberg's social Trinity with its mutual relations, its intermeshing of God and creation, and its loose identification of the divine essence with love. At times it appears, as Molnar contends, that love is the subject and God's freedom to love is the predicate.[166] It is good that he says that God's lordship is based in eternity, where "in the eternal fellowship of the Son with the Father the Son subjects himself to the Father as the King of eternity. The divine lordship is not first set up in God's relation to the world. It has its basis in his trinitarian life."[167] But then he conflates this with the subjection of the creatures to the Creator.[168] So when discussing love in God, he states, "This power [love] can thus give existence to creaturely life because it is already at work in the reciprocity of the trinitarian life of God as in eternity each of the three persons lets the others be what they

162. Ibid., 1:335.
163. Ibid., 1:335–36.
164. Ibid., 1:421.
165. Ibid., 1:429.
166. Molnar, *Divine Freedom*, 153.
167. Pannenberg, *Systematic Theology*, 1:421.
168. Ibid.

are."[169] He seems to say that love is the divine essence.[170] Love has power over persons, including the Trinitarian persons.[171] The Trinitarian concept of person is like the human one, since the persons are constituted ecstatically (in relation to others).[172] The differences are that the divine persons are constituted in relation to only two others, and their identity is defined exclusively by the relation to the others.[173] Therefore, both the personal distinctions and the unity of the Father, Son, and Spirit are grounded in the concrete reality of divine love.[174] It is hard to see how, on this basis, God is one being and not three.

So, in Pannenberg's social doctrine, dynamically conceived, there are three subjects, the unity of which is love. Like Moltmann, he is close to tritheism. Again, the creation seems to be necessary for God. His hold on the deity of the Son seems shaky. His polemic against relations of origin simply substitutes relations of opposition and elevates them to primacy.

169. Ibid., 1:427.

170. Ibid., 1:428.

171. Ibid., 1:430.

172. See John D. Zizioulas, *Being as Communion: Studies in Personhood and the Church* (Crestwood, N.Y.: St. Vladimir's Seminary Press, 1985); John D. Zizioulas, "Human Capacity and Human Incapacity: A Theological Exploration of Personhood," *SJT* 28 (1975): 401–47.

173. Pannenberg, *Systematic Theology*, 1:431.

174. Ibid., 1:432.

Returning East: Bulgakov, Lossky, and Staniloae

We now return to the East. With increased communications in the modern world, leading Eastern philosophers and theologians began to draw on certain lines of thought in the Western tradition. This trend was particularly marked in Russia, especially after the Bolshevik Revolution in 1917, when many leading intellectuals were forced into exile and ended up in Western Europe. A creative tension arose between their Orthodox tradition and Western culture. Again in recent years there has been an explosion of interest in Western Christianity in the theology and worship of the Orthodox Church. We will confine our attention to three leading Eastern theologians. The first, Sergius Bulgakov, was a prominent exponent of Russian love mysticism that built on certain medieval Western thinkers, including Richard of St. Victor, and in turn resonates with the interests of Jürgen Moltmann and contemporary feminist theologians. Bulgakov, a maverick, is not viewed in an entirely favorable light by the guardians of Orthodox theology. Our second figure, Vladimir Lossky, another Russian emigré in Paris,[1] appropriates the tradition of Gregory Palamas and has been very influential in the West. He is a leading representative of those who base

---

1. Rowan Williams remarks that "for most of the twentieth century, the story of Orthodox theology is the story of Russian theology, both in Russia itself before 1917 and in the emigration afterwards (especially in Paris)." Rowan Williams, "Eastern Orthodox Theology," in *The Modern Theologians*, ed. David F. Ford (Oxford: Blackwell, 1989), 152.

their theology self-consciously on the Fathers, and he has found a more ready acceptance by the church in Russia. The third figure we will consider is the Romanian, Dumitru Staniloae.

Sergius Bulgakov

Sergius Bulgakov (1871–1944) was a professor of political economy at the University of Moscow when he was converted from Marxism to Christianity. In 1918 he entered the priesthood of the Russian Orthodox Church. Exiled by the Bolsheviks in 1923, he taught economics at the Russian University in Prague before becoming dean of the newly founded Russian Theological Institute (St. Sergius Institute) in Paris. Under his leadership, it became the major center of Russian theological studies in the twentieth century. Paris was the focal point for exiled Russian intellectuals, and there Bulgakov came into direct contact with mainstream Western scholarship. However, his work stands at the zenith of a long process in which Russian philosophers and theologians drew on certain strands of Western mysticism. His work straddles both East and West, but in crucial ways is fully acceptable to neither.

The Background to Bulgakov's Thought

The lines of thought that led to Bulgakov's Trinitarian theology are traceable in the more immediate context to the seminal Russian personalist thinker Vladimir Solovyov (also spelled Solovyev or Soloviev) (1853–1900) and, after him, the husband-and-wife team of Dmitry Merezhkovsky and Zinaida Hippius with their strongly existential slant, the mystical philosopher Nikolai Berdiaev (1874–1948), and the theologians Pavel Florensky and Lev Karsavin (1882–1952), the last of whom applied kenoticism to the Trinity.[2] These thinkers begin their discussion of the Trinity from an analysis of personhood. They understand persons, not as individual entities, but in communion with others. From this, they see the Trinity as a communion of

---

2. See Michael Aksionov Meerson, *The Trinity of Love in Modern Russian Theology: The Love Paradigm and the Retrieval of Western Medieval Love Mysticism in Modern Russian Trinitarian Thought (from Solovyov to Bulgakov)* (Quincy, Ill.: Franciscan Press, 1998), for a detailed analysis of the development of this movement.

love. This is, of course, nothing new. It has antecedents in the West, with Richard of St. Victor (see chapter 11). Richard is clearly a source for this movement, and for Bulgakov in particular, for he too considered the Trinity to be three divine persons in a communion of love. It is no accident that St. Sergius Institute is only a stone's throw from the Abbey of St. Victor. We have seen how this theme has surfaced in the West at a much later date. Jürgen Moltmann sees the Trinity as a communion of love, with three subjects. In various ways, he, LaCugna, Walter Kasper, and other Westerners have drawn on Bulgakov and their common source in Western love mysticism. Both the Russians and the Westerners make a major paradigm shift from a center in God (which is what Barth stressed and what the tradition in general followed) to a base in human experience—to what Meerson describes as "the anthropocentric premises of modern philosophy."[3] Thus, the human person is the gateway to understanding the Trinity. This is so, it is thought, because there is a basic congruity between human beings and God, demonstrated by the Incarnation.

Solovyov argued that the human mind can arrive at knowledge of the absolute, which is love and supreme goodness.[4] It can attain this through logical deduction. God is self-differentiating love. The absolute and creation coincide as opposites in Jesus Christ, for Christ is the mediating principle between God and creation. Here, God's humanity gives meaning to all that exists. The divine and human interact in ceaseless communion. Solovyov does not identify human thinking with the absolute, as Hegel does—there are parallels, but not an identity. Rather, Solovyov puts the person at the heart of his philosophy and makes personhood the link between God and human beings. The person constitutes being. Being is not an absolute category, but person is being and constitutes being.[5]

3. Meerson, *Trinity of Love*, xiii-xiv.
4. Solovyov's ideas on God-manhood and Sophia can be found in Vladimir Soloviev, *La Sophia et les autres écrits français*, trans. and ed. François Rouleau (Lausanne: La Cité: L'Age d'homme, 1978); Vladimir Soloviev, *Lectures on Divine Humanity*, trans. Boris Jakim (Hudson, N.Y.: Lindisfarne Press, 1995); Vladimir Sergeyevich Solovyev, *Vladimir Solovyev's Lectures on Godmanhood*, trans. Peter P. Zouboff (New York: International University Press, 1944); Vladimir Sergeyevich Solovyov, *A Solovyov Anthology*, arr. S. L. Frank, trans. Natalie Duddington (Westport, Conn.: Greenwood Press, 1974). See also Vladimir Sergeyevich Solovyov, *Godmanhood as the Main Idea of the Philosophy of Vladimir Solovyev*, trans. Peter P. Zouboff (Poughkeepsie, N.Y.: Harmon Printing House, 1944).
5. Meerson, *Trinity of Love*, 21–26.

Not surprisingly, some regard Solovyov as a pantheist. He rejects the accusation, and it appears that he is more a panentheist, for he argues that God contains everything in himself and that creation is rooted in the life of the Trinity. He deduces God's triunity from the idea of absolute goodness and love, worked out on the basis of the human experience of love and by logical reasoning. Indeed, the Trinity is as much a truth of speculative reason as of revelation, and the Fathers who denied it to be a truth of reason may have been weak in their philosophical understanding. The doctrine is "fully intelligible from the side of logic" and is simply the crown of pre-Christian religious wisdom, for Philo and Plotinus held it every bit as much as Origen and Gregory the Theologian.[6] From this he concludes that God contains all things in himself. Solovyov has constructed God in the image of man and then asserted that *this* God contains all that exists. This is in line with the blurring of Creator and creature seen much later in the Westerners who follow Rahner's axiom and correlate God and creation. Bulgakov himself recognizes that "Soloviev's doctrine of Sophia is undoubtedly syncretistic," for he combines Orthodox tradition with elements of ancient Gnosticism and his own poetic mysticism.[7] For Solovyov, love constitutes the unity of God, and this he calls Wisdom (Sophia). Creation and human history unfold the eternal love of the Trinity in three forms—truth, goodness, and beauty. While God contains the whole creation, it is principally the human person that meets God. God's humanity in Jesus Christ reveals the conformity between divine and human persons. God as a person is the exemplar of the human being as a person. Since love is personal, absolute personality takes the form of the love of God. Thus, human love (especially erotic love, directed toward another human subject who is different in every respect, being of the opposite sex) is grounded in the Trinity and bears the image of the Trinity.[8] Bulgakov will adopt and adapt each of these themes from the perspective of a theologian. Solovyov's influence is vividly clear, as Bulgakov himself agrees. "Soloviev's religious outlook had an inescapable influence on the

---

6. Soloviev, *Divine Humanity*, 73–77, 89–92; Solovyev, *Philosophy of Solovyev*, 141–55.

7. Sergius Bulgakov, *The Wisdom of God: A Brief Summary of Sophiology* (London: Williams and Norgate, 1937), 23–24.

8. Meerson, *Trinity of Love*, 26–47.

thought of subsequent generations, whether those who submitted to it did so consciously or not. Personally, though I do not share his gnostic tendencies, I regard Soloviev as having been my philosophical 'guide to Christ' at the time of change in my world-outlook." Indeed, "all the living Russian religious thinkers of our time have been influenced directly or indirectly, positively or negatively, by sophiology."[9]

Anthropocentrism

The problem with patristic theology, as Bulgakov sees it, is its impersonalism. The Greek word *hypostasis* signified not only persons, but things. Instead, he approaches the Trinity in terms of interpersonal relations.[10] This follows the lines mapped out by Solovyov, from a starting point in human experience. Ironically, as Meerson points out, in this Bulgakov also follows the archenemy of religion, Ludwig Feuerbach (1804–1872). Feuerbach had pronounced in 1841, "But this distinction between what God is in himself, and what he is for me . . . [is] an unfounded and untenable distinction. I cannot know whether God is something else in himself or for himself than he is for me; what he is to me is to me all that he is."[11] Feuerbach proceeded to argue that God is the human projection of pure love. In effect, love is God. Bulgakov, on the other hand, takes this focus on love and adapts it to Trinitarian theology. However, it is a focus based on man and beginning with man. He correlates human beings with God. Human experience in creation is the channel to knowledge of God. Bulgakov himself was spurred to his focus on Sophia by a mystical experience when he first visited Hagia Sophia in old Constantinople.[12] Underlying these assumptions is the orthodox belief that God created man in his own image with a compatibility with himself. Thus, the Incarnation is possible.[13] However, this is a different twist. Instead of beginning with God, who reached down to us in the Incarnation, Bulgakov moves in the opposite direction, from human experience to God.

9. Bulgakov, *Wisdom of God*, 24–25.

10. Meerson, *Trinity of Love*, 161–63.

11. Ludwig Feuerbach, *The Essence of Christianity*, trans. George Eliot (New York: Harper Torchbooks, 1957), 14, cited by Meerson, *Trinity of Love*, 164.

12. Bulgakov, *Wisdom of God*, 13.

13. Meerson, *Trinity of Love*, 165–69.

Personalism, Love, and Perichoresis

For Bulgakov, God and man are compatible since they are persons. So our first task is to understand what human persons are. Then we will be able to inquire about divine personality. At root, human persons are related to others. This relatedness finds expression in love, whereby persons go out of themselves to the other. The self, the "I," does not exist by itself, but for others. It is aware of itself (*hypostasis*) and its nature (*ousia*). Yet the human self is limited, for it develops, becomes, and is in process. These limitations do not apply to divine personality.

The consciousness of the self is conciliar (*sobornyi*). Existence is relational, and love is the essence of relationality. Thus, God is love, each person surrendering himself in love to the others. The Trinity is "the eternal act of self-surrendering and kenosis in divine love of the three divine persons."[14] This is an I-thou-he relation, "a conciliar structure of personality," or "a tri-personal *sobornost* [conciliar relations]."[15] Meerson correctly points to the similarities of this thinking with Richard. It is this I-thou-he relation that gives rise in Bulgakov's thinking to the Trinity. Personal consciousness is not something in isolation, but is trihypostatic. At the same time, Bulgakov carefully excludes the tritheistic danger. There is no "they" in God. The Trinity is not a society, but "an eternal act of self-positing through love" in a ceaseless movement of perichoresis.[16]

Sophia

To appreciate Bukgakov's Trinitarianism, it is vital to understand his sophiology, by which the divine world and the created world are united. Following Solovyov's lead, he builds his theology around the concept of Sophia (Wisdom). As Bobrinskoy says, "It runs through his great theological works like a watermark."[17] He wants to avoid an impersonal view of the being of God. This is most evident in "the ontological absurdity, the heresy, which characterizes all varieties of imper-

14. Ibid., 174.
15. Ibid., 175; Sergius Bulgakov, *A Bulgakov Anthology* (Philadelphia: Westminster Press, 1976), 143.
16. Meerson, *Trinity of Love*, 177.
17. Boris Bobrinskoy, *The Mystery of the Trinity: Trinitarian Experience and Vision in the Biblical and Patristic Tradition*, trans. Anthony P. Gythiel (Crestwood, N.Y.: St. Vladimir's Seminary Press, 1999), 36n17.

sonal conceptions of the Holy Trinity (beginning with that of St. Augustine)."[18] Behind these failures lies the fact that "the doctrine of the consubstantiality of the Holy Trinity, as well as the actual conception of substance or nature, has been far less developed [than that of the three *hypostases*] and, apparently, almost overlooked."[19] Indeed, the terms *substance* and *consubstantiality* are not biblical, but are adapted from the philosophy of Aristotle.[20] *Substance*, both in the East and in the West, is interpreted "purely as a philosophical abstraction, and utilized to achieve a logical solution of the trinitarian dogma." It remains a sealed book as far as we are concerned.[21] However, all is not lost. The Bible does reflect on this when it applies to the doctrine of the substance of God the biblical revelation of Wisdom (Sophia) and the Glory of God. Bulgakov refers to Proverbs, Job, and Ecclesiasticus.[22] The NT also has plenty to say about Wisdom.[23] In biblical theology, there is, side by side with a revelation of the personal being of God, a doctrine of divine wisdom either in God or with God. But also in the OT there is another striking figure—the Shekinah, the Glory of God, in the midst of which God manifests himself.[24]

What does this mean in relation to God? Bulgakov concludes that the Glory of God is a divine principle which, "though it differs from God's *personal* being, yet it is inseparably bound up with it: it is not God, but Divinity."[25] These divine substances must belong to the Holy Trinity, for there are no grounds to limit them to any one particular person.[26]

This leads immediately to a further question, concerning the precise relation between the dogmatic conception of the divine substance as it has been traditionally understood (*ousia* or *physis*) and the figurative revelations concerning Wisdom (Sophia) and Glory. Is there any reason to distinguish them?[27] Further, do Wisdom and Glory differ

18. Bulgakov, *Wisdom of God*, 83–84.
19. Ibid., 44.
20. Ibid., 44–45.
21. Ibid., 46.
22. Ibid., 47–49.
23. Ibid., 50.
24. Ibid., 50–52.
25. Vladimir Lossky, *The Mystical Theology of the Eastern Church* (London: James Clarke & Co., 1957), 52.
26. Ibid., 53.
27. Ibid.

from each other? Yes, there is a distinction, insofar as Wisdom refers to content, and Glory to manifestation, but they are inseparable. There is but one Godhead expressed at once in Wisdom and Glory.[28] If *ousia* differs from them, then it becomes empty, abstract, metaphysical. Monotheism postulates the identity of these two principles—*ousia* and Sophia. "*Ousia* stands precisely for Wisdom and Glory."[29] Therefore *ousia*, Wisdom, and Glory can be used interchangeably. So there is no reason to distinguish Wisdom from God's being. Thus, following Trinitarian dogma, *ousia*-Sophia is distinct from the *hypostases* (persons), but cannot exist apart from them and is eternally hypostatized in them.[30]

Bulgakov moves on to ask the question to which his argument is leading: what *is* God? He answers:

> God is Love—not love in the sense of a quality or a property pecu-liar to God—but as the very substance and vigour of his life. The tri-hypostatic union of the Godhead is a mutual love, in which each of the Hypostases, by a timeless act of self-giving in love, reveals itself in both the others. However, the divine Hypostases alone do not con-stitute the only personal centres of this love, for Ousia-Sophia like-wise belongs to the realm of God's Love.[31]

The aspects of love in the Trinity vary in each of the persons, and "besides that which is personal there can be a love which is not." So we can speak of love in the mutual relationship of the three *hypostases and* in the relationship of God to his Godhead, "but in like manner in the love of the Godhead for God. Thus if God loves Sophia, Sophia also loves God."[32] God is a living and loving substance, ground, and principle. But, we may ask, *exactly how many are there* in God? Bulgakov recognizes the three *hypostases*. He discourses at length on the one being of God, preferring Sophia to *ousia*. But here he also mentions the Godhead and distinguishes it from God and from the three persons. This seems alarmingly like an emerging pantheon. Bulgakov

28. Ibid., 54–55.
29. Ibid., 55.
30. Ibid., 56–57.
31. Ibid., 57–58.
32. Ibid., 58.

is aware of the problem that his language causes. Does this not lead to the conception of a fourth *hypostasis*? Certainly not, he protests. For this principle—Sophia—is nonhypostatic, though capable of being hypostatized in a given hypostasis. Nor does it lead to another God, for God possesses the Godhead, or he is the Godhead, is *ousia*, is Sophia. Nor do the three persons possess a common substance, such as in collective ownership, for this would lead to tritheism. There is one wisdom, one glory, not three.[33] He insists on the full ontological reality of *ousia*-Sophia, "an ontological reality analogous to that of a body informed by a reasonable soul in its relation to the spirit incarnate in it."[34] It is not a mere quality. He wants to avoid reducing the essence of the Godhead "to the shadowy existence of a logical abstraction."[35] This at least shows Bulgakov's awareness of the problem and his wish to be Trinitarian. However, he wants to have his cake and eat it too. Sophia is his solution to an impersonal view of the being (*ousia*) of God. Yet in answer to this question of a fourth person, he retreats by saying that Sophia is nonhypostatic, nonpersonal. If Bulgakov is correct here, then his case for Sophia collapses and his original criticism of the tradition is undermined.

How, then, does the divine Sophia relate to the persons of the Holy Trinity? One and the same Sophia is possessed in a different way by each person. "We should learn to think of the divine *Sophia* as at the same time threefold and one."[36] Hence, Sophia is not limited to the person of the Son. Wisdom belongs to the Father, the first principle, the divine subject. With respect to the Father, Sophia connotes *ousia*, since the Father is only revealed in the other persons by the power of his self-denying love.[37] Thus, Sophia reveals the whole Trinity and each person severally. As the Son and the Holy Spirit reveal the Father, so the double figure of Wisdom-Glory reveals the Godhead. The Father alone possesses Wisdom-Glory, and the two revealing *hypostases* manifest it in themselves.[38] Here we note the Eastern order, with the Father primary. Does Sophia divide the Trinity thus, with a

33. Ibid., 59–60.
34. Bulgakov, *Wisdom of God*, 92–93.
35. Ibid., 87–89.
36. Ibid., 63.
37. Ibid., 64–68.
38. Ibid., 80.

radical distinction between the Father, on the one hand, and the Son and the Spirit, on the other? No, Bulgakov contends, since "the *ousia* is one and undivided in the Holy Trinity, and . . . the Holy Trinity itself, by a triune act, possesses it in common in its one life."[39] So Sophia belongs to all three persons, both in their triunity and in their separate being and to each one in a way peculiar to himself. The entire Trinity is Sophia, just as the three persons are in their separateness.[40] He repeats that Sophia is not a *hypostasis*, but a quality belonging to a *hypostasis*. The Father, the Son, the Holy Spirit, and the Holy Trinity are either *ousia* or Sophia. But the statement cannot be reversed. The statement "*Ousia*-Sophia is the Father, Son, etc." would be untrue or contain the heresy of impersonalism.[41]

Lossky is strongly critical of Bulgakov. He refers to the danger inherent in the Eastern insistence on the monarchy of the Father, namely, placing the persons before the nature. This is evident if the nature is given the character of a common revelation of the persons, which is what Bulgakov's sophiology does. His teaching reveals the snares into which the Russian thinker is prone to stumble, for "Father Bulgakov regarded God as a 'person in three hypostases', who reveals himself in the ουσια—Wisdom."[42] However, "the Orthodox tradition is as far from this eastern exaggeration as from its western antithesis."[43] As Lossky argues, Bulgakov's fundamental error is to identify the energy of Wisdom (Sophia) with the essence (*ousia*) of God, making an attribute of God the very principle of the Godhead. God is not determined by any of his attributes. All determinations are inferior to him, Lossky continues, logically posterior to his being in itself, in its essence. Moreover, the Holy Spirit can never be assimilated into the mutual love between the Father and the Son.[44] Lossky is right. We saw how Bulgakov argues that the Spirit unites the Father and the Son, implying that they are divided. Whatever abstract quality may be proposed as basic to any understanding of God's being, even if it purports to com-

39. Ibid., 81.
40. Ibid., 82.
41. Ibid., 83.
42. Lossky, *Mystical Theology*, 62, citing Bulgakov's *Agnus Dei* from its French translation, *Du Verbe incarné* (Paris: Aubier, 1943), 13–20.
43. Lossky, *Mystical Theology*, 62–63.
44. Ibid., 76–77.

bat impersonality, the Trinity is undermined. Such proposals are ultimately based on rationalism, not revelation. Here Barth provides an effective criticism, for by beginning with God the temptation to extrapolate abstract qualities or personal attributes back into God is avoided.

Divine Humanity (God-Manhood)

A central theme in Bulgakov, following Solovyov, is God-manhood. This refers to the compatibility of God and man, which finds clearest expression in the Incarnation, but embraces the whole of creation and redemption. This is Sophia finding expression through the Word and the Holy Spirit.

Bulgakov's panentheism is clear in his discussion of creation. God created *ex nihilo* (from nothing). Thus, there exists no other principle of creation outside of God or apart from God. There can be no source of the world but God.[45] What this means for Bulgakov is not that there was nothing besides God, but that he created "nothingness" (being in the state of becoming). Creatureliness exists in a fusion of being and nothingness, being and nonbeing. The world gets its capacity to exist from God.[46] Creation is not something new for God, for if it were there would be "a certain incompleteness in God without creation." Thus, God creates the world "out of himself." There is nothing new for God.[47] He points to some of the Fathers, who held that the divine world is a prototype of the creaturely world, and also argues on the basis of Proverbs 8 that Wisdom is a prototype of creation, not as a quality, but ontologically "as the ever present power of God, the divine essence, as the Godhead itself."[48] Thus, "God in his three Persons created the world on the *foundation* of the Wisdom common to the whole Trinity."[49] The different persons of the Trinity participate differently in creation. The Father alone acts hypostatically, while the Son and the Spirit "abandon themselves to the will of the Father as his word and action" and participate not hypostatically but "sophianically, revealing themselves in Wisdom."[50]

45. Bulgakov, *Wisdom of God*, 96.
46. Ibid., 97–98.
47. Ibid., 98–99.
48. Ibid., 100–102.
49. Ibid., 104.
50. Ibid., 105.

This, Bulgakov is careful to add, is not pantheism. Creation exists by the power of God, it is outside of God, it belongs to God, and it finds the foundation of its reality in God, but it is not the same as God.[51] Instead, it is panentheism—"God confers on a principle which originates in himself an existence distinct from his own. This is not pantheism, but panentheism." The created world is the creaturely Sophia, a principle of relative being in process of becoming, and in composition with the nonbeing of "nothing." This is what is meant when we say that the world is created by God from nothing.[52] There is, then, a need for a mediating principle between God and the world—since the world is distinct from God, yet participates in his being. The *hypostasis* of the Logos cannot provide it, for this principle is not to be sought in the being of God, but in his nature—Sophia in all its aspects, both divine and creaturely. "Sophia unites God with the world as the one common principle, the divine ground of creaturely existence."[53]

This brings Bulgakov to the Incarnation. Man as the image of God establishes both the divinity of man and the humanity of God. He refers to Acts 17:28 ("We are [God's] offspring"), to Ezekiel's vision of the glory of God in the form of "the image of heavenly manhood" (Ezek. 1:26), and to the Son of Man in Daniel 7:9–13. From this he concludes that the Incarnation "is closely connected with this heavenly or eternal manhood. There is something in man which is directly related to the essence of God. It is no one natural quality, but his whole humanity, which is the image of God."[54]

This compatibility between God and man is seen in a striking parallel between the Son and the Holy Spirit and a corresponding dyadic relation in man. Within the eternal God-manhood, we can distinguish the Logos as the God-man and the Holy Spirit as his divine humanity. There is thus a difference between the Logos and God-manhood, on the one hand, and the Holy Spirit and God-manhood, on the other. "But the Son and the Holy Spirit together constitute God-manhood, as the revelation of the Father in the Holy Trinity." God's image in man is not fully unfolded without the inter-

---

51. Ibid., 109.
52. Ibid., 110.
53. Ibid., 112–13.
54. Ibid., 117–18.

relation of these two principles. Man as husband and wife reflects this—two different exemplifications of human nature manifest in their unity the fullness of humanity and of the image of God enshrined in it. Their union is sealed by the dyad of the Son and the Holy Spirit, which reveals the Father. The reinstatement of man takes place only in God-manhood, in the Incarnation of the Word and the outpouring of the Holy Spirit.[55]

Bulgakov develops these two related themes at some length. "In view of the fall, the Incarnation . . . was obviously an atonement. But its purpose extends beyond this to the complete divinization of the creation, and the union of things in heaven and things on earth under the headship of Christ."[56] The creation of man underlies the Incarnation. There is some inalienable characteristic in man by which the possibility of the Incarnation is comprehensible.[57] He continues: "We must infer that, since the person of the Word found it possible to live in human nature as well as in its own, therefore it is itself in some sense a human person too." In order to serve as person to manhood, the divine person of the Word must itself be human "or, more exactly, co-human." Its union with human nature corresponds to the original relation between them. Man, on his side, must be capable of receiving and making room for a divine person in place of the human. So "man's original mode of being is theandric."[58] "The incarnation thus appears to postulate, on its hypostatic side at least, some original analogy between divine and human personality, which yet does not overthrow all the essential difference between them." The personal spirit of man has its divine, uncreated origin from "the spirit of God" (Gen. 2:7). It is a spark of the divine. Man is made a partaker of the divine nature and capable of divinization.[59] Man is theandric—the Word is the everlasting God-man (cf. 1 Cor. 15:47–49; Rom. 5:15). "Thus it is possible for the person of the heavenly God-man, the Word, to become the person of a created human nature, and so realize its original God-manhood."[60] It was natural for

55. Ibid., 119–21.
56. Ibid., 125.
57. Ibid., 126.
58. Ibid., 129.
59. Ibid., 129–30.
60. Ibid., 130–31.

the Word to take the place of the human personality of the human nature of Christ.

Thus, the union of the two natures in Christ rests in their mutual relationship as two variant forms of divine and created Wisdom. The dogma of Christology rests on sophiological foundations.[61] There is a kenosis (self-emptying) by Christ (cf. Phil. 2:7), but our Lord never ceased to be God. The kenosis occurred through God-manhood, "that unity of eternal and created manhood which is Sophia, the Wisdom of God."[62] While thus united, the two natures remain distinct to eternity.[63]

In turn, Pentecost also has a direct connection with God-manhood.[64] While the content of Sophia is the Word, its life is the Spirit.[65] What was new at Pentecost was not the gifts of the Spirit of God, but God the Spirit coming in person. Here the third person of the Trinity, the personal Spirit of Wisdom, comes down to abide in the world.[66] The Spirit's personal descent completes the link between God and creation begun in the Incarnation. He is described as another Comforter—never is Christ separated from the Holy Spirit. So God-manhood is the work not of one person, but of two.[67] The Spirit, however, is not *united* to human nature as the Son is, but he *penetrates* it—always measuring his action in accordance with the weakness of the creature.[68] "This then is Pentecost; the fruit of the Incarnation, the penetration of the creature by Wisdom, the union of the divine and created Sophia in the power of the Spirit—God-man-hood." Its full significance will only be known at the Parousia of Christ and the transfiguration of the world.[69] Then will come a new revelation of Pentecost and the *personal* revelation of the third *hypostasis*, which at present we lack. This will be the full revelation of the divine Sophia.[70]

61. Ibid., 132–33.
62. Ibid., 134.
63. Ibid., 141.
64. Ibid., 149–69.
65. Ibid., 149.
66. Ibid., 157–59.
67. Ibid., 162–63.
68. Ibid., 166.
69. Ibid., 167.
70. Ibid., 168.

The Kenosis of God

Since the Trinity is love, the three persons are self-effacing. "The revelation of oneself through the other, the knowledge of oneself as the other . . . such a relationship in which every one exists only for the other and in the other, identifying oneself with him: such a life in the other is love. Love as reciprocity and mutual self-negation is the substantial relationship of the triune subject."[71] God is sacrificial love. The relations of the divine persons exemplify this. From this, Bulgakov deduces that the Cross is central to the being of God. The self-sacrifice of the Cross, the total identification of the Son with humanity, the cosuffering of the Father in abandoning the Son, and the suffering of the Spirit in leaving the Son demonstrate the kenosis of the Trinity. Long before Moltmann, Bulgakov wrote of the crucified God. He also operated with a fully developed Rahnerian axiom before Rahner.[72] Moreover, he saw creation itself as kenotic, as "an act of sacrificial love." The creation is unstable and so needs redemption, quite apart from any consideration of human sin. Thus, creation and redemption are ontologically identical and both express the sacrificial emptying of the Trinity.[73]

Transcending the Tradition?

Bulgakov is convinced that his model of self-sacrificial, perichoretic love can overcome the divisions in the church associated with the *filioque* controversy. Something new is needed to do this, he thinks. The patristic resources have been exhausted.[74] The personalist paradigm has the capacity to resolve the question. Both the Eastern and the Western positions on the clause are one-sided. He calls the dispute "une déformation et une partialité de la pensée dogmatique," a "logomachy . . . dogmatically obscure . . . entirely negative . . . carried on in the icy emptiness of scholastic abstractions."[75] He is unable to trace any impact from the question in the life of the churches, which would

71. Meerson, *Trinity of Love*, 177–78.
72. Ibid., 178–80.
73. Ibid., 181–82.
74. Bulgakov, *Anthology*, 139; Meerson, *Trinity of Love*, 185.
75. Bulgakov, *Anthology*, 139–40; Sergei Nikolaevich Bulgakov, *Le Paraclet*, ed. Constantin Andronikof (Paris: Aubier, 1946), 87.

certainly have been the case if heresy was involved.[76] It has not affected the worship of the Holy Spirit in either church. The first movement of the Spirit is from the Father *on* the Son. The Spirit rests on the Son. Then the second movement of the Spirit, as the hypostatic love of the Son for the Father, is from the Son to the Father. Both sides recognize a relation between the Son and the Spirit. As Bulgakov says,

> The Son, through his begetting, receives the Holy Spirit from the Father and, though being personally distinct, remains eternally insep- arable from the Holy Spirit; the Son, then, is begotten *ex Patre Spir- ituque*. In the same way, the Spirit proceeds from the Father and rests on the Son; this is what corresponds to both *per Filium* and *ex Patre filioque*. In all the interpersonal relationships within the Trinity, there is always an *and* and a *through*.[77]

He argues that not only is the *filioque* clause no reason for the schism, but that a variety of *theologoumena* should be tolerated in the church. However, he is critical of causal language here, which John of Da- mascus failed to avoid.[78] Bulgakov's proposals have not received wide- spread approval in the East. Bobrinskoy refers to his and Boris Bolo- tov's criticisms of the *filioque* controversy and points to Lossky's defense of the Eastern position.[79]

Assessment

Bulgakov's sophiology is dynamic, scintillating, and brilliant, with much profound insight. Bobrinskoy refers to "great riches" concealed here.[80] Bulgakov shows, in typically Eastern fashion, a refreshing absence of concern about the agnostic and skeptical crit- icism of the Enlightenment that has so bedeviled Western Chris- tianity. But, quite apart from his proving a fertile field for a later generation of panentheists like Moltmann, a number of obvious criticisms arise, besides those of Lossky. Bulgakov has very similar weaknesses to Moltmann. He follows Solovyov's approach to God

76. Bulgakov, *Paraclet*, 124–25.
77. Meerson, *Trinity of Love*, 183; Bulgakov, *Paraclet*, 143.
78. Meerson, *Trinity of Love*, 184.
79. Bulgakov, *Paraclet*, 87, 93–94, 124–25; Bobrinskoy, *Mystery*, 291–93.
80. Bobrinskoy, *Mystery*, 36.

through human experience. This leads directly to panentheism. He
has to clarify how he differs from pantheism. Moreover, his preoc-
cupation with Sophia—despite his protestations—effectively subjects the being of God to an attribute. His reductionist focus on Wisdom eliminates God's freedom. Despite his proper concern to
preserve the freedom of God in creation, he posits a state of nothingness that precedes and coexists with it. Moreover, the Cross is
integral to God's being since the Incarnation and all it entails flow
out of the divine Sophia. The end result is confusion between God
and the creature. Lossky points to Bulgakov's corresponding confusion between the church and the cosmos, when he comments that
the religious philosophy of Solovyov, the eschatological utopianism
of Fedorov, and the sophiology of Bulgakov, "which is an ecclesi-
ology gone astray," have the net result that "in these thinkers the
idea of the Church is confounded with that of the Cosmos, and the
idea of the Cosmos is dechristianised."[81] It comes as no surprise that
in 1937 Bulgakov was censured by the Moscow Patriarchate,
accused of intellectualism, gnosticism, an overactive imagination,
creating a fourth *hypostasis* (Wisdom), and infusing masculine and
feminine elements into the members of the Trinity.

Vladimir Lossky

Vladimir Lossky (1903–1958) was probably the greatest single
Orthodox influence in the West. Living in exile in France, he was able
to project Eastern theology to a Western audience. He considered himself to be building on the tradition of the Fathers, rather than on a line
of specifically Russian thought. He was also polemical. He opposed
the sophiological school of Bulgakov and also the *filioque* clause, seeing the West as having a distorted theology as a result. Indeed, as Del
Colle comments, "It is difficult in many passages of Lossky's work to
distill his constructive exposition of the Greek Fathers from his implicit
and explicit polemic against Latin theology."[82]

81. Lossky, *Mystical Theology*, 112; Bulgakov, *Wisdom of God*, 199–220.
82. Ralph Del Colle, *Christ and the Spirit: Spirit-Christology in Trinitarian Perspective* (New York: Oxford University Press, 1994), 23.

Apophaticism

At the heart of Lossky's theology is the axiom that God is unknowable in his essence and transcends his revelation.[83] Thus, theology is effectively identified with contemplation. Negation, not affirmation, is the way to proceed in relation to God. Basing his approach on the *Areopagitica* of Dionysius the Areopagite, Lossky says:

> Dionysius distinguishes two possible theological ways. One—that of cataphatic or positive theology—proceeds by affirmations; the other—apophatic or negative theology—by negations. The first leads us to some knowledge of God, but is an imperfect way. The perfect way, the only way which is fitting in regard to God, who is of his very nature unknowable, is the second—which leads us finally to total ignorance. All knowledge has as its object that which is. Now God is beyond all that is inferior to him, that is to say, all that which is. If in seeing God one can know what one sees, then one has not seen God in himself but something intelligible, something which is inferior to him. It is by *unknowing* . . . that one may know him who is above every possible object of knowledge. Proceeding by negations one ascends from the inferior degrees of being to the highest, by progressively setting aside all that can be known, in order to draw near to the Unknown in the darkness of total ignorance. For even as light, and especially abundance of light, renders darkness invisible; even so the knowledge of created things, and especially excess of knowledge, destroys the ignorance which is the only way by which one can attain to God in himself.[84]

God thus transcends all affirmations and negations. One can have no concepts relating to God, only signs.[85] This apophatic approach to *theologia* means that knowledge of God is not knowledge as we usually understand it, but rather total ignorance. It is not intellectual knowledge at all, but mystical ecstasy. As Lossky insists, theology and mysticism go together.[86]

83. Vladimir Lossky, *In the Image and Likeness of God*, ed. John H. Erickson and Thomas E. Bird ([Crestwood, N.Y.]: St. Vladimir's Seminary Press, 1974), 89.

84. Lossky, *Mystical Theology*, 25.

85. Alar Laats, *Doctrines of the Trinity in Eastern and Western Theologies: A Study with Special Reference to K. Barth and V. Lossky* (Frankfurt am Main: Peter Lang, 1999), 83–84.

86. Lossky, *Mystical Theology*, 7–22.

The Equal Ultimacy of the Persons and the Essence in the Trinity

In the Trinity, neither the three persons nor the unity is prior to the other, for God is "absolutely one according to his nature, absolutely three according to his persons," "a primordial antinomy of absolute identity and no less absolute diversity."[87] The essential identity of the three and their hypostatic diversity are equally ultimate.

The Essence and the Energies

According to Lossky, the Eastern church distinguishes in God the one nature or essence, three *hypostases* or persons, and the energies. We are unable to participate in either the essence of God or in the three *hypostases*. We cannot become the *hypostasis* of the Son. Yet the apostle Peter says that we are made to share the divine nature (2 Peter 1:4). "We are therefore compelled to recognize in God an ineffable distinction, other than that between his essence and his persons, according to which he is, under different aspects, both totally inaccessible and at the same time accessible." This is the distinction between his essence or nature and the energies or divine operations. These latter are forces inseparable from God's essence "in which he goes forth from himself, manifests, communicates, and gives himself." In this way, the divine nature communicates itself to us through its energy.[88] This corresponds to the distinction between the Trinity (the immanent Trinity) and the economy. Lossky refers to Basil, among others,[89] in support of this view. We saw in chapter 7 how Basil left some hostages to fortune, and this is one. The energies are outpourings of the divine nature, "for God is more than his essence," and "God exists both in his essence and outside of his essence."[90] The energies are "an exterior manifestation of the Trinity."[91] Failure to distinguish between God's being and his work will lead to a confusion between God's being and his acts, so that both the procession of the persons and the creation of the world will equally be acts of the divine nature or essence. "The Son and the Spirit are, so

87. Ibid., 88; Lossky, *Image and Likeness*, 80.
88. Lossky, *Mystical Theology*, 70.
89. Others include Maximus the Confessor, Dionysius, John of Damascus, and Gregory Nazianzen.
90. Lossky, *Mystical Theology*, 73.
91. Ibid., 80.

to say, personal processions, the energies natural processions. The energies are inseparable from the nature, and the nature is inseparable from the three Persons."[92] The obvious root of Lossky's teaching here is Palamas (whom we criticized in chapter 11).

God is inaccessible in his essence, as is clear in Lossky's espousal of apophaticism. However, he is present in his energies "'as in a mirror,' remaining invisible in that which he is; 'in the same way we are able to see our faces, themselves invisible to us in a glass', according to a saying of St. Gregory Palamas."[93] God totally reveals himself in his energies. Yet his nature (essence) is in no way divided, for the distinction between essence and energies merely signifies two different modes of the divine existence. The energies are "the *natural* processions of God himself," akin to the distinction between the sun and its rays.[94] For the moment, we will leave aside the question of whether or not Lossky has divided God in two. However, there is a vital point to note in this distinction. For Lossky, it appears that, on the one hand, God is wholly unknowable and we are to devote ourselves to a process of mystical negation by which we arrive at the darkness of total ignorance. On the other hand, in his energies God has totally revealed himself.[95] The net effect of this is that God is reduced to nothing. On the one hand, he is unknowable and cannot in any particular detail determine the course of our life. On the other hand, since he has wholly revealed himself, we can be the masters of this revelation, and so can determine for ourselves the details of what we can and ought to be and do. Lossky's total agnosticism concerning who God *is* sounds pious, but in reality it is quite the reverse.

This distinction between essence and energies, Lossky maintains, enables us to appreciate how the Trinity can be incommunicable in essence and yet come to dwell within us. This presence is not causal, the result of omnipotent action by God. In this, he rules out the view of God's omnipotent grace held by Aquinas and Calvin. Nor, he proceeds, is God's presence in accordance with his essence, for this is unknowable and incommunicable. Rather, "it is a mode according to

92. Ibid., 85–86.
93. Ibid., 86.
94. Lossky, *Image and Likeness*, 54–55.
95. Ibid., 55–56.

which the Trinity dwells in us by means of that in itself which is communicable . . . by the energies which are common to the three hypostases, or, in other words, by grace," which the Holy Spirit communicates to us. He who has the Spirit has also the Son and the Father.[96] The union with God to which he calls us, signified in 2 Peter 1:4, is union with God in his energies, not in his essence or persons. "In deification we are by grace (that is to say, in the divine energies), all that God is by nature, save only identity of nature. . . . We remain creatures while becoming God by grace, as Christ remained God in becoming man by the Incarnation."[97]

The Economy

Christ's person is that of the second person of the Trinity. In the hypostatic union, the two natures permeate each other. But this permeation is unilateral, coming from the divine side. Yet it enables the human nature to be pervaded by the divine energies from the moment of the Incarnation, as iron is permeated by fire, becoming fire while remaining iron.[98]

The divine dispensation has two sides to it. Negatively, it consists of salvation and redemption from sin. Positively, it consists of deification, God's ultimate goal for humanity.[99] Both elements are necessary. The positive side needs to be taught because of the work of the Holy Spirit. The Holy Spirit is inseparable from the Son, and so too are their respective operations. Lossky is highly critical of the West for its exclusive focus on redemption, the juridical, the work of Christ, his death and resurrection. As a result, the Spirit's work suffers neglect. This trend goes back to Anselm. In contrast, the Bible presents a range of metaphors signifying our full redemption—the bucolic, where the Lord is seen as the good shepherd; the juridical, on which the West focuses; the military, denoting the conquest of Satan; the medical, or healing from sickness and corruption; and the diplomatic, the divine stratagem by which the devil is deceived. However, the West builds its theology on only one of them. It misses the

96. Lossky, *Mystical Theology*, 86.
97. Ibid., 87.
98. Ibid., 145–46.
99. Lossky, *Image and Likeness*, 110.

end goal of deification and so diminishes the work of the Spirit at the expense of the work of the Son.[100]

Notwithstanding this, the Incarnation is certainly the ontological foundation of the whole of salvation. In it there is a twofold kenosis (self-emptying). In the first place, the Son submitted his will to the will of the Father. This is actually the will of the whole Trinity, for the Father's will is the source of will, the will of the Son is expressed in obedience, and the will of the Spirit is expressed in accomplishment. The Son's submission led to his incarnation. Second, there is also the kenosis of the deified humanity of Christ, by which he submitted to the fallen condition of humanity, which entailed suffering and death.[101] The first kenosis is the basis of the second. Both have as their ultimate end the union of humanity with God.[102]

However, of equal significance is the economy of the Holy Spirit. The goal of Christ's work is the deification of human nature,[103] achieved by the Spirit granting grace to us inwardly. Through this, the Holy Trinity dwells within us. In this, the Spirit does not suppress human personality, but rather confirms it.[104] "Within the church the Holy Spirit imparts to human hypostases the fullness of deity after a manner which is unique, 'personal', appropriate to every man as a person created in the image of God."[105] The Holy Spirit has a twofold role in the economy, first toward the church (John 20:19–23), and second in relation to human persons (Acts 2:1–5).[106] The Spirit is never considered by the East as the bond of love between the Father and the Son, as in Western Trinitarianism after Augustine. Nor is he the bond uniting Christ and the church.[107] This would make the Spirit secondary to the other two persons, his work merely ancillary to the Son's. Besides, love is a property of the divine nature, an attribute

---

100. Ibid., 98–110. This stress on both the incarnation of the Son and the work of the Spirit is common to the Orthodox, although others, such as John Zizioulas, stress more than Lossky two dimensions of the one work of God. See John D. Zizioulas, *Being as Communion: Studies in Personhood and the Church* (Crestwood, N.Y.: St. Vladimir's Seminary Press, 1985), 123–42.

101. Lossky, *Mystical Theology*, 144–46.

102. Ibid., 154–55.

103. Ibid., 172–73; Lossky, *Image and Likeness*, 97–110.

104. Lossky, *Image and Likeness*, 108; Lossky, *Mystical Theology*, 166–68.

105. Lossky, *Mystical Theology*, 166.

106. Ibid., 166–68.

107. Ibid., 243–44.

common to all three persons, not something peculiar to the person of the Holy Spirit.

The kenosis of the Son and the Spirit is evident in that not one of the three persons reveals himself. Instead, each one manifests the others. The Father does not make himself known, but allows the Son to reveal him. The Son does not draw attention to himself, but leads us to the Father. The Spirit bears witness to the Son and not to himself. Each one "acts in concourse" with the other two,[108] for they "do not themselves assert themselves, but one bears witness to another."[109] Laats calls this view of Lossky's "ascetic."[110] It entails the renunciation of existing for oneself, freeing oneself from one's nature. This is what the ascetics and mystics attempted. This, Lossky maintains, is characteristic of God and, in turn, on our level, is involved in deification.

The Immanent Trinity

Lossky, following the fourteenth-century Eastern councils, makes a major distinction between the trihypostatic existence in itself (the relations of the persons of the Trinity in itself) and the trihypostatic existence "outside the essence" (in the economy). In his hypostatic existence, the Holy Spirit proceeds from the Father alone. However, in order of manifestation, the Spirit proceeds from the Father through the Son.[111] Here the difference between the immanent Trinity and the economic Trinity is obvious. Lossky appears to qualify this elsewhere, but only in appearance, not reality, for through the Incarnation we catch "a glimpse"—no more—of the interior relations of the Trinity.[112] This difference mirrors the gap between the essence and the energies. While there is continuity with the Son, in the Trinity and in his incarnation, at root the essence of God remains unknowable.

This ineffability also affects the persons. The divine persons are in community. Their perfection lies in kenosis. Each reveals the other

---

108. Ibid., 85.
109. Ibid., 160.
110. Laats, *Doctrines of the Trinity*, 115–19.
111. Lossky, *Image and Likeness*, 93ff.
112. Vladimir Lossky, *The Vision of God* (London: Faith Press, 1963), 66.

and opens himself to the other;[113] none asserts himself.[114] However, it is impossible to define positively what a person is. Apophaticism applies here also. Lossky admits that he has not found such a doctrine in patristic theology. Indeed, it cannot be conceptualized.[115] The divine persons are unique, irreducibly different,[116] "ineffably distinct."[117] They are "three consciousnesses but a single Subject."[118]

The Monarchy of the Father

For Lossky, as for the entire East, the Father is the *principium*, the source and fountain of deity. Thus, he contends against the West, the origin of the *hypostases* is not impersonal, since it is based on the *person* of the Father, not on the divine essence.[119] Thus, every divine energy comes from the Father. In the manifestation, in the economy, there is an order (*taxis*), in which every energy comes from the Father, is expressed in or through the Son, and goes forth in the Holy Spirit. This order must be clearly distinguished from the hypostatic procession (the intra-Trinitarian relations) from the Father alone.[120] This raises the acute problem of the faithfulness of God, for his revelation in the economy does not reflect who he is eternally. This introduces Barth's specter of a *Deus absconditus* (a hidden God) lurking in the shadows behind his revelation to threaten us.

Lossky charges the West with advocating an impersonal divine essence, impairing the monarchy of the Father. Grounding the unity of the Trinity on the common nature or essence, as in the West, means that the essence "overshadows the persons and transforms them into relations within the unity of the essence."[121] In consequence, "the hypostastic characteristics . . . find themselves more or less swallowed up in the nature or essence." The persons are then identified with the relations between them and so are reduced to relations, as in

113. Lossky, *Image and Likeness*, 106.
114. Lossky, *Mystical Theology*, 144.
115. Lossky, *Image and Likeness*, 111–14.
116. Ibid., 107–13.
117. Lossky, *Mystical Theology*, 61.
118. Lossky, *Image and Likeness*, 192.
119. Lossky, *Mystical Theology*, 58ff.; Lossky, *Image and Likeness*, 81ff.
120. Lossky, *Image and Likeness*, 91–94.
121. Lossky, *Mystical Theology*, 58.

Aquinas.[122] The West is rationalistic, and its doctrine actually ends up with nothing more than a monad. "Where the Trinity is concerned, we are in the presence of the One or of the Three, but never of two." A personal God cannot be a monad, but neither can he be a dyad, which is an opposition of two terms and cannot signify an absolute diversity.[123] Instead, the three persons are absolutely different. By speaking of the Son as wisdom and the Holy Spirit as will (or love), the West introduces external qualities into the Trinity, whereas the Trinity is prior to all the qualities in which God manifests himself.[124] The energies cannot characterize the divine persons. One cannot transmute the relations of the persons in the manifestation of the Trinity into the Trinity itself. In fact, one cannot know the Trinity in itself.

Criticism

Apophaticism. Right at the heart of Lossky's theology is total agnosticism. We have remarked that the total unknowability of God as he *is*, together with his total accessibility through his energies, is far from the pious construction that it appears to be. It affirms either that God is nothing since we cannot know him, or that he is totally knowable, in which case we can be masters of his revelation. In both instances, God is reduced to nothing and we are everything.

Essence/energies. Here our earlier criticisms of Palamas again apply. Lossky introduces a division in God, rather than a distinction. Classic Trinitarian dogma held that God is one being or *ousia*, and three persons or *hypostases*. There is no interposed third element, such as the energies. Moreover, the NT teaches that we can know God. We cannot know him in his fullness, but we may know him truly. This is because he has revealed *himself* to us and, by the Holy Spirit with his Word, we can know him.[125]

---

122. Ibid., 56–57; Lossky, *Image and Likeness*, 77ff.

123. Lossky, *Image and Likeness*, 84–85.

124. Ibid., 86.

125. See, *inter alia*, T. F. Torrance, *The Hermeneutics of John Calvin* (Edinburgh: Scottish Academic Press, 1988), 86ff.; T. F. Torrance, *Theology in Reconstruction* (Grand Rapids: Eerdmans, 1975), 76–98; Thomas F. Torrance, "Intuitive and Abstractive Knowledge: From Duns Scotus to John Calvin," in *De doctrina Ioannis Duns Scoti: Acta Congressus Scotistici Internationalis Oxonii et Edimburgi 11–17 Sept. 1966 celebrati* (Rome: Curae Commissionis Scotisticae, 1968), 4:291–305.

It is clear, as Illtyd Trethowan indicates, that Lossky makes a distinction in God other than that of the persons. The net result, Trethowan concludes, is "disastrous. For it seems to destroy God's unity."[126] Lossky is aware of this charge, since it was brought against Palamas himself by his opponents in the fourteenth century. He defends himself against it.[127] But it seems to me that this idea of the energies depends on the essence of God being beyond knowledge, on a comprehensive ignorance, an ignorance of total darkness. However, such a postulate cannot make sense, for it assumes that we know enough about God's essence to judge it unknowable!

The distinction also introduces the idea that Laats describes as "levels of the trinity." There are three of these: first, that which is immanent in God—the three persons in the divine essence; second, the Trinity in manifestation—the three persons in the energies, the eternal overflow of the essence; and, third, the economy—the three persons at work in the creation through the energies. Of these, the second and third levels are congruent, but the first is not.[128] No such levels are present in the classic Trinitarian dogma of the East, where the essence and the persons are mutually exhaustive.

Moreover, there is also Lossky's puzzling distinction between the essence of God and that which is "outside the essence." God is greater than his essence or being! He operates "outside his essence." This seems to mean that God's essence is somehow limited. If so, what does this do for God's immanence—and transcendence? In any case, how can Lossky or anyone say this, if it is impossible to know anything about God's essence? Here it would seem that the argument for the utter ineffability of the essence of God collapses on itself.

Laats draws attention to a further problem. Because of the gap between essence and energies, God is free in creation, for it is not the work of his nature. However, since the energies are the overflow of his nature, it would seem that in terms of his energies he is not free to be or not be in relation to what is not God.[129] This leads us back to our earlier criticism that Lossky's position has the problem of a *Deus*

126. Illtyd Trethowan, "Lossky on Mystical Theology," *DRev* 92 (1974): 243, cited by Laats, *Doctrines of the Trinity*, 75–76.
127. Lossky, *Mystical Theology*, 76–77.
128. Laats, *Doctrines of the Trinity*, 91.
129. Ibid., 121–22.

absconditus, a radical cleavage between God as he is and God as he has revealed himself.

Lossky's doctrine of the divine essence, which after all is what gives rise to the teaching on the energies and is most basic to his theology, actually contradicts the historic doctrine of the Trinity. The essence is above the persons and the Trinity itself, as Lossky presents it. It is superessential. Yet Lossky can also say that God is greater than his essence. Lossky wants to have his cake and eat it too.[130] Trethowan comments that "to place a real distinction within God himself other than that of the Persons is surely not only uncalled-for but also disastrous. For it seems to destroy God's unity."[131] Dorothea Wendebourg has said as much, commenting that if the essence-energies distinction is real, as the Orthodox claim it is, the persons have no soteriological functions.[132] Lossky's Trinitarian doctrine contains crippling problems.

Dumitru Staniloae

Dumitru Staniloae (1903–1993) taught at the Theological Institute in Bucharest, Romania, from 1947 until his retirement in 1973. During that time, he was imprisoned for five years by the regime, spending much of this period in a concentration camp. He remarked in later years that "to carry one's cross in this way is the normal condition of the Christian, and so there is no need to talk about it."[133] Laats argues that, in contrast to Lossky, Palamas was not a leading influence on Staniloae.[134] However, it is clear that he was influenced by many of the same figures as Lossky—Dionysius the Areopagite, the Cappadocians, John of Damascus, Maximus the Confessor, and Palamas, all of whom he cites repeatedly, especially the Areopagite.

---

130. See the comments of Catherine LaCugna and Polycarp Sherwood, recorded by Laats, *Doctrines of the Trinity*, 124.

131. Cited by Laats, *Doctrines of the Trinity*, 76,

132. D. Wendebourg, "From the Cappadocian Fathers to Gregory Palamas: The Defeat of Trinitarian Theology," *StPatr* 17, no. 1 (1982): 196.

133. Kallistos Ware, foreword to *The Experience of God*, by Dumitru Staniloae, trans. and ed. Iona Ionita and Robert Barringer (Brookline, Mass.: Holy Cross Orthodox Press, 1994–2000), 1:xiii.

134. Laats, *Doctrines of the Trinity*, 87n67.

On the other hand, he is more moderate, nuanced, qualified, and balanced than Lossky.

The Knowledge of God

Staniloae's greater carefulness is seen in his treatment of the crucial Eastern view of the unknowability of God. He agrees that God is not known in his essence, whether through cataphatic or rational knowledge or by the superior apophatic or ineffable knowledge. However, rational knowledge is not to be renounced; rather, it must be deepened through apophatic knowledge. Again, apophatic knowledge must come to expression in rational terms. However, apophatic knowledge is different from the *via negativa* of Western theology. The latter is based on reason and is a negative intellectual theology, whereas the apophaticism of the East is knowledge by direct experience. In Eastern terms, the two approaches are not mutually exclusive, but complementary. They differ in degree rather than kind. What is peculiar to apophatic knowledge is that God is experienced as *person*.[135] In Staniloae's own words,

> That cleansing from the passions and the acute sense of one's own sinfulness and insufficiency are necessary conditions for this knowledge shows that it is not a negative, intellectual knowledge as has been understood in the West, that is, the simple negation of certain rational affirmations about God. It has to do with a knowledge that comes through experience. In fact, the Eastern Fathers prefer the term "union" to "knowledge" when dealing with this approach to God.[136]

God is not identical to any of his qualities—infinity, eternity, simplicity—for he infinitely transcends them. They are "around God's being." As God is person, between him and us a relationship of love exists that maintains both God and ourselves as persons. Thus, our knowledge of God makes us seek to know him more, while our love for him stimulates us to an even greater love. Yet in this, apophaticism reigns in its two forms: what is experienced but cannot be defined, and

135. Staniloae, *Experience of God*, 1:95–100.
136. Ibid., 1:101.

what cannot even be experienced.[137] Since no person can be defined, since a person is alive, how much less can the supreme personal reality be captured in human notions. If anyone thinks he knows God by his own notions, he is spiritually dead.[138] However, for the Fathers both intellectual affirmations and negations have a basis in our experience of God's operations in the world. So a distinction between intellectual and apophatic knowledge that is too rigid is misplaced. As Dionysius the Areopagite commented, God transcends negations even more than affirmations, for he is supremely positive reality. For Dionysius, even the term "darkness," cited by Lossky, is unsuitable to God. God is not knowable, but the one who believes can experience him in a sensible and conscious manner.[139]

The intent of all this is to preserve the sense of mystery, which includes reason, but is deeper than that. It stresses the incomprehensibility of God, that he transcends all human reason or experience.[140] Indeed, he transcends existence itself. Hence, God is not *a being* or *an essence*. He is superessential, of an order entirely different from all created being.[141] He cannot be defined, for he is supremely apophatic, self-existent.[142] God has revealed of himself only that which relates to how he stands in relationship to the world.[143]

How does the Incarnation fit into this paradigm? Despite Staniloae's more cautious and balanced account, does not this Eastern bifurcation in the knowledge of God imply a Nestorian understanding of Christ? If God is not knowable as he is, and all that is possible for human beings is a knowledge of those things that are "around him," namely, his uncreated energies or attributes,[144] how can the humanity of Christ have real personal union with the second person of the Trinity? It seems to me an inescapable conclusion that there can be no hypostatic *union* in Christ if God is like that. The two natures were—and still are—unbridgeably distant.

137. Ibid., 1:103.
138. Ibid., 1:108–9.
139. Ibid., 1:112.
140. Ibid., 1:117.
141. Ibid., 1:129–31.
142. Ibid., 1:134–38.
143. Ibid., 1:211.
144. Ibid., 1:126.

Moreover, a second and allied question arises. T. F. Torrance has argued that Calvin overcame the late medieval dilemma of abstractive and intuitive knowledge of God by his theology of Word and Spirit. To grasp what Torrance means, we must recall that the Roman Catholic Church, by identifying knowledge of God with vision, reduced knowing God in this life to assenting to the teaching of the church, for here and now we cannot see God. Calvin, on the other hand, placed knowledge of God more in hearing than in sight. It is true that we cannot see God, but we can hear him. He speaks to us in his Word, preached and read. The Holy Spirit accompanies the Word and graciously grants us direct intuitive knowledge of God as we hear him in faith. The East has never addressed this vital point of Calvin's.[145]

Staniloae, like others in the Palamite tradition, is left without true knowledge of God. We cannot know the Trinitarian persons, for they are apophatic. What we can experience to some extent, namely, the dynamic manifestations of God, are "around his being" and are not identical with him. Yet at the same time God "in his entirety makes himself known to us" and causes us to experience him through each operation.[146] This dialectic reduces God to an unknowable nothing *in se* and at the same time elevates ourselves to a position where we can fully know his manifestations.

Intra-Trinitarian Love and Perichoresis

In Eastern Christianity, the sense of salvation is determined by the intra-Trinitarian love of God.[147] Each person in the Trinity knows himself and actualizes himself perfectly and eternally because of the "dynamic reciprocal interiority of the persons," or perichoresis. We must not understand this as a physical interiority; rather, it means that "each person is intentionally open to the others and directed towards them in a love which is total and infinite, and that each person holds on to nothing for himself, but is given wholly to the others. It is a total and infinite spiritual *perichōrēsis* of conscious love."[148] Staniloae explains:

---

145. Torrance, "Intuitive and Abstractive Knowledge"; Torrance, *Theology in Reconstruction*, 76–98; Torrance, *Hermeneutics of John Calvin*, 86ff.
146. Staniloae, *Experience of God*, 1:127–28.
147. Ibid., 1:192.
148. Ibid., 1:203.

Only this complete Trinitarian unity and knowledge explain the joy God has in knowing and loving other persons too, and in turn the joy these other persons have in knowing God and one another in a union without confusion. . . . If there were no Trinitarian love, neither would there be knowledge of God or any possibility of knowledge and love between God and created persons. The striving for knowledge comes from interpersonal love, and this comes from the holy Trinity.[149]

Staniloae argues that the divine love is seen in God's movement toward his creatures, toward union with them. This follows from the fact that there is in God "a community of persons among whom love is manifested."[150] He continues:

The fullest loving going out towards creatures was carried out by God through the incarnation of his Son, who assumed human nature. But simultaneously the Son filled human nature with his divine love for the Father. Through love the Holy Spirit unites us with God and among ourselves and becomes the bearer of love from God to us and from us to God and one another, just as God's incarnate Son is too. The Spirit moves us from within through his love which he has from the Father and brings to us the love of the Father, while at the same time implanting in us too his own love for the Father and for all men.[151]

The intra-Trinitarian love highlights the divine persons. "Love always presupposes two 'I's' who love one another" in a reciprocal relationship. Apart from the perfect love of the persons of the Trinity, there can be no accounting for love among human beings. This Trinitarian love does not produce the divine persons, as Catholic theology says it does, for by making love prior to persons they make it—and so the Trinity—impersonal. Instead, according to the East, divine love presupposes the divine persons, and so is entirely personal.[152]

This intra-Trinitarian love is the foundation of our salvation and deification, "the extension to conscious creatures of the relations that obtain between the divine persons." Through his incarnation, the Son

149. Ibid., 1:204.
150. Ibid., 1:240.
151. Ibid., 1:243.
152. Ibid., 1:245–47.

introduces us to filial communion with the Father, while through the Spirit we pray to the Father or speak with him as sons. In prayer, the Spirit draws us into his own prayer, creating between us and the Father, through grace, the same relation he has with the Father and the Son by nature. The incarnate Son as man expressed his filial love of the Father as an obedient love, while the Father was affirming his love to us as Father. For his part, the Holy Spirit deified the Son's humanity, making it fit to participate in the love that the Son has for the Father. Thus, we are drawn through the Holy Spirit into the relationship that the Son has with the Father. We are raised "into communion with the persons of the Holy Trinity."[153]

Staniloae powerfully emphasizes the three persons and their perichoretic communion of love. He also avoids the excesses into which Moltmann falls. He writes of the three persons as three subjects, for each loves the others, but he is also careful to safeguard the divine unity. There is no divine being lying behind the three, for being can only exist in a *hypostasis*, so God does not exist apart from the three persons. God is "a community of subjects who are fully transparent."[154] The divine essence is subject or threefold subject,[155] at one and the same time unity and relation, relation in the very heart of unity.[156] Thus, as three subjects, the three "compenetrate each other" and are "perfectly interior to one another," in full and perfect communion. Thus we can speak of a single God and three "I's." Staniloae is careful to safeguard the unity of the Trinity. This means that, in the generation of the Son and the procession of the Spirit, both the Son and the Spirit joyfully participate "along with the other—though from his own position—in living that act whereby the other comes forth from the Father."[157] Staniloae argues strongly that each "I" never asserts himself over another "I," but regards only the other, or sees himself only in the other. "In this self-forgetting of each person for the other perfect love is manifested and only this makes possible that unity which is opposed to individualism."[158] Citing Basil, he affirms that God tran-

153. Ibid., 1:248–49.
154. Ibid., 1:256.
155. Ibid., 1:260.
156. Ibid., 1:258.
157. Ibid., 1:260–62.
158. Ibid., 1:264.

scends the numbers one and three in our experience, for "the three subjects are so interior in their unity as Being that knows no dispersal that they can in no way be separated so as to be counted as three entities having a certain discontinuity between them."[159]

Summary

Duncan Reid explores in far greater detail than we can do here the differing lines between the Eastern and Western doctrines of the Trinity. The West is marked by what he calls "the identity principle," by which the Trinity is held to be as it is revealed in the economy of salvation. We have stressed this throughout as a vital principle. The West here points to the faithfulness and reliability of God. Reid adds that the East, by contrast, with its doctrine of energies, "postulates a *superessential* doctrine of the trinity, that is, one in which the trinitarian hypostases are regarded as fundamentally independent of economic functions or motifs."[160] Thus, there is no assurance that God is not other than he has revealed himself to be.

The Eastern doctrine of the Trinity requires different Trinitarian levels, undermines our knowledge of God, and, in so doing, implicitly questions the faithfulness and reliability of God. Largely due to its isolation from the West, the East has had no medieval period, no Renaissance or Reformation, and no Enlightenment, and so has never had to grapple with the vital epistemological breakthrough achieved by Calvin, to which Barth in his own way held, of direct auditory, intuitive knowledge of God. Moreover, its view of salvation, centered on incarnation, resurrection, and deification, leaves little room for the Atonement and justification. Its distinction between essence and energies, we must say again, is a major flaw. As Reid points out, the Orthodox regard this as a *real* distinction, not merely a rational one. However, a real distinction of this kind can hardly avoid questioning the simplicity of God.[161] It creates a situation where it is necessary to postulate a variety of levels in God, since God's actions are separate from his being.

159. Ibid., 1:265–66.
160. Duncan Reid, *Energies of the Spirit* (Atlanta: Scholars Press, 1997), 67.
161. Ibid., 88ff.

On the other hand, Eastern criticisms of the West should be heeded. The West, from Augustine, has had problems with the Holy Spirit. By asserting that the Spirit is the bond of love and union between the Father and the Son, it has tended to reduce the Spirit to less than a person. Behind this is the underlying problem of starting with the premise of the unity of the divine essence. Since the persons in some way follow, the essence is inherently impersonal. By contrast, the East begins with the persons, "reserving the concept of essence to denote God's beyondness."[162] By focusing on the persons, the East is able to develop with great vigor the living personal relations of the Trinity, which Western theologians have found exceedingly difficult. It is along these lines that a positive and effective challenge to Islam can be mounted.[163] Nevertheless, many misconceptions need to be clarified along the way. An example is the claim made by Staniloae that "while Western Christianity has represented more a mistrustful brake on humanity's path towards progress, the Orthodox Churches have always supported the people's aspirations for progress," in view of their doctrine of the Trinity, resurrection, and deification.[164] It seems that differing views of the Trinity mask still further divergences, including such things as the meaning of "the people's aspirations for progress."

162. John Meyendorff, *St. Gregory Palamas and Orthodox Spirituality* (Crestwood, N.Y.: St. Vladimir's Seminary Press, 1974), 126.

163. For further exploration of these themes, see, e.g., Reid, *Energies of the Spirit*.

164. Staniloae, *Experience of God*, 1:191.

Thomas F. Torrance

Thomas F. Torrance (1913–) is arguably the most significant theologian in the English-speaking world of the past fifty years or more.
After parish ministry and a brief spell as professor of church history
at New College, in the University of Edinburgh, he became professor
of Christian dogmatics there in 1952, and remained in that post until
his retirement in 1979. Since then he has produced a welter of publications. His main areas of interest are the connection between theology and natural science, particularly physics, ecumenical engagement
with the Orthodox churches, and the doctrine of the Trinity. Raised
in a missionary home deep in mainland China, he has seen himself as
a theological evangelist to the whole of Western culture.[1]

At first, Torrance's writings on the Trinity were scattered articles
in a range of books that reflect his wide interests across the whole field
of dogmatic and historical theology. Some of these articles were col-
lected and republished in *Trinitarian Perspectives* (1994).[2] Earlier *The
Trinitarian Faith* (1988) expounded the Trinitarian theology of the
church as it reached its resolution of the fourth-century crisis. Beyond

1. An outstanding account of Torrance's life and work is found in Alister E. McGrath, *Thomas
F. Torrance: An Intellectual Biography* (Edinburgh: T & T Clark, 1999). Torrance's younger
brother, David W. Torrance, provides a more personal account in "Thomas Forsyth Torrance:
Minister of the Gospel, Pastor, and Evangelical Theologian," in *The Promise of Trinitarian Theology: Theologians in Dialogue with T. F. Torrance*, ed. Elmer M. Colyer (Lanham, Md.: Rowman & Littlefield Publishers, 2001), 1–30.

2. Thomas F. Torrance, *Trinitarian Perspectives: Toward Doctrinal Agreement* (Edinburgh:
T & T Clark, 1994).

this, Torrance projected a multivolume dogmatics, but has been able to produce only one installment. However, this volume, *The Christian Doctrine of God: One Being, Three Persons* (1996), is perhaps his greatest single work.[3] Recently Elmer M. Colyer produced an excellent introduction to Torrance's theology and edited a symposium in which leading contemporary theologians interact with him on the doctrine of the Trinity.[4]

Major Influences on Torrance

In 1937, Torrance went to Basel for doctoral studies under Karl Barth. Barth's theology was to have a profound impact on him. However, it would be a serious mistake to call Torrance a Barthian, even if such creatures could be said to exist. Torrance is too powerful a thinker to be labeled by another man's theology. Indeed, his contribution to the volume edited by Donald McKim, *How Karl Barth Changed My Mind*, is better called "how I changed Karl Barth's mind."[5] Besides Barth, his teacher at Edinburgh, H. R. Mackintosh, had a significant impact on Torrance. Yet the impetus that both of these men provided was to drive Torrance back to the classic theological sources of the Reformation, particularly Calvin, and to the Fathers. His doctoral thesis at Basel was published as *The Doctrine of Grace in the Apostolic Fathers* (1946).[6] Thereafter, Torrance established himself as a major authority on Calvin and developed an encyclopedic knowledge of patristics. In particular, he drew extensively on the work of the Alexandrians, Athanasius, and Cyril, as well as Gregory Nazianzen.

At the same time, Torrance is no mere antiquarian. His philosophy teacher at Edinburgh, A. E. Taylor, made much use of contemporary science in his work, and Torrance was to follow in his steps. The Hungarian-born chemist and philosopher of science, Michael Polanyi,

---

3. Thomas F. Torrance, *The Christian Doctrine of God: One Being, Three Persons* (Edinburgh: T & T Clark, 1996).

4. Elmer M. Colyer, *How to Read T. F. Torrance: Understanding His Trinitarian and Scientific Theology* (Downers Grove, Ill.: InterVarsity Press, 2001); Elmer M. Colyer, ed., *The Promise of Trinitarian Theology: Theologians in Dialogue with T. F. Torrance* (Lanham, Md.: Rowman & Littlefield Publishers, 2001).

5. This is a phrase coined by Tony Lane in a review of the volume.

6. Thomas F. Torrance, *The Doctrine of Grace in the Apostolic Fathers* (Edinburgh: Oliver & Boyd, 1946).

developed a theory of knowing that had a kinship with Torrance's own thought, which he saw as applying to the theological field as well as to the natural sciences. Here two independent streams coalesced, for Torrance had already worked out his own epistemological approach by the time he encountered Polanyi.[7] Like Polanyi, Torrance recognizes that to know in a scientific way (*scientia* = knowledge), the knower must submit himself to the object of knowledge and allow it to disclose itself. This entails an attitude on the part of the knower akin to faith and obedience, whereby all preconceptions are to be subjected to the critical scrutiny of the one or the thing known.[8] Torrance points to the practice of James Clerk Maxwell as exemplifying this approach, and holds that it is reinforced by the theories and practice of Albert Einstein. In theology, it is not hard to see how this basic hermeneutic is compatible with the strong stress on revelation and the centrality of God taught by Barth—and, we may add for good measure, by Calvin.

Torrance's concern for the present and the future is connected to his work on the past. His interest in the Greek fathers drew him into dialogue, on behalf of the World Alliance of Reformed Churches, with the Greek Orthodox Church. After many years of discussions and partial agreements, a highly significant landmark was reached in 1991 with the signing of the "Agreed Statement on the Holy Trinity," published in 1993. The importance of this is underlined by the fact that the Greek Church had invited the fourteen other Orthodox communions to participate. Its weakness (see chapter 10) is that there were no representatives present who were committed to the Augustinian model. It is an agreement among those predisposed to agree. It is less than a major ecumenical breakthrough. To say, with Gary Deddo, that "in principle the 1,000-year-old schism over the *filioque* has been resolved" is a trifle premature, since the schism was between Orthodoxy and Rome, not between Orthodoxy and the World Alliance of Reformed Churches![9]

7. On the use that Torrance makes of Polanyi, see McGrath, *Thomas F. Torrance,* 228–32; Colyer, *How to Read T. F. Torrance,* 332–33.

8. For Polanyi, see Michael Polanyi, *Personal Knowledge* (Chicago: University of Chicago Press, 1958); Michael Polanyi, *The Tacit Dimension* (Chicago: University of Chicago Press, 1958).

9. Gary W. Deddo, "The Holy Spirit in T. F. Torrance's Theology," in *The Promise of Trinitarian Theology,* ed. Colyer, 107.

The Main Structures of Torrance's Trinitarianism

In Torrance's theology, the Trinity "is both the *ultimate ground* of our salvation and knowledge of God and the *basic grammar* of Christian theology."[10] This at once points us to the integral connection of theology and worship. Torrance is careful to ground the most developed and refined theological concepts relating to the Trinity in basic Christian experience of the gospel. However, this does not mean that he derives these concepts or his theology from our own experience. In fact, the very reverse is the case. What it does mean is that there is an unbreakable connection between theology and Christian faith and worship, both grounded in God's sovereign action in revelation and salvation.

This is clear when he asserts that *God may be known only through God*. We cannot know God apart from his saving actions.[11] As with Barth, there is no path to God by natural theology, for all is dependent on revelation. Here Torrance undercuts the contemporary predilection, following Rahner, to base knowledge of God, including God as triune, on human experience. We saw how this leads to pantheism or panentheism. For Torrance, this approach is impossible, for "there is no God other than the self-revealed God, and no self-revelation of God apart from the fulfilment of his eternal purpose in his saving and reconciling acts in the life, death and resurrection of Jesus proclaimed to us in the Gospel."[12] This revelation is through Jesus Christ and in the Spirit, so that in the Holy Trinity we have to do with God himself. God is intrinsically triune and cannot be truly conceived otherwise.[13] Jesus Christ is "the all-important bridge between God and man and the one place in space and time where we human beings may share in God's knowledge of himself and really know him and believe in him in accordance with his own self-interpretation."[14] Thus, revelation is "not the revealing of something about God, but God revealing himself out of himself in such a way that he who reveals and he who is revealed are one and the same."[15] Torrance also undercuts the

10. Colyer, *How to Read T. F. Torrance*, 287.
11. Torrance, *Christian Doctrine of God*, 13.
12. Ibid.
13. Ibid., 15–16.
14. Ibid., 17.
15. Ibid., 22.

Western approach since Aquinas by introducing the Trinity right away. God is one being, three persons. The three persons are one God, and God is the three persons. Hence, "to admit any other than a trinitarian way of thinking about God is in fact not only to relativise and question the truth of the Trinity but to contradict the Trinity and to set aside the Gospel."[16]

Torrance spells out the integral connection between theology and worship further by considering the way, from our side, that we are drawn into knowing God. Here the connections with Polanyi are evident. *We need to indwell the NT as a whole and in all its parts* so as to allow the message to be interiorized in the depths of our mind.[17] The metaphor of indwelling was one that Polanyi used. It has roots in the Johannine concept of indwelling, and both Polanyi and Torrance himself draw on this. When we do this, Torrance argues, we find that the overwhelming stress in the NT is on the deity of Christ, on the unbroken relation between the Son and the Father,[18] which was forced on Jesus' followers by his resurrection.[19] Speaking of "the whole coherent evangelical structure of historical divine revelation given in the New Testament Scriptures," Torrance says, "It is when we indwell it, . . . absorb it in ourselves, and find the very foundations of our life and thought changing under the creative and saving impact of Christ, . . . that we believe in him as Lord and God." In the Crucifixion and Resurrection, we are led to distinguish between Christ the Son of God and God the Father, and so to think of a distinction, as well as oneness, between the Father and the Son, between God and God. Further, in the light of Pentecost, when the Holy Spirit promised by the Father was poured out on the church, ground is given for the discernment of God as intrinsically triune.[20]

However, the doctrine of the Trinity developed in the course of church history. How do the creeds fit into the picture? Torrance argues that there is a clear biblical basis for them, since, according to Paul, access to knowledge of God as he is in himself has been provided for us through the reconciliation with God brought about by the Cross of

16. Ibid., 24.
17. Ibid., 37.
18. Ibid., 49.
19. Ibid., 52.
20. Ibid., 53–54.

Christic.[21] The connection between theology and worship is again relevant, for the worship and doctrine of the Trinity belong together.[22] Theological statements point to the transcendent reality of God, and thus can never be abstracted from a context of worship and adoration. For instance, the *homoousios* expresses the truth that "God's revelation of himself as Father, Son and Holy Spirit in the incarnate economy of salvation was grounded in and derived from God as he is in his own eternal Being and Nature."[23] The *homoousios* is the theological key that the church needs to unlock the implicit doctrine of the Trinity in the NT and to bring it to explicit formulation. In the mystery of God's self-revealing, there is an inarticulate ingredient, as well as an articulate ingredient. The former governs the latter. "We know of him more than we can ever tell."[24] This clearly corresponds to Polanyi's tacit dimension of knowledge.

Levels of Knowledge

There are, in Torrance's estimation, three levels of knowledge. He describes this as "a stratified structure comprising several coordinate levels" and "different levels of truth in their cross-level coordination with each other." The most basic level, the ground level, is the level of evangelical apprehension and experience. This level of knowledge is open to the higher level of the revealing and saving acts of Christ in his incarnate economy and is dependent on it to be what it is. This higher level, in turn, is open to the transcendent level of the Trinitarian relations in God himself and is dependent on it to be what it is.[25] This three-level structure corresponds to the three levels of thought in scientific knowledge as expounded by Einstein and Polanyi: a basic level of ordinary, everyday experience, a secondary level of scientific theory, with the search for the logical unity of empirical and conceptual factors, and a tertiary level of a more refined and higher logical unity with a minimum of refined concepts and relations. This highest level is marked by a "logical economy and simplicity," such as is seen in the theory of rel-

21. Ibid., 68.
22. Ibid., 74.
23. Ibid., 80.
24. Ibid., 81.
25. Ibid., 83.

ativity.[26] This hierarchical system of truths is open upwards, but not reducible downwards, ruling out all reductionism. As a direct consequence, "any meaningful rational system must have indeterminate areas where its formalisations break off and retain their consistency only through controlling organisation from a higher frame of reference."[27] This also applies to doctrinal formulations. These require cross-level reference to a higher level in order to be ontologically significant as well as theologically consistent. No dogmatic system contains its own truth-reference. What this means is that theological statements point to the transcendence of God and so entail and require worship. Moreover, they cannot be reduced to the laws of logic. Here we come face-to-face with the single greatest difference between theology and the natural sciences. The living God is the supreme truth. We are summoned to respond to him in a way that is utterly different than in natural science. Moreover, the structure must be understood from the top down, not the other way around, as in science.[28]

What does this mean in detail? First, at the ground level of religious experience and worship, we learn more in the church than we can ever say, reinforced by constant reading and study of the Bible within the community of the faithful. This is the *sine qua non* of all the other levels, which can never be detached from this, their root.[29] Second, at the theological level we are able to use theological knowledge to apprehend more fully the economic and ontological and Trinitarian structure of God's revealing and saving acts in Jesus Christ.[30] Here the *homoousion* is the vital hinge, for the key is the identity of Jesus Christ with the being of God.[31] Third, at the higher theological level our thinking enters more deeply into the self-communication of God in the saving and revealing activity of Christ and in his one Spirit. Here too the *homoousion* is of primary significance, with the insight that what God is toward us in Jesus Christ he is inherently and eternally in his own being. Thus, our knowledge of God in the gospel is

26. Ibid., 84–85.
27. Ibid., 86.
28. Ibid., 87.
29. Ibid., 88–90.
30. Ibid., 91.
31. Ibid., 93–98.

grounded in who he is in himself, in the being of God. But the *homoousion* does not allow us to read back into God what is human and finite.[32]

The Personal Nature of God

With the Trinity, we have to do with God in his internal, intelligible, personal relations. With the *homoousion* and the hypostatic union, the concept of perichoresis, or mutual containing, helps us hold together the identity of the divine being and the intrinsic unity of the three divine persons. In line with this is what Torrance calls an onto-relational concept of the divine persons, which includes the relations of the persons in what they are. In fact, the development of the doctrine of the Trinity brought about a radical transformation of the Greek concept of being, from an impersonal to a personal sense. It "revealed the profound personal nature of God's being." It is not that the three persons are *in* the being of God (as though the persons were not identical with God's being), but that the three persons *are* the one God. God is "a fullness of Personal Being in himself . . . a communion of Persons." The one being of God is not some abstract essence, but the intensely personal "I am." The divine being and the divine communion are to be understood wholly in terms of one another.[33] The hypostatic union, the *homoousion*, being and person, and perichoresis are a coordinated set of theological concepts on three interrelated levels. They are the way in which the Trinity, implicit in Scripture, comes to explicit articulation.

The Immanent Trinity and the Economic Trinity

Torrance is critical of Rahner's axiom, and in line with Barth he preserves the sovereign freedom of God. The Incarnation involved no surrender of God's transcendence "or any compromising of his eternal freedom," for it was not necessary for God to be God and live as God.[34] There is, of course, a right and a wrong way to take Rahner. Rahner's axiom has value if all it is taken to imply is that the economic Trinity

32. Ibid., 98–99.
33. Ibid., 102–4.
34. Ibid., 108.

is a reliable indicator of who God is in himself. This is the value that
Torrance sees in it. However, Rahner asserted that the identity between
the economic Trinity and the immanent Trinity worked in both directions. Not only is the economic Trinity equated with the immanent
Trinity, but the immanent Trinity is equated with the economic Trinity. This has encouraged the belief that the economic Trinity is all there
is and that talk of the immanent Trinity is pure metaphysical speculation. The consequence is that creation is viewed as correlative with God.
God is not free, but is bound up with the world in an ongoing mutual
history. The Incarnation was not the result of a decision freely made by
God, but instead overflowed out of his being. This way of thinking
leads to pantheism or panentheism. It is the route taken by Moltmann,
LaCugna, Elizabeth Johnson, and Robert Jenson.

The Centrality of the *Homoousion*

Torrance argues pervasively that the *homoousion* expresses the
central content of the NT witness to Jesus Christ.[35] The identity of
Jesus Christ with God, which the term affirms, means that faith in
Christ perfectly coincides with faith in God.[36] This recognition at
Nicaea was an absolutely fundamental, irreversible, and inerasable
event in the history of the Christian faith, "a decisive step in deeper
understanding of the Gospel, giving precise expression to the all-
important relation between the incarnate Son and God the Father."
The Nicene formulation is akin to some of the great events in the history of science "in which the rational structure of human knowledge
of the created universe has been profoundly revised in a way upon
which we cannot go back."[37] It brought about a revolution in the way
we think about God. God is not alien and unknowable. He has communicated with us. He himself is a living, dynamic, personal being
and has revealed himself to be so. He loves us and has enabled us to
know him.[38] The *homoousion* "expressed the fact that what God is

35. See Colyer, *How to Read T. F. Torrance*, 70–81.
36. Thomas F. Torrance, *The Trinitarian Faith: The Evangelical Theology of the Ancient
Catholic Church* (Edinburgh: T & T Clark, 1988), 117; Thomas F. Torrance, *The Mediation of
Christ* (Grand Rapids: Eerdmans, 1983), 53.
37. Torrance, *Christian Doctrine of God*, ix-x.
38. Ibid., 3–4.

'toward us' and 'in the midst of us' in and through the Word made flesh, he really is in himself; that he is in the internal relations of his transcendent being the very same Father, Son and Holy Spirit that he is in his revealing and saving activity in time and space toward mankind."[39] It is "the supreme evangelical truth by which the Church stands or falls."[40]

As Gunton comments, "It would be difficult to exaggerate the importance for him [Torrance], in all aspects of his work, of the principle of the *homoousion*."[41] In particular, Gunton points to the crucial place of the *homoousion* of the Holy Spirit for Torrance. It enables a move to be made from God's economic action to his eternal being while, at the same time, preventing us from reading into God the kind of causal connections that we find in the created world. It keeps our knowledge of God spiritual and maintains the priority of a center in God, rather than in human experience.[42] Here again we see how Torrance stands out from much contemporary theology, which seeks knowledge about God from human experience and rejects any doctrine of an immanent Trinity. Instead, for Torrance, the *homoousion* compels us to read back into the immanent Trinity what is given in the economy, for in Christ and in the Spirit the inner being of God is, in some measure, disclosed.[43]

Perichoresis

Torrance understands perichoresis in a dynamic way as the mutual indwelling and interpenetration of the three persons "in the onto-relational, spiritual and intensely personal way" in which he expounds the Trinity. It involves "mutual movement as well as a mutual indwelling," in which "their differentiating qualities instead of separating them actually serve their oneness with each other." It is "the eternal movement of Love or the Communion of Love which the Holy Trinity ever is within himself." This corresponds to the teaching on

39. Torrance, *Trinitarian Faith*, 130.
40. Ibid., 132.
41. Colin Gunton, "Being and Person: T. F. Torrance's Doctrine of God," in *The Promise of Trinitarian Theology*, ed. Colyer, 116.
42. Ibid., 120.
43. Ibid., 122–23.

mutual coinherence of Epiphanius, Cyril of Alexandria, Athanasius, and Gregory Nazianzen,[44] although Torrance is quick to point out that it was pseudo-Cyril who first applied the term *perichoresis* to the persons of the Trinity (a claim recently refuted).[45]

Torrance argues that perichoresis offsets the danger of remnants of Origenist subordinationism. Since the three mutually contain one another, the Trinity is an indivisible wholeness. There is consequently no place for the Father to be underived deity, while the Son and the Spirit receive deity from the Father.[46] Rather, it asserts the full equality of the three persons as *autotheos* (God in themselves, not God by derivation), while also affirming their real distinctions. The Father, the Son, and the Holy Spirit share everything except the individual characteristics that differentiate them. The priority or monarchy of the Father must not be taken to imply a priority or superiority in deity. The "inner trinitarian order is not to be understood in an ontologically differential way," for it applies to the mysterious disposition or economy that the three have in the unity of the Godhead, "distinguished by position and not status, by form and not being, by sequence and not power, for they are fully and perfectly equal."[47] Here perichoresis rules out any ideas of before and after or of degrees of deity. In this perichoretic way, we can think of the Father as the Father, but not as the deifier of the Son and the Spirit.[48]

This leads us to Torrance's distinctive proposal concerning the divine monarchy. His position flows directly out of his teaching on perichoresis. As a corollary of this dynamic, mutual indwelling and communion, the Trinity may be known only as a whole in a circular movement from unity to trinity and from trinity to unity. Because of this, for Torrance the monarchy is that of the whole Trinity, not just the Father. Gregory Nazianzen taught this view, Torrance has advocated it, and the agreement between Orthodox and Reformed churches adopts it.[49]

44. Torrance, *Christian Doctrine of God*, 171–72.

45. Thomas F. Torrance, "Thomas Torrance Responds," in *The Promise of Trinitarian Theology*, ed. Colyer, 316; see Vassa S. Conticello, "Pseudo-Cyril's *De Sacrosancte Trinitate*: A Compilation of Joseph the Philosopher," *OCP* 61 (1995): 117–29.

46. Torrance, *Christian Doctrine of God*, 173–74.

47. Ibid., 175–76.

48. Ibid., 179–80.

49. Ibid., 181–85.

As a result of this understanding of the monarchy, Torrance argues that the procession of the Spirit rests on a deeper basis, originating in the *being* of the Father that is common to the Spirit and the Son, thus undercutting the *filioque* controversy.[50] He also launches a powerful critique of Palamism, arguing that, due to its strong distinction between the procession and the mission of the Spirit, it "drive[s] a wedge between the inner Life of God and his saving activity in history."[51]

One Being, Three Persons: Three Persons, One Being

Torrance points to the agreement between Athanasius and the Cappadocians at the Council of Alexandria (362) that God consists of one being and three persons as crucial in establishing that "the one and the three" and "the three and the one" are the obverse of each other. Here he notes the stark contrast to the Augustinian-Western conception of the Trinity, which begins with the one essence of God and only then moves on to the three persons. Instead, there should be no question of separating the trinity from the unity or the unity from the trinity.[52] Torrance's realism shines through when he points to reality having priority over our language, in contrast to today's postmodern agenda, as Colyer points out.[53]

Thus, in the intensely personal communion we have with God, we cannot have communion with the Father, or with the Son, or with the Holy Spirit, without having communion with all three, for they are who they are precisely as one indivisible being and three inseparable persons, or three inseparable persons and one indivisible being. In the doxologies of the church, there is no division in the worship of the Father, the Son, and the Holy Spirit, for they are homogenous and indivisible in their being and nature and are worshiped together as one God. They are three active persons, but are worshiped, not as a trio of divine objects, but as intrinsically and eternally triune, as one. So when we pray, we do not pray specifically to one person, divide our worship between them, or direct our devotion separately to the three

50. Ibid., 190ff.
51. Ibid., 187.
52. Ibid., 112–13.
53. Ibid., 116; Colyer, *How to Read T. F. Torrance*, 303n79.

persons, for in worshiping and praying to each person we worship and pray to the whole undivided Godhead.[54] Torrance, in seeking to avoid the Western tendency toward an impersonal essence, talks about the being of God as "fulness of personal being."[55]

The name *Father* may refer to the whole Godhead or instead to the person of the Father.[56] The Son proceeds from the being of the Father, not from the person of the Father. It is not always easy to distinguish the difference, Torrance agrees. The Father is the principle of the Godhead, but when he is considered in his inseparable oneness with the Son and the Holy Spirit as one being, the monarchy is identical with the Holy Trinity.[57] Here Torrance introduces an innovation. He wants to avoid the idea of Basil and Gregory of Nyssa that the person of the Father is the principle, or unifying center, of the Trinity. This leads, he says, to the Son and the Holy Spirit deriving their deity from the Father. However, he differs here from Calvin. His position also lends support to Gunton's criticism of a modalist tendency, for does not Torrance tend to blur the irreducible distinctions between the persons?

Torrance strongly maintains the unqualified oneness of the Father and the Son.[58] God has communicated his divine self to us in Jesus Christ, and thus now lives his divine life in our human life.[59] Absolutely, the Son is true God of true God, whole God of whole God. In himself he is very God. Relatively, toward others (*ad alium*), he is distinct from the Father and the Spirit.[60] In turn, the Holy Spirit absolutely is whole God of whole God, while relatively the Spirit is distinct from the Father and the Son.[61] The Spirit is not directly known in his own person, for he is hidden behind the revelation of the Father and the Son, which he mediates through himself. As spirit, he confronts us with the mystery of God. But he is not unknown or unknowable, for he takes us into communion with himself.[62]

54. Torrance, *Christian Doctrine of God*, 133–34.
55. Ibid., 102–4.
56. Ibid., 140.
57. Ibid., 141.
58. Ibid., 142.
59. Ibid., 142–43.
60. Ibid., 145.
61. Ibid., 147–48.
62. Ibid., 151–52.

The three persons are, Torrance maintains, substantive relations. They are more than "modes of being," as Basil and Gregory of Nyssa taught.[63] When thinking of the Trinitarian persons, we must set aside all analogies from the visible world. Instead, we must think of the Father and the Son as imageless relations. The persons are what they are not only in distinction from the others, but in relation to them. The differentiating characteristics (fatherhood, sonship) not only distinguish them, but also unite them. The Father stands in an ineffable relation as Father to the Son. The Holy Spirit must be understood in a spiritual and a completely genderless way.[64] We can affirm the real and intimate relation between the Father and the Son while exercising "a measure of apophatic reserve in our use and understanding of the words 'father' and 'son' as applied to God, for the truth they signify even in divine revelation lies beyond the limits of the terms used to signify it. They are intended to denote God in the inner relation of his Being as Father and Son in ways that elude our imagination and conceptual grasp."[65] Hence, "It would be a serious mistake . . . to interpret what is meant by 'Person' in the doctrine of the Holy Trinity by reference to any general, and subsequent, notion of person, and not by reference to its aboriginal sense." It must be understood "in an utterly unique way appropriate to his eternal uncreated and creative Nature, but it also may be applied to human 'persons' made in the image of God in a very different creaturely way." Just as we may not understand the fatherhood of God by analogical projection out of human fatherhood, so also may we not understand God as personal √ in terms of what human persons are. Human persons must be understood in relation to the creative personhood of God, not vice versa.[66]

The *Filioque* and East-West Division

We have seen that Torrance attempts to get beyond the East-West division on the *filioque* clause.[67] This he does by claiming, following Gregory Nazianzen, that the monarchy is the *being* of the Father. This

63. Ibid., 157.
64. Ibid., 157–58.
65. Ibid., 159.
66. Ibid., 160.
67. Ibid., 186–91.

means that the whole Trinity, not the person of the Father, is the one monarchy of God. Torrance does this because of his overwhelming emphasis on the *homoousion* and on perichoresis. All three persons are each and together the whole God. They mutually indwell and interpenetrate each other. Therefore, no one person can be before the others, and neither can any one person be after the others. Hence, the Spirit proceeds out of the *being* of the Father, the one identical being which is the being of all three persons.[68] We shall comment on this in a moment.

Criticisms

Colin Gunton, while strongly appreciative of Torrance's achievement, makes some definite criticisms of his approach to the Trinity. In particular, he points to the powerful central role of the *homoousion*. This obviates any idea of subordinationism for Torrance. Gunton is in agreement with this result. However, Gunton also says that it downplays the monarchy of the Father. There is clearly some economic subordinationism in the Scriptures. The Son obeys the Father. Gunton refers to Barth, who reads this up into the eternal Trinity, where the economic subordination, without being taken away, becomes an immanent equality of being. So Barth can say that it is as godlike to be humble as to be exalted, and that there are elements of commanding and obeying within the being of God. For Torrance, Gunton points out, the homoousian drive of his thought minimizes such elements.[69] We will explore this area in the next chapter. In short, we will argue that while great care must be taken to avoid reading into the eternal being of God elements that belong to the humanity of the incarnate Christ, nevertheless it is sound to consider whether there is something about the Son that made it fitting that he become incarnate. Moreover, we must also ask how, if that were not the case, a Nestorian disjunction between the Son and the assumed human nature could be avoided. The point here is that Torrance seems to smooth out any potential wrinkles unduly.

Gunton also criticizes Torrance for veering toward a Western concept of person by adopting the Augustinian principle of the indivisibility of the works of God. Contrary both to East and West, at least

---

68. Torrance, *Trinitarian Perspectives*, 112, 141.
69. Gunton, "Being and Person," 120–21.

as far as they are widely understood, the being of God and the persons are given together (equally ultimate) for Torrance. He moves from perichoresis to person, arguing that by virtue of perichoresis there developed a new concept of person in which the relations belong to what the persons are.[70] Torrance veers here to the Western concept of person and appeals to Augustine's principle that the works of God are undivided. He says, following G. L. Prestige, that *ousia* refers to the being of God in respect of its internal reality, while *hypostasis* refers to the being of God in its outward reference. But, Gunton asks, can we distinguish between inner and outer like this? Do not being and person refer to God in both inner and outer terms? Surely there is no being of God that is not that of three persons in mutually constitutive perichoresis.[71] Torrance vigorously denies this criticism.[72]

More pertinent, to my way of thinking, is Gunton's question of "whether the immense stress on the *homoousion* does not run the risk of flattening out the particularities, so that divine *being* tends to be stressed at the expense of the divine *persons*. Another way of putting it would be to ask whether the Eastern fathers have been read rather too much through Western eyes."[73] Again, he argues that Torrance's vision is rather more patristic than biblical, for "it is remarkable how little exegesis of Scripture . . . is to be found." Moreover, the texts that Torrance cites all support his thesis. Gunton asks whether Torrance gives sufficient attention to passages like 1 Corinthians 15 and some of those in the Fourth Gospel—texts that lend support to the subordinationist elements of the economic Trinity. They seem to counter his main thesis and so deserve careful attention.[74] This is an interesting criticism, considering our earlier note in chapter 9 on Gunton's own lack of biblical exegesis!

Gunton also questions Torrance's claim that the monarchy is that of the whole Trinity. He asks whether Athanasius really supports this thesis, and whether he and the Cappadocians express the particular being of the three persons rather more clearly than does Torrance.[75] If

70. Ibid., 124–25.
71. Ibid., 127–28.
72. Torrance, "Thomas Torrance Responds," 317.
73. Gunton, "Being and Person," 129–30.
74. Ibid., 130.
75. Ibid., 130–31.

the underlying dangers of modalism are to be removed, more attention needs to be paid to the concrete ways in which the particular persons of the Trinity present themselves to our experience in the economy of creation and salvation.[76]

Gunton and Torrance approach the matter from different angles,
Gunton largely aligning with John Zizioulas, and Torrance with the
faculty of theology of the University of Athens, to which Zizioulas's
views are not acceptable.[77] For Zizioulas, divine personhood transcends human limitations.[78] He thus rejects all Western conceptions of
the person. Instead, personhood is an open-ended concept, and can
only be understood in terms of being related to others. This applies
both to divine and human persons. In his 1985 book, he develops these
ideas further. Personhood is what constitutes beings, and so the being
of God is identified with personhood.[79] As Alan Torrance (T. F. Torrance's nephew) suggests, the problem with Zizioulas is that he follows Basil and Gregory of Nyssa in arguing for the person of the Father
as the unifying principle in God.[80] This ends up projecting a causal
relationship into God.[81] Zizioulas says that God exists because of a
person, rather than a substance.[82] This tends to subordinate the Son
and the Holy Spirit, and creates the specter of unipersonality rather
than impersonality. He makes the Father the cause of the divine substance, with the *hypostases* of the Son and the Holy Spirit being derivative and contingent. Indeed, the Father is the cause of the communion.[83] Alan Torrance suggests that this makes the Father the primordial
reality, not the Trinity.[84] So there is a principial divide here between
the Torrances, on the one hand, and Zizioulas and, to some extent,
Gunton, on the other hand.

76. Ibid., 134.
77. See Torrance, "Thomas Torrance Responds," 314ff.
78. John D. Zizioulas, "Human Capacity and Human Incapacity: A Theological Exploration
of Personhood," *SJT* 28 (1975): 401–47.
79. John D. Zizioulas, *Being as Communion: Studies in Personhood and the Church* (Crestwood, N.Y.: St. Vladimir's Seminary Press, 1985).
80. Ibid., 41.
81. Alan J. Torrance, *Persons in Communion: An Essay on Trinitarian Description and
Human Participation with Special Reference to Volume One of Karl Barth's Church Dogmatics* (Edinburgh: T & T Clark, 1996), 288–89.
82. Zizioulas, *Being as Communion*, 41–42.
83. Ibid., 17.
84. A. Torrance, *Persons in Communion*, 292.

In our judgment, there is a slight hint in T. F. Torrance of a modalist tendency. He has an overpowering, overwhelming stress on the homoousial and perichoretic relations of the persons. But he does not place similar stress on the irreducible distinction of the persons. In a rounded doctrine of the Trinity, there should be equal stress on the one being and the three persons. With Torrance, the balance is somewhat one-sided. Regarding the *filioque*, for instance, he concludes that the Spirit proceeds from the being (*ousia*) of the Father. The being of the Father is identical to the being of the Son, and so to the being of the Spirit himself. Thus, if indeed the Spirit proceeds from the perichoretic communion of the three, he proceeds from himself as well as from the Father and the Son. How then can the outcome be avoided that the personal distinctions are blurred or even eclipsed?

This concern is reinforced when Torrance, again following Augustine's principle of the indivisibility of the works of the Trinity *ab extra* (that is, with reference to the created world), argues that the whole undivided Trinity is present and active in the incarnate Son.[85] While there is a sense in which this is both correct and essential to affirm, the crucial point is that it is only the Son who took human nature into personal union in the Incarnation—which the Father and the Holy Spirit have never done. Colyer comments that "Torrance notes that it is not possible for us to delineate sharply between the distinctive activities of the trinitarian persons, for the coactivity of the persons perichoretically contain and interpenetrate one another and even pass over into each other."[86] Torrance himself concludes, as a result, that the law of appropriations "falls completely away."[87] It would be ludicrous to call Torrance a modalist, but, like a car that tends to pull over to one side, the dominant direction of his thought is biased away from the distinctiveness of the three persons. However, all this is not to deny that Torrance's treatment of the Trinity is probably the best one to date.

85. T. F. Torrance, *Christian Doctrine of God*, 108.
86. Colyer, *How to Read T. F. Torrance*, 320.
87. T. F. Torrance, *Christian Doctrine of God*, 200.

Critical Issues

I've often reflected on the rather obvious thought that when his disciples were about to have the world collapse in on them, our Lord spent so much time in the Upper Room speaking to them about the mystery of the Trinity. If anything could underline the necessity of Trinitarianism for practical Christianity, that must surely be it!

—*Sinclair Ferguson, personal e-mail*

The Trinity and the Incarnation

Toward a Resolution of the Problems of East and West

In chapters 10 and 11, we discussed the weaknesses of both Eastern and Western doctrines of the Trinity. Let us summarize the main problems. The East, from the fourth century, has held that the person of the Father is the center of divine unity. The main danger of this is a subordinationist tendency. If the Father is the guarantor of unity in the Godhead, it is only a short step to the Son and the Holy Spirit having a derivative status. On the other hand, the West since Augustine has begun with the divine essence. It has had difficulty accounting for the real eternal distinctions between the persons. With the essence prior to the persons, a less than fully personal view of God has resulted. The bias here is in a modalist direction. Seeing this, some in the West, like Moltmann, have argued that the Trinity is a community of three equal persons. However, since they lack a full doctrine of the immanent Trinity and correlate the Trinity with human history and experience, their conclusions veer toward tritheism and pantheism, often being explicitly panentheistic. On the other hand, T. F. Torrance, going back behind the Cappadocians and Augustine and following clues from Athanasius and Gregory Nazianzen, argues that the monarchy is to be seen as the whole Trinity, understood in a homoousial and perichoretic manner. However, he does not give equivalent emphasis to the distinctiveness of the three persons.

Overall, the Western approach to the Trinity has created problems. It is obvious that the Trinity is not a vital part of Western worship. It is seen by Western Christians as a mathematical conundrum,
a matter for advanced philosophers, not ordinary believers. There are
powerful tendencies toward an impersonal view of God and a subordinate position for the Holy Spirit. This has bred agnosticism and atheism. The East, on the other hand, has maintained the Trinity as a vital
part of the worship of the church. Its liturgies are pervaded by Trinitarian prayers and doxologies. However, especially since Palamas, its
separation of the unknowable divine essence from the uncreated energies, with a corresponding eclipse of the persons, undermines our
knowledge of God. We cannot know God as he is. The eternal and
immanent Trinity is ineffably other than what is revealed to us.

Where do we go from here? It is clear that we need to preserve
both the unity and identity of the one indivisible being of God and, at
the same time, the irreducible differences among the three persons.
Here Gregory Nazianzen is brilliantly helpful. In the passage in which
Calvin found vast delight, he says:

> This I give you to share, and to defend all your life, the one Godhead
> and power, found in the three in unity, and comprising the three sep-
> arately; not unequal, in substances or natures, neither increased nor
> diminished by superiorities or inferiorities; in every respect equal, in
> every respect the same; just as the beauty and the greatness of the
> heavens is one; the infinite conjunction of three infinite ones, each
> God when considered in himself; as the Father, so the Son; as the
> Son, so the Holy Spirit; the three one God when contemplated
> together; each God because consubstantial; one God because of the
> monarchia. No sooner do I conceive of the one than I am illumined
> by the splendour of the three; no sooner do I distinguish them than
> I am carried back to the one. When I think of any one of the three I
> think of him as the whole, and my eyes are filled, and the greater part
> of what I am thinking escapes me. I cannot grasp the greatness of
> that one so as to attribute a greater greatness to the rest. When I con-
> template the three together, I see but one torch, and cannot divide
> or measure out the undivided light.[1]

1. Gregory Nazianzen, *Orations* 40.41.

Gregory oscillates back and forth from the one to the three. When he considers the one, he is illumined by the splendor of the three. When he distinguishes the three, he is carried back to the one. Gregory points to the dangers of building our doctrine of the Trinity *either* on the one being of God in isolation *or* on the three persons (or any one of them) in isolation. These dangers are demonstrated thoroughly in the subsequent history of the church.

Gregory's hermeneutic, as he expresses it in this passage, is strikingly modern. Physicists working at the atomic level oscillate in thought between waves and particles. The reason for this is that on the atomic level matter has both a wave character and a particle character, the so-called wave-particle duality of matter. Thus, an electron acts both like a particle and like a wave, as also does light. As a result, it is not possible to measure both the speed and the position of such particles. The most famous, and perplexing, aspect of the wave character of particles is seen in the double slit experiment. When an electron is fired at a metal target with two small slits in it, suitably spaced, it appears that the electron goes through both slits, and produces an interference pattern just like a light wave does on the opposite side of the target. Thus, at a fundamental level—because of the wave character of particles— it is impossible, no matter how many observers there may be, to determine both the position and the velocity of an atomic particle. Thus, to do physics at the atomic level, it is necessary to oscillate in thought between waves and particles.[2] There is a parallel to this in the field of gestalt psychology, from which we learn that as we gain a grasp of the whole, we tend to lose connection with the parts, while if we focus on the parts, we lose our grasp of the whole. Another way of putting it is to think of what happens when you focus your gaze on a particular object. Try doing it. Notice that when you look intently at this or that, the rest of your field of vision becomes blurred and indistinct. Then if you look away from the object of your former gaze and attend to the background, which now comes into clear focus, your former object of attention becomes a blur.

In this connection, the limitations of logic are apparent. James Loder and the late W. Jim Neidhardt have pointed out, in what

2. I am indebted to Dr. John Dishman, formerly of Bell Laboratories, for this information.

T. F. Torrance in the foreword calls "an altogether remarkable book
with unusually fresh creative thinking," that, while logic is of value in
everyday life or in "trivialities" (as they call them), when we approach
the boundaries of the universe, it breaks down. They point to a wide
range of areas where creation is not reducible to neat laws of thought.
Among other things, physics, mathematics, psychology, and human
development all manifest this feature.[3] They illustrate the point with
Escher's famous line drawings, including his _Möbius Strip II (Red Ants)_
(woodcut, 1963). This is based on the "strange loop" discovered by
the grandfather of the psychoneurologist Paul J. Möbius. The Möbius
band, through a 180° twist, has only one side and one edge, although
two are evident in any cross-sectional view. Escher's work shows ants
crawling along the surface of a two-sided Möbius band. As the eye
follows the ants around the band, the two sides are disclosed to be
only one side.[4] If a reductionist elevation of logic is impermissible in
dealing with matters of creation, how much less is it to be followed in
relation to the Holy Trinity? T. F. Torrance insists that the proper course
in seeking to know is to submit our minds to the object of knowledge
so as to allow it to disclose itself on its own terms. It follows that
knowledge in science is to be based on the reality of what is. Logical
deductions from premises are good within certain parameters, but, if
absolutized, can prevent us from knowing. In theology, this means we
must faithfully submit ourselves to God's revelation and allow our
thoughts to proceed on the basis of who he discloses himself to be.

Let us return now to the question of the Trinity. We saw that it
is inadequate to make the basis of our inquiries the one essence of God
apart from the three persons. Calvin, in contrast, started from the three
persons. This is what Gerald Bray wants us to do.[5] It is more in line
with the way in which God has revealed himself in the Bible and in
the history of salvation. It mirrors our own experience in prayer, as
we shall consider in the next chapter. However, if we pay heed to the
method of Gregory, we will want to give equal consideration to the
three and the one, the one and the three. As Alan Torrance puts it,

3. James E. Loder and W. Jim Neidhardt, _The Knight's Move: The Relational Logic of the Spirit in Theology and Science_ (Colorado Springs: Helmers & Howard, 1992).

4. Ibid., 36–43.

5. Gerald Bray, _The Doctrine of God_ (Leicester: Inter-Varsity Press, 1993), 197–224.

"The doctrine of the Trinity demands a conception of the triune persons which integrates their distinctness and particularity, on the one hand, and their radical union and communion, on the other."[6] Distinctness and particularity, union and communion—both are equally ultimate and equally necessary. Therefore, both should equally be the focus of our attention. These parameters should be equally balanced in the way we view the Holy Trinity: unity and diversity, identity and difference, equality and order, union and particularity.

Vital Parameters

One being—three persons, three persons—one being. Like Gregory Nazianzen, we need to recognize the equal ultimacy of the being of God and the three persons. God is a fully personal being—we might say that he is far more than that, for he is personal being *par excellence*. He is the creator of human persons. Thus, he is supremely personal—indeed, more than personal, as C. S. Lewis argues.[7] He is in fact a communion of three persons. However, we must give equal weight to the distinctness of the persons and to the oneness of God's being. Both sides of the picture must be seen. God is three irreducibly distinct persons in indivisible union, and he is one God in three inexpressibly different ways. If we were to stress the three irreducibly distinct or different persons, we would veer toward tritheism. If we were to stress the one indivisible union, we would be in imminent danger of modalism. Both must be equally weighted. In the words of Staniloae, "The entire divine essence, a spiritual essence subsistent in threefold fashion, possesses the quality of being subject or threefold subject. The subsistence of the divine being is nothing other than the concrete existence of divine subjectivity in three modes which compenetrate each other, hence in a threefold subjectivity." They possess themselves "as the consciousness of three subjects perfectly interior to one another." "That is why we can speak of a single God and three 'I's.'"[8] These twin

---

6. Alan J. Torrance, *Persons in Communion: An Essay on Trinitarian Description and Human Participation with Special Reference to Volume One of Karl Barth's Church Dogmatics* (Edinburgh: T & T Clark, 1996), 281–82.

7. C. S. Lewis, *Mere Christianity* (San Francisco: Harper, 1960), 160.

8. Dumitru Staniloae, *The Experience of God*, trans. and ed. Iona Ionita and Robert Barringer (Brookline, Mass.: Holy Cross Orthodox Press, 1994–2000), 1:260–61.

statements comprise the doctrine of the Trinity at its most basic level: There is one God; in God there are three persons—the Father, the Son, and the Holy Spirit, each of whom is God. By placing these two statements side by side as equally necessary, the dangers of one-sidedness can be offset.

The three persons are homoousios. The Father, the Son, and the Holy Spirit are identical in being. Each person is the whole God. The three together are not more God than any one by himself. Since all three are one identical being, no one person is of higher or lesser status than any other. There are no gradations of deity. Thus, all three together are worshiped, as the Niceno-Constantinopolitan Creed (C) holds.

The three persons mutually indwell one another in a dynamic communion. The doctrine of perichoresis affirms that the three persons of the Trinity occupy, in Gerald Bray's words, the same infinite divine space. Since each is wholly God and fully God, no one person is any greater than any other, while the three together are not greater than any one. Thus, the three mutually indwell each other. This is not an indwelling that submerges the particularities of any of the three. It is dynamic, with living relations. Here the focus of Bulgakov and Staniloae on love, following Richard of St. Victor, is very helpful. We were highly critical of Moltmann in chapter 14, but he makes the positive point that the Trinitarian persons are bound together in love. In chapter 19, we will explore how this is so important now that Islam has reappeared on the radar in a big way.

The three persons are irreducibly different from one another. That the three persons of the Trinity are not simply subsistent relations is demonstrated by the Incarnation. In becoming flesh, the Son took a human nature into personal union, and that for eternity. This the Father and the Holy Spirit did not do. The Son is forever united to humanity, which is not the case with the Father and the Spirit. This points to the fact that the three are different from each other, irreducibly different, in ways that we cannot understand. The Son is eternally different from the Father and the Holy Spirit. Likewise, we can rightly conclude, the Holy Spirit is different from the Father and the Son. This is so forever, while at the same time the work of the Trinity *ab extra* (that is, with reference to the created world) is indivisible. The three work together as one since they are one being.

There is an order among the persons. Within the parameters mentioned above, there is also an order (*taxis*) among the three. This order is not to be understood in terms of human arrangements, such as rank or hierarchy, but in terms of an appropriate disposition.[9] The most common order in terms of the outworking of salvation, both in the NT and in the early church, is *from the Father through the Son by the Holy Spirit*; the reverse movement in our response to God's grace is *by the Holy Spirit through the Son to the Father.* However, the NT presents variations. The apostolic benediction has the order of Son, Father, and Holy Spirit. We saw other such patterns in chapter 3. This shows the equality of the three—each is the whole God. It points to their identity of being. But the baptismal order of Father, Son, and Holy Spirit is obviously the most common, being repeated every time a baptism is administered. In its context in the gospel of Matthew, it expresses the new covenant name of God. As such, it points to an irreversible *taxis.* For instance, despite the elements of mutuality reflected in these different orders, the Father sends the Son, and the Son never sends the Father. The Holy Spirit proceeds from the Father, but the Father never proceeds from the Holy Spirit or the Son.[10]

A doctrine of the Trinity that is to be faithful to the Bible from which it emerges must give equivalent expression to each of the above parameters. These parameters are mutually defining. The three persons are irreducibly different, *and* they are one identical being. There is an order among them, *and* they mutually indwell each other, are equal in status, and are one in being. They mutually indwell one another, *and* they are irreducibly different. And so on and so forth.

Note on Eternal Generation and Eternal Procession

Since Irenaeus, the church has held that the Father begat the Son in eternity. This comes to expression in C and is repeated in later confessions, such as the Westminster Confession of Faith. This doctrine has come under fire on both biblical and theological grounds. Since the nine-

9. See our comments in footnote 60 on the patristic use of the word ταξις (*taxis*). p. 400.
10. See "Note on Eternal Generation and Eternal Procession," below.

teenth century, many NT scholars have held that this teaching does not find biblical support since the Greek word *monogenēs* in passages like John 3:16, while translated "only begotten" in older English translations of the Bible, simply means "only" or "one and only." It is also held that the passage in Psalm 2:7, "You are my Son; today I have begotten you," is cited in the NT with reference to Jesus' resurrection (Acts 13:33) and so does not refer to the relation between the Father and the Son in eternity. Furthermore, from the theological angle it is argued that the eternal generation of the Son either implies or entails a subordinate status for the Son, and it is even claimed that this view comes from Neoplatonism. Similar arguments have been advanced in opposition to the doctrine of the eternal procession of the Holy Spirit from the Father.

Let us look first at the biblical criticisms. As we do so, it is with the strong caution that the doctrine of eternal generation does not depend on the meaning of any one word, nor even on strict biblical exegesis alone. It is a theological predicate grounded in the eternal relations of the Son and the Father in the one being of God. However, since some debate has surrounded lexicography and exegesis, we are compelled to give an account of it. First, the older understanding of *monogenēs* has never been eclipsed. Although B. F. Westcott, B. B. Warfield, and the majority of twentieth-century exegetes abandoned it,[11] the idea that it means "only begotten" has continued to receive support from, among others, F. Büchsel, J. V. Dahms, C. H. Dodd, M. J. Lagrange, F. F. Bruce, John Frame, and Roger Beckwith.[12] More-

11. Robert L. Reymond, *A New Systematic Theology of the Christian Faith* (New York: Nelson, 1998), 326ff.; Raymond E. Brown, *The Gospel According to John (i-xii)*, Anchor Bible (Garden City, N.Y.: Doubleday, 1966), 13–14; Brooke Foss Westcott, *The Gospel According to St. John: The Greek Text with Introduction and Notes* (London: John Murray, 1908), 1:23; B. B. Warfield, "The Biblical Doctrine of the Trinity," in *Biblical and Theological Studies*, ed. Samuel G. Craig (Philadelphia: Presbyterian and Reformed, 1952), 52; C.H. Turner, "Ο ΥΙΟΣ ΜΟΥ Ο ΑΓΑΠΗΤΟΣ," *JTS* 27 (1926): 113–29; D. Moody, "God's Only Son: The Translation of John 3:16 in the Revised Standard Version," *JBL* 72 (1953): 213–19; Otto Betz, *What Do We Know About Jesus?* (London: SCM, 1968).

12. John V. Dahms, "The Johannine Use of Monogenēs Reconsidered," *NTS* 29 (1983): 222–32; M. Theobald, *Die Fleischwerdung des Logos* (Münster: Aschendorff, 1988), 250–54; F. Büchsel, "μονογενης," in *TDNT*, 4:737–41; C. H. Dodd, *The Interpretation of the Fourth Gospel* (Cambridge: Cambridge University Press, 1953), 305; M.-J. Lagrange, *Évangile selon Saint Jean* (Paris: Gabalda, 1948), 413; F. F. Bruce, *The Gospel of John* (Grand Rapids: Eerdmans, 1984), 65n26; John M. Frame, *The Doctrine of God* (Phillipsburg, N.J.: P&R Publishing, 2002), 710–11; Roger Beckwith, "The Calvinist Doctrine of the Trinity," *Churchman* 115 (2001): 308–16.

over, before writing off the older view, it is important to pay heed to the contexts in which the word occurs. *Monogenēs* appears in Hebrews 11:17 and in Luke 7:12, 8:42, and 9:38 with reference to an only child. Moulton and Milligan consider that if "only begotten" had been the intended meaning, then another word, *monogennētos*, would have been used, since the *-genos* ending refers to kind, rather than derivation.[13] However, Büchsel disputes this assertion.[14] The term refers to the Son of God only in the writings of John—in John 1:14, 18; 3:16, 18; 1 John 4:9. Each of these passages relates to Christian believers being born or begotten by God. The verb *gennaō* (to beget or to give birth) is used in each place.

John 1:14 reads, "And the Word became flesh and lived among us. And we saw his glory, glory as of the *monogenēs* from the Father, full of grace and truth" (my translation). This refers to the Son's incarnation and to his life and ministry. In the immediately preceding context, John records that those who believed in his name were given authority to become children of God. These believers or children of God were born of God (*ek theou egennēthēsan*). The focus here is on the spiritual rebirth of believers, which John sharply distances from physical birth or generation. The idea of birth or begetting (either the male or the female part in generation or birth) is pervasive. John understands it in a spiritual manner, of rebirth by the Holy Spirit in regeneration. God's Son is directly connected with this. He is the *monogenēs* from the Father; they are the children (*tekna*) of God. As God has become the Father of believers in their generation or birth, so the Word stands in relation to the Father as his *monogenēs*. It is his relation to the Father that is in view, not any particular event in his life or in the work of salvation. Moreover, it is impossible to eradicate the idea of begetting from this description.

A few verses later, in John 1:18, the Word is described as "the *monogenēs* God [*or* Son], who is at the Father's side," and who has made the unseen God known to us. Here the same contextual considerations apply, and again the *monogenēs* is said to be in the closest

---

13. James Hope Moulton and George Milligan, *The Vocabulary of the Greek New Testament: Illustrated from the Papyri and Other Non-literary Sources* (London: Hodder and Stoughton, 1963), 416–17.

14. Büchsel, "μονογενης."

and most immediate proximity to the Father. His relation to the Father self-evidently transcends the purely temporal.

In John 3:16–18, John's comments follow his account of Jesus' interview with Nicodemus. Jesus has confronted Nicodemus with his need, as a leading teacher of Israel and a member of the Sanhedrin, for a radical rebirth by the Holy Spirit. Unless he is born from above, or born again, by water and the Spirit, he will not see the kingdom of God (that is, eternal life). The regenerative work of the Spirit is necessary to gain eternal life. The similarities with 1:14–18 are obvious. In both passages, God is the author of life or a new status for his children. The verb *gennaō* (to give birth or to beget) occurs seven times in verses 4–7. Jesus stresses that he is talking about a spiritual reality, birth, or begetting by the Spirit, mysterious and inscrutable. These are heavenly things, not earthly ones (v. 12), connected with his own incarnation, crucifixion, and ascension (vv. 13–14). In this context, John says that God the Father sent his *monogenēs* Son to give eternal life to all who believe (v. 16). Lack of faith in the *monogenēs* Son of God will debar a person from life (v. 18). John uses the term, as in chapter 1, to refer to the Word or Son in relation to the Father, and brings it into immediate connection with the outset of spiritual rebirth to life by the Holy Spirit.

In 1 John 4:7–9, John urges his readers to love one another. Everyone who loves has been begotten by God (again the verb is *gennaō*) and so knows God. Again, the spiritual reality of begetting by the Holy Spirit is in view. It is the outset of spiritual life. In contrast to those begotten by God, those who do not love do not know God, since God is love (v. 8). Then John says, "In this the love of God is made known among us, that God sent his *monogenēs* Son into the world that we might live through him" (my translation). The same features are present here too. The *monogenēs* Son is in relation to God, in particular the Father. Believers, or those who love and who know God, receive life from God, compared to being begotten.

There is one further passage, 1 John 5:18. There John says that "everyone who has been begotten (*gegennēmenos*—perfect tense) of God does not sin, but he who was begotten of God (*gennētheis*—aorist tense) keeps him, and the evil one does not touch him" (my translation). The difference in tense between the perfect, referring clearly to those begotten to new life by God, and the aorist supports the idea that the latter refers to a different subject than the former, and thus to Christ. The reference again would be to eternity, where the relation between the Father and the Son is based.[15]

In each of these cases, no particular episode in the Son's work of salvation is in view. Peter does connect our regeneration with the resurrection of Christ, since we are raised to new life in union with him, who was himself raised from the dead (1 Peter 1:3), and so too does Paul (Rom. 6:1–11). But John—and he is the one who uses the term—has as his prime focus the Son's relation with the Father, a relation existing throughout his earthly life and ministry and in effect when he was sent into the world to be our Savior. Moreover, this relation—as John consistently maintains—is eternal, preceding creation (John 1:1–3, 18; 8:58; 20:31). Besides, the invariable connection with spiritual begetting or birth makes it impossible to eliminate any reference to begetting when it comes to the Son. Of course, this is not understood in a physical sense—apart from anything else, Jesus had no human father. While the doctrine of eternal generation does not stand or fall on this one word, it is important to recognize that claims that it has no bearing on the question are greatly exaggerated.

As for the statement in Psalm 2:7, "I will tell of the decree: The LORD said to me, 'You are my Son; today I have begotten you,'" this undoubtedly comes to full expression in the resurrection of God's Son to reign over his enemies. This is the way Paul cites it in his speech in Acts 13, and it is the probable sense in Hebrews 1:5. However, Psalm 2:7 itself refers to the relation between Yahweh and the one whom he calls "my Son," which is governed by the nature of the one who speaks (Yahweh) and the one who is addressed (Yahweh's Son). Thus, while it reaches fulfillment in Jesus' resurrection, it can hardly be limited to that.

The attacks on the eternal generation of the Son on biblical grounds need to be reconsidered. Moreover, are not those best quali-

---

15. See the translations of the RSV (1946, 1952), NEB, and NIV; J. R. W. Stott, *The Epistles of John: An Introduction and Commentary* (London: Tyndale Press, 1964), 192; Kenneth Grayston, *The Johannine Epistles*, New Century Bible Commentary (Grand Rapids: Eerdmans, 1984), 145. In Stott's words, "It is the high privilege of the Christian to be like Christ . . . begotten of God and therefore sons of God." He adds that our begetting and sonship are different from his, which are unique and eternal, but they are sufficiently similar to make it possible for John to use nearly identical expressions to cover both.

fied to assess the meaning of a first-century Greek word native Greek speakers of the centuries closest to the time? The Greek fathers understood *monogenēs* in these Johannine passages to mean "only begotten." Were they less qualified to determine its meaning than people living nearly two millennia later who speak a different language? Nonetheless, the doctrine of eternal generation does not stand or fall on the basis of this one word. Its validity is based on the teaching of the eternal sonship and the relation of the Son to the Father in the undivided being of God.

In addition, criticisms have been made of eternal generation on theological grounds. It is claimed that the teaching posits a lesser status for the Son, making him an emanation from the Father in Neoplatonic guise. However, this is not how the framers of C understood the matter.[16] Indeed, we saw in chapter 4 that it is difficult to make a clear-cut case that Origen himself saw it that way. His intent was to counteract gnostic ideas of emanation and to assert the Son's identity of being with the Father. Widdicombe observes that Origen stressed the Son's real, individual existence and also his sharing of the divine nature of the Father. He aimed to keep a balance between these two fundamental ideas.[17] The Fathers, including Origen, consistently urged that all ideas of human generation be removed from the picture. Human begetting entails a beginning of existence. A human father exists before his son is begotten. This is not the case here, they urged. The Father is always the Father, and the Son is always the Son.[18] In the *Expositio fidei*, a work attributed to Athanasius,[19] but with all the marks of Marcellus of Ancyra,[20] the author states that the Son is "true God of true God . . . omnipotent from omnipotent . . . whole from whole" (*theon alēthinon ek theou alēthinou . . . pantokratora ek pantokratoros . . . holos ex holou*).[21] This reflects the language of the creed of Nicaea (N) and was to be the basis of the relevant

16. Cf. Gregory of Nyssa, *Against Eunomius* 3.4.

17. Peter Widdicombe, *The Fatherhood of God from Origen to Athanasius* (Oxford: Clarendon, 1994), 85–86.

18. On the eternal generation of the Son and its application to the relations of the persons, not to the divine essence, see Francis Turretin, *Institutes of Elenctic Theology*, ed. James T. Dennison Jr. (Phillipsburg, N.J.: P&R Publishing, 1992–97), 1:278–302, esp. 292–302.

19. PG 25:199–208.

20. R. P. C. Hanson, *The Search for the Christian Doctrine of God: The Arian Controversy 318–381* (Edinburgh: T & T Clark, 1988), 231.

21. PG 25:201.

section in C, connected with the eternal generation of the Son. Marcellus of all people can hardly be accused of subordinationism, but the argument is not materially affected if Athanasius was the author. Later Photius argued too that the creedal statements connected with eternal generation underline the *homoousios* of the Father and the Son.[22]

Similar principles apply when we consider the eternal procession of the Holy Spirit. It is often claimed that the *locus classicus*, John 15:26, refers purely to the history of salvation, to the coming of the Spirit at Pentecost, and so any projection back into eternity is not only exegetically improper, but speculative. However, while Jesus' comments do clearly refer to Pentecost, they cannot be restricted to it. He uses the future tense (*pempsō*) to refer to his sending of the Spirit at that particular time, but uses the present tense to say of the Spirit that he "proceeds" (*ekporeuetai*) from the Father. The Spirit's sending at Pentecost, in which the Son is the sender, is distinct from the Spirit's procession, which is continuous and for which the Father is the spirator. This may be a Hebraic parallelism, but we are nonetheless again in the realm of the relation between two distinct agents, the Father and the Holy Spirit, and it is the nature of these agents that should govern our view of the relation between them. As D. A. Carson states, the early creedal statement on the procession of the Holy Spirit is "eminently defensible," since the clause here in John 15:26 (allowing for John's theology as seen throughout this gospel) presupposes this ontological status.[23] The parameters that we noted above indicate clearly that neither the Son nor the Holy Spirit is subordinate in being or status, and that the begetting and the procession apply to their relations as persons.

How Does the Incarnation Impinge on the Trinity?

We must now ask how the Incarnation relates to the Trinity. Here is something quite extraordinary. The Word who was with God and

22. Photius, *On the Mystagogy of the Holy Spirit*, trans. Holy Transfiguration Monastery (n.p.: Studion, 1983), 92, 170. For other examinations of the question, see Paul A. Rainbow, "Orthodox Trinitarianism and Evangelical Feminism," available at www.cbmw.org/resources/articles/orthodox_trinitarianism_feminism.pdf; and Lee Irons, "The Eternal Generation of the Son," available at www.members.aol.com/ironslee/Private/monogenes.htm.
23. D. A. Carson, *The Gospel According to St John* (Leicester: Inter-Varsity Press, 1991), on 15:26.

was God became flesh and lived in this world as man. For us and our salvation, he became obedient to death on the cross, and then rose from the dead, ascended into heaven, and now sits at the right hand of God the Father. From there he will come to judge the living and the dead. The assumption by the Son of human nature into personal union is permanent and eternal. There are a number of questions that this raises.

Could Any of the Three Persons of the Trinity Have Become Incarnate?

It is sometimes asked whether any of the persons of the Trinity could have become incarnate. Often it is said that God became man, as if the whole Trinity became incarnate, or as if any one of the three persons might have taken on the task. Why was it that *the Son* became man? Did it have to be the Son? T. F. Torrance argues that the Son had to be made incarnate rather than either of the other two persons because that is what happened. It "sets aside as evangelically and theologically unentertainable any other alternative such as the possibility that the Father or the Holy Spirit could have or might have become incarnate."[24] However, he goes on to say that the whole Trinity is present, since in all the works and ways of God all three persons work together inseparably.[25] On the other hand, Anselm considers that it was necessary that the Son become incarnate for ontological reasons.[26] The incarnation of the Son shows that the distinctions of the persons are irreducible. Only the Son became incarnate and is now united to humanity. Neither the Father nor the Holy Spirit is personally united to man. Here there is an obvious difference that distinguishes the Son for all eternity.

This is pertinent when we recall that salvation ultimately entails union with God. This has been called deification in the East. Harnack convinced most scholars that the West, following Augustine, rejected this idea. However, Gerald Bonner and others have shown that Augustine in fact accepted the teaching and that it percolated down from

24. Thomas F. Torrance, *The Christian Doctrine of God: One Being, Three Persons* (Edinburgh: T & T Clark, 1996), 199.
25. Ibid., 200.
26. See chapter 11 and Anselm, *De fide Trinitatis et de incarnatione Verbi* (PL 158:276–79, 283–84); G. R. Evans, *Anselm* (London: Geoffrey Chapman, 1989), 56–57.

him in Latin theology to the time of the Reformation.[27] Recent Finnish scholarship has drawn attention to similar themes in Luther, while Carl Mosser has pointed to Calvin's acknowledgment of deification.[28] In the West, a classic statement of Protestant theology, the Westminster Larger Catechism, describes salvation as "union and communion with Christ in grace and glory." This union is spiritual and mystical, but real and inseparable.[29] It means that we will "enjoy [God] for ever," according to the Westminster Shorter Catechism.[30] Therefore, since salvation consists of union with Christ, the incarnation of the Son, rather than the Father or the Holy Spirit, is appropriate.

While only the Son became man, the Incarnation nevertheless reveals the whole Trinity. Jesus' prayers to the Father reveal a living, dynamic relation, a vital union and communion. These are two distinct subjects. They are not merely "relations subsisting in the divine nature," as Aquinas defined divine persons.[31] Jesus' baptism makes known all three persons. The Holy Spirit descends as a dove and rests on Jesus, while the Father's voice declares Jesus to be his beloved Son. Again, these are three distinct persons. Jesus' words in <u>John 14:6ff.</u> are crucial. He alone is the way to the Father. He who sees the Son sees the Father. He is both identical with, and distinct from, the Father. The Gospels are full of the fact that Jesus is the Son of God who reveals the Father and lives in the power of the Holy Spirit. It leads to the confession that God is just like Jesus. If we want to know what God is like, we need look no further. Jesus' whole life and ministry is revelatory—healing the sick, giving sight to the blind, giving hearing to the deaf, preaching good news to the poor, weeping over Jerusalem, preparing his disciples for the task that lay ahead, living in obedient faithfulness to the Father under the direction of the Holy Spirit.

27. Gerald Bonner, "Deification, Divinization," in *Augustine Through the Ages: An Encyclopedia*, ed. Allan D. Fitzgerald (Grand Rapids: Eerdmans, 1999), 265–66; A. N. Williams, *The Ground of Union: Deification in Aquinas and Palamas* (New York: Oxford University Press, 1999); Panayiotis Nellas, *Deification in Christ: Orthodox Perspective on the Nature of the Human Person*, trans. Norman Russell (Crestwood, N.Y.: St. Vladimir's Seminary Press, 1987).

28. Carl Mosser, "The Greatest Possible Blessing: Calvin and Deification," *SJT* 55 (2002): 36–57. See esp. p. 40, where the author cites Calvin's comment on 2 Peter 1:4 that "it is the purpose of the gospel to make us sooner or later like [*conformes*] God; indeed it is, so to speak, a kind of deification [*quasi deificari*]."

29. WLC, QQ. 65–66. See the entire section, QQ. 65–90.

30. WSC, Q. 1.

31. Thomas Aquinas, *ST*, Pt. 1a, Q. 29, art. 4.

How Far Does the Incarnate Son Reveal the Eternal Son?

In recent years, the question has been asked how far it is permissible to argue back from the human obedience of the incarnate Christ to the place of the Son in the immanent Trinity. This question was originally generated by some observations of Barth. He argued that the obedience of Christ reflects a comparable attitude on the divine level, in which the Son lives in loving submission to the Father. This is so since, as Molnar observes, in Barth's thought "Jesus' human actions are never merely the actions of a human being who was not also the eternal Son of God."[32]

Recently, the feminist debate has brought such considerations to the forefront. With a feminized doctrine of God rising to prominence, there has followed a strong movement to eliminate anything appearing to give credence to submission by the Son to the Father in the Trinity. A thoroughgoing homogenization of the persons in fully mutual relations is the overpowering tendency. By this means, a complete reciprocity between male and female in human society can be underpinned ontologically. Overtly feminist theologians like Elisabeth Schüssler Fiorenza, Elizabeth Johnson, and Catherine Mowry LaCugna, as well as feminist sympathizers like Jürgen Moltmann, come into this category. However, the drift has extended further afield, affecting many who identify themselves as conservative or evangelical.[33]

Human obedience to God is not servile, but godly: Jesus' human obedience saves us. Moltmann comments that talk about obedience to God encourages a mentality of slavishness. "The idea of the almighty ruler of the universe everywhere requires abject servitude, because it points to complete dependency in all spheres of life."[34] One can appreciate how Moltmann, born and raised in Nazi Germany, might with compatriots of his generation be especially sensitive to authoritarian-

---

32. Karl Barth, *CD*, IV/1: 192–205; see IV/1: 157–357; IV/2: 42–43, 170; Paul D. Molnar, *Divine Freedom and the Doctrine of the Immanent Trinity: In Dialogue with Karl Barth and Contemporary Theology* (Edinburgh: T & T Clark, 2002), 294.

33. Gilbert Bilezikian, "Hermeneutical Bungee-Jumping: Subordination in the Trinity," *JETS* 40 (1997): 57–68; Kevin Giles, *The Trinity and Subordinationism* (Downers Grove, Ill.: InterVarsity Press, 2002).

34. Jürgen Moltmann, *The Trinity and the Kingdom: The Doctrine of God* (London: SCM, 1991), 191–92.

ism in all its many forms. However, we must assert without equivo-
cation that human obedience to God is most definitely not slavish. It
is the fulfillment of being human. What strips us of our humanity is
disobedience, seen in Adam and the whole race thereafter. To the contrary, obedience is godly (and thus godlike, acting in the image of God,
who is Jesus Christ). The Bible is full of God's requirements that his
people obey him (cf. Josh. 24:15; Ps. 119). It is a question of whom
we obey—God or mammon (Matt. 6:24), God or idols (Josh. 24:15ff.),
for if we think that obedience to our loving, gracious, and merciful
God is slavish, then we are instead devoting ourselves to a truly
demeaning slavery, that of sin and willful self-assertion, obeying ourselves, setting ourselves up as the yardstick of what is right. This is
idolatry. A rejection of obedience to God on principle leaves no coherent basis to distinguish between the morals of Mother Theresa and
those of Adolf Hitler. Instead, Jesus obeyed the Father (John 17:4; Heb.
10:5–10; Rom. 5:12–21; 1 Peter 2:21–24). His human obedience won
us salvation.[35] Slavish indeed! As for me and my house, we will serve
the Lord. The Collect for Peace in the liturgy for Morning Prayer in
the 1662 *Book of Common Prayer* of the Church of England speaks
of God, "in knowledge of whom standeth our eternal life, whose service is perfect freedom."

Is the Son's humanity limited to the time of salvation only? It is
often claimed that the Son's obedience is restricted to his humanity
and his incarnate state. For example, Gilbert Bilezikian writes of
Christ's obedience as "a task-driven, temporary phase of ministry."[36]
Certainly, there are many passages in the Gospels that are to be understood of Christ simply according to his human nature. His sufferings
and death are obvious examples of these, often attributed to God in
the theology of the past generation, but correctly undergone by Christ
as man.[37] Certainly, we must avoid extrapolating everything back from
the gospel records into the immanent life of God. However, as Augustine outlined, the NT not only refers to Christ as God and to Christ

35. See Robert Letham, *The Work of Christ* (Leicester: Inter-Varsity Press, 1993), esp. 105–21,
130–32.
36. Bilezikian, "Hermeneutical Bungee-Jumping," 61.
37. Thomas G. Weinandy, *Does God Suffer?* (Notre Dame, Ind.: University of Notre Dame
Press, 2000).

as man, but also speaks of Christ as the Son in relation to the Father.[38] Moreover, Christ's incarnate state continues for ever. He remains man and always will be so. He did not jettison his humanity at the Resurrection, like a booster rocket, as the Jehovah's Witnesses claim.[39] Even now, he makes intercession for us as our great high priest (Heb. 7:25). As Paul says, "For we know that since Christ was raised from the dead, he cannot die again; death no longer has mastery over him" (Rom. 6:9, my translation). Our salvation consists of union with Christ, and so our resurrection is a sharing in his human resurrection and is part of the same reality.[40] He was not raised from the dead in order to bring his humanity to a terminus at some later date. His humanity can no more be abandoned than can ours. If it was sheared off, our salvation would go too. The reality is that he has taken human nature into union with himself for all eternity. Union between God and man is permanent. It is based on union with the Son. In the words of Christopher Wordsworth's great hymn for Ascension Day:

> You have raised our human nature in the clouds to God's right hand;
> There we sit in heavenly places, there with you in glory stand:
> Jesus reigns, adored by angels, man with God is on the throne;
> Mighty Lord, in your ascension we by faith behold our own.

Is it congruous for the Son as such to unite to himself a human nature that yields obedience to the Father? This leads us to ask a further question. Is there something about the Son that makes it compatible for him to unite to himself a human nature that lives in obedience to the Father? Is there something in the Son *as Son* that makes this union with an *obedient* human nature fitting? Before we say no to this question, we need to pause and note the dangers of replying in that way. If there is nothing about the Son *as Son* that makes personal union with an obedient human nature appropriate and fitting, then we would be in peril of a Nestorian separation between the Word incarnate, for whom submission to the Father would be inappropriate, and

---

38. Augustine, *De Trinitate* 2.1.1–3; 5.4.5–16.17.
39. WSC, Q. 21; WLC, Q. 36. Sergius Bulgakov, *The Wisdom of God: A Brief Summary of Sophiology* (London: Williams and Norgate, 1937), 141, points out that the two natures of Christ remain distinct for eternity.
40. Letham, *Work of Christ*, 75–87, 211–23.

the assumed humanity, which does submit to the Father. Such a separation is ruled out by orthodox Christology.[41] The ecumenical councils of Chalcedon (451) and Constantinople II (553) both affirmed the hypostatic union. Chalcedon pronounced that there is just *one* person of Christ, existing in two natures—without confusion, *without separation*. The Second Council of Constantinople then laid down, in the dogma of *anhypostasia*, that the human nature of Christ has no independent existence apart from the union effected by the Word. In the twin dogma of *enhypostasia*, it held that the Word provides the personalizing center in the incarnate Christ.[42] Thus, the Word (the eternal Son) is the personal center of Christ. As Paul writes, "*God* was in Christ" (2 Cor. 5:19, my translation). Consequently, all actions of the incarnate Christ according to both natures are attributed to the person of the Son. This follows from the fact that while it is impossible for humans to reach out to God, it is gloriously possible (and even more gloriously actual) for God to reach down to us and encompass our humanity in personal union. Thus, the Word *incarnate* obeys the Father. At the same time, it is the *Word* incarnate who obeys the Father.

The same conclusions follow when we consider the two wills of Christ. Historically, the church has maintained that his will is a property of the natures, not the person. Thus, Christ has two wills, a divine will and a human one. This is known as *dyotheletism*, in contrast to the rejected option of *monotheletism* (only one will), which the church considered would eclipse Christ's humanity. However, an unavoidable corollary is that the two wills, divine and human, nonetheless coincide. There is no discrepancy, as if one will worked against the other, or as

---

41. For the same reasons, also out of order is the idea advanced by Bilezikian that the obedience of the Son of God is limited to the economy of salvation and must accordingly be understood to refer to his humanity only. If this were so, either his humanity need not continue to obey God after salvation is complete, or else his humanity is to be abandoned at the consummation of salvation. Either way, immense Christological problems ensue. See Bilezikian, "Hermeneutical Bungee-Jumping."

42. Herbert M. Relton, *A Study in Christology: The Problem of the Relation of the Two Natures in the Person of Christ* (London: SPCK, 1917); Aloys Grillmeier, *Christ in Christian Tradition*, vol. 2, *From the Council of Chalcedon (451) to Gregory the Great (590–604)*, part 2, *The Church of Constantinople in the Sixth Century*, trans. John Cawte (London: Mowbray, 1995), 438–62; Basil Studer, *Trinity and Incarnation: The Faith of the Early Church*, trans. Matthias Westerhoff, ed. Andrew Louth (Collegeville, Minn.: Liturgical Press, 1993), 224–29; G. W. H. Lampe, ed., *A Patristic Greek Lexicon* (Oxford: Clarendon Press, 1961), 485–86, 666; B. Studer, "Enhypostasia," in *EECh* (1992), 1:272.

if the human will obeyed and the divine will did not, Jesus would then have been some kind of schizoid. Of course, there is a sense in which Christ according to his humanity needed to learn and to align his will with the divine plan. His intense prayers in the garden of Gethsemane are a case in point (Heb. 5:7–10). However, since the wills belong to the natures, they coincide, since the two natures themselves are united hypostatically. The two wills exhibit one united will. We repeat, it is impossible to separate the human obedience of Christ from who he is.

Here Sergei Bulgakov has some important things to say. He argues that the creation of man underlies the Incarnation. There is, he says, some inalienable characteristic in man by which the possibility of the Incarnation is comprehensible.[43] This characteristic is found in the person of Christ. Following the Christological controversy and its resolution, "we must infer that, since the person of the Word found it possible to live in human nature as well as in its own, therefore it is itself in some sense a human person too." By this Bulgakov is not proposing some mixture of divine and human. Rather, in order to serve as person to manhood, the divine person of the Word must itself be human "or, more exactly, co-human." Bulgakov's intention is to attest the fullest compatibility between the eternal Word and humanity. He argues that the union of the Word with human nature corresponds with the original relation between them. Man, on his side and for his part, must be capable of receiving and making room for a divine person in place of the human. "The incarnation thus appears to postulate, on its hypostatic side at least, some original analogy between divine and human personality, which yet does not overthrow all the essential difference between them." He points to the account in Genesis 2:7, where the personal spirit of man has its divine, uncreated origin from "the spirit of God." It is a spark of the divine. Man is made a partaker of the divine nature and capable of divinization. "Thus it is possible for the person of the heavenly God-man, the Word, to become the person of a created human nature." So, Bulgakov concludes, it was natural for the Word to take the place of the human personality of the human nature of Christ.[44]

43. Bulgakov, *Wisdom of God*, 126.
44. Ibid., 129–31.

The human obedience of Christ has a basis in the Son of God himself. Avoiding Nestorianism, we affirm that the obedience of Christ as man has a basis in the Son of God himself. This is the argument of Karl Barth, spelled out in detail in part of his *Church Dogmatics*[45] and argued extensively throughout the section "The Obedience of the Son of God."[46] He takes up the theme elsewhere too.[47] He claims that "for God it is just as natural to be lowly as it is to be high," for "even in the form of a servant, which is the form of his presence and action in Jesus Christ, we have to do with God himself in his true deity." The truth and actuality of the Atonement depend on this being so, for unless the one who reconciles the world is God himself, we could not be reconciled with God. If this were something that had no basis in God, then God would be acting in an arbitrary manner.[48] Barth acknowledges that this is a difficult matter, and he warns against subordinationism, which dissolves the deity of Christ. He also rejects the idea that this is restricted to "a kind of forecourt of the divine being," that this takes place only as "a worldly form" of God, something "purely economic," as if it was intended only to rescue us in the work of salvation, for if God's economy of revelation and salvation is distinguished from his proper being, then God has not brought us into touch with himself, but "he has only acted as though he had done so. But if he has not, how can there be on this theory any reconciliation of the world with God?" Barth rightly castigates as modalism this refusal to acknowledge that Christ's obedience is grounded in his being as the Son. "For if in his proper being as God God can only be unworldly, if he can be the humiliated and lowly and obedient One only in a mode of appearance and not in his proper being, what is the value of the true deity of Christ, what is its value for us?"[49] The point is that when we have to do with Jesus Christ we have to do with God. His presence in the world is identical with the existence of the humiliated, obedient, and lowly man, Jesus of Nazareth. Thus, the humiliation, lowliness, and obedience of Christ are essential in our conception of God. Not only can we speak of an obedience in God, but we have to do so. In

45. Barth, *CD*, IV/1: 192–205.
46. Ibid., IV/1: 157–357.
47. Ibid., IV/2: 42–43, 170.
48. Ibid., IV/1: 192–94.
49. Ibid., IV/1: 196–97.

stark contrast, the modalistic view, as Barth says, presents us with a Christ whose proper being remains hidden behind an improper being, an "as if."[50] Barth concludes that the unity of God "consists in the fact that in himself he is both One who is obeyed and Another who obeys."[51] The incarnate obedience of Christ is grounded "in his own being, in his own inner life," for "as the One who is obedient in humility he wills to be not only the one God but this man, and this man as the one God." Thus, "he is in time what he is in eternity." "He is as man what he is as God," for "that is the true deity of Jesus Christ, obedient in humility, in its unity and equality, its *homoousia*, with the deity of the One who sent him and to whom he is obedient."[52] Geoffrey Bromiley comments that "obedience is not alien to the Son. Barth suggests that even in his eternal deity as the Son, Christ is obedient to the Father. Nor does this imply either subordinationism or modalism."[53] Berkouwer, citing Bavinck in support, also points to the submissiveness of the Son to the Father as antedating the Incarnation, deriving "from the depth of the trinitarian being of God."[54]

Emphatically, this obedience must *not* be understood on the basis of our human obedience, however godly, but rather on the basis of the submission of the Son eternally. Even more, all suggestions of slavishness, arising from the sinful structures of a fallen world, must be eliminated from consideration at this point. This form of analogical predication is as misplaced as it is to think backward from human generation to the generation of the Son in eternity. It rules out talk of "command structures," "hierarchy," and "boss-servant relationships" that some throw out emotively to cloud the matter.[55] Rather, the Son's relation to the Father is the model for our relation to the Father. What is his by nature is ours by grace. By this, all actual human relationships are under judgment. None can claim ultimate

50. Ibid., IV/1: 198–200.
51. Ibid., IV/1: 201.
52. Ibid., IV/1: 203–5.
53. Geoffrey W. Bromiley, *An Introduction to the Theology of Karl Barth* (Grand Rapids: Eerdmans, 1979), 181.
54. G. C. Berkouwer, *Divine Election*, trans. Hugo Bekker (Grand Rapids: Eerdmans, 1960), 163.
55. Bilezikian, "Hermeneutical Bungee-Jumping," 57–68.

validity or immunity from criticism.[56] For a discussion of this in Barth, see Jüngel.[57]

This is not subordinationism. This must be distanced from subordinationism. Some conservative evangelicals have openly defended what they term "the eternal subordination of the Son." At best, language like this is misleading. Some credence has been given to this phraseology by Charles Hodge, who argued that the Son is subordinate to the Father in terms of personal subsistence.[58] In these cases, the intention is orthodox, but the language is open to misunderstanding. Subordinationism proper posits the erroneous belief that the Son is somehow less than the Father. It argues for gradations of deity. In its most extreme form, Arius argued that the Son was created. Beyond that, the idea that the Father is the origin of the deity of the Son and the Holy Spirit, evident to an extent in Basil and Gregory of Nyssa, implies that the latter are less than the Father in some way. The points we must maintain and preserve are clear. *In terms of his being*, the Son is identical to the Father and the Holy Spirit. *In terms of his status*, he is equal. *In terms of relation*, he is from the Father. The matter before us concerns *the relations* between the Father and the Son. It *is a matter of order*—an order that we will explain, as far as we can, in a moment.

The Son's obedience is not inferiority, any more than the invisibility and anonymity of the Holy Spirit make him of less significance than the Son or the Father. To see it as a matter of superiority and inferiority is to view the Holy Trinity according to human analogies. The same criticism applies to talk of this entailing a "chain of command."[59] The orthodox fathers consistently oppose that form of ana-

---

56. This applies to patriarchal systems and practice as well as to feminism, as I argue in "The Man-Woman Debate: Theological Comment," *WTJ* 52 (1990): 65–78, and in "The Hermeneutics of Feminism," *Them* 17 (January-April 1992): 4–7.

57. Eberhard Jüngel, *Karl Barth: A Theological Legacy*, trans. Garrett E. Paul (Philadelphia: Westminster Press, 1986), 127–38.

58. Charles Hodge, *Systematic Theology* (Grand Rapids: Eerdmans, 1977), 1:554, 460–68, 474.

59. Nor is the relationship between man and woman to be construed as "a chain of command," as some evangelical feminists falsely accuse me of teaching. This is to use a human relationship, a military metaphor, to govern the doctrine of the Trinity—*exactly the reverse* of what I argue in "The Man-Woman Debate" and in "Hermeneutics." The point is that the Trinity is three irreducibly different persons in indivisible union, one in being, equal in status, indwelling in mutual love, in an order (not a rank). Human beings, made in God's image, exemplify a sim-

logical predication. They insist that we cannot move from human generation to divine, for the generation of the Son by the Father transcends anything that we can possibly know. Nor can the relation
between the Father and the Son be compared to other creaturely realities, for it is eternally prior to each and every one of them. The matter concerns the *order (taxis)* among the persons—their relations, not
their deity. It is a question of order, not rank. We recall that the orthodox and the Arians used the word *taxis* in different ways. The Arians used it to support their heretical idea that the Son was of lesser
rank or status than the Father. The pro-Nicenes used the word in the
sense of a fitting and suitable disposition, not a hierarchy.[60] In short,
the relation between the Father and the Son must be seen in terms of
the full *homoousion*, for all three persons are of the one identical
being, in loving perichoresis. Thus, as Calvin says, the Son, as God,
is of himself (*ex seipso*), while in terms of his person he is from the
Father (*a Patre*).[61] T. F. Torrance explains that in this "irreversible
relation" between the Father and the Son, in which "the Father 'naturally' comes first," the Son is all that the Father is, except for being
the Father. The Father is the Father of the Son, but he is not his deifier. This inner-Trinitarian order is distinguished "by position and not
status, by form and not being, by sequence and not power, for they
are fully and perfectly equal."[62] From the East, Bobrinskoy comments
that the obedience of Jesus "is the hinge of his double relation to the
Father: as eternal Son and suffering servant. It represents the eternal
and 'terrestrial' aspect of love of the Son, who came to do the will of
the Father" (John 6:38). "Although he was a son, he learned obedience through what he suffered" (Heb. 5:8). This obedience of Jesus,

ilar unity in diversity, created for loving communion, in equality and with irreducible differences. The evangelical feminists neglect the order between the persons. It is a modalist error.

60. The word τάξις has a range of meanings. It was often used in military contexts and had
the idea of rank, entailing a hierarchy of some kind. This fitted in well with the Arian view of a
gradation between the Father and the Son, with the latter having a lower and subordinate status. However, it was also used of role, office, class, orderliness and regularity of the stars, order
in the church or monastery, or an ordered constitution. It is in the sense of order, not rank, closer
to what is fitting and suitable, rather than any sense of hierarchy, that the orthodox use the term.
See Lampe, *Lexicon*, 1372–73.

61. John Calvin, *Institutes of the Christian Religion*, trans. Ford Lewis Battles, ed. John T.
McNeill (Philadelphia: Westminster Press, 1960), 1.13.19, 25.

62. Thomas F. Torrance, *Christian Doctrine of God*, 176.

who "in the days of his flesh . . . offered up prayers and supplications, with loud cries and tears, to him who was able to save him from death" (Heb. 5:7), derives therefore from his eternal condition of Son; it is rooted, with the Cross and the death of the Lamb, in divine love itself (see Rev. 13:8; 1 Peter 1:19–20). His unconditional obedience to the Father, Bobrinskoy says, "opens the path of salvation to humans, which the Son actualizes "in the days of his flesh.""[63]

It is undergirded by the faithfulness of God. Moltmann's strictures concerning the economic Trinity and the immanent or ontological Trinity are pertinent and, at this point, agree with my argument here. He questions the claims of the East that the mission of the Holy Spirit differs from his eternal procession. The East has used this distinction to preserve its opposition to the *filioque.* It concedes that in the economy of salvation the Spirit is sent by the Father and the Son, but maintains in contrast that in the immanent Trinity the Spirit proceeds from the Father only. Moltmann challenges this dichotomy, affirming that the economic Trinity is a reliable gauge of the immanent Trinity, owing to the faithfulness of God. "One cannot say, therefore, that something holds true in God's revelation, but not in God's being."[64] By the same token, we point to the obedience of the incarnate Son in the economy of salvation, reflecting his eternal relation to the Father in loving submission, in identity of being and equality of status. The faithfulness of God also undercuts the suggestion made by Warfield—only a suggestion, for he does not pursue it—that certain aspects of the relation between the Father and the Son in the history of salvation may have been due to a "covenant" between the persons of the Trinity by which the Son submitted himself temporarily to the Father, intending to abandon such submission upon the completion of our salvation.[65] If this were so, the Son could not have revealed God to us.

John Thompson asks if Barth is in danger of attributing inferiority to the Son, and so teaching subordinationism. Can the Son be

63. Boris Bobrinskoy, *The Mystery of the Trinity: Trinitarian Experience and Vision in the Biblical and Patristic Tradition,* trans. Anthony P. Gythiel (Crestwood, N.Y.: St. Vladimir's Seminary Press, 1999), 118.

64. Jürgen Moltmann, "Theological Proposals Towards the Resolution of the *Filioque* Controversy," in *Spirit of God, Spirit of Christ: Ecumenical Reflections on the Filioque Controversy,* ed. Lukas Vischer (London: SPCK, 1981), 165–66.

65. Warfield, "Biblical Doctrine of the Trinity," 53–55.

God as such if this is so? Thompson rejects these charges, arguing that the Son's obedience is *as Lord*—"one must not, therefore, see obedience (in the Son) as indicating an inferiority to the Father but rather as the expression—the central expression—of their relationship. These distinctions indicate that the Father is primarily majestic in commanding love and the Son primarily obedient to the Father, but each shares in the being and work of the other."[66] He cites W. Kreck, who says that God, who "is not only in the heights but also in the depths, not only the Lord but also servant, rules not only in power but can, at the same time, meet us in weakness." These are not trifling speculations or "metaphysical phantoms" when a distinction is made between "one who commands and one who obeys."[67] Karl Rahner asks a pertinent question when he says, "May we really say without more ado that from the concept of the Son of the synoptic Jesus we must eliminate his obedience to the Father, his adoration, his submission to the Father's unfathomable will? For we eliminate them when we explain this kind of behavior in him only through the hypostatic union as such. They are then properties of the Son, but not constitutive moments of his sonship."[68]

The Son's submission to the Father is compatible with his full and unabbreviated deity. Therefore, we may rightly say that the Son submits in eternity to the Father, without in any way breaking his indissoluble oneness with the Father or the Holy Spirit, and without in any way jeopardizing his equality. Being God, he serves the Father. Being God, the Father loves the Son and shares his glory with him (John 17:1–4, 22–24). The Son's obedience is in relation to the Father—he acts as both the judge and the judged; as Son he goes into the far country. Laats says of Barth's construction of this argument, "The basis of the determination of the Son to become a human being and thus the

66. John Thompson, "On the Trinity," in *Theology Beyond Christendom: Essays on the Centenary of the Birth of Karl Barth, May 10, 1886*, ed. John Thompson (Allison Park, Pa.: Pickwick Publications, 1986), 17–19.

67. Walter Kreck, *Grundfragen der Dogmatik* (Munich: Chr. Kaiser, 1970), 84, cited by Thompson, "On the Trinity," 19. See also P. T. Forsyth, *Marriage: Its Ethic and Religion* (London: Hodder and Stoughton, 1912), 70, and Rowan Williams, "Barth on the Triune God," in *Karl Barth: Essays in His Theological Method*, ed. S. W. Sykes (Oxford: Clarendon Press, 1979), 175.

68. Karl Rahner, *The Trinity*, trans. Joseph Donceel (New York: Crossroad, 1997), 62–63.

basis of his humility and obedience is in the immanent Trinity. The Son is obedient already antecedently in the Trinity."[69]

This sounds all very well, but does it have support from Scripture? Admittedly there is very little in the Bible that allows us to peer into the life of the immanent Trinity. However, that is not to say that there is *nothing* that can help us. First, Paul grounds his great exhortation in Philippians 2:5ff. to live as Christ did on the way he conducts himself as God. "Being in the form of God, he did not use his status of equality with God for his own advantage,[70] but emptied himself, taking the form of a slave" (my translation). The Son's self-emptying was not a subtraction of his deity, for he continues to be in the form of God (present participle: *huparchōn*). Rather, it involved an addition, the addition of human nature. He emptied himself by becoming man and following a path of obedience that led to the death of the cross. He added the form of a slave to the form of God. However, his decision to do this was made prior to his doing it. His determination not to exploit his true and real status for his own advantage was made in eternity. His self-emptying on earth flowed from his refusal to pursue self-interest in eternity. His human obedience reflects his divine submission.[71] The latter no more detracts from his full deity than does his postresurrection exaltation diminish his full humanity. Since his obedience on earth did not curtail his deity, neither does his self-effacement in eternity.

Again, the author of the letter to the Hebrews points to Christ not seeking to be our great high priest, but being appointed by the

69. Alar Laats, *Doctrines of the Trinity in Eastern and Western Theologies: A Study with Special Reference to K. Barth and V. Lossky* (Frankfurt am Main: Peter Lang, 1999), 48; Barth, CD, IV/1: 170, 177, 192–94; IV/2: 42–43.

70. The word *harpagmos* has been the subject of intense debate down through the years. See Roy W. Hoover, "The *Harpagmos* Enigma: A Philological Solution," *HTR* 64 (1971): 95–119; Ralph Martin, *Philippians*, New Century Bible (Grand Rapids: Eerdmans, 1980), 96–97; N. T. Wright, "ἁρπαγμός and the Meaning of Philippians 2: 5–11," *JTS* 37 (October 1986): 321–52.

71. Lossky comments that there is a twofold kenosis (self-emptying). In the first place, the Son submitted his will to the will of the Father. This is actually the will of the whole Trinity, for the Father's will is the source of it, the will of the Son expresses it in obedience, and the will of the Spirit expresses it in accomplishment. The Son's submission led to his incarnation. Second, there is also the kenosis of the deified humanity of Christ, by which he submitted to the fallen condition of humanity, which entailed suffering and death. The first kenosis is the basis of the second. Vladimir Lossky, *The Mystical Theology of the Eastern Church* (London: James Clarke & Co., 1957), 144–46.

Father (Heb. 5:4–5). The author proceeds to say that Christ's high priesthood occupied "the days of his flesh" (v. 7). It included his being tempted in all points as we are. This took place throughout his life. There was no point at which he suddenly switched into a priestly mode.[72] His entire course of human obedience is in view, although most evidently the time in the garden of Gethsemane, when he offered "prayers and supplications, with loud cries and tears." His appointment to the work of high priest is prior to the work itself and so prior to his incarnation. The idea is that at this time the Son "did not exalt himself." He did not seek this task for his own advantage. He did not claim the office. He was appointed to it, and his appointment was made by the Father. As Calvin wrote, with the Father is the beginning of activity.[73] And, so we may say, with the Son is the loving, joyful, faithful acceptance of the Father's initiating plan.[74]

The Trinity and the Work of Christ

Augustine was right to emphasize that in all the works and ways of God there is an engagement of all three persons of the Trinity. Since the three mutually coinhere, they all work together—in harmony, we might say, rather than in unison, for each is irreducibly distinct. Calvin puts it well when he says that to the Father "is attributed the beginning of activity, and the fountain and wellspring of all things; to the Son, wisdom, counsel, and the ordered disposition of all things; but to the Spirit is assigned the power and efficacy of that activity."[75] The same applies in all aspects of our salvation. From its beginning in the eternal counsel of God to its completion at the eschaton, our salvation is rooted in the Trinity. The Father chose us in Christ before the foundation of the world, and to him is attributed the beginning of action. In the Incar-

72. Letham, *The Work of Christ*, 24, 105–21.

73. Calvin, *Institutes*, 1.13.18.

74. Rainbow, "Orthodox Trinitarianism," 8, points out that "the very theologians who forged the Homoousios formula were also led by their understanding of scripture to confess in various ways that the Son *qua* Son honors the Father, and that this honor obtains both before and after the Incarnation, both at creation and in the eschaton—indeed that it is integral to the timeless relation of the two Persons." He produces an extensive list of NT scholars in support of this view, including B. F. Westcott, G. R. Beasley-Murray, H. A. W. Meyer, F. Godet, C. K. Barrett, A. Robertson and A. Plummer, L. Joseph Kreitzer, and Karl Rahner.

75. Calvin, *Institutes*, 1.13.18.

nation, the Son takes human nature, lives, dies on the cross, is raised from the dead, ascends to the right hand of the Father, and will return to consummate our salvation. In turn, the Holy Spirit is sent at Pentecost to indwell and to pervade his people, to render us suitable for union and communion with God. Thus, the grand sweep of salvation follows a Trinitarian structure. However, in each aspect all three persons are integrally involved, while one in particular is directly evident. Thus, only the Son became incarnate, but he was sent by the Father and conceived by the Holy Spirit according to the flesh. Thereafter his ministry was pursued in dependence on, and obedience to, the Father, while the Spirit directed him and empowered him. When it came to the climactic moment of the Cross, he offered himself up "through the eternal Spirit" to the Father (Heb. 9:14). On the third day, the Father raised him from the dead by the power of the Holy Spirit (Rom. 8:11). In turn, the ascended Christ received from the Father the promised Holy Spirit and poured him out on his church (Acts 2:33–36), including within that action all that the Spirit did thereafter in giving faith, love, obedience, and perseverance to Christ's people.

In particular, let us consider the work of Christ the Son. All he did "for us and our salvation" he did according to both natures. As God, he had the strength to suffer and to make atonement for us. As man, he lived an obedient and sinless life and in our human nature offered himself up to the Father as a pure and sufficient offering for sin. His obedience, active and passive, his perfect fulfillment of God's law on our behalf, and his suffering the penalty of the broken law in our place, secured our deliverance from the wrath of God and our entrance into eternal life by God's grace, received through faith.[76] His whole, undivided person brought about our salvation, both as man and as God. From what we have argued, this entailed a full engagement of the eternal Son in securing salvation. This was not, in Barth's words, something involving merely "the forecourt of God's being"— as if this was a singularity that did not reflect who God really is. That would be a form of Nestorian Christology, so separating the deity and humanity of Christ that the integrity of his person is threatened. That would not be incarnation, but merely a deity indwelling a man. It could not bring about salvation, for it is only through God living *as man*

76. See Letham, *The Work of Christ*, 105–57.

that this could be achieved. Furthermore, since there was a full engagement of the eternal Son in the Incarnation, so much so that Jesus Christ
as the Son of God truly revealed God, all three persons of the Trinity
in their distinct ways were operating in the life and ministry of the
incarnate Christ, while it was specifically the Son who lived and suffered as man. When we consider the lengths to which the Son went,
the whole Trinity indivisibly accompanying him, we bow ourselves in
worship and praise. This will be the theme of the next chapter.

*Let all us faithful, speaking devoutly of him from whom we have
received sanctification, in company with the Angels perpetually glorify the Father, Son, and Holy Spirit: for he is a Trinity in Persons, but
one in Essence, one God; to whom also let us sing: Blessed be thou,
O Lord God forever!*

*In Jordan was the Trinity made manifest; for the Most Divine Person
of the Father himself proclaimed: He that is baptized, the same is my
beloved Son. And the Spirit descended upon him that was like unto
himself. Him do men bless and exalt unto all the ages.*

*When in Jordan thou wast baptized, O Lord, the worship of the Trin-
ity was made manifest. For the voice of the Father bare witness unto
thee, calling thee his beloved Son, and the Spirit, in the form of a dove,
confirmed the steadfastness of that word. O Christ our God, who didst
manifest thyself, and dost enlighten the world, glory to thee.*[77]

---

77. Epiphany: Canticle VII-VIII; Antiphon III, Tone I, *Service Book*, 186, 188.

The Trinity, Worship, and Prayer

The dogma of the Holy Trinity is not only a doctrinal form, but a living Christian experience which is constantly developing; it is a fact of the Christian life. For life in Christ unites with the Holy Trinity, gives a knowledge of the Father's love and the gifts of the Holy Spirit. There is no truly Christian life, apart from knowledge of the Trinity; this is abundantly witnessed in Christian literature. —Sergius Bulgakov, *The Orthodox Church*

The Neglect of the Trinity in the Western Church

God-centered worship (can worship be anything else?) must, by definition, give center stage to what is distinctive of Christianity, the high-water mark of God's self-revelation in the Bible.[1] Yet Trinitarian theology has had a wider impact on the piety of the Eastern church. Eastern liturgies are permeated with Trinitarian prayers and doxologies. In the West, the Trinity has in practice been relegated to such an extent that most Christians are little more than practical modalists. As Laats comments, "Instead of being in the centre of christian worship and thinking it has been marginalised."[2]

---

1. This chapter is based on a lecture given at Mid-America Reformed Seminary on 10 November 1999, published in *MJT* 13 (2002): 87–100 and republished with permission.

2. Alar Laats, *Doctrines of the Trinity in Eastern and Western Theologies: A Study with Special Reference to K. Barth and V. Lossky* (Frankfurt am Main: Peter Lang, 1999), 160.

Colin Gunton suggests some reasons for this.[3] He points the finger at Augustine, the seminal Trinitarian of the Western church. Augustine, beginning from the premise of the unity of God, had difficulty with the concept of theophany and Incarnation. Thus, he did not build his Trinitarian thought on the basis of historical, biblical revelation as the Cappadocians did. His famous psychological analogy was thereby flawed. It was ahistorical and failed to do justice to the persons of the Trinity. It has made the Trinity problematic in the West, a recondite mystery for the theologically advanced, and has bred the atheism and agnosticism we see around us.

These criticisms carry weight, although we noted in chapter 9 that they are overdone. The early chapters of *De Trinitate* are full of biblical exposition, and much of Augustine's other writing on the Trinity is found in the course of his *Tractates on the Gospel of John*. However, allowing for those caveats, Gunton's strictures strike close to home. Consider some of the traditional works of systematic theology produced in the Western Reformed tradition. Charles Hodge plows through some 250 pages on the doctrine of God before turning his attention to the Trinity. Louis Berkhof follows the same pattern—page after page on the existence of God, the knowability of God, the being and attributes of God, and the names of God. Only then does he consider the Trinity.[4] On the more popular level, J. I. Packer's best-seller *Knowing God* (1973) has only seven pages out of 254 on the Trinity.[5] He recognizes that for most Christians it is an esoteric mystery to which lip service may be paid once a year on Trinity Sunday. However, after his chapter is over, he carries on as if nothing has happened. Contrast this with the great theologian of the Eastern church, John of Damascus. His *De orthodoxa fidei* starts off on a Trinitarian footing as early as 1.1–10. In the West, the two Reformation and post-Reformation theologians who, in my estimation, have been most helpful in focus-

3. Colin Gunton, "Augustine, the Trinity, and the Theological Crisis of the West," *SJT* 43 (1990): 33–58; Colin Gunton, *The Promise of Trinitarian Theology* (Edinburgh: T & T Clark, 1991).

4. Charles Hodge, *Systematic Theology* (Grand Rapids: Eerdmans, 1977), 1:191–441 on the existence, nature, and attributes of God, and 1:442–82 on the Trinity; Louis Berkhof, *Systematic Theology* (London: Banner of Truth, 1958), 19–81 on the existence and attributes of God, and 82–99 on the Trinity.

5. J. I. Packer, *Knowing God* (London: Hodder and Stoughton, 1973), 256–63.

ing worship in a clearly Trinitarian manner have a distinctly "Eastern" feel to them in certain crucial respects. Both John Calvin and John Owen strongly stress the distinctness of the three persons. Much of their writing on the Trinity is spent discussing the deity of the Son and the Holy Spirit and, in Owen's case, arguing forcibly for the distinct worship of the three.[6]

We noted in the introduction a striking example of the muddle in Western Christianity as seen in a letter to the *Times* (London) in June 1992 by David Prior, a well-known evangelical Anglican vicar in London. Prior recounted how he was preparing a sermon for Trinity Sunday on the Trinity, searching for some intelligible comparison to help his congregation. He found it on television watching cricket, the Second Test Match between England and Pakistan at Lord's. Ian Salisbury, the English leg spinner, bowled successively a leg break, a googly, and a top spinner. There, said Prior, was a perfect analogy—one person expressing himself in three different ways! Full marks to Prior for spotting the importance of cricket—a pity about the theology. Before I had opportunity to send off a response to the editor, a half dozen or so others had pounced to point out that his letter should be signaled "wide," for he had resurrected the ancient heresy of modalism. Modalism, we remind ourselves, is the idea that the Father, the Son, and the Holy Spirit are merely ways God revealed himself and do not represent eternal antecedent personal realities in God himself. They are temporary appearances, like an actor assuming different roles at different times. The problem with this, of course, is that if it were so, we would have no genuine knowledge of God, for he would be something in himself other than what he has revealed himself to be.

This general bias in Western Christianity is in stark contrast to Gregory Nazianzen, who speaks of "my Trinity" and who, in his *Oration on the Theophany*, states, "When I say God, I mean Father, Son, and Holy Ghost."[7] In the West, on the other hand, philosophers of

6. John Calvin, *Institutes of the Christian Religion*, trans. Ford Lewis Battles, ed. John T. McNeill (Philadelphia: Westminster Press, 1960), 1.13. John Owen, *Of Communion with God the Father, Son, and Holy Ghost, Each Person Distinctly, in Love, Grace, and Consolation* (1657), in *The Works of John Owen*, ed. William H. Goold (reprint, London: Banner of Truth, 1965–68), 2:1–274.
7. Gregory Nazianzen, *Orations* 38.8 (PG 36:320).

religion who are also Christian customarily refer to a generic "God" all the time, the Trinity going without mention.[8]

Examine any hymnbook or chorus book you can find, and search for compositions that are clearly Trinitarian. You won't find many. Ask yourself, as you do so, how many items could easily be sung by Unitarians, orthodox Jews, or Muslims. You will be surprised. Let's name a few—and these are traditional favorites that have stood the test of time and by dint of usage have established themselves as part of the canon of Anglo-Saxon hymnody. "My God, How Wonderful Thou Art," "Praise My Soul, the King of Heaven," "Immortal, Invisible, God Only Wise," "Praise to the Lord, the Almighty, the King of Creation," and even (dare I say it?) "Great Is Thy Faithfulness" are only theistic, at best implicitly binitarian. "How Great Thou Art" is at best binitarian. We could go on. Of course, we may bring Trinitarian assumptions to these texts and so interpret them, although I daresay only a very few may do so, but this is not present in the texts themselves. Since theology and worship are integrally connected, as the Fathers taught,[9] this is a serious problem.

Only God Can Make God Known and Determine How We Relate to Him

Naming in the ancient Near East denoted the sovereignty of the one who named over the one named. Thus, for example, Adam names the animals (Gen. 2:19–20) in fulfilling the creation mandate of Genesis 1:28ff. to exercise dominion over the animal world. However, only God ever names God. Never is a name given to him by humans. Only he has the right to name himself, for he as the Creator is not subject to any other being. Moreover, the covenant community is to have no other gods than he (Ex. 20:1–3). Contemporary feminists notwithstanding, human attempts to reimagine God or to name him are simply that—figments of the imagination, idols made in a human image,

8. Cf. the pertinent comments along these lines of Nick Needham, "The *Filioque* Clause: East or West?" *SBET* 15 (1997): 161.

9. Cf. Hilary of Poitiers's claim that God cannot be known except by devotion. Origen held that *theologia* and *eusebeia* (piety) mutually condition each other. Prosper of Aquitaine coined the seminal formula: *Legem credendi lex statuat supplicandi* (the rule of prayer establishes the rule of faith—and vice versa).

without validity. *It follows that God is sovereign in his self-revelation.* This is clear in Exodus 33:18–34:7, where Yahweh refuses Moses' request to see his glory, which is impossible. Instead, he affirms his utter authority, placing Moses in a cleft in the rock while granting him a new revelation of his name.[10]

Further, God is sovereign in granting us knowledge of himself by the Holy Spirit. The additional factor of human sin places us in total reliance on God to make himself known. Paul insists that we were dead in sin, helpless to do anything to put right our rebellion against God and unwilling to do so, for the dead cannot will or do anything to change their situation (Eph. 2:1–2). He also says that unbelievers are blinded by the god of this age, so they cannot see the light of the gospel of the glory of God in Christ (2 Cor. 4:4). As Jesus taught, we trust him only as we are drawn by the Holy Spirit (John 6:44). Hence, humanity's predilection for new objects and forms of worship is rebellion against the true and living God, the Holy Trinity. Only by the gracious action of the Trinity, breaking into our darkness and death and arousing us to new life, can we ever know him.

The God who has made himself known for our salvation has revealed himself to be triune. He unfolds his revelation progressively in covenant history. At each stage, he names himself. In the Abrahamic covenant, he makes himself known as El Shaddai (God Almighty) (Gen. 17:1). In the Mosaic covenant, he names himself Ehyeh (Ex. 3:14; cf. y'vah, 6:3). At the apex of redemptive history, Jesus comes to fulfill the promises of the OT. Matthew records how Jesus inaugurates the kingdom of heaven, promised to Abraham long before. The covenant is no longer restricted to Israel, but extends to the whole world. Indeed, many Israelites will be cast out of the covenant community while the Gentiles are now to be part of it (Matt. 8:11–12). As the Mosaic covenant was inaugurated with the sprinkling of covenantal blood, so the new covenant is founded in the blood of Jesus (Matt. 26:27–29). At the end of his gospel, Matthew recounts how the nations are to be made disciples, with the new covenant sacrament of baptism. This baptism is into *the one name of the Father, and the Son, and the Holy*

10. See Thomas F. Torrance, "The Christian Apprehension of God the Father," in *Speaking the Christian God: The Holy Trinity and the Challenge of Feminism*, ed. Alvin F. Kimel Jr. (Grand Rapids: Eerdmans, 1992), 120–43.

Spirit. Thus, Jesus the Son names God as the one God who is the Father, the Son, and the Holy Spirit, in connection with the new covenant sacrament, baptism. This is God's crowning revelation of himself—all that went before points to this. Retrospectively, it casts light on all that led up to it (like a detective mystery that discloses in the final scene the clues that make sense of the entire story).

So the triune God alone grants us access to himself and determines how we are to relate to him and approach him. In the Mosaic covenant, Moses was required to construct the paraphernalia of Israel's worship exactly as Yahweh told him. Jesus announced that no one comes to the Father except through him. Access to the Father is exclusively through the mediation of the Son. These are terms laid down by the triune God.

Christian Worship Is Distinctively Trinitarian

> When we look at the Godhead . . . that which we conceive is One; but when we look at the persons in whom the Godhead dwells, and at those who tirelessly and with equal glory have their being from the first cause[11]—there are three whom we worship. (Gregory Nazianzen, *Orations* 31.14)

> . . . one essence, one divinity, one power, one will, one energy, one beginning, one authority, one dominion, one sovereignty, *made known in three perfect subsistences and adored with one adoration* . . . united without confusion and divided without separation. (John of Damascus, *De orthodoxa fidei* 1:8)

> The proper and peculiar object of divine worship and invocation is *the essence of God*, in its infinite excellency, dignity, majesty. . . . Now this is common to all three persons, and is proper to each of them; not formally as a person, but as God blessed for ever. All adoration respects that which is common to all; so that in each act of adoration and worship all are to be adored and worshipped. (John Owen, *Of Communion with God the Father, Son, and Holy Ghost,* in *The Works of John Owen*, ed. W. H. Goold, 2:269)

11. Here is the characteristic Cappadocian teaching on the Father as the fountain of deity.

The Basis and Ground of Worship

The church's worship is grounded in who God is and what he has done. The Father has sent the Son "for us and our salvation." This is prominent in John, chapters 5, 10, and 17, but Paul also directs our attention to it in Romans 8:32. In turn, the Father together with the Son has sent the Holy Spirit to indwell the church. The focus of the Spirit's ministry is to speak of Christ the Son. This is summarized clearly in Galatians 4:4–6: "When the fullness of time had come, God sent forth his Son, born of woman, born under the law, to redeem those who were under the law, so that we might receive adoption as sons. And because you are sons, God has sent the Spirit of his Son into our hearts, crying, 'Abba! Father!'" Here lies the basic premise of all God's actions—*from the Father through the Son by the Holy Spirit.* As Cyril of Alexandria states in his *Commentary on John*, "All things proceed from the Father, but wholly through the Son in the Spirit."[12] These words of Paul, and this order which is so evident in the Fathers, encapsulates the whole of redemptive history. Not only is our salvation a work of God, not only is it Trinitarian through and through, but it is initiated by the Father, accomplished by the Son, and applied by the Holy Spirit. Of course, Augustine was right in that all aspects of this great drama of redemption are put into effect by all three persons of the Trinity working together in harmony—*opera Trinitatis ab extra indivisa sunt.* However, Calvin's description holds true, both as a general principle and as an image of what has actually happened in human history, that with the Father "is attributed the beginning of activity, and the fountain and wellspring of all things; to the Son, wisdom, counsel, and the ordered disposition of all things; but to the Spirit is assigned the power and efficacy of that activity."[13] The Father sent the Son; then, following the Son's death and resurrection, he sent the Spirit of his Son.

Our Response

John Owen comments that our communion with the Trinity rests on the union we have with Jesus Christ, for "communion is the mutual communication of such good things as wherein the persons holding

12. PG 74:477.
13. Calvin, *Institutes*, 1.13.18.

that communion are delighted, bottomed upon some union between them." Thus, our communion with God consists "in his *communication of himself unto us, with our returnal unto him* . . . flowing from that *union* which in Jesus Christ we have with him."[14]

Ephesians 2:18. Paul has pointed out that Christ made reconciliation by the Cross (v. 14), tearing down the dividing wall between God and ourselves due to sin, and between Jew and Gentile due to the ceremonial law. He goes on to say that both Jew and Gentile have identical means of access to God in Christ. "Through him [Christ] we both [Jew and Gentile] have access in one [Holy] Spirit to the Father." Access to God is ultimately access to the Father. This is through Christ, the one mediator between God and man (1 Tim. 2:5). It is the Spirit who gives us life in place of death (cf. v. 1), raising us in Christ (vv. 6–7) and graciously granting us faith (vv. 8–10). Calvin held that the principal work of the Holy Spirit is to give us faith.[15] It is a cardinal teaching of Scripture that saving faith is the gift of God, given by the Spirit (John 6:44; Eph. 2:1–10; 1 Cor. 12:3). Here is the reverse movement to that seen as the ground of the church's worship—*by the Holy Spirit through Christ to the Father.* This encompasses our entire response to, and relationship with, God—from worship through the whole field of Christian experience.

From this it follows that prayer is distinctively Trinitarian. The Christian faith exists in an atmosphere saturated by the Trinity. At its most basic level, each and every Christian believer experiences in an unarticulated form communion with the Holy Trinity. It is the Holy Spirit who creates a desire to pray and worship God. It is he who brings us to faith and sustains us in a life of faithful obedience. In turn, our access to the Father is exclusively through his Son, Jesus Christ. No one comes to the Father except through him (John 14:6). Now that he has offered the one perfect sacrifice for sins for all time, we have access to the holy place, the presence of God (Heb. 10:19–20), and so can approach with confidence the throne of grace, knowing that our great high priest is there to intercede for us, he who has experienced to the full the struggles of human life in a fallen world and so can sympa-

14. Owen, *Of Communion with God*, in *Works*, ed. Goold, 2:8–9.
15. Calvin, *Institutes*, 3.1.1.

thize with us in our weakness (Heb. 4:14ff.). Indeed, Jesus introduces us to the same relation he has with the Father. He is the Son by nature; we are children by grace. We now call on God as "our Father." Moreover, the Spirit brings us into his own intercession for us (Rom. 8:26–27). He thus eliminates the distance between us and God, creating in us the same relation he has with the Father and the Son.[16] Prayer and worship are thus an exploration of the character of the Holy Trinity. It is urgent to ensure that our theology is in line with this most basic Christian experience. For the lack of it, the faithful are misled and their ability to articulate and understand in measure what they tacitly believe and confess is stunted.

John 4:23–24. The Samaritan woman's question concerns the proper place of worship, whether at Jerusalem (which the Jews insisted YHWH required) or Mount Gerizim (where the Samaritans worshiped). Jesus supports Jerusalem, indicating that the Jews worshiped according to knowledge, while the Samaritans did not. Both the Bible and history support this. The Samaritans were a mixed race, formed from remnants of the ten northern tribes together with settlers from other nations brought in by the Assyrians after the destruction of the northern kingdom. Their religion was syncretistic, combining elements of the worship of YHWH, based on the Samaritan Pentateuch, together with aspects of the ancestral religions of the various imported nations. However, Jesus says, now the time has arrived when the distinction between Israel and Samaria, between Jerusalem and Mount Gerizim, is superseded. True worshipers now worship the Father in spirit and in truth.

What does Jesus mean? This hardly means merely that a particular location is completely irrelevant, or that true worship can now occur anywhere, although that may be entailed in what he says. Nor is "spirit" a reference to the human spirit, as if true worship were purely inward and externals were of no consequence. Rather, we should remember the extensive teaching in the fourth gospel on the Holy Spirit, concentrated later in chapters 14–16. Every reference to *pneuma* (spirit) in this gospel, bar probably two, points to the Holy Spirit. In this con-

16. See Dumitru Staniloae, *The Experience of God*, trans. and ed. Iona Ionita and Robert Barringer (Brookline, Mass.: Holy Cross Orthodox Press, 1994–2000), 1:248–49.

nection, Jesus means that true worship is directed to the Father in the
Holy Spirit. In the words of Basil the Great,

> It is an extraordinary statement, but it is nonetheless true, that the
> Spirit is frequently spoken of as the place of them that are being sanc-
> tified. . . . This is the special and peculiar place of true worship. . . .
> In what place do we offer it? In the Holy Spirit. . . . It follows that
> the Spirit is truly the place of the saints and the saint is the proper
> place for the Spirit, offering himself as he does for the indwelling of
> God, and called God's temple.[17]

Again, with reference to "truth," do we have to look any further than
John's record of Jesus as the embodiment of truth (14:6), as the true
light coming into the world (1:9), "full of grace and truth" (1:14), who
as a result brought grace and truth into the world (1:17)? Is not Jesus
pointing to himself, implying, as Paul, that new covenant worship is
Trinitarian? We worship the Father in the Holy Spirit and in the fullness of truth, his incarnate Son.[18]

In summary, Gregory Nazianzen puts these passages in context
with his comment, "This, then, is my position . . . to worship God the
Father, God the Son, and God the Holy Ghost, three persons, one Godhead, undivided in honour and glory and substance and kingdom."[19]

Putting it another way, from the side of God, *the worship of the
church is the communion of the Holy Trinity with us his people.* We are
inclined to view worship as what we do, but if we follow our argument,
it is *first and foremost* something the triune God does, our actions initiated and encompassed by his. The author of Hebrews refers to Christ
offering himself up unblemished to the Father "in or by eternal spirit,"
a probable reference to the Holy Spirit. Since our salvation is received
in union with Christ, what is his by nature is ours by grace. Thus, in his
self-offering to the Father, he offers us his people in him. We are thereby
enabled to share in the relation he has with the Father ("Our Father in
heaven," we pray—our Father by grace, because he is first Jesus' Father
by nature). Jesus, we remember, ascended to his Father and our Father,

---

17. Basil of Caesarea, *On the Holy Spirit* 26.62 (PG 32:184).
18. See Athanasius, *Letters to Serapion on the Holy Spirit* 1.33 (PG 26:605–8), for a similar explanation.
19. Gregory Nazianzen, *Orations* 31.28 (PG 36:164–65).

to his God and our God. By his cross and resurrection, and the ascension that followed, he brought us into the same relation he has with the Father. Thus, Christ is, in reality, the one true worshiper,[20] and our worship is a participation in his. A focus on our worship, on what we do, is inherently Pelagian. Further, our worship is *by the Holy Spirit* in Christ. As John Thompson puts it, "If one understands the New Testament and the view it gives of how we meet with and know God and worship him as triune, then worship is not primarily our act but, like our salvation, is God's gift before or as it is our task."[21] This should reassure us, for, as Owen reminds us, while "the love of God is like himself,—equal, constant, not capable of augmentation or diminution; our love is like ourselves,—unequal, increasing, waning, growing, declining."[22]

The worship of the church is thus not only grounded in the mediation of Christ, but takes place in union with him and through his mediatorial work and continued intercession. Cyril of Alexandria comments:

> Being still endued with human shape, he molds accordingly the form of his prayer, and asks as though he possessed it not. . . . [I]n him, as the first fruits of the race, the nature of man was wholly reformed into newness of life, and ascending, as it were, to its own first beginning was molded anew into sanctification. . . . Christ called down upon us the ancient gift of humanity, that is, sanctification through the Spirit and communion in the divine nature.[23]

Behind this lies the Incarnation (the Son of God did not simply indwell human nature, but came *as man*, permanently assuming unabbreviated human nature—sin apart), the vicarious humanity of Christ (he took our place in every way—even in worship, since as man he owed it to the Father), his full and complete obedience to the Father by the Holy Spirit, and his continuing high priestly intercession as expounded

---

20. A. M. Ramsay, *The Glory of God and the Transfiguration of Christ* (London: Longmans, 1949), 91ff.

21. John Thompson, *Modern Trinitarian Perspectives* (New York: Oxford University Press, 1994), 99–101.

22. Owen, *Of Communion with God*, in *Works*, ed. Goold, 2:29–30.

23. Cyril of Alexandria, *Commentary on the Gospel according to St. John* (London: Walter Smith, 1885), 481, 484, 496, 536, 538 (PG 74:477–78, 481–82, 495–96, 542–46).

in John 17 and Hebrews.[24] Therefore, since Christian worship is determined by, initiated by, shaped by, and directed to the Holy Trinity, *we worship the three with one undivided act of adoration*. I want now to say something, however tentative, about our worship of the three, while at the same time remembering that the three coinhere, mutually indwelling each other in the unity of the undivided Trinity. Once more, we recall the vital point made by Gregory Nazianzen—"No sooner do I conceive of the one than I am illumined by the splendour of the three; no sooner do I distinguish them than I am carried back to the one."[25]

It is often said that the only distinction of the persons is the ineffable eternal generation and procession. This is not so. Only the Son became incarnate, not the Father or the Holy Spirit. Only the Holy Spirit came at Pentecost, not the Son or the Father. Only the Father, not the Holy Spirit, sent the Son. As we argued before, these economic activities point back to immanent relations. If the Incarnation could equally have taken place with the Father or the Holy Spirit as the subject, would God not be arbitrary? We have argued that there is something *appropriate* in the Son *qua* Son becoming incarnate. We might ask whether this irreducible distinctiveness lends sharpness to our worship.

The Bible indicates that the Father determined that his kingdom would be established and advanced principally by the Son. In this sense, it is the Son who occupies center stage. This is entirely in accord with the purpose of the Father. "'Tis the Father's pleasure we should call him Lord." The Father sent the Son with the intention that he receive the glory and praise for our deliverance. His exaltation following his resurrection, by which he is given "the name that is above every name," is to the glory of God the Father, in pursuance of his eternal plan (Phil. 2:9–11). In turn, the Son will, after the economy of salvation is complete, hand the kingdom back to the Father (1 Cor. 15:28). Again, the Holy Spirit works anonymously in the background, not speaking of himself or bringing glory to himself, but testifying of Christ, the Son. He hears the Son and witnesses of him. He works unseen. Gregory of Nyssa writes of "a revolving circle of glory from like to like. The Son is glorified by the Spirit; the Father is glorified by the Son; again the Son has his glory from the Father;

24. See Robert Letham, *The Work of Christ* (Leicester: Inter-Varsity Press, 1993), 105–32, 155–57.
25. Gregory Nazianzen, *Orations* 40.41 (PG 36:417).

and the Only-begotten thus becomes the glory of the Spirit. . . . In like manner . . . faith completes the circle, and glorifies the Son by means of the Spirit, and the Father by means of the Son."[26]

Thus, there are good reasons (both economic and ontological) for worshiping *in one act of adoration* the three in their distinct persons and relations with one another. A living relationship with God requires that each of the persons be honored and adored in the context of their revealed relations with each other. The nature of our response in worship is to be shaped by the reality of the one we worship. We worship the Father, who chose us in Christ before the foundation of the world, who planned our salvation from eternity, who sent his Son into the world and gave him up for us. We worship the Son, in filial relation to the Father, who willingly "for us and our salvation" was made flesh, who submitted himself to life in a fallen world, who trod a path of lowliness, temptation, and suffering, leading to the cruel death of the cross. We worship him for his glorious resurrection, for his ascension to the right hand of the Father, for his continual intercession for us, and for his future return to judge the living and the dead and to complete our salvation. As John says, "Our fellowship is with the Father, and with his Son Jesus Christ" (1 John 1:3). We worship the Holy Spirit, who gives life and breath to all, who grants us the gift of faith, who sustains us through the difficulties of life as Christians in a world set in hostility to God, and who testifies of the Son. And, as Gregory would urge us, we worship with one act of adoration the one undivided Trinity, for as we cast our minds and hearts before the three persons of the Holy Trinity, we at once are enlightened by the one. As Staniloae says, the three are "wholly interior to one another."[27]

No one has expressed this better than John Owen. He writes that "the saints have distinct communion with the Father, and the Son, and the Holy Spirit (that is, distinctly with the Father, and distinctly with the Son, and distinctly with the Holy Spirit)." This is evident in the distinct ways in which Scripture refers to the three persons, particularly in the communication of grace to us.[28] However, as Owen is quick to point out, when we hold distinct communion with any one person,

26. Gregory of Nyssa, *Dogmatic Treatises, Etc.*, in *NPNF*[2], 5:324.
27. Staniloae, *Experience of God*, 1:255.
28. Owen, *Of Communion with God*, in *Works*, ed. Goold, 2:9–17.

the other two persons are also included. We may have communion with one person principally, but the other two are included secondarily, "for the person, as the person, of any one of them, is not the prime *object* of divine worship, but as it is *identified* with the nature or essence of God." He refers here to the Augustinian principle *opera Trinitatis ab extra indivisa sunt*. Thus, whenever we have communion with any one person, there is an influence from every person in that act. Moreover, communion with God, Owen acknowledges, is broader than this, for we have communion with the whole deity as such.[29]

As we consider this, we are struck by our ignorance. These are matters beyond us. It is like the old illustration of dipping a teacup into the ocean. Beside the vastness of the Atlantic, the water in our teacup is infinitesimal. But yet, the water in the teacup *is* the Atlantic ocean, insofar as it is a true sample. It is true that we don't know the inner workings of the Trinity and can never know them beyond what is revealed. It may be better to remain silent. But we do know what the Son is like. We know that "being in the form of God, he did not count equality with God something to be exploited for his own advantage, but he emptied himself, taking the form of a servant, becoming in the likeness of men. And being found in form as a man, he humbled himself, becoming obedient to death, even the death of the cross" (Phil. 2:5–8, my translation). We know also that he created and sustains the laws of physics. We also know something of what the Holy Spirit is like, for we know that in the midst of the turmoil of everyday life, love, joy, peace, patience, kindness, goodness, faithfulness, meekness, and self-control are the fruit of the Spirit, hallmarks of his own character produced in us on a creaturely level. We know that the Father chose that his kingdom be initiated and advanced by the Son and the Spirit. We know, in Pannenberg's words, that

> as Jesus glorifies the Father and not himself . . . so the Spirit glorifies not himself but the Son, and in him the Father. . . . The Father hands over his kingdom to the Son and receives it back from him. The Son is obedient to the Father and he thereby glorifies him. The Spirit fills the Son and glorifies him in his obedience to the Father.[30]

29. Ibid., 2:18–19.
30. Wolfhart Pannenberg, *Systematic Theology*, trans. Geoffrey W. Bromiley (Grand Rapids: Eerdmans, 1991), 1:315.

We also know, as Calvin puts it, that the will of the Father differs not in the slightest from what he has revealed in his word. And as we think of the three in their distinctness, we recall that they indwell each other in undivided union.

Some Specific Matters

This should affect the way we treat people. Worship and reconciliation go together. Christian worship is focused on the Holy Trinity and controlled by the Trinity. God is the undivided Trinity, in which the three indwell each other in love, seeking the interests of the others. Worship entails the whole person submitting to, becoming conformed to, the one worshiped. If Philippians 2 was true of Christ the Son at all times, it must become true of us too. We will develop this point in chapter 20, but for now we note the connection.

Worship, perichoresis, and the charismatic movement. Richard Gaffin, in a recent article, points to a tendency in the charismatic movement to separate the Holy Spirit from Christ. He counters by pointing to the close connection that Paul draws between Christ and the Spirit.[31] This argument is undergirded by the patristic teaching on perichoresis, the mutual indwelling of the three persons, all occupying the same divine space. The Father is *in* the Son, the Son is *in* the Father, the Holy Spirit is *in* the Son and the Father, the Father is *in* the Holy Spirit, and the Son is *in* the Holy Spirit. Thus, to worship one person at the expense of the others is to divide the undivided Trinity. Worship of any one of the three at once entails worship of all three and worship of the indivisible Trinity. An undue emphasis on one person, whether it be the focus on Jesus in pietism or the concentration on the Holy Spirit in charismatic circles, is a distortion. Owen, in his discussion, is careful to guard against this danger.

General theistic worship is defective worship. We referred to the common focus on "God," undefined and undifferentiated, particularly evident in philosophy of religion circles. How much of what passes for Christian worship falls into this category? If the hymnody we noted is anything to go by, the vast majority of the worship of the Western church

---

31. Richard B. Gaffin Jr., "Challenges of the Charismatic Movement to the Reformed Tradition," *Ordained Servant* 7 (1998): 48–57.

does. Still less do entertainment-oriented church services, or man-centered, seeker-sensitive "worship," pass muster. Here the borderline with idolatry is often hard to discern. Entertainment, evangelism, and worship are distinct and different things. They should not be confused.

There is a need to refocus Western hymnody. We need more Trinitarian hymns. There was an outpouring of such hymns following the Trinitarian crisis, but by the high Middle Ages this had slowed to a trickle, eventually to dry up altogether. Our brief summary at the start of the chapter shows how far short the common stock of Western hymnody falls of the fullness of the biblical teaching about God, let alone the identity of the triune God we worship. This applies to the argument for exclusive use of the Psalter in church worship. The Psalms are the Word of God in human words, and so should feature strongly in the worship of the NT church, as they did in the later part of the OT. In this, we share in Christ's use of the Psalter in praise to the Father. However, the Psalms do not explicitly reflect the full range of Trinitarian revelation, and so cannot be the sole diet of the church without truncating its worship.

Prayer is—among other things—exploration of the Holy Trinity. Christian experience is Trinitarian, prayer very centrally included. One wonders how much of the decline in appreciation of the Trinity is due to unguided extemporaneous prayer. At times of theological strength and spiritual vitality, this may be fine, but when decline sets in, there is nothing then to check it. Here the great prayers written or compiled by Thomas Cranmer, the ancient *Te Deum*, and the rich liturgies of the Eastern church can be our guides. We need to remind ourselves that in prayer we are engaging directly with our three-personed God—with "our Trinity," to borrow again from Gregory Nazianzen. In the words of Lukas Vischer, "in our calling upon him the mystery of the Trinity itself is actualized. So we pray with Christ and in the power of the Spirit when we call on God his Father as *our* Father."[32] Staniloae adds that the intra-Trinitarian love is the foundation of our salvation, "the extension to conscious creatures of the relations that obtain between the divine persons." Through his incarnation, the Son introduces us to filial communion with the Father, while through the Spirit we pray to the Father or speak with him as sons. In prayer, the Spirit draws us into his own prayer, creating between us and the Father,

32. Lukas Vischer, ed., *Spirit of God, Spirit of Christ: Ecumenical Reflections on the Filioque Controversy* (London: SPCK, 1981), 10.

through grace, the same relation he has with the Father and the Son by nature. The incarnate Son as man expressed his filial love of the Father as an obedient love, while the Father was affirming his love to us as Father. For his part, the Holy Spirit sanctified and pervaded the Son's humanity, making it fit to participate in the love the Son has for the Father. Thus, we are drawn through the Holy Spirit into the relationship the Son has with the Father. We are raised "into communion with the persons of the Holy Trinity."[33]

We need to recover Calvin's and the Westminster Confession of Faith's view of the Lord's Supper and develop it further in a Trinitarian direction. An effective Zwinglianism has dominated American Protestantism, including, sad to say, Presbyterianism. According to Calvin and the Westminster Assembly, in the Eucharist the faithful feed on Christ in faith by the Holy Spirit, and thus in union with Christ the Son we share in his access to the Father. This is worlds apart from an act of mental recollection of the human Jesus.[34]

Chief of all, the Trinity must be preached and must shape preaching. Preaching is the high point of worship. Not only must the Trinity be preached, but *all* preaching must be shaped by the active recognition that the God whose word is proclaimed is triune. A Trinitarian mind-set must become as integral to the preacher as the air we breathe. As Peter Toon comments, "Preachers and teachers need so to communicate the Faith and so direct public worship that they really and truly give the impression that the Holy Trinity is God and God is the Holy Trinity."[35] This will come only as preachers give explicit recognition in their prayers and sermons to God as triune, and so encourage their congregations to think, pray, and live in that light. We recall the comment of Sinclair Ferguson, mentioned in the introduction, that when Jesus gave his Upper Room Discourse to his disciples about to be plunged into grief and stress, he instructed them not on stress management techniques, but on the Trinity. The most practical preaching is that which enables us to advance in our knowledge of the God who is three persons.

---

33. Staniloae, *Experience of God*, 1:248–49.

34. See Robert Letham, *The Lord's Supper: Eternal Word in Broken Bread* (Phillipsburg, N.J.: P&R Publishing, 2001); Keith A. Mathison, *Given for You: Reclaiming Calvin's Doctrine of the Lord's Supper* (Phillipsburg, N.J.: P&R Publishing, 2002).

35. Peter Toon, *Our Triune God: A Biblical Portrayal of the Trinity* (Wheaton, Ill.: BridgePoint, 1996), 234.

We must work toward a correspondence between tacit and artic-ulated knowledge and experience. Michael Polanyi argues for the exis-tence of what he calls tacit knowledge, a basic level of prearticulated knowledge.[36] He suggests that we know more than can be expressed. This explains how we can think and work toward a solution of a prob-lem, the identity of which we cannot clearly put in words. In Polanyi's terms, the experience of the Christian church *is* Trinitarian, even if its assimilation into forms of teaching and worship is less than it might be. Our argument is that this needs to be brought to expression more thoroughly and pervasively, so that it becomes part of the church's articulated consciousness. In time, there will then be a correspondence between the reality itself, on the one hand (God the Holy Trinity), and what is confessed, believed, and taught, on the other—and finally what is tacitly believed and known.

The effects of this may be far-reaching—not only on worship and prayer, but also on our worldview, our view of creation, and the way we treat people, missions, and all work for the kingdom of God. We will consider some of these matters in the final chapters.

> *Glory to thee, our God; glory to thee.*
> *O heavenly King, the Comforter, Spirit of Truth, who art in all places*
>   *and fillest all things; Treasury of good things and Giver of*
>   *life: Come and take up thy abode in us, and cleanse us from*
>   *every stain; and save our souls, O Good One.*
> *O Holy God, Holy Mighty, Holy Immortal One, have mercy upon us.*
> *O Holy God, Holy Mighty, Holy Immortal One, have mercy upon us.*
> *O Holy God, Holy Mighty, Holy Immortal One, have mercy upon us.*
> *Glory to the Father, and to the Son, and to the Holy Spirit, now and*
>   *ever, and unto ages of ages.*
> *O all-holy Trinity, have mercy upon us. O Lord, wash away our sins.*
>   *O Master, pardon our transgressions. O Holy One, visit and*
>   *heal our infirmities, for thy Name's sake.*
> *Lord, have mercy.*
> *Lord, have mercy.*
> *Lord, have mercy.*
> *Glory to the Father, and to the Son, and to the Holy Spirit, now and*
>   *ever, unto ages of ages. Amen.*[37]

36. Michael Polanyi, *The Tacit Dimension* (Chicago: University of Chicago Press, 1958).
37. The All-night vigil service, the third hour, *Service Book*, 43.

N I N E T E E N

The Trinity, Creation, and Missions

Biblical Basis

Let us remind ourselves of the first paragraphs of chapter 1 on the work of creation as we find it in the first chapter of Genesis and what it tells us about God the Creator. It portrays the creation and formation of the world and the ordered shaping of a place for the human race to live. It presents man as head of creation, in relation to, and in communion with, God his Creator. The act of *creation* itself is direct and immediate (vv. 1–2), distinct from the work of formation that follows.[1] The result is a cosmos that is formless, empty, dark, and wet—unfit for human life. The rest of the chapter describes the world's *formation* (or *distinction*) and *adornment*—God introducing order, light, and dryness, making it fit for life to flourish. First, God creates light and sets boundaries to the darkness (vv. 2–5). Second, he molds the earth into shape, so that it is no longer formless (vv. 6–8, 9–10). Third, God separates the waters and forms dry land, so that it is no longer entirely wet (vv. 9–10). Following this, he populates the earth, ending its emptiness (vv. 20–30), first with fish and birds, then with land animals, and finally, as the apex of the whole, with human beings made in his image. This God is not only almighty, but also a master planner, artist, and architect supreme. This order is clear from the parallels

1. Herman Bavinck, *In the Beginning: Foundations of Creation Theology*, ed. John Vriend and John Bolt (Grand Rapids: Baker, 1999), 100ff. See also the discussion in Thomas Aquinas, *ST*, Pt. 1a, Q. 66, art. 1–4, and the entire section QQ. 66–74 in general.

425

between the two groups of days, the first three and the second three.[2] In all this he shows his sovereign freedom in naming and blessing his creation, and sees it is thoroughly good. At the end comes the unfinished seventh day, when God enters his rest which he made to share with man, his partner, whom he created in his own image. Entailed is an implicit invitation for us to follow.[3]

Particularly striking is God's sovereign and variegated ordering of his creation. In particular, he forms the earth in a threefold manner. First, he issues direct fiats. He says, "Let there be light," and there is light (v. 3). So too he brings into being with seemingly effortless command the expanse (v. 6), the dry ground (v. 9), the stars (vv. 14–15), and the birds and the fish (vv. 20–21). Each time it is enough for God to speak and his edict is fulfilled. Second, he works. He separates the light from the darkness (v. 4), he makes the expanse and separates the waters (v. 7), he makes the two great lights, the sun and the moon (v. 16), and sets them in the expanse to give light on the earth (v. 17), he creates the great creatures of the seas and various kinds of birds (v. 21), he makes the beasts of the earth and reptiles (v. 25), and finally he creates man—male and female—in his own image (vv. 26–27). The thought is of focused, purposeful action by God, of divine labor accomplishing his ends. However, there is also a third way of formation, in which God uses the activity of the creatures themselves. God commands the earth to produce vegetation, plants, and trees (vv. 11–12). He requests the lights to govern the day and the night (vv. 14–16). He commands the earth to bring forth land animals (v. 24). Here the creatures follow God's instructions and contribute to the eventual outcome. This God, who created the universe, does not work in a monolithic way. His order is varied—it is threefold, but one. His work shows diversity in its unity and unity in its diversity. This God loves order and variety together.[4]

---

2. See chapter 1. As I noted there, this pattern was discerned at least as long ago as the thirteenth century. See Robert Grosseteste, *On the Six Days of Creation: A Translation of the Hexaëmeron*, trans. C. F. J. Martin, Auctores Britannici Medii Aevi (Oxford: Oxford University Press for the British Academy, 1996), 160–61 (5.1.3–2.1); Aquinas, *ST*, Pt. 1a, Q. 74, art. 1. See Robert Letham, "'In the Space of Six Days': The Days of Creation from Origen to the Westminster Assembly," *WTJ* 61 (1999): 149–74.

3. Cf. Heb. 3:7–4:11.

4. See Francis Watson, *Text, Church, and World: Biblical Interpretation in Theological Perspective* (Edinburgh: T & T Clark, 1994), 142–43.

This reflects what the chapter records of God himself. The triadic manner of the earth's formation reflects who God, its Creator, is. He is a relational being. This is implicit from the very start. We notice distinctions among God, who created the heavens and earth (v. 1), the Spirit of God, who hovers over the face of the waters (v. 2), and the speech or word of God, issuing the fiat "Let there be light" (v. 3). His speech recurs frequently throughout the chapter. While it is most unlikely that the author and the original readers would have understood the Spirit of God in a personalized way, due to the heavy and insistent stress in the OT on the uniqueness of the one God, Wenham correctly suggests that this is a vivid image of the Spirit of God.[5] The later NT personalizing of the Spirit of God is a congruent development from this statement.

With the creation of man there is the unique deliberation, "Let us make man in our image," which expresses a plurality in God (vv. 26–27). Von Rad says that this signifies the high point and goal to which all of God's creative activity is directed. In chapter 1, we argued that, since Scripture has a fullness that goes beyond the horizons of the original authors, the many Fathers who saw this as a reference to the Trinity were on the right track. While this was concealed from the original readers and from the OT saints as a whole, and was not how it was understood then, the Fathers were certainly not at variance with the trajectory of the text. Rabbinical commentators were often perplexed by this passage and similar ones referring to a plurality in God (Gen. 3:22; 11:7; Isa. 6:8). The NT gives us the principle that the OT contains in seed form what is more fully made known in the NT, and on that basis we may look back to the earlier writings and see richer meaning in them. This is much like rereading a detective mystery and finding clues that we missed the first time through, but which now are given fresh meaning by our knowledge of the whole. In terms of the *sensus plenior* (the fuller meaning) of Scripture, these words of God attest a plurality in God which came later to be expressed in the doctrine of the Trinity. The original readers would not have grasped this, but we, with the full plot disclosed, can revisit the passage and see the clues there.

I have written elsewhere, commenting on Genesis 1:26–27:

5. Gordon J. Wenham, *Genesis 1–15*, Word Biblical Commentary (Waco, Tex.: Word, 1987), 15–17.

Man exists as a duality, the one in relation to the other. . . . As for God himself . . . the context points to his own intrinsic relationality. The plural occurs on three occasions in v. 26, yet God is also singular in v. 27. God is placed in parallel with man, made in his image as male and female, who is described both in the singular and plural. Behind it all is the distinction God/Spirit of God/speech of God in vv. 1–3. . . . [T]his relationality will in the development of biblical revelation eventually be disclosed as taking the form of a triunity.[6]

I refer there to kindred comments by Karl Barth.[7]

In short, this God who made the universe—establishing an order with a vast range of variety, with human beings as the crown of his creation, representing him as his image bearers—is relational. Communion and communication are inherent in his very being. In creating the world, he has made us for himself, to enter into communion with him in a universe of ravishing beauty and ordered variety. By his creation of the seventh day, he ceased from his works in contemplation of their ordered beauty and goodness, and invites us to join him. The first chapter of Genesis says to all who read it that Yahweh, the God of Israel, the God of Abraham, Isaac, and Jacob, the God of Moses, is also the Creator of all things. He who made his covenant with his people Israel is not merely a territorial divinity, but the one to whom all nations are accountable, for he is their maker. There is a clear unity between creation and redemption. The mandate in Genesis 1:26–29 to multiply and subdue the earth embraces the whole creation and is also the basic building block for the unfolding structure of salvation after the Fall. Reflecting on this implicitly Trinitarian structure of Genesis 1, Athanasius writes of creation being *in Christ*.[8] Since Genesis (no less than every other part of the Bible) is to be read in the context of the whole of Scripture, we can see references in the NT to the roles of Christ and the Holy Spirit in creation as reinforcing this (Col. 1:15–20; Heb. 1:3; 11:3; John 1:1ff.).

This is underlined by other—unmistakably poetic—accounts of creation in the OT. In Psalm 33:6, creation is said to have taken place

6. Robert Letham, "The Man-Woman Debate: Theological Comment," *WTJ* 52 (1990): 71.
7. Karl Barth, *CD*, III/1: 196.
8. Athanasius, *On the Incarnation* 1, 3, 12, 14 (PG 25:97–102, 115–22).

"by the word of the LORD . . . and by the breath of his mouth." In Proverbs 8:22ff., a passage much used and abused in the debates of the early church, Wisdom is personified and eulogized as sharing with the Lord in the creation of the heavens and the earth. Job acknowledges that the Spirit of God made him (Job 33:4; cf. 26:13), and the psalmist also talks of God's Spirit as Creator (Ps. 104:30). It is impossible to think of creation (*this* creation, *this* multifaceted and coherent creation, the only one we know and the only one there is[9]) occurring apart from its maker being relational, and so in accordance with his full revelation as triune, as Bavinck so cogently argues.[10] Bavinck goes even further, arguing that "without generation [the generation of the Son by the Father] creation would not be possible. If in an absolute sense God could not communicate himself to the Son, he would be even less able, in a relative sense, to communicate himself to his creature. If God were not triune, creation would not be possible."[11]

The NT develops this further by its unequivocal claim that Christ, the eternal Son of God, is the Creator. All things were made by him and for him. He is the one who holds everything together. God's ultimate purpose for the universe is that Christ be the Head, the one in supreme authority over the redeemed and renewed cosmos (Col. 1:15–20; Eph. 1:10; John 1:1–3; Heb. 1:1–3). This is the background to those events in the Gospels where Jesus demonstrates his authority over creation. For example, by walking on the water and calming the raging storm, he demonstrates that he has the full authority of Yahweh, of whom the psalmist says, "Your way was through the sea, your path through the great waters; yet your footprints were unseen" (Matt. 14:21–33; Ps. 77:19). Athanasius has a graphic illustration of this when he compares the relationship between created and divine wisdom with the printing of the name of a king's son on every building of the town his father builds, implying that the Son's name is imaged throughout creation.[12] Athanasius is right and biblical. The name of Christ is engraved on the whole creation. Hallmarks of the Trinity are evident throughout. "The heavens declare the glory of God, and the sky above

---

9. The hypothesis that there are a potentially infinite number of parallel universes is speculation for which there exists no evidence.

10. Bavinck, *In the Beginning*, 39–45.

11. Ibid., 39.

12. Athanasius, *Orations Against the Arians* 2.79 (PG 26:314).

proclaims his handiwork" (Ps. 19:1), and that glory and that handi-work belong to the Father, the Son, and the Holy Spirit, ever one God, unto the ages of the ages.

Basic Principles

Colin Gunton lists a number of central features in the Christian account of creation. In its historical context, the teaching of creation *ex nihilo* is unique, "one of the most momentous developments in all the history of thought."[13] This asserts that creation is an act of divine sovereignty, and that the universe has a beginning in space and time. It is not eternal or infinite. There are only two categories of reality—God and everything else.[14] This is in stark contrast to all forms of monism, such as ancient Gnosticism and today's New Age spiritual-ity. Moreover, this act of God was not arbitrary, but purposeful, deriv-ing from his love (hence the Trinity) and heading somewhere. It con-trasts vividly to the Islamic doctrine of fate, which cannot be derived from love, since Allah is conceived as unitary, with dominant power and will. A Trinitarian theology of creation enables the universe to be closely related to God, but free to be itself. It opposes deism, which pictures a remote God who has no day-to-day contact with his cre-ation, and scientific materialism, which posits purely immanent causes for all that is.

Gunton points out that an allegorical approach to Genesis under-mines history and has pagan, gnostic origins. Instead, the Bible asserts that God created time, and because of this our world and its history have ultimate value. Origen and Augustine succumbed to an ahistor-ical approach through flirtations with Neoplatonism, undermining the direct involvement of God in matter by positing a higher value to the nonmaterial. In contrast, Gunton argues, creation, incarnation, and resurrection underline the fact that, to God, matter matters.[15] At the other end of the spectrum from Origen, a literalist view draws too shal-

---

13. Colin Gunton, *The Triune Creator* (Grand Rapids: Eerdmans, 1998), 65–66.
14. This, we saw in chapter 4, was the background to Origen's vital distinction between gen-eration and creation, two ideas that were identified in Gnosticism and Neoplatonism.
15. Gunton, *Triune Creator*, 44–50, 57–61.

low a picture. It reduces the rich complexity of the Bible's teaching on creation to a wooden one-dimensionality.

What we need, as Gunton declares, following Irenaeus's refutation of the gnostics, is a *theological* interpretation of creation. By this he means an account of creation that integrates the whole biblical witness, not just Genesis alone, and sees it in the light of its triune maker.[16] To understand creation in a way that is appropriate to God's whole revelation in Scripture and redemption, we need to see it from an explicitly Trinitarian perspective. This means that a theology of creation does not, and must not, limit its biblical basis to Genesis 1 alone. Like Irenaeus, we need to listen to the whole of Scripture in the light of what happened in Jesus Christ.[17] This is a very important argument, in line with classic Reformed theology and its sixteenth-century confessions.[18] In summary, since the triune God created the universe, we cannot understand it apart from the historical reality of the incarnation in Jesus Christ, and of the Holy Trinity who made it.

This line of thought follows a basic principle of biblical interpretation: Every passage of Scripture must be seen in the light of the whole. Just because Genesis 1 comes first in the Hebrew, Greek, and English Bibles does not mean it can be viewed in isolation. In fact, it is likely that Job was compiled before Genesis, in which case Job 38 could claim to be read first if we were to adopt that procedure. In fact, Job 38 forces our own limitations and God's own utter sovereignty and inscrutability into the foreground:

> [The LORD said:] Where were you when I laid the foundation of the earth? Tell me, if you have understanding. Who determined its measurements—surely you know! Or who stretched the line upon it? On what were its bases sunk, or who laid its cornerstone, when the morning stars sang together and all the sons of God shouted for joy? . . . Have you commanded the morning since your days began, and caused the dawn to know its place? . . . Have you entered into the springs of the sea, or walked in the recesses of the deep? . . . You

16. Ibid., 62–64.
17. Ibid., 64.
18. Letham, "In the Space of Six Days," 149–74.

know, for you were born then, and the number of your days is great! (Job 38:4–21)

Both biblically and theologically, the Christian view of salvation cannot be separated from a Christian view of creation. Irenaeus strongly affirms the goodness of creation, including matter, and has a clearly Trinitarian perspective, God (the Father) creating by means of his two hands (the Son and the Holy Spirit), needing neither angels nor any other inferior power to assist him.[19] Despite the pre-Nicene subordinationism, which seems to treat the two hands as instruments of the Father, the positive point is that, for Irenaeus, God does not require intermediaries between himself and the universe to achieve his ends. There are two realities only—God the Creator and his creation. The creation is real, but only in relation to the God who upholds it by his two hands. *It is precisely Trinitarianism that enables Irenaeus to affirm creation out of nothing.*[20] Because creation is a work of the Holy Trinity, it is not only an act of will and power, but an act of love. This is radically counter to Islam, as we shall consider shortly. God the Father enters into personal relations with the created order through his two hands, the Son and the Holy Spirit. Underlying the work of creation is the eternal union and communion of Father, Son, and Holy Spirit.

Moreover, creation is relatively perfect. It is good, but destined for fulfillment at the end (implying the possibility of a fall and redemption). This is different from the Big Bang theory, where an expanding universe will eventually wind down and collapse back into nothingness.[21] By contrast, without the providence of the Holy Trinity, the cosmos has no power to prolong its existence in the slightest. A biblical and Trinitarian view of creation entails that the cosmos was not made to lapse back into nothingness, but to become something even greater than it was at first.

Sadly, this Trinitarian view of creation was lost. Augustine found it difficult to see real value to time—so he considered creation to have been instantaneous. Possibly, Neoplatonic influence may have led him to distrust matter. His doctrine of the Trinity was not grounded in

19. Irenaeus, *Against Heresies* 2.2.4 (PG 7:714–15).
20. Ibid., 4.20.1 (PG 7:1032).
21. *Contra* Stephen W. Hawking, *A Brief History of Time: From the Big Bang to Black Holes* (New York: Bantam Books, 1988).

human history, but in human psychology, in which mind is primary over matter. In contrast, Gunton points out that the eternity of the Creator and the time of the creature meet in the incarnate Christ, in human time.[22] The link between creation and the Incarnation is something I have explored elsewhere.[23] Augustine was, of course, dominant in the West for centuries. The effective exclusion of the doctrine of the Trinity from the Christian doctrine of creation is therefore at the root of the apparently mutual exclusion of theology and science, Gunton argues. With the emergence of Aristotelian influences in medieval times, abstract causality (logic) replaced a personal relation between God and the world as the basis of creation.[24] The Reformers, especially Calvin, regained some ground. Calvin saw the world in a semiotic manner, as a sign pointing beyond itself to its maker. But this insight was soon lost.

So creation and redemption are in continuity, in contrast to the gnostic separation of the two, with the god of creation different from the god of salvation. Rather, Christ is the mediator of creation as well as of redemption. Herman Bavinck argues that creation presupposes a triune God. By eternal generation, God communicates his full image to his Son, while by creation he communicates a weak image to the creature. The latter depends upon the former, as both prior and eternal. Without generation, creation would be impossible, and so if God were not triune, creation would not be possible.[25] The procession of the Spirit from the Father and the Son is the basis of the willing of that world. The creation proceeds from the Father through the Son in the Spirit in order that, in the Spirit and through the Son, it may return to the Father.[26] At the same time, this continuity allows room for genuine distinction, thus avoiding the cosmic soup into which New Age pantheism mixes everything.

Christianity stresses the Incarnation as God's supreme affirmation of his creation. The Resurrection clinches this. The Apostles' Creed and C both summarize the plan of salvation, grounded in the Trinity. However, this entails the renewal of creation. God the Father created

22. Gunton, *Triune Creator*, 68–96.
23. Robert Letham, *The Work of Christ* (Leicester: Inter-Varsity Press, 1993), 197ff.
24. Gunton, *Triune Creator*, 116, 147.
25. Bavinck, *In the Beginning*, 39.
26. Ibid., 45.

all things (C makes the Trinitarianism explicit); the Son became incarnate, died on the cross, and rose for us and our salvation (in this God reaffirms his creation by taking part of it into personal union); while the Resurrection is itself the renewal of creation and the beginning of the kingdom that shall have no end. There is an unbreakable unity between creation and redemption—seen clearly in such passages as Colossians 1:15–20. All things declare the glory of the Holy Trinity. All things will be brought to their ultimate purpose of glorifying the Holy Trinity. The Holy Spirit is remaking the created order. Jesus Christ the Son is reigning and will reign, to the glory of God the Father.

Vestigia Trinitatis?

The Bible attests that all creation reveals the glory of God. The Psalms are full of comments to this effect. Psalm 19:1–6 speaks vividly of the creation as an icon (*eikōn*, or image), as something through which we perceive the reality of God. It is not itself God, but it points to him. "The heavens declare the glory of God, and the sky above proclaims his handiwork" (v. 1). Paul, in Romans 1:19–20, also reflects on creation in this way. The invisible things of God are clearly visible in the world around us, he says, through the things that have been made, leaving human beings without excuse for rejecting him.

Calvin, in his commentary on Genesis, emphasizes that God reveals himself in creation. Moses' intention is "to render God, as it were, visible to us in his works." The Lord, "that he may invite us to the knowledge of himself, places the fabric of heaven and earth before our eyes, rendering himself, in a certain manner, manifest in them." The heavens are "eloquent heralds of the glory of God, and . . . this most beautiful order of nature silently proclaims his admirable wisdom." He "clothes himself, so to speak, with the image of the world . . . magnificently arrayed in the incomparable vesture of the heavens and the earth." In short, the world is "a mirror in which we ought to behold God."[27] There is a symmetry in God's works to which nothing can be added.[28] The divine artificer arranged the creation in such a

---

27. John Calvin, *Commentaries on the First Book of Moses Called Genesis*, trans. John King (reprint, Grand Rapids: Baker, 1979), 1:58–62.

28. Ibid., on Gen. 1:31.

wonderful order that nothing more beautiful in appearance can be imagined.[29] In the Catechism of the Church of Geneva (1541), he foreshadows his comments on Genesis in saying that the world is a kind of mirror in which we may observe God. The account here is given for our sake, to teach us that God has made nothing without a certain reason and design.[30]

In considering the separation of light from darkness on the first day, and reflecting on the differences in the ancient world in reckoning when the day actually ends and begins, Calvin says that Moses accommodated his discourse to the received custom. God accommodated his works to the capacity of men, fixing our attention and compelling us to pause and reflect. There is nothing here but that which relates to the visible form of the world, the garniture of that theater which he places before our eyes.[31] This is in line with Calvin's overall claim that God accommodates himself to our capacity in all of his revelation. Indeed, it has been persuasively argued that, for Calvin, God not only accommodates his revelation to our level, but also accommodates himself, speaking to us in the prattling babble of baby talk (*balbutire*, "to prattle," is a favorite verb of Calvin's in this connection).[32]

If the world was made by the Holy Trinity, and it also declares the glory of God, it seems reasonable to suppose that there will be hints all around us in creation that point to the Trinity. Ever since Augustine propounded his Trinitarian illustrations, this has been a matter of close debate. Proofs for the Trinity were used extensively in the Middle Ages and also in the eighteenth century. We have seen the weaknesses of this approach. Illustrations drawn from the world do not and cannot *prove* the doctrine of the Trinity. In fact, rather than establishing the Trinity, they point to some form of heresy. For example, a clover leaf is often cited as an illustration of the Trinity. It has three parts, yet is one leaf. However, each person of the Trinity is not

---

29. John Calvin, *Institutes of the Christian Religion*, trans. Ford Lewis Battles, ed. John T. McNeill (Philadelphia: Westminster Press, 1960), 1.14.21.

30. John Calvin, *Calvin: Theological Treatises*, trans. and ed. J. K. S. Reid (Philadelphia: Westminster Press, 1954), 93–94.

31. Calvin, *Genesis*, on Gen. 1:3–5.

32. See David F. Wright, "Calvin's Accommodating God," in *Calvinus sincerioris religionis vindex: Calvin as the Protector of the Purer Religion*, ed. Wilhelm H. Neuser, Sixteenth Century Essays & Studies 36 (Kirksville, Mo.: Sixteenth Century Journal Publishers, 1997), 3–19.

one third of it, but rather possesses the entire divine essence. The three indwell one another, occupying the same divine space. The most that analogies like this one yield is evidence of diversity in unity and unity in diversity. There are hints of the relationality of God, and of his own unity in diversity, all around us. However, these do not constitute a logical or mathematical proof, nor do they adequately portray the Trinity as such.

In her book *The Mind of the Maker*, Dorothy L. Sayers argues that "the Trinitarian structure of activity is mysterious to us just because it is universal—rather as the four-dimensional structure of space-time is mysterious because we cannot get outside it to look at it." She suggests that, as the mathematician can to some extent observe space-time from without, "we may similarly call upon the creative artist to extricate himself from his own activity far enough to examine and describe its threefold structure."[33] She illustrates her point from the mind of the creative writer, but points out that what is true of writing is true of other forms of creativity. She talks of the creative idea, timelessly beholding the entire work in one instant, as corresponding to the Father; the creative energy or activity begotten by that idea, working in time from the beginning to end of the work, being the image of the Word; and the creative power, the meaning of the work, resembling the image of the indwelling Spirit. And, she says, "these three are one, each equally in itself the whole work, whereof none can exist without the other: and this is the image of the Trinity."[34] Much of the rest of her book is an unfolding of such Trinitarian imagery. It is highly suggestive and superbly expressed, but one cannot escape the conclusion that these three elements are the outworkings of a single mind and do not possess distinct personal existence of their own. As expressions of the diversity in unity that God has stamped upon creation, they are helpful, but as mirrors of the Trinity they are defective—as were the illustrations of Augustine, whom Sayers cites with approval at the start of her discussion.

John Frame suggests a number of Trinitarian analogies. He points to a wide range of triadic patterns drawn from a broad spectrum. While his argument bears careful consideration, none of the analogies exactly

33. Dorothy L. Sayers, *The Mind of the Maker* (San Francisco: HarperCollins, 1979), 36.
34. Ibid., 37–38.

reflect all the contours of the church's doctrine of the Trinity, nor does he claim that they do.[35] Frame does succeed in demonstrating that all around us, wherever we look, is inescapable and overwhelming evidence of unity in diversity and diversity in unity. On the other hand, at the opposite end of the spectrum, Barth's rejection of the *vestigia Trinitatis* flows so much from his programmatic rejection of natural theology that equal caution is needed in the face of his consistent negativity on this matter.

Icons and General Revelation: Creation as an Icon

However, we return to the clear biblical teaching that creation points us to God, and that God is triune. In what ways does the creation testify of the Holy Trinity? Reformed theology has taught that the creation reveals God. It does not bring salvation to us in our fallen condition, but it does not leave God without witness. Consequently, the human race is left inexcusable for its continued rejection of its Creator.[36] Creation itself is, as Calvin said, an *eikōn* (image), a window through which we can perceive something of its maker, a mirror by which we can see God. While the Trinity as such may not be directly discerned, Paul has pointed to God's "eternal power and divine nature" (Rom. 1:20) as clearly evident. I have suggested that, in particular, his unity in diversity and diversity in unity are clearly displayed throughout the universe. The relationality of the cosmos points unmistakably to its relational Creator.

Eastern Christianity is particularly identified with the use of icons. These are not intended to be worshiped.[37] They are teaching devices, windows through which to perceive greater realities that lie beyond. Thus, Leontius of Neapolis said that icons are "opened books to remind us of God."[38] Reformed theology believes in icons too! However, it

---

35. See John M. Frame, *The Doctrine of God* (Phillipsburg, N.J.: P&R Publishing, 2002), 726–32, 743–50. This is the best case I have yet encountered for this position. See especially the article he cites by Vern S. Poythress, "Reforming Ontology and Logic in the Light of the Trinity: An Application of Van Til's Idea of Analogy," *WTJ* 57 (1995): 187–219.

36. WCF, 1.1.

37. Timothy Ware, *The Orthodox Church* (London: Penguin Books, 1969), 38–40, 41ff., 277–78; John Meyendorff, *Byzantine Theology: Historical Trends and Doctrinal Themes* (New York: Fordham University Press, 1979), 42–53.

38. PG 94:1276a, cited by Ware, *Orthodox Church*, 40.

regards the Eastern view as far too restrictive. For the Reformed, the whole of creation is an icon. All around us, the natural world cries out with a loud roar, or quietly and soothingly breathes a gentle whisper, to the effect that "the hand that made us is divine." The creatures and natural phenomena are not to be worshiped, for God made them. But since God did make them, he reveals himself through them. These are the clothes that God wears to display his glory. The clothes are not the person, nor is the world God, but as the clothes adorn the person, so the world testifies with a powerful and beautiful voice to its triune Creator.

Yes, art and music are spheres in which we can praise our Creator, and which can display his glory. In a certain sense, they are revelatory. As developed in cultures permeated by Christian influence, they readily disclose the unity in diversity to which we have referred. In my own experience, the monumental Eighth Symphony of Anton Bruckner enabled me, when a teenager, to realize that the human race was not, after all, an inconsequential speck of cosmological dust, and so to overcome doubts as to the existence of God. Particularly important was the masterful recorded interpretation of Eugen Jöchum and the Berlin Philharmonic Orchestra, as well as a live performance at a Sir Henry Wood Promenade Concert at the Royal Albert Hall in London in August 1965 conducted by Gennadi Rozhdestvensky, at which I was standing only six feet behind the conductor! It could not bring salvation, for only Christ does that in his gospel. But its magnificent sonority, its vast, cathedral-like structure, and the profundity of its affirmation of faith in the midst of a maelstrom of struggle and doubt (for, as one critic wrote, it stands "at the place where music, philosophy, and theology meet") point to the utter majesty of God. Bruckner was a Christian, and Beethoven was not—yet there is a sublimity of almost superhuman quality about some of Beethoven's music, particularly the late string quartets. Who can listen to the Piano Trio in B-flat, Op. 97 (the "Archduke"), especially the third movement—the *andante cantabile*—and not be led beyond the mundane? The question of Beethoven's beliefs is beside the point. It is irrelevant. He was a man, made in God's image, the master of a creative medium that God himself has made for our good and as a vehicle to glorify him. He was working within a genre that owed its development to the Christian faith. The whole notion of developing a theme, of moving progressively and purposefully to a goal, of returning after a myriad of complex modulations to a resolution, of a variety of instruments playing different notes that are all part of a single score, is based on the matrix of realities found in the created order, which the Holy Trinity put there in the work of creation itself, and which reflects who he is. The turbulent rationalist Beethoven, the angst-ridden Mahler, the syphilitic Schubert, the scatological Mozart, as well as the pious Bruckner and Johann Sebastian Bach, all testify—whether deliberately, as in the case of the last two, or unwittingly, as with the others—to the triune God who made them and the world around them, to his unity in diversity, purpose, structure, and beauty, which such human creativity mirrors.

Unity in Diversity and Diversity in Unity

In particular, then, it is in its unity in diversity and its diversity in unity—evident everywhere—that the creation points to the Trinity. In this, even though it does not prove the Trinity in a mathematical or logical sense, it bears witness as in a mirror. Let us consider one universal element of creation—color. Color is from one perspective a certain combination of molecules. That is, various colors are formed by particular molecular arrangements. However, this does not fully explain the phenomenon. If a chemist argued that this is the *only* defining characteristic of color, he would be engaging in reductionism and simply be wrong. An explanation also exists in terms of physics: light waves measured by a spectrometer. Moreover, the appearance of color is affected by light. Any particular molecular combination will look different in different light. This can be seen on any day when there is a combination of sunshine and clouds, or if we compare the colors of trees at midday and at dusk. Furthermore, no two people have identical perceptions of color. For example, some people think turquoise is mainly green, while others say it is mainly blue. In addition, the same color will seem different when surrounded by different colors. All this does not exactly parallel the Trinity, but it does display both unity in diversity and also the relational character of the universe, which in turn reflect the character of God, the Holy Trinity.[39]

39. I am indebted to Dr. John Van Dyk, a research chemist and a member of my congregation, for this and the following examples.

In addition, when a beam of (colorless) light is passed through a prism, it fans out into a series of colors—from red to orange, yellow, green, blue, indigo, and violet. This process is reversible. If red, green, and blue lights are mixed in the appropriate relative amounts, colorless or "white" light results.

Again, if we wish to match the red paint on a barn, we can use one or more of the many hundreds of available pigments or dyes. Our barn paint, examined with a spectrophotometer (a spectrometer that measures spectral reflectance or transmittance), will have a definite spectrum (a two-dimensional plot, looking like a series of hills and valleys, that shows the intensity of light at different wavelengths). If we make five paints that visually match our barn, we will probably find that they all have different spectra, none of which matches that of the barn paint. If these five paints, which match the barn's color in normal daylight, are taken indoors and observed in incandescent or fluorescent light, there is a good chance they will no longer match the color of the barn or of each other! The environment, the illuminants, the colorants, and the spectral sensitivity of normal observers each contribute to color.[40]

Staniloae expresses the unity in diversity of the world well when he says,

> There was a time when the coincidence of opposites was considered incompatible with reason. Whenever a synthesis of such a kind was encountered—and the whole of reality is like this—reason would break it up into irreconcilable and contradictory notions, setting up some elements over against others or trying to melt them all down by force into one new element. In the understanding of reality, however, reason has now become accustomed to unifying the principles of distinction and unity to such an extent that it is no longer hard to see the antinomic model of being that characterizes the whole of reality. It is an accepted fact for reason that plurality does not break apart unity, nor does unity do away with plurality. In fact, plurality necessarily exists within unity, or, to express it another way, unity is manifest in plurality. It is a fact that plurality maintains unity and unity main-

40. For further reading, see Roy S. Berns, *Billmeyer and Saltzman's Principles of Color Technology*, 3rd ed. (New York: John Wiley & Sons, 2000), esp. 15, 25–29, 152. Berns refers to an experiment of Roland Derby in which two dyed wool fabrics, one green and one brown in incandescent light, appear the same color in daylight around 6500° K and reverse their colors under skylight around 10,000° K!

tains plurality, and that the decline of either of them mean the weakness or disappearance of the life or existence of any individual entity. This conception of the mode of being of reality is recognized today as superior to former ideas of what was rational, while under the pressure of reality the idea of what is rational has itself become complex and antinomic. Assertions formerly considered irrational because of their apparently contradictory character are now recognized as indications of a natural stage towards which reason must strive, for the understanding of this stage constitutes the natural destiny of reason, and the stage is itself an image of the supernatural character of that perfect unity of what is distinct within the Holy Trinity. Today many see the plurality of the entire creation as something made specific in all manner of trinities. Bernhard Philberth, for example, declares that the whole of creation is a threefold reflection of the Trinity.

For Staniloae, "the most suitable image for the Holy Trinity is found in human unity of being and personal distinction."[41]

Strikingly, Rabbi Jonathan Sacks, obviously not a Trinitarian, recognizes the unity in diversity of God's creation. He writes:

> God is in the details. Sometimes I am asked as a Jew—members of other faiths may have had the same experience—why our faith has so many laws and prohibitions, such intricate prescriptions of what we may or may not eat, may or may not do on the Sabbath and so on. Surely, they airily imply, God is above that sort of thing. I hope he isn't, because if he were, we would never have had the ordered complexity of life on earth; the 3.1 billion letters of the human genome, an error in any one of which could spell fatal handicap; the three million species of living things; the astonishing capacity of the human brain or much else of the meticulous diversity of creation. To be a true artist is to have a passion for detail. I think of Beethoven endlessly revising his scores, sometimes taking years before a musical idea reached the perfection he required, or Monet in his eighties painting the water-lilies in his garden time and again in his attempt to capture for eternity the sunlit sensation of a moment.[42]

41. Dumitru Staniloae, *The Experience of God*, trans. and ed. Iona Ionita and Robert Barringer (Brookline, Mass.: Holy Cross Orthodox Press, 1994–2000), 1:250.

42. *Times* (London), 22 February 2003. Sacks is the chief rabbi of the United Hebrew Congregations of the Commonwealth.

Music demonstrates unity in diversity very clearly. We noted how Western classical music emerged in a culture formed by Christianity and how its central features mirror the works of God—purpose, movement toward a goal, and resolution. Its unity in diversity is heard in a variety of instruments combining to play one integrated piece. This is particularly obvious in chamber music, where the various instruments can be heard distinctly within the overall score. String quartets feature this prominently, especially those of the classical period (Haydn, Mozart, and the early Beethoven), which were composed in a conversational style, the voices interacting. However, it is also obvious as the genre develops, with the radical changes made by Beethoven.[43] I suppose a trio mirrors the Trinity even more evidently than a quartet. We referred to Beethoven's "Archduke" trio earlier, but this is merely one example, albeit a particularly wonderful one.

The two major challenges to the Christian faith today—the postmodern thinking of our own culture and Islam—are both deviations from the created order of unity in diversity and diversity in unity that the Holy Trinity has embedded in the world. In order for Christian missions to be effective in both settings, this root question must be effectively addressed. Unless this is done, the ministry of the gospel in these contexts will be blunted. The same applies to each and every setting in which the gospel is to be preached, but these are the two most prominent contexts in which readers of this book will find themselves.

Islam: Unity Without Diversity

Islam's doctrine of God leaves room neither for diversity, diversity in unity, nor a personal grounding of creation, for Allah is a solitary monad with unity only.[44] The Islamic doctrine of God is centered on power and will. There is virtually no room for love. The kind of

43. See Robert Winter and Robert Martin, eds., *The Beethoven Quartet Companion* (Berkeley: University of California Press, 1994), especially the article by Joseph Kerman, "Beethoven Quartet Audiences: Actual, Potential, Ideal," 7–27.

44. As Toon comments, "The Christian understanding of personhood flows from the Christian doctrine of the Three Persons who are God. . . . If God is simply a monad then he cannot be or know personality. To be personal otherness must be present together with oneness, the one must be in relation to others." Peter Toon, *Our Triune God: A Biblical Portrayal of the Trinity* (Wheaton, Ill.: BridgePoint, 1996), 241.

love the Qur'an attributes to Allah—and it does so rarely—is a love for those who are just, who purify themselves and fight for his cause. It has no conception of a prevenient love for sinners, or of the supreme being himself providing the way self-sacrificially for sinners to return to him.[45]

Islam began with a rejection of the Trinity as repugnant to reason. Jesus Christ, according to Mohammed, was simply a human prophet. Allah is one and has no need of a son. It is not befitting to the majesty of Allah that he should beget a son.[46] The doctrine of the Trinity is blasphemous.[47] Mohammed had been raised in an area where heretical Christian groups lived. Possibly he learned about both Judaism and Christianity from merchants on the trade routes from Arabia to Syria. This may explain his extremely limited grasp of both. He had a smattering of knowledge of the OT and NT, of a most rudimentary and distorted kind. It is clear he had no contact with orthodox Christianity. For example, the Qur'an refutes the notion that Mary was part of the Trinity.[48] With his explicit repudiation of the Trinity, Mohammed denies that Jesus died on the cross.[49] The Qur'an scoffs at the idea that God would let a prophet die by crucifixion—according to the common belief of the Arab world at the time of Mohammed, God's favor is evidenced by success.

The Trinity is a crucial element in outreach to Islamic people. It is often avoided because objections immediately arise. However, the

45. Qur'an 2:195, 222; 3:134, 148, 159; 4:42; 5:13, 93; 9:4, 7, 108; 19:96; 49:9; 60:8; 61:4.
46. Qur'an 19:35.
47. "O People of the Book! Commit no excesses In your religion: nor say Of Allah aught but the truth. Christ Jesus the son of Mary Was (no more than) A Messenger of Allah, And His Word, Which He bestowed on Mary, And a Spirit proceeding From Him: so believe In Allah and His Messengers. Say not "Trinity": desist: It will be better for you: For Allah is One God: Glory be to Him: (Far Exalted is He) above Having a son. To Him Belong all things in the heavens And on earth. And enough Is Allah as a Dispenser of affairs" (Qur'an 4:171). "They do blaspheme who say: Allah is one of three In a Trinity: for there is No god except One God. If they desist not From their word (of blasphemy), Verily a grievous penalty Will befall the blasphemers Among them" (Qur'an 5:73).
48. "And behold! Allah will say: 'O Jesus the son of Mary! Didst thou say unto men, "Worship me and my mother As gods in derogation of Allah"?' He will say: 'Glory to Thee! never could I say What I had no right (To say). . . . Never said I to them Aught except what Thou Didst command me To say, to wit, "Worship Allah, my Lord and your Lord"'" (Qur'an 5:116–17).
49. "That they said (in boast), 'We killed Christ Jesus The Son of Mary, The Messenger of Allah'—But they killed him not, Nor crucified him. But so it was made to appear to them, And those who differ Therein are full of doubts, With no (certain) knowledge, But only conjecture to follow, For of a surety They killed him not" (Qur'an 4:157; see also 5:110).

implications of the Islamic view of Allah are far-reaching. Because of it, Islam has no way to explain or even to maintain human person-hood. Relationality among human beings cannot be founded on man being the image of God, since God himself is not and cannot be a rela-tional being. Moreover, love cannot exist in God. A monad cannot love. C. S. Lewis, while not specifically addressing Islam, points to the fact that God can only be love if, in effect, he is triune:

> All sorts of people are fond of repeating the Christian statement that "God is love". But they seem not to notice that the words "God is love" have no real meaning unless God contains at least two Per-sons. Love is something that one person has for another person. If God was a single person, then before the world was made, he was not love.[50]

And, we might add, if he were not love, he could not be personal, either.

From its doctrine of Allah, consequences have flowed in the his-tory of Islam. A unitary, monadic god produced a unitary community of his followers, the *ummah*. The followers of the Prophet are a sin-gle community "justly balanced,"[51] a brotherhood, "a single brother-hood."[52] The one nation of Islam is a unitary entity. This may help to explain why, from time to time, there have been attempts to unite exist-ing political entities—Egypt and Syria in the 1950s and early 1960s, and Gaddafi's offers of political union between Libya and other Arab countries. In turn, the monolith requires *dhimmitude*, a form of tol-erance for, but servitude of, the People of the Book (Jews and Chris-tians). It also calls for the extermination of outright infidels. As a corol-lary, political systems in Islamic countries do not recognize diversity. Uniformly they are authoritarian dictatorships, "tyranny tempered by assassination," with an increasing trend to impose Islamic law on soci-ety. This is seen in particular in the place given to women, over which it may be best to draw a discreet veil. The only predominantly Islamic country that does not fit this picture is Turkey, which was secularized in 1923 by Mustafa Kemal (Kemal Ataturk). There is a similar lack of

50. C. S. Lewis, *Mere Christianity* (San Francisco: Harper, 1960), 174.
51. Qur'an 2:143.
52. Qur'an 21:92; 23:52; 49:10.

differentiation between church and state in Islam. In fact, there is nothing that corresponds to the church in Christian societies. As an example, in Iran the religious leaders are part of the power structure of the state. At the outset of Islamic history, Mohammed conquered territories and became their ruler. The state and the church were and are identical, with Allah being the head and the Prophet his earthly representative. As such, the law is a given. There is no debate about it. It is simply to be administered. In turn, submission (*islam*) is required. It is only in countries influenced by Christianity that there exists a separation between these two spheres.[53]

Bernard Lewis points to the aversion of the Islamic world to polyphonic music—where different performers play different instruments from different scores, which blend together as one musical statement. "To this very day the Middle East—with the exception of some Westernized enclaves—remains a blank on the itinerary of the great international virtuosos as they go on their world tours."[54]

The church has historically made little ground against Islam. The territory of the Eastern church was largely overrun in the seventh and eighth centuries. Consequently, the church was forced on the defensive and struggled to preserve its inheritance. By the thirteenth century, Islam was culturally ahead of the Christian civilization of the West. Its philosophers, notably Avicenna and Averroes, produced the leading interpretations of Aristotle. This posed a major threat to the intellectual and doctrinal credibility of the Christian faith. Siger of Brabant may even have suggested, as a way to cope with the threat, the notion of "double truth"—that something could be false according to reason, but true in the realm of faith.[55] Aquinas tried to resolve this tension. His *Summa theologica* proposed the integration of reason and

53. Bernard Lewis, *What Went Wrong? Western Impact and Middle Eastern Response* (New York: Oxford University Press, 2002), 96–97.

54. Ibid., 136.

55. David Knowles, *The Evolution of Medieval Thought* (New York: Vintage Books, 1964), 270–77; Jaroslav Pelikan, *The Christian Tradition: A History of the Development of Doctrine*, vol. 3, *The Growth of Medieval Theology (600–1300)* (Chicago: University of Chicago Press, 1978), 289–90; Josef Pieper, *Scholasticism: Personalities and Problems of Medieval Philosophy* (New York: McGraw-Hill, 1964), 123ff.; Edward P. Mahoney, "Sense, Intellect, and Imagination in Albert, Thomas, and Siger," in *The Cambridge History of Later Medieval Philosophy: From the Rediscovery of Aristotle to the Disintegration of Scholasticism, 1100–1600*, ed. Norman Kreitzmann (Cambridge: Cambridge University Press, 1982), 602–22.

faith, refuting the idea of double truth. His *Summa contra Gentiles* was written as an apologetic in the face of the Islamic challenge. However, the problems of Aquinas's own Trinitarianism weakened the impact of this work. Aquinas held to the Trinity only with some difficulty. Moreover, he held back his treatment of the Trinity until long after discussing the doctrine of the one God. So although he achieved much in reestablishing a rational defense of the faith, he failed to challenge Islam at its roots.

Its doctrine of God is the major weakness of Islam. It is the root of all other problems. It is here that the Christian apologete and evangelist can probe, with sensitivity and wisdom. While the Trinity is one of the major stumbling blocks to Muslims turning to Christ, it must be presented with intelligence and skill. Here the love paradigm of Richard of St. Victor, rediscovered in modern Russian Orthodox theology and developed in differing ways by Moltmann and Staniloae, offers help. Only a God who is triune can be personal. Only the Holy Trinity can be love. Human love cannot possibly reflect the nature of God unless God is a Trinity of persons in union and communion. A solitary monad cannot love and, since it cannot love, neither can it be a person. And if God is not personal, neither can we be—and if we are not persons, we cannot love. This marks a vast, immeasurable divide between those cultures that follow a monotheistic, unitary deity and those that are permeated by the Christian teaching on the Trinity. Trinitarian theology asserts that love is ultimate because God is love, because he is three persons in undivided loving communion. By contrast, Islam asserts that Allah is powerful and that his will is ultimate, before which submission (*islam*) is required.

Today's Postmodern Culture: Diversity Without Unity

Developments in the West since around 1970 have moved in the opposite direction to Islam. Postmodernism allows (indeed, forces) diversity, but not unity, and thus has no room for diversity in unity. Today it pervades virtually every facet of life in the Western world. The stress on diversity in the corporate world and the media, the constantly shifting statements of leading politicians, the disintegration of large and seemingly impregnable countries, and the huge emphasis on the way people feel, are all expressions of postmodernism. It affects us all, every day of our lives.

In order to understand postmodernism, we first need to consider the modernism to which it is "post." The modern world was born in the Enlightenment, around 1700, and lasted at the popular level until about the third quarter of the last century. It had an optimistic belief in human progress, based on a high evaluation of reason, stemming from a rejection of the biblical and Christian worldview. Immanuel Kant (1724–1804) held that scientific knowledge is founded on observation by the senses. Religion, not based on empirical observation and verification, belongs in a different category than science. This led to the widespread myth of objective science and bred a deep bias against the supernatural. Miracles were unacceptable, and so the Virgin Birth, the Incarnation, the Resurrection, and the deity of Christ were rejected by those who shared this way of thinking. This worldview encouraged a split between faith and history. Faith belongs to the religious realm (the noumenal), beyond scientific or historical investigation. The claim that Christianity is a historical religion was opposed by the counterclaim made by the children of the Enlightenment that historical events cannot establish ultimate truth, and thus that the historical resurrection of Christ as the church proclaimed it could not establish the religious truth of the Christian faith. Moreover, the modern stress on reason was set against authority imposed from outside, such as Scripture. While reason, under the authority of God's revelation, is vital, the post-Enlightenment use of reason was autonomous, independent of the Bible and the teachings of the church. At its height at the end of the nineteenth century, liberalism focused on history and the historical Jesus, subjecting the gospel records to scientific, historical investigation, and looked askance at anything it could not fit into its own predisposed categories.

Evangelicalism was a reaction of Christianity to this worldview, and in many ways an adaptation to it. While right-wing fundamentalism ignored modernism, evangelicalism took over some of its features, stressing regeneration, sanctification, and evangelism—all good and necessary, but directed to the human end of the gospel, in contrast to the historic faith. The church historically had confessed faith in the Holy Trinity, the incarnation of Christ, and the church and sacraments.

There were, of course, many other elements to Christianity. The Bible, after all, talks of many things—of ships, shoes, and sealing wax, of cabbages and kings. Yet the focus of C—the Trinity, the Incarnation, the church and sacraments—was the hard core of the faith. Evangelicalism, responding to modernism, went down a new and different route, concentrating its energies on matters relating to man and personal salvation.[56]

A number of factors combined to undermine modernism. First, developments in physics destroyed Kant's assumption of two separate realms—the physical and observable, on the one hand, and the spiritual, religious, and ethical, on the other. The theories of relativity established that matter and energy are interchangeable approaching the speed of light, and so are part of a continuum. The observable and nonobservable are not two separate realms, for with light foundational to the universe, what is observed is interpreted by what cannot be observed; the space-time continuum is not something you can see, hear, or smell, and light is not so much something you see as it is a medium through which you see. Thus, the realms of science and the spiritual are distinct, but not separate. In addition, these advances disclosed the limitations of logic as one approaches the boundaries of the universe. Following the Michelson-Morley experiment of 1887, it became clear that light does not behave according to the rules of formal or symbolic logic.[57] Later, the coexistence of the wave and particle theories of light reinforced this—theories that appear to cancel each other out logically (how can light behave like discrete particles and also like continuous waves?), but are both nonetheless true. We can also point to the famous uncertainty principle of Heisenberg, which established the inexactitude of all human scientific measurements, and to Gödel's theorems in mathematics, which established that systems cannot simultaneously be consistent and comprehensive. In short, science and mathematics demonstrated the limits of logic. Nature is a given, and is not under the dominion of human reason.

Second, the Enlightenment's belief in human progress and the powers of reason was shattered by two world wars, by the horrors of

56. Robert Letham, "Is Evangelicalism Christian?" *EvQ* 67, no. 1 (January 1995): 3–33.
57. Michael Polanyi, *Personal Knowledge* (Chicago: University of Chicago Press, 1958), 9–15.

Auschwitz, Hiroshima, and other atrocities, and by a growing awareness of an emerging ecological crisis. Human nature no longer appeared benign. The Western world had bred monstrous deeds beyond belief. Confidence in human ability to shape and control the world so as to produce continuous progress and an increasingly fulfilling lifestyle was undermined. Many started to explore the nonrational. Eastern mysticism and the occult entered Western society in a big way, and the New Age movement emerged as a phoenix out of the ashes of hippiedom. With this sea change, emotion trumps reason and image triumphs over substance.

Third, the destructive effect of ideology seen in Nazism, Communism, and religious manipulation led to a deepening suspicion of strongly held truth claims. It seems to me no accident that some of the chief exponents of postmodernism are French, for continental Europe bore much of the brunt of destructive, intolerant ideology during the last century. But religion, including cults identified in some way with Christianity, is not exempt. The Jonestown massacre of 1978 stemmed from an originally Christian church. Many evangelical leaders have put spiritual and emotional pressure on their followers that has been described by one writer as comparable to a floodlit concentration camp.[58]

The world that has emerged is a very different one. It has a generally pessimistic view of human progress. The scientific and technological advances of previous centuries are frequently questioned, because of their negative impact. Additionally, the modern world's reliance on reason has been replaced by a preference for emotion. Successful athletes are asked less to analyze the game and more often questioned as to how they feel. The cardinal fault in interpersonal relations now is to hurt someone's feelings. Descartes' "I think, therefore I am" has been swept aside by postmodern man's "I emote, therefore I am." Again, distrust of ideology now has ideological status. Pluralism in society is reflected by the acceptance of the insights of disparate religious sources as more or less equally valid. In Christianity, the old evangelicalism has splintered with the demise of the Enlightenment. In its place has emerged the charismatic movement, reflecting a kinship with postmodernism in its reliance on emotion above reason, its replacement of linear, progressive hymns (characteristic of the whole

58. Graham Shaw, *God in Our Hands* (London: SCM, 1987), 31, 47.

Judeo-Christian tradition) with cyclical, repetitive choruses, and by its collapsing of the physical and the spiritual into one.

On the positive side, the old objections to Christianity no longer carry the weight they once did, for the cultural assumptions that supported them have crumbled. The scientific worldview made possible by James Clerk Maxwell (a devout elder in the Church of Scotland) and Albert Einstein is no longer inherently hostile to Christianity. But a new situation has emerged, creating other, potentially even more serious obstacles. While emotions are not to be shunned, for God created them and intended us to respond to him with our whole being, there are peculiar and sinister dangers in a world shaped not by considered thought, but by image and gut feelings. These dangers relate to civil society and the rule of law, and also to the church and its faithfulness to Christ. Ancient Israel faced similar temptations from Canaanite religion. God revealed himself to the whole person through the mind or understanding, but Canaanite religion was directed from somewhere below the head.

The modern world was shaped by philosophers like Descartes and Kant and by the natural science that developed from their assumptions, seen in people like Isaac Newton. With postmodernism, various earlier philosophies coined by Nietzsche, Marx, and Heidegger have been developed further. In the vanguard of this new world order are not so much scientists as literary critics. Its root feature is the view that the world is without objective meaning or absolute truth.[59] The thrust of much of the work of Roland Barthes (1915–80), Michel Foucault (1926–84), and Jacques Derrida (1930-2004) is that human language, whether spoken or written, does not refer to an objective world, but is instead a system of linguistic signs referring back to itself. There is no point in asking what the original speaker or author intended to say, for the author is forever lost to us. We simply have a text before us, to which you, the reader, can give any meaning you wish. There is no objective world beyond your own interpretation. Meaning itself is endlessly deferred. Indeed, according to Barthes, talk of an objective world is really an attempt by bourgeois elites to maintain power by manip-

59. In the next two paragraphs I am particularly indebted to Anthony C. Thiselton, *Interpreting God and the Post-Modern Self: On Meaning, Manipulation and Promise* (Edinburgh: T & T Clark, 1995).

ulation. All language (whether spoken or written) refers simply to itself. For Derrida, a text has no point of reference outside itself. Fixed meanings are generated by a mobile army of metaphors.

This has serious consequences, especially for claims of absolute truth—claims that such and such is true at all times and places. For postmodernism, truth claims are in reality attempts to manipulate people, bids for power and control. Historic Christianity comes clearly into this category. Postmodern critics seek to unmask the hidden agendas underlying claims of absolute truth by a procedure known as deconstruction. Like peeling an onion, they remove layer upon layer of surface claims to get at the real manipulative core underneath. Postmodernism is deeply suspicious of the advertising industry, which puts us all at the mercy of someone's desire to exert power over us economically in an inherently deceitful way. The Christian church is an obvious target for deconstruction, since it has wielded power over its adherents and, in some cases, whole cultures.

In fact, for postmodernists beliefs are simply the preferred options of a cultural group, like a taste for ice cream. You believe the way you do because the group with which you mix believes that way and you are happy and comfortable with it. Everything is culturally and socially conditioned. This fits well with a tolerant pluralism, in which any and all beliefs are more or less equally legitimate—all insights, that is, which cannot and do not claim to be true other than for the one who has them. No group can claim that it has *the* truth, since truth (if indeed there can be said to be any) is endlessly elusive. Christianity is personally and individually qualified, a matter of taste. Absolute truth is not possible. The Christian gospel cannot be objectively true or applicable to anyone who does not share a taste for it or for whom it is not a particularly helpful insight.

Second, postmodernism's world is one of instability, diversity, and fragmentation. Since postmodernism allows no objective truth, there can be no fixed point of reference to determine what we should believe or how we are to act. This lack of fixity entails a total lack of stability in everyday life. No basis exists for a commonly accepted morality. This world of constant flux fits a situation in which today's technology is dated within six months. In large American corporations, diversity is the name of the game. The workforce is taught to accept people of different ethnic backgrounds and of alternative lifestyles. Since there are no fixed moral standards, anything goes. In politics, we have been witnessing the fragmentation of large states formed during the modern era, when unity was rationalistically imposed on diverse peoples. In varying ways, the USSR, Yugoslavia, and Czechoslovakia fragmented. In the West, the politics of Canada have been dramatically regionalized. The United Kingdom was formed in the age of the Enlightenment, with central government imposed from Westminster on four nations, but now devolution is creating representative assemblies in Scotland, Wales, and possibly in the English regions, while the long-term continuance of the union is considered problematic. As for the USA, there are few Americans left, for everyone is a hyphenated American: an African-American, an Italian-American, a Jewish-American, a Korean-American—the list is endless. In each case, the stress on reason and the imposed unity of the modern age is replaced by postmodernist diversity and fragmentation. A major exception is the European Union, but there the bureaucratic, rationalistic push toward a federal superstate does not command popular support, and with its increasing size, due to new members from the east, it is unlikely to achieve its goals.

But if there is no absolute truth, who is to say that your insights are any better than those of Adolf Hitler? If everything is a giant language game, we have removed any basis for rejecting ideas that are morally repugnant. If there is no basis for morality, the immoral does not exist. Indeed, the world of postmodernism is entirely arbitrary. If the emotions trump reason, we have no rational grounds for anything. This mind-set is also riddled with inconsistencies. Is there an objective world for, say, Jacques Derrida to enable him to earn money? Does he accept a salary? Does he emerge from his language games to eat? What if someone listening to him lecture advanced to the podium and punched him in the face, giving him a bloody nose? Would there be an objective world then?[60] In short, postmodernism cannot stand the test of everyday life. It does not work and it will not work. It fails the test of Lud-

60. "There was a faith-healer from Deal,
Who said that pain wasn't real.
When he sat on a pin
He announced with chagrin
'I dislike what I fancy I feel.'" (source unknown)

wig Wittgenstein, who insisted that language and philosophy must have "cash value" in terms of the real world in which we go about our business from day to day. To do that, we assume that there is an objective world and act accordingly. If there were not, life could not go on. Wittgenstein himself compared such a situation to someone buying several copies of the morning paper to assure himself that what it said was true![61]

The way people conduct themselves in ordered societies can be explained only on the basis that they assume there to be standards of conduct that hold true across the board, in times and places other than their own. Moreover, postmodernism asks us to accept for itself what it denies to everything and everyone else. It denies and deconstructs absolute truth claims, yet its own claims are absolute, excluded from the relativism that it foists on the assertions of others. It claims that all human language refers only to itself. This is an absolute claim, applying to all human discourse, spoken or written. It is also reductionistic, reducing the whole of reality to one form, in this case a particular theory of language. Such reductionism is not a claim about language so much as a philosophy, a worldview, a fundamentally religious worldview. It elevates one branch of human activity and knowledge above all others and claims for it the ultimate reference point (almost divine status) that it argues does not and cannot exist. Its claims are self-destructive, rebounding upon itself. It also fails the test of Gödel's theorem, which determined that no system can be enclosed on itself. In reality, human beings cannot live without objective meaning or absolute truth. Life disintegrates without it.

In terms of instability and diversity, the postmodern world of constant flux is seeing insecurity, breakdown, and the rise of various forms of terrorism. As diversity rules, subgroups are divided against each other, tribe against tribe. With suspicion fueled by a deconstructionist mentality, each fragmentary unit looks to blame the other. A cult of the victim develops, and responsibility declines. This is a recipe for social breakdown, instability, and the unraveling of any cohesion that once existed. Thiselton argues that the postmodern self is predisposed to assume a stance of conflict.[62]

---

61. Ludwig Wittgenstein, *Philosophical Investigations* (Oxford: Blackwell, 1963), sec. 265, pp. 93–94.

62. Thiselton, *Interpreting God*, 131.

Arbitrariness in public life will mean the destruction of public justice. The rule of law emerged in the context of a Christian worldview. The great medieval jurist, Henry de Bracton (d. 1268), taught in his groundbreaking and seminal work *De legibus et consuetudinibus Angliae*, in which he systematized the laws of England, that the king was himself under the law—responsible to God, in the place of Jesus Christ, as God's vicar:

> For judgments are not made by men but by God, which is why the heart of a king who rules well is said to be in the hand of God. . . . [L]et no one unwise ascend the seat of judgment lest in the day of wrath he feel the vengeance of him who said "Vengeance is mine, I will repay. . . ." [O]n that day when they shall behold the Son of Man . . . who shall not fear that trial when the Lord shall be the accuser, the advocate and the judge?[63]

Additionally, modern science (and the prosperity accompanying it) was built on the capital bequeathed by the Protestant Reformation. Science cannot even exist in a world of mere language games, with no objective order. The battle against microorganisms requires vigorous scientific research. Prosperity cannot continue in a world of self-conscious anomie. As ethnic and interest groups press their own agendas with increasing vigor, discord and violence will increase.

The problem with Enlightenment rationalism was that it sought unity without diversity. Its glorification of human reason led it to impose order and unity. But set free from the authority of the Word of God, it failed to recognize the diversity that God had placed in creation. Postmodernism, in contrast, stresses diversity, but without unity. Fragmentation is built into its program. This is where all forms of unbelief go wrong. Christianity maintains unity in diversity and diversity in unity. God, our Creator, is triune. The Father, the Son, and the Holy Spirit are in eternal and undivided union as the one triune God. Cut adrift from biblical revelation, which is grounded in the eternal, antecedent reality of God himself, unbelief will always swing wildly from one pole to the other. How is the

63. Henry de Bracton, *On the Laws and Customs of England*, trans. and ed. Samuel E. Thorne (Cambridge, Mass.: Harvard University Press, 1968–77), 2:21, citing Rom. 12:19; Rev. 3:7; 18:9–10; John 5:22; Matt. 3:7; 12:36; 13:30, 41, 42.

church to combat postmodernism? How can we most effectively proclaim and live the gospel in this kind of world? Beyond that, how can we plan for the future, when postmodernism bites the dust, as surely it must?

Doing the Truth—an End to Manipulation

The criticisms of Foucault, Barthes, and others are not to be dismissed lightly. There are far too many floodlit concentration camps for comfort. The quiet atmosphere of a prayer meeting, the frenetic mood of evangelism and charismatic worship—now almost pervasive in conservative churches—are all vehicles for crass spiritual pressure and manipulation. How often do evangelists use music to get their audience into the right mood, to soften them up, so that they can influence them more easily and so change their behavior? This is reprehensible. In the search for statistics and success, lives are subordinated to an evangelist's or a preacher's ego. Much "worship" today is not worship at all, for it is not directed to the Holy Trinity, but to the advancement of hidden agendas, the bolstering of human pride, or the entertainment of seekers. Jesus prayed that his church might be one (John 17), not only in a spiritual sense or in heaven, but visibly in this world, "so that the world might believe" that the Father sent him. This unity is to mirror on a creaturely level the union in the Trinity. It is thus a unity grounded in truth—not a merely institutional or enforced unity, but a unity in deed and truth. It is not yet evident. To combat postmodernism, and for the furtherance of the worldwide advance of Christ's rule, it must come. We must work toward it in practical terms now, by abandoning manipulation, by teaching and doing the truth, and by seeking to promote the unity and catholicity of the church, as well as its purity and apostolicity.

Initial Spadework Necessary

Unless we start at square one, we might as well operate from a different universe. It is not simply that people today have little understanding of creation and the God who made it, like the pagans in Paul's day (Acts 17:16–34). Behind all that, as we have seen, the idea of truth itself is in question. We need to understand that Christ claims the whole of life, from church and prayer to family life, business, and education. In evangelism, this requires laying patiently the groundwork of the nature of God the Holy Trinity, creation, and the objectivity of truth. It is vital that we present people with the context in which an intelligent response to the gospel can be made. The message of God's grace must be grounded in creation, the reality of truth, and in the union and communion of the Trinity.

Trinity and Incarnation

Perhaps the most appropriate response to the postmodern suspicion of claims of objective, absolute truth is in our focusing on the manipulation-free, self-giving love of God. The incarnation of Christ demonstrates this beyond parallel. In Philippians 2:5ff. Paul stresses that even in eternity the Son did not count his equality with the Father something to be exploited for his own advantage. Instead, he received all things from the Father, including the honor of being our high priest (Heb. 5:5). In his incarnation, he emptied himself, not by ceasing to be God, but by adding the form of a servant, becoming man. Then, in his incarnate ministry, he freely humbled himself, serving others, ultimately giving himself up to the cursed death of the cross, reserved by the Roman authorities for the lowest of the low, and which the Philippians, priding themselves on their city's status as a Roman colony, under the protection of the *ius Italicum* (Roman law), would have readily seen as the most despicable way to die. Christ does not put pressure on us in order to realize his own hidden agenda. Instead, he gave himself up to death.

This shows us what God is like. The holy and undivided Trinity is a union of unbroken love. The Father, the Son, and the Holy Spirit do not manipulate each other for their own ends, nor can they be deconstructed so as to disclose that the real situation is other than it first appears. The Trinitarian love is pure and just, good and kind. The persons are distinct, and the union is undivided. There is no conquest of unity by diversity, nor of diversity by unity. The three are one, and the one is three. Here is the theological heart of the Christian faith, and this should also be our focus in the postmodern world. In missions of all kinds, it is imperative that we operate with a consistently biblical, Trinitarian doctrine of creation, salvation, and the future. The centrality of the Holy Trinity is not only vital to worship and prayer, but also in evangelism to individuals and cultures. At the heart of all this is the way we treat other people, for if God is relational and we are made in his image, at the center of the Christian faith is the way we deal with other human beings who share his image. This is the theme of our final chapter.

> *Glory to God in the highest,*
> *and peace to his people on earth.*
> *Lord God, heavenly King,*
> *almighty God and Father,*
> *we worship you, we give you thanks,*
> *we praise you for your glory.*
> *Lord Jesus Christ, only Son of the Father,*
> *Lord God, Lamb of God,*
> *you take away the sin of the world: have mercy on us;*
> *you are seated at the right hand of the Father; receive our prayer.*
> *For you alone are the Holy One,*
> *you alone are the Lord,*
> *you alone are the Most High, Jesus Christ, with the Holy Spirit, in*
> *the glory of God the Father. Amen.*[64]

---

64. *Gloria in excelsis* (Morning Prayer II), *The Book of Common Prayer and Administration of the Sacraments and Other Rites and Ceremonies of the Church Together with the Psalter or Psalms of David: According to the Use of the Episcopal Church* (New York: Church Hymnal Corporation, 1979), 94–95.

The Trinity and Persons

A good many people nowadays say, "I believe in a God, but not in a personal God." They feel that the mysterious something which is behind all other things must be more than a person. Now the Christians quite agree. But the Christians are the only people who offer any idea of what a being that is beyond personality could be like. All the other people, though they say that God is beyond personality, really think of him as something impersonal: that is, as something less than personal. If you are looking for something super-personal, something more than a person, then it is not a question of choosing between the Christian idea and the other ideas. The Christian idea is the only one on the market. . . .

All sorts of people are fond of repeating the Christian statement that "God is love". But they seem not to notice that the words "God is love" have no real meaning unless God contains at least two Persons. Love is something that one person has for another person. If God was a single person, then before the world was made, he was not love. —C. S. Lewis, Mere Christianity

Edmund Hill, in his introduction to his translation of Augustine's *De Trinitate*, voices concerns about the word *person* that have echoed down the years. Claiming the support of Augustine, but revealing a good dose of postmodernism, he suggests that any word could be used, since it is a pure convention or label. He cites Raimundo Pannikar, who expressed his admiration to some African bishops that their language had no word for "person."[1] This seems, to my mind, like an attempt to be clever. In reality, it is rather silly. Augustine's own confusion is in good measure due to his starting point with the one being of God, which, as we have seen, created problems for the distinct identity of the three, particularly the Holy Spirit. As C. S. Lewis says in the extracts above, love exists between persons. Where the person is held to be problematic, love will wither. It is true that there is a problem of defining exactly what a person is—not only a divine person, but even a human one. But that is inevitable. As the French personalist philosopher Emmanuel Mounier (1905–50) points out, "One can only define objects exterior to man, such as can be put under observation," while the person "is the one reality that we know, and that we are at the same time fashioning, from within. Present everywhere, it is *given* nowhere."[2] The essence of the person, Mounier insists, is indefinable. It is never exhausted by its expression, nor subjected to anything by which it is conditioned. It is not an abstract principle, but "a living activity of self-creation, of communication and attachment, that grasps and knows itself, in the act, as the *movement of becoming personal*." It is "the mode of existence proper to man."[3] It was only with the advent of Christianity that a decisive notion of personhood emerged, Mounier continues, and it was a scandal to Greek thought. Christianity brought the unthinkable notion that diversity and multiplicity, hitherto considered evil, was part of the world that God had created *ex nihilo*. The human person is an indissoluble whole, for God is personal and offers to each human being a relation of unique intimacy, of participation in his divinity. As such, man has freedom, and freedom is constitutive of his personhood.[4] "The absoluteness of the person neither cuts him off from the world nor from other men. . . . Even the conception of the Trinity . . . produces the astounding idea of a Supreme Being which is an intimate dialogue between persons, and is of its very essence the negation of solitude."[5]

1. Edmund Hill, introduction to *The Works of Saint Augustine: A Translation for the 21st Century: The Trinity*, trans. Edmund Hill, ed. John E. Rotelle (Hyde Park, N.Y.: New City Press, 1991), 52, 59.

2. Emmanuel Mounier, *Personalism* (Notre Dame, Ind.: University of Notre Dame Press, 2001), xvi-xvii.

3. Ibid., xviii-xix.

4. Ibid., xx-xxi.

5. Ibid., xxii.

Bishop Timothy Kallistos Ware writes along similar lines to Mounier:

> What is my true self? Who am I? What am I? The answers are far from obvious. The boundaries of each person are exceedingly wide, overlapping as they do with those of other persons, ranging over space and time, reaching out of space into infinity, out of time into eternity. In an important sense we do not know exactly what is involved in being a person.

He points out that there is a reason for this. "It is because the human being is made in God's image and likeness; since God is beyond understanding, his icon within humanity is also incomprehensible."[6]

Drawing on the teaching of the Fathers, Panayiotis Nellas argues that while he is a political and rational being—thoroughly earthly— "man realizes his true existence in the measure in which he is raised up towards God and is united with him."[7] For Paul, man's growth to full stature consists in his Christification, his union with Christ. Christ is the image of God, and man is the image of Christ, the image of the image.[8] Man is a creator because he is the image of the supreme Creator. He rules because Christ is the almighty Lord and King. He is responsible for the creation because Christ is the Savior of the human race, and he unites in himself matter and spirit, since Christ unconfusedly unites uncreated divinity and created contingency.[9] His destiny is union with Christ and God. "The category of biological existence does not exhaust man. Man is understood ontologically by the Fathers only as a theological being."[10] Christ, then, is the archetype, the epitome of human personhood, of what it is to be a true human being. Since he is the Son of God, he is God's revelation of what it is to be a divine person too.

---

6. Kallistos Ware, foreword to *Deification in Christ: Orthodox Perspectives on the Nature of the Human Person*, by Panayiotis Nellas, trans. Norman Russell (Crestwood, N.Y.: St. Vladimir's Seminary Press, 1987), 9.

7. Nellas, *Deification in Christ*, 15.

8. Ibid., 24; Philip Edgcumbe Hughes, *The True Image: The Origin and Destiny of Man in Christ* (Grand Rapids: Eerdmans, 1989).

9. Nellas, *Deification in Christ*, 26–27.

10. Ibid., 33–34.

The Trinity as Persons in Union and Communion

T. F. Torrance, drawing on his vast knowledge of the Fathers, points out that the persons of the Trinity are not merely relations (as Aquinas held), but persons in relation, and so he affirms that the relations between the persons belong to who the persons actually are. For example, the Father is the Father in his relations with the Son and the Spirit, and so on. He points throughout his works to similarities to field theory in the natural sciences, and particularly in particle physics. This teaches us that we need to form our thinking on the basis of who the divine persons are, rather than on what we experience of personhood on the human level, avoiding an obvious temptation to base our thought on human analogies, such as that of a natural father and his son. This was the mistake of the Arians, who reasoned that since a human son comes into existence at a certain point in time, so the Son of God began to be and so is not coeternal with the Father, but is of another being than he. Instead, as Torrance insists, these are imageless relations. Since God is Spirit (John 4:21–24), we must think of him in a spiritual manner, not in conformity with earthly analogies. For instance, he is not a sexual being.[11] Indeed, the Trinitarian relations transcend human relationships of paternity and filiation to an infinite degree.[12] God in his own being eludes our grasp. On the other hand, if he is entirely remote from anything we experience, will not the names he himself has used of himself be meaningless? Would God then be unknown and unknowable? The solution to this enigma is the Incarnation. God as Father is the Father of our Lord Jesus Christ. We know what the fatherhood of God is like, because he is Jesus' Father. The relation between the Son and the Father is the basis for our understanding of what human relationships should be like. We are to start from a center in God, and specifically from a center in his self-revelation—in his Son, Jesus Christ. As Jesus said to Philip, "Whoever has seen me has seen the Father" (John 14:9).

This reminds us of a kindred problem, that of trying to grasp how God can be *three* persons, based on what we know of human person-

---

11. Thomas F. Torrance, *The Christian Doctrine of God: One Being, Three Persons* (Edinburgh: T & T Clark, 1996), 157–58.

12. Dumitru Staniloae, *The Experience of God*, trans. and ed. Iona Ionita and Robert Barringer (Brookline, Mass.: Holy Cross Orthodox Press, 1994–2000), 1:246.

hood. Once Trinitarian theology introduced the idea of person, it "became a regular item in the furniture of our everyday thought" and inevitably came to have an independent history of its own, as Torrance observes.[13] The danger is that of importing modern concepts of personhood into our thinking on the Trinity. Once again, this is a mistake. We need to approach the matter from the other end. Personhood is to be understood (insofar as we can ever understand it) in terms of the way God is three. He is an eternal communion of three *hypostases* in undivided union. He creates human persons.[14] He is, in C. S. Lewis's terms, beyond personality, for he is, as it were, superpersonal. We must look to Jesus Christ, for he is God the Son, who has united with human nature. The person of the incarnate Son includes and encompasses humanity.

Furthermore, the vexing question of whether to start from and emphasize the one being of God or the three persons, is best approached by recognizing their equal ultimacy. As Torrance argues, "The one Being of God is identical with the communion of the three divine Persons and the Communion of the three divine Persons is identical with the one Being of God," for God is "intrinsically personal . . . completely personal."[15] This is what Van Til means when he writes that God is one person and three persons, although he expresses it in a confusing way. God is not one person in the relational sense in which the three persons are to one another. However, Van Til means that there is no question of God being less than personal.[16] Alan Torrance is prepared to talk in terms similar to those of Van Til.[17]

The three persons, then, are in eternal and joyful communion and union. As Staniloae puts it, "The three subjects are so interior in their unity as Being that knows no dispersal that they can in no way be separated so as to be counted as three entities having a certain discontinuity between them."[18] John D. Zizioulas wrote in 1975 that, according to the

13. Torrance, *Christian Doctrine of God*, 159–60.

14. Ibid., 160.

15. Ibid., 161.

16. Cornelius Van Til, *An Introduction to Systematic Theology* (Phillipsburg, N.J.: Presbyterian & Reformed, 1974), 229–30.

17. Alan J. Torrance, *Persons in Communion: An Essay on Trinitarian Description and Human Participation with Special Reference to Volume One of Karl Barth's Church Dogmatics* (Edinburgh: T & T Clark, 1996), 256–57.

18. Staniloae, *Experience of God*, 1:265–66.

Greek fathers, the human person transcends human limitations, going beyond the self toward another. Contrary to all Western conceptions of the person, it is open-ended, and can only be understood in terms of being related to others, whether one speaks of divine or human persons.[19]

Are, then, the divine persons more basic than the one being of God, as Zizioulas[20] and Colin Gunton[21] argue, and many in the East have held? Should we today place our stress on the three persons, as Gerald Bray wants us to do?[22] Or, alternatively, is the Western tradition, with its point of departure with the one being of God, to be preferred? Is divine being more basic than persons, or are persons prior to being? On many occasions, we have referred to this problem, with its attendant dangers of tritheism or modalism. We have argued for equal ultimacy. Staniloae again supports this when he says that the Fathers "do not conceive of the divine being separately from person."[23] From the West, as one favorable to Barth and T. F. Torrance, Molnar also stresses that we are to begin "neither with plurality *nor* with unity, but with the triune God who is simultaneously one and three." He goes on to say that "God's unity can neither be perceived nor known apart from faith in his Son, and without the operation of the Holy Spirit. Father, Son, and Spirit are not three subjects, just because God is essentially one and three and never is one first or three first."[24] This brings us back to Gregory Nazianzen:

> No sooner do I conceive of the one than I am illumined by the splendour of the three; no sooner do I distinguish them than I am carried back to the one. When I think of any one of the three I think of him as the whole, and my eyes are filled, and the greater part of what I am thinking escapes me. I cannot grasp the greatness of that one so as to attribute a greater greatness to the rest. When I contemplate

19. John D. Zizioulas, "Human Capacity and Human Incapacity: A Theological Exploration of Personhood," *SJT* 28 (1975): 401–47.
20. John D. Zizioulas, *Being as Communion: Studies in Personhood and the Church* (Crestwood, N.Y.: St. Vladimir's Seminary Press, 1985), esp. 41–42.
21. Colin Gunton, "Being and Person: T. F. Torrance's Doctrine of God," in *The Promise of Trinitarian Theology: Theologians in Dialogue with T. F. Torrance*, ed. Elmer M. Colyer (Lanham, Md.: Rowman & Littlefield Publishers, 2001), 115–37.
22. Gerald Bray, *The Doctrine of God* (Leicester: Inter-Varsity Press, 1993), 197–224.
23. Staniloae, *Experience of God*, 1:257.
24. Paul D. Molnar, *Divine Freedom and the Doctrine of the Immanent Trinity: In Dialogue with Karl Barth and Contemporary Theology* (Edinburgh: T & T Clark, 2002), 232–33.

the three together, I see but one torch, and cannot divide or measure out the undivided light.[25]

Along these lines lies the eventual resolution of the great division of the Christian church regarding the Trinity.

Union with God as the Goal of Our Salvation

Genesis 1:26–27 records that Adam was created in the image of God. Yet in the NT Paul insists that Christ is "the image of the invisible God" (Col. 1:15; cf. 2 Cor. 4:6). He frequently refers to Christ as the Second Adam, in a variety of contexts relating to old and new ages: to sin and grace (Rom. 5:12–21), to death and life (1 Cor. 15:20–58). Since the image of God looks forward to Christ as the Second Adam, there is much justice in the teaching of the Fathers that the human race was created in Christ, the true image of God. After the Fall, this relationship was marred. Now we are being renewed in Christ, the image of God (Eph. 4:24; Col. 3:10; 2 Cor. 4:4–6). Moreover, Genesis 1 presents God as a relational being (see chapter 1). "Let us make man in our image," he said. Man, made in the image of God, is also relational—male and female, in relation both to each other and to their Creator. The image of God is set in a context of relationality and communion of persons, to be realized eschatologically in Christ.

Hence, the goal of our salvation—our ultimate destiny—is union with Christ. The Western church focuses almost entirely on the way we become Christians in regeneration and justification, or on the process of living as Christian believers in today's world, in sanctification. We look back to the accomplishment of salvation in the cross and resurrection of Christ. In the work of Christ, we see atonement for our sins, ourselves redeemed from the power of sin and Satan by the sheer grace of God, and consequently freed to serve him, adopted as his children. We focus on our conduct in this world, our responsibilities as Christians in the home, church, workplace, and world. We are glad that God has made his covenant with his people in Christ, that his grace has been made known so wonderfully and dramatically.

25. Gregory Nazianzen, *Orations* 40.41 (PG 36:417).

However, here we are looking beyond all that to the future, to eternity, to what happens after Christ's return and the Last Judgment. We are looking to our ultimate destiny, to "the resurrection of the dead and the life of the world to come." This is the goal to which our salvation leads. What we experience of God and his salvation now is preparing for this and cannot be detached from it. For that reason, we cannot appreciate our place as members of the body of Christ here and now in today's world if our understanding of our future destiny is blurred. Our present journey is governed by our future destination. It is helpful to know where we are heading—and why we are heading there.

Union with God in Theological Context

Robert Grosseteste, who was bishop of Lincoln beginning in 1235, in his classic *Hexaëmeron*, wrote that at the heart of the Christian faith

> there seem to be grouped together the following unities or unions: the union by which the incarnate Word is the one Christ, one Christ in his person, God and man; the union by which Christ is one in nature with the church through the human nature he took on; and the union by which the church is reunited with him by a condign taking up, in the sacrament of the Eucharist. . . . These three unions seem to be grouped together in the One which is called the whole Christ. Of this One the apostle says, to the Ephesians [*sic*]: "For you are all one in Christ Jesus", or, as the Greek text has it: "You are all one person in Christ Jesus". That One of which it says: "That they also may be one in us" seems moreover, to add to the foregoing considerations that the Son, as Word, is one in substance with the Father, and hence with the Holy Spirit. . . . It adds also the unity of our conformity in the highest kind with the Blessed Trinity, through our reason. To this conformity and Deiformity we are led by the mediator, Christ, God and man, with whom we form one Christ.

Grosseteste goes on to say that "there is an orderly descent, through the unity of the Trinity and through the incarnate Word, through his body which is the church, to our being one, in a deiform way [or "one in God-form with the Trinity," as another possible reading goes]."[26] Grosseteste has put his finger on the pulse of the Christian faith. These unions are the very heartbeat of what God is and all that he has done for us.

First and foremost, God is one being, three persons, and three persons, one being. The indivisible Trinity consists of three irreducibly distinct persons. Their distinctness or difference is in no way whatever erased, obliterated, or eroded by the union. But the union is real, eternal, and indivisible. The three are one identical being.

Following this, God the Son became incarnate. He assumed into personal union a human nature, conceived in the womb of the Virgin Mary. This human nature is not merely contiguous with his deity, as the Nestorian heresy held, for that would not be incarnation, but merely indwelling. Such an indwelling could not save us. God would not then have come *as man*, and so man would not have been brought into union with God. In contrast, the Incarnation is an unbreakable *union* between God the Son and the assumed human nature—*without division, without separation*, as the Council of Chalcedon stated in 451. Moreover, this union continues forever. On the other hand, neither the deity nor the humanity loses its distinctness in the union. Chalcedon was careful to balance the above pair of descriptions with another—*without confusion, without mixture*—for Christ is not an amalgam. His deity and humanity are not like ingredients in an ontological soup which blend into a third substance. Just as the three persons of the Trinity remain eternally distinct in the one being of God, so the deity and humanity of Christ are forever deity and humanity while united without possibility of severance in his one person. This means that our humanity is forever united to God in personal union!

In turn, when it comes to our own salvation, we—all believers without exception—are united to Jesus Christ. This is the foundation of the entire working out of salvation. I have written elsewhere about how foundational is union with Christ.[27] It is central to Paul's theology, as is clear in Ephesians 1:3–14, where every single aspect of salvation is received "in Christ" or "in him." The Westminster Larger

26. Robert Grosseteste, *On the Six Days of Creation: A Translation of the Hexaëmeron*, trans. C. F. J. Martin, Auctores Britannici Medii Aevi (Oxford: Oxford University Press for the British Academy, 1996), 47–48.

27. Robert Letham, *The Work of Christ* (Leicester: Inter-Varsity Press, 1993), 75–87.

Catechism takes this position too, in questions 65–90, where it fits the whole *ordo salutis* under the umbrella of "union and communion with Christ in grace and glory." This union has substitutionary and representative dimensions to it, for Christ acted on our behalf in his life and ministry, death, resurrection, and ascension. Since God is just, there are legal aspects that undergird the atoning death of Christ. However, union with Christ is far wider than the legal or representative. For example, we are united with him in our sanctification. This is evident from passages like Romans 6:1ff. In union with him, we are adopted as God's children, given to share by grace in the relation with the Father that he has by nature, so that we now call on God as "our Father." So union with Christ has filial dimensions to it, and this brings us at once into the sphere of personal relations. Moreover, since the Son's relation to the Father is one of indivisible union, our relation to him—and consequently to the Father—is one of indivisible union too. Paul writes, in connection with the Lord's Supper, that we are one flesh with Christ, "members of his body" (Eph. 5:29–33). John records Jesus' prayer to the Father requesting that his people demonstrate visibly before the world a unity grounded in the union he has with the Father (John 17:21–24). It follows from our comments above that this union no more deprives us of our humanity than does the assumption of human nature by the Son negate the reality of the humanity he assumed. It erodes our personal distinctiveness no more than the indivisibility of the Holy Trinity erases the distinctiveness of the three persons. These unions preserve the diversity, as we saw in the last chapter.

Nellas refers to the fourteenth-century theologian Nicolas Kavasilas, who wrote that this union transcends all others that we may experience:

> The union of Christ with the believer is greater than that of a householder with his home, or of a branch with the vine, or of a man with a woman in marriage, or of a head with the members of a body. The last point was made by the martyrs, who preferred to lose their heads rather than Christ. And when the Apostle Paul prays that he should be cursed so that Christ may be glorified, he shows that the true believer is united more closely with Christ than with his own self.[28]

28. Nellas, *Deification in Christ*, 119.

So, in the words of Paul, "It is no longer I who live, but Christ who lives in me" (Gal. 2:20).

The Christ with whom we are in union is of the same—the identical—being as God. Strictly speaking, we are united to his humanity, but his humanity is inseparable from his deity, due to the hypostatic union. Thus, union with his humanity is union with his person. Moreover, since the person of Christ is that of the eternal Son,[29] we are united to God. Once again, this does not mean any blurring of the Creator-creature distinction, any more than the assumption of humanity by the Son in the Incarnation does. His humanity remains humanity (without confusion, without mixture). So we remain human, creatures. As Hughes comments, what is meant "is not the obliteration of the ontological distinction between Creator and creature but the establishment at last of intimate and uninterrupted personal communion between them."[30]

The Biblical Teaching on Union with God

A number of biblical passages point to our union with God. Probably the first that springs to most minds is 2 Peter 1:3–4. There Peter says, "His divine power has granted to us all things that pertain to life and godliness, through the knowledge of him who called us to his own glory and excellence, by which he has granted to us his precious and very great promises, so that through them you may become partakers of the divine nature." Through his precious and very great promises, we become sharers of the divine nature (*theias koinōnoi physeōs*)—this Peter presents as the goal of our calling by God. He has called us "to his own glory." Our destiny as Christians is to share the glory of God. This recalls Paul's comment that "all have sinned and fall short of the glory of God" (Rom. 3:23). Our proper place is to share God's glory, but by sin we fell short and failed to participate in his glory; however, in and through Christ we are restored to sharing the glory of God as our ultimate destiny. Glory is

29. This was affirmed as dogma by the Second Council of Constantinople (553). See Aloys Grillmeier, *Christ in Christian Tradition*, vol. 2, *From the Council of Chalcedon (451) to Gregory the Great (590–604)*, part 2, *The Church of Constantinople in the Sixth Century*, trans. John Cawte (London: Mowbray, 1995), 438–62; Herbert M. Relton, *A Study in Christology: The Problem of the Relation of the Two Natures in the Person of Christ* (London: SPCK, 1917), passim.

30. Hughes, *True Image*, 286.

what belongs distinctively and peculiarly to God. We are called to partake of what God is. This is more than mere fellowship. Fellowship entails intimate interaction, but no participation in the nature of the one with whom such interaction takes place. Peter's language means that this goes far beyond external relations. There is an actual participation in the divine nature.

In John 14:16ff., John records Jesus' teaching that the Holy Spirit, upon his coming at Pentecost, "will remain with you and shall be in you" (my translation). In the presence of the Spirit, the *Paraklētos*, Jesus himself will be present (John 14:16–17). He then declares that to those who love him and keep his word "my Father will love him and we shall come to him and take up our residence with him" (John 14:23, my translation). The word *monē* means "a place where one may remain or dwell"[31] and conveys the idea of permanence.[32] The coming of the Holy Spirit is, in effect, the coming of the entire Trinity. The Father, the Son, and the Holy Spirit take up residence with the one who loves Jesus. This residence is permanent—the three remain with the faithful. It involves the greatest possible intimacy—the three indwell the one who loves Jesus. The faithful thus have a relationship to the Trinity that is far closer than any that they enjoy with other human beings. This goes beyond fellowship to communion (or participation), and is strictly a union, a joining together that is unbreakable.

Further, John writes in 1 John 3:1–2:

> See what kind of love the Father has given to us, that we should be called children of God; and so we are. . . . Beloved, we are God's children now, and what we will be has not yet appeared; but we know that when he appears we will be like him, because we shall see him as he is.

The Father's love is such that we now share the relation to him that his Son has. We are now the children of God in Christ. Moreover, at his return, we will be transformed so as to be like Christ the Son. We

---

31. LN, 1:732.
32. Cf. LSJ, 2:1143.

shall see him in his glory. We shall share his glory. We will be in union with him.

We have referred to a few passages, but the whole tenor of Scripture points to it. God has made us for this. He created us in Christ, the image of the invisible God. Following our sin, and the Son's redemptive work, we are being remade in the image of Christ. The Trinity created us with a capacity to live *in him*, as creatures in and with our Creator. The Incarnation proves it. If it were not so and could not be so, then Jesus Christ—God and man—could not be one person, for the difference between Creator and creature would be so great that incarnation would not be possible. But now our humanity in Jesus Christ is in full and personal union with God, and so in union with Christ we are brought into union with God.

Thus, Laats hits the nail on the head when he expresses the idea that human personhood is to be seen in terms of communion with God. "A human person is one who is in principle open to the Holy Spirit and who is able to respond to him. Or to put it in other words: a human person is the one who can in principle be in communion with God."[33]

Incarnation, Pentecost, and Union with God

There are two decisive moments in this great and overwhelming sweep of God's purpose for us. First, in the Incarnation, the Son takes into personal union a single human nature. Second, the Holy Spirit comes at Pentecost and indwells or pervades myriads of human persons. There are clear differences here that reflect the differences between the persons of the Trinity. The Son unites a *single* human *nature*, while with the Spirit *countless* human *persons* are involved. With the Son there is a *personal union*, whereas the Spirit *pervades* or *indwells* us.

The Spirit, at Jesus' baptism, rested on him and led him in his subsequent faith, obedience, and ministry. In union with him, we are united with the Spirit who rests on him. The idea of indwelling denotes permanence, for he comes to remain in us forever. However, the word could connote a certain incompleteness, as in the case of a liquid poured into

33. Alar Laats, *Doctrines of the Trinity in Eastern and Western Theologies: A Study with Special Reference to K. Barth and V. Lossky* (Frankfurt am Main: Peter Lang, 1999), 162–63.

a bucket, where the bucket itself remains unaffected, since the liquid merely fills the empty spaces. Pervasion, on the other hand, complements the image of indwelling by pointing to the idea of saturation, of thoroughness. Once more, this does not take away or diminish our humanity. After all, Jesus is fully and perfectly man—the most truly *human* man—and as such he is the Christ (the Anointed One), on whom the Spirit rests, directing him throughout the course of his life and ministry. Rather, pervasion by the Holy Spirit *establishes* our humanity.[34] He makes us what we ought to be. He frees us from the grip of a sinful, fallen nature and renews us to be like Christ. This is what it means to be human.[35] Well does Staniloae comment when he affirms that only the Holy Trinity assures our existence as persons, and that it is only because God is triune that salvation can occur.[36] Salvation not only reveals that God is triune, but also proceeds from that reality.

The Western Church on Union with God

After Harnack, it was widely thought that Augustine turned the Western church away from the Eastern perspective on the Christian life as one of deification or participation in the divine nature.[37] However, recent scholarship has challenged this view. Gerald Bonner cites a range of places where Augustine refers to the Christian as deified—not according to substance, but by participation.[38] Lancel writes of the concept being part of his thought and vocabulary throughout his career.[39] We noted Grosseteste's description of our union with God as

34. This pervasion is somewhat akin to marriage, where the two become one flesh. Marriage unites a man and a woman, but it does not diminish either one or eliminate their proper characteristics.

35. Incidentally, this is why naturalistic evolution is incompatible with the Christian faith, for man is made to be in union with God—in Christ and permeated by the Holy Spirit. This, not a particular exegesis of a single word in Genesis 1, utterly demarcates Christianity from evolutionism.

36. Staniloae, *Experience of God*, 1:276, 248.

37. Adolf von Harnack, *History of Dogma*, trans. James Millar (London: Williams & Norgate, 1897), 3:165.

38. Gerald Bonner, "Augustine's Concept of Deification," *JTS* 37 (1986): 369–86; Gerald Bonner, "Deificare," in *Augustinus-Lexicon*, ed. C. Mayer (Basel: Schwabe & Co., 1986), 1:265–67; Gerald Bonner, "Deification, Divinization," in *Augustine Through the Ages: An Encyclopedia*, ed. Allan D. Fitzgerald (Grand Rapids: Eerdmans, 1999), 265–66; D. Meconi, "St. Augustine's Early Theory of Participation," *AugStud* 27 (1996): 81–98.

39. Serge Lancel, *Saint Augustine*, trans. Antonia Nevill (London: SCM Press, 2002), 132, 151.

"deiform," that is, as being conformed to the likeness of God and united with him.[40] A. N. Williams has explored in depth how the theme is preserved in Aquinas, a generation after Grosseteste, and she concludes that his doctrine of deification is compatible with that of Palamas. Her research undermines the claim that it is a peculiarly Eastern doctrine.[41] Recently, there has been a flurry of interest in Luther's teaching on deification, spearheaded by Finnish scholarship.[42] This has aroused much debate. Dennis Bielfeldt, for one, has called for greater conceptual clarity.[43] Carl Mosser directs attention to the theme in Calvin. In commenting on 2 Peter 1:4, Calvin writes of our "partaking of the divine nature" as "that than which nothing more outstanding can be imagined." In this we are raised up to God and united with him, "a grace the magnitude of which our minds can never fully grasp." The purpose of the gospel, Calvin says, is "to make us sooner or later like God." It is "a kind of deification" (*quasi deificari*).[44] But this is not all that he has to say on the theme. In fact, Mosser establishes that the theme occurs throughout his writings. Calvin addresses it while discussing man as the image of God, union with Christ the mediator (a topic central to his entire soteriology), baptism, the Lord's Supper, glorification, and the Trinity.[45]

Even the Westminster Assembly did not lose sight of this important point. While the Westminster Confession of Faith follows a strictly logical *ordo salutis* (effectual calling, justification, adoption, sanctification, saving faith, repentance, good works, perseverance), with only

40. Grosseteste, *On the Six Days of Creation*, 48.

41. A. N. Williams, *The Ground of Union: Deification in Aquinas and Palamas* (New York: Oxford University Press, 1999), passim, esp. 157–75.

42. See in particular Simo Peura, *Mehr als ein Mensch? Die Vergöttlichung als Thema der Theologie Martin Luthers von 1513 bis 1519*, Veröffentlichungen des Instituts für europäische Geschichte (Mainz: Verlag Philipp von Zabern, 1994). The pioneer of the Finnish school is Tuomo Mannermaa, who argues that deification (*theoÿamsis*) pervades Luther's thought until his last commentary on Genesis; see Tuomo Mannermaa, *Der im Glauben gegenwärtige Christus: Rechtfertigung und Vergottung zum ökumenischen Dialog* (Hanover: Arbeiten zur Geschichte und Theologie des Luthertums, 1989); Tuomo Mannermaa, "*Theosis* als Thema der finnischen Lutherforschung," in *Luther und Theosis: Vergöttlichung als Thema der abendländischen Theologie*, ed. Simo Peura (Helsinki: Luther-Agricola-Gesellschaft, 1990), 11–26.

43. Dennis Bielfeldt, "Deification as a Motif in Luther's *Dictata super Psalterium*," *SCJ* 28 (1997): 401–20.

44. Carl Mosser, "The Greatest Possible Blessing: Calvin and Deification," *SJT* 55 (2002): 40–41.

45. Ibid., 36–57.

the slightest nod in the direction of glorification, the Westminster Larger Catechism knows no such reticence. It is subtly different from the Confession, placing the entire *ordo salutis* under the umbrella of "union and communion with Christ in grace and glory."[46] The members of the invisible church "by Christ enjoy union and communion with him in grace and glory,"[47] which "is the work of God's grace, whereby they are spiritually and mystically, yet really and inseparably, joined to Christ as their head."[48] This union and communion is not merely symbolic or figurative. It is more than metaphorical. It is real. It is brought about by the Holy Spirit and, being mystical, defies attempts to explain it logically. It is also inseparable, for we can no more be severed from Christ than can he be severed from his humanity.[49] The Catechism then goes on to place the whole process of salvation in this life, from justification onward, under communion with Christ.[50] The entire series of questions from 65 to 90 is the working out of union and communion with Christ, in this life and beyond. Finally, at the Day of Judgment, the righteous (now acquitted and forever freed from sin and misery) "shall be made perfectly holy and happy . . . in the immediate vision and fruition of God the Father, of our Lord Jesus Christ, and of the Holy Spirit, to all eternity. And this is the perfect full communion, which the members of the invisible church shall enjoy with Christ in glory."[51] Our ultimate destiny, according to the Westminster divines, consists in unbridled fruition (enjoyment) of the Holy Trinity. This "fruition" is both communion and union. It is focused on Christ.

Let us put this in context. Regeneration, calling, and justification by faith all occur at the start of the Christian life. Redemption from sin and Satan by the blood of Christ is also a once-for-all event, but it is paired with our adoption as the children of God and so continues on during our life in Christ.[52] Sanctification occurs also when we are

46. WLC, QQ. 65–90.
47. WLC, Q. 65.
48. WLC, Q. 66.
49. Cf. WLC, QQ. 36–40.
50. WLC, Q. 69.
51. WLC, Q. 90.
52. Tim Trumper, "The Metaphorical Import of Adoption: A Plea for Realisation: I: The Adoption Metaphor in Biblical Usage," *SBET* 14, no. 2 (autumn 1996): 129–45; Tim Trumper, "The Metaphorical Import of Adoption: A Plea for Realisation: II: The Adoption Metaphor in Theological Usage," *SBET* 15, no. 2 (autumn 1997): 98–115.

separated from sin and made alive together with Christ,[53] but it is then a process throughout the rest of our lives, during which we are progressively conformed to the image of Christ. All these aspects of salvation relate to events here and now, to the path by which we travel to our final destiny. They are the means by which we are saved. On the other hand, glorification (in Western terminology), or deification (according to the East),[54] is brought to fruition at the eschaton and lasts for eternity, and so is the final goal of salvation. It is true that in some respects this has already begun. Paul uses the aorist *edoxasen* (glorified) in Romans 8:30, implying that it is so sure that it has, in effect, already happened.[55] This reminds us of the lines of Isaac Watts, "the men of grace have found, glory begun below." I have written elsewhere on how the Lord's Supper anticipates the great eschatological feast, the marriage supper of the Lamb. Here and now, in the sacrament, our union with Christ is cultivated and we are prepared for the ultimate goal of union with the Holy Trinity.[56] Nevertheless, since time is created by God and so is good, we should recognize that this is not to be realized fully until the future.[57]

The Trinity, Sharing God's Nature, and How We Treat Others

Toon sums up much of what we have said when he observes that "the Christian understanding of personhood flows from the Christian doctrine of the Three Persons who are God," and so "if God is simply a monad then he cannot be or know personality. To be personal

53. John Murray, "Definitive Sanctification," *CTJ* 2 (1967): 5–21.
54. Note that in the Bible "glory" is associated with God. It belongs strictly to him and sets him apart from his creatures.
55. Cranfield comments that the use of the aorist is "significant and suggestive." Glorification is already foreordained by God. He has decreed it. Christ is already glorified, and in him the glorification of justified people is already accomplished. C. E. B. Cranfield, *A Critical and Exegetical Commentary on the Epistle to the Romans*, International Critical Commentary (Edinburgh: T & T Clark, 1979), 1:433. Leon Morris agrees that Paul writes as if it were already accomplished. See Leon Morris, *The Epistle to the Romans* (Grand Rapids: Eerdmans, 1988), 333–34.
56. Robert Letham, *The Lord's Supper: Eternal Word in Broken Bread* (Phillipsburg, N.J.: P&R Publishing, 2001).
57. Hebrews 2:5–6 describes the human race as partners with God in the administration of the cosmos. Jesus, as man, fulfills Psalm 8 and is now crowned with glory and honor at the right hand of God. As the pioneer of our salvation, he is bringing us to that place, too, where the whole cosmos will be directed by Christ and all who are in him.

otherness must be present together with oneness, the one must be in relation to others."[58] This drives us inexorably to our conclusion that we are called to worship the Holy Trinity, to live in loving and joyful union and communion with the Holy Trinity, and—precisely because of that—to live in loving communion with other human beings.

Once again, we return to Philippians 2:5–11. Have this mind in you which was also in Christ, Paul says to the Philippians. The incarnate Christ followed a path of obedience and humiliation, leading to the cruel and—for those in Philippi, a Roman colony—shameful death of the cross. He looked not to his own interests, in contrast to the First Adam, but to those of others. This loving, self-sacrificial obedience was the fruit of his decision in eternity not to exploit his status of being "in the form of God."[59] This is what the eternal Son is like. We are to follow his example, for this is what God is like. When he seeks his glory, he is not pursuing self-interest like a celestial bully. It is not that he is more powerful than we are, and so his pursuit of his own glory wins out, come what may. Since he is an undivided union of three persons, a union of love, each seeking the interests of the other, we can follow him on a creaturely level. Hebrews 5 runs along similar lines, referring to Christ's refusal to claim the office of high priest for himself, but rather accepting his appointment by the Father. We noted earlier how this self-effacement cannot be restricted to his incarnate ministry, since the appointment to high priesthood preceded the high priesthood itself. v. 4-5 amp

Thus, the Father allows the Son to bring in the kingdom, the Son leads us to the Father, while the Spirit does not speak of himself but testifies of the Son.[60] This was pointed out originally by Gregory of Nyssa, when he wrote that in their mutual indwelling, the three seek the glory of the others. There is, he says, "a revolving circle of glory from like to like. The Son is glorified by the Spirit; the Father is glorified by the Son; again the Son has his glory from the Father; and the Only-begotten thus

---

58. Peter Toon, *Our Triune God: A Biblical Portrayal of the Trinity* (Wheaton, Ill.: Bridge-Point, 1996), 241.

59. On the phrase *en morphē theou*, see *inter alia* Ralph P. Martin, *Carmen Christi: Philippians ii 5–11 in Recent Interpretation and in the Setting of Early Christian Worship* (Grand Rapids: Eerdmans, 1983), 99–133.

60. Wolfhart Pannenberg, *Systematic Theology*, trans. Geoffrey W. Bromiley (Grand Rapids: Eerdmans, 1991), 1:315–17.

becomes the glory of the Spirit. . . . In like manner . . . faith completes the circle, and glorifies the Son by means of the Spirit, and the Father by means of the Son."[61] Eugraphe Kovalevsky similarly comments that "the character of the hypostasis of the Holy Spirit is to love by eclipsing himself, as the Father by forgetting himself loves the Son in whom he has placed all his joy, and as the Son is beloved because he puts off his own 'I' in order that the Father may be made manifest and the Spirit shine forth."[62] In a way similar to that of C. S. Lewis, Staniloae argues that perfect love requires many "I's" who love one another while remaining unconfused, and also requires the highest degree of unity among them. He argues that, apart from the existence of perfect eternal love, there can be no explanation for love in the world. This love does not produce the divine persons, but rather presupposes them.[63]

The priority of love is stressed by John. In the fourth gospel, his main theme is Jesus' identity with God. Jesus is equal to God and one with him. He and the Father indwell one another. Indeed, Jesus is the Word made flesh, the one who made the world and who himself is God. In 1 John he insists that Jesus, the Son of God, has come in the flesh. He who is from eternity is also true man. In turn, we who believe have fellowship with him. Following his comment that when Christ returns we shall be like him (1 John 3:2), John mentions "the message that you have heard from the beginning, that we should love one another" (1 John 3:11). This is the proof that we have passed from death to life (v. 14), and it takes practical form in meeting the physical needs of our brothers and sisters (vv. 17–18). Indeed, according to John, God's commandment is that we believe in Jesus Christ his Son and love one another (v. 23). There follows a possible citation of a hymn fragment, referring to love (1 John 4:7–10):

> Beloved, let us love one another, for love is of God,
> and everyone who loves has been born of God and knows God.
> He who does not love does not know God,
> because God is love.
> In this the love of God is made known among us,

61. Gregory of Nyssa, *Dogmatic Treatises, Etc.*, in NPNF², 5:324.
62. Eugraphe Kovalevsky, "Saint Trinité," *Cahiers de Saint Irénée* 44 (January-February 1964): 3, cited by Staniloae, *Experience of God*, 1:279n29.
63. Staniloae, *Experience of God*, 1:245.

that God sent his only begotten Son into the world
that we might live through him.
In this is love; not that we loved God
but that he loved us,
and sent his Son as propitiation for our sins.[64]

Since God himself is love (1 John 4:16), and we have fellowship and communion with him, love is the acid test of our discipleship. If we love others, we belong to Jesus Christ. If we lack love, we are not his at all. God is a triune communion of persons. Love is intrinsic to who he is. Attributes like grace, mercy, justice, and even holiness are all relative to creatures. His wrath is relative to sinners, as the expression of his holiness in response to human sin. Love, however, belongs to who he is in himself in the undivided communion of the three persons. The Father loves the Son. The Son loves the Father. The Father loves the Holy Spirit. The Holy Spirit loves the Father. The Son loves the Holy Spirit. The Holy Spirit loves the Son. This reciprocal love of the three persons exists in the unbreakable union of the undivided Trinity. In that we are enabled to be "partakers of the divine nature," "changed from glory to glory" by the Spirit of the Lord, we are brought into this communion of the love of God.

The unity and purity of the church require this. This is our calling as Christians. It stands in stark contrast to abusive churches, where the leaders hijack the congregation for their own personal agendas. Where individual believers are subject to dictation by those in power, there the purpose of the church is negated. Even more, it is definitively *ungodly*, for it is the opposite of what God is like and what human beings are to be as those who are in his image. This is a particular problem in conservative churches, where there is a serious attempt to follow the Bible. Here there is a temptation for the leaders to think that God is on their side in a whole range of matters, down to the fine print. In independent churches, where there exists no outside check, it is not uncommon, but no pattern of church government is exempt from the danger. The point is that the slippery slope to self-aggrandizement is something on which Jesus Christ, the servant of the Lord, did not travel. He emptied himself. He became obedient to the cross.

64. My translation.

The mission of the church to spread the gospel also requires the practice of love, of self-effacement, of looking to the interests of others. Without it, our preaching will be undermined. With it, it is reinforced. We have only to recall the comments of the primitive church's contemporaries, as recorded in Acts—"See how they love one another"—to understand that this is powerful reinforcement of the gospel message on a human level, and that the lack of it is the greatest single barrier to its advance. Especially in the context of engagement with Muslims, the love paradigm of Richard of St. Victor is pertinent, provided it is biblically based, rather than forged out of Richard's rationalism. We saw how, in the last century, it was adopted by Bulgakov, Lossky, and Staniloae in the East, and by Moltmann and others in the West. However, their respective theologies have sundry other defects, which are not to be copied. Notwithstanding, it is precisely with the question of love that the Islamic doctrine of Allah founders, and, with it, the Islamic doctrine of humanity. Again, when we think of the postmodern West, it is the nonmanipulative, self-sacrificial love of the Trinity, seen in the Incarnation and the atoning sacrifice of the Son that should be center stage. It is, then, the Trinity that "assures our continuance and perfection as persons to all eternity,"[65] and it is the Trinity that provides the sole basis for the greatest of all human tasks. Jerome records the story of the apostle John, being carried around in advanced age by his disciples and repeating over and over, "Little children, love one another." When asked why he only said these words, John replied, "Because it is the Lord's command, and if this only is done, it is enough."[66]

> *Almighty and everlasting God, who has given unto us your servants grace by the confession of a true faith to acknowledge the glory of the eternal trinity, and in the power of the divine majesty to worship the unity. We beseech you, that you would keep us steadfast in this faith, and evermore defend us from all adversities, who lives and reigns one God, world without end. Amen.*[67]

65. Staniloae, *Experience of God*, 1:247.
66. See J. R. W. Stott, *The Epistles of John: An Introduction and Commentary* (London: Tyndale Press, 1964), 49.
67. Collect for Trinity Sunday, *The Book of Common Prayer according to the Use of the Church of England* (Oxford: Oxford University Press, n.d.), 160 (personal pronouns modernized).

A P P E N D I X 1

Gilbert Bilezikian
and Bungee Jumping

In an article published in 1997,[1] Gilbert Bilezikian, professor emeritus at Wheaton College, takes me to task for an article that appeared in *WTJ* in 1990.[2] In particular, he attacks me—along with Wayne Grudem—for suggesting that there is an order among the persons of the Trinity that, on the grounds that man is made in the image of God, can help us understand the relationship between the human sexes. Men are entrusted with headship and authority in spheres such as the church and the family, yet men and women are equal, both made in the image of God. This mirrors the irreversible relations of the persons of the Trinity. The Father sends the Son, never vice versa, while the Son lovingly submits to the Father. Yet the three distinct persons are utterly equal in status and identical in being. What concerns us here are the Trinitarian issues that arise. Bilezikian's ideas are representative of a broad swathe of evangelical opinion. It is necessary first to see something of his criticism of me.

First, his article is full of misquotation and misinterpretation. I argue that the Bible says that the Father sends the Son. This reflects an irreversible order between the Father and the Son. Both are equal

---

1. Gilbert Bilezikian, "Hermeneutical Bungee-Jumping: Subordination in the Trinity," *JETS* 40 (1997): 57–68.
2. Robert Letham, "The Man-Woman Debate: Theological Comment," *WTJ* 52 (1990): 65–78.

479

in the unity of God, and this order exists in such a way as to be compatible with that unity and equality. Yet Bilezikian cites my statement, "In terms of God's actions in the history of redemption and revelation we note a clear order,"[3] in these words: "In terms of God's actions in the history of redemption and revelation we note a clear order [hierarchy]."[4] His insertion of the word "hierarchy" within the citation leads his readers to conclude that I advocate a hierarchy in the Trinity, despite my never using that word in the passage cited or in the entire article—or anywhere else, for that matter! Instead, I consistently use the word "order." This translates the Greek word τάξις (taxis). I use this term in the orthodox sense, denoting a suitable disposition, rather than in the Arian sense of rank.[5] Bilezikian attacks me for using it in the Arian sense. It leads me to wonder whether he is even aware of the different usages.

Following this, without citing any evidence (for which there is none), he attributes the term *subordination* to me—a term I never use and steadfastly deny. I never use *subordination* or *hierarchy* or their functional equivalents—indeed, I sedulously avoid them. With these distortions, Bilezikian writes of my "ontologically stratified, split-level Trinity," which apparently leads me straight into the trap of Arianism (!). I give lip service to the coequality of the members of the Trinity, while in the same breath denying this equality. "On the one hand, Letham cannot bring himself to sacrifice the oneness of the Godhead. On the other, he is driven to superimpose upon it an order of hierarchy."[6]

Bilezikian's problem seems to be the idea of an order in the Trinity, which he thinks "means an ontologically structured hierarchy."[7] Yet this is the classic form of Trinitarian theology. God is one being and three persons. The three are of the identical essence and indwell each other. None is more God, or less God, than the others. In relation to each other, the Father begets the Son, and the Father (and the Son) spirate the Spirit. In the economy, the Father sends the Son, and the Father (and the Son) send the Spirit. These relations are irreversible. An order exists. Both East and West recognize it, and it is to that order

3. Ibid., 68.
4. Bilezikian, "Hermeneutical Bungee-Jumping," 63.
5. G. W. H. Lampe, ed., *A Patristic Greek Lexicon* (Oxford: Clarendon Press, 1961), 1372–73.
6. Bilezikian, "Hermeneutical Bungee-Jumping," 64.
7. Ibid.

that I draw attention in the early part of the article. Bilezikian either ignores or rejects this order. This is not a split-level Trinity, nor is there a boss-servant relation.

Having imported by misinterpretation the idea of subordination, Bilezikian then paints me into a corner. The word *subordination* crops up repeatedly in his article, referring to my comments, although I never use it. He flatly ignores my statement that the order among the persons involves no question of superiority.[8] I repeatedly assert that this order is compatible with the full equality of the three persons in the undivided Trinity. With regard to the question of male and female in human society, I am vehement against the subjection of women, on the grounds that this is a sin against God, saying that "sinful domination by the man over the woman (or vice-versa) is a negation of the coequality with which man is to image God."[9] Elsewhere I have written that "the oppression of women is sin against women, men and God himself. . . . Evangelical feminists as well as patriarchal traditionalists will do well to consider this."[10] The basis of these conclusions is the unity and coequality of the Holy Trinity. Bilezikian has evidently not read carefully enough, but selectively culled a phrase here, a phrase there. This will not do. For example, he speaks of the efforts of Grudem and me "to assign a subsidiary role to the Son."[11] He should read my book entitled *The Work of Christ* to see whether I assign a subsidiary role to the Son.[12]

Emotive Phraseology

Bilezikian colors his writing by emotive turns of phrase. He writes of the order between the Father and the Son, as I expound it, leading to a "number two in the trinity," with the work of salvation imposed on the Son—his boss told him to do it, since it was a job no one else wanted to touch, with the result that he was dragged to death against his will.[13] This is a "split-level Trinity," he avers, with the Son being

8. Letham, "The Man-Woman Debate," 72.
9. Ibid., 73.
10. R. Letham, "The Hermeneutics of Feminism," *Them* 17 (January-April 1992): 7.
11. Bilezikian, "Hermeneutical Bungee-Jumping," 66.
12. Robert Letham, *The Work of Christ* (Leicester: Inter-Varsity Press, 1993).
13. Bilezikian, "Hermeneutical Bungee-Jumping," 59.

"a second-ranking officer of the trinity, the lower god in an Olympian hierarchy."[14] Bilezikian is enamored with his own rhetoric. He even suggests that I teach a functional autonomy of the Son from the Father![15] He says all this, despite my strong asseverations in the article that the relations in the Trinity are *not* to be understood in terms of human relations, let alone those existing in a fallen world. It is a relation "fully compatible with, and the appropriate expression of, full ontological equality."[16]

It seems I also reduce the work of salvation to "a particular limited purpose,"[17] thus belittling the grandeur of redemption. Bilezikian ignores the fact that I use this phrase to attack modalism, which reduces God's self-revelation in human history to a convention designed for our salvation, "a mode into which he had switched for a particular limited purpose, a form of being other than his own."[18] In short, what Bilezikian's fulminations lack in accuracy, they gain in vehemence and caricature. "Let us quit talking about subordination," Bilezikian fumes.[19] Yes, precisely.

Misunderstanding the Patristic Use of *Taxis*

Bilezikian does not appear to realize that an order (*taxis*) among the persons is part of Trinitarian orthodoxy. He states that after the Arian controversy "order or ranking" is excluded among the persons "concerning their eternal state."[20] He conflates two different concepts, one heretical, the other orthodox. The idea of rank is certainly heresy, of that we both agree. The Son and the Holy Spirit are not less than the Father, nor inferior to him. Each person is wholly God and the whole God. The three are no greater than any one. The Arians asserted that the Son was created and so is of a different being than the Father. Basil and Gregory of Nyssa at times implied that the three persons constitute a causal chain, with the Father being fully God, and the two

14. Ibid., 66.
15. Ibid., 67.
16. Letham, "The Man-Woman Debate," 73.
17. Bilezikian, "Hermeneutical Bungee-Jumping," 68.
18. Letham, "The Man-Woman Debate," 68.
19. Bilezikian, "Hermeneutical Bungee-Jumping," 67.
20. Ibid., 58.

others deriving their deity from him. However, the true order is not a rank, but an orderly disposition. In that order, with no diminution of deity or severance of unity or identity, the Father begets the Son and spirates the Spirit. In our salvation, the Father sends the Son. Never are these relations reversed. As Barth indicated, we can even argue—with caution—that the submission displayed by the Son while securing our redemption reflects eternal realities in God. This must be done in such a way as not to undermine the one being of God, in which all three persons completely inhere.

Bilezikian, however, argues that nowhere in Scripture is the Son said to obey the Father. This is not NT terminology, he insists.[21] This is rather surprising, since the gospel of John (the book that most emphatically declares the full deity of Christ) is full of statements by Jesus himself to this effect.

Viewing Christ's Functional Subjection as Temporary

Bilezikian argues that every passage in Scripture speaking of Christ's humiliation "pertains to his ministry and not to his eternal state."[22] In this he thinks differently than Augustine, who teaches that some statements in the Bible refer neither to the Son's deity nor to his humanity, but to him as the Son in relation to the Father. Moreover, Augustine expressly teaches that the Father sent the Son prior to the task about which the sending is concerned.[23] We saw in chapters 17 and 20 that Paul's statement in Philippians 2:5–11 about Christ's determination not to exploit his equality with God to his own advantage refers to the situation prior to his incarnation.

Bilezikian argues that if Christ's humiliation in his human life is not an event isolated from his eternal condition, his *kenosis* or self-emptying (Phil. 2:7) is stripped of its uniqueness. His incarnate condition, Belezikian contends, was contrary to everything that went before. If instead it is seen as reflecting eternal realities in God, it becomes normative.[24] Instead, Christ's "functional subjection is not

---

21. Ibid., 65.
22. Ibid., 60.
23. Augustine, *On the Trinity* 2.5.7–9.
24. Bilezikian, "Hermeneutical Bungee-Jumping," 65.

an eternal condition but a task-driven, temporary phase of ministry."[25]
We shall consider this far-reaching assertion in a moment.

Conclusions

Perhaps Bilezikian can tell us how he manages to avoid modalism, for he appears bent on erasing every distinction between the Father and the Son within the undivided and coequal Trinity. He points in that direction when he says (with historical inaccuracy) that the councils excluded every form of hierarchy, order, or ranking among the persons of the Trinity in their eternal state.[26] He is correct about excluding hierarchy and rank. However, the councils insisted that an order exists among the persons. Differences of opinion about this order have been the greatest single occasion of the rift between the Eastern church and Western church. How can Bilezikian say that the councils excluded that which both East and West, with different paradigms, affirm?

Moreover, Barth aptly comments that in the incarnation we have direct dealings with God. Jesus is really God the Son. We do not have to deal with some proxy, some "forecourt of the divine being."[27] For Bilezikian, however, it appears that the Son does represent a kind of "forecourt of the divine being," for we do not have to do with God the Son himself; rather, he acted as he did to facilitate "a task-driven, temporary phase of ministry," without saying anything about his eternal identity. Yet our salvation depends on the fact that we deal with God himself in Christ, not with some temporary transmogrification. If Jesus is not a true revelation of God, we are forever lost. This question of modalism is a crucial one, for it would seem that for Bilezikian Christ is only a temporary appearance. He does not reflect the eternal Son as he is. His obedience on earth is merely "a task-driven temporary phase of ministry."[28] This view leads to the conclusion that the Christ who walked the earth is not identical to the eternal Son of God. Bilezikian is distancing himself from the assumption of the Fathers that the way in which God has revealed himself in human history points

25. Ibid., 61.
26. Ibid., 66.
27. Karl Barth, *CD*, IV/1: 196–97, but also the whole of 192–205.
28. Bilezikian, "Hermeneutical Bungee-Jumping," 61.

reliably to who he is eternally. Henri de Lubac comments that "it is through the 'economy,' and only through it, that we have access to 'theology.'"[29] Bilezikian chooses to ignore or reject the phrases in C, the only ecumenical statement of faith there is, one confessed throughout the centuries, that the Son is "light *from light*, true God *from true God.*" As Rainbow says, no orthodox church father and no ecumenical church council has ever adopted Bilezikian's ideas.[30]

Bilezikian's position appears pious and plausible, since he so emphatically stresses the deity of Christ. However, it is subtly misleading. For one thing, it destroys prayer. In prayer, as Jesus taught us, we share by grace the relation he has by nature eternally with the Father. We call on God as "our Father," as he did. However, according to Bilezikian, the Son does not sustain the relation to the Father in eternity that he showed in his life on earth, since the latter is a "singularity,"[31] adopted temporarily in order to bring about our redemption. Is the relation into which we are brought by the incarnate One a "singularity" too?

Furthermore, Bilezikian's position shows striking similarities with some aspects of the theology of Marcellus of Ancyra. Marcellus, we recall from chapter 5, was an eager proponent of the Council of Nicaea at a time when its anathemas were more clearly supportive of a Sabellian interpretation. Later, when clarity of language emerged, his views were rejected.

First, Marcellus had such an overpowering focus on the unity of God that he had no room to accommodate personal distinctions. There was simply one God in one *hypostasis*. Before creation, the Logos was in God, but had no distinct existence of his or its own.[32] Bilezikian does not hold to this. However, he does focus on the unity and equality of the three at the expense of a corresponding emphasis on their distinctiveness. For Marcellus, like Bilezikian, the deity of Christ was (correctly) an axiom, the Logos being one with God, as a man is with his reason.[33]

29. Henri de Lubac, *The Christian Faith: An Essay on the Structure of the Apostles' Creed* (San Francisco: Ignatius Press, 1986), 91–92, cited by Paul A. Rainbow, "Orthodox Trinitarianism and Evangelical Feminism," available at www.cbmw.org/resources/articles/orthodox_trinitarianism_feminism.pdf, 8.

30. Rainbow, "Orthodox Trinitarianism," 9–10.

31. Ibid., 65.

32. Marcellus, "Die Fragmente Marcells," in GCS 14, Fr. 92, p. 207.

33. Henry Melvill Gwatkin, *Studies of Arianism* (Cambridge: Deighton Bell, 1900), 81–83.

Bilezikian and Marcellus agree that lowly titles given to Christ in the NT refer to his incarnate state only, not to his eternal state. Marcellus considers that Christ was called Son only after the Incarnation, and so the Father-Son relation cannot be read back into God prior to creation.[34] Where Paul, in Colossians, describes Christ as "the first-born of all creation" or "the image of the invisible God," Marcellus says that this concerns "the economy of his flesh,"[35] "his birth according to the flesh, not his original state as others say."[36] Statements such as these cannot be applied to eternity.[37] They refer to his lowly condition only. He is only called Son after the Incarnation.[38] Similarly, Bilezikian argues that Christ's humiliation in his incarnate state is a "singularity" that cannot be part of the immanent Trinity.

Bilezikian comes strikingly close to Marcellus on the temporary nature of the Incarnation. For Marcellus, the Logos is the Son only from his birth to the final judgment, when he will revert to his state as the Logos in God. The incarnate state will then end.[39] Christ's kingdom lasts from his resurrection until its terminus at the final judgment[40] (hence the refuting phrase in C that the Son's kingdom shall have no end). Similarly, for Bilezikian, Christ's functional subjection in his incarnate state was "a task-driven, temporary phase of ministry." His incarnate ministry and his eternal state are separate. The former is not normative for the latter.[41] For Marcellus, the Incarnation was merely for the conquest of Satan,[42] so once creation is delivered from bondage, there will be no further need for the form of a servant that the Logos adopted.[43]

Perhaps Bilezikian can also tell us how he avoids Nestorianism. His overwhelming focus on the unity of the Son with the Father cannot but serve—like Marcellus's—to loosen the unity of God and man in Christ.[44]

34. Ibid., 83.
35. Marcellus, "Die Fragmente Marcells," Fr. 4, p. 186.
36. Ibid., Fr. 5, p. 186.
37. Ibid., Fr. 6–8, p. 186.
38. Ibid., Fr. 31, p. 190.
39. Ibid., Fr. 103, p. 209.
40. Ibid., Fr. 101, p. 209.
41. Bilezikian, "Hermeneutical Bungee-Jumping," 60–65.
42. Gwatkin, *Studies*, 84.
43. Marcellus, "Die Fragmente Marcells," Fr. 106, p. 211.
44. Winrich A. Lohr, "A Sense of Tradition: The Homoiousion Church Party," in *Arianism After Arius: Essays on the Development of the Fourth Century Trinitarian Conflicts*, ed. Michel R. Barnes (Edinburgh: T & T Clark, 1993), 92.

Marcellus's view requires a theophany, rather than an incarnation,[45] and so it would seem does Bilezikian's. If we follow the argument in chapter 17, it is difficult to see how Bilezikian can preserve the unity and integrity of the person of Christ, if Christ's human nature obeys God, but his divine nature (and it is the Son who personalizes the incarnate Christ, according to Constantinople II[46]) does not and cannot render submission to the Father. In other words, it seems inescapable that in Bilezikian's Christology there is a split between the Son, whose eternal mode is free from obedience or submission to the Father, and the human nature, which does obey. The result is a person with two radically incompatible natures. Again, since humanity has been taken into permanent union with the Son of God, how on this basis can Bilezikian address the eternal consequences of the Incarnation, its permanent and ongoing existence? The hypostatic union still exists and does so forever. On the other hand, Bilezikian's claim—like Marcellus's—that Christ's incarnate submission is temporary and task-oriented, implies that once the task is done, the submission is discarded. If so, we could not be saved, for salvation is received and fulfilled in union with Christ and emphatically requires that the incarnate state be unbreakable and everlasting. Christ is risen, never again to die (Rom. 6:9). Bilezikian refers to Christology as "a theological issue all of its own." Perhaps this is the problem, for the Fathers did not share that view. For them, the doctrine of the Trinity and Christology were interlocking, and they saw both as impinging directly on our salvation.

The title of Bilezikian's article argues his case that my discussion was akin to bungee jumping, constructed to prove something. It seems to me that Bilezikian is the bungee jumper, and as he disappears rapidly into the yawning chasm below, his harness is worryingly frayed.

---

45. Gwatkin, *Studies*, 86.

46. Aloys Grillmeier, *Christ in Christian Tradition*, vol. 2, *From the Council of Chalcedon (451) to Gregory the Great (590–604)*, part 2, *The Church of Constantinople in the Sixth Century*, trans. John Cawte (London: Mowbray, 1995), 438–62; B. Studer, "Enhypostasia," in *EECh* (1992), 1:272, who comments, "Every concrete nature, while always being in a hypostasis, does not necessarily exist in its own hypostasis. . . . Hence in Christ the hypostasis of the Logos is both the subject of the properties of the human nature and the principle of the subsistence of this nature, thus uniting the human properties with the divine properties and distinguishing that man from all others."

Kevin Giles on Subordinationism

Kevin Giles. *The Trinity and Subordinationism*. Downers Grove, Ill.: InterVarsity Press, 2002.

Kevin Giles, vicar of St. Michael's Church in North Carlton, Australia, has for thirty years contended for the ordination of women. He has specialized in NT studies and is a graduate of Moore College, Sydney, the largest theological college in the country, with a strongly Reformed orientation and located in the most conservative diocese in the older countries of the Anglican communion. This book may become a major resource for those who share his views. It may well persuade others to join them. It is well written and covers a lot of ground.

Giles argues powerfully for the full equality of men and women. Both are created in the image of God. He targets conservative evangelicals who maintain a hierarchical view of the sexes on the basis of a presumed hierarchy of being, function, or role in the Trinity. By *subordinationism* he means the idea that the Son is eternally set under the Father. He is hostile to the 1999 Sydney Anglican Diocesan Doctrine Commission Report: *The Doctrine of the Trinity and Its Bearing on the Relationship of Men and Women*, which he includes in an appendix. He refers to Athanasius, the Cappadocians, Augustine, and the ancient creeds to claim that the idea that the Son is subordinate in function or personal subsistence is dangerously close to heretical and has no basis in the tradition of the church. Instead, the Trinity is a communion of three coequal persons. All forms of subordinationism are ruled out, both by Scripture and church tradition. From this it follows that arguments for the subordination of women cannot be buttressed by appeal to the Trinity.

Giles argues that there is a case study of a similar nature. Until the nineteenth century, Christians uniformly believed that slavery was ordained by God, but now hardly anyone holds to that opinion. Times have changed, Western culture has moved on, and with it our interpretation of Scripture has altered. So too in the case of women; since the 1960s, widespread education and new methods of contraception have caused massive social and cultural upheavals. Women have a radically altered place in today's world. With these changes, many evangelicals now read the Bible in a new light and, as with the old slavery tradition, see women's subordination not only as culturally outdated, but as theologically insupportable.

So much, in a nutshell, for Giles's case. He has some ready targets, for there has been some misguided language by some of his opponents—the phrase "the eternal subordination of the Son" is outside the boundaries of the tradition and Giles is right to point this out. This is a powerfully written and often compelling argument, the best I have read from his perspective. Why do I dissent from his conclusions?

First, his hermeneutics are open to serious questioning. Giles is right to argue that the Bible is to be read theologically (is there any other way?). However, he gives undue scope to what he calls "God's work in history." "Texts are not self-interpreting. They are only symbols on a page until a human agent gives them meaning" (p. 8). Thus, as "God's work in history" progresses, we may develop new interpretations of Scripture. Such applies to slavery and women. However, since God's work in history is dynamic and ongoing, who is to say that the next generation may not reject this generation's insights? Notably, Giles does not consider the intention of the original author, who has disappeared from the scene. His text is a piece of putty, to be shaped by each successive cultural epoch.

Moreover, this lack of fixity in biblical interpretation is matched by a similarly open-ended basis for ethics. We are not to look to the past for ethical guidance, Giles insists. The devil was present in creation. Instead, our conduct is to be shaped by eschatology. Requirements grounded in creation do not apply to us today. Present practice is to be based on our future destiny. "The ideal is in the future, in the age to come" (p. 177). The Bible is always to be interpreted in accordance with this forward-looking perspective (p. 202). To appeal to creation for the basis of social order "contradicts the overall teaching of Scripture" (p. 179). Hence, women are to be freed from all forms of submission. None of the biblical exhortations to women to be in submission apply today (pp. 203, 268), for Paul's statements are culturally conditioned and do not apply to us. Gene Haas, of Redeemer College, Ontario, is working on a major critical treatment of eschatological ethics, which we eagerly await. For now, the content of such ethics is hardly definable. It entails superseding the law, for the Decalogue is the republication and application of creation ordinances, which Giles invites us to leave behind. It tallies with his aversion to talk of obedience. Jesus is never said to obey the Father, he opines.

Giles is emphatic that "through the change in culture God is screaming out to us" (pp. 201–2). Not all the Bible is to be obeyed, but God "screams out to us" through changes in the world around us. Where, we ask Giles, is the word of God to be found? Out of which culture(s) of the world does God scream? Do his screams emanate from anywhere other than white, professional, Western circles at the start of the twenty-first century? When cultures clash, are God's sounds discordant? Who is to determine what cultural changes are canonical?

A second problem concerns Giles's selectivity. The classic doctrine of the Trinity affirms that the three persons are of one identical essence and are coequal eternally. The three mutually indwell one another, yet are irreducibly distinct. The Father is not the Son, the Son is not the Father, and so on. Moreover, there is an order (*taxis*) among them. This is not an order of rank, as the Arians and Eunomians argued, in which the three are arranged in some form of hierarchy. It is more akin to a suitable disposition, a well-arranged constitution (see G. W. H. Lampe, ed., *A Patristic Greek Lexicon*, 1372–73). Thus, the Father begets the Son and spirates the Spirit, the Son is begotten, and so on. In turn, the Father sends the Son, and the Father and the Son send the Spirit. These relations are not reversible, although the three have a mutuality since they are all equal, and are each—as well as together—the whole God. Giles has a strong and emphatic grasp of the consubstantiality of the Son and the Spirit with the Father, of that there is no doubt. However, while paying lip service to the order, he does not give anywhere near corresponding stress to the distinctions of the three persons.

His selectivity comes to the fore in his treatment of three theologians in particular. He accuses Charles Hodge of teaching that the Trinity is a hierarchy, the Father communicating the divine essence to the Son in generating him (pp. 71–74). This is a misreading of Hodge, who denies that derivation of essence is involved or that there is a difference in rank between the Father and the Son (*Systematic Theology*, 1:468–70). Giles states that Hodge approves Pearson's claim that the Father is preeminent, but Hodge cites Pearson as an example of *speculation* that goes far beyond the facts of Scripture, something the Reformers were not prepared to do. Moreover, Hodge refers to the Nicene fathers so as to distance himself from their speculations, not endorse them.

Giles, to his credit, does consider Barth's remarkable and stimulating discussion of the obedience of Christ (*CD*, IV/1: 192–205), in which he suggests that Christ's obedience during his incarnate ministry reveals something of a divine obedience in eternity (pp. 86–91). However, Giles prunes out anything that might undermine his own thesis. Throughout, Barth refers to Jesus Christ as the acting subject in the Incarnation, while Giles interprets this of God, the whole Trinity, on the basis of Augustine's dictum *opera Trinitatis ab extra indivisa sunt*. Most egregious is this citation from *CD*, IV/1: 202: "Therefore we have to draw the no less astounding deduction that in equal Godhead the one God is, in fact, the One and also Another, that he is indeed a First and a Second." However, Giles omits from this Barth's preceding sentence, the first of the paragraph, governing the words he does cite: "As we look at Jesus Christ we cannot avoid the astounding conclusion of a divine obedience." If Giles had included this sentence, it would have torpedoed his entire argument. He leaves it out.

Giles also refers to an article of mine in the *WTJ* in 1990, originally composed some years before. He accuses me of subordinationism and a hierarchical view of the Trinity. This despite the fact that in the early pages I state most emphatically the unity and coequality of the three persons, and—following Barth—that the submission or obedience of the Son in the Trinity is in terms of the order, the relations of the persons, and is *such as is fully compatible with their unity and equality*. I may have made an unfortunate turn of phrase at one point, but my only reference to subordination(ism) is wholly negative, and to superiority/inferiority in the Trinity (twice) is entirely dismissive, and of hierarchy or command there is not so much as a whisper. That does not stop Giles from labeling his opponents in the most lurid terms (although he concedes that Hodge, the Moore College faculty, and I are not true Arians!). In the last three years, I have been accused in print of anti-Welsh prejudice, of being an outspoken proponent of "the Shepherd-Gaffin theology" and now of subordinationism—all untrue, but what a heady mix!

Giles is trapped in the Trinitarian paradigm of the Western church. Augustine found some difficulty in doing justice to the three, in particular to the Holy Spirit. The West since has found this even more difficult. Giles cites approvingly Aquinas's definition of persons as subsistent relations (p. 74), but he is evidently unaware of the work of Christopher Hughes (1989), who argues that, with his powerful doctrine of the divine simplicity, Aquinas is scarcely able to be Trinitarian, and could at best accommodate a modified Sabellianism. Giles is similarly uncritical of Rahner, who has been widely accused of modalism. His treatment of Rahner's famous axiom (that the economic Trinity is the immanent Trinity, and the immanent Trinity is the economic Trinity) fails to see that it has been most commonly used to collapse the immanent Trinity, to support a form of pantheism or panentheism. Paul Molnar's fine volume on the immanent Trinity (2002) should be read here. Giles makes a few cursory references to Easterners—Lossky and Zizioulas—but shows little interest in their perspective. This is not surprising, since the Eastern stress on the Father as the *Archē* would not strengthen his case at all. He also lumps all recent Trinitarian theology together into one unified movement that has as its intent to eliminate all forms of subordinationism. In fact, it is far from monolithic. Molnar's work underlines that. It is good that Giles has read T. F. Torrance, but he makes no mention of Gunton's critical questioning of whether Torrance has paid sufficient attention to the distinctions between the persons. Moreover, if anything, the bulk of writing in this field has followed particular agendas: ecumenical, ecological, egalitarian. In part, Giles acknowledges this (p. 104). It can hardly be said uniformly to have favored theological orthodoxy. Much of it is panentheistic at best.

Additionally, I have some serious theological questions to ask. Hovering in the background are some troubling modalist tendencies. When an author is so vehement against one error, there is a good chance that he is in danger of the opposite. Has Giles come to terms with the Incarnation? He appears to suggest that it is temporary (pp. 30, 116). The diocesan report puts its finger on this point too, when it says that "the differences between the co-equal persons of the Trinity are not only voluntary or temporary" (p. 129). Since we are saved in union with Christ, if Christ's humanity is for a temporary phase only, we cannot be saved. That is how crucial this is. Does Giles properly appreciate the significance of the Incarnation? He says it is *only one scene* in the God-directed drama of creation, redemption, and consummation (p. 30). The Incarnation does not differentiate the Father from the Son, but indicates their unity (p. 31). Giles is right that all three persons are engaged in all of God's works and ways. However, *only* the Son—not the Father, nor the Holy Spirit—entered into hypostatic union with our humanity, and he did so forever. He is raised from the dead, never again to die (Rom. 6:9). The diocesan report is right when it warns that the approach favored by Giles leads to a case for *undifferentiated* equality (p. 136).

Along these lines, Giles says that Augustine precludes reading the Son's incarnate work back into the Trinity (p. 198). He is wrong. Augustine says that the sending of the Word precedes the work for which he is sent. "For the Son is from the Father, not the Father from the Son. And . . . the Son is not only said to have been sent because the Word was made flesh, but therefore sent that the Word might be made flesh." So the Word "was sent that it might be made man; because he was not sent in respect to any inequality of power, or substance, or anything that in him was not equal to the Father; but in respect to this, that the Son is from the Father, not the Father from the Son" (*De Trinitate* 2.5.7–9). His sending preceded his incarnation, and so his incarnate life and ministry can (as appropriate) reveal something of his eternal relations. If this were not so, we would be left with agnosticism, in flat contradiction to Jesus' own words that he who has seen him (in his lowliness) has seen the Father (John 14:9 et al.). Giles is certainly blind to the dangers of modalism. He does not seem to realize that the creed of Nicaea (325) was initially rejected by many because of its Sabellian associations—it anathematized those who denied the Son to be of the same *hypostasis* or *ousia* (p. 44). He also ignores the reference in the Niceno-Constantinopolitan Creed (381) to the relations of the persons (p. 46).

In the end, Giles's argument collapses. It is self-defeating. He has to point to the submission of Christ on earth as a paradigm for the mutual submission that he calls (rightly) on us all to display. So he says repeatedly that "voluntary subordination is godlike" (pp. 18, 31, 116, 117). Indeed, "what is Christlike is to subordinate oneself" (p. 117). Giles misses the point that if the Son submits to the Father in eternity, his submission could hardly have been imposed on him, for he is coequal with the Father, of the identical divine being. He submits willingly. The scholastics would call this the will of concomitance: it is this way and he wills it to be so, for the three have one united will. Giles even cites one of his heroes, Athanasius, to the effect that the divine Son willingly subordinated himself in the Incarnation (p. 37). But, we may ask, if he did so in the Incarnation without jeopardy to his deity, why is this not so in eternity? Since he has permanently united to himself the assumed human nature, does it not follow as something appropriate for the Son in his exaltation as well as in his humiliation, not as a slave to a master, but in the loving and willing communion of coequals?

Giles talks of women's inferiority being demonstrated by their exclusion from certain leadership responsibilities because of who they are (p. 17). His opponents' position traps a woman by her sexual identity. Who she is determines what she can do (p. 182). However, I too am similarly trapped. I cannot give birth to children, or nurse them, and so I am deprived of one of the most crucial tasks that God has given to the human race. Giles's problem is that he equates leadership with superiority, submission with something lesser. However, God has shown that loving, willing submission to others is superior. Those who are first will actually be last.

Finally, in discussing Adam and Eve, Giles never comes to grips with Romans 5:12–21 (p. 190). If they were created in a state of complete mutual reciprocity, exactly to the liking of the white, middle-class, educated, liberal-minded, early twenty-first-century intelligentsia, why does Paul say that all sinned *in Adam*? If the sin of Adam affects the whole race, it also affected Eve. If it affected Eve, then Adam was in some way her head and representative. If Eve was the first to sin, as the record of Genesis 3 indicates, or if, as Giles says, it was the fault of both of them, this is even more evident. Giles never discusses Romans 5. It would overturn his case. It is inconvenient for him. But I almost forgot—has the onward march of "God's work in history" superseded Romans 5?

Glossary

We cannot discuss the Trinity without using a range of theological terms. In order to help you as you read the book, I have listed below many words that may be unfamiliar if you have never studied theology formally.

adoptionism. An early heresy that held that Christ became the Son of God in his resurrection.

analogical predication. Argument based on analogy, where two things are similar, but not totally alike. This can take the form of attributing to God characteristics existent in creation (e.g., goodness), purging them of all created limitations and sinful inadequacies and extrapolating them to an infinite degree. Scholastic theology in the West often used this method in its consideration of God. However, Protestantism has generally rejected such an approach, basing talk about God on biblical revelation.

anhypostasia. The dogma that the human nature of Christ has no personal existence of its own, apart from the union into which it was assumed in the Incarnation. This means that the Son of God did not unite himself with a human being (which would entail two personal entities), but with a human nature.

anthropomorphic. Describing God in human terms.

apophatic. Knowing God (according to the dominant idea in the Eastern church) primarily through mystical contemplation, rather than through positive propositions or intellectual activity. Indeed, we are to empty our minds of logical and intellectual categories and pray in ignorance.

appropriation. Attribution of a divine work to one person of the Trinity. Since God is one, all three persons act together in all of God's works. Yet each work is particularly attributed (appropriated) to one person. Thus, only the Son became incarnate, and only the Holy Spirit came at Pentecost.

This does not deny that the other two persons were also involved in each of these acts.

Arians. Those who held views like, or similar to, those of Arius (*ca.* 276–337), who taught that the Son was a creature who came into being at some point, and who was the agent through whom the world was made, but was not coeternal with the Father, nor of the same being.

attributes. Particular characteristics of God, such as holiness, sovereignty, justice, goodness, mercy, and love.

being. Something that is—an existent.

binitarianism. The idea that the Son is God, along with the Father, but the Holy Spirit is not. Some statements in the NT appear binitarian, but these simply do not refer to the Spirit, rather than deny his participation in God. The *pneumatomachii*, in the fourth century, were binitarians, and their teaching was rejected by the church as heretical.

cataphatic. In Orthodox theology, cataphatic theology consists of positive affirmations (in contrast to apophatic theology, which is based on negations). According to Dionysius the Areopagite, this leads us to some knowledge of God, but is an imperfect way. The perfect way, the only way that is appropriate to God, who is of his very nature unknowable, is the apophatic method—which leads us finally to total ignorance.

Christology. Teaching relating to the person of Christ.

consubstantiality. The dogma that the Son and the Holy Spirit are of the same substance as the Father. This means that all three persons are fully God and are the whole God.

deification. According to the Eastern church, the goal of salvation is to be made like God. This the Holy Spirit effects in us. It involves no blurring of the Creator-creature distinction, but rather focuses on the union and communion that we are given by God, in which we are made partakers of the divine nature (2 Peter 1:4).

docetism. The early heresy that Christ's humanity was apparent and not real. The term is a derivative of the Greek verb *dokein,* "to seem or appear." This view is heretical because only a perfect, sinless man can atone for the sins of man.

doxology. An ascription of praise, normally to God.

dyotheletism. The doctrine that there are two (harmonious) wills in the incarnate Christ. This supposes that will is a property of the natures of Christ (divine and human), rather than of the person.

economic Trinity. The Trinity as revealed in creation and salvation—acting in our world, in human history.

energies. According to Gregory Palamas, the essence of God is unknowable. We have to do with God's energies, his powers at work in the creation.

enhypostasia. The dogma promulgated at the Second Council of Constantinople (553) that the person of the incarnate Christ is the eternal Son, who took into union a human nature conceived by the Holy Spirit in the womb of the Virgin Mary. Behind this lies the biblical teaching that man is made in the image of God and thus is ontologically compatible with God on a creaturely level. Thus, the Son of God provides the personhood for the assumed human nature.

eschatological. Relating to the last things, from the Greek word *eschatos* (last).

essence of God. What God *is*, his being (from *esse*, to be).

Eunomius. A fourth-century heretic who, like Arius, believed that the Son was created and so was not of the same being as the Father.

generation (eternal). The unique property of the Son in relation to the Father. Since God is eternal, the relation between the Father and the Son is eternal. This is not to be understood on the basis of human generation or begetting, since God is spiritual. It is beyond our capacity to understand.

hermeneutic. A principle of interpretation that governs how texts or realities are to be understood.

hypostasis. A Greek word meaning "something with a concrete existence." In terms of the Trinity, it came to mean "person." Thus, by the end of the fourth-century controversy, it referred to what is distinct in God, the way he is three, while *ousia* was reserved for the one being of God.

homoousios. "Of the same being," meaning that the Son and the Spirit are of the same, identical being as the Father.

homoiousios. "Of similar or like being," a term used by many who were afraid that the creed of Nicaea equated the Father with the Son. Many of these *homoiousians* gave their support to the settlement of the Trinitarian controversy in 381.

immanent Trinity (cf. "ontological Trinity"). The Trinity in itself, or the three persons as they relate to one another without regard to creation.

kenoticism. Based on the Greek verb *kenoō* ("to empty," Phil. 2:7), the idea that in the Incarnation Christ divested himself of certain divine attributes (omnipotence, omnipresence, omniscience).

liturgy. The order of worship in a church service, usually in the form of written prayers, responses, and ascriptions of praise to God.

Logos Christology. At the time of the early church, there was considerable speculation in Hellenistic and gnostic circles about a preexistent being,

filioque: "and from the Son."

the *Logos*. The apostle John uses this term in reference to the preincarnate Christ (John 1:1–18). Many of the ante-Nicene fathers used the term, but added some of these speculative concepts to it. This thinking tended to place the Son in a subordinate position in relation to the Father.

Macedonians. The putative followers of Macedonius, bishop of Constantinople from 342 until his deposition in 360. They denied the deity of the Holy Spirit. Macedonius himself may not have held this view.

modalism. The blurring or erasing of the real, eternal, and irreducible distinctions among the three persons of the Trinity. This danger can arise when the unity of God, or the identity in being of the three persons, is overstressed at the expense of the personal distinctions. It can also surface where there is a pervasive stress on salvation history, so as to eliminate any reference to eternal realities. When that is so, God's self-revelation in human history as the Father, the Son, and the Holy Spirit is no longer held to reveal who he is eternally in himself.

monarchy/monarchianism. Sole rule, the rule of one. It refers to the unity of God, his oneness (cf. Deut. 6:4). In the Eastern church, it was common to base the monarchy on the Father. However, this often led to the subordination of the Son and the Spirit—or else to modalism, by which the other persons were reduced to little more than attributes.

monistic. Reducing reality to one principle.

monotheism. Belief in only one God.

monotheletism. The idea that in the incarnate Christ there was only one will. This view was rejected by the church because "will" was regarded as a predicate of both of the two natures. If there was only one will, the human nature of Christ would be diminished or worse.

nature of God. What God is *like* (love, just, holy, omnipotent, etc.). The particular aspects of his nature are termed attributes. In the fourth century, the nature of God was sometimes used as a synonym for his essence or being.

Neoplatonism. A movement in the third and fourth centuries that built on and adapted certain aspects of Platonic philosophy, together with elements from other sources, including Christianity. This influenced to varying degrees Clement of Alexandria, Origen, and the pre-Christian Augustine. How far the latter extricated himself from the impact of Neoplatonism is a continued subject of debate.

notions. In Latin theology, notions are the defining characteristics of the divine persons. Thomas Aquinas held that there are five notions: unoriginatedness (innascibility), paternity, filiation, spiration, and procession.

ontological. Relating to being, that which is.

ontological Trinity (cf. "immanent Trinity"). The Trinity in itself, or the three persons as they relate to one another without regard to creation.

order (Greek, *taxis*). The relations between the three persons of the Trinity disclose an order: the Father begets the Son and sends the Holy Spirit in or through the Son. These relations are never reversed.

ordo salutis. The order of salvation, or the way we are brought to salvation by the Holy Spirit and kept there. It encompasses effectual calling, regeneration, faith and repentance, justification, adoption, sanctification, perseverance, and glorification, all of which are received in union with Christ.

ousia. Being (that which is). Since there is only one God, he has only one *ousia*. The word refers to the one being of God. However, before the Trinitarian crisis of the fourth century was resolved, this word had a range of meanings, and so there was much confusion. See chapter 5.

panentheism. The view that, while God and creation are distinct, God is in creation and the creation is in God. Thus, God is integrally bound up with creation and is as dependent on it as it is dependent on him. *p. 332*

pantheism. The view that identifies God with the creation. Thus, the creation is to be worshiped.

parallelism. Hebrew poetry rhymed not words but ideas. Often one statement is repeated in slightly different form. This is clear in the Psalms.

perichoresis. The mutual indwelling of the three persons of the Trinity in the one being of God.

persons. The Father, the Son, and the Holy Spirit. There has been much debate about whether *person* is an appropriate or adequate term for the three, since in its modern usage it entails separate individuals. However, no proposed alternative has succeeded in establishing itself, for they invariably yield a less than personal view of God.

pneumatomachii. The "fighters against the Spirit," who, while accepting the deity of the Son, did not hold that the Holy Spirit is God. Their rise to prominence in the fourth century occasioned the Council of Constantinople (381), which resolved the Trinitarian crisis and declared this view heretical.

polytheism. The belief that there is more than one divine being.

processions. The eternal begetting of the Son and the eternal procession of the Holy Spirit. These are matched by the *missions*, the historical sending of the Son and of the Spirit. The Eastern church considers it an error to call the Father's begetting of the Son a procession. For the East, this is a typically Western confusion of the Father and the Son.

procession, eternal. The eternal relation of the Holy Spirit to the Father (and to the Son, in the Western view).

properties. Paternity, filiation, active spiration, passive spiration (procession), and innascibility (see "notions").

protology. The doctrine of the first things (from the Greek *prōtos,* first). It can relate to creation or to the divine preexistence in eternity.

realism. The claim that universals (broad, general ideas or principles, such as whiteness) are real. This is contrary to nominalism, which maintains that only particulars (specific instances of, e.g., whiteness) are real.

relations. The relation between the Father and the Son, the Son and the Father, the Father/Son and the Holy Spirit, and the Holy Spirit and the Father/Son. These are considered differently in the Eastern church than in the West. The relations between the three persons differ, in that the Father is first, the Son second, and the Spirit third. The Father begets the Son and emits the Spirit; he neither is begotten nor proceeds. The Son is begotten and (according to the West) shares with the Father in the emission or sending of the Spirit, and does not proceed. The Spirit proceeds from the Father and from (or through) the Son, but does not beget and is not begotten. These relations are irreversible.

Sabellianism (see modalism). Sabellius held, heretically, that the one God revealed himself successively as the Father, the Son, and the Holy Spirit, and that these are not eternal personal distinctions.

social doctrine of the Trinity. An understanding of the Trinity that sees the three persons as a community, interacting with one another. Its basic premise is that the three persons have priority over the one being (essence).

sophia (wisdom). This is a theme developed by Russian Orthodox theology during the last two centuries. It has had an appeal to feminist theologians, on the irrelevant basis that the Greek *sophia* is a feminine noun.

soteriology. The doctrine of salvation (from the Greek *sōtēr,* "savior").

spiration. The defining characteristic of the Holy Spirit: his procession from (passive spiration), or his being breathed out by (active spiration), the Father. The West insists that the Spirit also proceeds from the Son (the *filioque* clause).

subordinationism. A teaching that the Son and the Holy Spirit are of lesser being or status than the Father.

substance. The "stuff" of which someone or something consists. There is one identical substance of which the Father, the Son, and the Spirit all consist, fully and absolutely.

theophanies. Appearances of God in the OT in human or other creaturely form.

tritheism. The belief that there are three gods. An exaggerated stress on the three persons of the Trinity can, it is claimed, lead to a belief that there are three gods, not one.

works of the Trinity *ad intra*. The actions that the three persons perform in connection with their own internal relations, without any reference to creation.

works of the Trinity *ab extra*. The actions that the three persons perform with reference to the world: creation, providence, and grace. These are free actions, since God was under no obligation to create or to bring about salvation following the Fall.

unbegotten/begotten. The property of the Son is that he is begotten by the Father from eternity. The Father is unbegotten. Begetting is qualitatively different from creating, refers to the eternal relations of the Father and the Son, distinguishes the Son from the creatures, and is beyond our capacity to understand.

Bibliography

Agreed Statement on the Holy Trinity Between the Orthodox Church and
the World Alliance of Reformed Churches. 1992. *Touchstone* 5 (winter): 22–23.

'Ali, 'Abdullah Yusuf, ed. 1997. *The Meaning of the Holy Qur'an*. 9th ed.
Beltsville, Md.: Amana Publications.

Anastos, M. V. 1981. Basil's Κατα Ευνομιου, a Critical Analysis. In *Basil of
Caesarea: Christian, Humanist, Ascetic: A Sixteen-Hundredth Anniversary Symposium*, ed. P. J. Fedwick, 67–136. Toronto: Pontifical Institute of Medieval Studies.

Anatolios, K. 1998. *Athanasius: The Coherence of His Thought*. London:
Routledge.

Anscombe, G. 1973. *Three Philosophers*. Oxford: Clarendon Press.

Anselm. *De fide Trinitatis et de incarnatione Verbi*.

———. *De processione Spiritus Sancti contra Graecos*.

Aquinas, Thomas. 1980. *Commentary on the Gospel of St. John*. Albany:
Magi Books.

———. *Compendium theologiae*.

———. *On Boethius*.

———. *Summa contra Gentiles*.

———. *Summa theologica*.

Arnold, C. 1993. Ephesians. In *Dictionary of Paul and His Letters*, ed. G. F.
Hawthorne, 238–49. Downers Grove, Ill.: InterVarsity Press.

Athanasius. 1951. *The Letters of Saint Athanasius Concerning the Holy Spirit*.
Trans. C. Shapland. London: Epworth Press.

———. 1980. *Select Writings and Letters*. Vol. 4 of NPNF[2].

———. *Defence of Dionysius*.

———. *Letters*.

———. *Letters to Serapion on the Holy Spirit*.

———. *Of Synods*.

———. *On Luke 10:22 (Matthew 11:27)*.

———. *On the Decrees of the Synod of Nicaea*.

———. *On the Incarnation.*

———. *Orations Against the Arians.*

———. *Statement of Faith.*

———. *To Epictetus.*

———. *To the Antiochenes.*

Augustine. 1991. *The Works of Saint Augustine: A Translation for the 21st Century: The Trinity.* Trans. Edmund Hill. Ed. J. E. Rotelle. Hyde Park, N.Y.: New City Press.

———. 1995. *On the Holy Trinity, Doctrinal Treatises, Moral Treatises.* Vol. 3 of NPNF[1].

———. *City of God.*

———. *Confessions.*

———. *De Trinitate.*

———. *Letters.*

———. *Of Free Will.*

———. *On Christian Doctrine.*

———. *On the Psalms.*

———. *On True Religion.*

———. *Sermon on Matthew 3:13.*

———. *Tractates on the Gospel of John.*

Azkoul, M. 1995. *St. Gregory of Nyssa and the Tradition of the Fathers.* Lewiston, N.Y.: Edwin Mellen Press.

Balthasar, H. U. von, 1992. *The Theology of Karl Barth: Exposition and Interpretation.* Trans. E. T. Oakes. San Francisco: Ignatius.

Bammel, C. P. H. 1990. *Der Römerbriefkommentar des Origenes: Kritische Ausgabe der Übersetzung Rufins: Buch 1–3.* Freiburg: Verlag Herder.

Barnes, M. R. 1993. The Background and Use of Eunomius' Causal Language. In *Arianism After Arius: Essays on the Development of the Fourth Century Trinitarian Conflicts*, ed. M. R. Barnes, 217–36. Edinburgh: T & T Clark.

———. 1993. Introduction to *Arianism After Arius: Essays on the Development of the Fourth Century Trinitarian Conflicts*, ed. M. R. Barnes, xiii–xvii. Edinburgh: T & T Clark.

———. 1999. Rereading Augustine on the Trinity. In *The Trinity: An Interdisciplinary Symposium on the Trinity*, ed. S. T. Davis, 145–76. Oxford: Oxford University Press.

Barr, J. 1988. 'Abbā Isn't "Daddy." *JTS* 39:28–47.

Barth, K. 1956–75. *Church Dogmatics.* Ed. G. Bromiley. Edinburgh: T & T Clark.

————. 1981. *Letters, 1961–1968*. Trans. and ed. J. Fangemeier and G. W. Bromiley. Grand Rapids: Eerdmans.

————. 1995. *The Theology of John Calvin*. Trans. G. W. Bromiley. Grand Rapids: Eerdmans.

Basil of Caesarea. *The Hexaëmeron*.

————. *Letters*.

————. *On the Holy Spirit*.

Bauckham, R. 1978. The Sonship of the Historical Jesus in Christology. *SJT* 31:245–60.

————. 1995. *The Theology of Jürgen Moltmann*. Edinburgh: T & T Clark.

Bauer, D. 1992. Son of God. In *Dictionary of Jesus and the Gospels*, ed. J. B. Green, 769–75. Downers Grove, Ill.: InterVarsity Press.

Bavinck, H. 1977. *The Doctrine of God*. Trans. W. Hendriksen. Edinburgh: Banner of Truth. (Orig. pub. 1951.)

————. 1977. *Our Reasonable Faith*. Ed. H. Zylstra. Grand Rapids: Baker. (Orig. pub. 1956.)

————. 1999. *In the Beginning: Foundations of Creation Theology*. Ed. J. Vriend and J. Bolt. Grand Rapids: Baker.

Beckwith, R. 2001. The Calvinist Doctrine of the Trinity. *Churchman* 115: 308–16.

Behr, J. 2001. *The Way to Nicaea*. Crestwood, N.Y.: St. Vladimir's Seminary Press.

Bellarmine, R. 1832. Secunda controversia generalis de Christo. In *Disputationum de controversiis christianae fidei adversus haereticos*. Rome.

Benoit, A. 1960. *Saint Irénée: Introduction à l'étude de son théologie*. Paris: Presses Universitaires.

Berkhof, L. 1958. *Systematic Theology*. London: Banner of Truth.

Berkouwer, G. 1960. *Divine Election*. Trans. H. Bekker. Grand Rapids: Eerdmans.

Berns, R. S. 2000. *Billmeyer and Saltzman's Principles of Color Technology*. 3rd ed. New York: John Wiley & Sons.

Betz, O. 1968. *What Do We Know About Jesus?* London: SCM.

Bielfeldt, D. 1997. Deification as a Motif in Luther's *Dictata super Psalterium*. *SCJ* 28:401–20.

Bilezikian, G. 1997. Hermeneutical Bungee-Jumping: Subordination in the Trinity. *JETS* 40: 57–68.

Bilz, J., ed. 1909. *Die Trinitätslehre des Hl. Johannes von Damaskus*. Paderborn: Ferdinad Schöningh.

Bobrinskoy, B. 1981. The *Filioque* Yesterday and Today. In *Spirit of God, Spirit of Christ: Ecumenical Reflections on the Filioque Controversy*, ed. L. Vischer, 133–48. London: SPCK.

———. 1999. *The Mystery of the Trinity: Trinitarian Experience and Vision in the Biblical and Patristic Tradition*. Trans. A. P. Gythiel. Crestwood, N.Y.: St. Vladimir's Seminary Press.

Bonner, G. 1986. Augustine's Concept of Deification. *JTS* 37:369–86.

———. 1986. Deificare. In *Augustinus-Lexikon*, ed. C. Mayer, 1:265–67. Basel: Schwabe & Co.

———. 1986. *St. Augustine of Hippo: Life and Controversies*. Norwich: Canterbury Press.

———. 1999. Deification, Divinization. In *Augustine Through the Ages: An Encyclopedia*, ed. A. D. Fitzgerald, 265–66. Grand Rapids: Eerdmans.

Bracton, H. de. 1968. *On the Laws and Customs of England*. Trans. and ed. S. E. Thorne. Cambridge, Mass.: Harvard University Press.

Bray, G. 1979. *Holiness and the Will of God: Perspectives on the Theology of Tertullian*. Atlanta: John Knox.

———. 1983. The *Filioque* Clause in History and Theology. *TynBul* 34:91–144.

———. 1993. *The Doctrine of God*. Leicester: Inter-Varsity Press.

Bromiley, G. W. 1979. *An Introduction to the Theology of Karl Barth*. Grand Rapids: Eerdmans.

Brown, P. 1967. *Augustine of Hippo: A Biography*. London: Faber and Faber.

Brown, R. E. 1966. *The Gospel According to John (i–xii)*. Anchor Bible. Garden City, N.Y.: Doubleday.

Bruce, F. F. 1984. *The Gospel of John*. Grand Rapids: Eerdmans.

Bucer, M. 1561. *In epistolam d. Pauli ad Ephesios*. Basel.

Büchsel, F. 1974. Μονογενης. In *TDNT*, 4:737–41.

Bulgakov, S. 1937. *The Wisdom of God: A Brief Summary of Sophiology*. London: Williams and Norgate.

———. 1946. *Le Paraclet*. Ed. C. Andronikof. Paris: Aubier.

———. 1976. *A Bulgakov Anthology*. Ed. J. Pain and N. Zernov. Philadelphia: Westminster Press.

Butin, P. W. 1995. *Revelation, Redemption, and Response: Calvin's Trinitarian Understanding of the Divine-Human Relationship*. New York: Oxford University Press.

Calvin, J. 1954. *Theological Treatises*. Ed. J. K. S. Reid. Philadelphia: Westminster Press.

———. 1959. *Calvin's Commentaries: The Gospel According to St John 1–10*. Trans. T. H. L. Parker. Ed. D. W. Torrance and T. F. Torrance. Edinburgh: Oliver and Boyd.

———. 1960. *Calvin's Commentaries: The Epistle of Paul the Apostle to the Corinthians*. Trans. J. W. Fraser. Ed. D. W. Torrance and T. F. Torrance. Edinburgh: Oliver and Boyd.

———. 1960. *Institutes of the Christian Religion*. Ed. J. T. McNeill. Trans. F. L. Battles. 2 vols. Philadelphia: Westminster Press.

———. 1961. *Calvin's Commentaries: The Epistles of Paul the Apostle to the Romans and to the Thessalonians*. Trans. R. Mackenzie. Ed. D. W. Torrance and T. F. Torrance. Edinburgh: Oliver and Boyd.

———. 1961. *Calvin's Commentaries: The Gospel According to St John 11–21 and the First Epistle of John*. Trans. T. H. L. Parker. Ed. D. W. Torrance and T. F. Torrance. Edinburgh: Oliver and Boyd.

———. 1963. *Calvin's Commentaries: The Epistle of Paul the Apostle to the Hebrews and the First and Second Epistles of St Peter*. Trans. W. B. Johnston. Ed. D. W. Torrance and T. F. Torrance. Edinburgh: Oliver and Boyd.

———. 1965. *Calvin's Commentaries: The Acts of the Apostles 1–13*. Trans. J. W. Fraser and W. J. G. McDonald. Ed. D. W. Torrance and T. F. Torrance. Edinburgh: Oliver and Boyd.

———. 1972. *Calvin's Commentaries: A Harmony of the Gospels Matthew, Mark and Luke*, vol. 3, *and the Epistles of James and Jude*. Trans. A. W. Morrison. Ed. D. W. Torrance and T. F. Torrance. Edinburgh: Saint Andrew Press.

———. 1979. *Commentaries on the First Book of Moses Called Genesis*. Trans. John King. 2 vols. Reprint, Grand Rapids: Baker.

———. 1983. Antidote to the Council of Trent. In *Selected Works of John Calvin: Tracts and Letters*, ed. H. Beveridge, 3:61–63. Grand Rapids: Baker.

———. 1983. Reply to Sadolet. In *Selected Works of John Calvin: Tracts and Letters*, ed. H. Beveridge, 1:37–38. Grand Rapids: Baker.

———. 2001. *Ioannis Calvini opera exegetica*, vol. 12/1, *Commentariorum in Acta Apostolorum liber primum*. Ed. H. Feld. Geneva: Droz.

Capes, D. 1997. Pre-existence. In *Dictionary of the Later New Testament and Its Developments*, ed. R. P. Martin and P. H. Davids, 955–61. Downers Grove, Ill.: InterVarsity Press.

Carson, D. 1991. *The Gospel According to St John*. Leicester: Inter-Varsity Press.

Catechism of the Catholic Church. 1994. London: Geoffrey Chapman.

Coakley, S. 1999. "Persons" in the "Social" Doctrine of the Trinity: A Critique of Current Analytic Discussion. In *The Trinity: An Interdisciplinary Symposium on the Trinity*, ed. S. T. Davis, 123–44. Oxford: Oxford University Press.

Coffey, D. 1999. *Deus Trinitas: The Doctrine of the Triune God.* New York: Oxford University Press.

Colyer, E. M. 2001. *How to Read T. F. Torrance: Understanding His Trinitarian and Scientific Theology.* Downers Grove, Ill.: InterVarsity Press.

———, ed. 2001. *The Promise of Trinitarian Theology: Theologians in Dialogue with T. F. Torrance.* Lanham, Md.: Rowman & Littlefield Publishers.

Conticello, V. S. 1995. Pseudo-Cyril's *De sacrosancte Trinitate*: A Compilation of Joseph the Philosopher. *OCP* 61:117–29.

Copleston, F. 1963. *Aquinas.* London: Penguin.

Cranfield, C. E. B. 1979. *A Critical and Exegetical Commentary on the Epistle to the Romans.* International Critical Commentary. Edinburgh: T & T Clark.

Crouzel, H. 1976. Les personnes de la Trinité sont-elles de puissance inégale selon Origène *Peri Archon* I, 3, 5–8? *Greg* 57:109–25.

———. 1989. *Origen.* Trans. A. Worrall. Edinburgh: T & T Clark.

Cullmann, O. 1959. *The Christology of the New Testament.* London: SCM.

———. 1962. The Reply of Professor Cullmann to Roman Catholic Critics. Trans. Robert P. Meye, *SJT* 15:36–43.

Cunningham, D. S. 1998. *These Three Are One: The Practice of Trinitarian Theology.* Oxford: Blackwell.

Cyril of Alexandria. *De sancta et consubstantiali Trinitate, Dialogus II.*

———. *In Joannis Evangelium.*

———. *Thesaurus de sancta et consubstantiali Trinitate.*

———. 1885. *Commentary on the Gospel according to St. John.* London: Walter Smith.

Dahms, J. V. 1983. The Johannine Use of Monogenēs Reconsidered. *NTS* 29:222–32.

Danielou, J. 1948. *Origene.* Paris: La Table Ronde.

Davies, B. 1992. *The Thought of Thomas Aquinas.* Oxford: Clarendon Press.

Deddo, G. W. 2001. The Holy Spirit in T. F. Torrance's Theology. In *The Promise of Trinitarian Theology: Theologians in Dialogue with T. F. Torrance*, ed. E. M. Colyer, 81–114. Lanham, Md.: Rowman & Littlefield Publishers.

De Margerie, B. 1982. *The Christian Trinity in History.* Trans. E. J. Fortman. Petersham, Mass.: St. Bede's Publications.

Del Colle, R. 1994. *Christ and the Spirit: Spirit-Christology in Trinitarian Perspective.* New York: Oxford University Press.

Dodd, C. H. 1953. *The Interpretation of the Fourth Gospel.* Cambridge: Cambridge University Press.

Dowey, E. A., Jr. 1994. *The Knowledge of God in Calvin's Theology.* Grand Rapids: Eerdmans.

Drecoll, V. H. 1996. *Die Entwicklung der Trinitätslehre des Basilius von Cäsarea.* Göttingen: Vandenhoeck & Ruprecht.

Driver, S. R. 1926. *The Book of Genesis.* London: Methuen.

Dunn, J. D. G. 1980. *Christology in the Making: A New Testament Inquiry into the Origins of the Doctrine of the Incarnation.* Philadelphia: Westminster Press.

—————. 1991. *The Partings of the Ways: Between Christianity and Judaism and Their Significance for the Character of Christianity.* Philadelphia: Trinity Press International.

Dvornik, F. 1948. *The Photian Schism.* Cambridge: Cambridge University Press.

Epiphanius. *Panarion.*

Erickson, M. J. 1995. *God in Three Persons: A Contemporary Interpretation of the Trinity.* Grand Rapids: Baker.

Esser, H. 1976. Hat Calvin eine "leise modalisierende Trinitätslehre"? In *Calvinus Theologus*, ed. W. Neuser, 20–24. Neukirchen-Vluyn: Neukirchener Verlag.

Eunomius. *Apology.*

—————. *An Apology for the Apology.*

—————. *The Confession of Faith.*

—————. *The Fragments.*

Eusebius of Caesarea. *Against Marcellus.*

Evans, G. R. 1989. *Anselm.* London: Geoffrey Chapman.

—————. 1999. Anselm of Canterbury. In *Augustine Through the Ages*, ed. A. D. Fitzgerald, 23–24. Grand Rapids: Eerdmans.

Fantino, J. 1994. *La théologie d'Irénée. Lecture des Écritures en réponse à l'exégèse gnostique: Une approche trinitaire.* Paris: Cerf.

Feuerbach, L. 1957. *The Essence of Christianity.* New York: Harper Torchbooks.

Fiddes, P. S. 1988. *The Creative Suffering of God.* Oxford: Clarendon Press.

—————. 2000. *Participating in God: A Pastoral Doctrine of the Trinity.* Louisville: Westminster/John Knox.

Ford, D. 1981. *Barth and God's Story: Biblical Narrative and the Theological Method of Karl Barth in the "Church Dogmatics."* Frankfurt am Main: Peter Lang.

Fortman, E. J. 1972. *The Triune God: An Historical Study of the Doctrine of the Trinity.* Philadelphia: Westminster Press.

Frame, J. M. 2002. *The Doctrine of God.* Phillipsburg, N.J.: P&R Publishing.

Furnish, V. P. 1984. *II Corinthians.* Anchor Bible. Garden City, N.Y.: Doubleday.

Gaffin, Richard B., Jr. 1978. *The Centrality of the Resurrection: A Study in Paul's Soteriology.* Grand Rapids: Baker.

————. 1998. Challenges of the Charismatic Movement to the Reformed Tradition. *Ordained Servant* 7:48–57.

Giles, K. 2002. *The Trinity and Subordinationism.* Downers Grove, Ill.: InterVarsity Press.

Goodwin, T. 1958. *An Exposition of Ephesians Chapter 1 to 2:10.* [Evansville, Ind.]: Sovereign Grace Book Club.

Grant, R. M. 1997. *Irenaeus of Lyons.* London: Routledge.

Grayston, K. 1984. *The Johannine Epistles.* New Century Bible Commentary. Grand Rapids: Eerdmans.

Gregg, R. C. 1981. *Early Arianism—a Way of Salvation.* Philadelphia: Fortress Press.

Gregory Nazianzen. 1989. *Select Orations of Saint Gregory Nazianzen.* Vol. 7 of *NPNF²*.

————. *Orations.*

Gregory of Nyssa. 1988. *Dogmatic Treatises, Etc.* Vol. 5 of *NPNF²*.

————. *Against Eunomius.*

Gregory Palamas. 1983. *The Triads.* Ed. John Meyendorff. Trans. Nicholas Gendle. New York: Paulist Press.

————. *Capita physica theologica.*

Grillmeier, A. 1975. *Christ in Christian Tradition*, vol. 1, *From the Apostolic Age to Chalcedon (451).* 2nd ed. Trans. J. Bowden. Atlanta: John Knox.

————. 1995. *Christ in Christian Tradition*, vol. 2, *From the Council of Chalcedon (451) to Gregory the Great (590–604)*, part 2, *The Church of Constantinople in the Sixth Century.* Trans. J. Cawte. London: Mowbray.

Grosseteste, Robert. 1996. *On the Six Days of Creation: A Translation of the Hexaëmeron.* Trans. C. F. J. Martin. Auctores Britannici Medii Aevi. Oxford: Oxford University Press for the British Academy.

Gunton, C. E. 1983. *Yesterday and Today: A Study of Continuities in Christology*. Grand Rapids: Eerdmans.

———. 1990. Augustine, the Trinity, and the Theological Crisis of the West. *SJT* 43:33–58.

———. 1991. *The Promise of Trinitarian Theology*. Edinburgh: T & T Clark.

———. 1998. *The Triune Creator*. Grand Rapids: Eerdmans.

———. 2001. Being and Person: T. F. Torrance's Doctrine of God. In *The Promise of Trinitarian Theology: Theologians in Dialogue with T. F. Torrance*, ed. E. M. Colyer, 115–37. Lanham, Md.: Rowman & Littlefield Publishers.

Guthrie, D. 1981. *New Testament Theology*. Leicester: Inter-Varsity Press.

———, and R. P. Martin. 1993. God. In *Dictionary of Paul and His Letters*, ed. G. F. Hawthorne, 354–69. Downers Grove, Ill.: InterVarsity Press.

Gwatkin, H. M. 1900. *Studies of Arianism*. Cambridge: Deighton Bell.

———. 1914. *The Arian Controversy*. London: Longmans, Green and Co.

Hanson, R. P. C. 1983. The Doctrine of the Trinity Achieved in 381. *SJT* 36:41–57.

———. 1988. *The Search for the Christian Doctrine of God: The Arian Controversy 318–381*. Edinburgh: T & T Clark.

Hapgood, I. F., comp. and trans. 1956. *Service Book of the Holy Orthodox-Catholic Apostolic Church*. 3rd ed. Brooklyn, N.Y.: Syrian Antiochene Orthodox Archdiocese of New York and All North America.

Harnack, A. von. 1896–99. *History of Dogma*. Ed. A. B. Bruce. 7 vols. London: Williams & Norgate.

———. 1990. *Marcion: The Gospel of the Alien God*. Trans. J. E. Steely. Durham, N.C.: Labyrinth Press.

Harrison, V. 1991. Perichoresis in the Greek Fathers. *StVladThQ* 35:53–65.

Haugh, R. 1975. *Photius and the Carolingians: The Trinitarian Controversy*. Belmont, Mass.: Norland.

Hawking, S. W. 1988. *A Brief History of Time: From the Big Bang to Black Holes*. New York: Bantam Books.

Hill, W. J. 1982. *The Three-Personed God*. Washington, D.C.: Catholic University of America Press.

Hodge, C. 1977. *Systematic Theology*. Grand Rapids: Eerdmans.

Hodgson, L. 1943. *The Doctrine of the Trinity*. Croall Lectures, 1942–1943. London: Nisbet.

Hoover, R. W. 1971. The *Harpagmos* Enigma: A Philological Solution. *HTR* 64:95–119.

Hopkins, J., ed. and trans. 1976. *Anselm of Canterbury*, vol. 3. Toronto: Edwin Mellen Press.

Hughes, C. 1989. *On a Complex Theory of a Simple God: An Investigation in Aquinas' Philosophical Theology*. Ithaca: Cornell University Press.

Hughes, P. E. 1961. *Paul's Second Epistle to the Corinthians*. New International Commentary on the New Testament. London: Marshall, Morgan & Scott.

———. 1985. The Christology of Hebrews. *SwJT* 28:19–27.

———. 1989. *The True Image: The Origin and Destiny of Man in Christ*. Grand Rapids: Eerdmans.

Hurtado, L. W. 1988. *One God, One Lord: Early Christian Devotion and Ancient Jewish Monotheism*. Philadelphia: Fortress.

———. 1993. Lord. In *Dictionary of Paul and His Letters*, ed. G. F. Hawthorne, 560–69. Downers Grove, Ill.: InterVarsity Press.

———. 1993. Pre-existence. In *Dictionary of Paul and His Letters*, ed. G. F. Hawthorne, 743–46. Downers Grove, Ill.: InterVarsity Press.

———. 1993. Son of God. In *Dictionary of Paul and His Letters*, ed. G. F. Hawthorne, 900–906. Downers Grove, Ill.: InterVarsity Press.

———. 1997. Christology. In *Dictionary of the Later New Testament and Its Developments*, ed. R. P. Martin and P. H. Davids, 170–84. Downers Grove, Ill.: InterVarsity Press.

Ignatius. *To the Ephesians*.

———. *To the Magnesians*.

Irenaeus. *Against Heresies*.

———. *The Demonstration of the Apostolic Preaching*.

Jenson, R. W. 1997. *Systematic Theology*, vol. 1, *The Triune God*. New York: Oxford University Press.

John of Damascus. *On the Orthodox Faith*.

Johnson, E. A. 1992. *She Who Is: The Mystery of God in Feminist Theological Discourse*. New York: Crossroad.

Jüngel, E. 1976. *The Doctrine of the Trinity: God's Being Is in His Becoming*. Edinburgh: T & T Clark.

———. 1986. *Karl Barth: A Theological Legacy*. Trans. G. E. Paul. Philadelphia: Westminster Press.

Justin. *Apology*.

Kannengiesser, C. 1988. Divine Trinity and the Structure of *Peri Archon*. In *Origen of Alexandria: His World and His Legacy*, ed. C. Kannengiesser, 231–49. Notre Dame: University of Notre Dame Press.

———. 1991. *Arius and Athanasius: Two Alexandrian Theologians*. Aldershot, U.K.: Variorum.

Kaspar, W., ed. 1993–2001. *Lexikon für Theologie und Kirche*. 3rd ed. 11 vols. Freiburg: Herder.

Kaufman, G. D. 1996. *God—Mystery—Diversity: Christian Theology in a Pluralistic World.* Minneapolis: Fortress Press.

Kearsley, R. 1998. *Tertullian's Theology of Divine Power.* Carlisle, U.K.: Paternoster.

Keith, G. A. 1988. Our Knowledge of God: The Relevance of the Debate Between Eunomius and the Cappadocians. *TynBul* 41:60–88.

Kelly, J. N. D. 1968. *Early Christian Doctrines.* London: Adam & Charles Black.

———. 1972. *Early Christian Creeds.* London: Longman.

———. 1983. The Nicene Creed: A Turning Point. *SJT* 36:29–39.

Kidner, D. 1967. *Genesis: An Introduction and Commentary.* London: Tyndale Press.

———. 1973. *Psalms 1–72: A Commentary on Books I–II of the Psalms.* London: Inter-Varsity Press.

———. 1975. *Psalms 73–150: A Commentary on Books III–V of the Psalms.* London: Inter-Varsity Press.

Kim, S. 1982. *The Origin of Paul's Gospel.* Grand Rapids: Eerdmans.

———. 2002. *Paul and the New Perspective: Second Thoughts on the Origin of Paul's Gospel.* Grand Rapids: Eerdmans.

Kimel, A. F., Jr., ed. 1992. *Speaking the Christian God: The Holy Trinity and the Challenge of Feminism.* Grand Rapids: Eerdmans.

Knowles, D. 1964. *The Evolution of Medieval Thought.* New York: Vintage Books.

Koopmans, J. 1955. *Das altkirchliche Dogma in der Reformation.* Munich: Chr. Kaiser Verlag.

Kopecek, T. A. 1979. *A History of Neo-Arianism.* 2 vols. Cambridge, Mass.: Philadelphia Patristic Foundation.

Kovalevsky, E. 1964. Saint Trinité. *Cahiers de Saint Irénée* 44 (January-February): 3.

Kuyper, A. 1975. *The Work of the Holy Spirit.* Trans. H. de Vries. Grand Rapids: Eerdmans.

Laats, A. 1999. *Doctrines of the Trinity in Eastern and Western Theologies: A Study with Special Reference to K. Barth and V. Lossky.* Frankfurt am Main: Peter Lang.

LaCugna, C. M. 1991. *God for Us: The Trinity and Christian Life.* San Francisco: Harper.

Lagrange, M.-J. 1948. *Évangile selon Saint Jean.* Paris: Gabalda.

Lampe, G. W. H., ed. 1961. *A Patristic Greek Lexicon.* Oxford: Clarendon Press.

Lancel, S. 2002. *Saint Augustine.* Trans. A. Nevill. London: SCM Press.

Lane, A. N. S. 1999. *John Calvin: Student of the Church Fathers*. Grand Rapids: Baker.

Larson, M. J. 2001. A Re-examination of *De Spiritu Sancto*: Saint Basil's Bold Defence of the Spirit's Deity. *SBET* 19 (1): 65–84.

Lawson, J. 1948. *The Biblical Theology of St. Irenaeus*. London: Epworth.

Lebreton, J. 1939. *History of the Dogma of the Trinity from Its Origins to the Council of Nicaea*. 8th ed. Trans. A. Thorold. London: Burns, Oates and Washbourne.

Leithart, P. J. 2000. "Framing" Sacramental Theology: Trinity and Symbol. *WTJ* 62:1–16.

Letham, R. 1983. The *Foedus Operum*: Some Factors Accounting for Its Development. *SCJ* 14:457–467.

———. 1989. Baptism in the Writings of the Reformers. *SBET* 7 (2): 21–44.

———. 1990. The Man-Woman Debate: Theological Comment. *WTJ* 52:65–78.

———. 1992. The Hermeneutics of Feminism. *Them* 17 (January–April): 4–7.

———. 1993. *The Work of Christ*. Leicester: Inter-Varsity Press.

———. 1999. "In the Space of Six Days": The Days of Creation from Origen to the Westminster Assembly. *WTJ* 61:149–74.

———. 2001. *The Lord's Supper: Eternal Word in Broken Bread*. Phillipsburg, N.J.: Presbyterian & Reformed.

———, and D. MacLeod. 1995. Is Evangelicalism Christian? *EvQ* 67 (1): 3–33.

Lewis, B. 2002. *What Went Wrong? Western Impact and Middle Eastern Response*. New York: Oxford University Press.

Lewis, C. S. 1960. *Mere Christianity*. San Francisco: Harper.

Lienhard, J. T. 1993. Did Athanasius Reject Marcellus? In *Arianism After Arius: Essays on the Development of the Fourth Century Trinitarian Conflicts*, ed. M. R. Barnes, 65–80. Edinburgh: T & T Clark.

———. 1999. *Ousia* and *Hypostasis*: The Cappadocian Settlement and the Theology of "One Hypostasis." In *The Trinity: An Interdisciplinary Symposium on the Trinity*, ed. S. T. Davis, 99–121. Oxford: Oxford University Press.

Lightfoot, J. B. 1881. *Saint Paul's Epistle to the Philippians: A Revised Text with Introduction, Notes, and Dissertations*. London: Macmillan.

Lincoln, A. T. 1990. *Ephesians*. Dallas: Word.

Loder, J. E., and Neidhardt, W. J. 1992. *The Knight's Move: The Relational Logic of the Spirit in Theology and Science*. Colorado Springs: Helmers & Howard.

Lohr, W. A. 1993. A Sense of Tradition: The Homoiousion Church Party. In *Arianism After Arius: Essays on the Development of the Fourth Century Trinitarian Conflicts*, ed. M. R. Barnes, 81–100. Edinburgh: T & T Clark.

Lorenz, R. 1979. *Arius judaizans? Untersuchungen zur dogmengeschichtlichen Einordnung des Arius*. Göttingen: Vandenhoeck und Ruprecht.

Lossky, V. 1957. *The Mystical Theology of the Eastern Church*. London: James Clarke & Co.

———. 1963. *The Vision of God*. London: Faith Press.

———. 1974. *In the Image and Likeness of God*. Ed. John H. Erickson and Thomas E. Bird. [Crestwood, N.Y.]: St. Vladimir's Seminary Press.

Louth, A. 2002. *St. John Damascene: Tradition and Originality in Byzantine Theology*. Oxford: Oxford Universtiy Press.

Lyman, J. R. 1993. *Christology and Cosmology: Models of Divine Activity in Origen, Eusebius, and Athanasius*. Oxford: Clarendon.

Mackintosh, H. R. 1912. *The Doctrine of the Person of Jesus Christ*. Edinburgh: T & T Clark.

Mahoney, E. P. 1982. Sense, Intellect, and Imagination in Albert, Thomas, and Siger. In *The Cambridge History of Later Medieval Philosophy: From the Rediscovery of Aristotle to the Disintegration of Scholasticism, 1100–1600*, ed. N. Kreitzmann, 602–22. Cambridge: Cambridge University Press.

Mannermaa, T. 1989. *Der im Glauben gegenwärtige Christus: Rechtfertigung und Vergottung zum ökumenischen Dialog*. Hanover: Lutherisches Verlagshaus.

———. 1990. *Theosis* als Thema der Finnischen Lutherforschung. In *Luther und Theosis: Vergöttlichung als Thema der abendländischen Theologie*, ed. S. Peura, 11–26. Helsinki: Luther-Agricola-Gesellschaft.

Marcellus of Ancyra [?]. 1906. Die Fragmente Marcells. In *GCS*, 14:183–215. Leipzig: J. C. Hinrichs'sche Buchhandlung.

———. *Expositio fidei*.

Marcus, W. 1963. *Der Subordinatianismus als historiologisches Phänomen*. Munich: M. Hueber.

Martin, R. P. 1980. *Philippians*. New Century Bible. Grand Rapids: Eerdmans.

———. 1983. *Carmen Christi: Philippians ii 5–11 in Recent Interpretation and in the Setting of Early Christian Worship*. Grand Rapids: Eerdmans.

———. 1992. *Ephesians, Colossians, and Philemon*. Atlanta: John Knox Press.

Mathison, K. A. 2002. *Given for You: Reclaiming Calvin's Doctrine of the Lord's Supper*. Phillipsburg, N.J.: P&R Publishing.

McCormack, B. L. 1995. *Karl Barth's Critically Realistic Dialectical Theology: Its Genesis and Development, 1909–1936.* Oxford: Clarendon Press.

McGrath, A. E. 1999. *Thomas F. Torrance: An Intellectual Biography.* Edinburgh: T & T Clark.

McGuckin, J. A. 2001. *St. Gregory of Nazianzus: An Intellectual Biography.* Crestwood, N.Y.: St. Vladimir's Seminary Press.

McInerny, R., ed. and trans. 1998. *Thomas Aquinas: Selected Writings.* London: Penguin.

McKee, E. A. 1989. Exegesis, Theology, and Development in Calvin's *Institutio*: A Methodological Suggestion. In *Probing the Reformed Tradition: Historical Studies in Honor of Edward A. Dowey, Jr.*, ed. B. G. Armstrong, 154–72. Louisville: Westminster/John Knox.

Meconi, D. 1996. St. Augustine's Early Theory of Participation. *AugStud* 27:81–98.

Meerson, M. A. 1998. *The Trinity of Love in Modern Russian Theology: The Love Paradigm and the Retrieval of Western Medieval Love Mysticism in Modern Russian Trinitarian Thought (from Solovyov to Bulgakov).* Quincy, Ill.: Franciscan Press.

Meijering, E. 1968. *Orthodoxy and Platonism in Athanasius: Synthesis or Antithesis?* Leiden: E. J. Brill.

Meredith, A. 1990. The Idea of God in Gregory of Nyssa. In *Studien zu Gregor von Nyssa und der christlichen Spätantike*, ed. H. R. Drobner and C. Klock, 127–47. Leiden: E. J. Brill.

———. 1995. *The Cappadocians.* Crestwood, N.Y.: St. Vladimir's Seminary Press.

Metzger, B. M. 1971. *A Textual Commentary on the Greek New Testament.* London: United Bible Societies.

———. 1973. The Punctuation of Rom. 9:5. In *Christ and Spirit in the New Testament: Studies in Honour of C. F. D. Moule*, ed. B. Lindars, 95–112. Cambridge: Cambridge University Press.

Meyendorff, J. 1974. *St. Gregory Palamas and Orthodox Spirituality.* Crestwood, N.Y.: St. Vladimir's Seminary Press.

———. 1979. *Byzantine Theology: Historical Trends and Doctrinal Themes.* New York: Fordham University Press.

Moingt, J. 1966. *Théologie trinitaire de Tertullien.* Paris: Aubier.

———. 1970. Le problème de Dieu unique chez Tertullian. *RevScRel* 44:337–62.

Molnar, P. D. 2002. *Divine Freedom and the Doctrine of the Immanent Trinity: In Dialogue with Karl Barth and Contemporary Theology.* Edinburgh: T & T Clark.

Moltmann, J. 1967. *Theology of Hope: On the Ground and the Implications of a Christian Eschatology.* Trans. James W. Leitch. London: SCM.

———. 1981. Theological Proposals Towards the Resolution of the *Filioque* Controversy. In *Spirit of God, Spirit of Christ: Ecumenical Reflections on the Filioque Controversy,* ed. L. Vischer, 164–73. London: SPCK.

———. 1991. *God in Creation: A New Theology of Creation and the Spirit of God.* San Francisco: HarperSanFrancisco.

———. 1991. *The Trinity and the Kingdom: The Doctrine of God.* London: SCM.

———. 1993. *The Crucified God: The Cross of Christ as the Foundation and Criticism of Christian Theology.* Minneapolis: Fortress Press.

Moody. D. 1953. God's Only Son: The Translation of John 3:16 in the Revised Standard Version. *JBL* 72:213–19.

Morris, L. 1988. *The Epistle to the Romans.* Grand Rapids: Eerdmans.

Mosser, C. 2002. The Greatest Possible Blessing: Calvin and Deification. *SJT* 55:36–57.

Moulton, J. H., and G. Milligan. 1963. *The Vocabulary of the Greek New Testament: Illustrated from the Papyri and Other Non-literary Sources.* London: Hodder and Stoughton.

Mounier, E. 2001. *Personalism.* Notre Dame: University of Notre Dame Press.

Murray, J. 1965. *The Epistle to the Romans.* Grand Rapids: Eerdmans.

———. 1967. Definitive Sanctification. *CTJ* 2:5–21.

Needham, N. 1997. The *Filioque* Clause: East or West? *SBET* 15:142–62.

Nellas, P. 1987. *Deification in Christ: Orthodox Perspectives on the Nature of the Human Person.* Trans. N. Russell. Crestwood, N.Y.: St. Vladimir's Seminary Press.

Niesel, W. 1980. *The Theology of Calvin.* Trans. H. Knight. Grand Rapids: Baker.

Nijenhuis, W. 1972. Calvin's Attitude Towards the Symbols of the Early Church During the Conflict with Caroli. In *Ecclesia Reformata: Studies on the Reformation,* by W. Nijenhuis, 73–96. Leiden: E. J. Brill.

Oberdorfer, B. 2001. *Filioque: Geschichte und Theologie eines ökumenischen Problems.* Göttingen: Vandenhoeck & Ruprecht.

O'Carroll, M. C. 1987. *Trinitas: A Theological Encyclopedia of the Holy Trinity.* Collegeville, Minn.: Liturgical Press.

O'Collins, G. 1999. *The Tripersonal God: Understanding and Interpreting the Trinity.* London: Geoffrey Chapman.

Old, H. O. 1975. *The Patristic Roots of Reformed Worship*. Zurich: Theologischer Verlag.

Olson, R. 1983. Trinity and Eschatology: The Historical Being of God in Jürgen Moltmann and Wolfhart Pannenberg. *SJT* 36:213–27.

Origen. 1998. *Homilies on Jeremiah: Homily on 1 Kings 28*. Trans. J. C. Smith. Washington, D.C.: Catholic University of America Press.

———. *Against Celsus*.

———. *Commentary on the Epistle to the Romans*.

———. *Commentary on the Gospel of John*.

———. *Homilies on Jeremiah*.

———. *On First Principles*.

Owen, J. 1657. *Of Communion with God the Father, Son, and Holy Ghost, Each Person Distinctly, in Love, Grace, and Consolation*. In *The Works of John Owen*, ed. W. H. Goold, 2:1–274. London: Banner of Truth.

Owen, P. 2000. Calvin and Catholic Trinitarianism: An Examination of Robert Reymond's Understanding of the Trinity and His Appeal to John Calvin. *CTJ* 35:262–81.

Packer, J. I. 1973. *Knowing God*. London: Hodder and Stoughton.

Pannenberg, W. 1968. *Jesus—God and Man*. Trans. L. L. Wilkins. Philadelphia: Westminster Press.

———. 1991. *Systematic Theology*. Trans. G. W. Bromiley. Grand Rapids: Eerdmans.

Parker, T. H. L. 1952. *The Doctrine of the Knowledge of God: A Study in the Theology of John Calvin*. Edinburgh: Oliver and Boyd.

Pelikan, J. 1974. *The Spirit of Eastern Christendom*. Vol. 2 of *The Christian Tradition: A History of the Development of Doctrine*. Chicago: University of Chicago.

———. 1978. *The Growth of Medieval Theology (600–1300)*. Vol. 3 of *The Christian Tradition: A History of the Development of Doctrine*. Chicago: University of Chicago Press.

Person, R. 1978. *The Mode of Theological Decision Making at the Early Ecumenical Councils: An Inquiry into the Function of Scripture and Tradition at the Councils of Nicaea and Ephesus*. Basel: Friedrich Reinhardt Kommissionsverlag.

Peters, T. 1993. *God as Trinity: Relationality and Temporality in Divine Life*. Louisville: Westminster/John Knox Press.

Petterson, A. 1995. *Athanasius*. London: Geoffrey Chapman.

Peura, S. 1994. *Mehr als ein Mensch? Die Vergöttlichung als Thema der Theologie Martin Luthers von 1513 bis 1519*. Veröffentlichungen des Instituts für europäische Geschichte. Mainz: Verlag Philipp von Zabern.

Photius. 1983. *On the Mystagogy of the Holy Spirit*. Trans. Holy Transfiguration Monastery. N.p.: Studion.

Pieper, J. 1964. *Scholasticism: Personalities and Problems of Medieval Philosophy*. New York: McGraw-Hill.

Polanyi, M. 1958. *Personal Knowledge*. Chicago: University of Chicago Press.

———. 1958. *The Tacit Dimension*. Chicago: University of Chicago Press.

Prestige, G. L. 1940. *Fathers and Heretics*. London: SPCK.

———. 1952. *God in Patristic Thought*. London: SPCK.

Quasten, J. 1992. *The Ante-Nicene Literature After Irenaeus*. Vol. 2 of *Patrology*. Westminster, Md.: Christian Classics.

———. 1992. *The Golden Age of Greek Patristic Literature from the Council of Nicaea to the Council of Chalcedon*. Vol. 3 of *Patrology*. Westminster, Md.: Christian Classics.

Rahner, K. 1966. *More Recent Writings*. Vol. 4 of *Theological Investigations*. Trans. K. Smyth. Baltimore: Helicon Press.

———. 1967. Der dreifaltige Gott als transzendenter Urgrund der Heilsgeschichte. In *Die Heilsgeschichte vor Christus*. Vol. 2 of *Mysterium Salutis: Grundriss heilsgeschichtlicher Dogmatik*, ed. J. Feiner and M. Löhrer. Einsiedeln: Benziger Verlag.

———. 1978. *Foundations of Christian Faith: An Introduction to the Idea of Christianity*. Trans. W. V. Dych. New York: Seabury Press.

———. 1997. *The Trinity*. Trans. J. Donceel. New York: Crossroad.

Rainbow, P. A. 1987. Monotheism and Christology in 1 Corinthians 8:4–6. D.Phil. thesis, University of Oxford.

Ramsay, A. M. 1949. *The Glory of God and the Transfiguration of Christ*. London: Longmans.

Reid, D. 1997. *Energies of the Spirit*. Atlanta: Scholars Press.

Relton, H. M. 1917. *A Study in Christology: The Problem of the Relation of the Two Natures in the Person of Christ*. London: SPCK.

Reymond, R. L. 1998. *A New Systematic Theology of the Christian Faith*. Nashville: Thomas Nelson Publishers.

Reynolds, S. 1960–61. Calvin's View of the Athanasian and Nicene Creeds. *WTJ* 23:33–37.

Richard of St. Victor. 1979. *The Twelve Patriarchs; the Mystical Ark; Book Three of the Trinity*. Trans. and ed. G. A. Zinn. New York: Paulist Press.

———. *The Trinity*.

Ridderbos, H. 1975. *Paul: An Outline of His Theology*. Grand Rapids: Eerdmans.

Rist, J. M. 1981. Basil's "Neoplatonism": Its Background and Nature. In *Basil of Caesarea: Christian, Humanist, Ascetic: A Sixteen-Hundredth Anniversary Symposium*, ed. P. J. Fedwick, 137–220. Toronto: Pontifical Institute of Medieval Studies.

Ritschl, D. 1981. Historical Development and the Implications of the *Filioque* Controversy. In *Spirit of God, Spirit of Christ: Ecumenical Reflections on the Filioque Controversy*, ed. L. Vischer, 46–65. London: SPCK.

Roberts, A., ed. 1989. *Fathers of the Second Century*. Vol. 2 of *ANF*.

———. 1989. *Tertullian, Part Fourth; Minucius Felix; Commodian; Origen, Parts First and Second*. Vol. 4 of *ANF*.

———. 1993. *The Apostolic Fathers—Justin Martyr—Irenaeus*. Vol. 1 of *ANF*.

———. 1993. *Latin Christianity: Its Founder, Tertullian*. Vol. 3 of *ANF*.

Roldanus, J. 1968. *Le Christ et l'homme dans la théologie d'Athanase d'Alexandrie: Étude de la conjonction de sa conception de l'homme avec sa christologie*. Leiden: E. J. Brill.

Rousseau, P. 1994. *Basil of Caesarea*. Berkeley: University of California Press.

Rowe, J. N. 1987. *Origen's Doctrine of Subordination: A Study in Origen's Christology*. Berne: Peter Lang.

Sanday, W., and Headlam, A. C. 1905. *A Critical and Exegetical Commentary on the Epistle to the Romans*. International Critical Commentary. Edinburgh: T & T Clark.

Sayers, D. L. 1979. *The Mind of the Maker*. San Francisco: HarperCollins.

Schnackenburg, R. 1991. *Ephesians: A Commentary*. Edinburgh: T & T Clark.

Schwöbel, C., ed. 1995. *Trinitarian Theology Today: Essays on Divine Being and Acts*. Edinburgh: T & T Clark.

Scott, J. M. 1992. *Adoption as Sons of God: An Exegetical Investigation into the Background of Υἱοθεσία in the Pauline Corpus*. Wissenschaftliche Untersuchungen zum Neuen Testament. Tübingen: J. C. B. Mohr (Paul Siebeck).

Shedd, W. G. T. 1995. Introduction to *Latin Christianity: Its Founder, Tertullian*. Vol. 3 of *ANF*, 3–11.

Simonetti, M. 1975. *La crisi Ariana nel IV secolo*. Rome: Institutum Patristicum "Augustinianum."

Smail, T. A. 1986. The Doctrine of the Holy Spirit. In *Theology Beyond Christendom: Essays on the Centenary of the Birth of Karl Barth, May 10, 1886*, ed. J. Thompson, 87–110. Allison Park, Pa.: Pickwick Publications.

Solovyov, V. S. 1944. *Godmanhood as the Main Idea of the Philosophy of Vladimir Solovyev.* Trans. P. P. Zouboff. Poughkeepsie, N.Y.: Harmon Printing House.

————. 1944. *Vladimir Solovyev's Lectures on Godmanhood.* Trans. P. P. Zouboff. New York: International University Press.

————. 1974. *A Solovyov Anthology,* arr. S. L. Frank, trans. N. Duddington. Westport, Conn.: Greenwood Press.

————. 1978. *La Sophia et les autres écrits français.* Trans. and ed. F. Rouleau. Lausanne: La Cité: L'Age d'homme.

————. 1995. *Lectures on Divine Humanity.* Trans. B. Jakim. Hudson, N.Y.: Lindisfarne Press.

Speiser, E. A. 1981. *Genesis.* Anchor Bible. New York: Doubleday.

Staniloae, D. 1981. The Procession of the Holy Spirit from the Father and his Relation to the Son, as the Basis for Our Deification and Adoption. In *Spirit of God, Spirit of Christ,* ed. L. Vischer, 174–86. London: SPCK.

————. 1994–2000. *The Experience of God.* Trans. and ed. I. Ionita and R. Barringer. Foreword by K. Ware. 2 vols. Brookline, Mass.: Holy Cross Orthodox Press.

Stead, G. C. 1977. *Divine Substance.* Oxford: Clarendon.

————. 1990. Why Not Three Gods? The Logic of Gregory of Nyssa's Trinitarian Doctrine. In *Studien zu Gregor von Nyssa und der christlichen Spätantike,* ed. H. R. Drobner and C. Klock, 149–63. Leiden: E. J. Brill.

————. 2000. *Doctrine and Philosophy in Early Christianity: Arius, Athanasius, Augustine.* Aldershot, U.K.: Ashgate.

Stephens, W. P. 1986. *The Theology of Huldrych Zwingli.* Oxford: Clarendon Press.

Stott, J. R. W. 1964. *The Epistles of John: An Introduction and Commentary.* London: Tyndale Press.

Studer, B. 1984. Augustin et la foi de Nicée. *Recherches Augustiniennes* 19:133–54.

————. 1992. Enhypostasia. In *EECh,* 1:272.

————. 1993. *Trinity and Incarnation: The Faith of the Early Church.* Trans. M. Westerhoff. Ed. A. Louth. Collegeville, Minn.: Liturgical Press.

————. 1997. *The Grace of Christ and the Grace of God in Augustine of Hippo: Christocentrism or Theocentrism?* Collegeville, Minn.: Liturgical Press.

Stylianopoulos, T. 1982. The Biblical Background of the Article on the Holy Spirit in the Constantinopolitan Creed. In *Études théologiques: Le IIe Concile Oecuménique.* Chambésy-Genève: Centre Orthodoxe du Patriarcat Oecuménique.

————. 1986. The Filioque: Dogma, Theologoumenon or Error? In *Spirit of Truth: Ecumenical Perspectives on the Holy Spirit.* Brookline, Mass.: Holy Cross Orthodox Press.

————, and S. M. Heim, eds. 1986. *Spirit of Truth: Ecumenical Perspectives on the Holy Spirit.* Brookline, Mass.: Holy Cross Orthodox Press.

Tertullian. *Against Praxeas.*

————. *On Modesty.*

Tetz, M. 1995. *Athanasiana: Zu Leben und Lehre des Athanasius.* Berlin: Walter de Gruyter.

Theobald, M. 1988. *Die Fleischwerdung des Logos.* Münster: Aschendorff.

Theophilus of Antioch. *To Autolycus.*

Thiselton, A. C. 1995. *Interpreting God and the Post-Modern Self: On Meaning, Manipulation and Promise.* Edinburgh: T & T Clark.

————. 2000. *The First Epistle to the Corinthians: A Commentary on the Greek Text.* Grand Rapids: Eerdmans.

Thompson, J. 1986. On the Trinity. In *Theology Beyond Christendom: Essays on the Centenary of the Birth of Karl Barth, May 10, 1886,* ed. J. Thompson, 13–32. Allison Park, Pa.: Pickwick Publications.

————. 1994. *Modern Trinitarian Perspectives.* New York: Oxford University Press.

Toon, P. 1996. *Our Triune God: A Biblical Portrayal of the Trinity.* Wheaton, Ill.: BridgePoint.

Torrance, A. J. 1996. *Persons in Communion: An Essay on Trinitarian Description and Human Participation with Special Reference to Volume One of Karl Barth's Church Dogmatics.* Edinburgh: T & T Clark.

Torrance, D. W. 2001. Thomas Forsyth Torrance: Minister of the Gospel, Pastor, and Evangelical Theologian. In *The Promise of Trinitarian Theology: Theologians in Dialogue with T. F. Torrance,* ed. E. M. Colyer, 1–30. Lanham, Md.: Rowman & Littlefield Publishers.

Torrance, T. F. 1946. *The Doctrine of Grace in the Apostolic Fathers.* Edinburgh: Oliver & Boyd.

————. 1968. Intuitive and Abstractive Knowledge: From Duns Scotus to John Calvin. In *De doctrina Ioannis Duns Scoti: Acta Congressus Scotistici Internationalis Oxonii et Edimburgi 11–17 Sept. 1966 celebrati,* 4:291–305. Rome: Curae Commissionis Scotisticae.

————. 1975. *Theology in Reconciliation.* Grand Rapids: Eerdmans.

————. 1983. *The Mediation of Christ.* Grand Rapids: Eerdmans.

————. 1988. *The Hermeneutics of John Calvin.* Edinburgh: Scottish Academic Press.

———. 1988. *The Trinitarian Faith: The Evangelical Theology of the Ancient Catholic Church*. Edinburgh: T & T Clark.

———. 1992. The Christian Apprehension of God the Father. In *Speaking the Christian God: The Holy Trinity and the Challenge of Feminism*, ed. A. F. Kimel Jr., 120–43. Grand Rapids: Eerdmans.

———. 1993. *Theological Dialogue Between Orthodox and Reformed Churches*, vol. 2. Edinburgh: Scottish Academic Press.

———. 1994. *Trinitarian Perspectives: Toward Doctrinal Agreement*. Edinburgh: T & T Clark.

———. 1996. *The Christian Doctrine of God: One Being, Three Persons*. Edinburgh: T & T Clark.

———. 2001. Thomas Torrance Responds. In *The Promise of Trinitarian Theology: Theologians in Dialogue with T. F. Torrance*, ed. E. M. Colyer, 303–40. Lanham, Md.: Rowman & Littlefield Publishers.

Trigg, J. 1998. *Origen*. London: Routledge.

Trumper, T. 1996. The Metaphorical Import of Adoption: A Plea for Realisation: I: The Adoption Metaphor in Biblical Usage. *SBET* 14 (2): 129–45.

———. 1997. The Metaphorical Import of Adoption: A Plea for Realisation: II: The Adoption Metaphor in Theological Usage. *SBET* 15 (2): 98–115.

Turner, C. 1926. Ο ΥΙΟΣ ΜΟΥ Ο ΑΓΑΠΗΤΟΣ. *JTS* 27:113–29.

Turretin, F. 1992–97. *Institutes of Elenctic Theology*, ed. J. T. Dennison. Phillipsburg, N.J.: P&R Publishing.

Vaggione, R. P., ed. 1987. *Eunomius: The Extant Works*. Oxford: Clarendon Press.

———. 2000. *Eunomius of Cyzicus and the Nicene Revolution*. Oxford: Oxford University Press.

Van Til, C. 1974. *An Introduction to Systematic Theology*. Phillipsburg, N.J.: Presbyterian and Reformed.

Vischer, L., ed. 1981. *Spirit of God, Spirit of Christ: Ecumenical reflections on the Filioque Controversy*. London: SPCK.

Von Rad, G. 1961. *Genesis: A Commentary*. Rev. ed. Philadelphia: Westminster Press.

Wainwright, A. 1963. *The Trinity in the New Testament*. London: SPCK.

Ware, T. 1969. *The Orthodox Church*. London: Penguin Books.

Warfield, B. B. 1930. *Studies in Tertullian and Augustine*. New York: Oxford.

———. 1952. The Biblical Doctrine of the Trinity. In *Biblical and Theological Studies*, ed. S. G. Craig, 22–59. Philadelphia: Presbyterian and Reformed.

———. 1952. The Spirit of God in the Old Testament. In *Biblical and Theological Studies*, ed. S. G. Craig, 127–56. Philadelphia: Presbyterian and Reformed.

———. 1974. Calvin's Doctrine of the Trinity. In *Calvin and Augustine*, ed. S. G. Craig, 187–284. Philadelphia: Presbyterian and Reformed.

Watson, F. 1994. *Text, Church, and World: Biblical Interpretation in Theological Perspective*. Edinburgh: T & T Clark.

Weinandy, T. G. 2000. *Does God Suffer?* Notre Dame, Ind.: University of Notre Dame Press.

Wendebourg, D. 1982. From the Cappadocian Fathers to Gregory Palamas: The Defeat of Trinitarian Theology. *StPatr* 17 (1): 194–98.

Wendel, F. 1963. *Calvin: The Origin and Development of His Religious Thought*. Trans. P. Mairet. London: Collins.

Wenham, G. J. 1987. *Genesis 1–15*. Word Biblical Commentary. Waco, Tex.: Word.

Westcott, B. F. 1908. *The Gospel According to St. John: The Greek Text with Introduction and Notes*. London: John Murray.

Whybray, R. 1975. *Isaiah 40–66*. New Century Bible Commentary. Grand Rapids: Eerdmans.

Widdicombe, P. 1994. *The Fatherhood of God from Origen to Athanasius*. Oxford: Clarendon.

Wiles, M. 1993. Attitudes to Arius in the Arian Controversy. In *Arianism After Arius: Essays on the Development of the Fourth Century Trinitarian Conflicts*, ed. M. R. Barnes, 31–43. Edinburgh: T & T Clark.

Williams, A. N. 1999. *The Ground of Union: Deification in Aquinas and Palamas*. New York: Oxford University Press.

Williams, R. 1977. The Philosophical Structures of Palamism. *ECR* 9:27–44.

———. 1979. Barth on the Triune God. In *Karl Barth: Essays in His Theological Method*, ed. S. Sykes, 147–93. Oxford: Clarendon Press.

———. 1983. The Logic of Arianism. *JTS* 34:56–81.

———. 1987. *Arius: Heresy and Tradition*. London: Darton, Longman, and Todd.

———. 1989. Eastern Orthodox Theology. In *The Modern Theologians*, ed. D. F. Ford. Oxford: Blackwell.

———. 1999. De Trinitate. In *Augustine Through the Ages*, ed. A. D. Fitzgerald, 845–51. Grand Rapids: Eerdmans.

———. 2001. *Arius: Heresy and Tradition*. 2nd ed. Grand Rapids: Eerdmans.

Winter, R., and R. Martin, eds. 1994. *The Beethoven Quartet Companion*. Berkeley: University of California Press.

Witherington, B., III. 1997. Lord. In *Dictionary of the Later New Testament and Its Developments*, ed. R. P. Martin and P. H. Davids, 667–78. Downers Grove, Ill.: InterVarsity Press.

Wittgenstein, L. 1963. *Philosophical Investigations*, trans. G. E. M. Anscombe. Oxford: Basil Blackwell.

Wright, D. F. 1997. Calvin's Accommodating God. In *Calvinus sincerioris religionis vindex: Calvin as the Protector of the Purer Religion*. Sixteenth Century Essays and Studies 36, ed. W. H. Neuser, 3–19. Kirksville, Mo.: Sixteenth Century Journal Publishers.

Wright, N. T. 1986. ἁρπαγμος and the Meaning of Philippians 2: 5–11. *JTS* 37:321–52.

Young, F. 1983. *From Nicaea to Chalcedon: A Guide to the Literature and Its Background*. London: SCM.

Zizioulas, J. D. 1975. Human Capacity and Human Incapacity: A Theological Exploration of Personhood. *SJT* 28:401–47.

———. 1985. *Being as Communion: Studies in Personhood and the Church*. Crestwood, N.Y.: St. Vladimir's Seminary Press.

Index of Scripture

Acts

2:1–5—343
2:33–35—26
2:33–36—40, 405
2:33–39—70
5:3–4—61
7:59–60—47
8:29—60
8:39—60
9:14—47
9:21—47
13—387
13:1ff.—77
13:33—261, 384
16:6–10—60
17:16–34—455
17:28—333
22:16—47

Romans

1:1—52
1:1–4—64
1:3–4—39, 204n9
1:7—52
1:9—52
1:19–20—434
1:20—437
3:21–22—53
3:23—468
3:23–24—53
4:8—43n25
4:24–25—53
4:25—77
5—496
5:1—53, 64
5:5—64
5:12–21—393, 464, 495
5:15—334
6:1ff.—467
6:1–11—387
6:4—53
6:9—394, 487, 494
6:11—53

6:23—53
7:4–6—64
7:25—53
8—79, 263
8:1–3a—64
8:3—49
8:3b–4—65
8:5–11—65
8:9—61, 255
8:9–11—60
8:11—15, 204n9, 405
8:15—37
8:26–27—60, 415
8:30—474
8:32—77, 413
9:1–5—65
9:5—41, 47, 53
9:28–29—43n25
10:9—53
10:9–13—47
10:12–13—53
10:13—44n25
10:16—43n25
11:34—43n25
12:19—454n63
13:9ff.—66
14:5–9—53
14:11—255n18
14:17–18—65
15:5–7—53
15:8—53
15:11—43n25
15:16—65
15:30—61, 65
16:20—34n1
16:27—53

1 Corinthians

1:1–3—52
1:4—53
1:9—53
1:31—44n25
2—62

2:1–5—65
2:6–16—80
2:8–11—150
2:9–16—65
2:10–11—316
3:11–17—65
3:20—43n25
6:11—65
6:12–20—65
8:5–6—69
8:6—44, 53
10:1–5—65
10:26—44n25
11:3—54
11:31—53
12:1–3—47, 61
12:3—61, 65, 414
12:4–6—60, 61, 64, 68
12:13—65
15—371
15:20–58—464
15:24–28—40, 54
15:27–28—255
15:28—122, 125, 193, 316, 418
15:47–49—334
16:22—43, 47
16:22–24—53

2 Corinthians

1:1–2—52
1:3—53
1:21–22—65
2:14–17—53
3:4–18—66
3:17—61
4:4—53, 411
4:4–6—464
4:5—53
4:6—53, 464
5:1–10—66
5:10—45
5:16–21—53

Index of Subjects and Names

Wendel, F., 252
Wenham, Gordon J., 19, 34n1, 427
West, 176, 181, 250
Westcott, B. F., 384, 404n74
Westermann, C., 19, 20
Western church, 2–3, 7, 11, 176, 181,
    201, 250, 354–55
    conception of person, 372
    modalistic tendency of, 212, 377
    neglect of Trinity, 407–10
    rationalism of, 346
    tendency toward impersonal essence,
        367–68
    on Union with God, 471–74
Western mysticism, 323, 324
Westminster Confession of Faith, 383,
    423, 472–73
Westminster Larger Catechism, 391,
    466–67, 473
Westminster Shorter Catechism, 391
Whybray, R. N., 27
Widdicombe, Peter, 103n64, 107,
    138n55, 388
Wiles, Maurice, 110
Williams, A. N., 472
Williams, D. H., 109
Williams, Rowan, 115, 126, 185, 186,
    194, 249, 274, 275, 288, 322n1
Wisdom, 22, 30–31, 90, 102, 133, 227,
    328–31, 332, 335, 429
    Arius on, 112
    in creation, 93

Witherington, B., 43
Wittgenstein, Ludwig, 453
Wolleb, 277
women
    changing roles of, 490
    exclusion from leadership, 495
    freed from submission, 491
    ordination of, 489
Word, 30–31
    Arius on, 112
    in creation, 44, 90, 93, 95, 99
    and Spirit, 239
    threefold form of, 273
words, and reality, 137
Wordsworth, Christopher, 394
World Alliance of Reformed Churches,
    218, 358
worldview, 424
worship, 7–8, 151, 156, 162, 362, 407,
    455
    of the Holy Spirit, 173
    of Jesus, 46–47, 50
    of the Son, 137
    and theology, 359–61
    and Trinity, 250, 251, 378, 412–24

Yahweh, 26
YHWH, 27–28, 43, 415

Zizioulas, John, 343n100, 372, 462,
    463, 493
Zwingli, Ulrich, 423

Robert Letham is Senior Lecturer in Systematic and Historical Theology at Wales Evangelical School of Theology (WEST). He has advanced degrees from Westminster Theological Seminary and the University of Aberdeen.